Governing America

Major Decisions of Federal, State, and Local Governments from 1789 to the Present

Volume III

Paul J. Quirk
William Cunion

GOVERNING AMERICA: Major Decisions of Federal, State, and Local Governments from 1789 to the Present

Facts On File, Inc.
An imprint of Infobase Learning
132 West 31st Street
New York NY 10001

Library of Congress Cataloging-in-Publication Data
Quirk, Paul J., 1949–
Governing America : major decisions of federal, state, and local governments from 1789 to the present / Paul J. Quirk, William Cunion.
p. cm.
Includes bibliographical references and index.
ISBN 978-0-8160-7567-6 (hc : alk. paper) 1. Political planning—United States—History. 2. United States—Politics and government. 3. Policy sciences—History. 4. United States—Economic policy. 5. United States—Social policy. I. Cunion, William II. Title.
JK468.P64Q55 2010
320.60973—dc22 2010018157

Facts On File books are available at special discounts when purchased in bulk quantities for businesses, associations, institutions, or sales promotions. Please call our Special Sales Department in New York at (212) 967-8800 or (800) 322-8755.

You can find Facts On File on the World Wide Web at http://www.InfobaseLearning.com

Text design by Annie O'Donnell
Composition by Publication Services, Inc.
Cover printed by Yurchak Printing, Landisville, Pa.
Book printed and bound by Yurchak Printing, Landisville, Pa.
Date printed: May 2010

Printed in the United States of America

10 9 8 7 6 5 4 3 2 1

This book is printed on acid-free paper.

Contents

Volume II

SOCIAL POLICIES

Volume III
GOVERNMENT, LAW ENFORCEMENT, AND FOREIGN AFFAIRS

Volume III

GOVERNMENT, LAW ENFORCEMENT, AND FOREIGN AFFAIRS

Crime

capital punishment

Criminal offenders have been punished by death on American soil since colonial days. Nevertheless, many significant changes have occurred in capital punishment laws and practices over time. Death penalty policies are continuously evolving and they vary, often dramatically, within the contemporary United States. This article begins by sketching a brief history of the death penalty from the country's foundation through the mid-1970s, when landmark U.S. Supreme Court decisions caused major changes in capital punishment laws nationwide. It next describes significant developments in death penalty laws and their administration during the ensuing, modern era of capital punishment. Several lingering policy questions associated with capital punishment are then discussed, including issues that have assumed greater focus and immediacy as new evidence accumulates about them. Recent trends in administration of the death penalty and their potential implications for the future of capital punishment in America also are examined.

The first recorded execution in what is now the United States occurred in colonial Virginia in 1608, when George Kendall died by firing squad as punishment for spying for the Spanish. Since that time, it has been estimated that more than 20,000 criminal offenders have been punished by death under colonial, state, or federal jurisdiction. Capital sentences were imposed for a variety of crimes under colonial rule and during early statehood. Prisons did not exist in America until the late 18th century and local jails were ill-suited for long-term incarceration, making the death penalty the primary option for a range of felonies. Property offenses, such as larceny and counterfeiting, as well as burglary, arson, kidnapping, rape, murder, and other violent crimes commonly were punished capitally. Owing in part to the lack of meaningful alternative sanctions, death sentences followed automatically on an offender's conviction. The relatively liberal use of executive clemency ameliorated some of the harshness and inflexibility of mandatory capital punishment.

Beginning in the 1790s, the states began to narrow the range of capital crimes. Pennsylvania led the way by enacting legislation that for the first time created separate categories of murder: first-degree, which included "willful, premeditated, and deliberate" killings as well as killings committed during designated felonies; and second-degree, comprising other unlawful killings with malice. Only first-degree murder was punished by death. Other jurisdictions soon adopted similar reforms. As the 19th century progressed, the death penalty increasingly was reserved for the most serious forms of murder, offenses that threatened the security of the state, such as treason and espionage, rape (especially in states in the South), and a smattering of other crimes. Some states dispensed with the death penalty altogether. For example, Michigan abolished capital punishment for all crimes except treason in 1847, and Rhode Island (in 1852) and Wisconsin (in 1853) abandoned the death penalty for all crimes.

Further limiting the reach of capital punishment, mandatory sentencing laws gave way to legislation that allowed judges and juries the discretion to choose between life imprisonment and death. In 1838, Tennessee became the first state to allow juries sentencing discretion in murder cases. Other jurisdictions followed suit, with this trend finally culminating in 1963 when New York abandoned mandatory capital punishment for deliberate and premeditated murder. Death sentences imposed automatically on conviction were perceived as unjust, because they prohibited consideration of individual case factors relevant to culpability. They also precluded mercy and proved to be unworkable. Juries nullified mandatory death penalty laws with some regularity by refusing to convict clearly guilty offenders.

Executions were typically carried out during colonial times by shooting or hanging, although more dramatic and more painful methods, such as burning at the stake, were sometimes invoked, including to punish slaves or help quell threats of insurrection. As was the custom in England, executions in the nation's formative years were public events that attracted large and often raucous crowds. Only in the 1830s did the states begin removing executions from public squares to behind jail and prison walls, a process not completed until 1936 when the last public hanging was carried out in Owensboro, Kentucky. Hanging endured as the most prevalent method of execution throughout the 19th century. However, with the hope of identifying a more humane alternative, New York developed the electric chair and first put it to use in 1890 against convicted murderer William Kemmler. Kemmler's execution was a gruesome affair—he did not die on the first administration of electric current and his body was badly burned—but many other jurisdictions soon abandoned hanging in favor of the electric chair or the gas chamber, which was introduced in the 1920s.

The 1930s saw the most executions in recorded American history, averaging 167 annually, including 199 in the peak year, 1935. With many young men enlisting for military service during World War II, and amidst a growing distaste for lethal violence, executions declined during the 1940s, to approximately 129 a year. And although the United States population grew steadily, the number of executions fell even more sharply during the 1950s, to about 72 a year, with just 49 carried out in both 1958 and 1959. As the 1960s dawned, polls reflected that public opinion was almost evenly divided between support for and opposition to the death penalty. Legal developments harbingered dramatic changes for the country's capital punishment practices.

With the death penalty's roots running so deep in American history, the constitutionality of capital punishment had never been seriously challenged. Moreover, executions overwhelmingly resulted from state convictions, rather than federal or U.S. military offenses, which further insulated them from review under the federal Constitution. Prior to the 1960s, the states had substantial latitude to conduct trials and impose punishment pursuant to their own standards, subject only to the broad constraints of the due process and equal protection mandates of the Fourteenth Amendment. The specific safeguards governing criminal cases spelled out in the Bill of Rights, or first 10 amendments to the U.S. Constitution, originally applied only to federal proceedings. These policies changed radically with the "due process revolution" initiated by the U.S. Supreme Court under the leadership of Chief Justice Earl Warren.

During the 1960s, the Warren court ruled in a series of cases that nearly all of the Bill of Rights protections relating to criminal proceedings had to be observed in state cases just as they were in federal cases. Thus, for example, the justices decided that the Sixth Amendment was binding on the states and required that poor people charged with felonies be provided with court-appointed trial counsel (*Gideon v. Wainwright* [1963]). They ruled that evidence obtained in violation of individuals' Fourth Amendment rights was free from unreasonable searches and that seizures must be excluded from state criminal trials (*Mapp v. Ohio* [1961]), and they famously announced that the Fifth Amendment required both state and federal law enforcement officers to administer suspects their *Miranda* rights before securing confessions (*Miranda v. Arizona* [1966]). And in 1962, in a case that had nothing to do with the death penalty, the Supreme Court decided that the Eighth Amendment's prohibition against cruel and unusual punishments applied to state criminal proceedings (*Robinson v. California*).

These developments encouraged defense lawyers to begin challenging the constitutionality of capital punishment in the state and federal courts. Litigation slowed executions to a trickle and, following two carried out in 1967, they eventually came to a halt. In 1968, the Supreme Court limited the states' authority to deny jurors the opportunity to serve in capital trials simply because they harbored "conscientious scruples" against the death penalty (*Witherspoon v. Illinois*). Other cases questioned whether the sentencing decisions made in capital trials violated fundamental due process requirements. Almost all capital punishment jurisdictions at that time gave juries the discretion to impose either death sentences or life imprisonment, but offered no legal standards or framework to guide their choice. Sentencing decisions typically were announced simultaneously with guilty verdicts, giving juries no opportunity to consider evidence relating exclusively to punishment. Decisions that literally were a matter of life and death, defense lawyers argued, demanded greater procedural safeguards.

While executions continued to be held in abeyance, the justices confronted the due process–based challenge to capital punishment in 1971. In *McGautha v. California*, by a 6-3 vote, the Court rejected the argument that entrusting juries with virtually unlimited discretion in making capital sentencing decisions was unconstitutional. The majority opinion expressed skepticism that meaningful legal criteria could be developed to guide a jury's choice between a death sentence and life imprisonment. "The infinite variety of cases and facets to each case would make general [sentencing] standards either meaningless 'boiler-plate' or a statement of the obvious that no jury would need." The opinion continued: "To identify before the fact those characteristics of criminal homicides and their perpetrators which call for the death penalty, and to express these characteristics in language which can be fairly understood and applied by the sentencing authority, appear to be tasks which are beyond present human ability." Nor, in the majority's view, did due process require a separate hearing to allow evidence to be presented on matters bearing directly on punishment.

In light of this decisive rejection of the claimed irregularities in death sentencing procedures, many observers were surprised when the justices immediately agreed to consider another frontal assault on capital punishment, based on the Eighth Amendment's prohibition against cruel and unusual punishments. The subtle distinction between this theory and the due process challenge involved a shift in focus from process to outcome. The argument advanced was that the death penalty, when applied in the haphazard and essentially arbitrary fashion authorized under current law, represented a "cruel and unusual punishment" for those rare and capriciously selected offenders made subject to it. The Court considered the Eighth Amendment challenge in 1972, in *Furman v. Georgia*.

And in *Furman*, a landmark 5-4 decision that produced nine separate opinions and spilled over more than 240 pages, the justices ruled that the death penalty, as then administered, was indeed a cruel and unusual punishment. Two of the five concurring justices took the position that capital punishment was inherently unconstitutional. The other three, however, focused on irregularities in the death penalty's administration—including evidence that it was tainted by racial and economic discrimination, that it was applied in a wanton and freakish manner, and that it was carried out so infrequently that it could not possibly accomplish its intended objectives. In principle, these perceived deficiencies could be corrected.

The lengthy, multiple, and inconsistent opinions obscured the decision's governing rationale, but *Furman*'s import was clear. Death penalty laws throughout the nation were unconstitutional and could not be enforced. The more than 600 offenders then under sentence of death were spared execution and resentenced to life imprisonment. If the states and the federal government wanted to reinstitute capital punishment they would have to enact new laws that would correct the problems identified by the justices who had condemned the existing sentencing procedures.

Furman v. Georgia brought one era of American capital punishment to a close, although a new one would soon begin.

Legislative reaction to the Court's ruling in *Furman* was swift and decisive. The decision was criticized by many as an intrusion on the states' long-standing authority to administer their criminal laws and, more particularly, as undermining their ability to combat violent crime. Death penalty statutes were promptly reenacted in almost all jurisdictions where they had previously been in place, although the specifics of the new legislation varied significantly. Responding to concerns expressed in *Furman* that death sentences had been imposed inconsistently and unfairly, several states reverted to laws mandating capital punishment on conviction for crimes including first-degree murder and rape. Others sought to regulate capital sentencing discretion rather than eliminate it. Such "guided discretion" legislation typically required the prosecution to prove that an aggravated form of murder had been committed, called for a separate penalty hearing to allow evidence on aggravating and mitigating factors bearing on punishment, and then directed the jury (or judge) to choose between a death sentence and life imprisonment after considering those factors.

The Supreme Court considered the constitutionality of the new laws in 1976, reviewing capital murder cases from Georgia, Florida, and Texas, which relied on guided discretion statutes, and from North Carolina and Louisiana, which had enacted mandatory death penalty legislation. After reviewing the country's history with capital punishment, identifying textual references within the Constitution to the death penalty, interpreting legislative activity and jury sentencing practices as evidencing continuing societal support for capital punishment, and concluding that retribution and general deterrence rationally justified the death penalty, the justices rejected (by 7-2 vote) the argument that capital punishment was inherently unconstitutional. The Court upheld the guided discretion statutes under review in *Gregg v. Georgia, Proffitt v. Florida,* and *Jurek v. Texas.* However, the justices invalidated the mandatory death penalty legislation at issue in *Woodson v. North Carolina* and *Roberts v. Louisiana.*

The justices were of the opinion that guided discretion statutes succeeded in minimizing the risk of arbitrariness that had been condemned in *Furman.* The important new safeguards included creating separate guilt and penalty trials, narrowing the range of death-eligible crimes, incorporating specific aggravating factors to guide sentencing discretion, and allowing the jury to consider mitigating factors prior to making a punishment decision. Mandatory death penalty laws, on the other hand, precluded juries from considering too many variables relevant to an offender's culpability, and promised to undermine rather than promote rational capital sentencing practices. By a slim 5-4 margin, the justices concluded that such inflexible laws violated the Eighth Amendment.

Executions resumed in 1977, after a 10-year hiatus, when Gary Gilmore waived appeals following his capital murder conviction and death sentence and died before a Utah firing squad. Other death-sentenced offenders, however, pressed issues in their appeals that had not been resolved in the series of 1976 Supreme Court decisions. Many of them prevailed as the lower courts and the Supreme Court clarified and refined constitutional doctrine governing the new capital punishment laws in numerous case-specific rulings. As death rows swelled by upward of 150 to 250 new entries per year between 1978 and 1983, only 10 executions were carried out. This trend came to a halt in 1983 when Supreme Court rulings abruptly reversed course and began upholding death sentences, sounding notably impatient about litigation-related delays in the capital punishment process. An average of 18 executions a year occurred throughout the remainder of the 1980s, and annual executions increased steadily the next decade, topping at 98 in 1999.

The Supreme Court issued several important decisions affecting capital punishment law after generally approving guided discretion legislation in 1976. Procedurally, the justices required open-ended admission of relevant, individualized mitigation evidence at capital sentencing hearings (*Lockett v. Ohio* [1978]), a measure that, in the opinion of some members of the Court, clashed with *Furman*'s mandate for regularity and consistency in the death penalty's administration. They approved the practice of "death qualifying" jurors in capital cases (*Lockhart v. McCree* [1986]), a process used to identify and then disqualify from jury service individuals whose personal views about the death penalty compromised their willingness to consider imposing a capital sentence. They invalidated the practice followed in a few states of allowing judges, rather than juries, to make the sentencing decision in capital trials, at least when new facts that had not already been determined by the jury figured into the determination of punishment (*Ring v. Arizona* [2002]).

Substantively, the Court interpreted the Eighth Amendment to prohibit capital punishment for certain crimes and certain categories of offenders. The justices outlawed using the death penalty for rape of either an adult or child victim (*Coker v. Georgia* [1977]; *Kennedy v. Louisiana* [2008]). In doing so, they broadly suggested that the Constitution forbids using the death penalty for personal crimes short of aggravated murder. They also limited, but did not preclude in all circumstances, capital punishment for the "nontrigger person" in a felony murder, that is, for a participant (such as a lookout) in a felony whose co-felon actually killed the victim (*Enmund v. Florida* [1982]; *Tison v. Arizona* [1987]). And, overruling earlier decisions in each instance, the Court exempted mentally retarded offenders (*Atkins v. Virginia* [2002]) and juveniles younger than 18 (*Roper v. Simmons* [2005]) from death-penalty eligibility.

Many of the Court's decisions were controversial, including a highly significant 5-4 ruling in which the justices rejected claims that Georgia's capital punishment system was fatally tainted by racial discrimination. In this 1987 case, *McCleskey v. Kemp*, the Court considered the constitutional implications of a comprehensive study that examined how the death penalty had been applied in Georgia in the post-*Furman* era. The study revealed that race, and especially the race of the murder victim, played a significant role in capital charging and sentencing decisions. Specifically, in otherwise similar cases, the odds that a death sentence would be sought and imposed in white-victim murders were 4.3 times higher than in murders involving black victims. Black offenders who killed white victims (such as in *McCleskey*), the study suggested, faced the highest likelihood of execution. Notwithstanding those findings, which essentially challenged whether the guided discretion legislation that the Court had approved in 1976 was effective in practice to purge arbitrariness from Georgia's capital punishment system, the majority was not persuaded that the risk of racial discrimination was constitutionally significant.

At the federal level, Congress's first post-*Furman* death penalty legislation took effect in 1988. This law was limited in scope, applying primarily to murders carried out in connection with major illegal drug activities. Six years later, President Clinton—who had interrupted his initial campaign for the White House in 1992 to make a highly publicized return to Arkansas to preside as governor over an execution—signed into law the much more comprehensive Federal Death Penalty Act of 1994. This act, part of a broad anticrime initiative, authorized capital punishment for scores of federal offenses. With public support for the death penalty strong, crime high on the political agenda, and constitutional obstacles regarding capital punishment largely resolved, the federal law's passage was ensured when President Clinton backed it and moderate House Democrats, discerning its inevitability, approved it to forestall enactment of an even more expansive statute.

Quick on the heels of this sweeping legislation, Congress passed, and President Clinton signed, the Anti-Terrorism and Effective Death Penalty Act of 1996 (AEDPA). Motivated largely by the quest to expedite the processing of capital cases, AEDPA imposed several new limitations on the availability of federal habeas corpus to state prisoners. The most notorious offender executed in the modern era under federal law is certainly Timothy McVeigh, who was responsible for the 1995 bombing of the Alfred P. Murrah Building in Oklahoma City, in which 168 men, women, and children lost their lives.

Amidst continuing developments in capital punishment law, conspicuous changes in death penalty practices began emerging at the turn of the 21st century. Nationwide, beginning in 2000, annual numbers of entries to death row (reflecting offenders newly sentenced to death) as well as executions plummeted. In 1999, 284 offenders joined the ranks of the condemned, a total somewhat below the 306 new death sentences imposed the year before. In 2000, however, the nation's death rows added significantly fewer new offenders (235), followed by 167 additions in 2001. By 2007, new death row entries dipped to approximately 110, representing just 38 percent of the 1999 total. Annual executions also tumbled. They steadily declined from the modern era highpoint of 98 in 1999, to 85 in 2000, bottoming at 42 in 2007, or 43 percent of the tally at the end of the century.

It is too early to tell whether these changes portend long-term trends or whether they will be transitory and fleeting. They are at least eye-opening, in the short term, and they have potentially dramatic implications for the future of the death penalty in this country. The striking downturn in new death sentences and executions may find explanation in recent policy-related developments pertaining to capital punishment and its administration.

Support for and opposition to the death penalty tend to be driven by three general and occasionally overlapping policy considerations. One concern is largely normative, involving value judgments about the fundamental justice and morality of capital punishment. Such beliefs are typically grounded in views about the propriety and appropriate limits of retributive justice, and/or are bottomed on religious faith. As such, they may be largely immune to modification or refutation through logic or empirical evidence.

In contrast, the other principal policy considerations influencing opinions about capital punishment are primarily empirical in nature. Consequently, they may be subject to change depending on what relevant evidence reveals. One such set of concerns centers on the death penalty's utility, including its value as a general deterrent to murder, its role in incapacitating dangerous offenders, the relief it may offer to murder victims' survivors, and its cost effectiveness. A second set of fact-based policy considerations focuses on the death penalty's administration. Issues include the risk of wrongful convictions and executions, racial disparities and other sources of arbitrariness in charging and sentencing decisions, the composition and functioning of capital juries, the adequacy of court-appointed defense counsel, and concerns about methods of execution such as lethal injection.

Although voiced less prominently during the pre-*Furman* era, retribution—or "just deserts"—more recently has become the principal justification offered in support of capital punishment. Adherents to this philosophy argue that death is a deserved and proportionate response to serious crimes such as murder, and it is the only way that society can adequately condemn and express moral outrage over the wanton taking of innocent life. Sometimes associated with the principle of "an eye for an eye," retributive justice also serves as a limitation on punishment. It explains, for example, why the death penalty is not used for relatively minor crimes or against offenders, such as juveniles or the mentally retarded, who are less than fully responsible for their conduct.

Skeptics question the retributive justification for capital punishment. They argue that literal "eye for an eye" symmetry between crime and punishment is not a regular feature of the justice system and that murder should not be an exception. They point out, for instance, that rapists are not raped, arsonists do not have their homes burned down, and that most criminal homicides are not punished by death. They further contend that government must be limited in its response to serious crime so that it does not risk mirroring the deeds of criminal offenders, a premise enshrined in the Eighth Amendment's prohibition against "cruel and unusual" punishments. Thus, few would support using torture to execute a murderer who tortured his or her victim, and even if they did, the Constitution would check such tendencies. They maintain that the proportionality principle that is a part of retributive justice may require that society's most serious punishment be reserved for the most serious crimes, but it does not dictate what that punishment should be.

Views about the morality of capital punishment for many people are interwoven with religious beliefs. Several major religions have adopted formal policy statements in opposition to the death penalty or supporting its use only in the most extreme circumstances. The Catholic Church and several Protestant and Jewish denominations are among the faith groups that generally oppose capital punishment, while many adherents to Islam, Southern Baptists, and some other religious organizations espouse broader support for the death penalty.

Debate has raged for centuries about whether the death penalty is a necessary and effective weapon in society's war against crime. Much of the controversy has centered on its role as a general deterrent, that is, in discouraging prospective offenders from committing crimes because of the risk that they will be caught and executed. The logic of general deterrence is that death is a uniquely severe punishment that most people seek to avoid. As the costs associated with criminal activity go up (and they can go no higher than being executed), individuals' willingness to incur them should go down. Therefore, intuitively, the threat of capital punishment should discourage people from committing murder.

Yet implicit in classical deterrence theory is the premise that actors rationally calculate the likely costs and benefits of criminal activity before deciding whether to engage in or refrain from that activity. Critics scoff at the proposition that most murderers fit the model of a deliberate and rationally calculating actor at the moment they decide whether to kill. They further emphasize that if a rational assessment of benefits and costs is made, few prospective offenders would willingly accept punishment by life imprisonment without parole (LWOP), which alone should suffice to discourage their plans. In other words, if capital punishment has unique value as a general deterrent to murder, which in their view is unlikely, it is limited to its tiny and perhaps nonexistent efficacy beyond the threat already posed by the alternative sanction of LWOP.

Many studies have examined whether the threat of the death penalty appears to affect murder rates. The studies are complicated by the countless other factors that may contribute to crime rates, such as the economy and unemployment, the prevalence of gang and drug activity, differences between urban and rural areas, gun control laws, the size of age-specific cohorts, the likelihood of arrest, what alternative punishments are available, and many more. Although a few studies have reported finding evidence that executions do help discourage murder, they have been greatly outnumbered by studies concluding that the death penalty has no discernible impact on murder rates and that flaws in these previous studies suggest otherwise. Some research has even suggested that executions actually stimulate murder, through a "brutalization" effect by which criminal homicide is perceived as being legitimated by the example of government-sponsored killing.

Incapacitation—the protection of society against dangerous offenders through their execution—is another utilitarian justification advanced in support of the death penalty. There is no quarreling with the effectiveness of capital punishment to serve this function; executed murderers will not kill again. Nevertheless, serious objections have been raised about using the death penalty to protect society against convicted murderers. First, a less drastic alternative, life imprisonment without parole, is readily available that should be equally effective to safeguard society. Whatever risk is presented to prison staff and other inmates presumably can be minimized by taking appropriate security precautions. In addition, an overwhelming majority of convicted murderers do not repeat their crimes, and it is virtually impossible to predict the very small minority of offenders who will. Using the death penalty in the name of incapacitation would be akin to seeking to locate the proverbial needle in the haystack, with lethal consequences for the great many offenders who could effectively be incapacitated through incarceration.

Increased attention to the suffering that crime victims endure, first at the hands of offenders and, all too often, later through neglect or slights by actors in the justice system, occasioned reforms embodied in victim-centered laws and social services that gained momentum in the 1980s and thereafter. The victims' rights movement brought calls for using the death penalty to help surviving family members achieve "closure" concerning their loved ones' murder. Yet "closure" is an ill-defined concept, and one that is rejected by many victims' survivors when used to suggest that an offender's execution will somehow ease the pain he or she caused. Additionally, since executions occur rarely in response to criminal homicide—in just 1 to 2 percent of such cases—the death penalty can hardly benefit the vast majority of the victims' community, except perhaps vicariously. Moreover, like people generally, murder victims' survivors are divided in their support for capital punishment and many oppose its use in general and in their loved ones' cases.

The monetary costs of capital punishment are another consideration in assessing its social utility. Some death penalty supporters question why convicted murderers should be kept alive at taxpayer expense while serving life prison sentences. Yet perhaps surprisingly, studies carried out in several jurisdictions have concluded that the death penalty is significantly more expensive than life imprisonment.

For many reasons—the need to death-qualify jurors through prolonged questioning; the number of involved attorneys, investigators, motions, and expert witnesses; the fact that guilt and punishment are addressed at separate trials; as well as others—capital cases typically are considerably longer and more costly than noncapital cases. Extra time and expense will be incurred even if the trial does not result in a death sentence, an outcome that occurs in more than half of capital prosecutions in most jurisdictions. Death row confinement entails heightened security costs, and condemned offenders typically are incarcerated 10 to 12 years and sometimes far longer while their cases are on appeal. Since those appeals frequently result in an overturned conviction or sentence, these additional expenses are incurred in large numbers of cases that will not end in execution. Studies thus have estimated that jurisdictions using capital punishment expend millions of dollars—money that could be used for additional police officers, for health care, education, or other pressing social needs—beyond what would have been spent had life imprisonment been sought as punishment.

The risk that miscarriages of justice will result in innocent people being convicted and executed has affected death penalty debate and policies like no other issue in recent memory. DNA tests, not available at the time many inhabitants of death row were tried, have helped clear at least 16 of the 130 individuals in the modern era of capital punishment who were wrongly convicted of murder, condemned to death, and subsequently exonerated and released. It is disputed whether all 130 of those released from death row were factually innocent, but advances in science, proof of the true offender's identity, and other forms of evidence leave no doubt that many of them had nothing to do with the crimes for which they were convicted. Faulty eyewitness identification, perjured testimony, false confessions, ineffective defense counsel, prosecutorial misconduct, and forensic errors and misconduct are among the key factors contributing to such wrongful convictions.

National attention centered on the issue of innocence in 2000 when Governor George Ryan imposed a moratorium on executions in Illinois after it became apparent that the number of death-sentenced individuals exonerated in that state during the post-*Furman* era (13) exceeded the number executed (12). Ryan subsequently appointed a study commission to identify the causes of the miscarriages of justice and issue recommendations. After considering the commission's report, he determined that the risk of error in capital cases was substantial and endemic to the justice system. Unwilling to assume that risk, in 2003 he commuted the death sentences of all 167 offenders awaiting execution in Illinois to life imprisonment. He pardoned four additional individuals who had been sentenced to death.

Illinois was far from alone in experiencing the wrongful conviction and near execution of innocent people. Concerns about innocence gave rise to growing unease about the death penalty nationally. Study commissions were appointed in several other states. Many of the study commissions examined additional issues relating to the death penalty's fair administration. For example, research already had produced evidence of racial and geographic disparities in capital charging and sentencing practices in a number of jurisdictions. As in the Georgia study at issue in *McCleskey v. Kemp,* investigators in states as disparate as Florida, Maryland, California, Illinois, South Carolina, and others found evidence that white-victim murders were prosecuted capitally and resulted in death sentences far more frequently than otherwise similar murders involving nonwhite victims. Additionally, variation in prosecutors' charging and juries' sentencing practices proved to be so significant in many states that where a killing took place, for example, in an urban center versus a rural community, was a much more important determinant of whether the death penalty would be imposed than statutorily defined aggravating factors.

The composition and performance of capital trial juries also came under scrutiny. The accepted practice of "death qualifying" juries, that is, of disqualifying potential jurors whose personal opposition to capital punishment would interfere with their ability to consider voting for a death sentence on conviction, already was known to exclude disproportionately greater numbers of African Americans than whites from jury service. Further skewing the racial makeup of capital trial juries were abuses of the peremptory challenges allotted to prosecutors and defense attorneys. Although the Constitution forbids racially motivated peremptory challenges, discerning the true purposes behind discretionary jury strikes makes this prohibition difficult to enforce. It is not uncommon, and not necessarily unconstitutional, for all-white juries or juries with just a small number of minority group members to be impaneled in capital murder trials.

Other research, based on extensive posttrial interviews with former jurors in capital cases, suggests that the legal rules that have been carefully constructed in post-*Furman* Supreme Court decisions to harness sentencing discretion are ineffective in practice. This evidence reveals that capital jurors frequently fail to understand the rules they are legally obliged to follow in reaching sentencing decisions. Not surprisingly, according to the former jurors' reports, the procedures and reasons that in fact guided their decisions frequently deviated markedly from the assumptions embedded in governing law. If accurately reflecting what occurs behind the closed doors that shield jury deliberations from direct observation, these interview results suggest that capital sentencing decisions may be largely immune to legal guidance and hence remain arbitrary in the law's eyes.

Nearly all defendants charged with capital crimes are unable to hire their own lawyers and consequently must rely on court-appointed attorneys. The resources made available to court-appointed counsel in capital cases, including not only the fees they are paid but also funds to hire investigators and expert witnesses, vary widely throughout the United States. Minimum training and experience requirements also differ markedly. In some states, special capital defender units have been created and are appointed in death penalty cases unless they have a conflict of interest (such as when codefendants are on trial) or are overcommitted. Lawyers in those offices tend to be experienced and well-trained, with relatively generous operating budgets. Other states rely on public defenders, or individual court-appointed counsel.

The low fees paid in some jurisdictions discourage many capable lawyers from taking on the time-consuming and difficult work of capital litigation. And unfortunately, the attorneys who accept appointments to represent defendants in capital trials often have been found lacking in their commitment or capabilities. Some have appeared at trial intoxicated. Others have fallen asleep during trials. Still others have proven to be insufficiently experienced, knowledgeable, or capable to effectively represent a defendant on trial for his or her life. Recent Supreme Court rulings have begun to put more teeth in the expectations regarding constitutionally adequate defense counsel, but inequities involving the quality of representation available to poor people are another source of concern regarding the fair administration of justice in capital cases.

Questions involving not only whether, but also how individuals should be punished by death additionally have plagued capital punishment's administration. Lethal injection currently is the primary or exclusive method for carrying out death sentences in this country in all jurisdictions except Nebraska. (Legislation requiring use of the electric chair in Nebraska was invalidated by the state supreme court, leaving that state with a death penalty statute that presently cannot be implemented.) Originally thought to be a painless and surefire execution method, lethal injection came under challenge when contrary evidence mounted.

Critics charged that the three-drug sequence used for lethal injections often malfunctioned, paralyzing individuals subject to it, thus masking symptoms of distress, while causing excruciating pain associated with suffocation and cardiac arrest. Moreover, ethical constraints commonly preclude physicians, nurses, and others within the medical community from participating in the deliberate taking of life, leaving lethal injections to be carried out by "execution technicians" who lack commensurate training and experience. Compounding those problems, significant numbers of death-sentenced offenders abused drugs, causing the technicians difficulty in locating veins suitable for the lethal injection procedure. Concerns about lethal injection brought executions to a halt nationwide for several months beginning in 2007. Executions resumed midway through 2008, after the Supreme Court ruled that lethal injection was not an inherently cruel and unusual method for carrying out capital punishment (*Baze v. Rees*).

In the short term, and barring unforeseeable developments, the principal constitutional issues surrounding capital punishment in the United States appear to be fairly well settled. Pursuant to those principles, the states and the federal government are free to enforce death penalty laws consistent with the "guided discretion" procedures approved by the Supreme Court in 1976, and when applied for the most serious crimes and against the most highly culpable offenders. As a consequence, legislatures and, more generally, the public are left with choices about the desirability and utility of capital punishment as a public policy instrument. Many changes have occurred in death penalty policies throughout the nation's history and signs point to continuing change. However, the precise changes that will occur are difficult to predict and are unlikely to be uniform.

Death penalty practices across the United States reflect the country's diversity. At present, 14 states and Washington, D.C., do not authorize capital punishment, while 36 states, the federal government, and the U.S. military do. Even within death penalty jurisdictions, great variation exists in the laws' application. For example, death rows in 10 jurisdictions in the country presently house more than 100 offenders, topped by California with well over 600, and Florida and Texas with nearly 400. In contrast, 12 states and the U.S. military have 10 or fewer prisoners under sentence of death. Execution practices also are strikingly different. Of the more than 1,100 executions carried out in the post-*Furman* period, or since 1977, roughly 82 percent have occurred in states in the South. Texas is far and away the leading execution jurisdiction during this era, accounting for more than 400 of the total. Virginia, a distant second, has executed just over 100 offenders. Several jurisdictions with death penalty laws have executed no one, or have experienced five or fewer executions.

The death penalty is steeped with symbolism. To many, it signifies society's intolerance of violent crime and its willingness to protect and affirm the value of innocent life by exacting the ultimate punishment against those who deliberately and unlawfully take it. For others, it represents government's violation of the humanity that even guilty offenders retain, and a practice fraught with risks and plagued by unfairness, with little or no social utility. The future of capital punishment will largely be shaped by rational assessment of the death penalty's social benefits and costs, as well as views about its fundamental justice and morality.

Further Reading:

Acker, James R., Robert M. Bohm, and Charles S. Lanier, eds. *America's Experiment with Capital Punishment: Reflections on the Past, Present, and Future of the Ultimate Penal Sanction.* 2d ed. Durham, N.C.: Carolina Academic Press, 2003; Banner, Stuart. *The Death Penalty: An American History.* Cambridge, Mass.: Harvard University Press, 2002; Bedau, Hugo Adam, and Paul G. Cassell, eds. *Debating the Death Penalty: Should America Have Capital Punishment? The Experts on Both Sides Make Their Best Case.* New York: Oxford University Press, 2004; Paternoster, Raymond, Robert Brame, and Sarah Bacon. *The Death Penalty: America's Experience with Capital Punishment.* New York: Oxford University Press, 2007.

–James R. Acker

defendants' rights

This article examines the rights of a suspect in criminal proceedings. It begins with a brief discussion of the history of those rights, then proceeds into the rights of a suspect during investigation prior to the filing of formal charges, after formal charges are filed, and during trial. It concludes with rights after trial available to defendants, whether convicted or acquitted, and a summary of policy implications and concerns.

When the colonists arrived in America from Europe, most were schooled in some form of the English adversarial court system. This system guaranteed certain rights based on the 1689 English Bill of Rights. Those rights included prohibitions against excessive bail, excessive fines, and cruel and unusual punishment. At trial, defendants charged with high treason were assured the right to a trial by jury. Some other countries, but not all, included a presumption of innocence that protected defendants from having to prove a negative (that they didn't commit a crime).

When the colonists sought redress against the British government through the Declaration of Independence, they complained that they were being deprived of certain rights guaranteed them in Britain. Specifically, they alleged that the British government was depriving them of their right to a trial by jury, that "pretended offenses" were tried overseas and not where they were alleged to have been committed, and that the monarchy engaged in cruelty and tyranny.

The Constitution was adopted by convention of the states in 1787 and fully ratified by 1790. The original Constitution did not incorporate those rights initially; however, according to the government archives describing the history of ratification, many states ratified the Constitution with the understanding that those rights would eventually be incorporated. At the first congressional meeting in March 1789, 12 amendments were initially proposed. Of those proposed amendments, the first two were rejected and proposals three through 12 became the 10 enumerated amendments in the Bill of Rights. The Fourteenth Amendment later extended many of those rights to the states, requiring them to provide some of the same protections for citizens against intrusion by state governments that are provided in the Bill of Rights for citizens against intrusion by the federal government. For purposes of this brief overview of the topic, assume the rights discussed have been extended to state actions as well, unless noted otherwise.

The judicial branch has been instrumental in providing protection for citizens from unwarranted governmental intrusion when it has interpreted constitutional and legislative provisions. The Supreme Court decisions in *Gitlow v. New York* (1924) and *Mapp v. Ohio* (1961) are two of the many examples in which specific protections (First Amendment and Fourth Amendment) have been interpreted by the Court to be imposed upon state agencies. Other prominent examples of fundamental rights in the criminal justice system affected by court decisions include the oft-heard warnings developed in *Miranda v. Arizona* (1966) ("You have the right to remain silent . . ."), application of the death penalty in certain cases (*Furman v. Georgia* [1972], *Gregg v. Georgia* [1976], *Atkins v. Virginia* [2002], and *Roper v. Simmons* [2005]), confrontation of accusers (*Crawford v. Washington* [2004]), and the right to counsel in all criminal cases involving six months or more of jail time (*Argersinger v. Hamlin* [1972]).

Suspects in criminal cases have varying constitutional and statutory rights depending on the stage of any proceedings. The rights available prior to formal charges being filed are limited. Once formal charges are filed through an indictment or information (the two major terms for a document filed with a court to bring a criminal case), the rights available to a criminal defendant are more extensive.

The Fourth Amendment of the Constitution protects citizens, their houses, papers, and effects from unreasonable searches and seizures by federal government officials. This right has been extended to protect citizens from unreasonable searches and seizures by state officials as well through the Fourteenth Amendment of the Constitution and many state constitutions.

For an arrest, police must have probable cause to believe a crime has been committed and that the person being arrested is the person who committed it. Probable cause must be based on such facts and circumstances within an officer's knowledge, combined with that officer's training experience, that would lead a reasonable officer to conclude based on the totality of the circumstances that a crime has taken place.

Similarly, for a search, whether of a person, place, or thing, officers must have probable cause to believe that a crime has taken place, is taking place, or is about to take place, and probable cause to believe that evidence may be found at the location or on the person to be searched. For example, an officer investigating narcotics violations may combine his training and experience with facts learned during his investigation of a particular suspected seller's home to develop probable cause to obtain a search warrant for that home. Once inside that home, he may search anywhere narcotics may be found.

The Constitution requires officers to obtain a warrant based upon probable cause and have it signed by a neutral, detached magistrate (judge) to make arrests and conduct searches; however, this right is not absolute. Courts have interpreted extensive exceptions that allow officers to make arrests and conduct searches without a warrant; however, the presumption is that a warrantless search/seizure is invalid and the burden is on the government to prove that one of those exceptions applies in a given case. This determination is usually handled at a hearing once formal charges have been brought. Most of the exceptions are based on common sense, such as the arrest of a defendant immediately following a felony committed in the officer's presence, or the seizure of contraband that is found in plain sight by the officer.

It is pertinent to an understanding of confession law to discuss the basis for the *Miranda* warnings and how that has changed the face of investigative procedures. The Supreme Court in *Miranda v. Arizona* (1966) and a later case, *Dickerson v. U.S.* (2000), determined that specific admonishments must be given to defendants who are suspects and are in custody before an interrogation can begin.

The case stemmed from the rape and kidnapping charges levied against Ernesto Miranda after the victim identified him in a lineup. He was arrested and interrogated, acknowledging only that he understood his right against self-incrimination. His confession was subsequently used at trial. Miranda was convicted and he appealed the use of his confession. The Supreme Court decided that he should have been informed of other rights as well, and remanded the case for a new trial, this time without the introduction of his statement into evidence. (Ironically, he was convicted again at his second trial even without the confession.) The Court's opinion in *Miranda* clearly outlines the warnings used today.

The Fifth Amendment ensures due process of law, which the Court determined was denied to Miranda because he was not informed of all his rights at the time of the confession. The Fifth Amendment also ensures that an accused has a right not to incriminate oneself. What this means is that a person is not required to provide statements that tend to show that they could be guilty of a crime. In general, a person is free to choose whether to talk to the police or not. This right does not extend to basic identifying questions by the police, such as a person's name, date of birth, or address. The Fifth Amendment protection also does not extend to witnesses withholding evidence from police, obstructing a criminal investigation, or providing false information to police.

The *Miranda* warnings are legally required only if two requirements are met: (1) the suspect is in custody (most often this means they have been arrested), and (2) the police intend to interrogate the suspect by asking questions or making statements that are intended to elicit potentially incriminating information. The key aspects of these warnings are that an arrested suspect may remain silent and that a statement that is voluntarily given may be used against them. Due process considerations also require the warning that you have a right to have an attorney present during any questioning and that one will be provided. This is to provide an attorney's assurance that a person's Fifth Amendment right to remain silent is not violated through threats or coercion and to provide legal advice during an investigation. This due process aspect is a different issue from the Sixth Amendment right to counsel at trial that is discussed later in this article.

Persons who are not in custody, whether they are suspects or not, are not required to be given the *Miranda* warnings prior to any questioning by police. Likewise, persons who are arrested but not questioned by police after the arrest are not required to be given the warnings. This ensures that the police conduct a thorough investigation of all parties, including taking statements from a suspect if that person cooperates, prior to making a determination of whether to file charges or make an arrest in the case. Obviously this is not always possible and police must often make decisions in their investigations based on the evidence they do collect.

Until the filing of charges, the defendant is merely a suspect and is still free to go about his or her daily routine. However, arresting and charging a defendant formally requires this person to answer for the allegations that he or she has committed a crime, which suddenly invokes many obligations on the accused, as well as more federal and state constitutional and statutory protections. The Fourth Amendment still applies, as well as the Fifth Amendment privilege against self-incrimination. The Fifth Amendment also provides the right to a grand jury indictment in federal capital, or infamous, cases. This right has been extended by statutes, state constitutions, and by custom to all felony offenses at the federal and state levels. Also included in the Fifth Amendment is a privilege against governmental deprivation of life, liberty, or property without due process of law. "Due process of law" means that a person is entitled to have a hearing or trial before a tribunal (court or administrative judge) and have a legal determination made before the government may detain a person for an unreasonable length of time or forfeit their property over to the government. As discussed above, it also includes the right to be given certain warnings prior to a custodial interrogation.

The Sixth Amendment also plays a large role once an arrest has been made or formal charges have been filed. Approximately eight rights in criminal cases are guaranteed by the Sixth Amendment. Perhaps the most well-known is the right to counsel. Once a person has been arrested or charged, adversarial proceedings have begun, and at each "critical stage" a person is entitled to be represented by an attorney and to have one appointed if a court makes a determination that the accused is unable to afford an attorney. Critical stages prior to a trial include the presentation of the accused before a magistrate, a live lineup or showup (if formal charges have been filed), and any pretrial matters that must be heard before the trial court. The accused is also entitled to be informed of the nature and cause of the accusations.

When an accused is arrested, the Eighth Amendment provides that excessive bail may not be imposed. The federal Bail Reform Act, as well as many state constitutions and statutes, also address specific details of this right. However, circumstances exist in which courts are permitted to refuse a defendant bail, such as in the case of a person charged with capital murder who would be a flight risk, or in circumstances in which a determination is made that there is a serious risk that the defendant may threaten or obstruct a witness. In *United States v. Salerno* (1987), the Supreme Court held that there is no absolute right to bail. The main purpose of bail is to provide a financial guarantee to the court that the accused will appear in court if the person is released before trial, and it may take the form of personal recognizance (payment to the court of a fixed amount only upon the failure of the defendant to appear in court), cash, or surety (the use of a bail bondsman to guarantee both the appearance of the defendant and the funds should the defendant fail to appear).

Bail may also be used to protect the community and the victim of an offense, and terms of release known as "conditions of bond/bail" may be imposed upon a criminal defendant. For example, a defendant may be ordered to report for drug testing, to stay a certain distance away from a person or place, or to have a leg monitor. In setting the amount of bail and the conditions of release, courts consider many statutory and traditionally relevant factors. These include:

1. The nature and circumstances of the offense, in particular, whether it is an offense that is violent or nonviolent in nature, or involving narcotics;
2. The weight of the evidence against the person;
3. The history and characteristics of the person. This includes character (including physical and mental condition, family ties, employment, financial resources, length of time in the community, community ties, past conduct history relating to drug or alcohol abuse, criminal history, record of court appearances) and status (whether at the time of the current offense or arrest, the person was on probation, on parole, or on other release pending trial, sentencing, appeal, or completion of sentence for an offense under federal, state, or local law); and
4. The nature and seriousness of the danger to any person or to the community that would be posed by the person's release.

Additional factors that courts have considered include whether the amount of bail is sufficiently high to give reasonable assurance that the defendant will appear in court, yet not oppressive to the defendant; whether the defendant is able to make bail (although it is not required that bail be set at an amount that a defendant can make); and the future safety of a complainant.

The rights of a defendant that exist pretrial continue through until a formal disposition of the case is made, whether it is through a plea agreement or a trial. A defendant who decides to challenge the charges continues to have a Fifth Amendment privilege against self-incrimination; a judge or jury may not hold that person's silence against them in any way, nor may it be considered for any purpose.

A defendant is entitled throughout a trial to the presumption of innocence. The government has the burden of presenting enough evidence to convince a judge or jury beyond a reasonable doubt that the defendant is guilty of a crime. Proving a case beyond a reasonable doubt overcomes the presumption of innocence.

The Sixth Amendment right to counsel includes the right to have an attorney of the defendant's choosing if that person is retained, but the defendant does not get to choose who represents him or her if an attorney is appointed. A defendant may also choose to appear *pro se*. This means that upon an intelligent and knowing waiver in open court, a person may represent himself or herself.

The remainder of the Sixth Amendment rights not previously covered also come into play at the trial. A defendant is entitled to a speedy and public jury trial, to confront the witnesses against him or her, and to have a compulsory process for obtaining witnesses on his or her behalf (usually accomplished through a subpoena). A speedy trial does not mean that the trial must take place within a designated period of time, but the time it takes to bring a case to trial must be reasonable and the delays must not have been the result of wrongdoing on the part of the government. The court will review on a case-by-case basis a defendant's claim that his or her right to a speedy trial was violated, considering many factors. For instance, the intentional absence of the defendant from the jurisdiction would be a factor against the defendant in such a claim, whereas deliberate delays by the government would weigh in favor of the defendant. The purpose of a speedy trial is to improve the credibility of the proceedings by having witnesses testify as soon as possible when their memory is still fresh, as well as ensuring the availability of those witnesses. It also reduces anxiety for the defendant, reduces the length of pretrial incarceration, and avoids delays and conduct that might jeopardize the defendant's right to a fair trial or the defendant's ability to defend himself or herself.

A public trial is intended to protect a defendant from having an unfair proceeding behind closed doors. The trial is usually required to take place in the location where the offense took place, although, in certain circumstances, a defendant may not be able to receive a fair trial at that location due to pretrial publicity. In those cases either the government or the defendant may make a formal request to transfer venue, that is, to move the location of the trial to a place where it is more likely that the potential jury pool will be unaffected by the publicity surrounding a trial.

A defendant has the option of a jury trial or a trial before the judge, often known as a bench trial. Generally, the default position is that a jury will hear a case and both sides (the government and the defendant) must affirmatively waive, or give up, the right to have a jury for the case to be heard by the judge alone. The purpose of a jury trial is to have unbiased, disinterested persons hear the evidence in a given case and make a factual decision as to whether the government has proved beyond a reasonable doubt the guilt of the defendant. In cases for which a jury is waived, the judge makes this factual decision.

The right to a jury is nearly always waived in cases for which a plea agreement is reached with the government. A plea agreement is a process in which a defendant pleads guilty (or sometimes, *nolo contendere*, or no contest) in exchange for a recommended sentence from the government. Occasionally, a defendant decides that he or she wishes to plead guilty without the benefit of an agreed-upon sentence because it is believed that a judge or jury might give a more lenient sentence than the government's recommendation. In such cases, the "trial" would simply be a sentencing hearing without a determination of the factual question of the guilt of the defendant, because that issue would no longer be contested.

In general, the government is required to disclose a list of witnesses to the defense at some point prior to the trial. In some venues this is required to be done well in advance of the day of trial; in other venues this is required to be done not later than immediately prior to the jury selection process. In part, this is so that the defense has an adequate opportunity to investigate the witnesses. Another purpose for providing a witness list is so that, during the jury selection process, the prospective jurors may be informed who the potential witnesses will be so any conflicts can be brought to the court's attention prior to trial.

The confrontation clause of the Sixth Amendment, state constitutions, and federal and state statutes requires that witnesses in most circumstances must be physically present in the courtroom for the defendant and his or her attorney to be able to view them and cross-examine them in open court. Some exceptions to this general rule include witnesses who might be placed in physical danger if they are not minimally disguised, as in *U.S. v. Marzook* (2006), or child victims of sexual assault if it is shown that they would be traumatized to see the accused in court such that they would be unable to provide their testimony, as described in the Supreme Court decision in *Maryland v. Craig* (1990). In such cases, children have been permitted to testify through closed circuit television or other alternative means. In all cases in which an exception has applied, an important public policy is at stake and the reliability of the testimony was otherwise assured.

The Federal Rules of Evidence and all state rules generally restrict hearsay or secondhand evidence from being considered by a judge or jury. Hearsay is defined as an out-of-court statement (either oral or written) being offered for the truth of that statement. For example, if a statement by Bob that he claimed to be Elvis is being offered to show that he is, in fact, Elvis, that statement would be hearsay. However, if the statement is being offered to show that Bob is suffering from dementia, the statement is not hearsay because it is not being offered to show the truth of the statement itself. In that case, it would be admitted into evidence. Not all hearsay is excluded; a number of exceptions may still apply. These exceptions are long-standing in legal decisions as having some reliability beyond a typical statement, and they are generally listed in the specific rules of evidence of the jurisdiction hearing the case.

During sentencing, many of the same rules apply, but some rules of evidence are relaxed to permit the finder of fact to consider things such as prior criminal record of the defendant and the character of the defendant, good or bad, in assessing the appropriate punishment for the crime and the particular defendant on trial. The defendant's rights are still protected during the sentencing hearing through rules of procedure, evidence, and the constitutional prohibition against cruel and unusual punishment.

Different rights and relief are available to defendants after a trial has taken place. The specific rights and remedies depend on whether the "trial" was based on a plea agreement, was an actual trial resulting in a guilty verdict, or was a trial that resulted in an acquittal. Those remedies may include any or all of the following: motion for new trial, appeal, writ of habeas corpus, and (in the case of an acquittal or overturned conviction) expunction. Most of these rights and remedies are provided by federal and state statutes.

If a defendant is found guilty, either by a plea or by a trial, the presumption of innocence has been overcome and no longer applies. No specific burden of proof exists during sentencing in most cases, unless the evidence includes other bad acts or crimes committed by the defendant, in which case the judge or jury must believe beyond a reasonable doubt that those other acts occurred in order to consider them against the defendant at punishment.

If a plea agreement is reached, the defendant is found guilty and is sentenced in accordance with the agreement. As part of that agreement, the defendant ordinarily must waive any post-conviction relief, specifically appeal. In those cases, once the defendant is sentenced, the process ends and the defendant serves his or her sentence.

If there is a trial rather than an agreement, there is no waiver of those rights. A defendant may file a motion for a new trial in the interest of justice if the jury's verdict is so contrary to the great weight of the evidence that the verdict is unjust, or if there is newly discovered evidence. Most courts will not grant this motion, but, in certain circumstances, it is a prerequisite to filing some claims on appeal and the motion must be made and heard.

Appeals can be taken on numerous issues ranging from incorrect decisions by the trial court on the admission of certain evidence to the inclusion of certain jurors who should have been excluded (or exclusion of certain jurors who should have been included) to ineffective assistance of counsel. The first appeal of a conviction is a fundamental constitutional right for which the defendant is entitled to have counsel appointed. During appeal, depending on the jurisdiction and the sentence imposed, the defendant may or may not be entitled to have an appeal bond, which would release him or her from any sentence imposed while the appeal is pending.

Once a defendant has been convicted and has raised his or her issues on appeal, there may be situations not covered or allowed on appeal, such as the discovery of new evidence that could not have been discovered prior to trial, new forensic testing, or claims that the defendant is being treated cruelly and unusually. These types of claims must be handled through a writ of habeas corpus. A writ is a request that a court order someone to do something or refrain from doing something. These requests are specifically for a court to order the defendant's release based on the circumstances. These are very infrequently granted, but, in recent years, with new DNA technologies becoming available, many more writ cases are making the news because increasing numbers of exonerations of innocent people have been granted.

If a person is incarcerated, a writ might be filed if the person is not receiving credit for time he or she has already served on a case. Some people on probation attempt to file writs because additional terms and conditions of probation are added. Each case is considered independently and is decided on the facts of that specific situation. It is impossible to predict all the situations in which a defendant might feel entitled to this type of relief.

Another remedy available to some defendants in some situations is civil liability. For example, the prohibition against cruel and unusual punishment requires that inmates be provided adequate medical care. If inmates have been denied medical treatment, they may sue to have that provided for them. Likewise, inmates are entitled to have access to legal materials if they are not being represented by counsel. If an inmate is being denied access to legal materials, the government may be liable to that defendant.

Finally, defendants who are tried and acquitted, or who are convicted and successfully appeal their cases resulting in their convictions being overturned, may be entitled to an expunction. An expunction is a process in which a court orders that the records of any arrest, bail, incarceration, trial, or appeal shall be destroyed, and the defendant may legitimately claim that he or she has never been arrested or convicted of an offense. Most states have statutes and rules of procedure in place that address how an expunction should be requested and carried out.

A similar procedure may be available for defendants who receive a form of probation called deferred adjudication. The idea behind deferred adjudication is that a defendant can be rehabilitated by completing conditions of probation but without an actual finding of guilt if he or she successfully completes those conditions. Some jurisdictions provide that a defendant who successfully completes deferred adjudication may have those records sealed or "nondisclosed" from certain public records requests, but those records will not be destroyed. However, it may help those defendants who are starting their lives over if potential employers are unable to view those records.

Numerous debates are ongoing regarding the rights of defendants at different points during the criminal justice process, particularly regarding death penalty cases and claims of actual innocence. Human rights' advocates and advocates for victims' rights are at odds over balancing closure for victims of crime with the process of ensuring fair trials and accurate outcomes for defendants. These issues are not easily resolved. At some point, the judicial system has to draw a line in the sand and say that cases are decided and defendants have received a full and fair opportunity to litigate their cases. Having ongoing debate and appeals in the courts over years and years decreases certainty in trial outcomes and reduces overall confidence in the justice system.

Other strong considerations with no easy answer include unfunded mandates by court opinions that interpret "new" rights and statutes that increase the workload for already overworked public defenders and private practitioners who accept criminal court appointments. Their ethical duties to their clients are often compromised by the increased workload, potentially creating the Hobson's choice of being grieved with their local bar association (and therefore risking their license) because "they didn't do enough" or they "forced" their clients to take a plea agreement instead of going to trial, or refusing to engage in the practice of criminal law at all, leaving fewer attorneys to do the work.

Additionally, increasing mandatory judicial processes to ensure the rights of defendants in court, where dockets are already overwhelmed, takes a significant amount of time with no corresponding increase in judicial resources. Police agencies and prosecutors are also concerned with these issues because they are entrusted with following these ever-changing procedures and ensuring that the responsibilities of all parties are carried out.

It is impossible to address every legal issue, legal right, or policy concern that could be relevant in an individual case. This entry merely skims the surface of major rights and remedies available to criminal defendants; it is not intended to replace legal advice if a person is charged with a crime. It should also be noted that this is an area of law that is constantly evolving, and it will continue to develop through case law and statutes as society responds to scientific advances, changing mores, and the never-ending debate about how to balance the needs of law enforcement with the desire to protect the individual.

Further Reading:
del Carmen, Rolando V. *Criminal Procedure: Law and Practice*, 7th ed. Belmont, Calif.: Wadsworth, 2007; Lewis, Anthony. *Gideon's Trumpet*. New York: Random House, 1964; Senna, Joseph, and Larry Siegel. *Essentials of Criminal Justice*. St. Paul, Minn.: West Publishing, 1995; Stone, Geoffrey R., et al. *Constitutional Law*, 5th ed. New York: Aspen Publishers: 2005.

– *Gretchen H. Choe*

---

drunk driving

The consequences of combining alcohol consumption with being behind the steering wheel of a motor vehicle have been a persistent concern of government officials and the American public for some time. Whether referred to as drunk driving, alcohol-impaired driving, driving under the influence (DUI), or driving while intoxicated (DWI), it remains a persistent public health problem. Although even low levels of alcohol consumption can impair driver judgment and response, the National Highway Traffic Safety Administration (NHTSA) defines an alcohol impaired driver as a driver having a blood alcohol concentration (BAC) of 0.08 or higher. BAC level refers to the grams of alcohol per deciliter of blood (g/dL). For instance, a BAC of 0.08 equates to about 8 parts of alcohol per 10,000 parts of blood.

While impaired driving remains an important public issue, the amount of impaired driving in the United States is at its lowest level since the 1980s when the federal government began tracking the issue. A 2007 national roadside survey of alcohol use by weekend drivers conducted by NHTSA found that 2.2 percent had BAC levels at or above 0.08. This represents a large decline from the results of previous NHTSA-sponsored national roadside surveys: 1973, 7.5 percent; 1986, 5.4 percent; and 1996, 4.3 percent. The 2007 survey also found driving with a 0.08+ BAC level to be more common among men, late at night, and among drivers of motorcycles.

The consequences of impaired driving can best be illustrated by the number of lives it claims. While it is difficult to determine whether alcohol impairment actually caused a fatal crash to occur, a common indicator is the number of fatalities that occur in crashes involving a driver with a BAC of 0.08 or higher. While likely overstating the severity of the problem, these statistics provide an indication of the trend over time.

NHTSA estimates that for the period 1982 to 2007 fatal motor vehicle crashes involving an alcohol-impaired driver claimed 399,275 lives, accounting for 36 percent of all traffic fatalities. In 1982, 48 percent of traffic fatalities involved an alcohol-impaired driver, a rate that steadily declined to 30 percent by 1997 and has remained fairly steady since with 32 percent in 2007.

The fatality data indicate that drunk driving is more common at nighttime, on weekends, and during holidays. While drunk driving is most common among young adult drivers, it is by no means only confined to this group. Among drivers involved in fatal crashes in 2007, 35 percent of those 22 to 24 years of age were alcohol-impaired as compared to 29 percent of those 25 to 34 years of age, and 23 percent of those 45 to 54 years of age. Impaired driving also occurs among those not of legal age as 18 percent of drivers under 21 years of age in a fatal crash were estimated to be alcohol-impaired. Furthermore, of the 14,447 drivers with a detectable alcohol level, it is estimated that 84 percent had a BAC of at least 0.08 and 55 percent (7,794) had BAC levels of 0.15 or higher.

In an effort to further describe the toll of impaired driving, Lawrence Blincoe and his colleagues estimate that alcohol annually causes 13,750 fatalities (a third of all traffic fatalities) and over 360,000 nonfatal injuries, and imposes economic costs of nearly $40 billion.

The dominant depiction of the impaired-driving problem in public debate is the "killer drunk" definition. This definition regards the problem as the result of the irresponsible use of alcohol by a small portion of the drinking population. The impaired driver is portrayed as visibly inebriated and as an individual who shows a blatant disregard for society by getting behind the wheel of a motor vehicle and likely has a history of impaired-driving offenses. Drunk driving is the most common violent crime committed in America and the image of its perpetrators is that of social deviants culpable for their actions who respond only to punishment.

Under the killer drunk definition, the goals of government policy are retribution and deterrence. Because drunk driving is a violent act against society, it is sinful behavior for which the sinner deserves to be punished. It is further hoped that by being punished, the convicted drunk driver will be deterred from future recurrences, as will other potential sinners. Deterrence theory assumes that individuals are utility maximizers who engage in behaviors because the perceived benefits (or pleasure) outweigh the costs. Once the costs are judged to exceed any derived benefits, an individual will no longer choose to engage in the undesired behavior. Thus, the heart of the process is the perceived costs imposed by government sanctions. Government interventions increase the cost of undesired behavior by increasing the certainty, severity, and celerity (or swiftness) of punishment. Identifying and punishing the drunk driver are responsibilities of law enforcement and the courts, making the institutions of criminal law central actors in implementing antidrunk driving policy.

An alternative definition of impaired driving takes a public health perspective. It regards impaired driving as a predictable, unfortunate consequence of a society that embraces alcohol use in social situations and highly values the private automobile as the primary mode of transportation. As such, individuals who drink and drive may actually be adhering to the social norms of the groups and of the contexts in which they find themselves. The consequences are especially acute for underage drivers, who are inexperienced with both alcohol consumption and driving. Furthermore, for a segment of the population, impaired driving is a result of the disease of alcohol addiction.

This alternative problem definition regards impaired drivers as a heterogeneous group. Alcohol impairment is often difficult to detect and the drinking driver may not be aware of his level of impairment. Most impaired drivers lack prior convictions and primarily harm themselves and their passengers. This definition recognizes that the vast majority of impaired driving trips do not result in crashes and are undetected by law enforcement.

The target group is the entire population of drinkers, all of whom are potential impaired drivers, as any level of impairment raises the risk of a crash. For this reason, the definition is concerned with any behavior that involves a combination of alcohol use that induces impairment and driving a motor vehicle. The culpability of the act varies with the circumstance and retribution is not a relevant policy goal.

Reflecting the diversity of people and circumstances that leads to impaired driving, a wide range of countermeasures are espoused. First, deterrent-based policies are a part of this strategy as long as they can be demonstrated to be effective at reducing crashes, injuries, and fatalities. Second, it embraces alcohol-control policies that reduce consumption, especially in places where people are likely to drink and drive. A third set of policy interventions aim at reducing the social incentive to drink and then drive, such as educational campaigns that affect social norms and restrictions on the promotion and marketing practices of the alcohol industry. Fourth, policies focus on treatment for problem drinkers on the premise that alcohol addiction is a disease. A fifth category of policy options center around transportation policies to reduce reliance upon the private automobile for those who consume alcohol.

While both problem definitions have been present throughout debates on impaired driving, the killer-drunk definition has dominated. As sociologist Joseph Gusfield writes, "It is because of the *killer drunk*—that antisocial, hedonistic, uncontrolled menace—is believed to tear (or reel) around our roads, that criminal law enforcement directed at individual offenders is, and will remain, the major method for dealing with drinking-and-driving." The killer-drunk definition has held sway for several reasons. First, its dominance speaks to the influence of the antidrunk driving citizens' movement (e.g., Mothers Against Drunk Driving, Remove Intoxicated Drivers) and their ability to put a human face on the consequences of impaired driving. This influence has been magnified by media interest in these stories, which draw public attention.

Second, the rise of impaired driving on the public agenda coincided with the more conservative political mood of the nation since the 1980s. Portraying drunk drivers as culpable for the consequences of their behavior is compatible with the belief that social problems result from individual acts of social deviance, not the result of societal or structural forces. Third, the killer-drunk definition is supported by the alcohol beverage industry because it does not require the industry to accept responsibility or to change, as it is the small number of "social deviants" who need to act more socially responsible.

The licensing of motor vehicles and drivers, and the regulation of alcohol consumption and sales, are regarded as state prerogatives. Thus, state governments have the primary responsibility for crafting policy to mitigate the harmful effects of alcohol-impaired driving. Due to the dominance of the killer-drunk problem definition, the linchpin in the battle against drunk driving has been a reliance on a deterrence-based strategy. States attempt to discourage impaired driving by imposing sanctions that increase the severity, certainty, and celerity of punishment.

Increasing the severity of punishment for drunk driving requires little effort and symbolizes a state "getting tough" on criminal behavior. The primary sanctions that states impose are fines and jail sentences. Thirty-three states statutorily set a minimum fine for a first-time DUI conviction with the median fine being $300. Additionally, 24 states have established minimum jail sentences for first-time DUI offenders with the median sentence being two days. The severity of the sanctions typically increases with additional DUI convictions. For instance, 32 states provide for vehicle impoundment or forfeiture for some multiple offenders. Sanctions are also heavier in many states for convicted drivers with high BACs.

Tools that pertain to the certainty of punishment increase the probability that impaired driving will be detected or that punishment will be imposed. Most notable among these are illegal per se laws that define the operation of a motor vehicle by a driver with a BAC at or above a specified level as a criminal offense. Defining a BAC level as conclusive proof that a driver is impaired means that faulty driving need not be established and makes a legal challenge to an arrest more difficult. Initially, states typically defined a BAC of 0.10 or 0.15 as illegal but, as of September 2009, all states and the District of Columbia have a 0.08 BAC illegal per se law. Similarly, zero tolerance laws target young drivers by setting a lower BAC as the legal limit for drivers under the legal age. Since 1998, all states have had a zero tolerance law with a 0.02 BAC limit.

Implied consent laws, open container laws, and sobriety checkpoints are other tools used by states to increase the certainty of punishment. Implied consent laws stipulate that by applying for a driver's license it is inferred that an individual consents to submit to a field sobriety, breath, or other test to determine level of intoxication. Thirty-four states and the District of Columbia have enacted implied consent laws that require an arrest for refusing to submit to a test for alcohol impairment and an automatic suspension of a driver's license. Open container laws make it illegal to have an open container of alcohol in the passenger compartment of a motor vehicle. Thirty-eight states and the District of Columbia have open container laws that apply to everyone in a motor vehicle and an additional five state laws apply only to the driver.

In the late 1990s, statewide sobriety checkpoints began to be conducted by states, adopting a strategy used by local governments. These checkpoints are roadblocks set up along the side of a road through which motor vehicles must pass. When stopped, a law enforcement officer informs the driver about the purpose of the roadblock and asks a few questions. If the driver exhibits behavioral or physical characteristics of alcohol impairment, the officer administers field sobriety and/or breath tests to assess whether the driver's impairment or alcohol level warrants a DUI arrest. Sobriety checkpoints are permitted in 40 states and the District of Columbia. A study conducted by James Fell and his colleagues at the Insurance Institute for Highway Safety reported that only 13 states conduct sobriety checkpoints every week, while some conduct them only several times per year.

Lastly, the celerity with which punishment is meted out is increased by administrative license revocation (ALR, or administrative per se laws), whereby law enforcement is authorized to suspend a driver's license at the time of a DUI arrest. Forty-one states and the District of Columbia have such a law.

A second general strategy that states use is to regulate the consumption and sale of alcohol, at least in situations in which driving is likely to follow. The most prominent of these alcohol-control policies is restricting the alcohol access of young drivers. After the end of Prohibition, states generally regarded 21 years as the minimum legal drinking age (MLDA). But in the early 1970s, 29 states lowered the MLDA in keeping with the trend lowering the legal age for activities such as voting. By the end of the decade an increase in alcohol-related fatalities among young drivers led to a reversal of this trend. The push for higher MLDAs was given a boost in the form of federal government pressure on states and, by 1988, all had adopted a MLDA of 21 years of age.

Because drunk drivers are most likely to have had their last drink at a bar or restaurant, states also use alcohol-control policies to reduce overconsumption at commercial establishments. For instance, 22 states prohibit sales practices and promotions by commercial establishments that encourage excessive alcohol consumption by patrons. These "happy hour" laws prohibit offering reduced price or multiple drink specials, drinking contests, alcohol as a contest prize, or any practice or event that is expected to encourage excessive consumption. Also, 41 states have dram shop laws that establish the liability of businesses that sell or serve alcohol to an underage or clearly intoxicated patron, for the harm caused by the patron to a third party in an alcohol-related crash. Among the penalties an establishment may face under a dram shop law are alcohol license revocation, fines, and monetary damages.

A third general state strategy for combating impaired driving is education and treatment. Education and hortatory tools are designed to discourage drinking-and-driving behavior. Common among these efforts are mass media campaigns and public service announcements that oftentimes are funded with federal dollars. These campaigns contain messages about the legal consequences of impaired driving, or they focus on the social and health consequences of drinking and driving. Messages seek to increase knowledge, heighten fear, and/or model desired behavior.

Aside from serving as a law enforcement event, a DUI arrest provides the opportunity to identify individuals with alcohol abuse or dependency problems. Laws in 36 states mandate that those convicted of a DUI offense participate in alcohol assessment and treatment. The nature of these legal requirements varies significantly from state to state and depends on the nature of the offense. Typically states screen for alcohol abuse and dependency problems, require attendance at DUI school, and may refer the convicted driver to treatment.

While states are the primary makers of anti-drunk driving policies, the federal government has played an important secondary role. It has dangled grants-in-aid as "carrots" and wielded crossover sanctions as "sticks" to motivate states to adopt desired national policies. For instance, the Drunk Driving Prevention Act of 1988 established incentive grants for states that met specific criteria, including an under 21-year-old drinking prevention program and an open container law. The Safe, Accountable, Flexible, Efficient Transportation Equity Act-A Legacy for Users (SAFETEA-LU) of 2005 tripled the amount of funds offered under previous statutes and raised the minimum criteria states had to satisfy. Initially these incentive grants had little effect on state policy, but as successive statutes increased the amount offered under the grant program and expanded the eligibility criteria, states adopted more of the targeted policies.

More effective has been the federal government's use of crossover sanctions, which are penalties placed on grants-in-aid or privileges in one policy area for not complying with requirements in a different policy area. For instance, Congress passed the Federal Uniform Drinking Age Act in 1984 that authorized the secretary of transportation to withhold 10 percent of federal highway funds from any state with an MLDA lower than 21 years of age. The Consolidated Omnibus Budget Reconciliation Act of 1985 authorized this to be a permanent withholding of a state's highway funds and, by 1989, all had raised the legal age to 21 years, establishing a uniform national MLDA. Similarly, the Transportation Equity Act for the 21st Century (TEA-21) of 1998 threatened states without a 0.08 BAC illegal per se law with a loss of 2 percent of their federal highway fund allocation beginning in 2003, a penalty that would increase each year up to a maximum of 8 percent in 2007. Only 15 states had 0.08 BAC laws in effect prior to TEA-21 and, by 2005, all states had complied.

Another stick the federal government has used is to direct highway funds from highway projects to traffic safety programs. While a state still receives the specified federal funds, they lose discretion over the use of those funds. This type of provision was included in TEA-21 and required states to adopt an open container law or else have up to 3 percent of their allocation transferred to impaired driving programs. Ten states adopted open container provisions in anticipation of, or shortly after, the implementation of the diversion provision but 15 states continued to resist. SAFETEA-LU strengthened the diversion mechanism and resulted in 11 states having highway funds transferred to safety programs because of noncompliance with its provisions.

Local governments also play a key role in reducing drunk driving as they have the primary responsibility for enforcing state laws. It is local law enforcement agencies that are responsible for identifying and arresting impaired drivers. After an arrest is made, the prosecution of the offense is in the hands of local prosecutors and courts, who also make the decisions about punishment and mandated treatments. Similarly, any jail time is served in facilities operated by local law enforcement, and local government arranges or administers any treatment programs that are required. Amid fears that not all prosecutors and judges were equally concerned with impaired driving, some states have reduced punishment discretion with laws that prohibit plea bargaining in DUI cases and that establish minimum penalties for a DUI conviction.

Despite the emphasis placed on a deterrent-based approach built on severe sanctions, the general conclusion that emerges from the econometric-based evaluations is that punitive drinking-and-driving laws are not effective. The deterrent effect of severe sanctions is undermined by the low probability of an arrest on any impaired driving trip.

It is the certainty and celerity of punishment that are regarded as having the greater deterrent potential. The implementation of 0.08 BAC illegal per se and zero tolerance laws are typically associated with lower state alcohol-related fatality rates, an effect most pronounced for young adults and teens. While zero tolerance laws have not eliminated alcohol consumption for young drivers, it appears that these drivers consume less alcohol than was the case prior to the implementation of these laws.

Sobriety checkpoints are regarded as an effective tool for increasing perceptions about the certainty of detection. Although some impaired drivers do slip through, sobriety checkpoints that are highly visible and frequently conducted and that screen many drivers are the most effective at reducing crashes, especially those that are alcohol related. The constitutionality of this antidrunk driving strategy has been challenged as a violation of the Fourth Amendment's guarantee of protection against unreasonable search and seizure. However, in 1990, the U.S. Supreme Court ruled that, if administered properly, the public purpose of minimizing the harm caused by drunk driving justifies the minimal intrusion on civil liberties that results from checkpoint procedures.

Increasing the celerity of punishment with administrative license revocation also is effective at reducing drunk driving. Driver's license suspension is the most effective sanction for reducing DUI recidivism. While research has found that most continue to drive with a suspended license, they tend to do so less frequently and drive in a safer manner that will not attract attention. As a

A sobriety checkpoint in East Haven, Connecticut *(Photo by Versageek/ Used under a Creative Commons license)*

result, the implementation of ALR is associated with lower alcohol-related fatality rates.

Alcohol-control policies are among the most effective tools states have used to combat drunk driving. The most frequently studied of these policies is the MLDA (21 year old), which has been consistently found to have resulted in lower motor vehicle fatality rates. Also effective are dram shop laws, which are among the policies most strongly associated with reduced alcohol-related fatalities. In contrast, a general assessment of "happy hour" laws cannot be made due to a lack of research.

Results associated with education and treatment approaches are less well established and appear to be more moderate. This is in part because mass media campaigns typically are implemented in ways that do not permit easy evaluation and because treatment programs vary greatly in design and implementation. In terms of mass media campaigns, no single campaign has been identified as effective in reducing drunk driving, although many traffic safety experts regard these as a necessary component in a government response to affect attitudes toward drinking and driving gradually over time.

Regarding rehabilitation, treatment programs can have some effect at reducing DUI recidivism under certain circumstances. Important to achieving this effect is that treatment be used alongside of sanctions (e.g., license suspension), not in lieu of, that individuals be assigned to the proper type of program for their needs, and that offenders be motivated to participate in the program. The heterogeneous nature of the impaired driving population suggests that a variety of program types are needed.

An increased emphasis on the hard-core drunk driver (multiple DUI offenses, high BAC) is likely to characterize future debates on impaired driving. Despite the ineffectiveness of deterrent-based tools that increase the severity of punishment, citizen groups and traffic safety officials promote stiffer sanctions in the form of higher minimum fines and jail terms to deter the hard-core drunk driver. Additionally, vehicle impoundment or forfeiture, license plate impoundment, and ignition interlock devices are touted as important components of deterrence policy. This latter set of sanctions focuses more on the state's ability to not simply deter behavior, but to incapacitate the hard-core drunk driver.

The need to increase the subjective probability of the certainty of punishment is receiving attention. To increase perceptions of the likelihood of detection, greater emphasis on sobriety checkpoints is encouraged, as well as dedicated DUI patrols in areas where impaired driving is most likely to occur. Greater emphasis is also being placed on increasing the likelihood that punishment will incur if an arrest is made. More support is building for funding special prosecutors who have the training and resources to prosecute DUI offenders, and special DUI courts that will more swiftly and competently process DUI offenses.

The challenge that proponents of these policies face is that increasing the certainty that impaired driving is detected and punished is expensive to accomplish. Noticeably absent from discussions is the additional use of alcohol-control policies (e.g., alcohol taxes) and transportation policies that would reduce reliance on private automobiles as tools for reducing impaired driving.

Further Reading

Blincoe, Lawrence J., et al. "The Economic Impact of Motor Vehicle Crashes, 2000." DOT HS 809 446. Washington, D.C.: NHTSA, U.S. DOT, 2002; Compton, Richard, and Amy Berning. "Results of the 2007 National Roadside Survey of Alcohol and Drug Use by Drivers. Traffic Safety Facts: Research Note." DOT HS 811 175. Washington, D.C.: NHTSA National Center for Statistics and Analysis, 2009; Fell, James C., Susan A. Ferguson, Allan F. Williams, and Michelle Fields. "Why Aren't Sobriety Checkpoints Widely Adopted as an Enforcement Strategy in the United States?" Arlington, Va.: Insurance Institute for Highway Safety, 2001; Gusfield, Joseph R. *The Culture of Public Problems: Drinking-Driving and the Symbolic Order.* Chicago: University of Chicago Press, 1981; NHTSA. "Traffic Safety Facts 2007: A Compilation of Motor Vehicle Crash Data from the Fatality Analysis Reporting System and the General Estimates System." DOT HS 811 002. Washington, D.C.: U.S. DOT, NHTSA, 2009; Ross, H. Laurence. *Deterring the Drinking Driver: Legal Policy and Social Control.* Lexington, Mass.: Lexington Books, 1984.

– David J. Houston and Lilliard E. Richardson, Jr.

gun control

The debate over gun control and gun policy in America has long been one of the most contentious issues in American politics. It incorporates not only contemporary legal and political disputes over the extent to which the government should or should not regulate guns, but also encompasses ancestral and cultural attachments to guns, historical practices, criminological consequences, and the relationship between citizens, the military, and the government. While contemporary politics has been punctuated by sharp political disputes over various types of gun regulations, laws regulating guns and gun ownership have existed throughout American history, even predating the Revolutionary era. In recent decades, the political and policy debate has intensified while the nature of the controls contemplated has centered on relatively limited changes.

Gun possession in America extends back to its earliest settlements, beginning with Jamestown and Plymouth, where guns were used for hunting and protection. Yet guns were relatively rare, and were seldom associated with interpersonal violence. Most significant gun-related violence occurred between Native Americans and European settlers, and later as a primary tool of war. In early conflicts, including the Revolutionary War, limited gun availability among the general population proved to be a severe problem, as American military leaders, including General George Washington, regularly complained that service-eligible males lacked not only working firearms, but the basic knowledge of their use and maintenance. The relative rarity of guns in early America is attributable to several facts. Guns were expensive, as they were made mostly by hand by blacksmiths (the first gun factory in America did not begin operation until 1790), who might perhaps turn out a couple of dozen weapons in a year. They were made of iron, meaning that they rusted quickly without regular maintenance; they required parts and materials, like gunpowder, that were often difficult to obtain and deteriorated rapidly; they were cumbersome and dangerous to operate, requiring the operator to have considerable skill. A well-maintained firearm, used periodically, could be expected to last no more than about five years. And while some colonials hunted regularly for food and pelts, most were subsistence farmers who relied on agricultural produce and domesticated livestock for food. Guns were also imported from Europe at substantial expense, but as the Revolution neared, import became more difficult.

Gun ownership became widespread in America around the time of the Civil War, when millions of men became acquainted with the use of firearms during military service, and technological improvements in gun manufacturing and standardization of ammunition made guns safer and easier to operate, more reliable, more prolific, and less expensive. As early as the 1850s, gun manufacturer Samuel Colt aggressively marketed revolvers to the larger public, linking his guns through extensive advertising campaigns with romanticized and idealized visions of the American West. Colt's innovations in the machine production of revolvers allowed a high-quality product to be manufactured in large numbers. By the end of the 19th century, the glut of handguns in America spawned by Colt and his competitors began to prompt calls for government action to stem the rising tide of gun violence found mostly in cities in the East rather than on the American western frontier.

Almost from the start, gun possession was accompanied by gun policy. From the colonial era through the early Federalist period in America, possession of firearms was regulated in three primary ways. One type of regulation required eligible males to own guns as part of their militia service obligation, as militias provided the primary means for collective local defense. Longstanding concerns about the lack of firearms among the general population continued to be a primary concern to American leaders up through and after the American Revolution. In 1792, Congress passed the Uniform Militia Act, which required each militia-eligible man to "provide himself with a good musket or firelock, a sufficient bayonet and belt, two spare flints, and a knapsack, a pouch with a box therein to contain not less than twenty-four cartridges . . . each cartridge to contain a proper quantity of powder and ball." Within the next two years, all 15 states passed similar measures; yet, they lacked enforcement power, and these laws were widely ignored. In addition, states often reserved the right to take or "impress" guns, even if privately owned, if they were needed for defense, and to direct that guns be kept in a central location for rapid accessibility.

A second type of early gun control law barred gun ownership to various groups, including slaves, indentured servants, Native Americans, Catholics or other non-Protestants, non-property-owning whites, those who violated hunting laws, and those who refused to swear oaths of loyalty to the government. Laws barring distribution of guns to Native Americans were among the first such measures. As early as the 1600s, persons discovered selling guns to Indians could be subject to death. Pennsylvania went further than other states to take guns away from citizens deemed disloyal when it passed the Test Act in 1777, which specified that those who refused to swear an oath of allegiance to the government would be disarmed, referring specifically to "persons disaffected to the liberty and independence of this state." According to one historian, this law disarmed up to 40 percent of the state's adult white male population. Continuing governmental concern with the nation's ability to organize reliable military forces through its militias prompted it to conduct periodic gun censuses both before and after adoption of the Constitution of 1787. In 1803, for example, Secretary of War Henry Dearborn coordinated the most extensive and thorough such gun census ever conducted up until that time, concluding that about 45 percent of all militiamen (men between the ages of 18 and 45) had "arms," or about a quarter of the white male adult population. A similar census seven years later produced about the same results.

A third type of gun law incorporated measures regulating or restricting gun use very much in the way guns are regulated today. For example, the state of North Carolina enacted a law in 1778 criminalizing hunting in the woods at night by firelight, a practice barred in contemporary America because game, such as deer, freeze when hit by artificial light at night. Anyone who was caught was impressed into military service for three years. Tennessee enacted a law in 1821 that prohibited the carrying of certain named dangerous weapons, including pistols. Those convicted were required to pay a fine. In 1837, Georgia enacted a similar law, making it a crime to sell or possess certain named dangerous weapons, including pistols. Those convicted paid a heavy money fine. Several counties in Virginia passed an ordinance making it a crime to hunt "wild fowl" with a gun while doing so on a "skiff" (a shallow boat). The penalty for violation was that the defendant's gun was taken from him, sold, with half of the proceeds of the sale to be given to the government and the other half to be given to the person who reported the crime.

In the 19th century, westward expansion was accompanied by the enactment of various gun regulations. These regulations underscore the wildly exaggerated stories about the use of guns in the American West. While the West did witness gun violence, its extent and pervasiveness has been greatly overstated, a process that began when contemporary newspaper reporters and authors of pulp fiction dramatized, glorified, and invented stories of numerous wild shootouts.

The settling and "taming" of the West was primarily attributable to the advance of homesteaders, ranchers, miners, tradesmen, businessmen, and others who populated the region, worked the land, drove away Native Americans, and established towns and cities. Gun-slinging cowboys carrying six-shooters and rifles played a relatively minor role in this process. As many historians of the West have noted, far more people died in shootouts in movies than ever died in the real-life West. For example, during the height of lawlessness in the legendary Dodge City from 1876 to 1885, a total of only 15 persons died a violent death—an average of 1.5 deaths per year. In Deadwood, South Dakota, in its most violent year, four people were killed. In the most violent year in Tombstone, Arizona, home of the celebrated gunfight at the OK Corral, only five people were killed. From 1870 to 1885, the combined total number of killings reported in the cowboy towns of Abilene, Caldwell, Dodge City, Ellsworth, and Wichita was 45, and only six of those killings were from six-shooters; 14 killings were by police.

Even in the most violence-prone western cattle towns, vigilantism and lawlessness were only briefly tolerated. Laws against carrying guns within city or town limits were immediately enacted and strictly enforced by having cowboys or others with guns check them at some designated location, for which they would usually receive a metal token for identification and reclaiming purposes. As a consequence, few homicides occurred even during the heyday of gun violence in the 1870s, and most that occurred resulted from drunkenness and disputes over gambling. Ironically, the rise in citizen gun ownership after the Civil War occurred mostly in eastern cities, not in the "Wild West."

The gun disarmament that was routinely practiced in newly formed western towns was well understood as a sign of civilization and an improvement in public safety, especially as local businesspeople realized that fear of violence and disorder drove away settlers and customers. Ironically, such strict gun control measures provoke more political heat and outrage in 21st-century America than they did in the 19th century.

Two types of events spurred the frequent calls for tougher gun laws in the 20th century the spread and fear of gun-related crime, and the assassinations of political leaders and celebrities. Despite enduring popular support for tougher laws, new federal gun regulations have been infrequent and limited in scope.

The first modern push for gun control laws arose from the Progressive Era of the late 1800s and early 1900s. A dramatic rise in urban crime, seemingly linked to the proliferation of handguns, prompted reform groups, newspaper editors, clergy, and other civic leaders to press for new regulations. In 1903, for example, the New York City Police estimated that at least 20,000 citizens in the city carried handguns on a regular basis. Gun crimes received extensive press coverage, and states and localities throughout the country enacted laws barring the carrying of concealed weapons. The federal government did not intervene in early gun control policy efforts, based on the prevailing belief of the time that gun regulatory decisions should be left to the states and localities. In several legal challenges to gun regulations, however, the U.S. Supreme Court upheld their constitutionality.

Among the earliest, and most sweeping of these new state laws was that enacted in New York

State, the Sullivan Law of 1911. Spurred by spiraling urban violence and the attempted assassination of New York City mayor William J. Gaynor in 1910, the Sullivan Law (named after the state senator who championed the bill) subjected the sale, possession, and carrying of deadly weapons to strict regulation. In particular, pistol carrying was strictly licensed, with violation elevated to a felony by the new law. From that time to the present, New York State has maintained among the toughest handgun laws in the country.

At the federal level, the first successful effort to enact gun policy began with a 10 percent excise tax on guns passed in 1919, and a law prohibiting the sale of handguns to private individuals through the mail enacted in 1927. The rise of gun-fueled gangsterism in the 1920s and early 1930s, and the election of Franklin D. Roosevelt in 1932 (who was himself subject to an unsuccessful assassination attempt in 1933 that resulted in the shooting death of Chicago mayor Anton Cermak), boosted the prospects for new gun laws. The first significant national measure was the National Firearms Act of 1934, which strictly regulated gangster-type weapons, including sawed-off shotguns and machine guns. In its original form, this legislation had also included a system of handgun registration, but that provision was stripped out of the bill by gun control opponents. The Federal Firearms Act of 1938 established a licensing system for gun dealers, manufacturers, and importers.

No new federal gun control laws reached the president's desk until 1968, when a five-year push for tougher laws culminated in the enactment of the Gun Control Act. Momentum for new controls took shape in the aftermath of the assassination of President John F. Kennedy in 1963. His assassin, Lee Harvey Oswald, had purchased a rifle through interstate mail. By the mid-1960s escalating crime rates and the spread of urban disorder raised new fears about spiraling gun violence. Such fears peaked in 1968, as urban rioting continued, and when, in that same year, civil rights leader Martin Luther King, Jr., and Senator Robert Kennedy, were both assassinated. Those two murders provided the final impetus for passage of the Gun Control Act. The law banned interstate shipment of firearms and ammunition to private individuals; prohibited gun sales to minors; strengthened licensing and record-keeping requirements for dealers and collectors; extended regulations to destructive devices including land mines, bombs, and hand grenades; increased penalties for gun crimes; and regulated importation of foreign-made firearms. Cut from the bill was a provision, backed by President Lyndon Johnson, to enact blanket gun registration and licensing.

The next major gun law enacted by Congress, the Firearms Owners Protection Act of 1986 (also called the McClure-Volkmer Bill), rolled back many of the provisions of the 1968 law at a time when anticontrol forces, led by the National Rifle Association, exerted great influence over Congress and the presidency of Ronald Reagan. It allowed interstate sale of long guns (rifles and shotguns), reduced record keeping for dealers, limited government regulatory powers over dealers and gun shows (in particular, limiting inspections of gun dealers to one a year), and barred firearms registration.

Highly publicized incidents of mass shootings in the late 1980s and 1990s, combined with the election of control supporter Bill Clinton to the presidency, resulted in a new and successful effort to enact gun laws of limited scope. Yielding to public pressure, Congress enacted the Brady Law in 1993 and a ban on the sale and possession of certain, named types of assault weapons in 1994.

Named after President Ronald Reagan's press secretary, James Brady, who was seriously wounded in the 1981 assassination attempt against Reagan, the 1993 Brady Law required a five business day waiting period for the purchase of a handgun, during which time local law enforcement authorities were to conduct background checks on purchasers to weed out felons, the mentally incompetent, and others barred from handgun possession. It also increased federal firearms license fees, financed improved record keeping, and called for implementation of an instant, computerized background check to be instituted in 1998 (the waiting period provision lapsed at the same time). The background check system was implemented as the National Instant Criminal Background Check System (NICS); since then, handgun sales can be completed as soon as the check inquiry is cleared. Dealers have up to three days to verify that the applicant is eligible to purchase the handgun, although 95 percent of all purchases clear within two hours, according to the FBI. From 1994 to 2007, the Brady Law stopped over a million handgun purchases. Nineteen states still impose their own waiting periods regardless of when a potential sale clears. These periods range from a few days to several months. In New York State, for example, prospective handgun purchasers must first obtain a handgun permit that requires the filing of paperwork, payment of a fee, a police background check that includes interviews with persons known to the applicant, and an appearance before a judge during which the applicant must explain the reasons for handgun ownership. The entire process normally takes several months.

The law also had the effect of reducing the number of gun dealers from over 300,000 to fewer than 100,000. The relatively modest changes made by this law belied the fierce controversy over its enactment. After it was first introduced in 1987, supporters labored for six years to win enactment. Supporters considered the measure an obvious step to reduce gun access to those who nearly all agreed should not have ready access to handguns, especially since 80 percent of all gun crimes are committed with handguns. Opponents viewed the law as the first step on the slippery slope to burdensome gun laws that would hamper legitimate gun ownership and use. The political divide on this bill paralleled that of other gun measures: Control supporters tended to be Democrats, northerners, and from urban areas. Control foes tended to be Republicans, from the South, and from rural areas.

In 1994, Congress enacted a ban on 19 specified assault weapons, plus several dozen copycat models, which were distinguished from other semiautomatic weapons by virtue of their distinctive military features, including more compact design, short barrels, large ammunition clips, lighter weight, pistol grips or thumbhole stocks, flash suppressors, or telescoping stocks (traits that facilitate concealability and "spray fire"). The law also exempted from the ban 661 specifically named weapons. According to government studies, although assault weapons constituted only about 2 to 3 percent of all guns in America, they accounted for 6 to 8 percent of gun crimes. By 2004, seven states and several localities had enacted their own assault weapons bans. The federal ban was imposed for a 10-year period, and lapsed when Congress failed to renew it in 2004. Ban opponents felt that this measure was ineffective, that it arbitrarily banned a few types of weapons because of their appearance rather than firepower, and that it was a gateway measure inviting more expansive gun bans. Supporters considered the measure a reasonable restriction on weapons designed for military use.

In the late 1990s a series of seemingly inexplicable schoolyard shootings committed by school-age boys in small cities, towns, and rural areas around the country prompted renewed calls for stricter gun laws. This seeming crescendo of schoolyard mayhem reached its peak in 1999 when two high school boys shot and killed 13 people, and wounded 23 others, at Columbine High School in Littleton, Colorado. In the aftermath of the incident, national shock and outrage pressed Congress to respond. The U.S. Senate yielded to national pressure, despite the fact that its Republican leaders opposed new gun control measures, when it passed a bill that would have required background checks at all gun show sales, flea markets, and pawn shops (closing the "gun show loophole"). The bill also called for revoking gun ownership for those convicted of gun crimes as juveniles, invoked tougher penalties for juvenile offenders who used guns in crimes and also for those who provided such guns to juveniles, required sale of locking devices or boxes sold with all new handgun purchases, blocked legal immunity to those who sold guns to felons, and banned the import of high-capacity ammunition clips (those that could hold more than 10 bullets). After weeks of bargaining and delay, the measure was defeated in the House of Representatives. Foes of this measure charged that these new restrictions would not thwart gun crime, would impose undue burdens on legitimate gun owners, and would open the door to even more gun restrictions. Bill supporters considered the measure's provisions to be reasonable and limited restrictions on otherwise unregulated gun sales.

The election of George W. Bush to the presidency in 2000 marked the ascension of the most gun-friendly president in modern history. During his administration, access to federal gun purchase records, even by law enforcement officials, was sharply restricted. Bush's Justice Department provided a new interpretation of the Second Amendment's "right to bear arms" that greatly expanded its scope, in the process overturning existing government legal policy dating back more than 50 years. In 2005, Congress enacted the Protection of Lawful Commerce in Arms Act, which barred civil suits against gun manufacturers and dealers. Supporters argued that such lawsuits represented a backdoor effort to regulate guns. Opponents noted that the gun industry was unique in having such legal immunity, and that it provided unjustifiable legal protection to a single industry.

In an unusual show of conciliation, gun rights and control groups combined forces to win enactment of a law in 2007 to improve record keeping for those judged mentally incompetent (and therefore ineligible) to own guns. While such individuals had long been barred from gun ownership, most states did not keep or properly report such information, a fact dramatized when a student with a history of mental problems legally bought two handguns in Virginia and used them to kill 33 people on the campus of Virginia Tech State University in April 2007.

National gun control policy is implemented by the Bureau of Alcohol, Tobacco, Firearms and Explosives (ATFE). Long a part of the Treasury Department, the ATFE was transferred to the Department of Justice in 2003 as part of homeland security reorganization. The agency has had limited success in implementing full enforcement of national gun laws. Enforcement lapses have resulted from legislative restrictions on its authority, budget cutbacks, a tarnished reputation resulting from its handling of the confrontation with the Branch Davidian compound in Waco, Texas, in 1993, and political opposition and criticism from gun rights organizations.

National Rifle Association headquarters in Fairfax, Virginia *(Photo by Bjoertvedt/ Used under a Creative Commons license)*

Many interest groups have claimed a stake in the modern gun debate, but one organization has dominated the political landscape like no other—the National Rifle Association. The NRA is the nation's largest and oldest gun rights group. Formed in 1871 by two veterans dismayed at the poor marksmanship skills of Civil War soldiers, the NRA functioned in its early decades primarily as a sporting and marksmanship organization. While it played some role in gun politics throughout the 20th century, the NRA took a decidedly more political turn in the 1970s when a more hard-line faction of the organization took over the NRA leadership. Thereafter, it devoted more of its organizational resources to political activities, and adopted a more aggressive conservative political posture. These activities were aimed at its political agenda of opposing gun control measures and promoting the rights of gun owners. It alienated some of its traditional supporters when it downgraded its traditional emphasis on hunting and sporting activities and instead embraced a more political and stridently antigovernment rhetoric, aimed especially at the government agency charged with enforcing gun laws, the Bureau of Alcohol, Tobacco and Firearms, in the 1980s and early 1990s.

The NRA subsequently backed away from such harsh attacks on the government in the mid-1990s, and found a more moderate figure to head the organization when it tapped actor Charlton Heston to serve as president from 1998 to 2003. The NRA worked closely with President George W. Bush's administration to win new protections for gun manufacturers and gun owners. With a membership of 4 million, the NRA is considered one of the most effective lobby forces in national politics.

The largest pro–gun control interest group, the Brady Campaign to Prevent Gun Violence (formerly known as Handgun Control, Inc.) has not been able to match the NRA in size or influence, but it has logged its own political victories. It pressed successfully for some improved licensing and record-keeping provisions inserted in the McClure-Volkmer Bill in 1986, and won significant victories with the enactment of the Brady Law in 1993 (named after Brady campaign head Sarah Brady's husband, James) and the assault weapons ban in 1994. Groups like the Brady campaign have been helped by the fact that public opinion has consistently supported stronger gun laws since the late 1930s. Yet as is true of the interest group politics in many areas, policy decisions are often the product of decisive group pressures rather than the weight of public opinion.

The Supreme Court has mostly avoided hearing cases related to gun rights and the Second Amendment. In three cases dating to the 19th century, and in the 1939 case of *U.S. v. Miller*, the high court had interpreted the Second Amendment's right to bear arms as pertaining to citizen service in a government militia. As the amendment says, "A well regulated Militia, being necessary to the security of a free State, the right of the people to keep and bear Arms, shall not be infringed." Since the high court's 1939 ruling, nearly 50 lower federal court rulings also embraced the militia-based meaning of the amendment. Many of these verdicts were appealed to the Supreme Court, but it consistently declined to accept the appeals.

In 2007, however, the Supreme Court agreed to hear an appeal of a lower court ruling based on a challenge to the District of Columbia's strict law that barred possession of working handguns. In the 2008 case of *D.C. v. Heller*, the high court ruled 5-4 that the Second Amendment did, in fact, protect an individual right of civilians to own guns for the purpose of personal self-protection in the home. This decision represented the first time in American history that a federal court applied the Second Amendment to strike down a gun law and used it as a basis to protect civilian gun ownership. The decision left open many unanswered questions. In his majority opinion, Justice Antonin Scalia said that access to some guns could be restricted, such as M-16 rifles, but provided no further guidance. He noted that some regulations could be maintained, such as laws barring gun sales to the mentally incompetent or restricting the carrying of guns into some public buildings. But these brief statements went no further to explain what restrictions might or might not be considered legal. What legal protections, if any, might extend to gun dealers, for example? Not surprisingly, within hours of the decision, lawsuits were filed against gun regulations around the country. Without question, the courts will face a blizzard of new challenges to gun laws from the local to the national level in the months and years to come.

The gun issue continues to evoke strong feelings on both sides. With a favorable Supreme Court ruling, gun rights supporters can now say that at least some civilian gun ownership is protected by the Second Amendment's right to bear arms. Further, they argue that gun ownership suppresses crime and is an effective form of self-defense, facilitates legitimate hunting and sporting practices, and protects the country from political tyranny. Gun control supporters argue that the high court ruling is an erroneous anomaly from an ultraconservative court majority, that guns in civilian hands increase gun mayhem in society (including murder, suicide, and accident), that gun ownership is more likely to cause than prevent tyranny, that stricter gun regulations protect legitimate gun owners, and that the constitutional right to bear arms refers to citizen militia service, not private gun ownership.

Future gun control efforts are likely to be shaped by at least two different factors: changing gun habits and new technologies. While the number of guns in America continues to grow—around 250 million by some estimates—the percentage of households with guns continues to decline, from about half of all households reporting one or more guns in the early 1960s to about a third of households at the start of the 21st century. This decline is attributable to the continued decline in rural populations, the decline of hunting as other activities and hobbies become more accessible, and a growing feeling that guns pose inherent risks that do not justify their ownership. On the other hand, new gun technologies and marketing efforts continue to appeal to some, also raising the specter of new gun regulation. For example, pressures have increased to regulate civilian possession of .50-caliber sniper rifles. First developed in the 1980s for military use against motor vehicles and airplanes, these weapons can hit a target from over a mile away, and are capable of great destruction in the hands of terrorists or others. Why, critics ask, should civilians be able to purchase such weapons? As more Americans come to view guns with skepticism, such questions are likely to persist.

Further Reading:

Cook, Philip, and Jens Ludwig. *Gun Violence: The Real Costs*. New York: Oxford University Press, 2000; Cornell, Saul. *A Well-Regulated Militia: The Founding Fathers and the Origins of Gun Control in America*. New York: Oxford University Press, 2006; DeConde, Alexander. *Gun Violence in America*. Boston: Northeastern University Press, 2001; Goss, Kristin. *Disarmed: The Missing Movement for Gun Control in America*. Princeton, N.J.: Princeton University Press, 2006; Hemenway, David. *Private Guns Public Health*. Ann Arbor: University of Michigan Press, 2004; Kennett, Lee, and James LaVerne Anderson. *The Gun in America*. Westport, Conn.: Greenwood Press, 1975; Kleck, Gary. *Targeting Guns*. New York: Aldine deGruyter, 1997; Ludwig, Jens, and Philip J. Cook, eds. *Evaluating Gun Policy*. Washington, D.C.: Brookings Institution Press, 2003; Spitzer, Robert J. *The Right to Bear Arms*. Santa Barbara, Calif.: ABC-CLIO, 2001; ———. *The Politics of Gun Control*. Washington, D.C.: CQ Press, 2007; ———. *Gun Control: A Documentary and Reference Guide*. Westport, Conn.: Greenwood Publishing Group, 2009; Vizzard, William J. *Shots in the Dark*. Lanham, Md.: Rowman & Littlefield, 2000.

– Robert J. Spitzer

hate crimes

In response to calls by advocacy and civil rights groups, the first hate crime laws were enacted in the mid-1980s. These laws, in varying degrees, distinguished "ordinary" crime from those crimes motivated by specifically designated prejudices. The latter offenses were labeled a "hate crime" and subjected offenders to separate and more severe punishment based on their biased motivation. The resulting jumble of hate crime laws have sparked much debate among scholars, politicians, the media, and advocacy groups as to the scope, legality, and legitimacy of such laws. This article will provide an overview of the definitional, legal, and policy challenges surrounding the promulgation and enforcement of hate crime laws.

A hate crime is a crime that is motivated, in whole or in part, by the offender's bias or prejudice based on a victim's actual or perceived group affiliation. It is important to note at the outset that a hate crime does not require the presence of actual hate. Indeed, a thrill-seeking teenager who defaces a church may not have any real hatred against Christians, but certainly would be subject to hate crime charges. In contrast, a woman who hates her employer and kills him would certainly not.

Crimes are transformed into hate crimes based on the offender's biased motivation. Unlike hate crimes, most garden-variety offenses do not include motive as an element of the offense. It matters not that a man robbed a bank because he was greedy or because he needed money to buy medicine for an ailing relative. If the prosecution can establish that the man intentionally robbed the bank, then he is guilty of the offense. In the context of hate crime, however, motive is a central element that must be established by the prosecution beyond a reasonable doubt. This is no small burden. For instance, imagine a fight between a black man and a white man that takes place at a baseball game. The white man punches the black man in the nose after a scoreless inning, screaming "I hate the Boston Red Sox, you #$@." If the explicative was race-based, is an ordinary assault at a baseball game transformed into a hate crime? If the expletive was not race-based, can the assault be treated as a hate crime? What if the white man had racist thoughts, but said nothing beyond his comment about the Red Sox when he punched the black man? Does that change if the man made the same Red Sox comment but was a member of a white supremacist group? What if one accepts the argument, made prominent by scholar Charles Lawrence, that all members of this society are unconsciously racist? Should every interracial altercation be scrutinized as a potential hate crime?

In addition to the complexities regarding motive, state and federal legislatures have little consensus as to which enumerated prejudices should transform "typical" offenses into hate crimes. Indeed, hate crime legislation varies considerably between states, and between the states and federal government.

State statutes vary considerably in terms of which prejudices transform typical offenses into a hate crime. At the one extreme is Wyoming, which has no hate crime law at all. When Matthew Shepard, a gay student at the University of Wyoming, was beaten to death because of his sexual orientation, advocacy groups around the world called for greater hate crime protection. Yet, Wyoming has never enacted any form of hate crime law, which means that a crime motivated by bias in Wyoming will not be legally recognized as such. In sharp contrast, California's hate crime statute punishes a wide array of bias motivations, including race, ethnicity, religion, sexual orientation, gender, disability, political affiliation, age, and transgender identity. Other states, such as South Dakota and Montana, provide enhanced penalties for crimes based on race, religion, and ethnicity, but not for crimes committed because of gender or sexual orientation. Thus, an offense that is considered a hate crime in one state may well be treated as an ordinary offense in another.

One significant source of controversy involves the inclusion of sexual orientation in hate crime legislation. Conservative and right-wing religious groups argue that the inclusion of sexual orientation will send a message of endorsement. This message has gained traction. Indeed, when the Georgia Supreme Court in 2004 struck down that state's hate crime statute as unconstitutional, efforts to pass a new version stalled over whether to include sexual orientation. So too, the federal government under previous administrations failed to extend federal hate crime protections to crimes motivated by, among other categories, sexual orientation.

By way of background, federal hate crime statutes currently fall within federal civil rights laws. In 1871, the federal government, in response to ongoing violence against blacks by whites after the Civil War, passed the first Civil Rights Acts (CRA). The CRA enabled the federal government to prosecute individuals who, either working in concert with others or as an employee of the government, had deprived others of their civil rights. Congress also enabled individuals to sue a state or local government employee in federal court when that employee interfered with a civil or constitutional right. In 1969, Congress authorized the federal prosecution of people who "by force or threat of force willfully injures, intimidates or interferes with . . . any person because of his race, color, religion or national origin and because he is or has been" engaged in specific federally protected activities such as attending school, voting, or serving on a jury.

Congress, however, has limited enforcement authority under the CRA. The federal government is permitted to act only where the crime takes place on federal property or during a federally protected activity. Further, its protections extend only to victims selected based on "race, color, religion or national origin." To address these limitations, Congress has attempted to pass legislation that would expand federal jurisdiction, and would add sexual orientation as one of the enumerated protected classes. Due to staunch opposition by religious fundamentalists and conservative politicians, efforts in previous years to pass a federal hate crime bill that includes sexual orientation have failed. Indeed, Congress's 2007 failed attempt—and the 2009 successful attempt—to pass the Local Law Enforcement Hate Crimes Prevention Act, popularly known as "The Matthew Shepard Act," illustrates the politics underlying hate crime legislation.

The Matthew Shepard Act expands the categories of qualified motivations for federal hate crimes and expands the scope of federal jurisdiction over hate crimes. Powerful advocacy groups, such as Focus on the Family, called upon legislatures to vote against the Matthew Shepard Act because, it argued, the intent of the law "is to muzzle people of faith who dare to express their moral and biblical concerns about homosexuality." President George W. Bush voiced his intent to veto the proposed legislation, even after it was attached as a rider to the Department of Defense appropriations bill. Although both legislative houses had strong advocates who favored the bill, Congress ultimately did not have adequate votes for its passage and the amendment was removed from the DOD bill.

The election of President Barack Obama seemingly ensures passage of the Matthew Shepard Act. President-elect Obama proclaimed his support for the bill throughout his campaign. As president, he issued a statement urging Congress to pass the 2009 bill. Attorney General Eric Holder declared that passage of the legislation was one of his "highest personal priorities." Like its predecessor, the Matthew Shepard Act would expand federal hate crime protections to gender, sexual orientation, gender identity, and disability. It would eliminate limitations on federal jurisdiction, enable the federal government to investigate hate crimes in the absence of state action, increase funding to states, and require the tracking of crimes based on transgendered status. On April 29, 2009, the bill handily passed in the House. On July 23, 2009, the Senate passed the bill, which was attached as an amendment to the National Defense Authorization Act of 2010. The Senate version of the bill would enable federal prosecutors to seek the death penalty for hate-based murders, a somewhat ironic amendment given that Matthew Shepard himself opposed the death penalty and that his father, Dennis Shepard, specifically asked the court to spare the lives of the men who murdered his son. Although differences between the House and Senate versions of the bill must be resolved, President Obama is certain to sign it into law. The inclusion of sexual orientation, gender, and gender identity sends a strong symbol of support to the gay, lesbian, bisexual, and transgender (GLBT) community.

In addition to the civil rights laws, several other legal mechanisms exist for the prosecution of hate crimes. Penalty enhancement statutes, for instance, increase penal sanctions for crimes motivated by statutorily enumerated prejudices. Penalty enhancement statutes do not create a separate criminal offense. Rather, a defendant who commits a criminal offense, such as assault, may receive an increased sentence if the crime was motivated by a bias that is enumerated in the hate crime statute. Twenty-seven states and the District of Columbia have some form of a penalty enhancement statute. In Vermont, for instance, a defendant who has committed an offense that is punishable by a maximum of one-year imprisonment could receive double that sentence if the crime was motivated by hate.

The Supreme Court recently called into question the efficacy of penalty enhancement statutes. In *Apprendi v. New Jersey* (2000), a white defendant fired shots into the home of an African-American family that recently moved into his neighborhood. After the prosecution established by a preponderance of the evidence that the defendant's conduct was motivated by racial bias, the defendant was sentenced to 12 years in prison—two years more than the statutory maximum. The Supreme Court reversed Apprendi's sentence and ruled that the prosecution must prove motive beyond a reasonable doubt to the trier of fact before that motive can be relied upon for an enhanced sentence. Given the complexities of proving motive, this increased burden of proof may make it difficult for the prosecution to establish its case.

The federal government's penalty enhancement statutes have also been called into question by the Supreme Court. The U.S. Sentencing Commission authorized a three-level sentencing guideline increase for crimes in which the victim was selected "because of the actual or perceived race, color, religion, national origin, ethnicity, gender, disability, or sexual orientation of any person." Interestingly, although the selection of a victim based on sexual orientation does not constitute a federal hate crime, it can be the basis for an enhanced sentence. In *United States v. Booker* (2007), the Supreme Court declared that these guidelines are merely advisory. Whether federal judges will choose to apply the hate crime enhancement to already severe sentencing laws remains an open question.

Another form of hate crime law creates a distinct category of offense for hate crimes. The Anti-Defamation League (ADL) authored highly influential model legislation that provides for two main substantive offenses: bias motivated crimes and institutional vandalism. Under the ADL model legislation, a person commits a bias-motivated crime:

> if, by reason of the actual or perceived race, color, religion, national origin, sexual orientation or gender of another individual or group of individuals, he violates Section ______ of the Penal code (insert code provisions for criminal trespass, criminal mischief, harassment, menacing, intimidation, assault, battery and or other appropriate statutorily proscribed criminal conduct).

Thus, if a person commits an "ordinary" crime, but does so because of an enumerated prejudice, then an additional substantive crime has been committed. In that instance, the ADL recommends that criminal liability for the bias-motivated crime be "at least one degree more serious than that imposed for commission of the underlying offense."

In 2000, New York State passed a hate crime statute, originally modeled on the ADL's proposed legislation. Under the New York hate crime law, a person commits a hate crime when he or she commits a specified offense and either:

> (a) intentionally selects the person against whom the offense is committed or intended to be committed in whole or in substantial part because of a belief or perception regarding the race, color, national origin, ancestry, gender, religion, religious practice, age, disability or sexual orientation of a person, regardless of whether the belief or perception is correct, or
> (b) intentionally commits the act or acts constituting the offense in whole or in substantial part because of a belief or perception regarding the race, color, national origin, ancestry, gender, religion, religious practice, age, disability or sexual orientation of a person, regardless of whether the belief or perception is correct.

The specified offenses include varying degrees of assault, menacing, reckless endangerment, manslaughter, murder, stalking, sex offenses, larceny, trespass, and harassment. As a result of this statute, a bias-motivated defendant who commits nearly any "typical" crime can be prosecuted for both that offense *and* the separate offense of hate crime.

Another substantive offense proposed by the ADL is institutional vandalism. Institutional vandalism occurs when a person:

> knowingly vandaliz[es], defac[es] or otherwise damage[es]:
> (i) Any church, synagogue or other building, structure or place used for religious worship or other religious purpose;

(ii) Any cemetery, mortuary or other facility used for the purpose of burial or memorializing the dead;
(iii) Any school, educational facility or community center;
(iv) The grounds adjacent to, and owned or rented by, any institution, facility, building, structure or place described in subsections (i), (ii) or (iii) above; or
(v) Any personal property contained in any institution, facility, building, structure, or place described in subsections (i), (ii) or (iii) above.

The simple act of vandalizing or defacing a church falls within the statute irrespective of whether the offender was motivated by prejudice. The model statute authorizes penalties based on the cost of the damage caused, including the cost to repair that damage.

A final form of hate crime laws are data collection statutes. In 1990, the federal government enacted the Hate Crimes Statistics Act (HCSA), which calls for data collection of crimes "that manifest evidence of prejudice based on race, religion, disability, sexual orientation, or ethnicity, including where appropriate the crimes of murder, non-negligent manslaughter; forcible rape; aggravated assault, simple assault, intimidation; arson; and destruction, damage or vandalism of property." Each year, the FBI publishes the data provided to it under the HCSA. But because the HCSA is voluntary and has never enjoyed adequate fiscal or full state support and cooperation, the resulting data is inherently unreliable.

This, in part, reflects the fact that only 27 states and the District of Columbia authorize hate crime data collection. Any crime motivated by bias in a state that does not report hate crime data to the FBI is not included in the national statistics. Moreover, even within the states that authorize data collection, there is great disparity as to which enumerated prejudices are counted. And because reporting to the FBI is voluntary, police departments often opt not to participate. This can result in severe underreporting. Finally, because resources devoted to training are limited, even police departments who wish to participate often report inaccurate, incomplete, and even incorrect data.

Many objections to hate crime statutes turn on First Amendment considerations. Critics of hate crime laws, such as James B. Jacobs, argue that hate crime unconstitutionally punishes hateful thoughts and speech. For example, if one man punches a gay man wearing a New York Giants jersey, and screams "I hate gays," then surely he could be charged with a hate crime. But if that same man punches a gay man and screams "I hate the Giants," then no hate crime would have been committed. The unlawful conduct in the above scenarios are identical (the punch), but the speech is not. And if it is the speech that results in additional hate crime sanctions, then how can that be squared with the First Amendment?

Supporters of hate crime laws counter that hate crime laws are not impermissible content-based restrictions on thought or speech, but rather are regulations of unlawful conduct. The Supreme Court has accepted that argument in the context of hate crime penalty enhancement statutes. In 1993, in *Wisconsin v. Mitchell*, the Supreme Court unanimously upheld the constitutionality of penalty enhancement hate crime laws. In *Mitchell*, a group of African-American teenagers severely assaulted a white teenager who was selected because of his race. The defendant received a significantly increased sentence under Wisconsin's penalty enhancement statute. The Wisconsin State Supreme Court struck down the statute, concluding that the statute impermissibly targeted "offensive motive or thought" in violation of the Constitution. The U.S. Supreme Court disagreed. The Court determined that the statute punished criminal *conduct* and not constitutionally protected viewpoints, and therefore did not violate the First Amendment.

The Supreme Court in *Virginia v. Black* (2003) upheld legislation targeting offensive conduct in the context of cross burnings. In 2003, a defendant in Virginia was convicted of cross burning under a statute that allowed the jury to infer intent to intimidate from the act itself of burning a cross. The defendant argued that the statute abridged his First Amendment rights. Although the Supreme Court confirmed that cross burning is a symbolically protected form of speech under the First Amendment, it held that cross burning with the intent to threaten or intimidate is not. This case drew a distinction between cross burning that is expressive, such as that which may occur at a Ku Klux Klan rally, and that which takes place on private property, for instance, the lawn of a black family or church. The former may enjoy First Amendment protection, while the latter may not if it can be established that the burning was intended to intimidate or harass the recipient.

With the likely passage of the Matthew Shepard Act, the federal government will send a strong symbolic message that bias based on sexual orientation as well as gender and transgender identity is not acceptable. This is not insignificant. Scholars have consistently emphasized the symbolic function of hate crime law. As scholar Sarah Beale explains, hate crime laws are largely perceived as expressing "a general affirmation of the societal value of the groups targeted by hate crimes and a recognition of their rightful place in society. Hate crimes legislation is seen as reinforcing the community's commitment to equality among all citizens." However, while hate crime laws have the potential to send symbolic messages of inclusion and tolerance, they also can send a potent message of governmental dis-inclusion and bigotry. Indeed, the Hate Crimes Statistics Act of 1990, which included sexual orientation in its data collection statute, was passed only with the inclusion of compromise language, insisted upon by conservative senators, including Senator Jesse Helms (R-NC), which stated that "nothing in this Act shall be construed . . . to promote or encourage homosexuality." In other words, the HSCA, designed to capture the scope of hate crime in the United States, was accompanied by a governmental message of bigotry toward gays and lesbians.

Moreover, even if passage of the Matthew Shepard Act sends a positive symbolic message, it is questionable whether it will have significant practical impact. Most hate crimes will continue to fall within the jurisdiction of the states, where little consistency exists as to which groups are protected and whether those laws are enforced. Some states, such as California and New Jersey, have developed a robust hate crime law and enforcement scheme, while other states pay lip service to hate crime laws by passing narrowly defined statutes, and allocating limited or no resources to training and enforcement. Data collection continues to be voluntary, leading to federal hate crime statistics that are at best woefully inaccurate. Nearly 30 years after the passage of the first hate crime laws, it is virtually impossible to measure whether hate crime laws have had any real impact at all.

Further Reading:

Beale, Sarah S. "Federalizing Hate Crimes: Symbolic Politics, Expressive Law, or Tool for Criminal Enforcement?" *Boston University Law Review* 80 (2000): 1,227–1,281; Grattet, Ryken, and Vanessa Jenness. "Examining the Boundaries of Hate Crime Law: Disabilities and the 'Dilemma of Difference.'" *Journal of Criminal Law and Criminology* 91 (2001): 653–697; Jacobs, James B., and Jessica S. Henry. "The Social Construction of a Hate Crime Epidemic." *Journal of Criminal Law and Criminology* 86 (1996): 336–391; Jacobs, James B., and Kimberly Potter. *Hate Crimes: Criminal Law & Identity Politics.* New York: Oxford University Press, 1998.

–Jessica S. Henry

identity theft

The U.S. Federal Trade Commission defines identity theft as occurring when "someone uses your personally identifying information, like your name, Social Security number, or credit card number, without your permission, to commit fraud or other crimes."

Identity theft is not a new crime but the increased use of credit cards, online retailers, the Internet, and other high-tech amenities has contributed to a surge in identity thefts and related crimes. As many as 9 million Americans have their identity stolen each year. This occurs in a variety of ways. The tactics thieves use include dumpster diving (rummaging through trash looking for paper with your personal information), skimming (stealing credit/debit numbers with a special device), phishing (posing as legitimate enterprises and convincing you to reveal your personal information), changing your address (diverting billing statements with a change of address form), old-fashioned stealing (physically taking your wallets and purses, mail, checks, or tax information from you or your employer), and pretexting (posing as you when contacting those you do business with in an effort to obtain your personal information).

The losses associated with identity theft are staggering. In 2007, the Javelin Company estimated that the average consumer loss associated with identity theft amounted to $5,720 per victim. A study conducted by Utica College's Center for Identity Management and Information Protection in the same year found that the median dollar loss for each victim of identity theft was $31,356 when losses included costs to companies.

The problems caused by identity theft are not confined to individuals and private sector companies. The U.S. Department of the Treasury recently released a report documenting that the number of fraudulent tax returns linked to identity theft had increased 579 percent from 2002 to 2007. These thefts occur in one of two ways. "First, thieves may steal a victim's Social Security number, and file a fraudulent return in an attempt to receive a tax refund. In other cases, victims of identity theft discover that their 'income,' as reported to the IRS, is much higher than what they actually earned—and what they used in their tax return—because thieves have stolen their Social Security number and used their name to obtain employment."

Identity theft is on the rise. Losses to taxpayers, consumers, and businesses are in the billions of dollars. While the crime itself is not new, what has changed is the scale and scope of this criminal activity. Identity thieves have become more sophisticated and brazen, and it is not uncommon to find a single individual or group of individuals stealing the identities of thousands of victims in a short time period.

Despite the startling increase in identity theft, individuals may not be as at risk for personal loss as they may at first think. The Fair Credit Billing Act limits personal liability for fraudulent use of a person's credit card to $50 per credit card. A number of credit card companies go further to protect consumers against loss, promising "zero-liability" for fraudulent charges. The Consumer Federation of America recently reported that fraudulent use of a credit card is the most common type of identity theft crime committed against consumers.

Those concerned with identity theft sometimes turn to for-profit companies that offer identity theft protection. What is often misunderstood about these services though is that they do not actually deter identity theft. Rather, by monitoring various credit and noncredit databases, they can detect fraud. This will have the effect of minimizing damage but will not actually prevent the fraud from occurring in the first place. Additionally, some of the companies that provide this service will assist in cleaning up your credit history if you are a victim of identity theft. While these companies can provide a valuable service to consumers, they are not a substitute for strong laws to help prevent identity theft from occurring.

Regardless of the effectiveness of credit monitoring services, many consumers are understandably concerned about the security of their identity. This concern is amplified by high-profile cases of identity theft. For example, in 2008, Federal Reserve chairman Ben Bernanke's identity was stolen by an identity theft ring run by a man known as "Big Head."

The public is understandably concerned about identity theft and has urged lawmakers to enact strong laws to deter this criminal behavior. While Congress has acted (see below), some confusion exists as to what exactly does and does not constitute identity theft. To be guilty of identity theft, a person must intend to steal a particular person's identity. The Supreme Court recently helped clarify what this means when it ruled that prosecutors cannot charge illegal immigrants with identity theft when, in the course of applying for jobs, they present Social Security numbers that are false. The Court reasoned that since the identity-theft statute requires the defendant to knowingly use the identity of another person, it does not apply to those who use random numbers. While working in the United States without proper documentation is still a crime, it is not a form of identity theft.

Numerous federal and state laws deal with identity theft. Federal laws can be broken into three categories: credit, criminal, and privacy and information security. State laws deal with credit freeze, credit information blocking, criminal, and Social Security numbers. Federal government laws provide citizens with a guaranteed level of protection regardless of where in the United States they live. State laws protect only those living in that particular state.

Three major federal credit laws deal with identity theft. The Fair Credit Reporting Act establishes procedures for consumers to identify and correct errors on their credit record and requires credit-reporting agencies to take steps to ensure that consumer credit reports are provided only to third parties for legitimate business needs. The Fair Credit Billing Act establishes procedures for consumers to resolve billing errors with credit card companies and limits consumer liability to no more than $50 for each credit card. The Electronic Fund Transfer Act provides consumers with protections when using a debit card or electronic fund transfer and limits consumer liability for unauthorized electronic fund transfers. Together, these laws seek to protect consumers from credit fraud and to limit liability if credit fraud does occur.

The major federal law that seeks to address identity theft was passed by Congress in October 1998. The Identity Theft and Assumption Deterrence Act of 1998 (Identity Theft Act) was intended to address the problem of identity theft. The Web site of the Federal Trade Commission summarizes the legislation: "Specifically, the Act amends [a previous statute] to make it a federal crime when anyone: knowingly transfers or uses, without lawful authority, a means of identification of another person with the intent to commit, or to aid or abet, any unlawful activity that constitutes a violation of Federal law, or that constitutes a felony under any applicable State or local law. Violations of the Act are investigated by federal investigative agencies such as the U.S. Secret Service, the FBI, and the U.S. Postal Inspection Service and prosecuted by the Department of Justice." The Identity Theft Act requires that anyone convicted serve a two-year sentence in addition to any other sentence imposed for underlying crimes. For example, if a criminal stole a person's identity and used it to defraud another person, he or she would be charged with violating both fraud statutes and the Identity Theft Act. If convicted, the person would serve two years in jail beyond a sentence for fraud.

Four federal laws have been enacted to help protect consumer privacy and information security. The Driver's Privacy Protection Act of 1994 limits state departments of motor vehicles as to the amount of personal information in their records they can disclose and to whom. The Family Educational Rights and Privacy Act of 1974 (FERPA) limits agencies and institutions that receive federal funding as to what information can be disclosed to third parties. The Gramm-Leach-Billey Act of 1999 "requires the FTC, along with the Federal banking agencies, the National Credit Union Administration, the Treasury Department, and the Securities and Exchange Commission, to issue regulations, . . . ensuring that financial institutions protect the privacy of consumers' personal financial information. Such institutions must develop and give notice of their privacy policies to their own customers at least annually, and before disclosing any consumer's personal financial information to a nonaffiliated third party, must give notice and an opportunity for that consumer to 'opt out' from such disclosure." The final rule of the Health Information Portability and Accountability Act of 1996, which took effect in 2001, regulates the security and confidentiality of patient information held by health plans and providers.

All states (with the exceptions of Alabama, Michigan, and Missouri) have adopted security (or credit) freeze laws. These laws give consumers the right to deny access to their credit file by anyone seeking to open a new account in their name. An identity thief cannot open a consumer's account when there is a credit freeze in place, since banks and credit card companies will not have access to check the credit file. Consumers who use this service must take the additional step of temporarily lifting their credit freeze when they apply for a new credit card or loan. Those entities that have access to the consumer's account when the freeze is put into place are exempt from the freeze.

Eighteen states (Alabama, Arizona, California, Colorado, Connecticut, Georgia, Idaho, Louisiana, Maine, Massachusetts, Montana, Nevada, New Hampshire, New Mexico, Oklahoma, Rhode Island, Virginia, and Washington) have enacted credit information blocking laws. These laws give consumers the right to demand credit-reporting agencies to block inaccurate information listed that is the result of identity theft. While the laws vary by state as to how long the credit-reporting agency has to block the information from the time it receives documentation from the victim of identity theft, all the laws share a common goal of helping to ensure that victims of identity theft are not denied credit in the future due to the criminal actions of a third party.

All 50 states have one or more laws that define identity theft as a criminal act, although exact definitions of "identity theft" and the criminal sanctions associated with them vary by state. Thirteen states (Alabama, Arkansas, Illinois, Kansas, Maryland, Mississippi, Missouri, Montana, New Hampshire, New Jersey, North Carolina, South Carolina, and Virginia) have enacted laws that specifically require inaccurate arrest records created when an identity thief uses someone else's identifying information when arrested be expunged and corrected. Ten states (Arkansas, Delaware, Iowa, Maryland, Mississippi, Montana, Nevada, Ohio, Oklahoma, and Virginia) have passed laws that allow one or more state agencies to issue "identity theft passports" to victims of identity theft once they have filed a police report citing that their identity has been stolen. The passport can be used to prevent victims of identity theft from being detained or arrested for crimes committed by the person who has stolen their identity. Thirty-seven states (all except Alabama, Alaska, Idaho, Iowa, Kentucky, Massachusetts, Nebraska, New Hampshire, Ohio, Pennsylvania, Tennessee, West Virginia, and Wyoming) have laws that attempt to protect the confidentiality of Social Security numbers. These laws vary in design and include restrictions on: publicly posting Social Security numbers, requiring Social Security numbers on identification cards issued by the state, and the like.

Taken as a whole, federal and state laws seek to protect individuals from identity theft, prosecute criminals who steal the identities of others, and provide victims of identity theft tools to recover from the crime. This three-pronged approach has evolved over time and aims to stop identity theft from occurring whenever possible, holding identity thieves accountable for their actions, and assisting those who fall victim to the crime. Despite the number of laws, the strong stance against identity theft by law enforcement, and the efforts of private-sector companies who work to prevent identity theft from occurring, scant evidence exists of a significant drop-off in identity theft.

The plethora of laws relating to identity theft do cause burdens for some. This has led to the need for exceptions and new rules. For example, regulators in Massachusetts determined in August 2009 that state identity theft rules that require "that personal information be encrypted when stored on portable devices or transmitted wirelessly or on public networks" be delayed a second time. The rules were supposed to take effect on January 1, 2009, but began on March 1, 2010. The reason for the delay is the one-size-fits-all nature of the law, which required all businesses to employ the same level of security for all businesses, regardless of the kinds of records they maintain or the risk of identity theft posed by their operations. The newest version of the rules attempts to meet these concerns by increasing flexibility and taking the concerns of small business owners into account.

The problems Massachusetts has had with implementing its identity theft laws in a way that does not cause needless bureaucracy and delays is not unique. The growth of laws to protect consumers from identity theft, punish criminals, and provide avenues for individuals to recover after becoming victims of identity theft has led to problems for businesses. In recognition of this, some states have been cautious in adding additional consumer protections before gathering information on what effect the proposed law would likely have on businesses. This constitutes a balancing act that attempts to weigh the legitimate interest of enacting laws to minimize identity theft with the obligations the proposed law would place on others.

The August 24, 2009, edition of the *Michigan Lawyers Weekly* gave an excellent summation of the problem, and the solution that Michigan is employing to try to balance these competing needs. On the one hand, "much of the problem with Michigan's laws on identity theft is that they do next to nothing to keep it from happening. . . . The laws in the Identity Theft Protection Act (of 2004) do require things like a data breach notification, which requires businesses to inform people if their personal information has been hacked, but it leaves it within the discretion of the business as to whether or not the breach poses a risk." Michigan's legislature has not responded to the loophole in protection from identity theft by passing laws to address the problem directly. Instead, they are proposing a new law that would establish "an Identity Theft Protection Commission to advise the governor and state departments on state policies and laws about identity theft, and on best practices for business and government—including how to reduce the use of Social Security numbers." If this law passes, the commission will have until September 2011 to make recommendations to the governor.

Massachusetts and Michigan represent the two alternatives in dealing with the effects of identity theft laws. States can either adopt laws quickly to respond to the legitimate public need for enhanced identity theft security and address the consequences in a post-hoc fashion or wait until sufficient information is gathered about the effects of a proposed law are known before crafting the law. Both approaches have merit and both approaches have a drawback. Laws that are enacted quickly respond immediately to a crisis but may have unintended harmful consequences. Laws that are crafted after careful deliberation are less likely to have unintended harmful consequences but will expose consumers to more risk until the deliberation process is completed.

Those who study identity theft will have to deal with two major issues in future. First, as technological advances become widespread, the need for new laws or changes to existing laws will emerge. As technology changes and evolves, there is a growing need for modifying and improving laws aimed at protecting consumers from identity theft. Identity theft laws are generally written in response to an existing problem, so new problems will likely continue to affect consumers before responses can be put into effect. This is a phenomenon not unique to the issue of identity theft. However, the rapid pace of technological change and the opportunities that these changes provide for criminals seeking to steal the identities of others make it of particular importance for this topic.

Second, a balance must be struck between the need to respond quickly with new laws that address pressing concerns that individuals have regarding identity theft and the need to weigh the relative costs and benefits of the proposed laws. If laws are enacted without forethought, the unintended consequences can cause more harm than the law seeks to avert. However, the time needed to consider all potential factors and gather input from all affected parties can delay needed action for years in some cases. No single correct answer exists for how much attention should be given to the goal of a speedy response compared to a measured response. It will vary with each case and depend on several factors, including the potential harm of inaction, the likelihood of the behavior occurring, the nature of the activity, the ability of existing laws to mitigate the behavior in question, and the demands of citizens.

Further Reading:

Logweller, Cary, ed. *Identity Theft Breaches*. New York: Nova Science Publishers, 2009; McNally, Megan M., and Graeme R. Newman, eds. *Perspectives on Identity Theft*. Monsey, N.Y.: Criminal Justice Press, 2008; Mitic, Scott. *Stopping*

Identity Theft: Ten Easy Steps to Security. Berkeley, Calif.: Nolo 2009; National Crime Prevention Council. *Preventing Identity Theft: A Guide for Consumers*. Washington, D.C.: National Crime Prevention Council, 2005; Stickley, Jim. *The Truth about Identity Theft*. Upper Saddle River, N.J.: FT Press, 2009. Also see the State Security Freeze Protection Site. Available online. URL: http://www.consumersunion.org/campaigns/learn_more/003484indiv.html. Accessed September 20, 2009; and the FTC's Identity Theft Site. Available online. URL: http://www.ftc.gov/bcp/edu/microsites/idtheft/. Accessed September 20, 2009.

– *Walter Huber*

juvenile crime and gangs

The history of juvenile crime and juvenile justice in America begins with social notions of what it means to be "young." Prior to the 1800s in the United States, "juveniles" were not a recognized group. They were not a special or protected class, and, as such, few laws or policies existed that were tailored to them. There were few attempts to restrict employment, mandate care, or require education for minors. In short, youth, in social expectation and under the law, were ostensibly equivalent to adults. In the 19th century, academics began to embrace the notion that youth did not have the same mental and physical capacities as adults. Child development emerged as a legitimate school of thought. Society began to accept the notion that children would require socialization from their primary caregivers (most often parents) to grow into mature and well-adjusted adults.

Rapid urbanization, industrialization, and rampant poverty in the 19th century drove the American middle class to assess some children, primarily economically disadvantaged and minority youth, as a threat to the "morals of society." Delinquency was on the rise and the family, or the primary agent of socialization, was seen as failing. Citizens began to rally for legal changes that would mandate minimal requirements for the care of youth. Laws to limit child labor and requirements for youth education coincide with the move to handle juvenile offenders distinct from adults.

The first separation of juvenile offenders from adult criminals came with creation of the House of Refuge (New York) by the Quakers in 1825. The House of Refuge was the first of many reform institutions designed to simulate the family environment and socialize youth in desirable ways. Children, who were seen as in need of care, were taken from their guardians, housed in the institution, and educated or required to work. Despite critiques that Houses of Refuge were too disciplined for youth, the institutions existed for a century.

After the establishment of Houses of Refuge, middle-class advocates, thus known as the "Child Savers," began a movement to create a separate justice system for juveniles. The Child Savers saw delinquency, running away, neglect, and abuse all as indicators of the same fundamental problem, the lack of an appropriate familial influence as opposed to some innate criminality. At the time, young offenders convicted of a crime were imprisoned with adult criminals. Youth advocates rejected this practice and argued that the consequence of housing impressionable youth with hardened adult criminals would be a more sophisticated juvenile delinquent. The Child Savers proposed a separate system (with separate facilities) that could focus on the individual needs of any troubled youth.

Critics have argued that the Child Savers were not the humanists they alleged to be. Instead, some critique them for unfairly imposing middle-class notions of gender, race, sexuality, and income on marginalized populations. In other words, they were "reforming" youth that failed to conform to middle class ideals of "moral" behavior.

Regardless of the critiques, the vision of the Child Saving Movement did succeed. The Illinois Juvenile Court Act of 1899 established the first independent judicial system for minors. The original juvenile court did not distinguish between "children in need." The court's jurisdiction included minors who violated the penal code (i.e., juvenile delinquents) and abused or neglected youth. They also took responsibility for status offenders. "Status offenders" engaged in behaviors that are against the law only because of the age of the individual (e.g., underage drinking, running away). The court was designed under the *parens patriae* philosophy, or the belief that the government should act in the best interest of the child when guardians cannot or have not provided sufficient care. In contrast to the criminal court, the juvenile court was not designed to determine guilt. Court officials were afforded discretion to identify the needs of juveniles and provide rehabilitation (e.g., education, vocation, religion) in a nonadversarial format. By the same token, juveniles were not afforded the same constitutional safeguards as adults. Juvenile court proceedings and records were also kept private so as to limit the stigma of court appearances on youth. By 1917, all but three states in the United States had established a separate juvenile court system. There was, however, little consistency in the implementation and mission of juvenile courts across the nation.

In 1920, many juvenile court systems added incorrigibility and truancy to the list of types of status offense cases the court would handle. Incorrigible youth were those incapable of being controlled by their guardians. Common behavior of incorrigible youth, particularly females, was engaging in sexual behavior. Truant youths were those who failed to attend the mandatory schooling. Like abused, neglected, or delinquent youth, these types of behaviors were seen as indicative of a youth in need and that could be treated by the juvenile court.

Previously (1912), Congress had created the Children's Bureau to investigate and report on all aspects of the welfare of children. Specifically, the bureau was to be cognizant of youth mortality, desertion, orphans, juvenile courts, disease, employment, and legislation for youth. Beginning in the 1930s, the Children's Bureau began reporting on oppressive aspects of juvenile justice. They found that status offenders were often incarcerated for longer periods of time than delinquent offenders. The treatment promises of the juvenile justice system were not evident, and juvenile crime was on the rise. By the 1950s, the belief in juvenile rehabilitation was fading. Treatment was slowly being replaced by more punitive responses.

Though the original juvenile court did not distinguish between delinquents and other juveniles in need, states in the 1960s began to revise their delinquency laws. Concern grew about status offenders being treated in the same way as delinquent youth (given that status offenders' behavior was only problematic due to their age). As such, juvenile courts during this period began to distinguish between juvenile delinquents and other youth in need.

The original juvenile court was designed to be nonadversarial and, therefore, juveniles were not seen as needing the same constitutional due process rights afforded adults. This changed in the mid-20th century when the Supreme Court issued a series of decisions that changed the constitutional rights of juvenile offenders, and subsequently the structure and process of the juvenile court.

Perhaps the most significant case, *In re Gault* (1967), afforded minors basic due process rights. Gerald Gault was a 15-year-old boy arrested and charged with making indecent phone calls to a neighbor. He was placed in detention without his parents being notified. He went before the judge without the neighbor ever being called to testify. He was ordered to be placed in the juvenile training school until the age of 21. And he was not granted an appeal. All of these events were allowable by state law because of the wide discretion given to the juvenile court. The Supreme Court used its decision in this case to apply numerous constitutional rights to juveniles. Among the safeguards afforded were the right to counsel, the privilege against self-incrimination, the right to appeal, the right of cross-examination, and the right to confront an accuser.

Within the next two decades the Court gave juveniles all the same due process protections as adults with the exception of the right to bail and jury trial. These court rulings have since been cited as spurring the destruction of the rehabilitative ideal of the juvenile justice system. Some have argued that increasing procedural safeguards for juveniles has made the juvenile justice system substantively indistinguishable from the criminal justice system.

Nationally, both the executive and the legislative branches of government were also active in juvenile justice reform. Under President Lyndon Johnson, the Juvenile Justice and Delinquency Prevention and Control Act of 1968 allocated funds for states' juvenile justice systems. This act granted monetary and technical assistance from the federal government to states and local governments for juvenile justice training programs. Regardless of these programmatic and policy efforts, juvenile crime rates continued to rise through the 1960s and 1970s. In addition, numerous incidents of abuse were reported in juvenile training facilities.

In response, Congress and President Gerald Ford passed one of the most significant pieces of juvenile justice legislation, the Juvenile Justice and Delinquency Prevention Act of 1974 (JJDPA). The JJDPA replaced previous national legislation that had been refined and amended since 1968. This marked the first time a unified national program was created to deal with the issue of juvenile delinquency prevention and control within the larger criminal justice system. The legislation created the Office of Juvenile Justice Delinquency and Prevention (OJJDP) to oversee the distribution of federal funds for programs and research. It also implemented programs designed to reduce juvenile delinquency in constituting the government's attempt to coordinate all federal programs and provide assistance to states and local entities. In a significant change, JJDPA removed the possibility of incarceration for status offenses. It also required incarcerated juveniles to be separated by sight and sound from any adult offenders in correctional facilities.

The JJDPA passed Congress with very strong majorities in both the House and the Senate. It was considered a welcome departure from previous strategies, which were held to be disjointed. Seemingly, the only downside to the legislation was its potential costs. In a statement released immediately after his signing JJDPA, President Ford noted that, despite the national commitment to improve the situation of juvenile delinquency in the United States, he was particularly concerned about the fiscal effects of such a substantial overhaul of federal organizations and funding in a struggling economy. Therefore, despite the massive organizational shift, he did not allocate any new funding for the JJDPA. Instead, he relied on the $155 million already appropriated under current juvenile programs.

Regardless of its fiscally conservative start, the JJDPA has been reauthorized by the government ever since its inception in 1974. Each time the bill has received widespread, bipartisan support. Hundreds of interest groups continue to advocate for its continuation. Over time, the JJDPA has mandated removal of juveniles from adult jails (1980), increased programs to support families (1984), allocated resources to address minority overrepresentation (1988), defined and restructured gang intervention programs (1992), and offered special attention to juvenile sex offenders who were themselves victims of abuse and neglect (1992).

In the mid-1970s Robert Martinson publicized the results of a metaanalysis evaluating the effectiveness of criminal rehabilitation programs. His analysis with colleagues Lipton and Wilks concluded that, when it comes to rehabilitation programs, "nothing works." The widely read report symbolizes the sentiment of the time that rehabilitation was futile (despite the fact that the report was later widely discredited). Soon after, the United States experienced a significant upsurge in the rate of violent youth crime. In particular, violent offenses committed by juveniles with guns soared through the 1980s and peaked in the early 1990s.

Through the 1970s and 1980s both liberals and conservatives launched attacks on criminal justice policies. Liberal academics commonly argued that policies were being implemented with little consistency. They called for less discretion in sentencing. Conservative academics began a renewed emphasis on belief in the "rational" criminal. The deterrence framework of certain, severe, and swift sanctions regained popularity. Then, in the 1990s, a number of conservative scholars, such as James Q. Wilson, began to speculate about an upcoming wave of juvenile crime. They predicted that "super-predators," a wave of violent youth without conscience, would take over the nation's streets in 2000. This newfound prediction helped fuel policies designed to curb youth violence, both real and envisioned.

All of these forces aided in a shift of attitudes from rehabilitation toward "get tough on crime." Policies soon followed that increased accountability, deterrence, just desserts, and incapacitation. By the mid-1990s, 47 states had increased their sanctions for youth violence. One of the most common types of reform became to expand the methods in which juveniles could be prosecuted and sentenced in the criminal courts. In addition, legislatures began to allow more public access to juvenile court records and hearings. Despite juvenile arrests decreasing through most of the 1990s, punitive responses toward juvenile delinquents increased.

Even with the popularity of punitive policies, significant efforts continue to be made to reorient policies toward prevention and intervention. For example, the Office of Juvenile Justice Delinquency and Prevention (OJJDP) introduced Comprehensive Strategies for Violent and Chronic Juvenile Offenders in 1993. This marked a shift from only "get-tough" responses toward juvenile crime toward a more "balanced" model. The OJJDP response prioritizes juvenile offenders with histories of serious or violent offenses. The balanced approach uses multiagency collaboration to target delinquency prevention. It includes a component of immediate intervention to prevent chronic delinquency. And it still allows for a control-based response for the small group of juveniles who are serious, chronic offenders. The balanced approach to juvenile justice has gained more support in recent years.

Public concern over gang members and violence also took center stage during the rise in crime in the 1980s and 1990s. Like delinquency, gang crimes increased to unprecedented levels in the 1990s with precipitous declines thereafter. A "moral panic" concerning gangs fueled a series of punitive gang policies. This trend continues today. Historically, gangs have proved to be a formidable challenge for local, state, and federal agencies. Programs and policies aimed at gangs and gang members have been less successful than those designed for dealing with juvenile delinquents more generally. It has been repeatedly suggested that attempts to control or eradicate gangs have had the unintended consequence of increasing gang solidarity and cohesion as opposed to weakening the groups.

Suppression techniques, or responses that rely on increased law enforcement or justice system sanctions, are the most commonly reported method for dealing with gangs despite the fact they are also viewed as the least effective. Common suppression techniques include massive police roundups, the development of specialized gang units, and sentencing enhancements for gang-related crimes.

Beginning in the 1980s, many police departments took gangs out of the general police responsibility and created specialized gang units. By 1999, more than 55 percent of large American police departments had gang units. Police gang units are responsible for one or more of four principal functions: (1) intelligence, (2) enforcement/suppression, (3) investigation, and (4) prevention. Studies have found that gathering intelligence was the primary function of 83 percent of gang units across the country. This intelligence is generally maintained in databases designed to track gang members (e.g., CalGangs in California) and then used in the investigation, enforcement, and prosecution of gang crimes.

Law enforcement involvement in gang prevention often takes the form of public education programs for youth, such as the Gang Resistance Education and Training (GREAT) Program. The GREAT Program is the largest and mostly widely evaluated gang prevention program in the country. The program consists of elementary and middle school curriculums, a summer program, and training for families. From five regional centers, law enforcement officers are trained and dispatched to schools all over the country. The program is designed to develop students' interpersonal skills to help them avoid the use of violence or delinquency to solve conflict. Evaluations of the original program showed small, but consistent, reductions in victimization and improved attitudes toward the police, but did not show differences in gang membership, drug use, or delinquent involvement. The program was revised and reintroduced in 2003. Short-term effects (i.e., one year after participation) of the revised curriculum show lower rates of gang membership and self-reported delinquent offending in GREAT participants as compared to non-GREAT students. A longitudinal evaluation of the program is currently underway.

Like the police, prosecutors have also created specialized gang units. A number of district attorneys' offices organize their gang units around the "vertical prosecution" philosophy. This method ensures that the same prosecutors handle all aspects of a gang case from the charge to trial through sentencing. This manner of prosecution has been adopted to maximize the knowledge of the attorney trying the gang case, thereby increasing success.

Another popular mechanism used against gangs in court is to consider gang members a special type of criminal offender and to enhance the sentence for gang crimes. Prior to the 1980s, prosecutorial attempts to treat gang membership as a special class of criminal were generally ineffective. This was primarily because the courts ruled that the definition of a "gang" was far too vague.

This changed in 1988 when California enacted one of the most significant pieces of gang targeted legislation. The California Street Enforcement and Prevention (STEP) Act defines a "criminal street gang" as a group of three or more people (either formal or informal) that has the commission of (enumerated) crimes as a primary activity, has a common name or sign, and whose members, either alone or together, have a pattern of criminal gang activity. This more concrete definition allows for sentencing enhancements (i.e., increased punishments) for gang crimes. California's legislation opened the door for other states to target gang members in court without violating their constitutional rights. By 2008, 46 of 50 states had enacted statutes directed specifically at criminal gang activity. Thirty-six states and the District of Columbia have legislatively defined a "gang," and 21 states have defined "gang crime/activity." Laws in most states that have followed the California legislation have withstood court challenges.

In addition to criminal sanctions, states have also pursued gang members in civil court. Civil gang injunctions/abatements use public nuisance laws to prohibit gang behavior on behalf of the city or neighborhood. Civil injunctions have been used to prohibit gang members from committing crime and engaging in other gang activities. Other behaviors prohibited by injunctions have been a limit to gang members congregating in public, flashing gang signs, carrying pagers, possessing weapons, intimidating witnesses, and extortion. Civil gang injunctions have successfully withstood constitutional challenges (e.g., *People v. Acuna,* 1997).

The National Youth Gang Suppression and Intervention Program by OJJDP was the first national effort aimed at the U.S. gang problem and was launched in the early 1990s. The program was designed to develop model approaches that focused on community-wide responses to gangs. The result was the Comprehensive, Community-wide Approach to Gang Prevention, Intervention, and Suppression Program (a.k.a., Comprehensive Gang Strategy, or Spergel Model), now a driving force behind the OJJDP response to gangs. The program has five modalities of intervention: (1) community mobilization, (2) social intervention, (3) provision of social opportunities, (4) suppression, and (5) organizational change and development of local agencies and groups. Again, like OJJDP's stance on delinquency, this program focuses on a balanced and comprehensive approach to dealing with gangs.

In addition, the OJJDP now operates other programs and centers to assist in its response to gangs. They operate the National Youth Gang Center (NYGC) to compile and review relevant gang literature, assessments of national gang programs, and independent research. In 2006, the Department of Justice initiated the Youth Gang Prevention Initiative to provide support for prevention programs that target young offenders returning to the community and help them resist gang involvement and to increase enforcement to respond to gang-related violence.

In addition to the aforementioned strategies, federal, state, and local governments have sponsored the implementation of numerous programs targeting at-risk and gang youth. No shortage of programmatic attempts have been made to control gang members or gang-related crimes. Programs have been designed to address the problem from a variety of angles. Strategies have included providing social opportunities such as jobs and education (e.g., Safe Futures), targeting youth firearm usage (e.g., Youth Firearms Violence Initiative, Operation Ceasefire), combating drugs, implementing gang member databases (e.g., CALGang), comprehensive service provision (e.g., 8 percent Solution in Orange County, Illinois, Gang Crime Prevention Center), mediation of gun violence between gangs (e.g., CeaseFire), and curfew enforcement (e.g., Community-Oriented Policing Services). Unfortunately, to date, while programs have been shown to significantly reduce delinquent behavior, far fewer programs have proved effective in significantly reducing gang activity or preventing gang membership/formation.

Further Reading:

Fearn, Noelle E., Scott H. Decker, and G. David Curry. "Public Policy Responses to Gangs: Evaluating the Outcomes." In *The Modern Gang Reader*, edited by Arlen Egley, Cheryl L. Maxson, Jody Miller, and Malcolm W. Klein. 3rd ed. Los Angeles: Roxbury Publishing Company, 2006; Feld, Barry. *Bad Kids: Race and the Transformation of the Juvenile Court*. Oxford: Oxford University Press, 1999; Tanenhaus, David S. *Juvenile Justice in the Making*. Oxford: Oxford University Press, 2004.

– *Kristy N. Matsuda*

---

prisons and corrections

As of 2008, the United States had over 2.3 million adults behind bars, including 1.5 million adults housed in state or federal prison, and over 700,000 in jail. This marks a sevenfold increase in the U.S. prison population since 1970. These numbers also make the United States the world's leader in incarceration, ranking above countries such as China (1.5 million prisoners) and Russia (895,000 prisoners), ranked second and third in the world, respectively. Measuring the U.S. prison population in relation to the total size of the U.S. population, Americans are far more likely to be imprisoned than are their Chinese, Russian, or western European counterparts. The U.S. incarceration rate, for example, at 750 per 100,000 population, by far exceeds Germany's 93 per 100,000 population. Today, 1 in 100 American adults are behind bars.

For many, these numbers are striking. One can reasonably ask why is it that the United States, a country viewed by many around the globe as a symbol of freedom and individualism, has witnessed such a large increase in its prison population that it leads the world's nations in imprisonment? This article on prison and corrections policy in the United States is designed to help answer this question. To do so, it is necessary to examine a variety of corrections-related policies enacted over the past three decades and the problems and political forces that helped produce those policies.

To begin, it is important to note that prison and corrections policies encompass a wide swath of rules, regulations, and processes that can involve all three major branches of government, and each level of government (federal, state, and local). In many cases, corrections policies involve capital investments. Policies governing whether new prisons or jails will be built to meet a growing need for prison beds, or whether preexisting but outdated facilities will be updated with new beds and modern safety technologies, are all good examples of corrections policies revolving around capital investment decisions. In addition, corrections policies also structure the rules, responsibilities, and behavior of those working and living inside the nations' prisons and jail facilities themselves. Prisons are generally viewed as federal or state correctional facilities that confine offenders serving a criminal sentence of more than one year. Jails are correctional facilities typically found at the local (city and county governments) level and are generally reserved for confining individuals awaiting trial or those who are waiting to be transferred to other correctional facilities after a criminal conviction in a court of law. Policies that dictate rules regarding inmate supervision, quality of prisoner health care, education and drug and alcohol rehabilitation services, and the pay scales of prison wardens and correctional officers, are but a few examples of corrections policies that dictate life inside correctional facilities. For the most part, these decisions are made within the government budgeting process, whereby lawmakers at the federal and state levels of government decide how scarce correctional resources are best used. Should scarce correctional dollars be used for building new prison facilities or might they be spent more efficiently by updating outdated facilities? To what extent should correctional dollars be allocated for prisoner education or drug and alcohol rehabilitation programs? These are just several questions that policy makers may ask themselves during the annual or biannual budgeting process, with the end result all representing clear cases of corrections policies.

But correctional policies also stretch into areas such as criminal sentencing, which includes controversial issues such as the death penalty and laws that structure the length of time (if any time at all) one must spend behind prison walls for a given criminal act. By proxy, these policies also structure the rules and regulations that govern a prisoner's release (in many cases a process known as parole), and whether an ex-prisoner will be monitored by corrections officials upon his return to society. From an even broader perspective, corrections policies can spill over to influence what might traditionally be viewed as "social policies," that is, policies that affect employment, marriage, or familial bonds. Because those who are sent off to prison often leave behind a spouse and children—those who are often reliant on that individual for their livelihood—a trip to prison has important, and in many cases, detrimental implications for a wide net of people, and not just for those individuals actually serving time. Time spent in prison can also carry with it a lasting stigma of a criminal record, which can often affect an ex-convict's ability to gain employment upon release given many employers' unwillingness to hire a convicted criminal. A criminal conviction that requires an extended separation away from family and friends increases the probability of failed marriages and may lead to family structures that are permanently broken. Corrections policies viewed from this broad conception cannot all be sufficiently addressed in a single article. But taken as a whole, prison and corrections policies encompass much more than those policies directly pertaining to governing what goes on behind prison walls.

Prison and corrections policies in the United States often tug at the center of a long-standing debate surrounding the government's role in relation to two often competing goals—promoting and protecting individual liberty and the maintenance of public safety. Maintaining public safety—that is, preventing or protecting the general public from events or actions (such as with cases of criminal activity like assault, murder, rape, and burglary, among others) that pose significant danger, injury, or harm—has long been viewed as a core function of government. But imprisonment, and the state's ability to take away an individual's freedom for acts that threaten public safety, also represents the height of state power, posing a direct challenge to individual liberty. Given this, it is not surprising that debate has been lengthy about how the government should wield its powers in the pursuit of public safety. How should the government use its coercive powers of imprisonment in the name of maintaining public safety? Under what conditions, that is, for what types of crimes, should the government imprison individuals, and for how long? What is the "right" punishment for a given action? All of these strike at the heart of the debate about how to best balance the need for public safety while also protecting citizens' individual liberties.

Corrections policies in the United States, like many other policy areas, have changed over time, reflecting a dynamic policy-making process. In the United States, throughout much of the 18th and 19th centuries, prisons and correctional facilities themselves were designed to punish those who committed acts that threatened public safety.

But the term "correctional facility"—what we might think of today as a prison or jail—got its very name from the fact that in these years, correctional institutions were intended to "correct" individual behavior. Thus, the idea was to place a real emphasis not only on punishment, but also on individuals' rehabilitation and successful reintegration into mainstream society.

To the extent that rehabilitation occurred is a mixed picture at best. Even during colonial times, punishments could be severe and long lasting. In many of the early colonies, convicted offenders, having served out their criminal sentence, found themselves with restrictions on their ability to enter into marriage or business contracts, obtain certain jobs, or invoke their right to vote. Lacking many of the rights enjoyed by "full" citizens, these policies made it difficult for many to reenter free society. In contrast to the sanctions widely imposed during the 18th and 19th centuries, a short period of reform characterized prison and corrections policies during the 1950s and 1960s, when political actors both inside and outside of government (including the Presidential Commission on Law Enforcement, the American Bar Association, and the American Law Institute) relied on the more ideological liberal courts of the 1960s to restore greater civil rights for convicted criminals and placed a renewed emphasis on prisoner rehabilitation and reintegration rather than simple punishment. Corrections reform efforts at the national level spilled over to the state legislatures by the early 1970s. These reforms are perhaps best represented by the growth in the number of state laws that required an automatic restoration of criminal offenders' rights after completing their sentence.

Even with the successful reforms of the 1960s and 1970s, the overarching tendency in the last three decades has been to place *more* punishment and restrictions on those convicted of criminal acts, not less. As will be discussed in greater detail below, corrections policies have become much more punitive over the past generation—the effects of which are perhaps best reflected in the burgeoning prison population in the United States.

When considering some of the changes in U.S. corrections policies, perhaps most striking is the dramatic punitive shift in U.S. criminal sentencing policies beginning in late 1970s and early 1980s. The punitive nature of these policies is perhaps best exemplified by the presence and use of the death penalty and the enactment of a variety of tough sentencing policies, including "mandatory minimum" sentences and "truth-in-sentencing" laws. Those in favor of tough sentencing policies argue that the threat of execution or long-term incarceration helps promote public safety by deterring potential criminals and repeat offenders from committing criminal acts because they can be certain of their sentence if caught. Others suggest that such punitive measures do little to deter crime and have led to overcrowding in jails and prisons that place a large strain on states' fiscal resources.

With the U.S. Supreme Court's reinstatement of the death penalty in 1976, relative to other advanced western democracies, the United States is the only country to retain and use the death penalty for certain capital offenses. At the state level, the presence and use of the death penalty varies across state correctional systems. State governments have significant discretion in deciding not only whether to enact a death penalty law, but, among those states that have such a law, how often and under what conditions criminal offenders are sentenced to death. These differences in states' propensities to enact death penalty laws and the rate in which executions are carried out is largely determined by the level of political support for the death penalty among citizens, elected officials, and judges within each state. Currently 38 of the 50 U.S. states retain the death penalty; combining each of the state's death row inmates brings the total number of death row inmates across the states to over 3,000. Of the nine states that carried out death penalty executions in 2008 (all by lethal injection), Texas had the greatest number with a total of 18, while Kentucky had the fewest with 1.

The increasingly punitive nature of sentencing policy in the states is also reflected in the growth and diffusion of "mandatory minimum" and "truth-in-sentencing" policies. To understand the nature of these policies, a larger focus on more general changes in criminal sentencing policy is instructive. Prior to the late 1970s, criminal sentencing in the United States primarily followed what is called an "indeterminate sentencing" model. Under this broad sentencing model, after an individual had been arrested and convicted of a criminal crime, the courts typically prescribed a *sentence length* that included a minimum and maximum time (e.g., two to five years). Prisoners were generally not eligible for parole (that is, they were not eligible for release to society) until they had served at least the minimum sentence prescribed by the court. Parole boards could not hold someone in prison longer than their maximum sentence, but, importantly, parole boards based upon a subjective evaluation of a prisoner's record (i.e., if a prisoner had good behavior in prison, participated in rehabilitation programs, or showed sufficient remorse for crimes committed) had significant discretion to release prisoners prior to that maximum sentence time.

But with crime rates (mainly street crimes) beginning to rise in the late 1960s, many lawmakers began to be pressured to "do something" about the crime problem. Rising public concern about crime—partly driven by media stories about paroled prisoners participating in new criminal acts upon release—led to consistent complaints, particularly from the conservative right, that judges and parole boards were "too lenient" on criminal offenders. In short, ideological conservatives argued that, in many cases, criminal punishment was often too soft. The assault on indeterminate sentencing was heard not only from the political right. Many on the political left, with concerns about racial and ethnic inequality, argued that parole boards and judges treated racial and ethnic minority prisoners differently from white prisoners. Racial and ethnic minorities, it was believed, were more likely to receive longer criminal sentences and less of a chance for parole.

By the mid-1970s, then, the indeterminate sentencing model was under attack from the political left and right, but for different reasons. These political forces helped lead to what is called a "determinant sentencing" model in which *legislative* institutions introduced mandatory minimum sentences for specific types of criminal acts (i.e., drug offenses, weapons offenses, or repeat offenses) via the enactment of legislation, placing severe constraints on what types of sentences judges could issue and the conditions under which prisoners could be paroled. Moreover, in many states, the parole boards had their power seriously curtailed or were eliminated outright. Thus, under the indeterminate model of sentencing, the bulk of the power, when it came to criminal sentencing and release decisions, rested in the hands of judges and parole boards. In contrast, under the determinant model, power shifted to elected lawmakers in legislative institutions, who imposed much more stringent minimum sentencing guidelines for specific types of crimes, based on what they perceived was appropriate.

In a similar vein to the use of mandatory minimums imposed by legislatures, by the mid-1980s, a number of states began enacting "truth-in-sentencing" laws. These laws vary significantly by state, but they focus largely on making violent offenders serve a greater proportion of their maximum sentence by eliminating, or severely curtailing, the ability of prisoners to earn early release. To a large degree, states began to impose these truth-in-sentencing laws because of political fiscal pressures passed down from the federal government stemming from enactment of the 1994 Violent Crime Control and Law Enforcement Act. This act dramatically expanded federal funding for hiring additional police officers in cities across the country, imposed a strict ban an assault weapons, and provided over $9 billion in additional funds for new prison construction. However, for the states, there was a catch. If states wanted federal dollars for prison construction, they were required to enact truth-in-sentencing laws that required violent offenders to serve not less than 85 percent of their prison sentence. By 2001, 30 states, including the District of Columbia, had enacted such laws, while others, including the state of Texas, required violent offenders to serve at least 50 percent of their sentence. Perhaps the most stringent form of mandatory minimums and truth-in-sentencing laws have come in the form of "three strikes and you're out" laws adopted by dozens of states during the mid-1990s. California, the largest state in the union, and the state with the largest prison population in the country (in part due to its own "three strikes" law passed in 1994), perhaps best exemplifies the punitive nature of three-strikes laws. Under the California law, a criminal offender convicted of a felony, but who also has two prior convictions for "serious or violent felonies," is sentenced to three times the normal presumptive term (to be served consecutively), or 25 years to life, whichever is longer.

As one might expect, adoption of mandatory minimums and truth-in-sentencing laws has had a profound impact on the length of time prisoners remain behind bars. Discretionary releases based on parole board decisions have dropped precipitously over the past two decades; 55 percent of prisoners were released by parole boards in 1980, but only 25 percent by 2001. With fewer "early" releases, more prisoners today are likely to serve out their entire prison sentence. In 2001, the number of state inmates serving their full sentence was six times greater than was the case in 1980.

Without doubt, the significant changes in U.S. criminal sentencing policies have contributed to the ever-growing prison population in the United States described in detail above. The overall effect of large prison populations is only now being fully felt—with the biggest burden placed on state governments who must find ways to pay for the housing of hundreds of thousands of additional state prisoners, many of whom are serving for longer periods. This has proven to be a difficult challenge, particularly as state governments have faced severe economic constraints in the immediate aftermath of the terrorist attacks of September 11, 2001, and, to a greater degree, after the collapse of the housing and banking industries in 2007 and 2008.

Prisons and jails are very capital intensive. They require large, highly trained staffs, and they operate 24 hours a day, seven days a week. Inhabitants of prisons and jails are more troubled and sicklier than is the general population. The growing prison population necessarily means more people to feed, clothe, house, and supervise. While the cost varies between states, the average cost of incarceration per prisoner in the United States in 2005 was $23,876. If one were to add these costs over, say, an inmate's 10-year sentence in the "average" state, it would total $238,760. The high average costs of incarceration are reflected in states' overall corrections-related spending. In 2007, the states spent over $49 billion on corrections-related expenditures, while only $12 billion 20 years earlier.

Year by year states' rising corrections costs are taking more out of their general revenue funds. This means fewer resources are often left for other important goals and needs valued by the public, including health care, education, or environmental protection, among others. On average, according to a 2008 Pew Center for the States report, states spent about 6 percent of their general revenues on corrections during the 2007 fiscal year—or 1 out of 15 general fund (discretionary) dollars. Forty-two of the 50 states have seen their overall corrections budgets (as a percentage of their overall budget spending) increase over the past 20 years. Corrections expenditures have gotten so large in some states, that they now spend more money each year on corrections than they do on higher education spending. Based on 2007 data, five states (Vermont, Michigan, Oregon, Connecticut, and Delaware) spend as much, or more, on corrections than they do on higher education. Some policy makers are questioning the benefit of spending an ever increasing slice of the state budget on incarceration. For example, are taxpayers getting their money's worth? Is there a "good return" on corrections' investments in the form of greater public safety? Could this money be better spent? This article will return to these questions at its conclusion, but a key question remains: How exactly did we get here? We know, for example, that prison populations are larger than ever, and that part of the story behind the prison population boom revolves around some of the dramatic changes in criminal sentencing policies. But what specific social or political forces led the United States down this path?

Lansing Correctional Facility in Kansas *(Photo by Americasroof/ Used under a Creative Commons license)*

Certainly one possibility is that crime rates have increased significantly in the United States over the past three decades, leading policy makers and citizens alike to support greater efforts at putting criminal offenders behind bars and expanding the use of "tough on crime" corrections policies. Research, however, shows that this is not the case; in fact, the rise in punitive correction policies has been largely independent of the crime rate in the United States. The answer, many experts believe, involves politics, and the many political benefits that elected officials received from being viewed by the public as "tough on crime." To best understand how politics has played such a critical role in the rise in tougher corrections-related policies, it is helpful to take a quick look back at recent political history.

Corrections policy before the early 1960s was generally viewed as a subject reserved for practitioners and technocrats—those who had the greatest amount of expertise on the subject—while elected leaders gave it little public attention. However, as street crime rates began to rise in the 1960s, the crime issue was first introduced into national partisan politics beginning with the 1964 presidential election. Barry Goldwater, the Republican presidential nominee of that year, warned of the "growing menace in our country . . . to personal safety, to life, limb, and property." He argued further that crime and rising disorder in the wake of the Civil Rights movement threatened freedom that must be "balanced so that liberty lacking order will not become the license of the mob of the jungle." Even with this rhetoric, the issue of crime in the mid-1960s failed to resonate with most voters; public opinion polls indicated that only about 4 percent of the public said crime was among the country's "most important problems," ranking far below other foreign policy and domestic issues.

Yet it was during this time that the Democratic Party and the Republican Party appeared to follow two divergent paths over how best to solve the crime problem. Many Republicans, taking the lead from Goldwater, increasingly used crime as a "wedge" issue as a way to secure support from more conservative Democratic voters who (along with conservatives) tended to blame rising crime rates on bad choices made by individuals, lenient judges, and soft punishments. For example, in his 1970 State of the Union Address, Richard Nixon effectively declared war on the "criminal elements which increasingly threaten our cities, our homes, and our lives." Wanting to be viewed as "tough on crime," Republicans advocated policy prescriptions that followed a deterrence and incapacitation approach, which promoted increased arrests, higher rates of incarceration, stricter probation and parole monitoring, and mandatory sentencing aimed at dissuading criminal activity by removing offenders from the larger community. In contrast, liberal Democrats tended to view the crime problem as a result of structural components such as urban poverty and the decline of urban manufacturing jobs. Because of this, they promoted policies aimed at fixing the so-called root causes of crime, not necessarily tougher sanctions.

With the election of Ronald Reagan as president, corrections policies became further detached from their technical, less political roots of the 1950s, emerging front and center in America's "morality politics" fights of the 1980s. In the process, the crime issue became closely connected to an ongoing cultural debate in America about what social ideals were most valued and what it meant for citizens to lead "just" and "righteous" lives. As part of this debate, the crime issue has often been portrayed by elected leaders, interest groups, and the media in broad, politically polarizing ways. Crime was used to help define what it meant for individuals to act responsibly or irresponsibly, and what constituted moral or immoral behavior. In short, the debate surrounding the crime issue became emotionally charged, and, as a result, support for punitive policies such as increased arrests, incarcerations, and longer sentences—all driven by emotional, symbolic rhetoric—became the norm.

Not wanting to be caught on the "wrong" side of a salient political debate laced in moralistic terms, risk-averse Democrats concluded that the only way to defend against law and order politics as defined in the 1980s and into the 1990s was to "get to the right of Republicans." In other words, many Democrats felt that to gain public support on the crime issue, and to win elections, Democrats had to be perceived as tough, or tougher, than Republicans on the issue. Many liberal Democrats, for example, had opposed the death penalty since its resumption in 1976, but, by the 1990s, Democratic congressional members introduced a variety of bills with multiple new capital offenses. There seemed to be a quasi competition within the Democratic Party about who could outdo the other when it came to being "tough on crime." In 1991, Senator Joseph Biden (D-DE) boasted that his crime bill called for the death penalty for 51 different offenses while President Clinton's proposal included only 46 offenses. Overall, this "shift" created a convergence on the crime issue among Democrats and Republicans, lending enough political support to form legislative majorities in support of the tough corrections policies described in detail above.

It is these political forces that, most agree, have largely structured the U.S. corrections and prison policies of today—policies that, as discussed above, have placed severe economic strains on state budgets. But even with the high economic costs associated with the punitive corrections policies promoted by *both* major political parties since the 1980s and 1990s the question remains: Are they worth it? One way to answer this, of course, is to measure whether they have markedly improved public safety. For example, if crime has dropped precipitously throughout the "tough on crime" era, then it could be argued that regardless of the cost involved, the public is "better off" because of improved public safety, and, with that, the public's overall quality of life. The 1990s, particularly, witnessed a substantial drop in violent crimes. Between 1993 and 2001, the number of violent crimes per 1,000 population dropped nearly 50 percent. Property crime rates (per 1,000 population) during this period dropped 47 percent. Violent and property crime rates have remained relatively low during much of the 2000s as well. Estimating the *independent* effects of rising incarceration rates on the decline in crime rates over this period has proven to be a highly complicated process because researchers have to also account for a large list of alternative factors that may have contributed to the decline in crime. These might include changes in unemployment levels, reductions in drug use (or certain types of drugs such as crack cocaine), or changes in demographic characteristics over time. Given this, researchers attempting to isolate the effects of rising incarceration rates on the decline in crime have often published a wide-ranging set of estimates. However, studies using the most rigorous statistical techniques, that is, those that should be viewed as the most reliable, suggest that about 2 to 5 percent of the total decline in crime during the 1990s can be attributed to the growth in imprisonment. If these numbers are correct, this suggests that 95 to 98 percent of the total drop in crime during the course of the 1990s would have occurred even without the prison boom.

Regardless of some of these statistics, for many, the drop in crime over the past decade provides an important signal about the efficacy of punitive corrections policies. From this perspective, the public is better off, and indeed "more safe," as a result of the policies enacted and implemented over the past three decades. But for opponents of the increasingly punitive corrections paradigm, the relatively small effect that higher imprisonment rates appears to have had on the decline in crime simply isn't worth the cost. Opponents are quick to point to the high economic costs associated with corrections mentioned above as reasons for their objections, but they are also increasingly pointing to the unequal distribution of punishment across racial groups and socioeconomic classes. For example, while blacks comprise about 12 percent of the U.S. general population today, they comprise nearly 50 percent of the U.S. prison population. It terms of a black/white imprisonment ratio, blacks are about eight times more likely to be incarcerated than whites. These disparities have led to heated debates about principles of equality and civil rights and will likely continue to do so in the years ahead.

In conclusion, a logical question remains: What will prison and corrections policies look like over the next decade or two? In the short run, with more states faced with overcrowded prisons, there is likely to be a growth in U.S. prison construction to help meet the demand. This is much easier said than done, however, as construction of new prisons often comes to a grinding halt due to local political concerns and the NIMBY (Not in My Back Yard) problem. The NIMBY problem occurs in situations in which the public supports a policy in a general sense—say, the building of a new prison—but locals do not want it built in their neighborhood. Thus, in many local communities, building new prisons is widely unpopular because of concerns about local public safety. Some states, unable to increase prison capacity sufficient to meet the demand, have been forced to begin releasing some less-violent prisoners back to the community earlier than planned.

While still in a relatively early stage of development, a growing chorus of voices argues that building more and more prisons to house more and more prisoners is not sustainable over the long run. Rather, policy makers need to find better ways to protect public safety at a much lower cost. High rates of recidivism among offenders released from prison after serving their sentences is one issue that has received considerable attention at both the state and federal levels of government. Although tracking recidivism rates can be technically difficult, the latest data from the Bureau of Justice Statistics shows that approximately 25 percent of prisoners released from prison are rearrested and returned to prison with a new sentence within three years after being released. To help reduce this "revolving door" effect, advocates of corrections reform suggest that correctional systems need to do a better job of preparing prisoners for reentry into community life by providing prisoners greater access to drug rehabilitation, job training, and other education programs while serving out their sentences. The extent to which states provide rehabilitation and "reentry" programs to prisoners varies widely across the United States. Corrections systems in some states have high quality reentry programs that are used by a large number of prisoners, others have programs but are poorly run and underutilized, while still others have no programs at all. Fiscal capacities and support for rehabilitation programs among elected leaders and prison officials explain much of the variation in access to prisoner reentry programs across correctional systems among the states.

However, in the past few years, several states, including Texas, Ohio, and Washington—states viewed as among the "toughest on crime" in the country—have instituted a set of new policies designed to reduce their prison populations and lower corrections costs. In 2007, Texas dramatically expanded its in-prison and community drug treatment funding, while Washington and Ohio have established a number of groundbreaking prisoner "reentry" programs that place a greater emphasis on providing services (drug rehabilitation, job training, housing, life skills training, and medical care) that advocates say prisoners need to improve their chances at successfully reentering society. In 2008, Congress took a dramatic step to expand prisoner reentry services by enacting the Second Chance Act, which provides millions of dollars in grants to states to expand their prisoner rehabilitation and reentry services. Many analysts have noted that a bill such as the Second Chance Act would not have been politically feasible even just a few short years ago. The overall drop in crime and a corresponding decline in the salience of the crime issue have provided some political space for "softer" corrections and crime policies to reach the governing agenda. Overall, it is too soon to know if this newfound emphasis on prisoner reentry has had any real or lasting effects on reducing states' prison populations, or its larger impact on public safety. Officials in the state of Texas have been encouraged with the early results. For the first time in over two decades, the state witnessed a small decline in its prison population in 2008. If prison reentry programs prove to be successful, even marginally so, U.S. prison and corrections policy over the next decade or two may place a much greater emphasis on rehabilitation than has been the case in the past.

Further Reading:

Beckett, Katherine. *Making Crime Pay: Law and Order in Contemporary American Politics.* New York: Oxford University Press, 1997; Pastore, Ann L., and Kathleen Maguire, eds. *Sourcebook of Criminal Justice Statistics.* Available onlins. URL: http://www.albany.edu/sourcebook/. Accessed on August 16, 2010; Smith, Kevin B. "The Politics of Punishment: Evaluating Political Explanations of Incarceration Rates." *Journal of Politics* 66 (2004): 925–938; Tonry, Michael, "Why Are U.S. Incarceration Rates So High?" *Crime and Delinquency* 45 (1999): 419–437; Travis, Jeremy. *But They All Come Back: Facing the Challenges of Prisoner Reentry.* Washington, D.C.: Urban Institute Press, 2005; Western, Bruce. *Punishment and Inequality in America.* New York: Russell Sage Foundation, 2006.

– Garrick L. Percival

---

sex offenders

Much of criminal law policy is made and implemented at the state level. As a result, policies related to sex offenders have been established primarily by state and local legislative action. In the mid-20th century, most criminal law was still shaped by a low-profile coalition of legal experts and prosecutors, with some input from law enforcement officials and defense attorneys, reflecting the view that law reform should depend more on professional expertise than on political judgment or influence. This process began to change later in the 1960s, as crime rates began to rise and "law and order" became a "hot button" political issue, particularly in state and national campaigns.

In 1960, the national rate of serious violent crimes, as reported in the FBI's *Uniform Crime Reports*, was 161 per 100,000 people. The reported rate for forcible rape was 9.6 per 100,000 people. Because forcible rape, unlike other violent crimes, was defined by law as a crime that could be committed only against women, reporting a rate based on total population was misleading. There was also general agreement that the crime was underreported by victims, with estimates ranging from 1 in 3 to 1 in 10 rapes being reported to the police.

The 1960s marked the beginning of a rise in reported crime that lasted for more than 20 years, with reported rapes rising from 9.6 per 100,000 people in 1960 to 18.7 in 1970, 36.8 in 1980, and 41.2 in 1990. Beginning in the 1990s the overall crime rate began to decline. By 2000, the number of forcible rapes had declined to 32 per 100,000. By 2007, the rate was 30 per 100,000, the lowest reported level in almost 30 years. But crime, particularly violent crimes by strangers against women and children, continued to serve as a polarizing issue in many political campaigns. The 2008 presidential campaign was the first in 40 years in which crime was not a major campaign issue.

Major organizations that focused on the treatment of women and their legal rights formed as the Women's Movement emerged in the 1960s and 1970s. The most prominent national organization was the National Organization for Women (NOW), founded in 1966. More women were elected to state and national legislatures, where they began to work together on issues of particular interest to them. In 1977 women in the House of Representatives formed the Congresswomen's Caucus, now the Congressional Caucus for Women's Issues, to work on shared legislative interests. Many state legislatures established committees on the status of women or comparable bodies to gather information on the problems facing women and to propose legislative responses.

Rape crisis centers began to appear in 1972, when the DC Rape Crisis Center, in Washington, D.C., and Rape Relief in Seattle were founded. By 1974, centers existed in 43 states. By 1976, more than 400 centers were open across the country. Initially formed to provide support and assistance to rape victims, they quickly began to focus on changing provisions of the criminal law that made it difficult to successfully prosecute rape cases. Local organizations soon formed statewide alliances and loosely organized national groups that shared program information and political strategies. The first of these was the National Coalition of Women Against Rape, later the National Coalition Against Sexual Assault (NCASA).

At its 1973 national conference, NOW established the National Rape Task Force, charged with researching existing laws and developing a model statute for rape reform; the actual model statute was approved at the 1974 conference. In 1975, the American Bar Association passed a resolution supporting broad changes in state rape laws and improvements in the treatment of rape victims. The first National Women's Conference, held in Houston in 1977, also endorsed major changes in existing rape laws.

The first major reform of rape law occurred in Michigan in 1974. Rape crisis centers, the Michigan Women's Task Force on Rape, and the Michigan State Women's Commission worked with prosecutors on a comprehensive reform of the law to improve the chances of successful prosecution and to eliminate provisions that put the victim on trial. The Michigan Criminal Sexual Conduct statute became a model for rape law reform, and, by the late 1980s, every state had enacted at least some of its reform elements. They included:

1. Rape shield laws to restrict the ability of defense attorneys to pose questions about the victim's sexual history or reputation.
2. Identifying rape as a crime of violence by changing the name from rape to criminal sexual conduct (as Michigan did) or sexual assault.
3. Gender-neutral language that encompassed male and female perpetrators and victims and included a broader range of abusive actions.
4. Multiple degrees of the crime based on the actions committed, the amount of force used or threatened, and the age of the victim. Michigan law created four degrees of criminal sexual conduct involving either sexual penetration or sexual contact.

5. Emphasis on force or intimidation by the assailant and lack of consent by the victim, without requiring physical resistance.
6. Elimination of corroboration requirements that required witnesses to the crime.

Many of these changes were incorporated into federal law in the Sexual Abuse Act of 1986, which used the term "sexual abuse" to refer to rape and other crimes of sexual violence. Introduced without success in 1984 and 1985, the proposal was sponsored in 1986 by Representative John Conyers, Jr. (D-MI), and Senator Charles Grassley (R-IA), and passed in both houses by a voice vote. By 1986, its provisions were relatively noncontroversial.

Most states had based their rape statutes on the English common law crime, which defined rape as an act that could be committed only by a man against a woman "not his wife." Until 1976, when Nebraska changed its law to eliminate this "marital exemption," a man who raped his wife could not be prosecuted. Married men had, in the words of David Finkelhor and Kersti Yllö, a "license to rape." In Oregon, one of the earliest states to change its law, the 1978 trial of John Rideout for the rape of his wife Greta drew national attention and generated serious public debate on the issue. Although Rideout was acquitted in a jury trial, the case helped to mobilize efforts to abolish the marital exemption throughout the country.

By 1993, at least some forms of marital sexual assault had been criminalized in all 50 states and the District of Columbia. In many states, the marital rape exemption was simply eliminated. Some states amended their laws to explicitly reject marriage as a defense to rape charges. Several states created separate offenses that applied to spouses or cohabiting parties, but they imposed special reporting requirements on the victim or limited prosecution to the most serious offenses.

The effort to eliminate the marital exemption was organized by advocacy groups that worked with victims of rape and domestic violence, supported by legal support groups and feminist organizations with a broader policy focus. Prosecutors, who had supported the earlier reforms, generally viewed this campaign as an impractical effort that would result in few successful prosecutions, and they feared that women would take advantage of the law to threaten their partners with false charges. Some state legislatures had established subcommittees, or special committees, that were aware of the difficulties faced by rape victims and supported reform. But legislators were often unsympathetic, as evidenced by the flippant comment reportedly made by California state senator Bob Wilson, chair of the State Senate Judiciary Committee: "If you can't rape your wife, who can you rape?"

The overall strategy was two part, seeking change through state-by-state legislation and challenging existing laws in selected court cases. The state-level lobbying involved the same groups that were already working on rape reform, including mainstream organizations such as the American Association of University Women, the YWCA, and the National Council of Jewish Women. This coalition had become stronger and better organized as a result of earlier reform efforts. Statewide organizations coordinated the efforts of local rape crisis centers and shelters, and larger budgets now allowed full-time employees to be paid in a reliable manner. Activists within the rape and domestic violence movements increasingly worked together as it became clear that domestic violence often involved both physical and sexual violence. Testimony by marital rape victims had a dramatic impact at legislative hearings.

National organizations were particularly helpful in challenging the marital exemption in the courts. In addition to the American Civil Liberties Union (ACLU), whose Women's Rights Project was founded in 1972 by Ruth Bader Ginsburg (appointed to the U.S. Supreme Court in 1993), and the Center for Constitutional Rights, legal arguments were developed and argued by the National Center on Women and the Law and the NOW Legal Defense and Education Fund (now known as Legal Momentum). The National Clearinghouse on Marital and Date Rape provided invaluable research materials and other assistance; its founder, Laura X, worked tirelessly on these issues for 20 years.

Cases challenging the marital exemption were carefully chosen to highlight the brutality of marital rape. One of the first was *Commonwealth of Massachusetts v. Chretien* (1981), decided by the Supreme Judicial Court of Massachusetts. The defendant broke into the residence of his wife, who had filed for divorce, and forcibly raped her. After police allowed him to leave, he returned that same night and raped her again. In *People of the State of New York v. Liberta* (1984) the defendant beat and repeatedly raped his estranged wife in the presence of their two-year-old son. The *Liberta* decision by the New York Court of Appeals was the first to strike down a state's marital exemption as an unconstitutional denial of equal protection to women. By 1986, the elimination of the marital exemption from federal law (as part of the Sexual Abuse Act of 1986) drew almost no notice.

Although the law now permits prosecution for sexual assault within a marriage, most criminal prosecutions are brought against spouses and cohabiting partners who have already separated. The campaign to end the marital rape exemption and to expand the definition of "rapist" to include husbands and intimate partners has changed the public perception of sexual assaults and sex offenders. Acquaintance rape (or "date rape") was rarely prosecuted in the 1970s and legally excluded from prosecution in some states; 20 years later it was perceived as a serious crime that could successfully be prosecuted.

The Violence Against Women Act of 1994 (VAWA), reauthorized in 2000 and 2006, was first enacted as Title IV of the Violent Crime Control and Law Enforcement Act of 1994. Senator Joseph Biden (D-DE) was the principal sponsor and moving force behind the bill, introducing it in 1990 and in each subsequent session of Congress until it was passed. The bill was originally limited to domestic violence, and the first hearings before the Senate Judiciary Committee that Biden chaired were dominated by testimony on domestic violence from victims, researchers, and service providers. Mary Beth Carter, president of NCASA at this time, recalls: "We questioned why you could call this 'violence against women' and not include rape." NCASA and the NOW Legal Defense and Education Fund worked with committee staff to make the bill more inclusive. By 1993, when the bill finally made it out of committee, it included provisions that increased the penalties for federal sex crimes, required convicted offenders to pay restitution, strengthened the federal rape shield act, and authorized grants for law enforcement, prosecution, and victim services. Title III of the bill, "Civil Rights for Women," allowed the victim of a crime of violence motivated by gender and due, at least in part, to "animus based on the victim's gender" to bring a civil lawsuit in the federal courts.

Senator Biden sought, and received, bipartisan support for VAWA from the start. The bill also received strong support from a wide range of women's groups. The National Task Force to End Sexual and Domestic Violence Against Women brought together dozens of national organizations, ranging from the National Center for Victims of Crime and the National Association of Women Judges to Business and Professional Women (BPW) and the General Federation of Women's Clubs. The task force also worked with activists and local grassroots organizations across the country to build support for VAWA and reached out to civil rights groups, churches, labor unions, antipoverty groups, and business organizations to build support beyond the usual core of feminist organizations.

In 1992 and 1993, the committee staff issued two reports that dramatically documented existing levels of violence against women and the problems rape victims encountered within the criminal justice system. Public opposition to VAWA was generally muted. Rather than directly opposing legislation for crime victims, opponents focused on the cost of its programs and the likelihood of wasteful "pork." The ACLU was almost alone in opposing provisions that authorized harsher treatment of arrestees and longer sentences for convicted offenders. It also opposed the "Civil Rights for Women" section, arguing that "gender-motivated violence" was so broadly defined that the right to sue could be abused. This section was also opposed by the Judicial Conference of the United States, made up of judges from the federal district and appellate courts. Chief Justice Rehnquist, speaking for the conference, criticized the legislation for federalizing actions that should be addressed in state courts. But the section stayed in the bill.

The VAWA statute was enacted as Title IV of the Violent Crime Control and Law Enforcement Act of 1994, the omnibus anticrime legislation supported by President Clinton. The provision allowing federal lawsuits in cases of violence motivated by animus based on gender was soon challenged in court. Christy Brzonkala, who filed the suit, was represented by attorneys from the NOW Legal Defense and Education Fund. In the Supreme Court case (*U.S. v. Morrison* [2000]), numerous amicus curiae briefs were filed. The VAWA provision was supported by 36 states, the National Network to End Domestic Violence, the Association of Trial Lawyers of America, and numerous women's organizations and civil rights groups. Senator Joseph Biden also filed an amicus curiae brief.

Morrison, the lead defendant, was represented by the Constitutional Center for Individual Rights. Briefs arguing that the VAWA provision was unconstitutional were filed by Alabama (the only state to take this position) and a number of conservative legal and political groups. Lawyers on these briefs included Edwin Meese III, attorney general under President Reagan, and Jay Bybee, soon to be the assistant attorney general for the Office of Legal Counsel under President George W. Bush.

Chief Justice Rehnquist, writing for a 5-4 majority in *U.S. v. Morrison*, agreed with the lower courts that Congress had exceeded its power under the constitution's commerce clause, because violent acts against women are essentially criminal (a matter of state law) rather than economic. Justice Souter, in an opinion joined by the other three dissenting justices, argued that Congress had gathered a "mountain of data" on the economic and social effects of sexual assault and domestic violence, and emphasized that the 36 states supporting the statute had recognized that "the current system for dealing with violence against women is inadequate."

Because of the Supreme Court's decision in *U.S. v. Morrison*, the "Civil Rights for Women" section was eliminated from VAWA when it came up for reauthorization later in 2000. The new VAWA legislation again had bipartisan support. It had become a symbol of a tough stance on crimes against women, and was difficult to oppose directly. However, pressure from sponsors and supporters was required to end Republican delays and ensure a floor vote before the end of the congressional session. VAWA was eventually combined with other legislation in the Victims of Trafficking and Violence Protection Act of 2000, and approved by votes of 371-1 in the House and 95-0 in the Senate. Although Republicans might be opposed to some of the programs that VAWA funded, they were unwilling to vote on the record against a bill for victims of violence and abuse.

By 2005, VAWA was supported by most members of Congress as pro-victim legislation that was also anticrime. While Senator Biden remained the chief sponsor and moving force behind the bill, it was also supported by conservative senators Orrin Hatch (R-UT) and Jeff Sessions (R-AL). Despite the addition of a controversial amendment to establish a national DNA registry of anyone detained by the police, even if they were not arrested or charged, VAWA 2005 was approved 415-4 in the House and by unanimous consent in the Senate, and was signed into law by President Bush in January 2006.

Gender neutral language in the reform laws acknowledged the possibility of male rape victims, and feminists coined the phrase "same sex rape" to replace the demeaning and suggestive "homosexual rape." But throughout the 1970s and 1980s little attention was given to the possibility of adult male victims. The men most likely to be assaulted, those incarcerated in jail or prison, were almost completely ignored in the campaign against rape. Sexual assault in prison was the subject of jokes, and was accepted as an inevitable part of incarceration. Prison was a brutal place; weaker men were raped, "owned" by stronger inmates and made available to other prisoners in return for payment or favors. On occasion, the family of a prisoner who was injured or became suicidal as a result of rape would ask why correctional institutions could not or would not protect vulnerable inmates, but little came of these individual complaints.

Feminists first addressed the problem of sexual abuse of women prisoners, primarily by guards and others in positions of authority. The 1974 case of Joanne Little, who killed a jail guard as he raped or attempted to rape her, drew national attention to the issue. The Southern Poverty Law Center helped to defend her when she faced murder charges, and 28 members of Congress, led by Representative Elizabeth Holtzman (D-NY), asked the Attorney General to investigate charges that sexual assaults on prisoners were common at the jail. More than 20 years later, Representative John Conyers, Jr. (D-MI) introduced the Custodial Sexual Abuse Act of 1998, which attempted to create federal law on sexual abuse by prison staff. He was unsuccessful in getting the bill attached to the VAWA reauthorization bill or in moving it out of committee on its own.

Without federal legislation, the issue had to be addressed on a state-by-state basis. Feminist organizations and groups supporting women prisoners kept the issue in the public eye and pushed for statutory reforms. Prison administrators and unions generally opposed legislation, offering the internal disciplinary process as an alternative. But the principle of these proposals, protecting prisoners against sexual abuse and exploitation, was difficult to oppose. By 2005, all but two states had criminalized custodial sexual contact in some way.

Although the laws were written in gender neutral terms, they were applied almost exclusively to female prisoners. Male prisoners were most likely to be victimized by other prisoners, although their abuse was sometimes condoned or encouraged by guards. Documenting the dimensions of the problem has been difficult. Carl Weiss and David J. Friar, authors of the sensationally titled *Terror in the Prisons* (1974), used anecdotal evidence to estimate that as many as one in five male prisoners would be raped. A carefully designed study of inmates in the Midwest state prisons by the Struckman-Johnsons, published in 2000, found that 7 percent of male prisoners reported being raped, and over 20 percent reported some form of coerced sexual contact. In the "Findings" section of the Prison Rape Elimination Act of 2003, Congress accepted "conservative estimates" that at least 13 percent of inmates in the United States have been sexually assaulted in prison.

Stop Prisoner Rape, founded in the 1990s and headed by Stephen "Donny" Donaldson and Tom Cahill, was the most active of several organizations working to end sexual assault in prison and to help survivors. Donaldson published an opinion column in the *New York Times* in 1993 on "The Rape Crisis Behind Bars," and he was the principal author of an amicus curiae brief on prison rape for the case of *Farmer v. Brennan* (1994). In that case, the Supreme Court ruled that correctional officers are obligated to protect prisoners from violence, including sexual assault at the hands of other prisoners, and that officers may be held liable if they act with "deliberate indifference" to threats to the safety of prisoners.

In the 1990s, the National Prison Project of the ACLU, along with Amnesty International USA and Human Rights Watch (HRW), became involved in efforts to document and prevent prison rape. By 2003, when the Prison Rape Elimination Act (PREA) was approved, the issue was no longer treated with derision. Michael Horowitz, a fellow with the Hudson Institute in Washington, D.C., is credited with building an unusual coalition of liberal and conservative organizations in support of the bill, including evangelical and mainstream church organizations. After being stalled in 2002, PREA was unanimously passed by both houses of Congress and signed into law in 2003. No one wanted to be on record as favoring prison rape. But as one commentator noted, "The fact that the bill passed Congress unanimously should be proof enough that it lacks vigorous enforcement mechanisms." PREA has been criticized by activists for doing relatively little to actually prevent or eliminate prison rape. Even so, the passage of the legislation represented a major turning point in public perception, as congressional leaders acknowledged that prison rape was both widespread and unacceptable.

PREA emphasized research and education, creating the National Prison Rape Elimination

Commission (NPREC) to study existing practices and make recommendations. Under the authority of PREA, units within the Department of Justice have developed training programs and published annual reports on sexual violence in detention facilities. In 2009, NPREC issued a comprehensive report documenting the scope and impact of sexual abuse in prisons, which it described as "a serious concern with dire consequences." The report set forth national standards to prevent, detect, and respond to sexual abuse in prisons, jails, police lockups, immigration detention facilities, community corrections centers, and juvenile facilities. Under a sunset provision in PREA, NPREC must disband 60 days after it submits its report. To ensure continuing attention to the problem, NPREC presented a set of recommendations to the Department of Justice and Congress designed to institutionalize responsibility and expand funding for training, research, and new programs.

Many state legislatures passed child protective statutes during the early 20th century, but they were generally implemented through the emerging system of juvenile courts. The informal methods and the closed proceedings of these courts meant that most allegations of child abuse were handled out of the public eye. Only the most dramatic and violent cases, often involving abduction or murder as well as sexual assault, were tried in the criminal courts. A stereotypic view of the child sexual offender (or "child molester") emerged, comparable to the stereotypical rapist: a violent, dangerous, mentally unbalanced stranger. Sexual abuse within the family was ignored, or distanced with another stereotype of the uneducated, isolated hillbilly family.

The rape law reforms of the 1970s and 1980s expanded the definition of child sexual assault and increased the likelihood of successful prosecution. As incest and statutory rape were included in the general offense of sexual assault, the harmful effects on victims were more likely to be acknowledged. The reforms also included graduated penalties. Prosecutors had persuaded feminist advocates that severe penalties made young victims less willing to report an assault and juries less willing to convict.

Federal legislation in the 1980s focused on the problem of child abductions. When John Walsh's six-year-old son Adam was abducted from a Florida mall and murdered, Walsh and his wife launched a campaign in Adam's memory to create a national clearinghouse of information on missing children. This was the first of many campaigns that have been organized in the name of a particular victim whose abuse or death had received public attention. Putting the victim's name on proposed legislation and presenting the legislation as a way of memorializing the victim have been extremely effective ways of gaining publicity and support for proposed changes, and they continue to be used by proponents of legislation to prevent or punish child sexual assault.

The Walsh family's efforts eventually led to passage of the Missing Children's Act (in 1982), the Missing Children's Assistance Act (1984), and the creation of the National Center for Missing and Exploited Children. Although no organized opposition to these bills emerged, most law enforcement agencies did not actively support them because of the logistical and workload problems associated with creating and administering a national database.

The programs created by these laws certainly helped to locate some missing children and reunite them with their families. At the same time, they were criticized by feminist activists, scholars, and some law enforcement officials as largely symbolic efforts. These groups argued that by focusing on stranger abduction, the programs did little to address the more common risks posed to children by family members and friends. As required by the 1984 legislation, the Justice Department's Office of Juvenile Justice and Delinquency Prevention (OJJDP) commissioned a national study of missing children, published in 1990. The study found that close to half of all missing children were either runaways (often due to physical or sexual abuse at home) or "throwaways" (children who were ordered out of their homes or barred from returning). Although only a few thousand children, 2 to 3 percent of the total number of missing children, were abducted by nonfamily members, these cases continued to drive public policy.

In October 1993, 12-year-old Polly Klaas was abducted at knife point from her home in Petaluma, California. Her body was found two months later. Despite the adoption of the federal laws championed by John Walsh, there was still no effective national network for sharing information or organizing search activities. In 1994, Polly's father, Marc Klaas, formed the Klaas Kids Foundation to work on this problem and related issues.

In July 1994 another high-profile crime captured public attention. Seven-year-old Megan Kanka was sexually assaulted and killed by Jesse Timmendequas, a convicted sex offender who had recently moved in across the street from Megan's family in Hamilton Township, New Jersey. Believing that they could have protected their daughter if they had been aware of his record, Megan's parents circulated a petition for legislation that would require police to notify residents when a convicted sex offender moved into the area. Within a few months, the petition garnered more than 400,000 signatures. The New Jersey legislature quickly enacted a community notification law that required convicted sex offenders to register with the police. The campaign for the bill occurred primarily in the media; the legislature held no hearings and did not consult experts in the field. Less than three months after Megan Kanka's death, the legislation known as "Megan's Law" was signed into law.

New Jersey's law was not the first statute to require sex offenders to register with law enforcement, but it had a dramatic impact. Minnesota had adopted predatory offender registration and community notification laws in 1991 after an active lobbying campaign by Patty and Jerry Wetterling, whose 12-year-old son Jacob had been abducted at gunpoint in 1989. After 1991, the Wetterlings began to push for federal legislation requiring every state to have a sex offender registry. They were among a group of victims and family members, including Marc Klaas, who were invited to testify before the House Subcommittee on Crime and Criminal Justice as it considered President Clinton's proposals for what became the Violent Crime Control and Law Enforcement Act of 1994. Their proposal for a federal registration requirement became the Jacob Wetterling Crimes Against Children and Sexually Violent Offender Registration Act. It was approved as part of the larger act and signed by President Clinton on September 13, 1994, only six weeks after Megan Kanka's death.

Because criminal law is largely under state jurisdiction, the law did not directly order sex offenders to register. Instead, states were required to have an "effective registration program" as a condition of eligibility for various funding and grant programs included in the act. The federal Megan's Law, adopted in 1996, required states to make registry information available to the public. By the end of 1996, all 50 states had approved a sex offender registration statute.

This rapid compliance was due less to the threat of losing federal dollars than to the broad coalition supporting registration and community notification and the general popular appeal of the policies. The cases that brought the registry proposal into the mainstream had defined it first and foremost as a crime prevention measure that helped to protect innocent children from violent predators. The media attention given to these cases and the growth of Internet networking made it possible for local community residents to come together in support of a simple measure that appeared to protect their families and neighborhoods. "Law and order" politicians and groups that supported tougher penalties for crimes could also support the proposals. Registration imposed additional post-prison burdens on convicted sex offenders, made it easier for police and parole officers to monitor their actions, and provided a host of detailed regulations that could provide grounds for further incarceration if offenders were not in full compliance.

Opponents most often objected to specific details of a bill or its proposed implementation, not to the general policies of mandatory registration and community notification. For example, law enforcement agencies pointed out the difficulties of tracking sex offenders as they moved from one jurisdiction to another, and noted that police departments lacked the manpower needed to confirm addresses and other information. Not surprisingly, program evaluations have consistently found that a significant portion of sex offenders covered by these policies have either failed to register or have provided incomplete or inaccurate information. Many law enforcement agencies also objected to requirements for active community notification, preferring to retain control by making information available only on request or under specific circumstances.

Despite the general popularity of these policies, there was some opposition. The ACLU's National Prison Project opposed the growing number of restrictions that were added to the basic registration requirement. The ACLU argued that the restrictions imposed additional punishment on those convicted of sexual offenses that went beyond the authorized prison sentence and stigmatized offenders in very public ways. Many prison reform groups also took this position, emphasizing how some of the restrictions associated with the registration requirement made it difficult for convicted offenders, many of whom had families, to find employment and legal housing. Juvenile justice organizations opposed the sweeping nature of the registration laws, which required many young offenders convicted of relatively minor crimes to register as convicted sex offenders, in some states for life.

While most feminist organizations did not directly oppose the popular registration and notification laws, they made the point that the majority of sex offenders would go unidentified and undeterred by these measures. More than 70 percent of all victims of child sexual assault are abused by family members and friends, most of whom have not previously been convicted of a sexual offense. They pointed out that existing laws, all named as memorials to child victims, offered symbolic reassurance but did little to actually protect children against the risks they were most likely to encounter.

Legal challenges were brought against the registration and notification laws in several states, with mixed results. Two of the cases were eventually heard by the U.S. Supreme Court. In *Smith v. Doe* (2003) the Court, in a 6-3 decision, held that the Alaska Sex Offender Registration Act was not an unconstitutional ex post facto law because it was intended as a civil, nonpunitive measure. In *Connecticut Department of Public Safety v. Doe* (2003) the Court unanimously upheld the legality of the Connecticut registry process, which posted offenders' names, addresses, photographs, and personal descriptions on the Internet with unlimited access.

Over time, an increasing number of restrictions were imposed on sex offenders. Registered sex offenders were prohibited from living near schools and parks and excluded from certain occupations and public activities. In 2006, a California referendum (Proposition 83, also called Jessica's Law) was proposed by two conservative state legislators. The proposition would prohibit all registered sex offenders from living within 2,000 feet of any school or park, and require lifetime Global Positioning System (GPS) monitoring of some offenders. Despite opposition from legislators, judges, and a state criminal defense attorneys association, the measure was approved by more than 70 percent of California voters.

In 2005, Congress began to develop a comprehensive federal law to replace the existing patchwork of statutes that had been adopted and amended over more than 20 years. The new law, known as the Adam Walsh Child Protection and Safety Act, standardized the existing network of registration and notification laws in Title I, the Sex Offender Registration and Notification Act (SORNA). It also expanded the number of sex offenses that required registration, imposed stricter registration and verification requirements, and made failure to register a federal felony with a maximum punishment of 10 years in prison. The bill passed by unanimous consent in both houses and was signed in 2006 by President George W. Bush in a highly publicized signing ceremony attended by the Walshes.

As the debate over sex offenses continued, some argued that the options available to sentencing judges under existing laws were not sufficient to protect the public against the most dangerous offenders. One response has been to use civil commitment statutes to confine predatory sex offenders after the completion of their criminal sentences. This kind of policy, first adopted by Kansas, has raised concerns about the indefinite confinement of individuals who have served their sentences but are still believed to be dangerous. The Supreme Court upheld the Kansas Sexually Violent Predator Act by a vote of 5-4 in the case of *Kansas v. Hendricks* (1997), opening the door for other states to adopt similar statutes. Officials of 39 states joined a brief urging the Supreme Court to uphold the Kansas statute as a legitimate means of protecting the community from dangerous sexual offenders. Briefs presenting challenges to the statute were prepared by the ACLU, the National Legal Aid and Defender Association, and the National Association of Criminal Defense Lawyers. Mental health organizations were divided. The Menninger Foundation and the Association for the Treatment of Sexual Abusers supported the state of Kansas, but the legislation was opposed by the American Psychiatric Association and the National Mental Health Association.

In 1995, Louisiana adopted a law making rape of a child under the age of 12 a capital crime, in spite of an earlier Supreme Court decision that appeared to prohibit the death penalty in rape cases (*Coker v. Georgia* [1977]). Five other states subsequently extended the death penalty to child rape. The first death sentence under the Louisiana statute was appealed to the Supreme Court. An amicus curiae brief opposing the penalty was filed jointly by the National Alliance to End Sexual Violence, the National Association of Social Workers, and state Coalitions against Sexual Assault in Louisiana, Minnesota, New Jersey, and Texas. Their brief argued that imposing the death penalty in child rape cases would actually harm victims by making the crime even less likely to be reported. In its 5-4 decision in *Kennedy v. Louisiana* (2008), the Supreme Court ruled that the death penalty was unconstitutional in child rape cases, based on the Court's recognition of an "existing national consensus" against its use and the Court's own independent judgment of the issue. Justice Kennedy, writing for the majority, specifically mentioned the problem of underreporting raised in the amicus curiae brief. He also noted: "In this context, which involves a crime that in many cases will overwhelm a decent person's judgment, we have no confidence that the imposition of the death penalty would not be . . . arbitrary."

Despite this recent Supreme Court decision, public opinion on the whole continues to favor a strict and punitive approach to sex offenders. However, some reports have challenged the effectiveness of the registration and notification approach that has dominated U.S. policy since 1994. A study of Megan's Law in New Jersey released by the National Institute of Justice in 2008 found that the statute had no demonstrable effect on the number of sex offense victims or the types of offenses committed and did not reduce the number of rearrests for sex offenses. The study acknowledged the broad public support enjoyed by Megan's Law programs, but suggested there might be more effective ways to achieve the stated goal of protecting children from sexual assault.

A larger and more comprehensive study of sex offender laws in the United States was released by Human Rights Watch (HRW) in 2007. HRW expressed its concerns very carefully, acknowledging the "sense of concern and urgency" that prompted the laws and the importance of "promoting public safety by holding offenders accountable." Despite these good intentions, HRW reported, "Our research reveals that sex offender registration, community notification, and residency restriction laws are ill-considered, poorly crafted, and may cause more harm than good." The report also noted that proponents of the current laws "are not able to point to convincing evidence of public safety gains from them." Rather than recommend the elimination of programs that had recently received unanimous support from Congress, HRW made recommendations to improve the accuracy and focus of sex offender registries, modify registry procedures to meet law enforcement needs, and link residency restrictions to actual offender risk levels. The HRW report generally urged the development of policies that take individual circumstances into account, and the rejection of inflexible policies like those that had been adopted in the Adam Walsh Act.

As concerns about crime began to take a back seat to economic issues after 2008, an opportunity may exist to reconsider the policies of the last 25 years. Public and legislative support for these policies remains high, but indications are that supporters may be willing to consider whether the current registration and notification laws actually deliver the safety and protection they promise.

Further Reading:

Bevacqua, Maria. *Rape on the Public Agenda: Feminism and the Politics of Sexual Assault.* Boston: Northeastern University Press, 2000; Center for Sex Offender Management (CSOM). "Fact Sheet: What You Need to Know about Sex Offenders." 2008. Available online. URL: http://www.csom.org/pubs/needtoknow_fs.pdf. Accessed July 11, 2009; Donaldson, Stephen. "The Rape Crisis behind Bars." *New York Times*, December 29, 1993. Available online. URL: http://www.justdetention.org/en/news/pre2002/doc_01_nyt.aspx. Accessed June 21, 2009; Finhelhor, David, Gerald Hotaling, and Andrea J. Sedlak. *Missing, Abducted, Runaway, and Throwaway Children in America.* Washington, D.C.: U.S. Department of Justice, Office of Juvenile Justice and Delinquency Prevention, 1990; Finkelhor, David, and Kersti Yllö. *License to Rape: Sexual Abuse of Wives.* New York: Holt, Rinehart & Winston, 1985; Human Rights Watch. *No Escape: Male Rape in U.S. Prisons.* New York: Human Rights Watch, 2001. Available online. URL: http://www.hrw.org/legacy/reports/2001/prison/report.html. Accessed June 17, 2009; ———. *No Easy Answers.* New York: Human Rights Watch, 2007. Available online. URL: http://www.hrw.org/sites/default/files/reports/us0907webwcover.pdf. Accessed June 22, 2009; Marsh, Jeanne C., Alison Geist, and Nathan Caplan. *Rape and the Limits of Law Reform.* Boston: Auburn House Publishing, 1982; National Mental Health Association (NMHA). "Confining 'Sexual Predators' in the Mental Health System." Policy Statement 55, NMHA. 2006. Available online. URL: http://www.mentalhealthamerica.net/go/position-statements/55. Accessed June 29, 2009; National Prison Rape Elimination Commission. *Report*, 2009. Available online. URL: http://nprec.us/files/pdfs/NPREC_FinalReport.PDF. Accessed July 2, 2009; Nelson, Barbara J. *Making an Issue of Child Abuse: Political Agenda Setting for Social Problems.* Chicago: University of Chicago Press, 1984; Robertson, James E. "The Prison Rape Elimination Act of 2003: A Primer." *Criminal Law Bulletin* 40 (May 2004): 270–279; Spohn, Cassia, and Julie Horney. *Rape Law Reform: A Grass Roots Revolution and Its Impact.* New York: Springer Publishing, 1992; Stolz, Barbara A. "Congress, Symbolic Politics and the Evolution of the 1994 'Violence Against Women Act.'" *Criminal Justice Policy Review* 10 (1999): 401–427; Struckman-Johnson, Cindy, and David Struckman-Johnson. "Sexual Coercion Rates in Seven Midwestern Prison Facilities for Men." *Prison Journal* 80 (Winter 2000): 379–390; Winick, Bruce J., and John Q. LaFond, eds. *Protecting Society from Sexually Dangerous Offenders: Law, Justice, and Therapy.* Washington, D.C.: American Psychological Association, 2003.

– Barbara Hayler

sexual harassment

Before 1975, the term *sexual harassment* used to describe the forced sexual coercion of women in the workplace was nonexistent in American culture, Historians of "second-wave" feminism have long noted the importance of the women's movement in successfully naming grievances that women could identify with in order to promote change. Until feminist activists coined the term *sexual harassment*, the problem of women facing abuse at the workplace at the hands of their male supervisors and coworkers remained nameless. The presence of women working alongside men resulted in various forms of sexual mistreatment, ranging from lewd comments and petting to forced intercourse and pressure to provide sexual favors in exchange for promotions. Women's reactions to these problems ranged from guilt to fear. Because of 19th-century cultural attitudes that equated working women with morally loose women, victims of sexual harassment feared the social and economic repercussions of reporting the problem—social ostracism and loss of their jobs for speaking out. These ideas persisted into the 20th century, even as the number of women in the U.S. workforce grew at a steady rate. Often, women were left with few options when sexually harassed at work. Aside from attempts to define the problem in protective labor legislation, there were few efforts to make sexual harassment a legal issue. The problem then remained underreported and misunderstood as an individual one that women brought upon themselves and not as an issue of employment discrimination. It was seen as a "part of the job" that women risked if they chose to work outside the home. Once the feminist movement mobilized and brought women's issues to the forefront of political and social change, activists framed sexual harassment as an economic problem that limited all women's employment opportunities. They also sought to change the prevailing social attitude that blamed victims while pushing for legislative measures to protect women's access to well-paying jobs.

In giving the problem of sexual harassment a name, feminists devised a framework to protest how it limited women's workforce participation. They looked to civil rights legislation when arguing that sexual harassment constituted a form of employment discrimination under Title VII of the Civil Rights Act of 1964, as amended, which prohibits discrimination in the workplace on the basis of race, color, sex, religion, and national origin. Feminist activists, legal theorists, and individual women, in speak-outs and in court cases, argued that sexual harassment deprived them of working in jobs that were economically and socially gratifying. Many of the women explained how they had been fired for complaining about the problem or had quit their jobs rather than deal with it on a day-to-day basis. In 1979, one of the leading feminist legal theorists on the issue, Catharine MacKinnon, went a step further and defined two specific types of sexual harassment in her book *Sexual Harassment of Working Women: A Case of Sex Discrimination*: quid pro quo harassment and condition of work harassment. Quid pro quo harassment refers to demands for sexual favors in exchange for an employment benefit, whereas condition of work harassment includes more subtle forms of harassment intended to intimidate victims at work.

Five years after the term *sexual harassment* was coined, the Equal Employment Opportunity Commission (EEOC), as the federal agency responsible for enforcing Title VII, issued its first sexual harassment guidelines, stating that sexual harassment constituted illegal sex discrimination. This 1980 policy was the first federal policy of its kind and accomplished two of the feminists' goals: legally defining the problem for employers and providing women an avenue through which to seek redress. In 1981, the Office of Civil Rights of the United States Department of Education (OCR) followed this lead and issued its own guidelines and defined sexual harassment as illegal discrimination under Title IX of the Education Amendments of 1972, prohibiting discrimination in education institutions.

In a definition that remains unchanged today, the EEOC outlined sexual harassment in its 1980 guidelines as "unwelcome sexual advances, requests for sexual favors, and other verbal or physical conduct of a sexual nature." The EEOC's policy included provisions for both types of sexual harassment that MacKinnon outlined. Regarding quid pro quo harassment, the EEOC explained that such conduct violated civil rights legislation when "submission to such conduct is made either explicitly or implicitly a term or condition of an individual's employment" and when "submission to or rejection of such conduct by an individual is used as the basis for employment decisions affecting such individual." The EEOC also made condition of work harassment an illegal form of sex discrimination in its policy by stating that "such conduct has the purpose or effect of substantially interfering with an individual's work performance or creating an intimidating, hostile, or offensive working environment." Because of the EEOC's phrasing and how it has been mentioned in different court decisions, this type of harassment is more commonly referred to as hostile work environment harassment.

The OCR based its definition on the EEOC's and continues to define sexual harassment as "unwelcome conduct of a sexual nature," which "can include unwelcome sexual advances, requests for sexual favors, and other verbal, nonverbal, or physical conduct of a sexual nature."

By the time these two policies were issued, women had already been fighting for the recognition of sexual harassment as sex discrimination in federal courts. During the course of 1974–1981, their case proceedings became the site in which judges first tackled this issue. These include the following decisions: *Barnes v. Train* (1974), *Corne v. Bausch & Lomb* (1975), *Tomkins v. Public Service Electric and Gas Company* (1976), *Williams v. Saxbe* (1976), *Miller v. Bank of America* (1976), *Barnes v. Costle* (1977), and *Bundy v. Jackson* (1979, 1981). Because the earliest cases had been filed before sexual harassment even had a name, the judges' decisions do not make use of the phrase until after 1976. The *Williams v. Saxbe* case was the first in which a federal district court found that sexual harassment constituted an actionable offense under Title VII. While many of the women who brought these suits did not see the same successful result as the plaintiff in this case, Diane Williams, the legal pioneering of these women and their attorneys was followed by others. By the end of 1979, nine more cases of employment discrimination had been filed at the federal level.

During this time, the issue became more complicated as lawmakers grappled with not only the question of when sexual harassment was sex discrimination but also of how much responsibility for the behavior should be attributed to employers. For instance, if an employer had no way of knowing that a supervisor was sexually harassing an employee, should it still be held liable? In 1986, these questions as well as the question of whether or not both types of harassment—quid pro quo and hostile work environment—violated Title VII reached the Supreme Court in the landmark *Meritor v. Vinson* case. When weighing these questions, the Court turned to the EEOC guidelines and ruled that both forms of sexual harassment were actionable under Title VII. When determining employer responsibility, the Court looked to agency principles and ruled that employers should always be liable for quid pro quo harassment. The Supreme Court also set the precedent that employers would be held liable for hostile-environment harassment if they knew or should have known about the problem and failed to correct it or if they did not have a reasonable sexual harassment policy and complaint procedure in place.

The next Supreme Court case involving sexual harassment was the 1993 decision *Harris v. Forklift Systems, Inc.* This case was significant for two reasons. First, the Court decided that in order to claim hostile-environment harassment alleged victims did not need to prove that they had suffered psychological damage. Second, the Court's judgment in this case became the test that has been applied to all hostile-environment cases since *Harris*, and it remains the current test for this kind of sexual harassment. The Court stated that in order to determine whether an environment is hostile or abusive, courts must look at the totality of circumstances regarding the discriminatory conduct and the level to which it interferes with an employee's work performance. In other words, hostile-environment sexual harassment may include anything from only one or two very severe abusive actions to several mild ones over a long period of time, neither of which has to be psychologically damaging.

In the 1998 case *Oncale v. Sundowner Offshore Services, Inc.*, the Supreme Court made its first ruling on sexual harassment that was not between a man and a woman. Here we see the transformation of sexual harassment law from its original usage that protected women in the workplace to protecting anyone, regardless of sex. When making its judgment the Supreme Court turned to the *Meritor* and *Harris* decisions in order to determine whether or not Title VII's prohibition "because of . . . sex" protects men as well as women and found that it could not bar a discriminatory claim in cases of same-sex harassment. The Court reiterated that for behavior to be actionable under Title VII it must be based on sex, meaning situations in which one sex is disadvantaged over the other, regardless of whether the plaintiff and defendant are of the same sex.

The Supreme Court returned to hostile-environment harassment in the workplace and the question of employer liability in two 1998 cases that were decided on the same day, *Burlington Industries, Inc. v. Ellerth* and *Faragher v. City of Boca Raton*. Both cases dealt with the principle that employers were liable for hostile-environment harassment if they knew or should have known about the abuse and did nothing to stop it. Whereas the *Harris* case provided the test for determining if an environment constitutes sexual harassment and in which scenarios corporations are liable, in these cases the Court attempted to refine the "knew or should have known standard." As a result, the Court's decision became the test for when corporations can be protected from that liability related to sexual harassment, known as the affirmative defense. The affirmative defense is only available to corporations in hostile-environment claims and protects corporations from frivolous hostile-environment lawsuits, if the employers can prove the following: First, the employer has to show that it took care to prevent and correct sexual harassment, and, second, that the plaintiff employee failed to use existing employer procedures to correct or avoid the behavior. The affirmative defense cannot completely guarantee that employers will be free from liability, but it demonstrates that sexual harassment law has evolved from the EEOC's original position regarding liability to the point where female employees are not the only persons who can seek protection in these kinds of cases.

Sexual harassment in education became a political issue at nearly the same time it grew as a concern for working women. The first appellate court case on sexual harassment in education, *Alexander v. Yale*, was decided in 1980, the same year the EEOC issued its sexual harassment guidelines. While the federal court found no cause of action under sex discrimination law in this particular case, plaintiffs continued to use Title IX throughout the 1980s when bringing claims of sexual harassment in educational institutions. Eventually, just as with the development of sexual harassment in employment law, these cases reached the Supreme Court. In the landmark 1992 case, *Franklin v. Gwinnett County Public Schools*, the Supreme Court weighed the question of financial responsibility in Title IX cases in which teachers were accused of harassing students. Before this ruling, Title IX only allowed for the federal government to terminate its funding of institutions that practiced sex discrimination. In the *Franklin* decision, the Court ruled that victims of sexual harassment may sue their schools and receive monetary damages, similar to what employee victims could do under Title VII.

In the late 1990s, the Supreme Court ruled on two other important cases involving sexual harassment in schools. While in its *Franklin* decision the Court had determined that school districts can be held liable for damages in cases where a teacher sexually harasses a student, it had not stipulated the conditions of that liability. The Court turned to this question in the 1998 case *Gebser v. Lago Vista Independent School District* and in the 1999 case *Davis v. Monroe County Board of Education*. The product of these two cases is the current test for school liability in sexual harassment cases. The test stipulates that schools are responsible for damages when they have actual notice of the harassment and are deliberately indifferent in solving the problem.

All in all, the history of the development of sexual harassment law shows the relationship between a feminist issue and public policy. Despite the strides that were made in the law recognizing sexual harassment as a form of discrimination in employment and in education, another aspect of the feminist movement's naming of the problem, public awareness, did not see similar success throughout the 1980s. There had been little public discussion of the problem owing to the uncertainty surrounding the issue. Some questioned the need for such policies as the EEOC guidelines and dismissed the problem's severity, and still others argued that they were not sure when "no" meant "no." Much of this changed in 1991 with the Clarence Thomas–Anita Hill scandal. Hill accused Thomas, her former employer and nominee to the Supreme Court, of sexually harassing her 10 years prior to his nomination when they were both employed by the Department of Education. The significance of these allegations was the media circus that surrounded Thomas's nomination before the Senate Judiciary Committee, offering a sensational story to the American public that finally made the topic of sexual harassment the subject of widespread discussion in society. In the years following Hill's testimony describing her accusations against Thomas, the number of sexual harassment charges filed with the EEOC rose sharply, and employers around the country began designing their own policies and procedures concerning sexual harassment in order to address the issue.

This history illustrates that the feminist movement was successful in shaping a problem that became federal employment policy, yet sexual harassment remains an issue that is greatly misunderstood, and, despite its inclusion in federal employment law, many disagree as to the necessity of those policies. A closer look at the rationale behind current sexual harassment policy illustrates how it was defined and framed under Title VII, instead of other avenues for redress.

When civil rights activists began lobbying for a civil rights bill after World War II, they argued for the inclusion of African-American men in American workplaces or, in other words, an end to employment discrimination on the basis of race. Activists then championed the addition of Title VII to the bill. Originally, the policy made no mention of gender until a conservative representative from Virginia, Howard Smith, attempted to defeat the bill by adding the word "sex" to the list of Title VII prohibitions. While some treated this as a joke, others, such as Representative Martha Griffiths of Michigan, stood up and defended the inclusion of the word "sex" in the bill. The Civil Rights Act passed with the sex provision included in Title VII on July 2, 1964. The act also established the EEOC for the purpose of enforcing Title VII by processing individual discrimination complaints. As the feminist movement gained ground in the 1960s, activists looked to Title VII and to the EEOC to gain access to better employment for all women.

Feminists turned to civil rights activism as a model for their arguments regarding equal rights in the workplace, and many women also began filing complaints with the EEOC as soon as it opened its doors in 1965. Another relevant trend of the late 1960s was the growing number of women in the workforce. Recent scholarship has traced the origins of the modern working women's struggle for equality in the workplace to the years just after World War II. Despite the popularity of the story that tells of the thousands of "Rosie the Riveters" who kept American factories running during the war and who later returned to their homes and housewife duties after it ended, this is not an accurate account of the reality of many working women's lives. A great number of "Rosies" did not actually leave the workforce for good after the war. Overall, the number of women in the workforce grew during the late 1940s from 25 percent of all workers and throughout the 1950s so that the percent of women in the total labor force was 34 percent by 1961. Historically, women had made up just over 20 percent of the workforce in 1910. By 1920, the figure was 25 percent, where it stayed until the 1940s. In the 1970s, the number of women in the workforce had increased to 43 percent, and the number kept climbing until 1991 when 57 percent of U.S. women were working outside the home.

The feminists who first spoke out in favor of antidiscriminatory policies for sexual harassment were products of these two postwar developments, as many had prior experience in social activist groups, such as the civil rights and anti-Vietnam war movements. They were also working women and were thus represented in the increasing statistical trend of women in the workforce. This greatly influenced their view that sexual harassment was a form of sex discrimination and should be considered as such under the law.

On May 4, 1975, a group of women met at the Greater Ithaca Activities Center in Ithaca, New York, for the first ever speak-out on sexual harassment. A total of 275 working women attended and listened to 21 women address the audience. The event was organized by three Cornell University employees, Lin Farley, Karen Sauvigné, and Susan Meyer, who had recently formed the group Working Women United (WWU) to raise awareness about sexual coercion in the workplace.

After hearing stories about local women who were sexually harassed in their community, they began to plan the May speak-out, but they did not know what to call the problem when publicizing their event. Before they left this historic meeting, the women coined the term *sexual harassment* and pledged to work together on the issue.

Once the problem of sexual harassment acquired a name and the women from Cornell formed WWU, they worked quickly to raise awareness about the problem. On April 21, 1975, Farley testified before the New York City Commission on Human Rights (NYCCHR). The commission, under the leadership of civil rights and feminist activist Eleanor Holmes Norton, was investigating sex discrimination in the blue-collar and service industries. Norton, appointed to lead this agency in March 1970, moved it into the direction of women's rights within her first few months in charge by holding a weeklong round of hearings on the problems faced by working women. She continued this effort to magnify women's inequality throughout the early 1970s. When Farley addressed Norton and the other commissioners at the 1975 hearings, she explained the problem of sexual harassment and how women were often unwilling to come forward about their experiences because of embarrassment or fear of reprisal. Following the hearings, Norton oversaw the addition of a sexual harassment provision to the NYCCHR's affirmative action policy.

As the 1970s progressed, WWU and other feminist organizers, such as Boston's Alliance Against Sexual Coercion (AASC), began to make more sophisticated arguments that sexual harassment constituted sex discrimination. Catharine MacKinnon also made similar claims in her 1979 book when she located the fundamental issue of sexual harassment in the relationship of women and work. She argued that U.S. workplaces promoted practices that disadvantaged women and, as such, affected their sexual and economic freedom in a way that put women on an unequal footing with men. MacKinnon hoped the determination that sexual harassment was sex discrimination would fix this social inequality with regard to men and women at work. MacKinnon realized that policies stipulating that sexual harassment was an illegal form of sex discrimination would provide women opportunities to improve their social status in the workplace and their economic status as well.

For these reasons, MacKinnon went to great lengths throughout her work to support the claim that sex discrimination law was the best choice for this to become reality. She analyzed all of the existing non–Title VII legal options to sexual harassment policy available in the late 1970s, including tort law, labor agreements, the Occupational Health and Safety Act, and criminal law. MacKinnon proceeded to pick apart each possible approach and discarded all of them in favor of anti–sex discrimination policy as the only solution that would remove this barrier to women's full equality in employment.

The year 1979 thus marked a significant turning point in the history of sexual harassment policy. By this time, at least six federal courts had decided that sexual harassment constituted an actionable offense under Title VII of the Civil Rights Act of 1964; Catharine MacKinnon had published her groundbreaking work; and feminist activists around the country were raising the issue as one of economic citizenship rights by protesting its negative impact on their earning capabilities and arguing for policies to address the problem. By the end of that year, the federal government also responded to the issue of sexual harassment in the form of congressional hearings. On October 23, November 1, and November 13, 1979, the House of Representatives Subcommittee on Investigations of the Committee on Post Office and Civil Service held hearings on sexual harassment in the federal government. The hearings, called after an alarming report of widespread sexual harassment at the Department of Housing and Urban Development (HUD), were led by Representative James M. Hanley (D-NY), the subcommittee chair. These hearings represent the first major federal government response to the problem of sexual harassment, and, as a result, they had lasting implications for sexual harassment policy. Because of Chairman Hanley's investigation and hearings, the first sexual harassment policies for both the federal government and private business sectors were created when the subcommittee charged the EEOC with writing its sexual harassment guidelines.

The importance of the late 1970s political arena in giving rise to feminist activism that defined sexual harassment cannot be overstated, as politicians at the local and federal level began responding to the issue. Eleanor Holmes Norton took her experience in New York City to Washington, D.C., when President Jimmy Carter appointed her to lead the EEOC in 1977. When Chairman Hanley gave Norton's EEOC the task of writing the first sexual harassment guidelines in 1980, he had confidence in Norton because of her long record of leadership on the issue of anti-discrimination policy enforcement. That Norton would then get behind an issue such as sexual harassment is not surprising given her history of activism. As a law student in the 1960s, Norton participated in both civil rights and women's rights activities. Norton's experiences as an activist and an attorney later led to her appointment as chair of the New York City Commission on Human Rights in 1970, a position she held until President Carter appointed her to the EEOC. While Human Rights Commissioner, she encouraged women to use sex discrimination law and file complaints and chaired the first-ever hearings on women's rights in the United States in September 1970. On August 19, 1975, Norton presided over another historic round of hearings when the New York City Commission on Human Rights conducted hearings on sexual harassment, the hearings in which Lin Farley and others had testified about the widespread nature of the problem. The sexual harassment clause the commission adopted after the hearings was historic because it was one of the first local policy responses to feminist activism on the issue of sexual harassment. Indeed, Norton's leadership at the commission in equal employment opportunity enforcement and in ridding that agency of an ominous case backlog made her an ideal candidate in 1977 when it came time for President Carter to appoint a new EEOC chair. By 1980, Norton had turned the agency around and was leading it in new directions in upholding Title VII and in fighting for women's equal employment opportunities. Because of the leadership roles of Hanley, Norton, and feminist activists, sexual harassment was framed as an issue of fairness and gender, one rooted in the liberal politics of the Carter administration and the feminist successes of the 1970s.

The guidelines that Norton's EEOC issued in 1980 provided more than a definition for lawmakers to turn to when considering sexual harassment cases. They also accomplished feminists' goals of making employers liable for sexual harassment and encouraging education about the problem. The EEOC's policy consisted of five paragraphs that defined the behavior, stated how it would be determined as sexual harassment under Title VII, outlined when employers were responsible for the conduct of their employees, explained when employers were liable with regard to other persons not previously mentioned in addition to other agents or supervisory employees, and, finally, stipulated why employers should implement preventive training programs to eliminate the problem. This last provision addressed one of the main ideas to come out of Chairman Hanley's hearings: not just stopping the behavior, but preventing it from happening in the first place. The 1980 EEOC guidelines included language that encouraged employers to conduct training programs about sexual harassment as well as developing complaint procedures and penalties in order to create more equitable workplaces and to avoid liability for discriminatory practices. This policy was consistent with the legal climate of the late 1970s–early 1980s in which appellate courts were ruling that sexual harassment violated Title VII and that employers were liable for the acts of their supervisors, employees, and agents.

The policy was viewed as a feminist victory, but it was not without its critics. As the Carter administration gave way to the Reagan administration and a more conservative turn in U.S. politics, employers questioned both the necessity of the EEOC guidelines and the strict liability that they provided. Consequently, these developments resulted in a second round of congressional hearings on sexual harassment. Shortly after Ronald

Reagan won the 1980 election, Eleanor Holmes Norton resigned her position as EEOC chair, leaving the organization without strong leadership during this time. After much debate before Congress, including opposition from such notable antifeminists as Phyllis Schlafly, the guidelines remained, but the disagreements over the severity of the issue hampered feminist efforts to educate the public about the problem. Eventually, the EEOC's strict liability language was removed from its guidelines as a result of the 1998 *Burlington* and *Faragher* decisions. While the EEOC guidelines and judicial decisions have not ended sexual harassment at school or at the workplace, employers and educators today have been put on notice about the problem and have heeded the warning to provide policies to try to prevent sexual harassment or to confront it when it does happen.

One ongoing issue that the Hill-Thomas scandal illuminated—in addition to the increased awareness that the Thomas hearings brought—is the tension between feminists and antifeminists regarding the problem of sexual harassment and feminist issues generally. After Clarence Thomas was confirmed as a Supreme Court justice, antifeminist organizations, including Phyllis Schlafly's Eagle Forum, targeted any members of Congress who had voted against Thomas and pledged to stop their reelection. Similarly, feminist organizations went after senators who had not supported Anita Hill. The argument over sexual harassment policy recalled points that both sides had used during the debate over the Equal Rights Amendment, including issues of equality and women's roles. New groups of women on both sides of the debate were inspired by the hearings to take a more committed stance for their cause, as membership in both conservative women's groups and feminist groups such as the National Organization for Women grew in the following years. The scandal also led to new critiques of feminist public policy, including those from Daphne Patai, who argued that the fervor of reformers in what she termed the "Sexual Harassment Industry" was leading women to fear men at the workplace and at school. Patai included Catharine MacKinnon in that group and argued that it imposed a view of women as victims on American society. These debates reflect ongoing questions about sexual harassment policy. What was once viewed as a necessity for working women is now being challenged in the context of today's workplace and education politics, where the policies are seen as outdated or unfair.

Further Reading:

Baker, Carrie N. *The Women's Movement against Sexual Harassment.* Cambridge: Cambridge University Press, 2008; Bularzik, Mary. "Sexual Harassment at the Workplace: Historical Notes." *Radical America* 12 (July–August 1978): 25–44; Cochran, III, Augustus B. *Sexual Harassment and the Law: The Mechelle Vinson Case.* Lawrence, Kansas: University Press of Kansas, 2004; Farley, Lin. *Sexual Shakedown: The Sexual Harassment of Women on the Job.* New York: McGraw Hill, 1978; MacKinnon, Catharine A. *Sexual Harassment of Women on the Job.* New York: McGraw Hill, 1978; MacKinnon, Catharine A., and Reva B. Siegel, eds. *Directions in Sexual Harassment Law.* New Haven, Conn.: Yale University Press, 2004; MacLean, Nancy. *Freedom Is Not Enough: The Opening of the American Workplace.* Cambridge, Mass.: Harvard University Press, 2006; Patai, Daphne. *Heterophobia: Sexual Harassment and the Future of Feminism.* Lanham, Md.: Rowman & Littlefield, 1998; Stein, Laura W., ed. *Sexual Harassment in America: A Documentary History.* Westport, Conn.: Greenwood Press, 1999. See also the EEOC Web site: http://eeoc.gov/types/sexual_harassment. html.

— *Sheila Jones*

surveillance and privacy

Although human societies have had notions of "privacy" in the sense of shielding personal activities from unwanted scrutiny as long as history has been recorded, the specific concept of "privacy" is of comparatively recent origin. Its roots in the Anglo-American legal tradition can be traced to the writings of the political philosopher John Locke in the late 17th century. Influenced by the ideologically motivated persecutions that had taken place in the British Isles during the previous decades, Locke emphasized that the state must be restrained from invading the property or person of its citizens. He explained in his *Two Treatises of Government*, "Though the earth . . . be common to all men, yet every man has a 'property' in his own 'person.' This nobody has any right to but himself."

Over the following century, British legal authorities, relying on common law precepts concerning property rights infused with Lockean philosophy, refined protections against government intrusion. In 1765, British jurist Lord Camden, striking down a warrant to seize private papers, wrote, "We can safely say there is no law in this country to justify the defendants in what they have done; if there was, it would destroy all the comforts of society, for papers are often the dearest property any man can have."

These views influenced American political thinkers of the late 18th century and led to the inclusion of several provisions in the Bill of Rights to the U.S. Constitution aimed at limiting the ability of government to intrude into the private affairs of citizens. These restrictions were still primarily thought of in terms of protecting physical property. The protection of personal autonomy and information was collateral. It was not until the late 19th century that those subjects started to be viewed as meriting particular protection.

The landmark event in defining the concept of "privacy" was the 1890 publication of an article by Samuel D. Warren and Louis D. Brandeis titled "The Right to Privacy" in the *Harvard Law Review*. Reviewing the evolution of legal privacy protections, Warren and Brandeis concluded: "[T]he right to life has come to mean the right to enjoy life—*the right to be let alone*; . . . and the term 'property' has grown to comprise every form of possession—intangible, as well as tangible." This definition of privacy, "the right to be left alone," has come to dominate policy discussions of the subject and serves as the bedrock principle for virtually all constitutional, statutory, and common law privacy protections existing today.

The single greatest force shaping the policy discourse concerning privacy over the past century has been technological advancement. Both governmental and private actors have sought to exploit new technologies to further traditional goals—power and wealth—and public reaction to those efforts has driven policy in a comparatively predictable manner: New technologies are developed, instances of abuse become apparent, and political pressure leads to restrictions on their use or on the use of information collected through them.

Before discussing how technology has shaped privacy concerns, it is useful to consider that all information technologies can be divided into three major categories. "Connection" technologies are those that affect how information is collected and transferred. Improvements in these technologies lower transaction costs, but also facilitate greater collection and retransmission of information. "Processing" technologies add value to the raw data collected through connection technologies by sorting and collating the data. Finally, "disconnection" technologies are means to control access to information, whether employed by parties utilizing connection/processing technologies to shield information in their possession or by parties that wish to prevent the collection/processing of information in the first place. These categories of technology give context to privacy regulatory schemes, as such schemes generally target abuses relating to a particular category or promote one category as a solution to the misuse of another category.

In the private sector, the use of technology has focused primarily on how to exploit personal information for wealth generation. The earliest instances came in the form of newspaper reporting, which started to become widespread in the late 18th century and expanded in the 19th century as printing costs fell. Publishers discovered that salacious coverage of prominent individuals' personal lives sold newspapers and magazines. The development of photography and telegraphy in the mid-19th century further intensified this trend by allowing more invasive intrusions into the subjects' lives and wider dissemination of reporting. When Warren and Brandeis and their contemporaries, such as E. L. Godkin, discussed threats to personal privacy by market actors, it was this type of collection and publication of private facts they were principally concerned with. However, a more pervasive, albeit less spectacular, intrusion into individuals' private affairs was developing during this time.

While personal information has always been a potentially exploitable resource, prior to the industrial revolution it was rarely worth systematically collecting because most people lived at subsistence levels. The development of mass production starting in the late 18th century, and the corresponding rise of living standards, altered this situation. As people gained disposable income and leisure time, they became appealing subjects for marketing. Marketing developed into a science, as businesses increasingly sought to understand consumer preferences. While the ability to predict the preferences of a specific individual remained elusive, marketers discovered by the late 19th century that preferences were tied to easily quantified demographic data, such as sex or age. Yet, given the high cost of collecting, storing, and processing information manually, marketers were constrained to conducting surveys of limited numbers of individuals, and long-term storage of the raw data was out of the question.

The invention of computers and networking technologies solved this problem. Personal information could be collected and transmitted in ever greater volumes at ever lower costs. Motor vehicle records, voter registrations, medical files, court records, credit card activity indices, and personalized shopping data collected from "loyalty cards" joined traditional demographic information in databases. Each of these datapoints enables businesses to predict consumer preferences on an increasingly individualized level. As computer processing power continues to grow, marketers' need for additional information to provide more datapoints likewise increases.

In the public sector, the intersection between technology and privacy has been more straightforward. Governments have always sought means to protect their citizens and to perpetuate their own power. The development of new information technologies has permitted collection of personal information to that end on ever more invasive and larger scales. The first instances arose during the American Civil War, during which President Lincoln ordered telegraph messages to be monitored for communications by Confederate sympathizers and spies. Wiretapping technology evolved in parallel with the development of telephones, and, by 1928, Louis Brandeis, who had been appointed as a justice to the U.S. Supreme Court, warned in his dissent in *Olmstead v. United States* that the "progress of science in furnishing the government with means of espionage is not likely to stop with wire tapping."

Brandeis's warning proved to be prophetic as improvements, first in wiretapping and then other forms of collection technologies, have become more widespread. Improvements in processing technologies have, in parallel, made it possible to more efficiently collate and analyze personal information collected from these different sources.

Privacy protections at the federal level have evolved out of two principal sources: (1) the U.S. Constitution and (2) federal statutes.

The U.S. Constitution contains no express "right to privacy." But a number of the Constitution's amendments have been read to create protections that have the effect of shielding individual privacy. The First Amendment guarantees freedom in both religious and political matters, securing, in the words of Justice Joseph Story, the rights of "private sentiment" and "private judgment." The Third Amendment protects the privacy of the home from soldiers seeking quarters without the owner's consent, preserving "the perfect enjoyment of that great right, of the [English] common law, that a man's house shall be his own castle," as Justice Story explained. The Fourth Amendment provides that individuals have the right to be secure in their persons, houses, papers, and effects. Judge Thomas Cooley characterized this as another extension of the principle that "a man's house is his castle." The Fifth Amendment, by prohibiting compulsory self-incrimination, thereby guarantees the right to silence and protects the privacy of one's thoughts. The privacy protections derivable from these and other provisions of the Constitution fall into two major categories: "autonomy" and "control of information."

"Autonomy" in constitutional law refers to the right of persons to be free from unwarranted governmental intrusion into their private affairs. The U.S. Supreme Court's view of the constitutional status of privacy and autonomy evolved significantly over the course of the 20th century.

***Jacobson v. Massachusetts* (1905):** In *Jacobson*, the Supreme Court determined that a compulsory vaccination statute did not violate any recognized constitutional right. State governments' powers included the ability to enact laws for the protection of public health. Compulsory vaccinations were a reasonable measure to that end, and allowing individuals to opt out of the vaccination programs would undermine their purpose. While there was "a sphere within which the individual may assert the supremacy of his own will, and rightfully dispute the authority of any human government," the Court concluded public safety took precedence.

***Buck v. Bell* (1927):** In *Buck*, the Supreme Court upheld a statute permitting compulsory sterilization of mentally disabled persons. Relying on *Jacobson*, the Court concluded that the power of states to protect the public health extended beyond imminent health risks to identifying those persons who were "manifestly unfit" and forcibly stopping them from reproducing.

***Griswold v. Connecticut* (1965):** In *Griswold*, the Supreme Court declared unconstitutional a statute prohibiting the use and distribution of contraceptives. Sharply departing from *Jacobson* and *Buck*, the Court found that the right to privacy was a fundamental right. Avoiding questions of substantive due process (a form of constitutional jurisprudence that many considered discredited), the Court surveyed dozens of past cases that had invoked privacy as a constitutional value. The Court concluded a right to privacy was an implicit part of the Bill of Rights. The amendments create implied "zones of privacy" without which their facial language would be meaningless.

In a concurrence, Justices Goldberg, Warren, and Brennan argued that a right to privacy should be found in the Ninth Amendment's broad statement of unenumerated rights. Justices Harlan and White separately concurred, postulating a right to privacy could be derived from the Fourteenth Amendment. However, Justices Black and Stewart dissented, arguing that the Court's decision had no textual basis in the Constitution. Although many later commenters have agreed with the dissenters' criticism, subsequent Supreme Court decisions have repeatedly built their reasoning on *Griswold*, and it remains the touchstone for discussions of constitutional protections for personal autonomy.

***Roe v. Wade* (1973):** *Roe* is generally thought of in terms of its result—recognizing a constitutional right to abortion. But this conclusion flowed from the Supreme Court's analysis of the right to privacy. To prevent the conflicting concurrences of *Griswold*, Justice Blackmun's opinion avoided the question of the precise location of a constitutional right to privacy. Instead, the *Roe* Court concluded that, regardless of its origin, the right to privacy could be protected via the Fourteenth Amendment's due process clause.

***Bowers v. Hardwick* (1986):** *Bowers* upheld a law that criminalized private homosexual activity between consenting adults. The *Bowers* majority concluded that the right to privacy in the Court's earlier decisions did not protect private, consensual, homosexual conduct. The majority rebuffed the defendants' privacy argument, suggesting that *Griswold* and *Roe* did not recognize a right to privacy but should be viewed as part of a line of cases dealing with limitations on government interference with child rearing. The four dissenting justices, however, concluded that the ability of adults to engage in consensual sexual conduct could be protected under the Court's earlier personal autonomy privacy decisions.

***Planned Parenthood of Southeastern Pa. v. Casey* (1992):** Deviating from the suggestion in *Bowers* that there might not be a constitutional right to privacy, the Court reaffirmed in *Casey* that there was such a right. Reviewing *Griswold*, *Roe*, and other decisions, the *Casey* Court found that a statute requiring married women to obtain permission from their husbands prior to having abortions violated their privacy rights. The Court concluded, "Our precedents have respected the private realm of family life which the state cannot enter. These matters, involving the most intimate and personal choices a person may make in a lifetime, choices central to personal dignity and autonomy, are central to the liberty protected by the Fourteenth Amendment."

Lawrence v. Texas **(2003):** Overturning *Bowers*, the Court in *Lawrence* invalidated a law that prohibited persons from engaging in consensual homosexual activity, based on *Casey*'s holding. The Court found that "petitioners are entitled to respect for their private lives. The State cannot demean their existence or control their destiny by making their private sexual conduct a crime. . . . It is a promise of the Constitution that there is a realm of personal liberty which the government may not enter."

"Control of information" refers to the right of persons not to have information, particularly communications, collected or disseminated by government agents. While supporters of privacy rights have vigorously argued for decades that the Constitution should be interpreted to protect a right to control access to information, the Supreme Court's jurisprudence in this area has been far less consistent than the trend in its decisions concerning personal autonomy.

Olmstead v. United States **(1928):** *Olmstead* was the first major Supreme Court decision concerning privacy rights and control of information. The case challenged the constitutionality of evidence collected by wiretapping telephone conversations as a violation of the Fourth Amendment. The majority surveyed a number of earlier cases and concluded the protections of the Fourth Amendment applied only to physical objects and places. As long as law enforcement agents did not enter the property, "There was no searching. There was no seizure." Dissenting, Justice Brandeis argued the majority had taken an unduly narrow view of the Fourth Amendment, and concluded that "the right to be let alone" must be protected against "every unjustifiable intrusion by the government upon the privacy of the individual, whatever the means employed . . . ."

Katz v. United States **(1967):** Although Brandeis's argument failed to carry the day in *Olmstead*, it was substantially adopted by the Supreme Court in *Katz*. In *Katz*, the Court considered electronic eavesdropping on a conversation in a public telephone booth. While the Court warned that "the Fourth Amendment cannot be translated into a general constitutional 'right to privacy,'" it substantially overruled *Olmstead*, finding "[T]he Fourth Amendment protects people, not places. What a person knowingly exposes to the public . . . is not a subject of Fourth Amendment protection. But what he seeks to preserve as private, even in an area accessible to the public, may be constitutionally protected."

Justice Harlan, in a concurrence, coined the phrase "reasonable expectation of privacy," and explained in what circumstances an individual would have protection against unreasonable searches. It required a two part analysis in Harlan's formulation, "[F]irst that a person have exhibited an actual (subjective) expectation of privacy and, second, that the expectation be one that society is prepared to recognize as 'reasonable.'" *Katz* continues to serve as the basic framework for analysis of whether government action constitutes a Fourth Amendment violation.

United States v. White **(1971):** In *White*, the Supreme Court considered whether conversations between a government informant and another person were constitutionally protected. The Court concluded a person has no expectation of privacy in information voluntarily disclosed to someone else, absent some other form of privilege.

United States v. Miller **(1976):** Building on *White*, the Court held in *Miller* that a bank customer had no reasonable expectation of privacy in bank records. The Court found the information contained in transaction records was under control of the bank, not the customer, and that it was irrelevant that the recordkeeping requirement was created by a federal statute.

Whalen v. Roe **(1977):** *Whalen* addressed a law that required physicians to report drug prescriptions to a government agency. The petitioners argued the database of prescription holders infringed their right to privacy. The Court conceded that the database infringed the patients' privacy rights, but concluded the state's interest in minimizing the risk of prescription drug abuse outweighed the infringement.

***Smith v. Maryland* (1979)**: In *Smith*, the Court synthesized its rulings from *Katz* and *Miller. Smith* concerned the placement of a "pen register" at a telephone company's central office without a warrant for monitoring which telephone numbers a suspect was dialing. The Court found that this did not violate the rule from *Katz*. The Court distinguished the use of pen registers from wiretaps, or listening devices, on the grounds that pen registers acquire only a list of numbers, not the contents of communications. Then, relying on *Miller*'s holding that there is no reasonable expectation of privacy in information given to third parties, the Court concluded the protections of *Katz* would not apply because the caller knew the telephone company kept a record of numbers dialed anyway.

***Kyllo v. United States* (2001)**: *Kyllo* presented the question of whether the use of infrared imaging equipment could constitute a "search" under the Fourth Amendment. The Court approached the matter in light of *Katz* and articulated a rule based on considerations of technological advancement. The impact of "sense-enhancing technology" should be evaluated by reference to whether physical intrusion into the subject property would otherwise have been required. "This assures preservation of that degree of privacy against government that existed when the Fourth Amendment was adopted."

The U.S. federal government has pursued what is described as a "sectoral approach" to privacy law. Under this approach, privacy protections are addressed to specific types of information, subject areas, or agencies. Congress has been particularly active in regulating privacy in the context of financial and medical records (covered in entries on Banking and Finance and Medical Privacy), but other subjects have been covered as well. Federal privacy legislation has come in three major waves from the 1970s to the late 1990s.

In the late 1960s and early 1970s, a series of investigations, by both news outlets and the U.S. Congress, revealed the federal government had been conducting extensive domestic spying programs through both civilian and military agencies without statutory authorization or court approval. These investigations particularly showed the agencies involved often relied on obtaining personal information from other government agencies or private institutions that had earlier legitimately collected it from the subject. Reacting to this discovery, Congress enacted several reforms. Of particular significance were the Privacy Act of 1974 and the Family Education Rights and Privacy Act of 1974 ("FERPA"). The Privacy Act restricted the ability of federal agencies to use or distribute records containing personally identifiable information without the consent of the subject, while FERPA afforded similar protections to students at schools receiving federal funding.

Concerns about abuse of government surveillance powers continued throughout the 1970s and into the early 1980s. This period was marked by more revelations of domestic spying uncovered by the Senate Select Committee to Study Governmental Operations with Respect to Intelligence Activities, often called the "Church Commission," and media exposés of the surveillance techniques used by the FBI in the "ABSCAM" anticorruption sting. During the same period, a series of high-profile computer "hacking" incidents occurred. Although these attacks caused little actual damage, the novelty of the events attracted significant public attention to the potential for personal information stored on networked computers to be compromised. All of these events contributed to a series of legislative and regulatory efforts in the mid-1980s addressed to the security of electronic communications, the most significant of which was the Electronic Communications Privacy Act of 1986 ("ECPA"). The ECPA was novel in that it imposed limitations on both government and private actors. In most instances, law enforcement agencies would be required to obtain a warrant prior to accessing stored electronic communications, and private parties that engaged in unauthorized access could be subject to civil and criminal penalties.

A final wave of federal legislation addressed to privacy issues came in the 1990s with the rise of the Internet. Two principal concerns drove this wave of legislation. First, many state and local governments began making public records containing personal information available online. Although the existence of these records was not new, the ease with which they could be accessed raised fears about the risk of misuse. Second, the public became increasingly aware of the extent to which personal information could be collected by Web site operators from visitors. Reports on so-called cyber-stalking proliferated, with the alleged threat to children receiving particularly prominent attention. Reacting to these concerns, Congress passed a number of new statutes. Of particular significance were the Drivers Privacy Protection Act of 1994, which imposed requirements for the security of motor vehicle records, and the Children's Online Privacy Protection Act of 1998, which prohibited the unauthorized collection of personal information from children under age 13 through Web sites.

Following the 9/11 attacks, federal legislation concerning privacy rights went into a retrograde mode. The USA PATRIOT Act of 2001 substantially weakened the protections of the ECPA by permitting warrantless access to electronic communications in a broader set of circumstances, and financial institutions were required to collect and report more extensive information about customer activity than previously required. Through 2008, no major new pieces of legislation concerning individual privacy were enacted, although several bills seeking to restore part of the protections repealed by the USA PATRIOT Act were entertained by Congress.

Because of a lack of specific privacy protections in the U.S. Constitution and the generally slower pace of legislative activity at the federal level, states have traditionally been at the forefront of developments in privacy law. The earliest explicit recognition of a "right to privacy" came from state supreme courts relying on Warren and Brandeis's writings as the basis for establishing the so-called privacy torts. As a result, the main source of privacy protections under state law was historically the common law, but, in recent years, state constitutions and statutes have become increasingly important in defining such protections.

State courts have found privacy protections arising out of the common law on a number of different theories, but the most critical has been tort law. Several privacy torts are recognized, but the most significant are intrusion and wrongful publication of private facts.

The tort of intrusion protects individuals from unreasonable and outrageous violations of their privacy. The tort was first clearly articulated by the Kentucky Court of Appeals in *Rhodes v. Graham*, 37 S.W.2d 46 (Ky. 1931), which found that wiretapping a telephone line could constitute a tortious act even if no physical entry onto the plaintiff's property occurred. The court concluded, "The evil incident to the invasion of the privacy of the telephone is as great as that occasioned by unwarranted publicity in newspapers and by other means of a man's private affairs for which courts have granted the injured person redress." Also in the early 1930s, courts began to elaborate the tort of "wrongful publication of private facts"—the act of recklessly or willfully publicizing embarrassing facts about an individual, such as sexual relations and medical information. Unlike defamation, the tort of wrongful disclosure concerns the publishing of *true* information rather than *false* information. The roots of the tort are found in the decision of the California Court of Appeals *Melvin v. Reid*, 297 P. 91 (Cal. Ct. App. 1931), which permitted a plaintiff to bring suit based on the use of her actual name and embarrassing personal information in a film.

The use of the privacy torts peaked by the mid-20th century and they are infrequently used today. The legal decisions establishing the torts placed tremendous emphasis on the harm to privacy flowing from widespread dissemination of personal information through media outlets. However, the U.S. Supreme Court greatly expanded First Amendment free speech protections during the post–World War II era. This led courts to carve broad affirmative defenses into the privacy torts for constitutionally protected speech. Thus, the protections afforded by the privacy torts are now available in a much more limited range of circumstances.

State constitutions generally contain provisions mirroring the Bill of Rights to the U.S. Constitution, and thus most states generally afford their citizens the same degree of constitution-based privacy protection as has been established by the Supreme Court. However, certain state supreme courts have found their state constitutions provide greater privacy protections than the U.S. Constitution. These rulings typically arise in situations where the U.S. Supreme Court is perceived as having lowered the generally accepted standard of privacy protections for particular types of personal information. Thus, for example, in response to *United States v. Miller* finding no reasonable expectation of privacy in bank records, a number of state supreme courts reached contrary conclusions relying on their state constitutions. Examples include, *Charnes v. DiGiacomo* (Colo. 1980) (finding Colorado state constitution created reasonable expectation of privacy in bank records) and *State v. McAllister* (N.J. 2005) (same under New Jersey state constitution). Likewise, following the decision of *Smith v. Maryland*, which found no warrant was required for installation of "pen registers," several state supreme courts found pen registers were still subject to warrant requirements under state constitutions. Examples include *People v. Sporleder* (Colo. 1983) (finding Colorado state constitution created reasonable expectation of privacy in telephone numbers dialed) and *State v. Hunt* (N.J. 1982) (same under New Jersey state constitution).

During the 1990s and early 2000s, many privacy advocates became concerned that the federal government was not acting swiftly enough to address the privacy implications of large-scale data collection and processing by businesses. Of particular concern was the risk of "identity theft," which typically consists of using the personal information of a victim to borrow money or make purchases on credit and then default. Privacy advocates thus switched much of their lobbying efforts to the state level, with the result being that many states have enacted statutes aimed at protecting the privacy of individuals' information that has been collected for commercial purposes. These statutes generally fall into one of three categories: data protection, data destruction, and security breach notification.

As of 2008, five states—Arkansas, California, Nevada, Rhode Island, and Utah—required security measures be put into place for personal information held by private entities. These statutes do not impose specific technical requirements for security, but instead demand reasonable security procedures and practices appropriate to the nature of the information, that is, greater security is required for more sensitive information.

Through 2008, eight states—Arkansas, California, Kentucky, New Jersey, Nevada, North Carolina, Texas, and Utah—had enacted data destruction laws. An increasingly recognized component of data security is making certain that personal information and other data is destroyed once it is no longer needed. The longer data is held, the more opportunities develop for it to be compromised, whether deliberately or inadvertently. As with state data protection laws, data destruction statutes avoid specific procedures in favor of more generalized requirements that commercial entities take reasonable steps to destroy personal information that is no longer necessary to be retained.

Thirty-eight states had enacted data breach notification laws by 2008. The development of notification laws is a particularly important advancement for privacy interest because, in the absence of a disclosure requirement, individuals are often unable to determine where their personal information was compromised. Understanding the time and location of the breach better allows individuals to take steps to protect their creditworthiness and otherwise minimize the impact of identity theft. Data breach laws generally require a party controlling a commercial database or other collection of personal information to report breaches of the system's security to the individuals whose personal information was stored in the database.

As the first decade of the 21st century draws to a close, the challenges to individual privacy loom large. Technological advancement continues to make it easier for both government and commercial actors to collect, filter, and redistribute personal information and this trend will undoubtedly continue into the foreseeable future. The question for privacy advocates is what the public policy debate around those controversies will look like.

The principal challenge to privacy in the public sector is what the limitations to personal privacy are when juxtaposed with questions of national security. In its 1967 decision in *Katz*, the Supreme Court explicitly stated that it was not reaching the question of whether the Fourth Amendment applied to government investigations taken pursuant to national security concerns. Justices Douglas and Brennan warned in a concurrence that could be the exception which swallowed constitutional limitations on searches and seizures, but the legislative restrictions imposed on surveillance in the 1970s and early 1980s substantially addressed that critique. Post-9/11, however, Congress both broadened the scope of what constituted a "national security" issue and gave federal agencies greater information-gathering powers.

Although very few privacy advocates go as far as the *Katz* concurrence in arguing that full Fourth Amendment protections should be applied to surveillance for national security purposes, many do argue that reforms by Congress have unduly weakened the protections previously set up to guard against abuses of the executive branch's investigative powers. Supporters of the reforms generally argue that the putative existential threat of 21st-century terrorism requires pervasive surveillance and the ability to instantaneously react to potential threats, making older limitations unrealistic at best, and detrimental to public safety at worst. Whether privacy advocates will ever prevail again to the extent they did in the mid to late 1970s remains uncertain.

The challenges to privacy in the context of the marketplace are less dramatic, but all turn on a very thorny underlying question: Who owns an individual's personal information? The concept that information *qua* information (in contrast to a physical object containing information) can be "owned" is a comparatively recent development in legal history, but it has a profound impact on individuals' abilities to protect their privacy.

To the extent the question has been considered by the courts or legislatures, it has largely been assumed that information is owned by the party who collected and organized it. Thus, for example, individuals do not own their mailing addresses or birth dates, but a market research company that collects that information can treat the resulting compilation as a form of property. This means individuals are typically not able to control the use of their personal information once another party has collected it and, in most instances, will have no recourse if, for example, that party sells it to a third party for marketing purposes or through negligence allows the information to be compromised by identity thieves or other bad actors.

The solution to this problem, as privacy advocates see it, is to change the location of ownership of personal information from those who collect and organize it to those who generate it, that is, individuals. This would allow individuals to impose restrictions on the collection or use of their personal information and make a wider array of remedies available. Statutes requiring such things as free access to credit reports or security breach notifications are part of giving individuals "ownership" of their personal information. There is no systematic opposition to this view, but many commercial entities oppose such measures on the grounds that they would make existing business models unworkable and could expose them to tremendous liabilities for relatively trivial mishandling of information. How this contest plays out will depend in large part on the ability of privacy advocates to demonstrate to commercial entities that new, viable, business models could be created despite the fact that the entities would be significantly restricted in their ability to collect, process, or disseminate personal information.

Further Reading:

O'Brien, David M. *Privacy, Law, and Public Policy*. New York: Praeger Publishers, 1979; Organization for Economic Cooperation and Development. *OECD Guidelines on the Protection of Privacy and Transborder Flows of Personal Data*. Available online. URL: http://www.oecd.org/document/18/0,2340,en_2649_34255_1815186_1_1_1_1,00.html. Accessed July 10, 2009; Schoeman, Ferdinand David, ed. *Philosophical Dimensions of Privacy*. New York: Cambridge University Press, 1984; Solove, Daniel J. *Understanding Privacy*. Cambridge, Mass.: Harvard University Press, 2008; Soma, John T., et al. "Balance of Privacy vs. Security: A Historical Perspective of the USA PATRIOT Act." *Rutgers Computer and Technology Law Journal* 31 (2005); Warren, Samuel D., and Louis D. Brandeis. "The Right to Privacy." *Harvard Law Review* 4 (1890): 193–220.

– *Stephen D. Rynerson and John T. Soma*

torts and negligence

The most popular character in the television series, *Seinfeld*, was Cosmo Kramer, known for his herky-jerky movements and for barging into Jerry's apartment without knocking. In one famous *Seinfeld* episode, Cosmo spilled a hot coffee latte on his chest while smuggling it into a movie theater. Kramer retained the services of Jackie Chiles, a parody of Johnnie Cochran, one of O. J. Simpson's defense attorneys, to sue the shop for selling him the too-hot coffee. Kramer's injuries were so minor that his burns healed after a single application of a skin balm he received from his friend with the nickname, The Maestro. Jackie Chiles, his attorney, was outraged that Kramer's use of the balm ruined a completely good lawsuit: "You put the balm on? Who told you to put the balm on? I didn't tell you to put the balm on. Why'd you put the balm on? You haven't even been to see the doctor. If you're gonna put a balm on, let a doctor put a balm on." Kramer also spurned Jackie's advice and negotiated a settlement with Java World, which gave him a lifetime supply of lattes. When Jerry asked him about his lawsuit, Cosmo replied: "Oh, I can be quite litigious." Elaine was particularly critical of Kramer's lawsuit. "What I mean who ever heard of this anyway? Suing a company because their coffee is too hot? Coffee is supposed to be hot."

This *Seinfeld* episode spoofed the real McDonald's hot coffee case, which, on the surface, appears to be as outlandish as Cosmo Kramer's frivolous lawsuit. Very few Americans know the factual circumstances that led to the McDonald's verdict because this case has not been accurately reported. At least a thousand news stories reported that a clumsy elderly woman spilled coffee on her lap and later sued McDonald Corporation because the hot coffee she ordered was too hot. The case was the subject of monologues by late night talk show hosts Jay Leno and David Letterman. The true facts of the hot coffee lawsuit are in sharp contrast from the parody of the case portrayed in the *Seinfeld* episode and in the mass media. In Albuquerque, New Mexico, 79-year-old Stella Liebeck purchased coffee at the drive-through window of a McDonald's restaurant. Contrary to most of the news stories, Mrs. Liebeck was neither driving the car nor was the vehicle moving at the time of the coffee spill accident. Mrs. Liebeck's grandson pulled to the curb and the car was already at a complete stop when she placed the cup of coffee between her knees in an attempt to remove the plastic lid.

As she was in the process of removing the plastic coffee cup cover, the scalding coffee spilled onto her lap and was immediately absorbed by her sweatpants, causing immediate second-and third-degree burns. Mrs. Liebeck sustained full-thickness burns to the muscle and fatty tissue layers of her inner thighs, groin, and buttocks from the superheated coffee. She spent eight days in the hospital recovering from her burn injuries enduring painful debridement procedures by which dead skin and tissue are removed. Mrs. Liebeck was disabled for a period of two years and unable to work as a sales clerk, suffering severe pain and disability for a period of two years. The coffee sold to Mrs. Liebeck was held at a temperature between 180 and 190 degrees, which was hotter than beverages sold at other fast food chains. The plaintiff's expert biomechanical engineer testified that serving any liquid at this temperature posed an unreasonably dangerous risk to consumers. The plaintiff's medical expert on burns testified that human skin burns twice as fast for each degree centigrade above 140 degrees. He testified that coffee or any liquid contacting human skin will cause third-degree or full-thickness burns in two to seven seconds. In contrast, the coffee served at home is typically brewed at 135 to 140 degrees (*Liebeck v. McDonald's Restaurant* 1994).

Mrs. Liebeck initially sought only reimbursement for her medical bills, which totaled nearly $10,000. When McDonald's refused to settle the case, she filed a product liability lawsuit. The jury heard evidence that McDonald's served coffee hotter than other fast food restaurants for taste reasons and made a corporate decision not to warn consumers or lower the temperature even though it had knowledge of over 700 prior similar cases of customers spilling coffee and suffering severe burns to their genital area, perineum, inner thighs, and buttocks. McDonald's quality control manager acknowledged the risk of serious injury posed by hot coffee, agreeing that a reasonable consumer could not anticipate such serious burns. The plaintiff's theory of punitive damages held that McDonald's managerial personnel and officers of the corporation knew that its coffee was unfit for human consumption, but yet took no steps to lower the temperature. Mrs. Liebeck's attorneys contended that deterrence would require that McDonald's forfeit several days of coffee revenues, constituting millions of dollars per day. The jury also awarded the plaintiff $2.7 million in punitive damages, a judicial remedy intended to punish and deter McDonald's for reckless disregard of customer safety (*Liebeck v. McDonald's Restaurant* 1994).

The media did not report that the trial judge reduced the award 20 percent because of a jury finding that the plaintiff contributed to her injury. Nor did the media report that the New Mexico trial judge reduced the $2.7 million in punitive damages to $480,000. Eventually the parties reached a confidential post-verdict settlement, presumably for a substantially reduced dollar amount. In the end, punishment of McDonald's was the functional equivalent of a parking ticket. However, the McDonald's Corporation did change its corporate policies in the aftermath of the punitive damages litigation. McDonald's coffee is now served at a lower temperature with conspicuous warnings printed on each cup. Punitive damages in product liability cases such as McDonald's serve a larger social purpose of changing corporate policies and attitudes toward consumers.

After the hot coffee case media blitz, the popular view of the McDonald's hot coffee award was that it was a windfall award made by an out-of-control jury redistributing wealth from a deep-pocketed corporation to a careless old woman and her attorney. However, the New Mexico jury was following the instructions of the trial judge in this case. In a strict product liability case, the plaintiff need prove only that the manufacturer's product was excessively dangerous, causing damages. The jury determined that McDonald's should be liable for creating excessive preventable dangers based upon evidence entered into the trial record that Mrs. Liebeck's injuries could have been prevented. A product such as hot coffee may be dangerously defective due to (1) a manufacturing defect, (2) a design defect, or (3) a failure of a manufacturer to warn of a danger or instruction on the proper use of the product. Punitive damages were based upon evidence that McDonald's knew of the danger of superheated coffee but took no steps to protect the consuming public.

The McDonald's hot coffee case is portrayed by tort reformers as an example of a greedy plaintiff seeking a windfall recovery. The case has been cited hundreds of times by tort reformers to indict the U.S. tort system in legislative hearings as well as in newspaper editorials. The "infamous" McDonald's hot coffee case was cited frequently by tort reformers calling for tort reforms in the state legislatures and in Congress. Rather than focusing on the woman who spent more than a week in the hospital because of severe burns from needlessly overheated coffee, or on the 700 other serious burns, which had been previously reported to the restaurant chain, the mass media extended sympathy to the company. Tort reformers contended that McDonald's did not deserve punishment because the restaurant chain sold billions of cups of coffee with a relatively low rate of injury. The McDonald's case served as the poster child for policy makers seeking to limit tort remedies. Tort reformers characterized the McDonald's hot coffee case as a tort horror story, spurring legislatures around the country to limit tort damages.

Tort law remedies are well established under the Anglo-American system of civil justice. The word *tort* is derived from the Latin for *tortus* or twisted. Torts are based upon a corrective justice theory of righting wrongs. A tort is an act or omission, not a mere breach of contract that produces injury in another. Torts are distinguished from contracts in that a contract arises from the parties' agreement, whereas a tort is a duty fixed by law. An actor is civilly liable for tort damages if his conduct intended to cause harm or was negligent, or if he engaged in an abnormally dangerous activity that caused harm. Torts are largely about negligence. A survey of 378,000 tort case involving 1.4 million plaintiffs and defendants in the 75 largest counties in the United States found a majority of torts to be negligence-based automobile accidents. Punitive damages are rarely awarded except in the most egregious intentional tort cases. Empirical studies of tort damages show no torts crisis and provide little or no support for advocates of tort reform. All of the available research on punitive damages confirms that punitive damages are rarely awarded, proportional to compensatory damages, and frequently reversed or reduced on appeal.

The hot coffee case illustrates problems with the way in which civil juries award damages and how they are reported. The Oklahoma Supreme Court noted how the McDonald's coffee case was inaccurately portrayed as a "windfall" recovery, creating public sentiment against the American civil justice system and a belief "that punitive damages are out of control and make no economic sense." Regarding the tort system of recovery, such portrayals "have left many with the belief, albeit wrong, that punitive damages are out of control and make no economic sense" (*Harwick v. Dye* [1999]). Most tort cases have less compelling facts than the McDonald's hot coffee case.

In a typical tort case such as an automobile driving case, a plaintiff sues the other driver for personal injury or damages caused by his negligent or reckless operation of a motor vehicle. In general, tort remedies are monetary damages for personal injury, though a plaintiff may have a recovery for injury to personal or real property. In rare cases, a plaintiff may seek an injunction to enjoin hazardous conditions that impair the use and enjoyment of land. Tort damages are traditionally divided into *nominal, compensatory*, and *punitive damages*. Nominal damages affirm the merit of the plaintiff's tort claim, but leave her with empty pockets. Nominal damages are, in effect, a symbolic remedy awarded in intentional torts cases where the plaintiff is unable to prove actual loss or injury. Nominal damages, for example, could be imposed against a trespasser who crossed the boundaries onto the plaintiff's land without permission but caused no damages.

Compensatory damages are the damages awarded to a person as compensation, indemnity, or restitution for harm sustained by him. Compensatory damages are subdivided into economic losses such as lost earning capacity—categorized as special damages—and noneconomic damages, often referred to as pain and suffering damages. The purpose underlying compensatory damages is to make the plaintiff whole again in a pecuniary way, to the position he would have occupied had no tort been committed. The tort system gives the plaintiff pecuniary damages not only for what he has suffered but also what he will suffer in the future. Compensatory damages are based upon the concept of corrective justice to right wrongs. The jury awarded Mrs. Liebeck $200,000 in compensatory damages, which the judge reduced to $160,000 because the jury found Mrs. Liebeck partially at fault for the spill. Corrective justice dictated that McDonald's pay only the injuries it caused. Most U.S. jurisdictions reduce a plaintiff's award of compensatory damages for any contributory negligence. In a few jurisdictions, plaintiffs receive no damages if they are even 1 percent responsible for their own accident or injury.

Special damages typically encompass measurable economic losses that are direct, reasonable, and expectable items of loss from an injury. Past medical expenses are recoverable as special damages so long as they are direct, reasonable, and expectable items of loss from an injury caused by the defendant. Special damages are typically recovered for hospital care, rehabilitation, ambulance services, or funeral expenses. Mrs. Liebeck, the plaintiff in the hot coffee case, incurred thousands of dollars in medical bills classified as special damages. She did not even seek lost earnings, which are another item of special damages. For each item of loss, the fact-finder must determine the nature, extent, and duration of the plaintiff's special damages by a reasonable certainty.

Noneconomic damages, sometimes called general damages, are awarded for pain and suffering. Pain and suffering awards for reproductive injuries includes compensation for disfigurement or infertility. Plaintiffs frequently use experts to give the jury a basis for determining a plaintiff's loss of enjoyment of life or pain and suffering. Most of the compensatory damages in the hot coffee case were awarded to compensate Stella Liebeck for the severe conscious pain she suffered during the debridement and skin-grafting procedures and her overall loss of life's enjoyment during her period of rehabilitation. The purpose of special damages and noneconomic damages is to make the plaintiff whole again. While money can never make the plaintiff whole again, it is the best the civil justice system can do.

Punitive damages are awarded to further a state's legitimate interests in punishing a defendant's unlawful conduct and deterring its repetition. The deterrent theme that animates punitive damages is the unequivocal message to the industry that "tort does not pay." However, the $2.7 million awarded to Stella Liebeck represented only about two days' profit from the nationwide sales of McDonald's coffee. In contrast to compensatory damages, punitive damages are to punish and deter extremely aggravated misconduct by the defendant. The focus of the punitive damages issue is that a large deterrent award is required to reform corporate practices, as there are cases when an award proportionate to actual damages does not achieve that objective. Mrs. Liebeck's attorneys contended that McDonald's failure to take prompt remedial measures to protect the public constituted malicious, willful, and reckless conduct. All but a few states have enacted one or more punitive damages reforms. Louisiana, Massachusetts, Nebraska, New Hampshire, and the state of Washington do not recognize the tort remedy of punitive damages, unless it is specially provided for in a statute. Most countries outside the United States do not recognize the doctrine of punitive damages.

The iconic McDonald's hot coffee case has been at center stage in the tort reform policy debates. The Ohio legislature heard misleading accounts of the McDonald's hot coffee case in legislative hearings about tort reform. In 1999, the Ohio Supreme Court struck down Ohio's 1995 tort reform because it impermissibly prevented plaintiffs from receiving full compensation for their injuries. Ohio's tort reform statute capped the amount of pain and suffering damages in any tort actions at the greater of $250,000 or three times the economic loss, with some exceptions. The Ohio Supreme Court cited the tort reformers' misuse of the McDonald's hot coffee case as evidence that the legislative proposals were enacted without a solid foundation (*State ex rel. Ohio Acad. of Trial Lawyers v. Sheward* [1999]). Illinois enacted the Civil Justice Reform Amendments of 1995, which was a tort reform that limited pain and suffering damages to $500,000 and imposed other limitations on tort recovery. During the legislative hearings, the McDonald's hot coffee case was presented as a case study for why the legislature should enact tort reform. The Illinois Supreme Court struck down the tort reform, observing that it was based upon misleading anecdotes such as the "infamous" McDonald's hot coffee case. The court found that Illinois tort reforms lacked a rational relationship to important state policies.

The misuse of the McDonald's hot coffee case is emblematic of a larger political movement to roll back torts and remedies of American consumers. The Illinois Supreme Court cited social science studies confirming that there was little evidence, apart from misleading anecdotes, such as the hot coffee case, "to support the perceived deleterious effects of the present civil litigation system" (*Best v. Taylor Mach. Works* Ill. 1997). The Illinois

Supreme Court held that the tort reforms violated equal protection and due process as well as consumers' right to a jury trial by placing arbitrary limitations on compensatory damages. The hot coffee case is also emblematic of the role of tort law as a contentious public policy issue in American society.

William Prosser begins his classic treatise on the law of torts with a statement that torts are a battleground of social theory. In the 21st century, tort law continues to be a crucible for public policy debates. At both the state and federal level, the twin targets of tort reform are punitive damages and noneconomic damages, which were both at issue in the hot coffee case. The majority of states have enacted reforms limiting these remedies, including New Mexico, where the hot coffee case was tried. Congress has been considering federal limitations on these tort remedies nearly every legislative session since 1980. Punitive damages and pain and suffering recovery is at the heart of the public policy debate over reforming the U.S. civil justice system.

Punitive damages were first recognized in a 1763 English case in which government agents ransacked the offices of the *North Briton* newspaper after one of its editors wrote editorials criticizing the policies of the king. The English court ruled that the jury was right in awarding "exemplary damages" because of the outrageous actions of the government in conducting a warrantless search (*Huckle v. Money* 1763). In a companion case, *Wilkes v. Wood* (1763), the editor of the *North Briton*, falsely imprisoned by the king's agents, asked the jury to grant a large award of exemplary damages to punish and deter such outrageous warrantless searches. The English jury awarded the *North Briton* publisher 1,000 pounds, sending the deterrent message that even the king is not above the deterrent power of the law.

Punitive damages were exported from England to America during the colonial period. The extraordinary tort remedy functioned to keep the social peace and settle neighborhood disputes. Defendants were assessed punitive damages for such unjustified acts as shaving the heads of orphans or poisoning a neighbor's cattle. Punitive damages served chiefly as a mechanism of social control of intentional torts in the local community. The tort remedy vindicated family values by punishing defendants who committed intentional torts, such as seduction, breach of promise to marry, alienation of affection, and general property wrongs. With the rapid growth of industrialization after the Civil War, punitive damages evolved to confront corporate malfeasance that caused mass disasters, such as train derailments. The controversy over punitive damages first began in the late 19th century when corporations were assessed punitive damages for ultrahazardous conditions, such as the unsafe maintenance of railroad tracks, bridges, and other industrial infrastructure. The modern controversy over punitive damages arose when punitive damages were extended to product liability, professional negligence, and other actions impacting American business. Manufacturers and their insurers formed tort reform alliances to limit punitive damages, such as the American Tort Reform Association (ATRA) and the Washington Legal Foundation.

The large punitive damages award in McDonald's hot coffee case led to renewed calls to curb this remedy. ATRA argues that U.S. manufacturers are at a competitive disadvantage because the United States is one of the few countries to recognize the doctrine. In the McDonald's hot coffee case, tort reformers argued that Mrs. Liebeck received a "windfall" that belongs to the public treasury, not the plaintiff and her attorney. Critics of punitive damages contend that it is unfair for a jury to impose the functional equivalent of a death penalty on U.S. businesses particularly since juries receive little guidance in making punitive damages awards. The insurance industry contends that the threat of punitive damages stifles the creative impulse in U.S. industry and acts to deter innovation. The Washington Legal Foundation, a tort reform group, contends that excessive punitive damages harm society by encumbering businesses with an unjustifiable "tort tax."

The Washington Legal Foundation criticizes punitive damages for creating a multiple punishment problem. In a product liability action such as the hot coffee case, it is possible that a state will impose punitive damages for the same product, practice, or course of conduct even when prior awards have been granted. The "portfolio of punitive damages" problem frequently occurs in mass-product-design or failure-to-warn cases. In tobacco litigation, this problem arises when a company such as Philip Morris is subject to multiple punitive damages awards based upon the same course of conduct in marketing cigarettes. In asbestos mass tort cases, numerous manufacturers were bankrupted to shield themselves from multiple potential punitive damages claims. The tobacco and asbestos cases are two high-profile examples of the multiple damages problem. In the Dalkon Shield intrauterine device (IUD) litigation, A. H. Robins filed for a Chapter 11 reorganization bankruptcy to avoid multiple civil punishment problems. Theodore Olson presents a compelling case to reform punitive damages because of the risk of excessive, duplicative punishment for the same conduct. The portfolio of punitive damages problem can also arise out of corporate policies, such as in insurance bad faith cases or product liability actions, that create a windfall for the first plaintiffs to file actions. Tort reformers contend that juror passion may be stirred by improper motives, such as the wealth of the corporation, and that jurors will act in making awards excessively disproportionate to actual harm.

The defenders of punitive damages argue that this remedy is a necessary incentive to uncover "smoking gun" evidence of wrongdoing undetected by public authorities. American tort law is unique when compared to many countries because of the degree that punitive damages supplements public enforcement with prosecution by private attorneys general. Under the U.S. contingency fee system, punitive damages results in full compensation because the plaintiff is unable to recover the cost of attorneys' fees and discovery. The tort victim is not fully compensated by compensatory damages without punitive damages. Punitive damages are a necessary incentive to induce plaintiffs to sue wrongdoers and deter highly undesirable conduct. Punitive damages help provide a safer society by deterring the creation of unsafe products, services, and conduct. Product liability is a field of tort law that concerns the legal liability of manufacturers for injuries caused by defective products. To have product liability, a product must be defective in design or in warning or possess a manufacturing defect.

Manufacturers, seller's distributors, retailers, and others in the distribution chain are potentially liable if they market products posing unreasonable danger to users or consumers that cause injury or death. Defective products have deadly consequences, as evidenced by what happened to Valerie Lakey, a five-year-old North Carolina girl, who was playing in a community wading pool. The pool's drain cover, which constrains the strong hydraulic vortex, was somehow displaced and Valerie became lodged in the opening. The pool's suction exerted a force from the uncovered drain that eviscerated the child. Seventy-five percent of her bowels were pulled out of her anus and her life was saved only by the heroic efforts of the medical personnel at a North Carolina hospital. The little girl ultimately survived but endured years of surgeries, hospital stays, and consultations with specialists.

Valerie Lakey's parents hired John Edwards (later a candidate for vice president), a product liability specialist. The Lakeys filed suit against Sta-Rite Industries, a Wisconsin pool equipment manufacturer on behalf of their daughter. Valerie Lakey's attorneys used aggressive pretrial discovery to uncover what the manufacturer of the pool drain knew and whether there were prior similar incidents. In a dozen prior cases, children suffered catastrophic injuries or near-misses caused by broken or missing pool-drain covers. What did the company do in the wake of this developing profile of dangers? Too little, too late. The company failed to issue fortified warnings or make design changes until mid-1987. An internal report discovered by the plaintiff's counsel stated that such "accidents were more common—the pressure from open drains tearing rectums and disemboweling small children. Without the grate, the suction is unimpeded and can exert considerable force." Valerie Lakey's lawyers were able to win a $25-million punitive damages settlement directly based upon these smoking gun documents that it was Sta-Rite's failure to take safety steps after learning that the suction from open drains could be deadly. Only after the case was filed did the manufacturer change its warnings and instructions. The state of North Carolina also passed statutes requiring wading pool covers due to this litigation. Reports of the settlement led the entire swimming pool industry to recall drain covers. The U.S. Consumer Product Safety Commission published extensive guidelines to help pool operators avoid similar entrapment injuries in the future. Punitive damages play a unique role in American society in punishing conduct that is inimical to public safety.

The opponents of punitive damages contend that punishment in such cases as the Lakey case or the McDonald's hot coffee case gives the jury too much power to determine corporate practices and policies. The U.S. Supreme Court contends that punitive damages create a potential for arbitrarily depriving defendants of their property without due process (*Pacific Mut. Life. Ins. Co. v. Haslip* [1991]). The Court's concern is that punitive damages imposed indiscriminately can bankrupt the defendant. Justice Sandra O'Connor's dissenting opinion in a 1993 case pointed to the tendency of juries to redistribute wealth from deep pocket corporations to plaintiffs and their attorneys, thereby engaging in illicit wealth distribution (*TXO Prod. Cor. v. Alliance Res. Corp.* [1993]).

Prior to the McDonald's hot coffee case, most jurisdictions enacted one or more limitations on punitive damages. Forty-five out of the 51 U.S. jurisdictions either do not recognize punitive damages or have enacted one or more limitation on the remedy since 1980. Half of the states that recognize the remedy of punitive damages revamped their jury instructions in recent decades to provide additional protections. A growing number of states conceive of punitive damages as civil punishment where the dollar amount is set in a separate proceeding. At present, 14 states require that the amount of punitive damages be determined in a bifurcated judicial proceeding following determination of the defendant's liability for punitive damages. During the punitive damages phase, attorneys for both sides introduce evidence relevant to the level of punitive damages necessary to punish and deter the defendant.

Tort reformers have succeeded in increasing the standards for awarding punitive damages in all but a few states. The majority of states have now enacted judicial or legislative tort reforms increasing the standard of proof needed to prove punitive damages, from the usual civil standard of preponderance of the evidence to the heightened standard of "clear and convincing evidence," over the past quarter century. Colorado is the only U.S. jurisdiction where a plaintiff must prove punitive damages beyond a reasonable doubt. Twenty-five states require punitive damages be proven by the heightened burden of proof.

The Supreme Court of the United States has entered into the public policy debate over punitive damages, expressing concern over the size of these awards in a series of cases beginning in 1995 in which it placed guidelines on the size of punitive damages based upon a ratio of compensatory damages. In *Philip Morris USA v. Williams,* an Oregon jury awarded Jesse Williams, an ex-smoker, $821,000 in compensatory damages along with $79.5 million in punitive damages, finding the tobacco mogul negligent and deceitful in its advertisements about the health effects of smoking. The Supreme Court reiterated three guideposts in determining whether the punitive damage award in the tobacco products case was constitutional: first, the degree of reprehensibility of Philip Morris's bad acts; second, the disparity between the harm (actual and potential) suffered by Jesse Williams and the punitive damages; third, the difference between the punitive award and the civil or criminal penalties authorized or imposed in comparable cases.

The Court in *Williams* decided that the due process clause precluded the use of evidence of the tobacco companies' injuries to third parties for purposes of punishment. The Court reasoned that the due process clause of the U.S. Constitution prohibited Oregon from punishing a defendant without the opportunity to present every defense. The Court reversed the punitive damages award because the jury had considered cases in which the tobacco company harmed persons other than the plaintiff. The Court reasoned that nonparty evidence would add a "standardless" dimension to punitive damages. The Court found it inappropriate that the Oregon jury considered evidence that the tobacco mogul harmed other smokers in setting the amount of punitive damages.

Patterns of wrongdoing and evidence of harm to nonparties served as "smoking guns" leading to punitive damages in the McDonald's hot coffee case. The New Mexico jury awarded punitive damages based upon the restaurant chain's inaction, despite its knowledge of hundreds of prior severe burns caused by superheated coffee. In the wake of *Williams,* future courts will need to instruct juries that they may consider the defendant's substantially similar wrongdoing for reprehensibility. If the McDonald's hot coffee case was retried after Williams, the plaintiffs' attorney could not base punishment on McDonald's awareness of the risk of hot coffee from the more than 700 prior cases of hot coffee burns in its corporate files.

Tort law has many terms for suffering, including general damages, noneconomic damages, pain and suffering, mental anguish, impairment, loss of the enjoyment of life, and loss of companionship and society. In the McDonald's case, more than 90 percent of Stella Liebeck's recovery for compensatory damages arose out of her pain and suffering from superheated coffee. The New Mexico jury awarded Mrs. Liebeck hundreds of thousands of dollars for her pain and suffering caused by her burns. A Justice Department study completed during the Reagan administration advocated a $100,000 cap on noneconomic damages to curb a litigation explosion in claiming pain and suffering. In a 2005 speech in Scranton, Pennsylvania, President George W. Bush called for a cap on noneconomic damages in medical malpractice lawsuits. Tort reformers hope that the Court will next take aim at the constitutionality of noneconomic damages or pain and suffering. The American Tort Reform Association (ATRA) calls for greater control over the unguided discretion given juries in awarding noneconomic damages.

The chief criticism of noneconomic damages is that this remedy is simply too expensive for businesses. Moreover, juries are not given sufficient guidance in awarding pain and suffering damages for noneconomic loss. Noneconomic damages are perceived as a highly manipulable remedy in the hands of talented trial lawyers, exploiting the deep pockets of corporations in unjustly enriching the plaintiff. The American Tort Reform Association blames standardless noneconomic damages as the largest contributor to America's litigation crisis. Tort reformers contend that this remedy contributes to inequities and inefficiencies in the tort liability system. Reformers compare noneconomic damages to special damages, which are objectively verifiable. Critics argue that the plaintiff receives full compensation for injuries to her person or property and may include medical bills, past and future earnings, and other direct economic expenses.

Plaintiffs' attorneys complain that noneconomic damages are sometimes difficult to recover because they are perceived as intangible losses. Noneconomic damages are real damages that have long been recognized by the American legal system. Ms. Liebeck, they argue, was entitled to compensation for enduring so much unnecessary suffering due to McDonald's careless practices. The supporters of noneconomic damages acknowledge the difficulty of placing a dollar figure on pain and suffering. Measuring the mental pain of losing a limb or other disfigurement defies easy measuring sticks and it is unclear why Congress or the U.S. Supreme Court would be in any better position than a jury hearing all the evidence in deciding what is just and fair. Courts have recognized diverse methods for measuring noneconomic damages but it is unclear whether any method should serve as the gold standard.

Courts already impose limitations on noneconomic damages in the form of caps or limitations on evidence. Courts do not permit counsel for plaintiff to suggest to the jury that they place themselves in the position of the injured person and determine the sum of money that they would require to incur his injuries. The movement to cap noneconomic damages in the states has already gained steam. In 2005 alone, roughly half of the states capped noneconomic damages in medical liability cases: Alaska, California, Colorado, Florida, Georgia, Illinois, Indiana, Louisiana, Maryland, Massachusetts, Michigan, Mississippi, Missouri, Montana, Nevada, New Mexico, North Dakota, Ohio, Oklahoma, South Carolina, South Dakota, Texas, Utah, Virginia, West Virginia, and Wisconsin. Hawaii, Idaho, Kansas, and Maryland cap noneconomic damages in all substantive fields. The most common form of tort reform is to cap the amount of damages that a plaintiff can receive. California's $250,000 on noneconomic damages in medical malpractice cases is the model for federal legislation pending before Congress.

Between 1980 and 2008, the majority of states have enacted limitations on punitive damages and noneconomic damages. Yet, the public policy debate over the size of punitive and noneconomic damages continues. The U.S. Senate is considering a statute that will place a $250,000 limitation on noneconomic damages in medical malpractice cases. Proposals to cap punitive damages will continue to be advanced in Congress and in the states. The U.S. Supreme Court will likely consider future challenges to the imposition of punitive damages and noneconomic damages. Tort reformers will next ask the Court to revisit the role that wealth of the defendant plays in the punitive damages equation. The Supreme Court has suggested that it may be receptive to curbing the use of wealth in setting punishment. Moving forward, it is most likely that the Court will adopt some new rule of evidence for the admissibility of wealth or the financial condition of the defendant to curb jury discretion. Noneconomic damages are particularly vulnerable to the charge that they are "standardless" in that no clear test exists for measuring pain and suffering. Pain and suffering damages, like capital sentencing, inevitably reflect human judgments. If the Court does expand its constitutional analysis to noneconomic damages, it can begin by simply applying federal excessiveness rules and standards to noneconomic damages. Noneconomic damages in medical malpractices case will continue to be targeted.

Further Reading:

American Tort Reform Association, *Non-Economic Damages Reforms*. Washington, D.C.: American Tort Reform Association, 2008; DeCamp, Paul. "Beyond State Farm: Due Process Constraints on Noneconomic Compensatory Damages." *Harvard Journal of Law and Public Policy* 27 (2003–04): 231; Galligan, Thomas C., et al., *Tort Law: Cases, Perspectives, and Problems*. New York: LEXIS/NEXIS, 2007; Koenig, Thomas H., and Michael L. Rustad. *In Defense of Tort Law*. New York: New York University Press, 2002; Olson, Theodore B., and Theodore J. Bourtros, *The Constitutionality of Punitive Damages*. New York: Washington Legal Foundation, 1989; Prosser, William. *Handbook of the Law of Torts*. 4th ed. St. Paul, Minn.: West Publishing, 1971 ; Rustad, Michael L. *Everyday Law for Lawyers*. Boulder, Colo.: Paradigm Publishers, 2007; Rustad, Michael L., and Thomas H. Koenig. "Taming the Tort Monster: The American Civil Justice System as a Battleground of Social Theory." *Brooklyn Law Review* 68 (2002): 1–105.

– Michael L. Rustad

Defense and National Security

arms control

Arms control policy in the United States and the world predates the nuclear era. Nevertheless, the introduction of nuclear weapons to arsenals of the United States, and eventually eight other nations, redirected international and national priorities from general and complete disarmament to nuclear arms control and nonproliferation. Throughout the cold war, U.S. policy objectives were consistent and had wide bipartisan support. U.S. priorities were first and foremost to maintain supremacy over, or parity with, the Soviet Union and, second, to the extent possible, contain the proliferation of nuclear weapons to other states. Arms control was a means to enhance U.S. security.

Despite the policy emphasis on nuclear weapons, most U.S. administrations have built on the legacy of their predecessors in other areas of arms control as well. The United States has participated in a host of negotiations on other armaments. Many of these negotiations led to new treaties and obligations, such as the 1972 Biological and Toxin Weapons Convention (BTWC), the 1992 Chemical Weapons Convention (CWC), and the 1990 Treaty on Conventional Armed Forces in Europe (CFE). Other negotiations, such as the Treaty to Ban Land Mines, culminated in agreements that the United States has not yet signed. Still others have led to treaties that the United States has signed but not ratified, the Comprehensive Test Ban Treaty (CTBT) for example. Finally, some negotiations, such as the Fissile Materials Cutoff Treaty, are ongoing.

This article explains U.S. arms control policy in the nuclear age. It begins with a description of principal actors involved in setting arms control policy and the national and international processes leading to their fulfillment. A discussion of the issues and agreements that characterized the bilateral U.S.-Soviet nuclear relationship from 1945 until 1992 follows. In addition to the bilateral nuclear agreements that emerged during this period of time, the entry will go on to explore the Nuclear Non-Proliferation Treaty (NPT), a product of the cold war whose multilateral implementation and verification remains a vital issue today. The third section will examine the conventions that govern other weapons of mass destruction—the BTWC and the CWC—and discuss current implementation concerns. The fourth section of the entry discusses multilateral treaties that the United States has declined to sign even though they have broad international support, such as the Land Mines treaty and the Convention on Cluster Munitions (CCM). The concluding portion of the entry will analyze the trends in arms control over the past 60 plus years and set forth ongoing challenges.

The U.S. president, through the executive branch, directs arms control policy. The Constitution grants the president the power ". . . by and with the Advice and Consent of the Senate, to make Treaties. . . ." As such, treaties are negotiated by the executive branch of government and require ratification by two-thirds of the Senate before becoming U.S. law.

Throughout the latter half of the 20th century, arms control had strong and sustained bipartisan support. All U.S. presidents from Kennedy to Clinton negotiated and signed significant arms control agreements. The administration of George W. Bush is an exception to this general trend. Bush's withdrawal of the United States from the 1972 Anti-Ballistic Missile (ABM) treaty, his attempt to rescind the U.S. signature to the Comprehensive Test Ban Treaty, his rejection of the Biological and Toxin Weapons Convention (BTWC) Protocol, and his failure to sign the CCM all support the argument that Bush was skeptical or hostile to building on the arms control accomplishments of previous administrations. The one treaty that Bush did negotiate, the Strategic Offensive Reduction Treaty (SORT), also known as the Moscow Treaty, did not eliminate or reduce any actual weapons; it merely promised to remove them from operational deployment. The agreement did not require the destruction of any weapons. The weapons removed from deployment could be returned to stockpiles.

After the Soviet Union detonated its first nuclear weapon, in 1949, arms control became a much higher priority to the United States. While the U.S. nuclear arsenal was superior to that of the USSR in the early years of the nuclear age, that superiority waned quickly. Arms control policy was directed from the White House during the Eisenhower administration. President Kennedy, however, established an independent agency—the Arms Control and Disarmament Agency (ACDA)—to provide research and advice to the president on all arms control issues, to advocate for and negotiate arms control agreements, and to monitor compliance with treaties. ACDA's director reported directly to the president. Throughout roughly the next 35 years, ACDA did operate independently, advocating for the Nuclear Non-Proliferation Treaty when the State Department opposed it, for example. ACDA took the lead in negotiating a series of nuclear and non-nuclear treaties, including bilateral nuclear treaties with the USSR, the multilateral NPT, and the multilateral treaties banning the production of biological and chemical weapons. Yet the ratification of the CWC led to the demise of ACDA as a strong independent voice for arms control.

One of the last actions of President George H. W. Bush was to sign the CWC on January 13, 1993. Despite support from Bush and members of his administration, President Clinton faced considerable opposition within the Senate to ratification of the convention. In particular, Senator Jesse Helms (R-NC), as chairman of the Senate Foreign Relations Committee, was able to use bureaucratic maneuvering to keep the ratifying legislation in committee and delay a Senate vote on ratification. In negotiations with the Clinton administration, Helms agreed to allow the bill out of committee only if ACDA would be incorporated into the State Department. Since this deal was made in 1997, arms control policy in the executive branch has been under the purview of the undersecretary of state for arms control and international security.

The Senate has the most direct congressional role in arms control policy, and nearly all arms control treaties submitted to the Senate in the second half of the 20th century have been ratified by strong, if not overwhelming, majorities. Of the major arms control treaties ratified by the Senate from 1963 until 2000, only the Chemical Weapons Convention, ratified by a comfortable 74-29 margin, received less than 80 percent support from the Senate. There are important exceptions to this trend, however. President Carter was unable to secure ratification of the SALT II nuclear weapons treaty in 1979 after the Soviet Union invaded Afghanistan, and he withdrew the treaty from consideration before a vote was taken. In 1999, the Senate, on a 48 for, 51 opposed vote, rejected ratification of the Comprehensive Test Ban Treaty.

The Senate Foreign Relations Committee has principal responsibility for arms control. The committee chair and the ranking minority member are typically instrumental in commenting on and, at times, shaping arms control policy and agreements. In addition, most arms control measures require implementing legislation, which embeds treaties in domestic law. Such legislation requires passage by both houses of Congress.

The military and intelligence communities are also influential voices in developing arms control policy within the U.S. government. Arms control policy has a direct effect on the military and, therefore, the military has a direct interest in influencing policy. The Department of Defense (DOD) typically has constituencies that are invested in particular weapons programs that arms control policy makers elsewhere in government seek to limit, or eliminate. Arms control has the potential to decrease DOD budgets and staffing. At the same time, DOD civilian and military leadership have understood the importance of halting the nuclear arms race and restraining the proliferation of nuclear and other weapons of mass destruction. Thus, while influencing the shape of arms control agreements, they have usually not blocked their negotiation or Senate passage. The Joint Chiefs of Staff did oppose the CTBT, however. Both the military and the intelligence communities have responsibilities to monitor compliance with arms control agreements. Members of each group advise the administration and testify before the Senate on the capabilities of their organizations to effectively monitor compliance with specific provisions of treaties.

As is appropriate in a functioning democracy, both the executive and legislative branches of government are influenced by other societal actors in developing arms control policy. Defense contractors and other industry representatives play a role. The Chemical Manufacturers Association, for example, was an important supporter of the CWC and frequently advised members of the U.S. negotiating team. Civil society organizations can also influence arms control policy through research and advocacy. The Nuclear Weapons Freeze Movement is an example of such a group. The Nuclear Freeze movement swayed public opinion as well as candidates for office in the United States and around the world. Members of research organizations such as the Brookings Institution or the Heritage Foundation often lend their voices in support of or opposition to specific arms control initiatives.

The making of U.S. arms control policy is a complex endeavor involving numerous actors and institutions. The influence of all governmental actors, the press, and the public shape the arms control agenda and determine how the agenda is implemented through executive and legislative action. We now turn to specific arms control agreements and their legacy.

Although the United Kingdom, France, and China all developed and tested nuclear weapons by the early 1960s, the "arms race" and efforts to control its acceleration was largely a U.S.-Soviet affair. The arms race between the United States and the USSR was not a single race, but three races occurring simultaneously: (1) racing to make more weapons, (2) racing to make more powerful weapons, and (3) racing to make more reliable and more sophisticated ways of delivering warheads to their intended targets. Moreover, none of the races had a perceptible finish line. While the United States started the race ahead of the USSR, the launch of *Sputnik*, the first artificial satellite to circle the earth from outer space, in 1957 demonstrated Soviet superiority in the third of these races.

For 30 years, from the mid-1950s to the mid-1980s the United States and the USSR built massive nuclear stockpiles. In 1966, the size of the U.S. stockpile peaked at nearly 32,000 warheads. The Soviet stockpile of nuclear weapons peaked at well over 40,000 in 1986. Negotiations to limit the growth or reduce the number of U.S. and Soviet weapons and means of their delivery led to the negotiation and implementation of a number of agreements: the Strategic Arms Limitation Treaties (SALT) I & II, the Intermediate Range Nuclear Forces treaty (INF), the Strategic Arms Reduction Treaties (START) I & II, and the Anti-Ballistic Missile (ABM) treaty.

SALT I was a five-year bargain between the United States and the USSR that placed limits on the growth of delivery systems, but did not reduce any warheads. The agreement placed limits on fixed land-based intercontinental ballistic missiles (ICBM), freezing them to the number already deployed or in construction. The agreement also placed limits on submarines and submarine (or sea)-launched ballistic missiles (SLBM). The Soviet Union insisted on lower limits for U.S. ballistic missiles, and the United States accepted those limits for a number of reasons. U.S. NATO allies also possessed SLBMs, which were threatening to the USSR Moreover, in 1970 the United

States deployed the first Minuteman ICBM with the ability to deliver three nuclear weapons at a time, with the individual warheads aimed at different targets within a larger footprint. These "multiple, independently-targeted reentry vehicles" (MIRVs) were designed to overcome the antiballistic missile system the Soviets had put in place. Although MIRVs were discussed in SALT, neither side thought it was in their interest to limit MIRVs at that time.

The United States and the USSR continued talks on a long-term comprehensive agreement that would replace the SALT I interim agreement scheduled to last a mere five years. Starting six months after the signing of SALT I and the ABM treaty, SALT II negotiations lasted for seven years through three U.S. administrations before producing a treaty that would never be ratified by the U.S. Senate. Many issues in the negotiations were left unresolved by the interim agreement, such as MIRVed missiles, cruise missiles, and bombers.

In 1974, U.S. president Ford and Soviet leader Brezhnev agreed to a formula for a 10-year SALT II agreement that would limit each side to a ceiling of 2,400 weapons launchers. Each side could distribute its ceiling among ICBMs, SLBMs, heavy bombers, and long-range air-to-surface missiles. In addition, launchers with MIRVs were limited to 1,300. U.S. missiles based in Europe would not be included in the ceilings. In spite of this formula, negotiations dragged on for another five years. Among the thorny disputes were how to consider cruise missiles, whether certain Soviet aircraft would be considered heavy bombers, MIRV verification provisions, and throw-weight limits. Although President Carter sought much lower limits, the Soviets insisted on negotiating within the agreed upon formula. Ultimately, the 1974 formula was incorporated into the SALT II agreement along with other provisions, including a ban on construction of additional fixed ICBM launchers, a ban on air-to-surface ballistic missiles, a limit of 10 warheads on a new type of permitted ICBM, limits on the number of cruise missiles per heavy bomber, bans on new weapons systems such as long-range ballistic missiles on surface ships and ballistic missiles and cruise missiles on the seabed, and limits to the throw weight of strategic ballistic missiles. When the treaty was completed in June 1979, President Carter submitted it to the U.S. Senate for ratification, but, following the Soviet invasion of Afghanistan, he withdrew the treaty and it was never ratified.

The SALT process included discussions between the U.S. and Soviet delegations limiting defensive, as well as offensive, weapons. ABMs are methods of intercepting ballistic missiles in flight, preventing them from reaching their intended targets. The purpose of limits on ABM systems was to create a balance between the nuclear forces of the two cold war enemies so that neither one would achieve an advantage in a first strike, nor would either one have an incentive to initiate war. Signed on the same day as the SALT I interim agreement (May 26, 1972), the ABM treaty permitted the United States and the USSR to deploy only two ABM systems each. Each system was limited to 100 missile interceptors and coverage of an area with a 150-kilometer radius. One system was allowed to defend the capital of the nation; the other was allowed to protect an offensive ICBM site. The treaty defined the components of an ABM system and the two countries agreed to a broad prohibition against the development, testing, and deployment of any ABM system or any of its components based in the sea, in the air, or in space, as well as land-based mobile systems or components. The treaty placed limits on the number of intercept launchers at the allowed ABM sites and limited those launchers to one intercept each.

While implementation of the ABM treaty began in a promising fashion, President Reagan's Strategic Defense Initiative (SDI) and the discovery of an early warning radar installation at the Soviet site of Krasnoyarsk led to mutual accusations of treaty noncompliance. In 2001, President George W. Bush announced a plan to revive the moribund missile defense system and abandon the constraints of the ABM treaty. Bush gave formal notice to Russia that the United States would withdraw from the ABM treaty and the United States did so in 2002.

The INF treaty marked the first nuclear disarmament treaty, in contrast to treaties reducing or limiting the growth of arms. Nuclear weapons in Europe had long been an area of disagreement between the United States and the USSR. Although the United States deployed nuclear warheads in Europe beginning in 1954, they were to be delivered with bombers, not missiles. Meanwhile, the Soviet Union began to deploy ballistic missiles in Eastern Europe armed with nuclear warheads. In 1981, President Reagan publicly proposed the elimination of all ballistic and cruise missiles in Europe. This "zero option" had its origins in the antinuclear movement in Europe. When Reagan made the proposal, the United States did not have any ballistic missiles deployed in Europe, but had plans to deploy both ballistic and cruise missiles starting in 1983. The USSR, however, if it accepted Reagan's proposal, would have had to remove already deployed missiles.

The Soviet Union repeatedly rejected the U.S. proposal. Consequently, the United States proceeded with its planned deployment of missiles in Europe. In response, the Soviets refused to resume the INF talks. As a result of the political upheavals in the Soviet Union following Mikhail Gorbachev's consolidation of power, the talks recommenced under a new name and the Soviet Union accepted the zero option. The treaty called for the removal of 1,667 Soviet warheads and 429 U.S. warheads. The treaty required not only that the missiles be removed from European soil, but also that the missiles—but not their guidance systems—be destroyed. The treaty did not require that the nuclear warheads be destroyed. They could be returned to the respective country's stockpile or placed in other missiles, including ICBMs. The treaty entered into force on June 1, 1988. Three years later, the United States had destroyed its final ground launched missiles and the USSR had destroyed its last SS-20. A total of 2,296 missiles were destroyed.

START is a series of negotiations between the United States and the USSR to move beyond limiting nuclear weapons launchers and grapple with reducing the number of warheads. START I required each country to reduce its aggregate number of deployed ICBMs, SLBMS, and heavy bombers to 1,600 and warheads associated with these delivery vehicles to 6,000. The number of U.S. nuclear warheads associated with its strategic nuclear delivery vehicles peaked in 1987 at 13,685; Soviet warheads peaked at 11,529. START I obligated each side to reduce its delivery capabilities by one-third, and its warheads by roughly one-half.

The START negotiations began in 1982, were stalled by the U.S. deployment of ballistic missiles in Europe, and subsequently were revived in 1985 after Gorbachev took power. The START I treaty was completed and signed just weeks before Communist hard-liners attempted a coup to regain power in the USSR in July 1991. By the end of 1991 the USSR ceased to exist, fracturing into the Commonwealth of Independent States. The breakup of the Soviet Union delayed START I's entry into force. When the USSR disintegrated, Belarus, Kazakhstan, and Ukraine each had nuclear weapons on their territory as, of course, did Russia. Subsequently, these three independent republics transferred their nuclear weapons to Russia.

In 1992, Russia and the United States quickly concluded a follow-on treaty to START I, which would have further reduced strategic forces. START II required the two parties to reduce their strategic warheads from 6,000 to no more than 3,500 and established limits within the overall maximum for ICBMs warheads and SLBM warheads. These reductions were to be phased in with an initial reduction to 4,200. Russia delayed ratification of START II for several years and, when it did ratify the agreement in 2000, it did so contingent on continued U.S. support of the ABM treaty. Bush's withdrawal from the ABM treaty triggered a response by Russia in announcing that it would not be bound by START II. The treaty has never entered into force

Even though START II has not entered into force, President Clinton and Russian president Yeltsin agreed on a framework to negotiate further reductions, labeled START III. The framework called for reductions in warheads in the range of 2,000-2,500 warheads, warhead destruction, and transparency measures. Revived by the Obama administration, talks to further reduce and destroy nuclear warheads and delivery mechanisms are ongoing.

In a brief treaty concluded in 2002, Russia and the United States agreed to reduce deployed strategic nuclear weapons to no more than 2,200 each by the year 2012. The agreement is perhaps noteworthy for what it omits rather than for what it includes. Since it restricts only deployed warheads it does not mandate the destruction of any warheads or delivery vehicles.

Despite serious nuclear proliferation issues, the United States and Russia still possess the vast majority of the world's nuclear weapons. In two bipartisan and much-discussed opinions in the *Wall Street Journal* in 2007 and 2008, former secretaries of state George Schultz and Henry Kissinger, former secretary of defense Perry, and former senator Sam Nunn called for a nuclear weapons free world and outlined actions to achieve that goal. President Obama has emphasized "America's commitment to seek the peace and security of a world without nuclear weapons" and described several actions, including further reductions in nuclear arsenals not only with Russia, but also with all nuclear armed states. President Obama's commitment to nuclear disarmament, coupled with the bipartisan support evidenced in the *Wall Street Journal* articles and commentaries on them, bode well for continued nuclear weapons reduction and destruction agreements.

Testing nuclear weapons, or acquiring data from nuclear weapons tests, is an integral component of successful nuclear weapons programs. Consequently, eliminating nuclear weapons tests has long been a goal of arms control advocates and the non-nuclear weapons states. Indian prime minister Jawaharlal Nehru was the first world leader to call for a "standstill agreement" among the nuclear weapons states on nuclear testing following radiation exposure in the Pacific occasioned by a U.S. nuclear test in 1954. The Soviet Union proposed a halt to nuclear weapons tests at the United Nations Disarmament Commission in 1955.

Early negotiations took place among the five nations on the subcommittee of the Disarmament Commission—the United States, the United Kingdom, the Soviet Union, Canada, and France. Whether a ban on nuclear testing could be effectively verified in the absence of onsite inspections, which the Soviets steadfastly opposed, was a point of contention. Little progress was apparent in the negotiations over the next few years. By the early 1960s the nuclear powers had begun to conduct nuclear tests underground. In contrast to atmospheric testing, which could easily be detected, some underground nuclear explosions could not be distinguished from naturally occurring seismic events.

In 1963, the United States, the USSR, and the United Kingdom agreed to ban nuclear explosions of any kind in the earth's atmosphere, in outer space, and underwater. Ultimately signed by more than 100 states, the Limited (or Partial) Test Ban Treaty (LTBT) limited where nuclear explosions could take place but did not limit the number or size of nuclear tests as long as they took place underground. Indeed, with the United States in the lead with over 1,000 tests, more than 2,000 nuclear weapons tests have taken place since the first was conducted in 1945.

Developing nuclear weapons, or new nuclear weapons, is nearly impossible without testing them. Consequently, eliminating nuclear weapons tests has been integral to arms control and nonproliferation policy. Negotiations to end all nuclear tests dragged on for decades. A Comprehensive Test Ban Treaty (CTBT) was finally completed in 1996, but it faces enormous obstacles before it can enter into force. Most importantly, all nuclear weapons states and all states with nuclear technology capabilities as of 1996 must ratify the treaty before it enters into force. Three nuclear weapons states—India, Pakistan, and North Korea—have not signed the treaty, and all have tested nuclear weapons since the treaty has been open for signature. Three other nuclear weapons states—China, Israel, and the United States—and three non-nuclear weapons states—Egypt, Indonesia, and Iran—necessary for entry into force, have signed but not ratified.

The U.S. Senate voted against ratification of the CTBT when President Clinton submitted the treaty in 2000. Despite strong Senate Republican opposition to ratification, President Obama has pledged to resubmit the treaty for Senate approval.

Former secretaries of state Schultz and Kissinger's support for bringing the CTBT into force may be sufficient to persuade enough Senate Republicans to secure ratification.

In 1963, President Kennedy warned that as many as 25 states could acquire nuclear weapons by 1970 unless steps were taken to prevent their proliferation. Not until the Johnson administration, however, did negotiations on a treaty to staunch nuclear weapons proliferation become a political priority.

The NPT created separate obligations for non-nuclear weapons states (NNWS) and nuclear weapons states (NWS), defined as those that had manufactured and exploded a nuclear weapon or other nuclear device as of January 1, 1967. The initial obligations for NNWS and NWS mirrored each other. NNWS agreed not to manufacture, acquire, or receive nuclear weapons and agreed to accept safeguards on their nuclear energy facilities. The safeguards would be negotiated with the International Atomic Energy Agency (IAEA) to verify that the peaceful nuclear facilities complied with the NPT obligations. NWS were obliged neither to transfer nuclear weapons or control over them to any recipient nor to assist non-nuclear weapons states in acquiring them. NWS also agreed to pursue negotiations to end the nuclear arms race and to pursue nuclear disarmament. These disarmament obligations have often served as a topic of heated disagreement among the parties to the treaty. The NNWS have repeatedly insisted on a CTBT as a means for the NWS to signal their commitment to nuclear disarmament.

In addition to duties, the NPT provides benefits to NNWS as incentives to become a party. The treaty formally acknowledges the right of non-nuclear weapons states to produce and use nuclear energy for peaceful purposes. Moreover, the treaty requires all states parties to ensure that benefits from the peaceful uses of nuclear explosions be available to all other states parties.

The United Nations Security Council passed a resolution in conjunction with the NPT that provided additional security incentives to NNWS to become parties to the agreement. The resolution, number 255, states that the Security Council "above all its nuclear weapon State permanent members, would have to act immediately" if a NWS threatened to use or used nuclear weapons against a NNWS. The resolution also recognized that some states intended to provide assistance to NNWS in that situation.

The NPT entered into force in March 1970 with three nuclear weapons states—the United States, the USSR, and the United Kingdom—and 43 non-nuclear weapons states. Implementation of the NPT has had a mixed record. Membership in the NPT is one mark of its success. The number of states party to the treaty slowly grew to its present membership of 191, the largest number to any arms control agreement. Moreover, membership has grown among states that possessed nuclear weapons inherited from the Soviet Union, and those that considered or had nuclear programs in place—South Africa, Brazil, and Argentina. Nevertheless, Israel, Pakistan, and India have refused to sign the NPT and now are nuclear weapons states. North Korea, moreover, became a state party but withdrew its membership and has since become a nuclear weapons state.

Dissatisfaction of the non-nuclear weapons states with the pace of nuclear weapons disarmament continues to mar review conferences of the treaty. In spite of this dissatisfaction, the NPT was extended indefinitely in 1995 following its first 25 years of operation. The indefinite extension was one of a package of decisions that included a call for the completion of the CTBT by 1996 and a treaty banning the production of fissile material. The status of the CTBT—completed but not signed or not ratified by six of the nine nuclear weapons states—is a constant reminder that all is not well with the NPT. Failure to complete a fissile material cutoff treaty is also a thorn in the side of the non-nuclear weapons states.

Another serious problem with the NPT is what actions are appropriate when states withdraw from the treaty to pursue acquisition of nuclear weapons, as in the case of North Korea, or are found in violation of their obligations under the treaty. In 2003, an IAEA report charged Iran with conducting secret nuclear activities, which violated its NPT obligations.

The Nuclear Non-Proliferation Treaty is the key component in the regime to control the proliferation of nuclear weapons, but the other regime components—the norm against the use of nuclear weapons, the promises entered into at NPT review conferences, and support of NPT institutions such as the IAEA—are critical as well. Until all states, members and nonmembers of the NPT, seriously tackle questions of proliferation and national nuclear policy, the NPT is in danger of further erosion and the world faces the possibility of further nuclear weapons proliferation and an increasing likelihood that nuclear weapons will be used, either deliberately or accidentally.

While nuclear weapons issues have dominated the arms control agenda, the international community has concluded disarmament agreements that ban the very possession of biological, toxin, and chemical weapons.

In 1925, bacteriological (biological) weapons were added to the 1925 Geneva Protocol that bound the contracting parties to refrain from using chemical weapons in warfare. Chemical and biological weapons continued to be linked in disarmament discussions until the 1960s. After an internal review by the Nixon administration in 1969 concluded that the United States should discontinue its offensive biological weapons program, the United States joined a British initiative that would outlaw the possession, development, production, stockpiling, acquisition, and transfer of biological weapons. Although the USSR and its allies resisted separating biological from chemical weapons, they changed course in 1972 and shortly thereafter concluded the Biological and Toxin Weapons Convention (BTWC).

The implementation of the BTWC, like other arms control agreements, has been marked by accusations of noncompliance. Moreover, in 1995 the states parties to the treaty embarked on a seven-year effort to negotiate a legally binding protocol to the treaty that culminated in a draft protocol in 2001. The draft, however, was resoundingly rejected by the George W. Bush administration. The negotiation mandate for the protocol has remained in limbo since then. It remains on the books, but no action has been taken to fulfill the mandate.

In the meantime, beginning in 2003, the parties to the treaty have met on a yearly basis to discuss topics relevant to the convention. The meetings have been widely regarded as informative and useful and have led to national and other efforts to support biosecurity, education, raising awareness, assistance in passing national legislation supporting the treaty, and other topics. The Obama administration's support for arms control initiatives in general holds out the possibility that the states parties may once again find a way to fulfill the mandate of a legally binding instrument to strengthen the effectiveness of the convention and promote its universal implementation.

The text of the BTWC contains a commitment by the treaty parties to continue negotiations on a treaty to ban the possession of chemical weapons. The negotiations took place over nearly 20 years and were often deadlocked on the issue of onsite inspections. In contrast to the BTWC, a treaty without any provisions to verify compliance, the Chemical Weapons Convention (CWC), contains extensive verification provisions for the destruction of existing chemical weapons stockpiles and old chemical weapons production facilities. The convention requires thorough declarations by government and industry and routine inspections to verify the accuracy of the declarations. The CWC has provisions for short notice onsite inspections, called "challenge inspections," in the event of allegations of noncompliance. This provision has never been utilized, however.

As with other arms control agreements, the CWC has encountered a number of problems in its implementation. On the positive side, the CWC has an impressive 188 states parties. Only two states, Israel and Myanmar, have signed but not ratified. Nevertheless, five countries—Angola, Egypt, North Korea, Somalia, and Syria—have not signed or acceded to the convention, and some or all of them may possess chemical weapons.

Demilitarization, the process of destroying chemical weapons stockpiles and chemical weapons production facilities, has not been accomplished as quickly as drafters of the convention anticipated. Albania, India, and, according to official documents "another State Party" (widely believed to be South Korea), have destroyed all of their weapons. Although seven states declared stockpiles, the United States and Russia had by far the largest. All stockpiles were to be destroyed 10 years after the treaty entered into force in April 1997. Now, more than 12 years after that deadline, just over 44 percent of the world's stockpiles have been destroyed. Russia and the United States have been granted an extension of the destruction deadline until 2012. After many delays, destruction is finally well underway and is proceeding rapidly. As of April 2009, Russia had destroyed just over 30 percent of its stockpile and the United States had destroyed nearly 60 percent. As for the 70 declared chemical weapons production facilities, 62 have been irreversibly destroyed or converted to peaceful purposes.

At the end of 1997 following a whirlwind of activity, the Mine Ban Treaty (MBT), also known as the Ottawa Convention due to the leadership provided by the Canadian government in securing its passage, was completed and signed by 122 countries. The MBT entered into force less than 18 months later, according to Rutherford "the fastest major international agreement ever to enter into force." The rapid pace of the negotiations was attributed in part to the participation and influence of nongovernmental organizations (NGOs), particularly the International Campaign to Ban Land Mines (ICBL). Like the BWC and the CWC, the MBT bans the possession, development, and production of land mines. In addition, the MBT contains requirements to destroy mines in place, and it establishes means to assist mine victims and increase awareness of mines.

The history of the MBT negotiations is remarkable for its innovative process. Protocols I and II to the Geneva Conventions and the Convention on Certain Conventional Weapons regulated the use of land mines, attempting to limit their indiscriminate effects rather than to ban them completely. Their impact on the use of land mines was an abject failure, in part, because their provisions applied only to international conflicts and not civil wars. Frustrated with the ongoing casualties caused by land mines and the ineffective formal international response, several nongovernmental groups developed a strategy in the mid-1990s to achieve a total ban on the production and use of antipersonnel land mines. In October 1992, six NGOs formed the ICBL with a simple goal: an international ban on the use, production, stockpiling, and sale, transfer, or export of antipersonnel land mines; increased resources for humanitarian de-mining; and increased resources for land mine victim rehabilitation and assistance. Any organization that agreed to this principle could join as a member of the campaign.

Early meetings of a core group of medium-sized states—Austria, Belgium, Canada, Germany, Ireland, Mexico, Norway, Philippines, South Africa, and Switzerland—took place outside the traditional forum for arms control talks and were attended only by states favoring a ban on land mines—keeping those states who did not agree with that principle from delaying, vetoing, or weakening the ban. By all accounts the participation of NGOs, above all the ICBL, in the negotiations was extensive and unprecedented.

The United States has not signed the treaty. The United States was unable to commit to removing land mines from the demilitarized zone separating North and South Korea. Nevertheless, it is the largest financial contributor to de-mining activities. While the United States has a large mine stockpile, it has not produced mines since 1997 and has not used them since the 1991 Gulf War. The norm created by the MBT has had a lasting effect and the United States is unlikely to reincorporate land mines into its military activities.

Following its success in banning land mines, the ICBL took on the issue of cluster munitions, forming in 2003, with other civil society organizations, the Cluster Munition Coalition (CMC). Typically dropped from the air or exploded on the ground, cluster munitions break into several dozen to several hundred small bombs in order to cover a wide geographic area. With the government of Norway taking the lead, proponents of a ban on the production, stockpiling, transfer, and possession of cluster munitions followed the process originated in the negotiations on land mines. Negotiations took place in 2007 and 2008 and the CMC opened for signature in December 2008 with 94 states as original signatories. The treaty will enter into force after 30 countries have ratified it. The United States has not signed the CMC and it has made clear that it did not support the process that led to the treaty.

The process by which the MBT and the CMC were negotiated underscores what may be a new trend in arms control. Traditional U.S. allies in Europe, along with Canada, Australia, and New Zealand and many other countries, are coming together in ad hoc meetings to tackle arms production and use on a weapon-by-weapon basis. Frustrated by lengthy negotiations in traditional fora, these champions of arms control have openly welcomed nongovernmental organizations as important partners in developing political will and public support for banning weapons. From a U.S. perspective, a government working with NGOs on arms control and disarmament is an unlikely alliance but one the United States may accommodate, if not embrace, in the future.

The success of the MBT and CMC treaties was also due, in part, to the deliberate reframing of the issue as one of humanitarian law rather than as arms control. The advocates of banning these weapons focused on the unacceptably high civilian casualties and the lingering danger posed by unexploded ordnance.

Arms control and disarmament policy in the United States following World War II has been marked by a number of phases. Throughout most of this period, nuclear weapons dominated the agenda. During the cold war, the United States and the USSR simultaneously built enormous nuclear arsenals and consistently sought means to end the vicious spiral. Arms control during that era sought to improve security by lessening the likelihood that either side would initiate a conventional or nuclear war. The means to security was to have a combination of measures that limited the growth of weapons and delivery systems while leaving each side vulnerable to a retaliatory nuclear attack through placing limits on ABM systems.

Simultaneously, the United States sought to limit the proliferation not just of nuclear weapons but chemical and biological weapons as well. To gain the benefits of nuclear technology, most nations agreed to forgo the possession of nuclear weapons by joining the NPT. Yet unfulfilled obligations on the part of the nuclear weapons states to abolish their nuclear weapons have repeatedly strained the implementation of the NPT. The absence of verification procedures in the BTWC has called into question its effectiveness, and the destruction of chemical weapons stockpiles is behind schedule.

The United States has shown reluctance in the post–cold war era to enter into new arms control agreements. Although it signed the CTBT, the U.S. Senate voted against ratification and the United States has not signed the MBT or the CMC. Moreover, the United States withdrew from the ABM treaty. The rest of the world, including the strongest allies of the United States, however, has not sat idly by. They have engaged in an innovative and streamlined process to initiate the banning of inhumane weapons such as land mines and cluster munitions. Making disarmament universal, whether the weapons are nuclear, chemical, biological, land mines, or cluster munitions, remains a serious problem that defies easy solutions.

Further Reading:

Burns, Richard Dean. *The Evolution of Arms Control: from Antiquity to the Nuclear Age*. Santa Barbara, Calif.: Praeger, 2009; Hoffman, David. *Dead Hand: The Untold Story of the Cold War Arms Race and Its Dangerous Legacy*. New York: Doubleday, 2009; Hymans, Jacques E. *The Psychology of Nuclear Proliferation*. New York: Cambridge University Press, 2006; Thomson, David B. *A Guide to the Nuclear Arms Control Treaties*. Los Alamos, N.M.: Los Alamos Historical Society, 2001.

– Marie Isabelle Chevrier

homeland security

On September 11, 2001, 19 Arab men hijacked four American commercial airliners and, with 24,000 gallons of jet fuel aboard each, turned them into flying bombs. Two struck New York

City's signature Twin Towers, the buildings of the World Trade Center. One hit the Pentagon and another, intended for Washington, D.C., missed its target and crashed into a field in Pennsylvania after a passenger revolt. Approximately 3,000 people were killed, exceeding the toll of 2,400 dead after the Japanese surprise attack on Pearl Harbor. By the next day, media the world over had transmitted the now famous image of the second airplane plunging into the south tower of the World Trade Center and declared it a world-altering moment. The French newspaper *Le Monde*, often critical of the United States, ran a front-page headline reading "*Nous sommes tous Américains.*" In London, Buckingham Palace played the U.S. national anthem during the changing of the guard. The world's response brought home the unprecedented nature of the event.

In the immediate aftermath, the United States placed security forces on a high state of alert and—for the first time—suspended civilian air travel for three days. Shortly after the attacks, al-Qaeda, a militant Islamic group, and its leader, Osama bin Laden, claimed responsibility. President George W. Bush ordered a military offensive against the group, the first initiative in what came to be known as the "War on Terror." In October 2001, the United States invaded Afghanistan, where bin Laden and his conspirators were believed to be hiding.

At home, the United States investigated whether the attacks were preventable and began to build a bureaucracy around a novel term: "homeland security." Before 9/11, Pentagon bureaucrats used the term to refer to missile defense programs. After 9/11, "homeland security" became a household name referring to the collection of federal agencies engaged in defense against domestic and international terrorism. Civil servants in these agencies had never before seen their work as part of a collective counterterrorism enterprise, though federal agencies had been doing homeland security for at least half a century. The Central Intelligence Agency and Federal Emergency Management Agency both had ancestors in World War II and cold war bureaucracies that defended the United States against foreign attack. Immigration agencies had long been concerned about who was entering the country, though security missions were often buried under a host of other concerns. Similarly, the Federal Aviation Administration had always been responsible for aviation security, though safety was a more pressing concern until a rash of hijackings in the 1960s and 1970s put terrorism on the public agenda.

The aftermath of the attacks of 2001 focused attention around these agencies' collective responsibility to prevent and respond to terrorism. Congress and the president chartered commissions to investigate whether the attacks could have been prevented. Foremost among these, the 9/11 Commission published a best-selling record of its probe. Commissioners concluded that the United States was vulnerable to attack because of the failure of intelligence and law enforcement officials to "connect the dots" and piece together signs of a terrorist plot. Contradictory immigration policies and a broken border security system also contributed to U.S. vulnerability.

Not all blame levied at the bureaucracy is warranted. Popular accounts refer to September 11 as "the world's worst failure of airport security." That perception led Congress to create the Transportation Security Administration in November 2001 to perform tasks formerly handled by the Federal Aviation Administration. From then on, airport passenger screening was to be conducted by federal employees;—prior to that date, screening was conducted by private companies with lower standards for employment. Despite the belief that the poor quality of baggage screeners might be to blame, airport personnel followed the letter of the law on the day of the attacks. The hijackers subdued passengers and crew using small knives that were legal on airplanes; only knives with blades greater than four inches long were prohibited. The hijackers entered the United States legally on temporary tourist visas and all possessed drivers licenses and ID cards. Baggage screeners, though, were a convenient target—one that could be immediately federalized—while the more serious vulnerabilities would require coordinating diverse intelligence, law enforcement, immigration, and disaster response bureaucracies.

a bad name, such as the true stories about building a secret 112,544 square foot bunker under the Greenbrier resort in West Virginia to house Congress during a nuclear war. FEMA also lacked coordination in responding to natural disasters. For large disasters, FEMA's response could be slow and excessively bureaucratic. For small and medium-sized disasters, FEMA was often unclear about whether it should intervene at all, and its equivocation frustrated states and localities. Congress was to blame for some of the agency's schizophrenia. Until reorganization in 1993 and the repeal of the Civil Defense Act in 1994, FEMA reported to over a dozen congressional committees, including the Senate Armed Services Committee, which confirmed appointees to an associate director position. Congress attempted to give direction to the agency by passing the Stafford Act of 1988, but the legislation contained a broad mandate with only the most general guidelines about FEMA's role in disaster preparation and response, and the act itself was ambiguous about whether or not FEMA was a national security agency.

As the costs of disasters escalated and botched relief efforts made the news, public pressure led Congress to add coherence to the system of disaster preparedness and response. The Robert T. Stafford Disaster Relief and Emergency Assistance Act was enacted in 1988. The Stafford Act defines how federal disasters are declared, determines the types of assistance to be provided by the federal government, and establishes coordination mechanisms among levels of government. It was introduced by Republican representative Tom Ridge of Pennsylvania, who would later become the first secretary of the Department of Homeland Security. The act drew bipartisan support, and it passed by 368 to 13 in the House. The act's major provisions include:

- Establishing a 75-percent federal, 25-percent local cost sharing plan
- Providing government assistance for disaster mitigation and recovery, but primarily relief after declared disasters
- Clarifying how Department of Defense resources would be used in disaster assistance.

In the 30 years that would follow, FEMA would distribute an average of $2 billion in Stafford Act funds each year. Though the Stafford Act added congressional authority to federal government disaster relief, it did not solve the problems of defining what kinds of disasters the government was to prepare for, or what the role of the national government should be in a federal system.

FEMA's poor reputation in the late 1980s and early 1990s led some members of Congress to call for abolishing the agency. Rather than fold FEMA into another department, new director James Lee Witt led a reorganization in 1993 that secured greater independence for the agency and a newly focused disaster mission. With the advice of emergency management professional associations and a staff steeped in disaster work, Witt shrank the agency's top-secret national security division and obtained more resources to prepare for natural disasters more quickly.

In retrospect, it appears that FEMA's reputation had to hit bottom before it could achieve a consensus on how to reconcile its multiple missions and authorities. It is difficult to imagine the president, Congress, and the many factions within the agency agreeing on a major reform if all of the parties were not dissatisfied with the status quo and the agency did not face the threat of extinction. By 1992, FEMA's reputation and its employees' morale had reached their nadir. FEMA's response to Hurricane Andrew was so slow and so widely publicized as inadequate that President Bush, in the midst of an election campaign, sent nearly 20,000 navy, air force, and U.S. Coast Guard troops to Florida and asked the secretary of transportation to take charge.

Faced with a media uproar, Congress convened blue-ribbon panels and began investigations into FEMA's performance. The chief culprit for FEMA's poor planning and slow response, the reports found, was its national security division, which set policies that hampered natural disaster relief. For example, FEMA developed a cutting-edge information technology system, but political executives refused to allow it to be used for disaster responses because of national security concerns. The system would have proven useful in 1989 when the agency was overwhelmed with applications for assistance from victims of Hurricane Hugo and the Loma Prieto earthquake. At that time, FEMA dedicated about 38 percent of its staff and about 27 percent of its budget (about $100 million, excluding the disaster relief fund) to national security emergencies. Of FEMA's approximately 3,000 full-time employees, 1,900 held security clearances, creating (at least) two competing cultures.

Drawing on expert reports, Witt proposed a reorganization of FEMA that unambiguously positioned the agency as the clearinghouse for natural disaster preparedness and relief programs. Witt reduced security clearances by 40 percent and moved national security programs for civil defense and continuity of government into a single, smaller division. He made mitigation a central part of disaster preparedness, and he issued grants to states and localities to reduce risk before disasters struck by, for example, providing incentives to property owners to limit building in floodplains or to strengthen structures in earthquake zones. Studies show that a dollar spent on mitigation activities such as strengthening building codes or relocating structures from flood plains saves money that would have been spent on disaster response and recovery.

FEMA's reputation soared after 1993, as it demoted its national security division and delivered more money to states and localities through mitigation programs. From 1995 to 2002, major newspaper editorials mentioning the agency were all either positive or neutral, while in previous years they were nearly all negative. Media accounts captured the agency's improvements in preparation and response. While responding to floods in the Midwest in the summer of 1993, for example, FEMA used mobile communications vehicles that had previously been reserved for national security programs. Congress passed legislation authorizing the reorganization that reduced the number of committees responsible for FEMA and the power held by national security committees, as well as allowing FEMA to pre-position resources in anticipation of a disaster without waiting for a hurricane, for example, to make landfall.

The reorganization also granted FEMA more autonomy over policy decisions. Witt eliminated 10 presidentially appointed management posts in the agency, which had earned a reputation as a dumping ground for political appointees. "The White House didn't like that," Witt said, referring to the Democratic Party operatives who staffed the Presidential Personnel Office, "but the president didn't mind."

Almost a decade after FEMA's reorganization, the agency underwent another remarkable turnaround—in the other direction. After the terrorist attacks of 2001 and a change in presidential administrations, the new FEMA leadership looked for a way to organize the federal role in disasters around a security mission. The reshuffling of responsibilities in the agency coincided with weakening morale and the retirement of many of the agency's longtime staff members. FEMA was famously criticized for a poor response in Hurricane Katrina in 2005 as well as for waste, fraud, and mismanagement, though in Katrina there was plenty of blame to go around among agencies and individuals at all levels of government. By 2005, FEMA's capacity had deteriorated. The agency's attempt at defining its mission to match its capacities had fallen victim to two forces in contemporary government: bureaucratization and politicization.

Bureaucratization, sometimes known as the "thickening of government," refers to the growth in both the number of people in government and the layers of hierarchy that separate them. The federal government has 16 departments headed by Senate-confirmed presidential appointees, for example, secretary, deputy secretary, undersecretary, and administrator. Each of these executives has a staff of senior executives, which includes chiefs of staff, associate deputy secretaries, assistant undersecretaries, deputy assistant secretaries, and associate administrators. These men and women, appointed and civil servants, are the senior executives that make policy for the bureaucracy. The number of senior executives has increased from 451 in 1960 to 2,409 in 1992, 2,385 in 1998, and 2,595 in 2004. The number may grow in proportion to increasing government responsibility, because of politicians' desire for control, or for both reasons. Whatever the cause, the kudzu-like growth of political executives makes navigating the bureaucracy an increasingly complex endeavor.

While a desire for control and improved performance motivates bureaucratization, this "thickening" of government paradoxically frustrates control and accountability. After September 11, the new Department of Homeland Security was created to refocus the bureaucracy around terrorism-related missions to correct the perceived organizational failures leading up to the attacks. The department absorbed FEMA as well as 21 other agencies responsible for missions other than terrorism, including customs inspection and fisheries protection. Political scientist Mariano Florentino-Cuellar shows how new terrorism missions detracted from the Coast Guard's other legacy missions, and other critics blame the focus on terrorism for FEMA's shortcomings in Katrina. U.S. House representative Bill Shuster claimed that DHS's leaders allowed FEMA's capacities to deteriorate "because its disaster mission cannot compete with DHS' terrorism prevention mission." These critics imply that prevention and interdiction are categorically different from other "all hazards, all phases" preparedness tasks, and that when included in the same agency, prevention and interdiction of attack overwhelm other concerns.

Some observers speculated that the Bush administration intended to shrink the nonsecurity missions of homeland security agencies to fulfill a long-standing agenda to reduce the federal government's role in domestic policy. In addition to bureaucratization, Congress and the executive attempted to politicize FEMA, or substitute their policy preferences for those of career civil servants. The chief vehicles for politicization are appointments, policy statements, and reorganization. Joseph Allbaugh, the political campaign manager whom President Bush selected to replace Witt as FEMA director, began his tenure by reducing mitigation programs and proposing new programs for terrorism preparedness. September 11 catalyzed the trend toward a terrorism-focused mission, and a new class of political appointees at FEMA ensured that the agency would revise its policies.

Other observers blame FEMA's poor performance on politicization. The agency had 35 political appointees by the end of George H. W. Bush's term and, after the agency's reorganization but by the end of Bill Clinton's first term, it had only 22. By 2002, however, that number had grown to 38. Appointees filled top management positions, policy development and speechwriting jobs, and some presumably technical jobs in newly created positions in the External Affairs Directorate and Information Technology Services. Whereas many of the Witt-era appointees had long careers in emergency management, the George W. Bush administration filled FEMA's upper management with political appointees who lacked disaster experience

By then, FEMA's political appointees had to work through DHS appointees, and bureaucratization and politicization combined to make it difficult for career civil servants in FEMA to influence broad policy. The Witt-led reorganization drew on the knowledge of the emergency management profession to expand mitigation programs to reduce disaster risk and recommend the "all hazards" approach to get the most out of limited resources and claim authority for natural disaster preparedness against civil defense. By the time Katrina struck, however, FEMA professionals faced layers of political management, a political agenda that emphasized the terrorist threat, and entrenched state and local authority over disaster preparedness.

The aftermath of the attacks of 2001 focused attention around a set of agencies' collective responsibility to prevent and respond to terrorism. Immigration, customs, emergency management, secret service, and Coast Guard agencies were included in a new department devoted to homeland security, but other security agencies such as the Federal Bureau of Investigation, the Central Intelligence Agency, and the visa office of the Department of State were left out. What explains the logic behind the creation of the DHS?

After September 11, Congress and the president chartered commissions to investigate whether the attacks could have been prevented. Foremost among these, the 9/11 Commission, published a best-selling record of its probe. Commissioners concluded that the United States was vulnerable to attack because of the failure of intelligence and law enforcement officials to "connect the dots" and piece together signs of a terrorist plot. Contradictory immigration policies and a broken border security system also contributed further to U.S. vulnerability. President George W. Bush created an Office of Homeland Security to coordinate the government's efforts to prepare for and prevent future attack. Under public pressure, Congress and the president created the Department of Homeland Security in 2003 to institutionalize the tasks of homeland security.

Homeland security agencies should not be judged by September 11 alone, but the crisis provides a useful focal point: Some agencies were substantially reorganized following the crisis while others resisted reform imposed from the outside. Others innovated to address terrorism even before the attacks. What explains why some agencies were receptive to change while others were not? Recent studies of federal reorganizations are pessimistic about the effectiveness of massive reorganizations. Large reorganizations, because of their size, require compromise among many competing interests. This compromise can frustrate a new organization's ability to achieve the larger goal it was created for. Still, reorganizations are one way in which agencies adapt, and the reorganization creating the DHS was one in a long line of a history of reorganizations undergone by the department's component parts.

The crisis of September 11 is more than one of the most daring terrorist operations in history; it is a watershed that will shape how governments think about security in the coming decades. As with Pearl Harbor, members of an entire generation divide their lives according to the periods before and after the event. The chasm is especially palpable for federal agencies that, before the attacks, defined national security largely as something that occurred overseas through the projection of military force. After September 11, agencies had to come to grips with what national security might mean for defending the nation against a surprise attack at home in addition to other missions they might have had before the fall of the twin towers. Intelligence agencies, for example, were reluctant to single out vaguely suspicious green-card carrying Muslims in the United States before 2001; this respect shown to the liberties of noncitizens has been reinterpreted as a pre-September 11 mentality. The post-September 11 approach, in contrast, calls for vigilance and intervention, because even though the probability that any single individual might commit a terrorist act remains low, the perceived cost has become unacceptably high. After the terrorist attacks, security becomes part of the mission of agencies included in the new Department of Homeland Security and even of many agencies not included.

How might historians evaluate homeland security reorganization a generation later? To borrow a phrase uttered after Pearl Harbor, "September 11 never dies." The event will remain too deeply engrained in the consciousness of everyone who lived through it for the number of memorials and public references to abate any time soon. For all the scholarly accounts of organizational learning and complexity, the sheer immediacy of the event improved terrorism preparation afterward. Frontline workers notice suspicious persons, and their superiors take such persons seriously first and foremost because of the memory of September 11, aside from any organizational change.

Nevertheless, politicians and the public were not content to let the crisis pass without enshrining increased attention to terrorism in organizational structures. Some agencies made great structural and policy improvements following 2001, and many more still fell short of their goals. The literature on bureaucratic failure provides sensible reasons not to expect perfection from any large and complex organization. And yet with some historical distance, the major accomplishments of homeland security are apparent.

The emergency management profession has attempted in fits and starts to incorporate terrorism into the all hazards, all phases framework. The intelligence agencies made a number of improvements that have long been recommended

FEMA administrator Craig Fugate introduces Secretary of Homeland Security Janet Napolitano at FEMA Region II's meeting on December 3, 2009, in New York City. Secretary Napolitano's visit marks the first time a Department of Homeland Security secretary has visited the region. *(Photo by Elissa Jun/FEMA)*

but never enacted until the political pressure following September 11. The CIA improved communication across agencies and across levels of government. A new umbrella organization, the Office of the Director of National Intelligence, has begun coordinating intelligence activity across agencies. Within the DHS, the former immigration and customs agencies combined some of their functions, and they may further combine and cross-train personnel in both service and enforcement functions, supplemented by specialized agents to handle complicated trade and security issues. The establishment of the Transportation Security Agency centralized security functions that were long neglected in the FAA.

This chapter takes as its starting point not the creation of the Department of Homeland Security but the history of how the United States planned for catastrophic events inside its borders, whether armed attack or natural disasters. If the Department of Homeland Security is to be successful, it must ensure that homeland security involves more than terrorism. The reorganization began with the mistaken though understandable assumption that we are besieged by terrorists. In truth, terrorism remains a real but only moderate threat alongside many other dangers, including natural disasters, disease, and technological accidents.

Agencies might follow two routes in the future to avoid giving nonterrorism missions short shrift. In one, agencies fold terrorism into their existing set of missions structured around an organizing concept. FEMA's all hazards and all phases concept includes all of its missions so that none can be, in theory, completely neglected nor can one be privileged to the exclusion of others. In the other route, agencies create separate divisions to fulfill specific tasks so that no one task dominates all divisions. The president's creation of a separate National Security Service within the FBI to focus exclusively on terrorism follows this approach and may relieve other FBI branches of terrorism responsibility so that they can focus on organized and white-collar crimes. Perhaps FEMA could spin off a similar terrorism entity.

As with other crises in American history, one can expect a substantial amount of attempts at revisionism. The 9/11 Commission was remarkably careful in not attributing blame for the attacks to any one actor but subsequent inquiries may not be so restrained. Revisionism that compiles facts to remedy misunderstandings fulfills a useful purpose, but revisionism that lays blame haphazardly does a disservice. In the case of homeland security, laying blame on any one agency or profession, or the threat of such scapegoating, may lead innovators to be overly cautious in addressing new dangers. Potential innovators should be held accountable like anyone else, but too much blame and invective can discourage even moderate risk taking.

What value will homeland security have for future generations? Though the United States was spared major terrorist strikes in the years immediately following September 11, subsequent attacks around the world prove that terrorism will remain a threat in the future. Asymmetric warfare is too tempting to weak and disparate movements who cannot mount a traditional military or political campaign. Terrorism will take new forms in the future, but many of the concerns remain the same. Communication within and across agencies, adequate training, and sufficient intelligence and contingency plans will be necessary no matter what method terrorists use. At bottom, federal agencies must be able to adapt to new threats, in cooperation with state and local actors and private entities, while not neglecting former missions. The history of homeland security agencies provides examples of how some agencies managed to adapt and make real gains while other attempts at change and adaptation stalled. We must do more than prepare for the last attack, and to do so requires opening the black box of bureaucratic behavior and attempting to understand why agencies do what they do and, rather than assume bureaucracies are hobbled by standard operating procedure and thus doomed to fail, illuminating how agencies might adapt over time.

Further Reading:

Birkland, Thomas A. *After Disaster: Agenda Setting, Public Policy, and Focusing Events*. Washington, D.C.: Georgetown University Press, 1997; Florentino-Cuellar, Mariano. "Running Aground: The Hidden Environmental and Regulatory Implications of Homeland Security." *American Constitution Society for Law and Policy Issue Brief*, May 2007. Available online. URL: http://www.acslaw.org/node/4919. Accessed July 10, 2009; Hopley, Russell J. "Civil Defense for National Security." Report to the Secretary of Defense by the Office of Civil Defense Planning, October 1948; Light, Paul C. *Thickening Government*. Washington, D.C.: Brookings Institution Press, 1995; National Commission on Terrorist Attack. *The 9/11 Commission Report*. New York: W.W. Norton, 2004; Roberts, Patrick S. "FEMA and the Prospects for Reputation-Based Autonomy." *Studies in American Political Development* 20 (Spring 2006): 57–87; Wilson, James Q. *Bureaucracy*. New York: Basic Books, 2000.

– Patrick S. Roberts

intelligence

Since the founding of the republic, American leaders have employed secret intelligence in the pursuit of foreign policy goals. General Washington relied heavily on spies in the war of independence, writing of the war effort that "the necessity of procuring good intelligence is apparent, . . . for upon Secrecy, success depends." Over the next two and a quarter centuries, the need for secret government activities has ebbed and flowed to meet the requirements of new leadership and a changing world. Throughout much of this period, intelligence remained the purview of the military, subject mostly to decisions of war and the immediate demands of the battlefield. While the first official U.S. intelligence body, the Office of Naval Intelligence (ONI), was founded in 1882, it was not until the end of World War II and the outset of the cold war that the modern U.S. intelligence community began to take shape. This article describes the politics and policies that have defined the subsequent 65 years of U.S. intelligence, from the creation of the Central Intelligence Agency (CIA) in 1947 through recent reforms such as the establishment of the Office of the Director of National Intelligence (ODNI) in 2004. It begins by defining the scope and nature of U.S. intelligence activities, before providing a history of major episodes in intelligence policy making, and finally evaluating the current status of major debates in this crucial area of national policy.

The U.S. intelligence community currently comprises 17 separate bodies: the CIA, the ODNI, the Defense Intelligence Agency (DIA), the National Security Agency (NSA), the National Geospatial-Intelligence Agency (NGA), the National Reconnaissance Office (NRO), the intelligence arms of the four military branches and the Coast Guard, and divisions within the FBI, the Drug Enforcement Agency, and the Departments of the Treasury, State, Energy, and Homeland Security. Together, these organizations gather information using open and secret sources, analog and digital technologies, in offices both at home and abroad. They conduct covert (deniable) and clandestine (hidden) operations, support law enforcement actions, and protect U.S. interests from foreign spying. They support military operations as well as national foreign policy decision making. Consequently, although they share the goal of protecting national security, U.S. intelligence agencies embody myriad missions, structures, and cultures. Despite these differences, one characteristic frequently identifies an activity or agency as part of the intelligence community: secrecy. While intelligence community methods and objectives may differ significantly, the three fundamental components of the intelligence enterprise—intelligence collection and analysis, counter intelligence, and covert operations—all depend on secrecy to significant degrees.

Given the many activities conducted by the members of the U.S. intelligence community, a comprehensive definition of intelligence policy is difficult to reach. Perhaps it is most useful to think of intelligence as a process that involves people working to help policy makers make and execute foreign policy decisions. This process has often been described as an "intelligence cycle" comprising five stages: tasking, collection, analysis, dissemination, and policy making. While these steps do not always proceed sequentially, the intelligence cycle concept provides a helpful outline of what is involved in strategic intelligence.

First, when the president, cabinet officials, military leaders, or members of Congress find that they need additional information regarding an area of policy, they request support from the intelligence community. Intelligence collectors then deploy communications satellites, human assets, and other means to gather information relevant both to the questions posed by policy makers and to other areas of national interest. Once gathered, this raw intelligence is processed by analysts who assess its validity and translate it into useful terms for policy consumers. Finished intelligence from different analytical centers is then coordinated and distributed for use in policy making. Of course, intelligence community products are only one resource policy makers use in making decisions, and at this point intelligence analysis competes with personal perspectives, ideology, partisanship, bureaucratic politics, and other interests for policy influence.

It is important to include this final step—policy making—as part of the intelligence process. Doing so highlights the fact that intelligence success or failure is a function not only of those actors concerned with collecting, analyzing, and communicating information, but also of those who utilize this information in policy making. Moreover, understanding policy decisions as part of the intelligence process suggests the link between intelligence analysis and covert activities, which are often considered part of the intelligence mission. Decisions to employ covert or clandestine policy tools, such as espionage, sabotage, and paramilitary operations, generally demand extensive support from intelligence analysis. The shared need for secrecy among intelligence providers and covert actors has brought these groups together in the same agencies, particularly the CIA.

While dozens of important developments in intelligence policy have taken place over the last 233 years, this entry will focus on three periods that have defined the contemporary intelligence landscape in the United States. The initial period, 1946 to 1950, saw the creation of the first peacetime civilian intelligence agencies, including the CIA, and the establishment of the set of tools and missions that define modern U.S. intelligence. During the second period, 1974 to 1979, policy makers were driven by conflict over the proper role of intelligence following allegations of illegal activities by the CIA. These activities included efforts to spy on Americans and assassinate foreign leaders, and both Congress and the White House moved to rein in what Senator Frank Church (D-ID) called the "rogue elephant" of U.S. intelligence. A final period of reform followed the attacks of September 11, 2001. This era has been striking for both the swiftness and the scope of changes in intelligence policy, most notably the domestic spying provisions of the USA PATRIOT Act and the creation of the Office of the Director of National Intelligence.

In each of these periods, three questions have stood at the center of the debate over U.S. intelligence policy. First, what is the proper place of secrecy in a democratic republic? That is, how much should the public and its elected representatives know about intelligence activities, when such exposure can limit the effectiveness of these activities and might endanger not only the lives of individual operatives but also the security of the entire country? This dilemma suggests a basic trade-off in intelligence between the protection of national security interests and the promotion of transparency and oversight in government. In this area, critics of U.S. intelligence activities have been particularly troubled by secret paramilitary and, more recently, interrogation activities conducted overseas.

A second question also relates to the proper balance of security and liberty in intelligence policy: What powers should intelligence agencies be given to collect information about U.S. citizens within America's borders? Early in the history of U.S. civilian intelligence, fears of an "American Gestapo" helped to establish a legal wall between intelligence collectors and domestic law enforcement. Recent reformers have pointed to this division as one of the fundamental problems in combating terrorism on U.S. soil, making surveillance a key issue in current intelligence debates.

Finally, intelligence policy has been driven by questions of resource allocation and bureaucratic control. The 17 agencies of the U.S. intelligence community are together responsible for $45–50 billion in annual funding and approximately 150,000 personnel. (Approximately 8 percent of the intelligence budget goes to agencies located within the Department of Defense, including the DIA and the technology-heavy NSA, NGA, and NRO.) These organizations are expected to play a central role in protecting American interests and security. Indeed, the two deadliest foreign attacks on U.S. soil—Pearl Harbor and 9/11—have been described foremost as "intelligence failures," and intelligence organizations also have been singled out for blame in crises ranging from the Korean War to the fall of the shah in Iran and the collapse of the Soviet Union. With so much at stake, and such heavy consequences for failure, policy decisions about funding, personnel, and authority for intelligence are fraught with conflict and uncertainty. Given limited budgets and sometimes redundant missions, intelligence agencies must compete for the attention of policy makers—attention that can bring additional resources and stature. This competitive environment has helped to define the politics of each of the three major periods of U.S. intelligence reform.

The three questions presented above have driven policy debates over intelligence since the founding of the modern U.S. intelligence community in 1947. That year saw the establishment of the CIA alongside the modern Department of Defense and the National Security Council as part of the National Security Act. These reforms reflected a general belief among U.S. policy makers that the world created in the aftermath of World War II would require fundamental changes to the country's national security structures. Intelligence in particular had been overlooked as a tool of national power over the preceding 170 years of the republic. This began to change when President Franklin Roosevelt and an enterprising war hero of World War I, Colonel William "Wild Bill" Donovan, established the Office of Strategic Services (OSS) during World War II. Roosevelt and Donovan had observed the successful role intelligence was playing in the British war against the Axis powers. After the United States joined the war, OSS was created and evolved into a wide-ranging outfit conducting espionage and covert actions across the globe.

After the war, and with the threat of a cold war with the Soviet Union looming, President Harry Truman saw a need to extend the intelligence mission into peacetime. Truman initially disbanded OSS before issuing a presidential directive establishing the Central Intelligence Group (CIG), the first civilian intelligence body in the nation. Staffed mostly by former OSS agents, CIG started with a limited mission to coordinate information from the State Department, Justice Department, military, and other agencies. By the end of 1946, however, CIG had grown nearly 20-fold, from 100 members to over 1,800, and it had carved for itself a broader niche, including expanded analytical and espionage responsibilities.

CIG's expansion did not come without a fight. The army in particular objected when its espionage assets were moved to the new group, and many at the State Department felt that informing the president of developments overseas was their exclusive purview. When President Harry Truman announced that intelligence would be part of a comprehensive military restructuring bill, to be presented to Congress at the start of the 1947 term, the battle over U.S. central intelligence began in earnest.

It was in the debate over Truman's military reorganization bill—what would become the National Security Act—that policy debates over secrecy, domestic surveillance, and the distribution of intelligence resources would first be undertaken publicly. The legislation, coming so soon after the defeat of Hitler's Third Reich, touched off fears among some members of Congress that Truman might be creating an "American Gestapo" in his efforts to formalize CIG into a new Central Intelligence Agency. These objections led to language in the bill prohibiting the CIA from any domestic security or law enforcement functions. Another potential area of disagreement—secret espionage and covert activities—was so controversial it was left out of the bill altogether. Rather than make public the government's intent to use such tools in the fight against communism, the National Security Act simply charged the CIA with performing "other functions and duties related to intelligence affecting the national security." This provided the CIA with flexibility to conduct secret operations if necessary, without broadcasting to the world that this was the case. (Two years later, the CIA Act of 1949 would establish a more formal authority for the CIA to engage in spying and other such activities.)

The National Security Act was signed into law on July 26, 1947, making the CIA the first statutory civilian intelligence agency in U.S. history. In the 20 years following the creation of the CIA, U.S. intelligence continued its evolution as a major component in America's cold war arsenal. This period saw a number of significant intelligence reforms, such as the creation of the National Security Agency in 1952; the establishment in 1961 of the Defense Intelligence Agency, which provided an all-source analysis capability within the Department of Defense; and the development of photo reconnaissance capabilities, utilizing both high-altitude airplanes such as the U-2, first launched in 1955, and satellites such as the "CORONA" program, established in 1962. While the political dynamics of these initiatives were not inconsequential, the new programs were generally driven by technological advancements and new collection and analysis requirements, rather than by a changing public policy environment. The next round of major reforms in U.S. intelligence would not come until the mid 1970s. These occurred in a period characterized by sharp partisan disagreements over the appropriate place of intelligence in a free society, and, more broadly, of America's place in the world.

In 1968, President Richard Nixon had arrived in Washington skeptical of the CIA and looking for cost-cutting opportunities among the national security establishment. After four years of struggling to rein in a resistant intelligence bureaucracy, including significant funding cuts and efforts to drive out "Ivy League liberals" and others Nixon deemed disloyal to his administration, the president decided to install his own man at the head of the CIA. His choice, James Schlesinger, was seen by many in the CIA as a Nixon loyalist who cared little for the culture and history of the intelligence community. These views were only reinforced when Schlesinger forced the resignation or retirement of 1,500 employees and enacted a painful reorganization of the intelligence estimates process. Yet these internal reforms were not Schlesinger's most lasting legacy in the intelligence community. Concerned about reputed connections between the CIA and the Watergate break-in during Nixon's 1972 reelection campaign, Schlesinger asked that a report be drawn up outlining any potentially illegal projects that had been undertaken by the agency. This report, nicknamed the CIA's "family jewels," would help kick off the most dramatic reform proceedings in the history of U.S. intelligence.

In the fall of 1974, Seymour Hersh of the *New York Times* caught wind of a secret document cataloging possible crimes perpetrated by U.S. intelligence agencies, including widespread surveillance of American citizens. The allegations centered around Operation CHAOS, a program initiated under President Nixon to spy on and infiltrate antiwar and other dissident groups in the early 1970s. Soon, Hersh had confirmed enough details to publish and expose detailing abuses perpetrated by the U.S. government. Not surprisingly, the "family jewels" story led to a firestorm of criticism leveled at the intelligence community by public officials and the news media. Three separate investigations were launched, one in each chamber of Congress—led by Otis Pike (D-NY) in the House and Frank Church(D-ID) in the Senate—and a separate "blue ribbon" panel named by President Gerald Ford and headed by Vice President Nelson Rockefeller.

The three bodies took different approaches in their investigations. All, however, operated under the attentive eyes of a public eager to learn more about the hidden world of U.S. intelligence, and an intelligence community equally committed to keeping those secrets tucked away. The administration group, nicknamed the Rockefeller Commission, was seen by some as an attempt to whitewash the controversy by setting a short timetable for its efforts, asking easy questions, and demurring when members of the intelligence community declined to answer questions in the name of national security. When new allegations of plans to assassinate foreign leaders surfaced, the commission's mandate was extended, but not so far that it was able to complete its investigation into the alleged plots. The Senate's Church Committee was more aggressive, while still attempting to maintain civil working relations with members of the intelligence community. After many months of investigations, it released 14 reports detailing its findings, although no new legislation came directly out of the committee. The Pike Committee was far less disciplined. This was due, at least in part, to the rancorous atmosphere created in the House by the 75 members of the "Watergate Class" elected in 1974 with a mandate to bring reform-minded change to Washington. Prone to sensationalism and damaging leaks of classified intelligence, the Pike Committee would eventually be closed down by a vote of 246 to 124 in the full House, which also opted to withhold Pike's final report from public release. (This would not prevent its publication, however, as most of the Pike Committee report was leaked to *The Village Voice* and published.)

In the end, several important intelligence reforms emerged during this period. While the Rockefeller Commission held no statutory authority itself, its recommendations and those of the Church Committee contributed to President Ford's Executive Order 11905, which strengthened internal oversight of the intelligence community, banned agencies from infiltrating domestic organizations, and forbade assassination as a tool of U.S. national policy. Later reforms also built on the recommendations of the Rockefeller and Church groups. New permanent oversight committees were created in both houses of Congress, and, in 1978, the Foreign Intelligence Surveillance Act (FiSA) created a new set of procedures governing intelligence surveillance within the United States. FiSA required intelligence agencies to secure approval from a new Foreign Intelligence Surveillance Court (FiSC) to conduct surveillance of U.S. nationals, permanent residents, or corporations. While such approval was not required for collecting intelligence on foreign entities within the United States, such activities had to be reported to FiSC by the attorney general. FiSA would later be amended by several post-9/11 reforms, including the USA PATRIOT Act (described below).

The aftermath of the intelligence investigations of the 1970s was felt for many years. The highly public and damning nature of the charges brought against the intelligence community reduced morale among the agencies and turned many in the country against them. President Jimmy Carter and his director of central intelligence (DCI), Admiral Stansfield Turner, sought to instill a more transparent and by-the-book culture within the community, efforts which did little to shore up belief in embattled intelligence organizations. The Ronald Reagan and George H. W. Bush presidencies shifted some autonomy back to the intelligence services, but during the 1980s intelligence seldom held an active spot on the policy agenda.

With the fall of the Soviet Union in 1991, many in Washington saw an opportunity to begin deconstructing the cold war national security infrastructure, including what they perceived as a bloated and increasingly irrelevant intelligence system. Funds for intelligence activities were cut, in some areas by as much as 25 percent. Still, this period did not include fundamental changes in the way the United States conducted its intelligence operations. Despite a dramatic shift in the scope and nature of threats facing the country, few policy makers were galvanized to pursue significant intelligence reforms.

This would change on September 11, 2001. Following devastating terrorist attacks on the World Trade Center and the Pentagon, policy makers sought to understand what went wrong and how similar tragedies could be avoided in the future. Subsequent legislation and executive initiatives revolutionized how the United States conducts its intelligence activities. These reforms mark the most recent stage in America's intelligence evolution, and they help to highlight the crucial questions that remain in intelligence policy today.

For many, the 9/11 attacks highlighted numerous problems with the U.S. intelligence community. Among the chorus of voices calling for intelligence reform was the National Commission on Terrorist Attacks Upon the United States, popularly called the 9/11 Commission. The 9/11 Commission investigation found several deficiencies in U.S. intelligence performance, including poor cooperation among agencies, a lack of expertise and human intelligence assets for key areas of the world, and a "failure of imagination" on the part of community leaders and policy makers. The commission's report, along with an investigation conducted jointly by the two intelligence committees in Congress, generated support among both policy makers and the American public for significant changes in U.S. intelligence policy.

The most important of these reforms would be the Intelligence Reform and Terrorism Prevention Act (IRTPA) of 2004. This law created a new bureaucracy, the Office of the Director of National Intelligence, to oversee and coordinate operations throughout the 16 other agencies of the intelligence community. Reformers had long been calling for more unified leadership within the community, including centralized control of budgets and personnel decisions, but had always been resisted by agencies—particularly those in the Defense Department—seeking to protect their bureaucratic autonomy. In the charged atmosphere that followed 9/11, such objections were overruled by policy makers in Congress and the White House who wanted to show that they were committed to real organizational change in intelligence. IRTPA also created new centers to coordinate efforts in combating terrorism and nuclear proliferation. While the performance of these centers has met with mixed reviews, they represent attempts to break down the organizational "stovepipes" that had long kept intelligence agencies from cooperating effectively with one another. Critics of the IRTPA reforms argue that adding new layers of bureaucracy on top of an already complex set of agencies will only hinder intelligence performance even more. So far there is evidence to support both sides of this debate, and the net effects of the IRTPA reforms remain to be seen.

Whereas IRTPA reordered control of intelligence resources, other post-9/11 reforms addressed the balance of security and liberty in U.S. intelligence operations. As policy makers and the American public came to see international terrorism as a grave threat to national security, many felt that protecting civil liberties was now less important than defending against future attacks. The USA PATRIOT Act, passed just six weeks after 9/11, amended FiSA and other existing laws to provide government agencies with sweeping new powers to gather information about the activities of American citizens and others within the United States. Specifically, it removed some restrictions on the types of information law enforcement can collect and retain about individuals, allowed for the extended detainment and deportation of immigrants suspected of terrorist activities, and gave new powers to the Treasury Department to regulate financial activities. The USA PATRIOT Act passed with only one dissenting voice in the Senate and a handful in the House. These reforms would have been far more controversial had Americans not been caught up in the aftereffects of 9/11. In the charged atmosphere of late 2001, however, only a vocal minority challenged the legislation, and intelligence policy took a swing toward privileging security over liberty concerns. A bipartisan group of senators did manage to attach sunset clauses to some of the most contentious provisions, requiring that they be renewed after four years. Despite growing concerns about government infringements on civil liberties, however, efforts to let these policies expire in 2005 were defeated, and the core provisions of the USA PATRIOT Act were retained by Congress. Opponents have been more successful in the courts, where several elements of the law have been stricken following successful constitutional challenges.

Other post-9/11 reforms, such as the creation of the Department of Homeland Security and new rules for holding and interrogating prisoners, have also impacted U.S. intelligence operations. Overall, the first eight years of the new millennium have demonstrated notable shifts in how U.S. policy addresses questions of secrecy, domestic surveillance, and the composition of the intelligence community. The final section below considers how these concerns might play out in future policy making.

U.S. intelligence policy must navigate a number of difficult trade-offs. For example, providing intelligence agencies with additional surveillance powers may require limiting Americans' privacy and other civil liberties. Greater transparency in intelligence operations can reduce their effectiveness, while too little oversight can lead to abuses such as those uncovered in the investigations of the 1970s. Resources for intelligence are limited, yet reducing intelligence support for warfare can cost lives on the battlefield, while fewer resources for national policy making can lead the president and Congress to make ill-informed decisions. Policy makers will continue to face these and other dilemmas in intelligence policy for the foreseeable future. How intelligence proceeds will be determined by three factors.

First, the nature of threats to the country will influence how policy makers approach intelligence. In times when foreign threats are perceived to be great, such as the start of the cold war and the immediate post-9/11 era, policies will tend to favor greater resources and autonomy for intelligence agencies. In more peaceful periods, intelligence capabilities are likely to be scaled back, as was seen at the end of the cold war. Today, the threat posed by international terrorism has generated significant new powers for U.S. intelligence. As the experience of 9/11 recedes and no new attacks take place on the homeland, efforts to limit these powers in favor of greater transparency and civil liberty protections may become more and more successful.

Second, the performance of intelligence agencies will help to determine future policy directions. U.S. intelligence is tasked with protecting national security while operating within the bounds of the law. The illegal activities outlined in the CIA's family jewels report generated wide-reaching reforms that changed the nature of U.S. intelligence for decades. At times, current debates over harsh CIA interrogation techniques and other efforts in the battle against terrorism have echoed those of the 1970s. Recent policy changes banning some of these activities suggest that further reforms may be forthcoming.

Finally, like any area of public policy, intelligence will remain subject to the politics of the times. Shifts in partisan control of Congress and the White House influence the rules governing intelligence activity and the resources allocated for its provision. Unlike other spheres of government policy, however, the secret nature of intelligence changes the political landscape in which these decisions will be made. It is frequently observed that intelligence failures are obvious and widely scrutinized, while intelligence successes remain hidden from public view. Moreover, starting with the National Security Act in 1947, many key policy discussions surrounding intelligence have taken place behind closed doors. Such secrecy can limit opportunities for position taking and credit claiming by policy makers, reducing the benefits of partisanship in intelligence policy. Yet it can also provide cover for politicians making sensational claims about intelligence abuses, or seeking to blame the intelligence community for their own faulty decisions. These political dynamics provide a unique environment for continuing debates over security, liberty, and the ongoing role of intelligence in a democratic society.

Further Readings:

Andrew, Christopher. *For the President's Eyes Only: Secret Intelligence and the American Presidency from Washington to Bush.* New York: HarperCollins, 1995; Betts, Richard. *Enemies of Intelligence: Knowledge and Power in American National Security.* New York: Columbia University Press, 2007; Commission on the Roles and Responsibilities of the U.S. Intelligence Community. *Preparing for the 21st Century: An Appraisal of U.S. Intelligence.* Available online. URL: http://www.gpoaccess.gov/int/index.html. Accessed August 21, 2009; Sims, Jennifer, and Burton Gerber, eds. *Transforming U.S. Intelligence.* Washington, D.C.: Georgetown University Press, 2005; Zegart, Amy. *Spying Blind: The CIA, the FBI, and the Origins of 9/11.* Princeton, N.J.: Princeton University Press, 2007.

– Brent Durbin

transportation security

Transportation systems are an integral and critical part of any society. Transportation is vital to the functioning of modern economies, provides the benefits of mobility for individuals within society, and is a major employer. More than almost any other sector of the economy, transportation is ubiquitous, used on a daily basis in some form by virtually everyone in society. Transportation systems provide the necessary connectivity to link providers and customers, raw materials and finished products, workers and worksites, travelers and destinations. They are the circulatory system of our national and global economies. As such, their critical nature in defense and security is incontestable, and only made more evident since the attacks on the air transport system on September 11, 2001. How we secure and protect our transportation systems is critical to national defense and homeland security.

Protection of transportation systems can be traced to the beginning of the republic, with the military charged to consider the protection of critical infrastructure, including transportation, part of its mission. During times of war the protection of transportation was given serious attention. In the Civil War, and again in World War II, enemy agents attempted to sabotage critical rail systems. However, in times of peace few actual security programs were in effect, in large part because there was no identifiable force or threat assumed to have a direct interest in harming the nation's transportation systems.

Even before 9/11, the growing menace of international terrorist groups provided a motive for the federal government to pay attention to the possibility of terrorist attacks on critical infrastructure, including the nation's far-flung transportation network. The President's Commission on Critical Infrastructure Protection (PCCIP) was created by President Bill Clinton in the wake of terrorist attacks on the World Trade Center in 1993 and the Federal Building in Oklahoma City in 1995. The commission issued its final report in 1997, and, in 1998, the Clinton administration issued Presidential Directive PPD 3, *Protecting America's Critical Infrastructures,* based on the commission's report, which included transportation among one of eight categories of infrastructure critical to national security.

The September 11 attacks showed the vulnerability of transportation to terrorism. The commercial air industry was the vehicle used for the attacks, and the immediate response was to focus on the vulnerability of the air transport system first, but with a recognition that all modes of transportation pose an attractive target for terrorist acts (as shown by the government decision to close the nation's rail system briefly after 9/11 and again during the first military strikes in Afghanistan in October 2001).

In the aftermath of 9/11, the problem of transportation security centered on several interrelated questions:

- What is homeland security, and what role does transportation security play in a comprehensive approach to security? Is it to be reactive, based on past events, or forward-looking and proactive, based on intelligence, planning, and threat assessment? Is it separate from national security, or should it be seen as an element of an overall strategy of national defense?
- What roles must be played in securing and protecting transportation systems, and how are they assigned to various government agencies, levels of government, private sector operators and users of the transportation system, and the citizenry?
- How will the programs be funded? What are the costs and benefits of transportation security?

The 9/11 attacks made evident the need for government to address transportation security as a national priority. Studies showed that transportation—buses, railroads, aircraft, urban mass transit—was a common and often deadly target of terrorists. But protecting the vast transportation system of over 300,000 miles of roads, thousands of commercial and general airports, and a sprawling interstate highway system was a daunting task. Specifically, how could the government organize itself and also be at the center of a network of private sector transportation organizations, state and local governments, and other first responders to provide the necessary intelligence and response capacity to meet the new challenge posed by terrorist groups?

Looking to past practice was not an option. Most transportation policy and administration was couched in terms of specific transportation modes: air, rail, marine, pipeline, highway, urban mass transit. Transportation policy and program administration has historically been mode-specific, as shown by the organization of federal agencies and programs that tend to concentrate on a specific means of conveyance: the Federal Aviation Administration for commercial air transport, the Federal Railroad Administration (FRA) for freight rail systems, the Federal Transit Administration for urban mass transit, the Federal Highway Administration for highways, and the Federal Maritime Administration for shipping. Both the organization of regulatory agencies and program agencies within the U.S. Department of Transportation (DOT) illustrate this "silo" approach to programming. The 9/11 attacks and the creation of the U.S. Department of Homeland Security in their aftermath required a rethinking of the traditional mode-centric approach. Transportation systems posed a tempting target for terrorists, and the interconnectivity of transportation modes became more evident.

Transportation security issues post-9/11 were also seen in light of globalization of trade and commerce. Not only international aviation but also intermodal shipping (which brought into consideration other modes engaged in intermodalism, especially ports and freight railroads) was seen as especially vulnerable to terrorism. Less than 3 percent of cargo containers entering ports were being checked. The production, storage, and movement of hazardous materials became another major focus after nonterrorist related accidents showed the potential danger of moving such goods, in rail cars, trucks, or containers, in particular in densely populated urban corridors. Securing the nation's ports requires international cooperation as well as securing operations in and around the port areas in the United States.

Thus, from the outset the post-9/11 approach has stressed cooperation, collaboration, and networking among public and private sector organizations and across national boundaries. The complexity of transportation security as a public problem by necessity involves networks of organizations, including state and local governments, first responders, and private sector transportation suppliers and users and the associations that represent them, such as the Association of American Railroads (AAR), the American Trucking Association (ATA), other similar trade associations, labor unions, and citizen groups.

As is the case with homeland security generally, transportation security is not seen by most in a partisan or ideological light. However, the deregulation of most transportation modes since the 1970s and 1980s has created fears within deregulated industries, for example, the freight railroads, that security issues would move government more directly into their operations, or mandate costly changes to business practices. Industry groups favored approaches that involved public-private cooperation in networks sharing information and planning, and lobbying groups such as the AAR and ATA. By organizing private sector efforts soon after 9/11, in recognition of both the economic risks terrorist threats posed to their operations and to effectively preempt strictly governmental programs that might limit their autonomy, they set in motion a collaborative approach to transportation security that continues to be a powerful alternative to public assumption of all aspects of securing the transportation system.

Transportation security legislation and executive action immediately after 9/11 enjoyed bipartisan support and was not seen as a contentious or ideologically driven issue. However, that changed quickly, as Congress and the Bush administration began to diverge in their preferred approaches to transportation security. After creation of the Department of Homeland Security, which it initially opposed, the administration favored an executive-centered strategy, using executive orders and annual budgets to direct DHS and other executive agencies concerned with transportation security to plan and implement security efforts. Congress, especially leaders of both parties in the Senate and House Democrats, favored an approach that would build on statutory requirements for security initiatives. While retaining some elements of partisan debate, much of the politics was institutional, pitting the congressional viewpoint against that held by the administration. However, even Congress was divided, with transportation committees and the newly formed homeland security committees vying for influence.

Transportation policy is provided by legislation and executive orders. Before the recognition that terrorist groups provided the major threats to domestic infrastructure, preparedness for emergencies involving transportation envisioned threats emanating from enemy nation-states or natural disasters. Examples in the pre-9/11 period include the Federal Civil Defense Act of 1949, which, until its repeal in 1994, was intended to guide efforts to protect the nation from foreign attack; and in the area of natural disaster prevention and mitigation, such as the Disaster Relief Act of 1974 and the Stafford Act of 1988. Reorganization of a cluster of federal programs involved in emergency and disaster management led to the creation of the Federal Emergency Management Agency (FEMA) in 1979. FEMA's creation was due mainly to threats of natural disasters, in particular hurricanes, rather than foreign or domestic terrorism.

The events of September 11, 2001, triggered new policy directives from both the legislative and the executive branches of government. Several pieces of legislation were drafted in the immediate aftermath of the tragedy, many directed at, or impacting, transportation security. The cornerstone of the nation's overall plan for combating terrorism was the USA PATRIOT Act, Pub. L. 107-56, passed by Congress and signed into law by President Bush on October 26, 2001. Title VIII identified terrorism to include transportation-related crimes, including attacking mass transportation systems and using biological agents and toxins as weapons.

Reacting to the use of aircraft as weapons in the 9/11 attacks, the first mode of transportation to be given new policy directives was aviation. It was, as Harold Relyea pointed out, an example of homeland security migrating from "symbolic status to that of a policy concept." The result was passage of the Aviation and Transportation Security Act of 2001, Pub. L. 107-71, signed into law by President Bush on November 19, 2001. The act established the Transportation Security Administration (TSA) within the Department of Transportation and gave it the responsibility to oversee security of all modes of transportation. TSA, however, was swept up in meeting a variety of responsibilities to provide aviation security, and neglected other modes for several years as it focused on air security. The legislation was specific in terms of new security measures to be employed, ranging from hiring and training 28,000 new federal screeners to flight crew training, arming flight deck crews and reinforcing cockpit doors, and screening baggage for explosives and other dangerous devices.

At roughly the same time as the USA PATRIOT Act and aviation security legislation was being considered, the question of how to organize and coordinate the range of homeland security programs was under consideration by both Congress and the administration. On October 8, 2001, President Bush issued Executive Order 13228, which established the Office of Homeland Security and the Homeland Security Council within the Executive Office of the President. The role of the OHS director, former Pennsylvania governor Tom Ridge, was to coordinate, not manage, homeland security policy and practice. Ridge was also given the title of assistant to the president for homeland security. However, leaders in Congress were unhappy with Ridge's role as a presidential adviser, which by executive privilege exempted him from testifying before Congress, and, in general, they questioned the wisdom of assigning homeland security to a coordinating function. The administration also rethought its position and sent Congress a draft of a bill proposing a new Department of Homeland Security in June 2002. The House and the Senate developed different versions of legislation designed to create the new department, with the House version closely tied to the president's proposal and the Senate version reflecting the leadership supplied by Senator Joseph Lieberman (D-CT). After Republican gains in Congress in the 2002 elections, the Senate passed the House version, H.R. 5005, by a 90-9 vote. The House had earlier passed the measure by a vote of 299-121. The new department became operational on March 1, 2003.

Creation of DHS had major consequences for transportation security. It positioned DHS, not the Department of Transportation, as the major responsible federal agency in charge of overall transportation security programs and planning. It included transportation as one of the major categories of infrastructure for planning and programming purposes. However, the immediate need to task the TSA with operational responsibilities for airport screening hindered the agency's ability to deal with other transportation modes or to balance operational needs with long-term planning and strategy.

Running second to air security as a perceived transportation threat has been port and maritime security. With over 80 percent of the world's global commerce moving over the oceans, maritime transportation is critical to the world economy, and disruptions would paralyze commerce and threaten shortages of oil, food, and manufactured goods worldwide. The nation's 361 ports are also the nodes at which different transportation modes connect, with much of the traffic moving from ships to trucks and trains in standard containers. With few containers subjected to checks at either the point of embarkation or point of entry, and with containers especially providing an inviting target for terrorists to use as conveyances for weapons of mass destruction, legislation to protect ports and maritime shipping was viewed as critical.

The Maritime Security Act of 2002, Pub. L. 107-295, addressed security concerns of vessels containing dangerous materials, such as liquefied natural gas (LNG) and oil, and others such as cruise ships that have been shown to be attractive targets for terrorist groups. The act charged the secretary of transportation to identify vessels that pose a high risk of involvement in a security incident to have certified security plans and meet the International Ship and Port Security Code. It also required U.S. ports determined to be at risk, such as facilities for LNG, fossil fuels, and cruise ships, to have an approved security plan. The four marine terminals handling LNG all had approved security plans by July 2004. In addition to the security plan provisions, the act also authorized grants for research and development, requires crew members of foreign-flag vessels to present proper identification, and established a National Maritime Security Advisory Committee to advise the secretary of transportation and Congress on maritime security matters. Although the language of the bill implies that the secretary of transportation is the lead player in maritime and port security, in fact the operational tasks are assigned to the U.S. Coast Guard, a component of DHS.

Continuing concern for the security of the nation's ports led to the SAFE Port Act, Pub. L. 110-53, enacted in October 2006. This legislation codified two programs administered by Customs and Border Protection in DHS, the Container Security Initiative and the Customs-Trade Partnership Against Terrorism; mandated the creation of interagency operational centers at selected ports; required that containers be screened for radiation; and required more information for customs officials to use in inspecting containers.

The largest elements of the nation's transportation system—its highway and rail networks—have received less attention by policy makers than the air and marine/port sectors. Surface transportation nonetheless provides terrorists with opportunities to cripple the nation's economy, inflict massive casualties through targeted attacks on vehicles and facilities, disrupt global commerce, and instill fear in citizens using the nation's roads, commuter rail systems, and urban mass transit. Surface transportation attacks may also be more difficult to prevent than attacks on other modes, and they offer terrorists a greater probability of escape and nonapprehension.

Legislation targeted at surface transportation security lagged behind air and port concerns in the first years after 9/11. This may be attributed in part to the enormity of the nation's rail and highway networks and the impossibility of ensuring security by traditional means of surveillance and policing. In the case of the freight rail industry—seven major railroads and several hundred smaller regional, short-line, and terminal railroads, almost entirely privately owned and operated—it was also attributable to the proactive stance taken by the industry to enhance security of operations, share information, and coordinate private security efforts with those of government. Although numerous studies indicated the possible use of rail freight as a means of conveying weapons of mass destruction, legislation directed at rail security languished in Congress and did not gain high priority in the DHS.

Attention to passenger rail security has increased in response to terrorist attacks on passenger trains outside the United States. The RAND Institute calculated that 181 attacks worldwide on trains and rail facilities took place between 1998 and 2003, resulting in 431 deaths. Perhaps surprisingly, one such attack, on Amtrak's *Sunset Limited* in Arizona on October 9, 1995, happened in the United States and was attributed to domestic terrorists. One person was killed and over 100 injured as the speeding train derailed and toppled into the desert 59 miles southwest of Phoenix.

Interest in passenger rail security followed directly from two prominent attacks on rail systems outside the United States, the London subway bombings on July 7, 2005, and the Madrid commuter rail bombings on March 11, 2004. Both led to significant loss of life and the temporary closure of key urban transportation systems vital to the life of major national capital cities. Neither represented highly sophisticated operations and did not involve weapons of mass destruction, but each showed the vulnerability of urban rail systems designed to move large numbers of people—in the United States, annually about 3.5 billion individual riderships—quickly and efficiently, without the feasibility of the elaborate screening and security apparatuses used for airports.

The TSA has responded to the threat to passenger rail and urban mass transit by awarding grants to mass transit systems through the Transit Security Grant Program. The bulk of grant money has gone to eight metropolitan areas, with the New York City region receiving roughly 40 percent of the total in recognition of its heavy reliance on rail transportation. DHS has also done testing of security plans at major transit locations, trained canine explosive detection teams, and deployed over 100 security inspectors to perform Security Analysis and Action Programs. It also works with local governments to provide antiterrorism and security training for local law enforcement officials.

Leaders in Congress complained that the amount of funding provided through the DHS budget for surface transportation funding was inadequate, measured both against the risks identified and the funding provided for air transportation security.

Calendar years 2006 and 2007 were watershed years for transportation security policy. Several major factors led to a reexamination of transportation security policy in 2006. One was the expanded interest of the Transportation Security Administration in securing modes other than commercial air transport, which had been its major focus since 9/11. In the area of freight rail policy, TSA partnered with the Office of Infrastructure Protection of DHS to create the National Capital Region Rail Security Corridor Pilot Project and a pilot project for a Rail Protective Measures Study Zone for the seven-mile stretch of greatest vulnerability through the District of Columbia. It has also worked with other units of DHS and DOT to conduct High Threat Urban Areas Corridor Assessments in 10 major urban areas where considerable movements of hazardous materials occur.

TSA followed up its initial studies with the circulation of draft Security Action Items to the freight rail industry. During the spring and summer of 2006, TSA and FRA representatives worked with industry to identify specific security items. In a memorandum titled "Recommended Security Action Items for the Rail Transportation of Toxic Inhalation Hazard Materials," dated June 23, 2006, DHS and DOT jointly identified a set of 24 security action items related to toxic inhalation hazard materials movement. These were divided into three categories: system security, access control, and en route security. Taken as a whole, these efforts in the freight rail area constituted examples of TSA moving to fulfill its legislative mandate to be the lead agency for transportation security in all modes.

The shift in power in Congress after the 2006 elections, with Democrats able to use their newfound strength to pass legislation to implement the 9/11 recommendations, provided a sharper focus on transportation security. The result was an omnibus bill, H.R. 1, called the Implementing the Recommendations of the 9/11 Commission Act of 2007. Passed by large majorities in both houses of Congress, it was signed into law by the president on August 3, 2007. The comprehensive bill amended much existing transportation security legislation and represented a major shift away from the executive-centered approach to planning in favor of a highly specific statutory approach. It is much too detailed to discuss in all its parts in this short article. Six separate titles, XII through XVII, spelled out in great detail actions to be taken by DHS and other federal agencies to enhance transportation security. Separate titles for transit, surface transportation, air transportation, and maritime transportation created or enhanced programs for training, planning, inspections, and other aspects of security. The balance had clearly shifted from an executive-centered approach to one in which Congress was dictating specific policy outputs from DHS. The act remains the primary legislative basis for transportation security planning and programming.

What measurable effects have the policies and programs in transportation security had? Most obviously, there have been no major attacks and no loss of life attributable to terrorism in any of the nation's transportation modes. Whether this is due to the effectiveness of security policy and programs or the disinterest of terrorist groups to attack the nation's transportation system is unknowable.

Second, transportation security requirements have not significantly reduced the nation's transportation systems from fulfilling their primary tasks. Even with the economic downturn since mid-2008, the global economy, the air transport system, and the movement of goods and people on a daily basis remain largely unhindered by the security arrangements drawn up post 9/11.

Third, indications are strong that the collaborative capacity-building approach taken has led to strong relationships between agencies at different levels of government and between public and private sector organizations. The flow of information between and among different parties in these networks is much greater than it was before 9/11 and the formation of DHS. Training and simulations of terrorist events have produced a much greater likelihood that such tragedies can be avoided or, if they occur, the effects can be mitigated.

Fourth, virtually all parties involved in transportation security have moved to embrace a risk- and threat-based approach, recognizing that not all facilities, operations, and infrastructure can be secured using surveillance and policing tactics. Intelligence is seen to be the key to effective security, and the accumulation, sharing, and analysis of pertinent information is the basis for the risk-based approach.

What issues remain? Clearly, transportation security, as is the case with homeland security in general, has progressed enormously in the short time since the 9/11 attacks galvanized attention on this formerly overlooked policy question. Congress has refined the initial approaches to transportation security enacted shortly after 9/11 in light of the growing body of knowledge related to security issues. Major questions remain, however, including at least these:

- Is the current structure of DHS, and in particular the assignment of the major role in transportation security to the TSA, still optimal, or does there need to be a fundamental reexamination and perhaps reorganization of the department?
- Should homeland security, including those aspects related to transportation, be seen as a separate policy realm or merged with national security, perhaps through an expanded view of the role of the National Security Council to include integration of national and homeland security?
- How do we balance demands for greater transparency and accountability with the requirements for secrecy and the withholding of information that can be used by terrorists? Should we maintain the concept of threat levels, or move to a more open system in which citizens are apprised of potential threats?
- How do we continue planning and modeling for response to, and impacts of, potential threats to the transportation system?
- What are the international impacts of U.S. policy and the role of international bodies in policy development? How much can we learn from terrorist events in other nations, and work with them to avoid such tragedies in the future?
- How can we protect specific modes of transportation while at the same time moving to a more integrative or holistic approach to securing the entire transportation network?
- How can we apply models of planning and mitigation of terrorist events to natural disasters such as hurricanes and floods?
- Is the funding provided adequate to deal with the requirements for planning transportation security programs, providing training and research, and assisting state and local governments and transportation industry providers?

Transportation security, like homeland security in general, has been and remains a relatively uncontentious arena of public policy. Partisan differences are not as strong as in most other areas of domestic policy, as shown by the overwhelming majorities that have voted to pass major security legislation. Institutional politics—the vying for relative power by Congress and the White House—has been more characteristic than vigorous ideological or partisan conflict. The immersion of transportation security within DHS has created to some degree a measure of interdepartmental rivalry between DHS and DOT, but DHS has emerged as the primary agent for both legislative and executive policy promoting transportation security.

The lack of conflict may hide the biggest policy question—the adequacy of funding and the development of capacity within the system to provide the level of security we desire for our transportation system. Funding for homeland security in general and transportation security in particular lags far behind the funds provided for national security. Much of the work has been done by state and local governments and private organizations, in part a reflection of the inadequacy of funding to provide services from the national government. As we enter a period of hard economic times, the ability of advocates of enhanced transportation security to compete for scarce funds will be challenged, unless external events alter the equation and produce a reactive approach to security needs.

Transportation systems will continue to be among the most vulnerable institutions in our society to natural and man-made disasters. Nothing can be done to ensure 100 percent safety for the entire transportation network. The impact of catastrophic events can be only roughly anticipated, and the resulting effects on the economic, social, and political life of the nation only partially inferred from the past. Policies can make the world marginally safer, but nothing can ensure safety in such an interconnected and dangerous world.

Further Reading:

Ervin, Clark Kent. *Open Target: Where America Is Vulnerable to Attack.* New York: Palgrave Macmillan, 2006; Flynn, Stephen. *America the Vulnerable: How Our Government Is Failing to Protect Us from Terrorism.* New York: HarperCollins, 2004; Johnston, Van R., and Jeremy F. Plant. "Rail Security after 9/11: Toward Effective Collaborative Regulation." *Public Works Management and Policy* 13 (2008): 12–21; Johnstone, R. William. "Not Safe Enough: Fixing Transportation Security." *Issues in Science and Technology* 23 (2007): 51–60; National Commission on Terrorist Attack. *The 9/11 Commission Report.* New York: W.W. Norton, 2004; Relyea, Harold. "Organizing for Homeland Security." *Presidential Studies Quarterly* 33 (2004): 602–624; Sweet, Kathleen M. *Transportation and Cargo Security: Threats and Solutions.* Upper Saddle River, N.J.: Pearson Education, 2006; Waugh, William L. Jr. "Securing Mass Transit: A Challenge for Homeland Security." *Review of Policy Research* 21 (2003): 307–316.

–Jeremy F. Plant

veterans' benefits

The founders of the nation originally conceived of a limited government that would nurture independence by interfering as little as possible in the lives of its citizens. Almost from the beginning, veterans of America's wars, however, were treated differently. After the American Revolution, soldiers were compensated for war-related disabilities, but it took decades for further benefits to be offered. Following the Civil War, at the urging of veterans groups and because of political expediency, government policy makers steadily increased veterans benefits until in 1890 virtually every Union Army veteran was eligible for a service pension, regardless of health. Because the distribution of these funds eventually came to be associated with political corruption, Congress was much less generous with World War I veterans. In 1932, the Hoover administration violently broke up an encampment of veterans seeking a promised bonus. To avoid a similar conflict for the millions of returning World War II veterans, the Franklin Roosevelt administration planned a modest benefits package. Again a veterans group led public opinion to increase these benefits, resulting in the much more generous "G.I. Bill." These benefits were widely distributed to white, male veterans and helped create a surge in the growth of the middle class. Veterans of the Korean War and the Vietnam War received benefits similar to the G.I. Bill with some modifications. Since the Vietnam era, veterans' benefits have been tied to the retention of the all-volunteer army. Veterans of Afghanistan and Iraq are facing their own challenges returning to civilian life, such as injuries from so-called improvised explosive devices and many cases of post-traumatic stress syndrome.

The volunteer army that fought the British in the American war for independence was composed of ordinary citizens from all over the colonies. Because of their experience with the British army, however, many Americans of the Revolutionary War generation distrusted standing armies, including their own Continental Army. During the war, injured soldiers were pensioned and many were offered land grants on the frontier, but they were expected to return to civilian life with the nation's thanks, and little else.

Years after the war ended, the public grew nostalgic about these ex-warriors and wanted to care for the impoverished veterans among them. This public sentiment coincided with federal coffers that were swollen with excess money collected in tariffs. Thus, in 1818, with the support of most Americans, President James Monroe proposed pensions for indigent Revolutionary War veterans. The debate in Congress split between House members who agreed with this public desire to provide for poor veterans, and a few senators who still held the traditional republican attitude that, because all citizens had helped win the war, no one group should be singled out. The resistant senators were outnumbered, however, and, in March 1818, President Monroe signed a bill into law that any veteran who had served at least nine months and could prove indigence would receive a pension. Enlisted men would receive $96 per year and officers $240 per year. In 1832, almost a half-century after the British surrender at Yorktown, all living Revolutionary War veterans, including militiamen, were granted full pensions regardless of financial need.

The Civil War changed the size and scope of the U.S. federal government forever, and veterans' benefits grew as well. Because of the magnitude of the conflict—2 million men fought for the Union and 750,000 for the Confederacy—both in treasure and in lives, the federal bureaucracy increased exponentially, and Americans looked to the federal government to do more for them as well. The government had to expand not only to accommodate thousands of burials and injuries to Union soldiers, but also payments to their wives and children. In February 1862 pension benefits were awarded for disabilities directly linked to military service and graded according to rank. Widows, orphans, and other dependents of deceased soldiers received pensions at the same pay rate that the soldier would have received.

After Appomattox, the huge number of highly politicized Union veterans that returned to homes across the country created a powerful social and political force. Veterans' groups formed so that the victorious Yankees could keep track of comrades and fight for even greater veterans' benefits. One such group, the Grand Army of the Republic, at its peak membership in the early 1890s boasted about 400,000 members and helped pass the massive 1890 federal pension law. The Dependent Pension Act granted service pensions to Union veterans—many of them still in their fifties. This law covered any honorably discharged veteran who had served at least 90 days in the Union army or navy and had any disability that incapacitated him from manual labor no matter when or how he got it.

In the decades following the Civil War, the Republican Party used its image as the savior of the Union to great political advantage. The Democrats in the U.S. Congress fought more generous pension laws, but they were badly outnumbered. Between the end of the Civil War and the Great Depression, the Grand Old Party lost only three presidential elections to the Democrats. This domination of the levers of government allowed the Republican Party to use veterans' benefits as a tool to win elections until well into the 20th century.

By the end of the Civil War, close to 180,000 African-American men had fought in the Union army—nearly 10 percent of the total force in 1865. Black Union veterans were also ostensibly eligible for the same pension benefits as white veterans. In practice, however, it was more difficult for these men to collect benefits. Besides institutional racism that put them at a disadvantage in the application process, black veterans had to contend with other factors that made collecting a pension more difficult. First, because most black veterans were ex-slaves, many of them were illiterate, which created obstacles to negotiating the application process, black veterans' applications were questioned and rejected more often than whites. Verifying last names, birth dates, and even birthplaces was more difficult when the soldier had once been enslaved. Because antebellum slave marriages were not officially recognized by states, determining the legitimacy of a widow's application was often problematic, requiring multiple witness depositions and more delays. Nevertheless, the admittedly lower amount of pension funds that reached these veterans was a great help to them in their old age, especially for the majority who lived in the states of the old Confederacy.

The Confederate soldiers that trudged home after Appomattox had no federal government help to alleviate their poverty or tend to their injuries. Though they were ineligible for U.S. federal pensions and hiring preferences, individual southern states eventually provided as much support for their veterans as they could manage. Sixteen states of the former Confederacy built so-called soldier's homes for the wounded and indigent veterans, and some southern states provided modest pensions, as well. In 1889, delegates gathered at New Orleans to form the United Confederate Veterans (UCV), which, by 1903, numbered about 80,000 members. Instead of engaging in national politics, however, the UCV tended memorial shrines, graves, and battlefields to honor their fallen Confederate comrades. Southern veterans also tended to a Lost Cause memory of the war that helped alleviate some of the pain of the surrender at Appomattox.

Approximately 4.5 million American men served in Europe during World War I. Unfortunately for veterans of the Great War, U.S. policy makers associated the massive Civil War pension system with graft and party politics. All four postwar presidents—Wilson, Harding, Coolidge, and Hoover—believed that the country's obligation to these veterans was fulfilled at their demobilization. Because of this attitude, shared even by many veterans themselves, government policy makers offered World War I veterans only modest benefits, such as the option of buying low-cost insurance, some vocational training, and medical care only for disabled veterans. In 1921, the Veterans' Bureau was created to administer medical aid to the many veterans struggling with shell shock and the effects of exposure to poison gas, but as the economy boomed in the 1920s, able-bodied veterans began demanding more for their wartime sacrifices.

In 1924, Congress promised to at least make up for the difference in civilian wages that soldiers missed out on during the war. They issued bonds to the veterans that would be payable when they matured in 1945, but, with the onset of the Great Depression in the early 1930s, veterans understandably wanted this bonus earlier and in cash. In the summer of 1932 about 15,000 veterans peaceably marched on Washington, D.C., to protest the government's refusal to pay these bonuses early. When some members of this "Bonus Army" would not leave their encampment, President Hoover ordered the veterans to be removed by force. Led by Douglas MacArthur, armed federal troops accompanied by five tanks attacked the protesters and drove them out of D.C. at bayonet point. The World War I veterans did get full payment in 1936, but Hoover's treatment of the Bonus Army veterans contributed to his defeat in November 1932.

In 1941, when the United States was drawn into World War II, millions of Americans swelled the ranks of the U.S. military. Policy makers in the Franklin D. Roosevelt administration, with memories of the Bonus Army debacle still fresh, began planning as early as 1943 how to accommodate the more than 15 million veterans that would return when the war ended. The spirit of social reform that had infused the New Deal was already waning by the mid-1940s, but President Roosevelt understood that a massive influx of laborers returning from war could swamp the fragile economic recovery. More importantly, he felt the country owed these veterans a leg up when

The Wilking Building located at 1512–14 H Street NW, in downtown Washington, D.C. In 1932, the U.S. government purchased the building and used it as office space for the Veterans' Bureau. *(Library of Congress)*

they came home. "We have taught our youth how to wage war," he said. "We must also teach them how to live useful and happy lives in freedom, justice, and democracy."

The bill that President Roosevelt submitted to Congress, however, did not go very far toward providing unemployment or educational benefits to veterans. Reaction to Roosevelt's weak version of the veterans' bill came from an unlikely source, the American Legion, a conservative organization typically opposed to expansive government programs. Nevertheless, the legion led the charge to widen benefits for soldiers returning for the second time in a little over two decades from European battlefields. Relenting to the more generous bill, on June 22, 1944, FDR signed the Servicemen's Readjustment Act of 1944, or the "G.I. Bill," that provided World War II veterans with substantial benefits. Honorably discharged veterans of at least 90 days of service qualified for low-interest home, farm, or business loans, financial aid for additional education or training, and unemployed veterans could qualify for benefits of $20 per week for up to one year.

The effect of the G.I. Bill on the growth of the American economy in the second half of the 20th century cannot be overstated. By 1947, almost half of all American college students were veterans. Eventually 2.2 million veterans had attended college under the G.I. Bill. Housing loans created a construction boom, such that by 1955 nearly one-third of new housing starts nationwide were backed by the Veterans Administration.

African-American and female veterans did not receive this government aid in proportion to their numbers. Many African-American veterans of World War II went on to lead the civil rights struggles of the 1950s and 1960s. Nevertheless, the foresight of policy planners in enacting this legislation helped create a postwar period of economic growth for the American middle class that has never been equaled since. Furthermore, the G.I. Bill created a public policy entitlement for veterans that foreshadowed the growth of the social welfare state in the 1960s.

Over 6 million Americans served in the armed forces during the era of the Korean War (1950–53), and approximately 2.5 million men and 800,000 women served in Vietnam. Compared to veterans of World War II, who were celebrated for their defeat of global fascism, veterans of Korea and Vietnam received little adulation from Americans when they came home. Policy makers extended some benefits to Korean War veterans as that conflict entered its long stalemate phase. In 1952 Congress enacted the Veterans' Readjustment Assistance Act, which provided veterans with educational benefits similar to, but less than the G.I. Bill's benefits. In 1966 the Veterans' Readjustment Benefits Act extended such provisions to all who served in the armed forces, even in peacetime. Four years later Congress passed the Veterans' Education and Training Amendments Act of 1970, the first of a series. By 1979, 740,000 veterans were enrolled in education or vocational training under these acts.

But this financial aid often did not address the unique physical and psychological challenges that especially Vietnam veterans endured. Due to the stress of guerrilla-style warfare, about 30 percent of Vietnam veterans developed post-traumatic stress disorder (PTSD) in the years after the fighting ended. Policy makers in Congress were slow to accommodate these veterans, however. The House Veterans' Affairs Committee delayed a readjustment counseling bill for years, eventually passing it in 1979. In the 1980s and 1990s Congress passed legislation recognizing the devastating effects of Agent Orange exposure on Vietnam veterans as well. Thirty years after the Vietnam War ended, policy makers of the post-9/11 era would be only slightly better prepared for the devastating physical and psychological wounds of guerrilla-style combat.

When Congress abolished the military draft in 1973, military recruiters began to entice new enlistees with benefits such as college financial aid. After the terrorist attacks of September 11, 2001, the wars in Iraq and Afghanistan put this relatively small, all-volunteer fighting force under significant strain. As with veterans of past wars, Iraq and Afghanistan veterans face many challenges upon returning home. Because traumatic brain injuries from roadside explosives are the signature injury of the Iraq war, veterans' access to sophisticated health care is a pressing issue for policy makers. Also because this kind of guerrilla fighting produces many cases of post-traumatic stress syndrome in American veterans, psychological intervention and counseling have been debated as well.

In 2008, Senator Jim Webb (D-VA) proposed legislation that would bring veterans' benefits in line with the dramatically increased educational costs of the 21st century. This new G.I. Bill received wide support from many Democrats and Republicans in the House and Senate, but it was opposed at first by President George W. Bush. President Bush and others reasoned that if educational benefits were too generous, more soldiers would leave the military earlier to take advantage of this benefit. Veterans groups, such as the Iraq and Afghanistan Veterans of America (IAVA), also supported Senator Webb's bill. After a compromise was reached on transferability of benefits to relatives, President Bush signed the bill in June 2008 and it went into effect in August 2009.

Policy makers of the 21st century face many challenges in caring for our military veterans. Because more soldiers are surviving significant battlefield injuries, politicians will be pressured to increase spending on proper health care and rehabilitation for these wounded warriors. Similarly, early and effective psychological intervention for returning veterans will have to be addressed by policy makers. Finally, because the return of a military draft is very unlikely, policy makers will be faced with providing sufficient inducements to keep the all-volunteer military fully staffed for America's future needs.

Although the founders of the nation did not foresee this level of intervention for military veterans, they understood the special obligations that America owes these ex-soldiers. Starting with the modest numbers of Revolutionary War veterans through the massive mobilizations of the Civil War, two world wars, Vietnam, and post-9/11 veterans, the United States has gradually increased its support for its veterans in a variety of ways. In a society that prides itself on being egalitarian, the American public long ago decided that military veterans are a distinct class of citizens who deserve to be compensated for their sacrifices.

Further Reading:

Bailey, Beth. "The Army in the Marketplace: Recruiting an All-Volunteer Force." *Journal of American History* 94 (June 2007): 47–74; Keene, Jennifer D. *Doughboys, the Great War, and the Remaking of America*. Baltimore and London: The Johns Hopkins University Press, 2001; Logue, Larry M., and Michael Barton, eds. *The Civil War Veteran: A Historical Reader*. New York and London: New York University Press, 2007; McConnell, Stuart. *Glorious Contentment: The Grand Army of the Republic, 1865–1900*. Chapel Hill and London: University of North Carolina Press, 1992; Mettler, Suzanne. *Soldiers to Citizens: The G.I. Bill and the Making of the Greatest Generation*. Oxford and New York: Oxford University Press,

2005; Resch, John. *Suffering Soldiers: Revolutionary War Veterans, Moral Sentiment, and Political Culture in the Early Republic.* Amherst: University of Massachusetts Press, 1999; Rosenburg, R. B. *Living Monuments: Confederate Soldiers' Homes in the New South.* Chapel Hill and London: University of North Carolina Press, 1993; Shaffer, Donald R. *After the Glory: The Struggles of Black Civil War Veterans.* Lawrence: University Press of Kansas, 2004; Wecter, Dixon. *When Johnny Comes Marching Home.* Cambridge, Mass.: The Riverside Press, 1944.

– Daniel O'Sullivan

---

war powers

Seeking to restructure the governing institutions of a fledgling nation forged in the crucible of the Revolutionary War, the delegates to the Constitutional Convention in Philadelphia confronted many challenges, but perhaps none was more explosive than the question of the proper distribution of war powers between the legislative and executive branches. Having sacrificed so greatly to free themselves from one tyrannical despot, the framers of the nascent republic's first government, the Articles of Confederation, went to the greatest lengths to prevent the emergence of another by creating a national government lacking an independent executive altogether. Instead, all of the executive powers of government were vested within the Continental Congress. This weak executive authority proved one of the key barriers to effective governance under the articles. The very first plan brought before the Philadelphia Convention—Edmund Randolph's Virginia plan—quickly distinguished itself as something more than a simple revision of the articles by proposing the creation of a new and independent executive branch of government.

Many of the most intense objections to the idea were centered on the concern that this new, independent executive, like the British Crown before it, would wield power over questions of war and peace. South Carolina's Charles Pickney warned that transferring the executive power of the Continental Congress to the new national executive "might extend to peace and war which would render the Executive a Monarchy, of the worst kind, to wit an elective one." Madison's notes from the convention record other delegates echoing Pickney's concerns. One of the strongest champions of an independent executive at the convention, Pennsylvania's James Wilson, sought to allay such fears by assuring his peers that the powers of war and peace were legislative, not executive in nature, and as such they would naturally fall under the purview of Congress.

Ultimately, of course, the framers did embrace the call for an independent, unitary national executive by creating the American presidency. However, the balance of enumerated war powers in Articles I and II of the Constitution reflects the fears of executive martial power articulated by many at the convention. Article I, Section 8, entrusts to Congress alone the authority to declare war, to raise and appropriate funds for armies and navies, and to make rules to regulate and govern these forces. Congress was also granted the power to call forth the militia into national service in exigent circumstances and to arm, regulate, and govern them. Finally, Article I entrusted Congress with the responsibility of protecting the nation from piracy and offenses against the Law of Nations, and gave it sole authority to grant Letters of Marque and Reprisals, 19th-century instruments authorizing limited warfare on the high seas. By contrast, the sole enumerated war power entrusted to the executive in Article II is that making the president "Commander in Chief of the Army and Navy of the United States, and of the Militia of the several States, when called into the actual Service of the United States."

As with much of the Constitution, ambiguities in the text relating to war powers have opened the door for strikingly different interpretations of the framers' original intent. Drawing on a myriad of contemporary documents from the founding period, the constitutional text itself, and early jurisprudence, a conventional interpretation has emerged for congressional primacy in military affairs. Such arguments begin by emphasizing that the power to declare war was vested exclusively in the legislature. The nature of this power evolved over the course of the convention. The initial wording proposed giving Congress the power "to make war"; however, Massachusetts delegate Elbridge Gerry proposed substituting "declare" for "make" so that the executive would have the authority to repel sudden attacks. Madison's notes of the ensuing debate in the Committee on Detail reveal some confusion in the discussion over the relative merits of the two verbs; however, most scholars contend that the basic intent is clear and that the power to initiate wars, with the exception of repelling sudden attacks and invasions, was to be vested exclusively in Congress. Moreover, contemporary English and international precedents as well as the framers and early American jurists themselves used the two verbs interchangeably. For example, no greater advocate of presidential power than Alexander Hamilton wrote, in defense of President Washington's Proclamation of Neutrality: "If the legislature have the right to *make* war on the one hand—it is on the other the duty of the Executive to preserve Peace till war is declared." Similarly in 1806, Justice Paterson wrote concerning the limits of presidential war power in *United States v. Smith*: "Does he possess the power of *making* war? That power is exclusively vested in the legislature."

The declare war clause gave Congress alone the authority to wage "total" or "perfect" wars, but what of more "limited" or "imperfect" military conflicts? Citing numerous judicial precedents from the years immediately following ratification, scholars in the conventional mold argue that Congress alone also held power to sanction limited military engagements. For example, in the 1801 case *Talbot v. Seeman* Chief Justice John Marshall wrote: "The whole powers of war being, by the Constitution of the United States, vested in Congress, the acts of that body alone can be resorted to as our guides . . . Congress may authorize general hostilities . . . or partial war."

Finally, the conventional view asserting legislative primacy in war powers minimizes the importance of any authority granted to the president stemming from his Article II role as commander in chief. While contemporary presidents have repeatedly drawn on this clause to justify taking the initiative militarily in various crises across the globe, the 18th-century meaning of the term was decidedly more limited. Alexander Hamilton addressed the issue explicitly in the 69th Federalist and rejected any suggestion that the commander in chief clause would convey upon the president tyrannical military powers: "In this respect his authority would be nominally the same with that of the King of Great Britain, but in substance much inferior to it. It would amount to nothing more than the supreme command and direction of the military and naval forces, as first General and admiral of the Confederacy; while that of the British king extends to the *declaring* of war and to the *raising* and *regulating* of fleets and armies—all which, by the Constitution under consideration, would appertain to the legislature."

As commander in chief the president would sit at the top of the military chain of command of the troops in the field. However, James Madison made clear that the Constitution entrusted all of the critical decisions about a war's initiation, continuation, and conclusion to the legislature: "Those who are to *conduct a war* [i.e., presidents by virtue of the commander in chief clause] cannot in the nature of things, be proper or safe judges, whether *a war ought* to be *commenced, continued* or *concluded*. They are barred from the latter functions by a great principle in free government, analogous to that which separates the sword from the purse, or the power of executing from the power of enacting laws." On every account, presidential war powers would appear subordinate to those of the legislature.

However, a number of revisionist scholars contend that the constitutional distribution of war powers between the branches is not nearly so clear cut. For these scholars, including former Bush administration Office of Legal Counsel official and Berkeley law professor John Yoo, the semantic shift from "make" to "declare" is very important. Madison's notes from the ensuing debate on August 17, 1787, show considerable confusion among the delegates about whether the language shift would expand or limit presidential war powers. For revisionists, this confusion in the records is evidence that no consensus existed among the framers about the precise ramifications of the wording change for the interbranch balance of war powers.

Instead of the debates providing clear guidance, we must instead turn to the meaning of the constitutional text itself, and here many revisionists argue that in 18th-century legal parlance the power to "declare" war was distinct from the power to "make" or "commence" it. A declaration served to clarify the legal status of two belligerents as being in a state of "perfect" war. However, military hostilities could be commenced, and indeed were repeatedly begun, in the absence of a declaration of war.

The power to "make" war, by contrast, revisionists argue was understood as an *executive* function according both to the political theories of Locke and Montesquieu and to the shared precedents of Anglo-American history. As a result, war powers, including the power to commence military hostilities short of total war, are granted broadly to the president through the vesting clause of Article II, subject only to the explicit restrictions on this power, such as the power of the purse and the sole power of Congress to legally declare a "perfect" war.

The great legal scholar Edward Corwin wrote in the early 20th century that this balance of constitutional war powers has served for the president and Congress as "an invitation to struggle" for primacy over the nation's foreign affairs. Through debates over ambiguities in the meaning of key constitutional words and phrases as well as the records from the constitutional and ratification conventions and early historical precedents, constitutional law scholars have certainly engaged in this struggle throughout our nation's history. And given these competing constitutional claims, the two branches of government themselves have also repeatedly done battle for influence over the direction of the nation's military affairs.

The earliest episodes of American military history under the new Constitution triggered a string of judicial decisions circumscribing presidential war power. Although the alliance with France proved indispensable to winning American independence, a set of naval confrontations on the high seas in the late 1790s brought the United States and its erstwhile ally to the brink of war. In a series of cases, the Supreme Court firmly established the authority of Congress not just to declare total war, but also to authorize limited military engagements, and it struck down military orders issued by President Adams as exceeding the war authority granted by Congress. Having already decided in *Talbot* that the "whole powers of war [are] by the Constitution of the United States, vested in Congress," the Court in *Little v. Barreme* (1804) ruled President John Adams's instructions to seize ships sailing *from* French ports in the Caribbean unconstitutional, as Congress had only authorized the seizure of vessels sailing *to* French ports.

Confronted with a similar situation several years later, President Thomas Jefferson held back in his confrontation with the Barbary pirates. When American vessels in the Mediterranean sea came under enemy fire, they returned fire and disabled a ship from Tripoli. Jefferson summarized his actions in a message to Congress: "Unauthorized by the Constitution, without the sanction of Congress to go beyond the line of defense, the vessel, being disabled from committing further hostilities, was liberated with its crew. The Legislature will doubtless consider whether, by authorizing measures of offense also, they will place our force on an equal footing with that of its adversaries." It was not until several months later, after Congress authorized offensive action against Tripoli, that Jefferson pursued more vigorous offensive action against the Barbary threat.

As the 19th century continued, however, presidents pushed against these bounds on executive war powers, and, by the 1840s, President James K. Polk would use his commander in chief powers to order the American military into positions along the disputed Rio Grande border with Mexico in the hopes of provoking a military confrontation. When Mexican troops opened fire on American forces, Polk rushed a war bill to Congress and demanded that it authorize military action and provide the needed funds for war. In the mind of John C. Calhoun, Polk had not simply repelled a foreign attack on American soil; instead, he had engineered a crisis and presented Congress with a fait accompli: "[Polk's action] sets the example, which will enable all future Presidents to bring about a state of things, in which Congress shall be forced, without deliberation, or reflection, to declare war, however opposed to its convictions of justice or expediency." When the opposition Whigs seized control of Congress two years later, even though the Mexican capital had fallen to American forces, they continued to attack the allegedly illegal machinations by which Polk brought the country into war. One of many congressmen leveling such accusations was a young freshman representative from Illinois, Abraham Lincoln, who introduced his now famous "spot resolution" that demanded from the administration "all the facts which go to establish whether the particular spot of soil on which the blood of our citizens was so shed, was, or was not, *our own soil*." If the president should refuse to answer, Lincoln suggested that his silence would serve as evidence "that he is deeply conscious of being in the wrong—that he feels the blood of this war, like the blood of Abel, is crying to Heaven against him."

Less than 20 years later, Lincoln found himself mired in a conflict that remains the bloodiest in American history. Confronted with a mortal threat to the very existence of the Union, Lincoln took a host of actions, from blockading Southern ports to calling-up a 75,000 man militia to combat the insurrection to suspending unilaterally the writ of habeas corpus, without prior congressional consent. For at least some of these actions, Lincoln acknowledged that he may have violated constitutional limits on presidential war power. However, Lincoln repeatedly sought congressional approval for his actions after the fact, and he defended his actions as necessary and justified only given the mortal threat to the Union itself.

After a lull during an era of congressional dominance, presidents again began to assert themselves more forcefully in the international arena at the dawn of the 20th century. Flexing his muscle in foreign affairs, when mediating the Russo-Japanese War, President Theodore Roosevelt, unbeknownst to Congress, warned other European powers that if they entered the war on behalf of Russia, Roosevelt himself would intervene in support of the Japanese. Moreover, under the aegis of his Roosevelt corollary to the Monroe Doctrine, which articulated a greater American role in the internal and foreign affairs of troubled governments in the Western Hemisphere in danger of defaulting on debts to European powers, Roosevelt repeatedly resorted to gunboat diplomacy and projected American military might throughout the region. Perhaps most famously, after having failed to secure a treaty from Colombia for the right to build a canal through the isthmus of Panama, Roosevelt changed course and backed Panamanian independence, even dispatching the *Nashville* to Colón harbor to dissuade Colombian attacks on the Panamanian rebels.

The 1917–18 American involvement in World War I also greatly swelled the president's role in military affairs. While Wilson frequently justified his actions with explicit reference to powers delegated to him by Congress, like his predecessors Wilson also on occasion pushed the bounds of presidential wartime authority. For example, in 1918 Wilson dispatched American troops into the nascent Soviet Union during the Russian Revolution, despite the new government's neutral status in the war, before yielding to congressional pressure to withdraw the troops.

Despite a growing executive role in leading military affairs, presidential primacy in military policy making was far from complete. As late as World War II, Franklin Roosevelt felt himself powerfully constrained by an isolationist Congress from increasing American military involvement in the struggle against Nazi Germany. To be sure, Roosevelt did not stand idly by; the president did all that he could to aid the effort of the Allies despite passage by Congress of the Neutrality Acts. In early 1941, Roosevelt succeeded in winning congressional approval for the Lend-Lease program, which made the United States an "arsenal of democracy." And that September he went even further and unilaterally ordered American naval and airborne forces to protect all merchant ships, regardless of national origin, from Axis attacks in key sea lanes. However, Roosevelt's private correspondences repeatedly stressed his frustration with congressional unwillingness to sanction further military intervention on behalf of the Allies. Even in the immediate aftermath of Pearl Harbor and much to the chagrin of British prime minister Winston Churchill, there were concerns in the Roosevelt administration that Congress might balk at declaring war on Japan's ally, Germany. The day after, Congress declared war against Japan, but not Germany, President Roosevelt took to the airwaves in a fireside chat linking Germany's fate in Europe to the fate of the Pacific war with Japan and urging the American people to "remember always that Germany and Italy, regardless of any formal declaration of war, consider themselves at war with the United States at this moment just as much as they consider themselves at war with Britain or Russia." While he stopped short of calling for a declaration of war against Germany, FDR reminded the public: "We expect to eliminate the danger from Japan, but it would serve us ill if we accomplished that and found that the rest of the world was dominated by Hitler and Mussolini." Fortunately for the Allies, Hitler solved the political and constitutional conundrum facing Roosevelt by declaring war on the United States two days later.

While presidential war powers had undoubtedly expanded over time, the critical turning point for many scholars was President Harry Truman's decision to order American troops to defend South Korea pursuant only to a resolution of the United Nations Security Council and without seeking a declaration of war or any other authorization for his actions from Congress. Many in Congress, including the Republican leader Robert Taft (R-OH) pledged their support for a resolution authorizing a military response, but denounced Truman's maneuver as illegal. Truman considered going to Congress for its backing, which appeared would be forthcoming. However, he fatefully decided against it and instead issued a bulletin from the State Department justifying his actions as pursuant to the president's authority as commander in chief. In stark contrast to Hamilton's definition of the commander in chief powers in Federalist 69, the State Department argued that "the President, as Commander in Chief of the Armed Forces of the United States, has full control over the use thereof" and it proclaimed a "traditional power of the President of the United States to use the Armed Forces of the United States without consulting Congress."

While Truman also justified the constitutionality of his decision by arguing that the Senate's ratification of the UN Charter authorized him to take action pursuant to a UN mandate, his successors would latch on to the assertion of inherent presidential powers as commander in chief. Since Korea, presidents have cloaked themselves in the mantle of commander in chief powers and assiduously maintained their authority to order American troops abroad to pursue a variety of policy goals independent of any prior congressional authorization.

In contemporary politics, it is virtually impossible to argue that presidents are not the preeminent actors guiding the nation's military policy. However, considerable scholarly debate remains about the capacity of the other branches of government to exert a check on unbridled exertions of presidential war powers.

Presidential war powers reached their zenith in the 1960s and 1970s during what historian Arthur Schlesinger, Jr., labeled the "imperial presidencies" of Lyndon Johnson and Richard Nixon. Both presidents asserted unbridled commander in chief powers to wage the war in Vietnam as they alone saw fit, even when, as in the case of Nixon's extension of the war into Cambodia, their policies directly contradicted the will of Congress. To combat such assertions, in the waning days of Vietnam, Congress began drafting a new legislative tool—the War Powers Resolution—designed to give the legislature a greater role in decisions of when to send and when to withdraw American military forces abroad.

The War Powers Resolution had two primary objectives. First, it required presidents to consult with Congress "in every possible instance" before dispatching American troops abroad and to continue such consultations throughout the course of the deployment. Second, and perhaps more importantly, the resolution provided a mechanism for Congress to end a military venture of which it disapproved without having to use the power of the purse to cut off funding for the troops. Supporters of the resolution pointed to the need to prevent another Vietnam. In the words of Hawaii Democrat Spark Matsunaga, "If we have learned but one lesson from the tragedy of Vietnam, I believe it is that we need definite, unmistakable procedures to prevent future undeclared wars. 'No more Vietnams' should be our objective in setting up such procedures."

Some liberal Democrats opposed the bill and argued that it implicitly recognized the president's right to initiate military action subject to time limits, a power not granted to the executive in Article II. However, the bulk of the opposition in both chambers came from congressional Republicans. These Republicans had few objections to the resolution's first aim—encouraging further consultation. However, a number objected to the resolution's second goal—creating a new mechanism to terminate presidential uses of force. In the House version, this took the form of a provision that required the president to terminate automatically any military engagement he began at the end of 120 days unless it was explicitly authorized by Congress. The Senate version forbade presidents from initiating any military action absent a congressional declaration of war, except for a narrow subset of actions, such as responding to an attack on the United States. For these cases, the Senate proposed a 30-day time limit, after which the mission would be terminated automatically unless authorized by Congress. House Minority Leader Gerald Ford (R-MI) contended that members of Congress should "have the guts and the will to stand up and vote" to end a military engagement, "instead of saying 'You cannot do it' by doing nothing." Championing a Republican alternative, Representative David Dennis (R-IN) echoed Ford: "We should have the authority . . . to require the executive to terminate his [military] action, but . . . we should be required to take some vote affirmatively to terminate [it]." However, for the resolution's architect in the House, Clement Zablocki (D-WI), the automatic withdrawal clock was both intentional and critical. Without it, Zablocki noted, presidents could veto any resolution attempting to end an overseas military commitment.

Congressional Democrats had more than enough votes to pass the resolution; however, without more Republican support, they could not override the veto looming from the White House. After many months of bargaining and political compromises, the Democratic majorities in both chambers succeeded in winning enough Republican support to override the president's veto and the War Powers Resolution became law in November 1973. At the time, the resolution was hailed as a potent check on presidential war powers. However, whether because of poor drafting or of political compromises necessary to court a veto-proof majority, the final language of the Resolution creating the mechanism for terminating unauthorized military actions left a giant loophole for presidential abuse.

Section 4 of the War Powers Resolution requires the president to report his actions to Congress whenever ordering American troops abroad under one of three conditions. If he has sent American troops into a zone of "hostilities" or "imminent hostilities," then the president is to issue a report under section 4(a)(1). After a report "is submitted or is required to be submitted pursuant to section 4(a)(1)," section 5 of the resolution requires the president to terminate the military venture within 60 days, plus an additional 30 if he certifies it is necessary to achieve the safe withdrawal of American forces, unless Congress has declared war or authorized an extended action by statute. This is the provision opposed by Ford and other Republican leaders that would terminate a military action, absent any affirmative action by Congress.

However, the resolution also allows the president to issue other types of reports under sections 4(a)(2) and 4(a)(3) that describe deployments posing less immediate danger to American forces: the dispatch of American forces into foreign theaters while equipped for combat, and the substantial increases of preexisting overseas commitments of American forces, respectively. Reports under these conditions do *not* trigger the automatic withdrawal clock. The resolution still provides a mechanism for Congress to compel the president to withdraw American forces for military actions reported under these criteria; however, it requires affirmative action by Congress in the form of passing a resolution demanding the withdrawal.

Has the War Powers Resolution served as a viable constraint on presidential war power? In its first 31 years on the books, presidents submitted 114 reports "consistent" with the War Powers Resolution. However, in only one case, President Ford's rescue of the *Mayaguez*, has the president acknowledged that American forces were deployed into a zone of hostilities and reported under the condition that automatically triggered the withdrawal clock (Section 4(a)(1)). Even in this case, the report was made after the military operation had concluded. In some cases, presidents have simply refused to report under the War Powers Resolution altogether. And in many other instances, even when American troops were drawing fire, presidents from Reagan to Clinton have resisted acknowledging that the troops were in a zone of hostilities to avoid triggering the automatic withdrawal clock.

As a result, while some hailed the War Powers Resolution as the primary achievement of a "resurgent" Congress in the early 1970s, since then most analysts have lamented its failure to reestablish congressional influence over making war. Because the resolution affords presidents multiple options to report their military actions, chief executives have simply chosen to report under one of the conditions that does not trigger the automatic withdrawal clock and to place the onus on Congress to act affirmatively to overturn them. Moreover, because of a Supreme Court decision in the early 1980s, there are constitutional questions about whether a simple concurrent resolution can compel the president to withdraw forces, or whether a joint resolution of both houses—which, as Congressman Zablocki feared, is subject to the president's veto—is required. If it is indeed the latter, then Congress would have to assemble veto-proof majorities in both chambers to use the resolution to compel an end to a presidential war.

Because of these difficulties, Congress has only once successfully invoked the withdrawal clock on its own—when it deemed that President Reagan's dispatch of marines to Lebanon in the early 1980s required a report under the section covering military operations in zones of "hostility." However, even this case was a result of a compromise with the Reagan administration, which agreed to an 18-month authorization for the marine force. Because the War Powers Resolution granted the president flexibility in reporting that allows him to avoid triggering the automatic withdrawal clock, and because congressional efforts to invoke it are so difficult in a charged partisan political environment and may even be subject to a presidential veto, it has failed to serve as the direct check on presidential war power envisioned by its drafters.

The Constitution itself grants Congress a further check on presidential actions as commander in chief: the power of the purse. Indeed, even advocates of expanded presidential war powers who reject the constitutionality of the War Powers Resolution acknowledge Congress's funding power as a viable legislative check on presidential war power. On several occasions, opponents of the president's policies in Congress have succeeded in using the power of the purse to constrain the president's flexibility as commander in chief. For example, in the early 1970s, Congress enacted a series of appropriations bills that placed restrictions on the number of American troops fighting in Vietnam, terminated the extension of the war into Cambodia, and ultimately forbade the reintroduction of American ground troops into Vietnam. In a similar vein, more than 20 years later, after the death of 18 American servicemen in Mogadishu, Congress used the power of the purse to cut off funding for military actions in Somalia after March 31, 1994. In other cases, such as when President Ford considered military action to help battle Communist rebels in Angola in 1976, Congress has used the power of the purse to forestall a presidential use of force altogether.

However, the power of the purse is a blunt instrument, the exercise of which can generate tremendous political costs. For example, Democratic majorities in the 110th Congress voted to use the appropriations process to mandate a timeline for American withdrawal from Iraq. However, when confronted with a presidential veto, they were unwilling to pay the political costs of withdrawing funding for the troops altogether to achieve their aims. As a result, in only the rarest of cases has Congress successfully used the power of the purse to assert itself in interbranch battles over war powers with the president.

From this record of the repeated failure by Congress to use the formal legislative tools at its disposal to compel the president to abandon a military course of which it disapproves, most scholars have decried congressional weakness, bordering on impotence in military affairs. Indeed, if Congress can retain a check on presidential war powers only by enacting legislation compelling the president to change course, then in all but the rarest of cases Congress is weak indeed.

However, a growing body of scholarship has begun to challenge these assertions of congressional weakness. To be sure, Congress is not the dominant player or even the coequal partner in war powers that the framers intended. However, through a variety of informal pathways, Congress may continue to affect presidential decision making when initiating and conducting wars, even when it cannot pass legislation proscribing or mandating a specific course of action.

Although Congress has repeatedly failed to write its military policy preferences into law, this does not mean that Congress is inactive in the military arena. Indeed, throughout American history Congress and its members have actively engaged questions of military policy both in Washington and in the larger public sphere. Even if the prospects for passage are slim, Congress frequently introduces, debates, and votes on legislation to alter the course of military policy. Its committees hold hearings to uncover new facts on the ground, investigate the administration's conduct of combat operations, and put forward an alternate perspective on military affairs to the public. And its members frequently speak out on major martial matters and engage their constituents in public debates of military policy. None of these actions alone can legally compel the president to change course. However, each of them holds the potential to affect the president's decision-calculus indirectly by sending signals of domestic unity or disunity to foreign actors or by raising or lowering the political costs the president stands to incur from pursuing a military action.

From an international relations signaling perspective, when Congress publicly supports the president, it sends important signals of American resolve to the target of a military action. When presidents threaten a foreign actor with force, congressional support greatly increases the credibility of that threat, and should make the foreign foe more likely to comply with American demands to avoid a military showdown. Once an action has begun, continued domestic support discourages a target state from intensifying its resistance in the hopes of outlasting American domestic willingness to fight. By contrast, when Congress opposes the president's policies, it undermines the credibility of presidential threats, and, during a military action, it sends important signals of American lack of resolve on the home front.

Actions taken in Congress can also have important domestic political ramifications and affect popular support for the war and the commander in chief. Visible signs of congressional support for the president and his policies can provide the White House with invaluable political cover. The desire for this support, coupled with the important signals it sends to foreign actors, helps explain why presidents often seek prior congressional authorization for planned military actions—as both George H. W. Bush and George W. Bush did for their campaigns against Iraq in 1991 and 2003—while assiduously maintaining that they possess the constitutional authority to order military action independent of Congress.

In a similar vein, public congressional opposition to the president and his policies—on the floor, in the committee room, or in the mass media—can weaken presidential support among the public and raise the political costs of staying the course. By challenging the administration's interpretation of events, congressional opposition can influence national policy debates and sway public opinion against the commander in chief. Moreover, by forcing the president to expend political capital defending himself from congressional challenges on the military front, Congress can weaken the administration's hand on other priorities in both the foreign and the domestic arenas. Thus, even when they fail to legally compel the president to change course, members of Congress may so raise the political price tag of launching or continuing a military venture that it may outweigh the benefits that the president initially hoped to obtain by acting militarily.

The primary difficulty such informal mechanisms pose for scholars is measuring their influence. With legislation, it is possible simply to count up the number of occasions on which Congress has passed laws to constrain the military powers of the commander in chief. These alternative means of indirect influence cannot be measured so simply; moreover, much of their influence on presidential decision making may be anticipatory. Knowing the potential strategic and political costs congressional opposition can generate, presidents may seek to avoid provoking opposition in Congress and adjust their conduct of military affairs accordingly.

Despite the difficulties of measurement, a number of recent studies have found evidence strongly consistent with the idea that Congress does continue to influence the presidential use of force, even though its legislative tools are cumbersome and frequently ineffective. For example, scholars have found that presidents facing a strong partisan opposition on Capitol Hill use force less frequently than their peers who enjoy strong co-partisan support in Congress. As a result, even when Congress does not affirmatively act to forbid a military response to an opportunity to use force abroad, calculations about the likely reaction of Congress still appears to influence significantly the president's decision of whether or not to intervene militarily.

Moreover, new analyses of historical use of force data suggest that congressional influence over military policy making continues even after American troops are deployed in the field. Presidents facing a strong opposition party are not only less likely to use force in the first place, but when they do resort to military measures they also choose missions that are systematically smaller in scope and shorter in duration than do their peers who enjoy stronger co-partisan majorities on Capitol Hill. Furthermore, during the course of a military operation presidents appear to adjust their conduct of a use of force in response to actions in Congress. When Congress debates and votes on legislation to curtail a military venture, holds critical hearings of the administration's conduct of an operation, or speaks out against a use of force, the expected duration of that military action decreases.

Thus, the congressional check may not be as strong or direct as that anticipated by the framers; however, in certain political circumstances, Congress can continue to exert an important, if often indirect, check on presidential war powers.

While scholars and analysts alike routinely focus on the capacity of Congress to check presidential war powers, the courts also possess the constitutional authority to strike down presidential actions that exceed the limits of their Article II authority. In *Marbury v. Madison* (1803) Chief Justice John Marshall famously declared that it was the "province and duty of the judicial department to say what the law is." Given the "invitation to struggle" inherent in the constitutional division of war powers, throughout American history political actors have looked to the Supreme Court as an arbiter to resolve interbranch disputes in the military arena.

In the early 19th century the Supreme Court decided a number of cases involving the scope of the national government's war powers and their locus within the governing framework. In every instance, this early jurisprudence gave primacy to Congress. In the estimation of the great legal scholar Edward Corwin, "The language of the Justices in these early cases implies that any act of war, to be entitled to judicial recognition as such, must be ascribed to congressional authorization."

President Lincoln's bold assertion of war powers in the Civil War again brought the question of military authority front and center. In 1861, the U.S. Circuit Court, knowing that Lincoln was unlikely to comply with its ruling, nevertheless struck down Lincoln's unilateral suspension of the writ of habeas corpus in *Ex Parte Merryman* (1861). Two years later, the high court finally ruled on the constitutionality of Lincoln's blockading of southern ports prior to any authorization by Congress. In *The Prize Cases* (1863), the Court ruled that the Confederate attack on Fort Sumter had moved the country into a de facto state of war, even if it had not yet formally been recognized by Congress, and thus Lincoln's actions were constitutional. Yet, the Court was careful to distinguish between Lincoln's actions in response to the southern attack and the right to commence a military engagement. Indeed, the government's own lawyer in the case made clear Lincoln's action was strictly distinct from "the right *to initiate a war, as a voluntary act of sovereignty.* That is vested only in Congress." And in 1866 with the war safely concluded, the Supreme Court took up the issue of the suspension of habeas corpus in *Ex Parte Milligan* (1866) and again ruled that it exceeded presidential powers even in a time of war.

While most 19th-century court rulings limited presidential war powers, in the early 20th century the Supreme Court actively contributed to the rebalancing of war powers favoring the executive with a number of decisions culminating in *United States v. Curtiss-Wright* (1936). In his decision for the Court, Justice Sutherland sweepingly proclaimed that the president was "the sole organ of the federal government in the field of international relations" and he described the president's powers in foreign affairs as "plenary and exclusive." Although the case itself involved only whether Congress could delegate certain foreign affairs powers to the president and much of Sutherland's language has been held not to carry precedential value for guiding future decisions, federal courts have repeatedly cited the case over the past 70 years to justify broad assertions of presidential war power.

The courts remained active in the field of war powers throughout World War II, and during the Korean conflict the Supreme Court famously struck down Truman's seizure of the steel mills, despite the president's claims that ensuring a continued supply of steel in the face of work stoppages was essential to the war effort and fell under the penumbra of his powers as commander in chief.

However, the Vietnam War and its aftermath witnessed a watershed change in war powers jurisprudence. Time and time again, the federal courts, including the Supreme Court, sought to avoid adjudicating interbranch disputes over war powers altogether. For example, in *Mitchell v. Laird* (1973) 13 members of Congress filed suit to stop American military operations in Indochina unless Congress explicitly authorized the continuation of military action. Congress had never declared war against Vietnam, and it had repealed the Gulf of Tonkin Resolution two years prior. The D.C. Circuit Court, however, avoided deciding the case by relying on the political questions doctrine—the idea that some controversies, even if the case involved the question of whether a branch of government has acted improperly, were of an inherently "political" character and could not be adjudicated by the federal courts. Although the courts had ruled on questions of the scope and exercise of presidential war powers repeatedly throughout the first 180 years of American history, in the Vietnam era the courts frequently resorted to the political questions doctrine to avoid entering inter-branch disputes.

Since Vietnam, federal courts have continued to rely on the political questions doctrine and other devices to avoid adjudicating disputes on the constitutional bounds of presidential war powers. In a host of cases covering American military interventions in Grenada, El Salvador, the Persian Gulf, Iraq, and Kosovo, members of Congress themselves filed suit in federal court asserting that presidents had overstepped their commander in chief authority by ordering American troops abroad absent prior congressional sanction. Yet, in most of these cases, the judiciary has ruled that individual members of Congress lack standing to sue and has hinted that the courts will intervene only if there is a true constitutional impasse pitting the legislature as an institution against a recalcitrant president refusing to obey a congressional directive. In a case involving the first Persian Gulf War, *Dellums v. Bush* (1990), the U.S. District Court ruled that the court may intervene in future cases, but only if a majority of Congress has acted to check presidential power and the president has refused to comply: "It is only if the majority of Congress seeks relief from an infringement on its constitutional war declaration power that it may be entitled to receive it."

Other cases brought by members of Congress have focused on the War Powers Resolution, specifically on the president's failure to report his actions under Section 4(a)(1), which would automatically trigger the 90-day withdrawal clock, even when American troops have taken fire and are indisputably in a zone of hostilities. However, the courts have repeatedly ruled that whether a military action falls under section 4(a)(1)'s purview for "imminent hostilities" is a political question beyond the purview of the judiciary.

As a result, most scholars have concluded that if Congress is unwilling or unable to defend its institutional prerogatives in foreign affairs, the courts are equally reticent to intervene on its behalf. The contemporary position of the courts was perhaps best captured in *Goldwater v. Carter* (1979): "If the Congress chooses not to confront the President, it is not our task to do so." Even if assertions of unilateral presidential war powers exceed those sanctioned by Article II of the Constitution, contemporary federal courts have repeatedly interpreted congressional silence—or at least the absence of opposition to the president's policies by a legislative majority—as tacit congressional consent to the president's actions.

In the wake of the terrorist attacks of September 11, 2001, the nation rallied behind President George W. Bush and embraced his calls for united, vigorous action to confront the new challenges posed by the terrorist threat. Congress swiftly enacted the Authorization for Use of Military Force (AUMF), which delegated to the president the power "to use all necessary and appropriate force" against "those nations, organizations, or persons he determines planned, authorized, committed, or aided the terrorist attacks that occurred on September 11, 2001, or harbored such organizations or persons, in order to prevent any future acts of international terrorism against the United States by such nations, organizations or persons." Pursuant to this authority, President Bush ordered American forces to invade Afghanistan and overthrow the Taliban regime that harbored the Al Qaeda terrorist responsible for the 9/11 attacks, a war that, despite lasting longer than American involvement in World War II, continues to enjoy widespread support both among the American people and the Congress.

However, drawing on assertions of inherent constitutional power as commander in chief and arguments that this authority was supplemented by Congress through the AUMF, President Bush has claimed a panoply of executive war powers in the war on terror, from the authority to order wiretaps on the international communications of American citizens without first obtaining warrants from the FiSA court as required by law, to the power to unilaterally establish military tribunals to try terror suspects and those designated enemy combatants independent of the federal judicial system, to the right to perform extraordinary renditions and transfer prisoners in American custody to foreign countries that practice torture. The scope of these asserted war powers has sparked some of the greatest interbranch clashes over war powers since the Vietnam era.

The federal courts, long reticent to intervene in war powers disputes, have proven surprisingly willing, in some instances, to engage terrorism cases and to issue rulings curbing both presidential and congressional power. Echoing the spirit of Civil War precedents, the Supreme Court in *Hamdi v. Rumsfeld* (2004), *Rumsfeld v. Padilla* (2004), and *Rasul v. Bush* (2004) struck down the Bush administration's policy of denying habeas corpus rights to detainees designated by the executive as enemy combatants, be they citizens or noncitizens alike. Writing for the plurality in *Hamdi*, Justice O'Connor declared that a state of war was "not a blank check for the president when it comes to the rights of the Nation's citizens." In *Hamdan v. Rumsfeld* (2006), the Supreme Court took aim at the Bush administration's unilaterally created system of military tribunals to try suspected terror subjects, and it ruled that the president's military order was in breach of both the Uniform Code of Military Justice (UCMJ) and the Geneva Conventions. And when Congress sought to strip from the federal courts its jurisdiction to hear habeas petitions from foreign detainees, the Supreme Court intervened again in *Boumediene v. Bush* (2008) and ruled the statute unconstitutional.

However, in other cases, the court's reticence to enter interbranch disputes was again on display. For example, in 2006 the U.S. District Court struck down the administration's warrantless wiretapping program as a violation of both congressional statute and the First and Fourth Amendments. However, the Circuit Court of Appeals, ruling that the plaintiffs lacked standing, overturned the District Court order and the Supreme Court declined to review the decision.

Congress, too, has taken a number of steps to confront bold assertions of unilateral presidential war powers, from demanding greater oversight of the NSA warrantless wiretapping program to banning the use of torture by American forces in the interrogation of terror suspects. This congressional resurgence culminated in the legislative attacks on the Bush administration's conduct of the Iraq War in the early days of the Democratic-controlled 110th Congress. Using a variety of vehicles, from the Webb amendment requiring minimum stateside rest and training periods between foreign deployments to war appropriations bills mandating a timeline for the withdrawal of American combat forces, the Democratic majority sought to undercut the Bush administration troop surge and to legislate an end to the war in Iraq. And even as their legislative initiatives failed to compel a change in course, Democratic committee chairmen continued to challenge aggressively the administration's conduct of the war through an unending string of high-profile investigations. While the Democrats failed to achieve their legislative aims, popular support for the war in Iraq remained surprisingly low throughout 2008, despite the reduction of American casualties and improvements in the security situation on Iraq in the wake of the surge. War support failed to rally, perhaps at least in part because of these Democratic efforts to remind the public of the war's continued costs in terms of men, materiel, military readiness, and American moral authority worldwide.

Contemporary events thus make plain that despite the ascendance of presidential war powers over the course of the 20th century, the constitutional "invitation to struggle" continues to fuel interbranch grappling over the balance of war powers in our system of separated institutions sharing power.

Further Reading:

Adler, David, and Larry George, eds. *The Constitution and the Conduct of American Foreign Policy*. Lawrence: University Press of Kansas, 1996; Fisher, Louis. "Judicial Review of the War Power." *Presidential Studies Quarterly* 35 (2005): 466–495; Hinckley, Barbara. *Less Than Meets the Eye: Foreign Policy Making and the Myth of the Assertive Congress*. Chicago: University of Chicago Press, 1994; Howell, William, and Jon Pevehouse. *While Dangers Gather: Congressional Checks on Presidential War Powers*, Princeton N.J.: Princeton University Press, 2007; Koh, Harold. *The National Security Constitution: Sharing Power after the Iran-Contra Affair*. New Haven Conn.: Yale University Press, 1990; Kriner, Douglas. *After the Rubicon: Congressional Constraints on Presidential Warmaking*. Boston University typescript, 2008; Schlesinger Jr., Arthur. *The Imperial Presidency*. Boston: Houghton Mifflin, 1973; Silverstein, Gordon. *Imbalance of Powers: Constitutional Interpretation and the Making of American Foreign Policy*. New York: Oxford University Press, 1997; Yoo, John. *The Powers of War and Peace: The Constitution and Foreign Affairs after 9/11*. Chicago: University of Chicago Press, 2005.

– Douglas Kriner

22 Diplomacy

foreign aid

Traditionally, U.S. foreign aid has focused on at least four enduring objectives: economic growth and development, eradication of poverty and disease, cessation of the destruction of the environment, and promotion of democracy and good governance. Following from this are four programmatic emphases to foreign aid: infrastructure development, social and economic development, humanitarian and security assistance, and support for democratic governance and political development. In the 20th century, foreign aid served a multiplicity of purposes: diplomatic, security, cultural, developmental, humanitarian, trade, and commerce. With the cold war's end, promotion of economic and social transitions in former socialist countries, support for democratic governance, conflict mediation, managing postconflict transitions, addressing environmental problems, and fighting international terror were increasingly important.

Democratic governance and political development have become particularly important in the last 15 years. As early as 1950, advocates of foreign aid made it clear that democratic governance was essential for development aid to succeed. Increasingly, since 1989, a concern has grown for the establishment of an international legitimacy for democracy, which has predominated at least conceptually in foreign aid debates.

This article examines U.S. foreign aid as it has evolved from its early antecedents to its contemporary applications in the broader context of foreign and security policy.

Any understanding of contemporary foreign aid must encompass the 18th, 19th, and early 20th centuries in Europe and the United States. Foreign aid has been governed by "the structural power patterns in the global system." Foreign aid policy has been a component of diplomacy and ultimately "a sophisticated instrument of control" or at least influence over its recipients. Foreign aid, like diplomacy, propaganda, or military action, is an instrument of statecraft.

A country's motivation for extending foreign aid variously includes national esteem, altruism, humanitarianism, military and strategic interests, political and diplomatic concerns, and commercial and collective or multilateral advantages. Although an important subtext links volunteerism, humanitarianism, and morality to assistance, virtually every donor country expects something in return: political support, military or strategic alliance, partnerships, and trade or commerce. Foreign aid has long been a burden and a privilege of leadership and power in world affairs.

Imperialism and colonialism defined foreign and security policy, and hence foreign aid over three centuries, still reminiscent of today. The British and the other European empires established the values of foreign aid, while the United States, an upstart imperial power, imbibed many of the racial, cultural, political, and economic assumptions of the Europeans after World War I. In the Philippines, for example, the American administration closely resembled British colonialism in Asia and Africa.

By the middle of the 18th century, the basis of international trade was the exchange of gold and silver, which evolved into a formal international monetary system at the end of the Napoleonic Wars. As a sign of friendship and alliance, states often loaned gold and silver at subsidized rates to less well-off countries. Loans under preferential conditions appeared as an instrument of foreign policy after the 1850s. In the last half of the 19th century, foreign loans, for example, were used in construction projects in Eastern Europe, Latin America, Asia, Africa, and the Middle East, including the Suez Canal.

British lending patterns were adopted by the United States, which had emerged from a debtor to a creditor nation after World War I. The availability of 19th-century loans to it meant a country would be admitted to a group with "securities" reliable enough to be traded on foreign markets. Access was controlled by European powers, and later the United States, or their banks. Ultimately these concessionary loans (and later grants) became the basis of contemporary official international assistance.

Foreign aid, narrowly viewed as concessionary monies, suggests that some government-funded financial or humanitarian assistance was extended before World War II, but the first broad transfer of funds in peacetime occurred with the Marshall Plan and later President Truman's Point Four Program.

The antecedents of foreign aid, prior to 1948, are important. Use of public resources for humanitarian relief began in the 19th century. Development funds for European colonies originated between the two world wars, and the United States, partially in response to the Nazi aggression, began to assist its Latin American dependencies in the 1930s.

In the British and the other European empires, development investment in the late 1800s and early 1900s spawned an interaction between government and nongovernmental organizations (NGOs) in Asia and Africa, particularly where missionary organizations were prevalent, and remain so today.

Governments in Asia and Africa, and earlier in Latin America, were heavily conditioned, often negatively, by their colonial heritage. State-centered industrial development focused on large-scale infrastructure projects (e.g., railroads, dams, highways, and ports) in India, Brazil, and Argentina and to some extent South Africa. There was seldom significant delegation of authority or significant local self-government granted by the colonial authorities, which for better or worse undergirded foreign aid contemporarily.

The historical definition of foreign aid is particularly important when one places the United States in the context of world imperial expansion represented in the 19th century by Manifest Destiny. U.S. imperial expansion was part of the country's perceived manifest destiny almost from the nation's founding, including cultural, social, and political values as well as geographical expansion. This was messianic in its vision, defined as isolationist prior to World War II, collectivist during much of the cold war, and unilateralist increasingly since the 1960s, culminating in the Iraq invasion in 2003.

U.S. foreign policy from the 1890s was based on isolationism, seeking to avoid European entanglements, but more assertive in the Western Hemisphere and the Far East, where the United States held stronger interests. The country's leadership sought to thwart threats to commercial activity in the Caribbean and the Pacific areas. Additionally, powerful aggressive expansionists in Congress, the business community, and the churches defined duty as "the obligation of a great nation to guide less fortunate persons, and bestow on them the enlightenment of her institutions and culture."

In August 1914, Herbert Hoover, chairman of the Commission of Relief in Belgium, articulated U.S. foreign aid principles that would define practices for the 20th century. He continued to play the role of war relief czar through the war and into the post–World War I period, first in the nonprofit sector, then in promoting the Pan-American Highway. In the aftermath of World War I, the United States came to believe its national values to be universal and exceptional, and Americans viewed their government and society as a model for the world.

Three legacies of World War I impacted foreign aid: self-determination, as defined by Woodrow

Wilson's Fourteen Points speech, became a watchword for developing and transitional states; humanitarian assistance required that NGOs feed the hungry and the displaced; and national governments would, because of the size of the problem, provide significant financial support.

Though funding was modest prior to 1948, foreign aid was important because it defined values and established processes whereby assistance is granted today. By 1940, the United States had a fully developed technical cooperation program in Latin America under the Good Neighbor Policy in agriculture, education, and health, and other foreign aid programs operated in China, Persia, and the Philippines.

The potentialities of overlapping if not of competing field activity may be illustrated most strikingly by reference to Latin America. A dozen or more U.S. government agencies were engaged in multiform aid enterprises, some of them dating from the 1930s. The United States also provided limited assistance to Liberia and Ethiopia in Africa and to Iran, the Philippines, and Thailand in Asia during the interwar period. However, prior to World War II, foreign aid provision was an unstructured process.

Origins of many foreign aid procedures and assumptions lay in the U.S. interventions in Latin America, Asia, and Africa prior to World War II and in competition with European colonial powers, particularly in East Asia. The Monroe Doctrine is important to that legacy: missionaries, concern with terms of trade, idealism, and balance of power calculations.

Chromolithograph of an allegorical female figure of America leading pioneers and railroads westward, by George A. Crofutt, ca. 1873 *(Library of Congress)*

President Franklin Roosevelt's establishment of a military and foreign assistance program for the Allied Powers during World War II and for the requirements of the war effort defined foreign aid parameters well into the postwar period. Operating under the hands across the sea (red, white, and blue) logo that still defines the U.S. Agency for International Development (USAID), the quasi-military nature of foreign aid procedures, and the links between military and civilian assistance, are testament to that period.

Foreign aid in its modern form dates from World War II when the U.S. responded to the Nazi invasion of Europe with Lend-Lease assistance to Great Britain. In early 1941, John Maynard Keynes, representing Britain, arrived in Washington to negotiate the Lend-Lease agreement, setting the stage for an elaborate aid system.

From World War II, foreign aid was linked to military as well as foreign policy. Its roots in organizations developed in that period, including the Foreign Economic Administration (1940) and Office of Lend-Lease Administration (1941). A third organization, the War Relief Control Board (1942), coordinated and provided funding for NGOs. Lend-Lease left behind a formative experience that impacted Allied leaders for a generation.

There were three components to the foreign aid system, beginning with the Marshall Plan, also known as the European Recovery Program (1948), and including the Mutual Defense Program (1949) and the Point Four Program (1950). The Marshall Plan was unique, even compared to subsequent aid programs. Its success can be understood, according to Vemon Ruttan, since it operated in a way that was easy for recipients to engage. European policy makers were able to control and manage the funds that they received.

Post–World War II foreign aid evolved through initial assistance to Greece and Turkey under the Truman Doctrine and modifications to the Marshall Plan. Contemporary foreign aid, primarily targeted to developing countries, began under Truman with the Technical Cooperation Administration (1950).

Truman proposed Point Four in his inaugural address in 1949, calling for a "'bold new program' for making the benefits of American science and industrial progress available to 'underdeveloped' countries." Assessments of Truman's speech made it clear that U.S. foreign aid had been a powerful instrument for strengthening orderly social processes in an era during which the exploitation of poverty, of bleak economic horizons, and of frustration of even modest national aspirations threatened both our own national security and the peace of the world.

During the 1950s, donors assumed foreign aid would provide a short-term boost to developing countries, filling the "finance gap" countries lacked to launch sustained economic development. Initially, the "magic formula" assumed aid should be invested in large-scale infrastructure.

In early years, a "state centric" focus characterized foreign aid both among donors and developing countries: building state capacity, particularly in development administration. The private sector, however, was seen as available to do development work.

By 1960, the foreign aid program faced difficulties. According to Walter Sharp, "There was almost a total lack of appreciation on the part of the host country personnel of what the [foreign aid] program was supposed to do." Not surprisingly foreign aid met up with the vagaries of political obstacles from the beginning of the post-war era. "Divergent views," he went on, "emerged as to where and how the line should be drawn between the exchange of technical knowledge and skills and the provision of capital investment. Which should come first? Or should they go hand in hand?" One factor slowing aid concerned congressional delays in appropriating funds.

Congress passed the Foreign Assistance Act of 1961, creating USAID ostensibly to draw together disparate aid programs under one agency and to focus aid on longer-term needs. In reality, though, Congress had grown frustrated with the ineffective management of aid by the State Department. USAID was viewed by the Kennedy administration as a "temporary agency" that would be disbanded once foreign aid had achieved its goals. USAID is still in operation. USAID's focus was to support health, education and training, transportation and agriculture, and economic development. Legislation called for the use of domestic federal agencies (and contractors and NGOs) to supplement USAID's activities.

Models developed during the Vietnam War influenced thinking about rural development and the relationship between aid and security into and beyond the 1970s. As Francis Fitzgerald notes, U.S. aid officials focused "almost exclusively on the development of policies and programs and [worked] with organization and reorganization.... In part, [this] came from the American—or Western—view of government as a complex machine."

Practical implications from the Vietnam involvement caused alarm. Picard and Buss have noted that the United States poured into Vietnam (with its fragile, simple economic system) enormous amount of money, people, and commodities. Critics suggested linking of defense and security with foreign assistance meant the United States had harkened back to an "old missionary tradition, [and] was obsessed by a zeal to improve Asia [and was] reanimated by the anti-Communist crusade."

Foreign aid continued to include funding for security, supporting assistance to countries playing a strategic role in U.S. interests. By the 1970s, USAID estimated that more than 1 million foreign police officers were trained or supplied through its "public safety" program. After 1975, the United States came under criticism for training police and security forces in repressive regimes.

Vietnam, ironically, became the model both for and against foreign aid and military assistance during the Iraq War. This duality suggested to critics a moral ambiguity to foreign aid as it related to recipient nations. From the Indochina period to the end of Vietnam, aid professionals cut their teeth on Southeast Asia programs.

Issues and perceptions of foreign aid are changing again, particularly in the areas of economic development and poverty reduction. Failure to reduce poverty and to grow economies over the past half-century has been validated by academic studies, argued ideologically, and reflected in changes in USAID priorities. Put simply, by 2000, "universal models of growth [did] not work well."

During the cold war (with the partial exception of Vietnam), the United States opted for collective action, a multilateral approach based on collegial action among allies, in its foreign policy. By 1971, foreign aid had been available to underdeveloped nations for close to 20 years, but foreign aid itself had become controversial. Contemporary foreign aid was significantly changed by the intervention in Vietnam in the 1960s and by the way the war shaped U.S. foreign aid after 1975, foreshadowing the Iraq War.

During the Ronald Reagan presidency, foreign aid went through a series of post-Vietnam reforms, including structural adjustment (i.e., sound monetary and fiscal policy, trade liberalization, deregulation, privatization) and conditionality requirements, questioning assumptions about state-sponsored development and looking toward private and nonprofit sectors to drive economic growth.

When he took office in January 1981, Reagan brought a new set of values to international affairs and initiated policy reforms that would define his presidency. Reagan's view of intervention was linked to Manifest Destiny and visions of a post–cold war "American Empire." Foreign aid (and security) policy toward Central America epitomized the issues, as did burgeoning developing country debt.

As we have argued elsewhere, "U.S. unilateralism [had become] simply the other side of the coin from U.S. isolationism." The year 1981 is important because that was when Robert McNamara stepped down as president of the World Bank, where international development policy was being defined by structural adjustment and public sector reform in many African, Central American, and Southeast Asian states. After his departure, it shifted to developing country debt.

Under structural adjustment, developing countries had their loans adjusted and then proceeded to borrow even more money from international organizations after debt relief. Not only was the debt crisis severe, but also much of foreign aid never reached target countries, having been siphoned off by creditors and development contractors.

In 1989, support for foreign aid declined largely out of "donor fatigue"—spending a lot of money with little to show for it, leaving many foreign aid watchers pessimistic about the future.

Over three decades ago, the United States ended a decade of involvement in the Vietnam War. After 2001, the United States invaded Afghanistan and Iraq, which necessitated long-term occupations. The Vietnam and Middle Eastern conflicts are often compared: Both represent conditions where foreign aid and military intervention were seen by many as unsuccessful.

President George W. Bush radically changed foreign policy and foreign aid programs in the wake of the attacks of September 11, 2001. Having found "a grandiose purpose" in foreign policy, Bush announced what he called his preemption doctrine: The United States would strike first in the event of an international threat to its security. This included the remilitarization of foreign aid in Afghanistan and Iraq and in the war on terror in general.

Increasingly, institutions of global or regional governance were asked to intervene during periods of social upheaval and political or economic collapse. As Stephen Brunne has summarized, "With less 'superpower' resolve to bring these crises to an end, and more of the world's wars resulting in deaths of civilians, aid organizations are increasingly involving themselves directly in social, political and even, at times, military matters."

Contemporary debates about foreign aid include discussions about unilateralism versus multilateralism, human security, support for democracy and governance, and links between foreign aid and trade and investment policy. Given the current global financial crisis, however, limited resources available for foreign aid have meant that Western powers cannot sustain the interventionist structures that had been maintained a generation earlier. To change, this would require a massive infusion of both military and foreign assistance in many different parts of the world. President Barack Obama moved to do just that in his first weeks in office in 2009.

Changes in foreign aid and a significant growth in the aid budget, however, occurred after September 11. Some evidence exists of increased cooperation internationally in foreign aid, at least outside of Iraq. In the aftermath of the attack, the United States is (reluctantly) enlisting in a global war on poverty. But only on its own terms. In the end, if there is to be a war against terror, the alleviation of poverty had to be based on a strategy of strong economic growth.

One initiative, the President's Emergency Plan for AIDS Relief (PEPFAR), launched in 2003, is a more collaborative approach to foreign aid. PEPFAR targeted $15 billion (over five years) in 15 countries to the prevention of 7 million new AIDS cases and provision of care for 10 million afflicted by the disease. PEPFAR fosters partnerships between the agency and recipient country, and to other international aid programs as well. PEPFAR, as with other aid programs, has its critics, but overall the program is widely acclaimed as a success.

While there have been limited foreign aid successes, when it fails, consequences can be catastrophic. Despite much pessimism, USAID continued to stress three overall concerns in 2005: conflict resolution and state transformation, development of civil society, and relief and development from a social and an economic perspective. Little had changed from a policy perspective.

Despite acceptance of structural adjustment by developing countries, by the mid-1990s foreign aid funding had plunged. Policy makers were concerned that impoverished people fed by religious fundamentalists and living in failed states would offer sanctuary and a breeding ground for terrorists. As a result, foreign aid surged under Bush, with allocations more than doubling in 10 years.

After September 11, 2001, the United States has increasingly struck back when threatened, refusing to accept international criticism. To Robert Kaplan, "A great philosophical schism has opened within the West, and instead of mutual indifference, mutual antagonism threatens to debilitate both sides of the trans-Atlantic community." The problem became more than a polemic, "The prevailing view focuses not on the dangers, but on the limited options for doing anything about them."

As a unilateralist proponent, Niall Ferguson, put it, "The hypothesis . . . is a step in the direction of political globalization, with the United States shifting from informal to formal empire much as late Victorian Britain once did," arguing that the United States should take up this global burden but fearing that the American Empire "lacks the drive to export its capital, its people and its culture to those backward regions which need them most urgently and which, if they are neglected, will breed the greatest threats to its [and the world's] security." Critics of unilateralism and aggressive multilateralism suggest that this smacked of colonialism.

Foreign policy and aid demonstrated the limits of unilateralism for the United States. There was still an absence of a clear strategy to deal with the some 50 or so weak and fragile states that were breeding spots for terrorism. With a new USAID administrator in early 2006, the fragile-states concept was dropped as concern grew about short-term conflict resolution and humanitarian aid. Fragile-states metaphors may have reminded the political leadership too much of the problems in Iraq and Afghanistan.

Unilateralism already has a retro feel, however, as the United States moves haltingly toward a post-Iraq world. After 2004, as the United States had become bogged down in Iraq, multilateralism began to make a comeback. As noted in late 2004, according to a *Washington Post* article cited by Picard and Buss, "Secretary of State Colin L. Powell [departed] on a weeklong trip to consult with an alphabet soup of European multilateral institutions and confabs, carrying a message that the second-term Bush administration [was] ready to work closely on forging what officials have dubbed 'effective multilateralism.'" Foreign aid became a part of this shift.

In late 2008, the Iraq story remained unfinished. Midterm elections returned the Democrats to power in the House of Representatives and the Senate. The popularity of the president was at an all-time low. The Iraq Study Group released its critical report. The military surge took Iraq from the headlines but it was replaced by an economic crisis, which came to dominate the 2008 presidential election. Issues of political, social, and economic development in Iraq (the gist of foreign assistance policy) were sidetracked.

And yet, despite the criticism, the focus remained on the limits of a military solution. Much more needed to be understood about the consequences for foreign aid. At least for the moment, unilateralism had been debunked. However, to what extent was foreign assistance a robust alternative? And could the United States return to the multilateralism that had allowed it to muddle through the cold war?

By 2008, some observers noted little commitment to involving USAID beneficiaries in policy development. There remained few mechanisms to monitor and evaluate foreign aid in terms of impact rather than output. However, agreement was general about the basic premise of reform of foreign aid and nation-building, that is, that institutions matter.

In late 2005, USAID, held discussions about the future of foreign aid. Rumors abounded that USAID would be restructured, linked to military activities, and folded into the State Department, thus ending its 45 years as an "independent agency." Andrew Natios, the USAID administrator, announced his resignation effective January 2006, allegedly in protest against the decision to incorporate USAID into State.

The new department of development assistance, located in the State Department, would be headed by a deputy secretary for development who would also, at least in the short run, serve as USAID administrator. USAID would be shorn of much of its economic development functions and would be directed away from long-term planning toward short-term goals, such as targeting conflict resolution, coordination with security objectives, and transitional assistance. Rumors portended an end to economic and social development assistance activity.

Some rumors were true. From a policy perspective, the institutional changes reflected the new international environment within the foreign policy and defense communities. Secretary of State Condoleezza Rice, in a speech at State, announced in January 2006 that a gradual process was beginning that would integrate USAID into State. Ultimately, this would bring foreign policy and foreign aid much closer together and link them to defense and security concerns, the so-called three Ds (defense, diplomacy, and development) or whole-of-government approach.

Secretary Rice spoke of transformational development that included reforms in governance, human capacity, and economic structures to build capacity for reconstruction and stabilization and to promote "fundamental changes in governance and institutional capacity, human capacity, and economic structure that enable a country to sustained further economic and social progress."

Close to one-fourth of foreign aid passed through the Defense Department by 2008. While much of traditional foreign aid would continue (at least in the short term), there would be a renewed focus on regime change, governance, and security issues, and, over time, a decline in interest in development. A number of foreign aid components were already operating outside of USAID.

By 2006, central to the debate about international assistance was whether and/or when should USAID as a coordinating mechanism for aid ultimately disappear? For several years, an autonomous HIV/AIDS office (PEPFAR) operated outside of USAID, and the Millennium Challenge Corporation (MCC) was organizationally completely independent from USAID and was designed to transfer major financial resources to a select number of democratic pro-growth and free trade–oriented developing countries. In all, there are 18–20+ foreign aid accounts, some in State and some in USAID, plus assistance programs (including nonmilitary programs) in Defense.

Critics of transformation diplomacy and the transition paradigm abound. Some suggest that developing countries are moving away from authoritarianism toward democracy, an assumption made by donors. But many developing countries remain in a "gray zone" for long periods of time, neither heavily authoritarian nor moving toward democracy. Movement toward democracy has been characterized by an "extremely gradual, incremental process of liberalization."

Ultimately, at issue in Secretary Rice's organizational and policy reforms was whether the changes at USAID marked the death toll for the traditional processes of foreign aid focused on economic development, what one critic calls a kind of "water torture," which was to be replaced by transformational diplomacy. The end of the traditional foreign aid mission implicitly assumes that antipoverty funds have been ineffective and should be terminated, to be replaced by funding that promotes strategic and political interests.

The goal of the Defense Department was to create civil and military transition teams in the field, based on models developed in Afghanistan that would play an increased role in postconflict situations. The model for control in Iraq was the Afghanistan model of regional security teams of military and civilians, with each team consisting of State Department officials, a USAID representative, and one or more military officers. These Provincial Reconstruction Teams (PRTs) were created by U.S. Ambassador Zalman Khalizad, an Afghan American, first in Afghanistan and later in Iraq, when he moved there in 2005.

In Afghanistan and Iraq, regional or PRTs were functioning outside of USAID (a model that seems likely to be replicated). By March 2006, there would be increasing linkages between State and USAID on the one hand and Defense on the other. Nation-building reforms came out of postwar planning for Iraq. According to Bob Woodward, "PRTs involved political and economic experts, aid workers and engineers who would go into the 18 provinces, set up posts, and help in the rebuilding."

In the field, USAID and State have encountered difficulties in staffing the civilian slots in PRTs. There were also financial constraints, particularly in Iraq, which delayed their implementation, and quarrels between State and Defense over control. Staffing of civilians in the newly created African Command (AFRICOM), which has also taken a whole-of-government approach to foreign and security policy, has also been problematic for some.

By the end of the Bush administration, central to the debate about aid was whether or when should USAID ultimately disappear? As of March 2009, President Obama has given little indication of how he will organize the aid function in his government.

As the United States entered the 21st century, foreign aid continued to play an important role in international relations. The "American way," according to General Wesley Clark, should not be "to rely on coercion and hard pressure but on persuasion and shared vision." Borrowing a term from Joseph S. Nye, Jr., at Harvard University, Clark said American power should be marked by "soft power" based on "diplomacy and persuasion."

Domestic influences in donor countries have played a role in the development of foreign assistance policy. Motivations for foreign aid have long been political and economic, as well as ethical and humanitarian in nature. Foreign aid can be successful from a developmental, diplomatic, and humanitarian perspective, but only if one understands the limits of foreign aid and is aware of the contradictions between aid and foreign and security policy.

Two conflicting models of foreign aid continued to compete in the marketplace of ideas: a top-down process of structural reform that emphasized political and economic transformation and bottom-up activities associated with NGOs, which emphasize poverty reduction and social empowerment through small-scale activities targeted at primary communities and directly at the individual poor family. USAID as an organization at various times relied on both. The motivation for foreign aid remains a combination of diplomacy (and security), commercialism, and a modicum of moralism, in part stimulated by an increasing involvement in the foreign aid debate by multiple actors among policy elites.

Ostensibly, the goals of foreign aid in 2009 remain what they were more than half a century ago. These include the reduction of material poverty through economic growth and the delivery of social services; the promotion of good governance through democratically selected, accountable institutions; and the reversal negative of environmental trends through strategies of sustainable development. U.S. priorities have become limited to economic growth efforts largely through MCC, political efforts at democratization, and finally a narrow focus on health issues, particularly HIV/AIDS.

To conclude, if not to caution, we can go back to Ralph Smuckler and Robert Berg's wise words in 1988: "The world of the 1990s, and that of the 21st century, will be substantially different from one in which a worldwide enterprise known as 'foreign aid' was launched forty years ago. New circumstances make the concept of foreign aid less appropriate. To much of Asia and Latin America, the concept of 'cooperation for development' fits better. By development cooperation, we mean that we share responsibilities widely and appropriately." Increasingly this principle should be applied to Africa and the Middle East as well.

It is important to remember that the goals of development policy can get mixed up because of the need of the organization to gain control over its social environment. There is a need, as Carol Lancaster points out, to reshape the organization and management of foreign aid: "USAID [had] one of the most elaborate and time consuming programming systems of any aid agency." Yet, despite or because of this, much of the foreign assistance provided by the United States has been ineffective.

A middle ground remains among critics, according to Chary Chang: "Between these critics and a steadily decreasing number of aid proponents are some analysts who contend that aid should not be terminated, but be concentrated on those countries that 'can be saved,' rather than on those desperately in need of it." An opposite view is that it should be limited to the poorest of the poor, or the "bottom billion" as one observer has put it. A saving model, however, according to Rondinelli, "consisted merely of transferring American administrative technology and 'know how' to less developed countries, much in the same way that industrial and agricultural technology and 'know how' were transferred through the Marshall Plan" (and Point Four).

Donors should provide foreign aid "only when the [recipient] national and local authorities are . . . clearly capable of receiving and using this aid through its own instrumentalities" in a manner that benefits the majority of its citizens. Developed countries also need to see that their self-interests are being met. In addition, civil society and nonprofit or private sector organizations should be able to utilize foreign aid to foster social, economic, or political development.

One constant has defined foreign aid over the last 50 years. Critics from developing countries suggest that the humanitarian and development goals of development policy have been distorted by the use of foreign aid for donor country commercial and political, or increasingly military, purposes. Given government in the 21st century, for foreign aid to succeed it would have to be perceived as in the self-interest of a country's leadership and the societies in both donor and recipient nations. That and a perception of the realities of the need for multilateralism are, if not a blueprint, a start in the debate about assistance in the future.

Further Reading:

Armitage, Richard L., and Joseph S. Nye. *A Smarter, More Secure America.* Washington, D.C.: Commission on Smart Power, Center for Strategic and International Studies, 2007; Buss, Terry F. *Haiti in the Balance: Why Foreign Assistance to Haiti Has Failed and What to Do about It.* Washington, D.C.: Brookings Institution Press, 2008; Chang, Larry. "Foreign Aid and the Fate of Less Developed Countries." Unpublished paper, 1986; Ferguson, Niall. *Empire: The Rise and Demise of the British World Order and the Lesson for Global Power.* New York: Basic Books, 2003; Fitzgerald, Frances. *Fire in the Lake.* Boston: Back Bay Books, 2002; Lancaster, Carol. *Foreign Aid: Diplomacy, Development, Domestic Politics.* Chicago: University of Chicago Press, 2007; Picard, Louis A., and Terry F. Buss. *A Fragile Balance: Re-examining the History of Foreign Aid, Security and Diplomacy.* Sterling, Va.: Kumaran Press, 2009; Picard, Louis A., Robert Groelsema, and Terry F. Buss, eds. *Foreign Aid and Foreign Policy: Lessons for the Next Half-Century.* Armonk, N.Y.: M.E. Sharpe, 2008; Sharp, Walter R. *International Technical Assistance.* Washington, D.C.: Public Administrator Service, 1952; Woodward, Bob. *State of Denial.* New York: Simon and Schuster, 2006.

– Louis A. Picard, Terry Buss, and Robert Groelsema

trade policy

Cordell Hull, President Roosevelt's secretary of state from 1933 to 1945, believed, as did President Woodrow Wilson before him, that trading nations foster international peace through economic exchange. Wilson and Hull stood at the dawn of an internationalist era in U.S. trade and foreign policies, which allowed the United States to embrace and shape global institutions to further its national interests. Nevertheless, trade policy has and will always respond to local concerns in the United States. Article 1, Section 8, of the U.S. Constitution empowers the Congress to "lay and collect" duties or tariffs and "to regulate commerce with foreign nations." The U.S. president is given delegated, rather than constitutional, authority in making trade policy. The United States Trade Representative (USTR), who negotiates trade agreements, is appointed by the president but must be careful to respond to congressional concerns. While Congress has not voted down any trade treaty in the post–World War II era, the passage of many has been difficult and others have not been presented to Congress for fears that they will be struck down. Despite the politics, the fact remains that nearly one in five to six jobs in the United States is directly related to trade, and the country's prosperity and international standing are inextricably linked to its stature as an open and trading nation.

Indeed international trade is as old as ancient history. Despite ups and downs, international trade has continued to grow throughout history. In the year 2007, total world merchandise trade was over $13.5 trillion, accounting for nearly 20 percent of the total economic product in the world. The U.S. share of world exports in 2007 was 8.5 percent and its import share was 14.5 percent.

The table below summarizes world trade and U.S. shares. However, international economic exchange is greater than these numbers, which do not show foreign direct investment or the trade in services. The latter includes trade in intangible products such as banking, tourism, telecommunications, and exchange of professional services. Including trade in services would add another $3.3 trillion to world trade in 2007 and $533 billion to U.S. exports and $336 billion to imports.

This article first provides a brief political economy of trade followed by a historical context for understanding U.S. trade politics before outlining the trade policies and their underlying politics and effects. Economics presents trade purely in terms of an exchange of goods and services and through its effects on the standards of living for people. However, religious, political, moral, and other sociocultural considerations have always been important in elevating or diminishing trade. One way of understanding these cultural considerations is to make explicit how trade is linked to everyday life and the cultural identity of people.

Trade is a natural component of human interactions. The late-18th century political economist Adam Smith's notion of division of labor laid the basis of prosperity through trade inasmuch as he opined that gains from economic exchange accrue to those who specialize in producing things for which they are most suited. These ideas from the late 18th century formed the basis of doctrines of comparative advantage in trade in the 19th century. Similarly, political theorists had begun to argue that as nations exchanged goods, they would be less likely to go to war with each other. This is best captured in French writer Frederick Bestiat's words that if trade does not cross frontiers, armies will.

But the case against trade is also made in economic and cultural terms. The *economic rationale against trade* rests on the thesis that economic specialization can make some nations too dependent on others or can result in an unequal exchange where one benefits at the cost of another. This argument is often cited in U.S. trade concerns with China. Cultural arguments against trade are many; the earliest ones were moral and philosophical. To the Greeks we owe the term *xenophobia*, or fear and dislike of foreigners. Christianity in general decried the profit motive that underlies commerce and trade. It was not until the modern era that such cultural notions regarding trade were questioned, but these arguments continue to be made. Trade wars are often portrayed in negative terms. Take, for example, the overly xenophobic tones in the United States against trade surpluses of East Asian countries. Many in the United States have fretted and fumed over Japanese trade surpluses from the mid-1970s to the mid-1990s, Chinese trade surpluses since the mid-1990s, and more recently over the controversies regarding outsourcing of jobs to India. Fueling these controversies are numbers such as

WORLD TRADE & SHARES OF THE UNITED STATES (2007)

	Exports $ million	Percentage of total	Imports $ million	Percentage of total
World	10,392,567	100	10,652,542	100
Low Income Countries	256,378	2.5	310,841	2.9
Middle Income Countries	2,785,199	26.8	2,551,288	24
High Income	7,351,037	70.7	7,790,420	73.1
United States	904,289	8.7	1,732,706	16.3

the ones shown in the table in which the total exports from the United States are $904 billion and imports are $1,732 billion, resulting in a merchandise trade deficit of $828 billion. This trade deficit is reduced with the U.S. trade surplus on services and its earnings from its foreign enterprises abroad. For example, around 25 percent of the total stock of foreign direct investment in the world comes from U.S. multinational corporations, which generate enormous amounts of earnings for the country. However, foreign direct investment is usually not considered part of international trade.

Historically, countries waver between participating actively in international trade and following more inward-oriented strategies. In the last century, the United States did not actively participate in international trade, despite the so-called rise of free trade in Western Europe, preferring instead to develop manufacturing industry in New England. Alexander Hamilton's 1799 *Report on Manufactures* outlined the intellectual argument to support the "infant industries" in New England. This led to a domestic conflict in the country whereby the Republican Northeast of the country supported protectionism in trade, while the cotton-producing South and corn-producing Midwest supported free trade. This factored into the Civil War (1861–1965) that ensued between the North and South, though the major issue in the war was abolition of slavery. After the Civil War, the fall in navigation costs and improvements in agricultural technologies further made the United States quite competitive in agriculture. Cheap corn exports to Italy, for example, threw hundreds and thousands of Italian farmers out of jobs, accounting, in turn, for the first wave of Italian immigration to the United States. Upon landing on U.S. shores, these farmers confronted hostility from the population for consuming U.S. economic resources.

In the 20th century, the United States strengthened its export profile with manufactured exports, but two world wars, the interwar years, and the Great Depression were not favorable to trade. Nevertheless, it was at this time, unlike the 19th century, that the United States began to express explicitly a preference for trade and also linked it to the cause of international peace. The famous Fourteen Points espoused by President Woodrow Wilson before Congress in 1918 included freedom of the seas and free trade as steps toward international peace. Secretary of State Cordell Hull was a strong advocate of free trade and, in a Wilsonian vein, he believed it to be a force for world peace. Hull also supported moves for the foundation of the United Nations in 1945. A particularly interesting episode in the interwar period was congressional enactment of the Smoot-Hawley protectionist tariff act of 1930, which sought to protect American jobs from import threats with hikes up to an average of 60 percent on imported goods during the Great Depression. Less than fours years later, as economic growth began to pick up, Congress enacted the Reciprocal Trade Act of 1934, authorizing the president to reduce tariffs by 50 percent on any product without congressional approval. The 1934 act also began a tradition by which Congress seeks to find ways to delegate its authority to the president.

At the end of World War II, as the global community went about designing international institutions, the need for creating one in international trade was led by the United States. Twenty-six influential trading nations met at the Havana Summit in 1947. Interestingly, the trade treaty that resulted called for an "International Trade Organization" that would have had wide-ranging powers. President Truman believed Congress would not ratify the ITO charter and pushed instead for ratification of the interim General Agreement on Tariffs and Trade (GATT), which became the de facto international trade institution. It is believed to have been enormously influential in boosting international trade. Between 1947 and 1994, GATT undertook eight rounds of multilateral trade talks among its member states to reduce tariffs or customs barriers. Starting with the Tokyo Round of 1974–78, GATT also undertook reductions in nontariff barriers (NTBs) among nations. These NTBs include nontransparent trade laws, quotas, and other quantitative restrictions, subsidies paid to domestic producers, and discriminatory government procurement practices.

GATT's Uruguay Round of trade talks, lasting eight years between 1986 and 1994, was important both for bringing new issues, such as intellectual property and services, into the international trade agenda and also for strengthening GATT itself with its transformation into the World Trade Organization (WTO), which came into being in 1995. WTO was given some teeth by the endowment of a formal dispute settlement body to adjudicate and settle trade disputes among countries. The new issues pushed by the United States revealed the sources of the country's competitive advantage in the world. This included trade in services, led by U.S. exports of telecommunications, banking, airline, hotels, and professional services. U.S. corporations also pushed for, and received, protections for intellectual property. The latter can be defined as creations of the human mind that are inputs into the manufacture of any product. Intellectual property protections include patents, copyright, industrial design, and trademarks. The primary concerns for the United States were global piracy of its products, ranging from luxury goods (such as fashion) to music and film videos.

The ninth round of multilateral trade talks currently under way since November 2001 is known as the Doha Round, named after the place where it was launched. However, at the time of this writing it has been slow going, chiefly because of factors within the United States and Western Europe. In the United States, Congress has been under tremendous pressure from domestic agriculture and some manufacturing sectors to not allow any more tariff and nontariff reductions. These sectors now believe that the United States would lose jobs and net gains would be little through further liberalization. The global financial crisis since 2007 has further emboldened protectionist quarters in the United States to argue that free and unregulated trade is inimical to economic prosperity. While President Obama has nominally committed himself to furthering multilateral trade negotiations, his first few months in office were taken up with domestic priorities and managing the fallout from the global financial crisis.

Three types of trade measures that are highly influential in U.S. trade politics are discussed next: Fast Track Authority, congressional ratification, and U.S. trade laws counteracting "harmful" export policies of other nations.

The previous discussion noted that since 1934 Congress has found ways to delegate its authority to the president to provide him with maneuvering room to reduce tariffs. The Trade Expansion Act of 1962 similarly provided leeway to the president to reduce tariffs unilaterally before the launch of GATT's so-called Kennedy Round of trade negotiations (1962–67). However, by the end of the Kennedy Round, it was apparent that the president would also need authority to negotiate nontariff trade barriers (NTBs) such as subsidies, quantitative measures such as quotas, and health and safety standards. Before the launch of the Tokyo Round (1974–78), Congress began to delegate Fast Track Authority (FTA) to the president with the Trade Act of 1974. FTA allows the president to sign treaties reducing tariffs and NTBs. The granting and workings of the FTA have allowed the U.S. president to sign and eventually get enacted multilateral trade treaties signed at the Tokyo Round and the Uruguay Round (1986–94), and to launch the Doha Round (2001–present). It has also enabled a host of regional and bilateral measures, such as the North American Free Trade Association or NAFTA ratified in 1994 and the DR-CAFTA with the Dominican Republic and five Central American economies ratified in 2005.

After the president notifies Congress, it can ratify only by an up or down vote on the measures and not amend specific provisions. However, FTA has posed increasing challenges. NAFTA had to be renegotiated when President Clinton came to office to institute labor and environmental provisions. President George H. W. Bush was granted FTA for the launch of the Doha Round by a narrow vote and only after enacting one of the highest hikes in subsidies to U.S. agriculture and steel industry to enable midwestern and northeastern members of Congress to enact the measure. The DR-CAFTA measure passed by one vote in the House. President Bush's FTA expired before the Doha Round negotiations were completed and President Obama lacks FTA to provide any kind of a boost to these stalled trade talks. One of the major issues in the Doha Round has been reluctance among major trading partners (United States, European Union, and India) to reduce agricultural subsidies.

Congressional ratification of trade treaties provides a major check on executive authority in trade, regardless of FTA and the office of the USTR. However, congressional oversight can also stall trade agendas at the behest of the local level pressures that Congress faces. In economic theory, offensive interests (those that gain from trade) are numerous and, therefore, hard to organize for collective action through legislative and executive bodies. On the other hand, defensive interests (those that gain from protection) tend to be less numerous, mobilized to act with fears of job losses, and therefore better organized. Protectionist lobbies such as textiles, sugar, and steel have a great deal of access to the U.S. Congress and it is hard for the USTR to grant any concessions to trading partners in these issues.

A variety of measures in U.S. trade laws also protect importers from perceived or actual harm. Section 201, or the "escape clause," allows temporary relief for industries if they can prove "serious injury" from imports, a recommendation made to the U.S. president from the bipartisan International Trade Commission (ITC). An analogous measure is the safeguards clause in the World Trade Organization. President Obama cited the WTO safeguards clause, rather than an ITC recommendation, recently in slapping 35 percent tariffs over an existing 4 percent on Chinese tires in September 2009, in responding to complaints from trade unions that they had lost 7,000 jobs in this sector as a result of a surge in imports from China from $453 million in 2004 to $1.8 billion in 2008. Historically, instead of facing 201 sanctions, many countries have also negotiated "voluntary export restraints" (VERs) toward U.S. markets.

Perhaps the most frequently employed measure is Section 301, which allows the United States to cite unfair trade practices such as "dumping" below fair price and "countervailing duties" enacted against unfair subsidies and other preferences given by exporting countries. Section 301 authorizes the ITC and the U.S. Department of Commerce to conduct its findings through due process and submit its recommendation within stipulated time periods. U.S. trading partners have complained that Section 301 is politically charged and provides an unfair advantage to U.S. manufacturers through production of data for ITC and access to legislators. Foreign manufacturers now regularly employ trade lawyers in Washington, D.C., to safeguard their interests against 301 complaints, though such remedies are expensive, especially for small developing countries. Mexico recently employed the law firm of Arnold and Porter to address antidumping complaints from U.S. tomato producers and successfully showed that it was not dumping its tomatoes on U.S. soil below a fair market value. In general, trading countries would rather utilize the dispute settlement mechanism at the World Trade Organization (WTO), which affords a more impartial hearing than the U.S. 301 laws.

Three ongoing issues, which arise from the effects of trade, are now discussed explicitly although references were made to them above. These are job losses and creation, old and new issues in trade, and preferential versus multilateral trade agreements.

A perennial fear of trade policy is that it would reduce jobs in the importing country. This is a valid proposition borne out theoretically and empirically. According to trade theory, countries should specialize in producing products from resources in which they are abundant. Import threats thus adversely impact products in which a country is comparatively disadvantaged and the prices of these products are usually high. At present, three-fourths of the U.S. population is employed in the service sector, 23 percent in manufacturing and industry, and 2 percent in agriculture. It would seem that the United States would be competitive in service sector jobs and products. Indeed, U.S. protectionist and trade relief measures have been largely in agriculture and manufacturing. During the 1992 presidential campaign, the fear of agriculture and manufacturing job losses to Mexico became a major concern. It was a central impetus for President Clinton to renegotiate some provision in the NAFTA agreement. In 2007, the U.S. trade deficit of $76 billion, and especially agricultural imports from Mexico—one of the three signatories of NAFTA—became targets of populist anger in the presidential campaign. Presidential candidate Hillary Clinton called NAFTA a mistake. The Economic Policy Institute calculated that, in the 1993–2002 period, NAFTA had helped to create 794,174 jobs and led to the loss of 1,673,435 jobs, with a net loss of 879,281. However, it is not clear if the net job losses would not have taken place as a regular effect of trade, regardless of NAFTA.

More recently, a generally pro-trade economist, Alan Blinder, argued that the United States would lose 40 million service sector jobs as all services became tradable and as countries such as India begin to provide these services with their offshore practices. In response, economist Brad Jensen responded that the United States comparative advantage did not lie in tradable versus nontradable services but in high-tech service jobs in which newly emerging countries cannot compete because of the skills and educational base in the United States. Indeed, the U.S. economy continues to generate surpluses in service sector trade.

The second issue of new versus old follows from the previous point. The U.S. comparative advantage is in services and technology-intensive products. The challenge for the United States has been to get its trading partners to purchase U.S. exports in these products. They counter that as long as the United States protects its agriculture and manufacturing jobs with protectionist trade measures and laws such as Section 301, it does not make sense for them to open their markets for U.S. products. Despite the opposition, the United States was able to get services and intellectual property issues on the Uruguay Round, leading to an agreement in both issue areas. Ironically, it was the United States and not India that wanted a services agreement. Twenty years later, as India becomes a services powerhouse, the United States wants to now protect its jobs in services (see discussion above). Intellectual property is defined as protections given in terms of royalty and other revenue payments to extract rents for creations of the mind. Specifically, many of the biggest exports from the United States—pharmaceuticals, entertainment industry products—gain from intellectual property protections. Again, the developing world opposed these moves but eventually, fearing trade sanctions from the United States, it reluctantly came along.

The final issue discussed is whether the United States best meets its national interest though preferential trade agreements (PTAs) with specific countries or multilateral agreements through the WTO. Especially in the current century, U.S. preference for PTAs has gone up as getting multilateral agreements through the WTO has become increasingly hard. Many of these agreements since the attacks of September 11, 2001, have been politically motivated with countries such as Morocco and Oman. Many of them have been with trading nations that only account for a small fraction of U.S. trade, such as with DR-CAFTA countries, Peru, and Colombia. At one time posited as building blocks toward a multilateral agreement, now PTAs are seen as obstructive toward one and enormously costly and time consuming for what they yield. However, the United States generally does well in bilateral negotiations with small countries in extracting concessions and, therefore, politically PTAs remain more attractive than multilateral talks where the United States must compromise more.

It is worth adding that various other groups have vehemently protested against free trade. Much of the developing world remains ambivalent and divided on free trade. Furthermore, many labor, environment, and human rights groups in the United States and abroad argue that the competitiveness among nations, which forms the basis of trade, also dilutes labor and environment standards as countries "race to the bottom" to reduce costs. The Doha Round was in fact supposed to be the Seattle Round, starting in 1999. However, protests in Seattle from advocacy groups delayed the start of the round.

U.S. politics continue to stall trade talks, yet world trade continues to grow. Between 2000 and 2005, world exports of merchandise grew by 10 percent, far greater than the growth in national incomes. This leads economists to believe that not only will trade not diminish in the future, but also that it will lead to economic growth. International trade rules such as those negotiated through GATT and WTO can facilitate the cause of trade, but negotiating these rules takes political will that has been forthcoming much more slowly in recent years. Ironically, international trade has grown despite the political slowdown, and will likely continue to do so in our increasingly "flat" world. Political pressures are strong, but market forces may be even stronger.

Further Reading:

Bergsten, C. Fred. *The United States and the World Economy: Foreign Economic Policy for the Next Decade.* Washington, D.C.: Peterson Institute, 2005; Blinder, Alan. "Offshoring: The Next Industrial Revolution." *Foreign Affairs* (March–April 2006): 113–128; Destler, I. M. *American Trade Politics*, 4th ed. Washington, D.C.: Institute for International Economics, 2005; Friedman, Thomas L. *The World Is Flat: A Brief History of the Twenty-First Century.* New York: Farrar, Straus and Giroux, 2005; Irwin, Douglas A. *Against the Tide: An Intellectual History of Free Trade.* Princeton, N.J.: Princeton University Press, 1996; Jensen, J. Bradford, and Lori G. Kletzer. "'Fear' and Offshoring: The Scope and Potential Impact of Imports and Exports of Services." Policy Brief, Peterson Institute for International Economics, January 2008. Available online. URL: http://www.iie.com/publications/interstitial.cfm?ResearchID=880. Accessed on August 16, 2010; Schott, Jeffrey J. *Free Trade Agreements: U.S. Strategies and Priorities.* Washington, D.C.: Peterson Institute, 2004; Singh, J. P. *Negotiating the Global Information Economy.* Cambridge: Cambridge University Press, 2008; Wolf, Martin. *Why Globalization Works.* New Haven, Conn.: Yale University Press. 2004; World Trade Organization. *World Trade Report 2007.* Geneva: World Trade Organization, 2007.

–J. P. Singh

23 Elections

campaign financing

Throughout much of American history, campaign financing for federal offices was left relatively unregulated and the public knew very little of candidates' campaign finance activity. Congress passed only a handful of laws relating to fundraising and spending in federal elections. For example, after President Theodore Roosevelt addressed the issue of corporations participating in campaigns in an annual message, Congress passed the Tillman Act in 1907, which banned corporations and national banks from making contributions to federal candidates. Congress also passed a series of laws in 1910 and 1911 imposing a narrow set of disclosure requirements and spending limits for congressional candidates.

After the Teapot Dome scandal in 1925, Congress passed the Federal Corrupt Practices Act, which provided the primary campaign finance framework until the reforms of the 1970s. This act closed some loopholes, revised spending limit amounts, and prohibited offering money in exchange for a vote. But its scope was otherwise narrow and the act provided for no enforcement mechanisms. Congress later added the Hatch Act in 1939, which prohibited federal employees from actively participating in political activity, and amended it the next year to limit fundraising and expenditures of multistate party committees, to limit the amount individuals could contribute to candidates, and to regulate primary elections. In addition, Congress enacted the Taft-Hartley Act, which banned political contributions from labor unions.

The largely unregulated framework for federal election campaign financing changed dramatically with the passage of the 1971 Federal Election Campaign Act (FECA), its amendments in 1974, 1976, and 1979, and the Revenue Act of 1971 and its 1974 amendments. The 1971 Revenue Act established public funding of presidential elections via the one-dollar-check-off box on income tax forms (later raised to three dollars). Presidential candidates could be eligible for public funds if they limited their spending (among certain other requirements). The 1971 FECA was a broad piece of legislation addressing many areas related to campaign financing. The act strengthened the existing bans on contributions by corporations and labor unions, but it also provided the legal basis for such organizations and others as well to form political action committees. The 1971 FECA further tightened campaign financing disclosure requirements and extended them to primary elections. Finally, it placed strict limits on media advertising by campaigns and on how much money individual candidates and their immediate families could contribute to their campaigns.

The break-in at the Democratic Party headquarters at the Watergate complex in 1972 and the ensuing scandal had many effects on the American political system, one of which was a call for greater reform of the government. As a result, Congress amended FECA in 1974 to provide the most comprehensive set of campaign finance laws adopted. The 1974 amendments to the FECA included the following provisions:

1. limits on direct contributions: from individuals, PACs, and party committees;
2. spending limits for political parties' expenditures on behalf of federal candidates: so-called coordinated expenditures;
3. candidate spending limits: for House, Senate, and presidential candidates, which replaced the media expenditure ceilings in the 1971 FECA;
4. limits on independent expenditures: for expenditures by individuals or interest groups made independently of a candidate's campaign to advocate the election or defeat of a federal candidate;
5. the Federal Election Commission: the FEC was created to implement and enforce the federal campaign finance laws;
6. new disclosure and reporting rules: requiring quarterly contributions and spending reports from candidates, with such reports made available publicly; and
7. amending the presidential election public funding system: to allow major party presidential nominees to receive public funds up to a preset spending limit provided they do not accept any additional private money and to establish a voluntary system of public matching funds in presidential primary campaigns.

The Supreme Court in 1976 significantly limited the scope of the 1974 FECA Amendments in *Buckley v. Valeo* (1976) by striking down certain provisions while letting other stand. For example, on the one hand, the Court upheld the limits on direct contributions from individuals, PACs, and political parties, reasoning that such limits were appropriate legislative mechanisms to protect against the reality or appearance of undue influence stemming from large contributions. On the other hand, however, the Court struck down the spending limits for expenditures by House and Senate candidates, the spending limits on independent expenditures, and the contribution limits for candidates and families to their own campaigns. Here, the Court saw the activities that Congress sought to limit as constitutionally protected political speech that could not be involuntarily limited and thus struck down the FECA amendments' restrictions as violating the First Amendment right to free speech. Nevertheless, the Court allowed the spending limits for presidential candidates who accept public funding to stand. Such limits were voluntary and thus different from those that the Court invalidated.

Advocates of campaign finance reform often criticize the Court's reasoning in *Buckley v. Valeo* because it equates money with speech (i.e., limits on campaign expenditures and independent expenditures are unconstitutional limits on free speech). They point to the unequal levels of money that candidates are capable of raising, for example, congressional incumbents who are able to raise more funding than their challengers, and to the unequal resources that individuals and groups control. Thus, so the argument goes, the *Buckley* decision implies an unequal right to free speech—the candidate who can raise more from the wealthiest individuals and groups receives "more speech" than most congressional challengers and the small individual contributor.

As a result of the *Buckley* decision, Congress amended FECA in 1976 to comply with the Court's rulings. In 1979, Congress further modified FECA to address unforeseen problems that arose in implementing the act and its previous amendments. For example, Congress streamlined candidates' reporting requirements, which were seen as too burdensome and costly. More significantly, Congress addressed concerns raised by party organizations that the spending limits imposed on them forced the parties to choose between election-related media advertising on candidates and traditional grass roots party-building activities such as voter registration and get-out-the-vote drives. In the 1979 FECA amendments, Congress exempted parties from spending limits for certain party-building activities, thus allowing such organizations to spend unlimited amount of federal (i.e., "hard") money on such pursuits.

Hard money must be raised from regulated sources such as PACs and individuals, and expenditures of hard money must be reported to the Federal Election Commission. Soft money, by contrast, consists of funds that parties collected in unlimited amounts for party-building activities, often from sources such as corporations and labor unions that are otherwise prohibited from participating directly in the campaign finance system. The advent of soft money did not come about from the 1979 FECA amendments, as is often believed to be the case, but instead from two FEC rulings interpreting those amendments. The dramatic increase since 1979 in the amount of soft money flowing into the political parties and the expenditures of soft money has been the subject of great concern for campaign finance reformers and one of the core components of reform efforts in Congress.

Such efforts were led in the Senate by Senators John McCain (R-AZ) and Russell Feingold (D-WI) and in the House of Representatives by Christopher Shays (R-CT) and Marty Meehan (D-MA). Their attempts to pass reform legislation focusing on banning soft money and regulating certain independent expenditures were met with mixed results. In the 105th and 106th Congresses, reformers were able to pass legislation in the House, only to meet defeat in the Senate. Finally, in the 107th Congress, both chambers of Congress approved campaign finance reform legislation, and President George W. Bush signed the bill (the Bipartisan Campaign Reform Act, or BCRA) into law. This legislation, among other provisions, bans soft money at the national level, prohibits state parties from spending soft money on federal candidates, increases the individual contribution limit to individual candidates from a fixed $1,000 to $2,000 indexed to inflation, and requires disclosure of expenditures by individuals and groups who spend at least $10,000 in a calendar year on electioneering communications.

BCRA immediately faced judicial challenge and, as a result of a special provision included in the legislation, received expedited appeal to the Supreme Court. In its decision in *McConnell v. Federal Election Commission* (2003), the Supreme Court upheld BCRA's primary provisions regarding issue advocacy and soft money, although it did strike down certain other provisions of the legislation. Despite calls over the years, including by Supreme Court justices, to overturn the *Buckley* decision, the Court reaffirmed *Buckley*. Further, the Court potentially expanded *Buckley*'s scope; although *Buckley* validated the goal of preventing corruption or the appearance of corruption as a constitutionally sufficient basis for certain campaign finance regulations, *McConnell* was expressly based on the premise of rooting out the appearance of corruption. BCRA, however, was the subject of a subsequent Supreme Court case, *Federal Election Commission v. Wisconsin Right to Life* (2007). In that case, the Court struck down a provision of BCRA related to funds spent by corporations on certain electioneering advertisements, but only on a basis as that provision applied to the advertisements in question rather than the provision being facially unconstitutional itself.

Throughout the over 30 years that the federal campaign financing system established by FECA (along with its amendments, and related regulations and judicial decisions) has been in effect, it has had a number of desirable and undesirable effects. As campaign finance expert Anthony Corrado contends:

> The new campaign finance system [created by FECA and its amendments] represented a major advancement over the patchwork of regulations it replaced. The disclosure and reporting requirements dramatically improved public access to financial information and regulators' ability to enforce the law. The contribution ceilings eliminated the large gifts that had tainted the process in 1972. Public financing quickly gained widespread acceptance among the candidates, and small contributions became the staple of presidential campaign financing.

Without limits on candidate expenditures, however, the cost of congressional campaigns has continued to rise, with all congressional candidates combined now regularly spending $1 billion or more every two years during each congressional election cycle. Moreover, many presidential candidates have forgone public financing so as to not be limited by spending limitations that accompany accepting public funds. This trend started with independently wealthy candidates Ross Perot and Steve Forbes spending their own money. When George W. Bush demonstrated during the 2000 and 2004 primaries that a candidate could raise significantly more money outside the public finance system, receiving public funding started to become a sign that a campaign was not viable if it could sustain itself on its own. In 2008, Barack Obama became the first major-party candidate to not use public funding in the general election; instead of receiving $84 million in public funding, Obama brought in over 3.5 times that amount during the general election period after September 1, 2008. As a result, the ever-increasing focus on fundraising—both at the presidential and at the congressional levels—has led many to believe that candidates for federal office are perhaps even more beholden to moneyed interests than in the unregulated pre-FECA days or that, at a minimum, the federal system of campaign finance is more ripe for scandal to arise.

FECA, BCRA, and their associated regulations apply to federal-level elections (i.e., president and Congress), but leaves open each state to decide for itself what campaign finance rules and regulations will govern the state-level elections for governor, other statewide elected offices, and the state legislature. States are sometimes referred to as laboratories where potentially up to 50 different approaches—or experiments—could be developed and tested for addressing public policy, and this certainly holds true for the issue of campaign finance.

An overview of regulations at the state level would show a wide range of approaches and regulatory frameworks in dealing with campaign financing for state elections, from minimal regulations to full public funding for qualified candidates in certain elections, and with a wide array of mechanisms utilized, such as contribution limits, bans on political activity by corporations and/or unions, and disclosure requirements. States are not the only laboratories either, as numerous cities have experimented with such mechanisms as full (Albuquerque, NM) or partial (New York City; New Haven, CT; Miami-Dade County, FL; Austin, TX; Boulder, CO; Tucson, AZ; and six cities in California, including Los Angeles, San Francisco, and Oakland) public financing, voluntary spending limits (Boulder, CO), and conflict-of-interest laws related to campaign contributions and the granting of government contracts (Westminister, CO, and Belmont, CA). Campaign finance laws also can be connected with other state-level reform efforts such as term limits, such as in Michigan. Further, a variety of social, demographic, and cultural factors also can influence the approach a state may take toward campaign finance regulations: factors such as population and geography (large state or small state; one or two dominant population centers or multiple), and a state's political culture and political philosophy regarding state regulation.

Given the variety of factors influencing state-level campaign finance regulations, one cannot easily summarize what constitutes the system of campaign financing in the states. Political scientist David Schultz, though, has identified four key lessons that can be drawn from the various states' experiences in campaign finance regulation. First, despite the wide array of campaign finance systems, the cost of campaigning for state-level elections has increased much like at the national level. As a result, the greater need for money puts more emphasis on each state developing a functional system of campaign finance regulation that works.

The second lesson that can be drawn from the states' experiences is that soft money has become a significant campaign finance issue. As was the case at the federal level, the amount of soft money received by state parties, and the variety of sources from where it was donated, increased throughout the 1990s and the 2000 election. Although BCRA banned soft money at the federal level, the legislation permits state, district, and local parties to continue to raise and spend soft money in accordance with state law so long as such funds are not spent on federal election campaign activity (except in very limited circumstances where a federal campaign may receive the incidental benefit of a voter identification, get-out-the-vote, or generic campaign activity). One way in which BCRA has impacted state parties, however, is that it cut off the flow of soft-money funds from the national political parties to the states. As a result, the state party organizations have had to find ways to replace the large amount of funds that the national parties had previously distributed prior to BCRA. According to one study by the National Institute on Money in State Politics, although state parties post-BCRA have not, in the aggregate, replaced all the funds that the national parties contributed prior to BCRA, they have become adept at raising soft money from other sources, including corporations, labor unions, individuals, and out-of-state donors who are no longer able to make large contributions to the national parties.

A third lesson, comparable to the second, is that independent expenditures and issue ads became prevalent at the state level just as they were at the national level before BCRA. Interestingly, though, is that the impact of independent expenditures and issue ads has been felt less in states that have no or lax limits on individual contributions to campaigns. This finding highlights the interconnectedness among the various components of a campaign financing system, where choices made with respect to one aspect of the system (e.g., whether to have contribution limits) affect what other issues may arise (e.g., whether issue ads become problematic).

All this ties into the fourth lesson that the pattern of campaign contributions and expenditures exhibited in any state is a function of both the regulatory framework within that state as well as the prominent local issues. As Schultz concludes, "The moral from state experiences can be used to confirm an old political adage that regulating money in politics is like a water balloon: if one squeezes one end of the balloon, the water will shift elsewhere. Regulations that seek to limit money in politics do not seem to prevent contributors from giving; they simply shift their donations to another venue."

This conclusion implies that no one solution will solve all problems arising out of the need for money in campaigns. But it also highlights the need for states to be able to experiment to determine what overall system works best for them. It also indicates that policy makers likely need to make choices by targeting what they feel are the most egregious problems (much in the way that BCRA's sponsors focused on soft money and issue ads at the federal level) while acknowledging that other, perhaps lesser, problems may persist.

One simple step that many states have taken is to increase the quality of disclosure of campaign finance information, in terms of the information both reported to the states and made available by the states to the public. The increased use of electronic filing has facilitated this trend. It has allowed the states to obtain more information on a timelier basis than traditional paper filing. In turn, states are able to incorporate the electronic filings they receive into easy-to-use searchable databases readily available via the Internet. According to a study performed by the Campaign Disclosure Project, as of December 2008, a majority of states require candidates to disclose the occupation and employer of their contributors; require timely reporting of last-minute contributions; require independent expenditures to be reported; require statewide candidates to file disclosure reports electronically (while nearly half—24—require both statewide and legislative candidates to file electronically); and to post-campaign finance data and provide searchable databases of contributions and expenditures on the Internet. Regardless of what regulatory framework a state employs, improved disclosure is seen as a core element in helping to prevent corruption or the appearance of corruption in campaign financing.

Although the states may be their own laboratories to determine the best campaign finance system for their own elections, they are still subject to the judicial framework governing campaign finance as set out in *Buckley* and its progeny cases at the Supreme Court level. Because the *Buckley* decision was based largely on the First Amendment, any state regulation on campaign finance cannot impermissibly restrict an individual's freedom of speech. Although the Court has applied the *Buckley* framework to state regulations, the results have not always produced clear directions for the states.

For example, in *Nixon v. Shrink Missouri Government PAC* (2000), the Court upheld Missouri's limitations on contributions to candidates for state office ($1,075). The *Shrink Missouri* court, in applying *Buckley*, asked "whether the contribution limitation was so radical in effect as to render political association ineffective, drive the sound of a candidate's voice below the level of notice, and render contributions pointless," and found the answer to be that the contribution limit did not exceed this outer boundary of permissible restrictions. Yet in *Randall v. Sorrell* (2006), when faced with a similar question regarding Vermont's contribution limits of $200 per candidate, the Court determined that this amount was too low to satisfy the above test. Further, whereas the *Shrink Missouri* court expressly rejected taking into account the effects of inflation between the *Buckley* decision and the present case, in *Randall* inflationary adjustments were used to demonstrate the impermissibility of Vermont's regulations.

Perhaps the best summary of the interaction between the application of the *Buckley* judicial framework and the promotion of allowing states to be laboratories for developing effective campaign finance policy came from prominent appellate court Judge Richard Posner of the Seventh Circuit of Appeals. In his opinion in *Majors v. Abell* (2004), Posner wrote, "Reluctant, without clearer guidance from the [Supreme] Court, to interfere with state experimentation in the baffling and conflicted field of campaign finance without guidance from authoritative precedent, we hold that the Indiana statute [in question in the case] is constitutional." So long as such experimentation is permitted and encouraged, states likely will continue to provide new and creative ways for addressing the ever-changing nature of campaign financing.

Further Reading:

Corrado, Anthony, Daniel R. Ortiz, Thomas E. Mann, and Trevor Potter, eds. *The New Campaign Finance Sourcebook*. Washington, D.C.: Brookings Institution Press, 2005; Farrar-Myers, Victoria A., and Diana Dwyre. *Limits and Loopholes: The Quest for Money, Free Speech, and Fair Elections*. Washington, D.C.: CQ Press, 2008; Schultz, David, ed. *Money, Politics, and Campaign Finance Reform Law in the States*. Durham, N.C.: Carolina Academic Press, 2002.

– *Victoria Farrar-Myers*

direct democracy

American politicians and lay citizens alike often boast of the glories of "our great American democracy," and indeed, American voters have directly decided issues from tax burdens to abortion to same-sex marriage in a host of statewide and local level elections over the years. But as many scholars point out, because the U.S. national government is more properly known as a "representative democracy" or "republic," we must look to the state and local levels of government for opportunities for "direct democracy." Here, opportunities for more direct citizen involvement in governance have been available to voters in some jurisdictions since before the Constitution's ratification and have been expanded in a number of states since the Progressive era at approximately the turn of the 20th century. This brief article will provide an overview of the origins of "direct democracy" and the political movements that helped established direct democracy options in the United States today, most notably the initiative, the referendum, and the recall. The essay will also discuss the resurgence of the initiative process in particular since the 1970s and will address several ongoing political controversies surrounding the tools of direct citizen policy making.

Direct democracy, understood as direct citizen discussions, development, and enactment of policy, dates back to at least ancient Greece, where it provided a cornerstone of governance for the city-state of Athens. Scholar Thomas Cronin also traces strains of direct citizen governance within the Roman Republic and later in Europe, most notably among the Swiss cantons, by at least the 12th century. The mechanisms of direct democracy utilized in Switzerland are typically credited as the guide for much of what developed in the U.S. state and local jurisdictions around the turn of the 20th century.

Elements of direct citizen governance were present in what is now the United States well before the American Revolution. The traditional New England town meeting, by which citizens could debate and determine for themselves certain local policies, could be found in some of the colonies' communities in the 17th century. While the U.S. Constitution's authors were clearly aware of the concept of direct democracy, the framers of the Constitution actively avoided direct democracy in their creation of the 1787 Constitution. While some Revolutionary leaders, most notably Thomas Jefferson, evidenced greater faith in the ability of "the people" to engage in at least some measures of self-governance, more conservative leaders, such as John Adams and Alexander Hamilton, were staunch opponents of more direct citizen input. Ultimately, Cronin credits the leaders of the founding era with seeking "not to establish a democracy but to establish a republic, which in Enlightenment thought had many definitions. But generally it embodied three principles: initial consent of the governed, rule by law, and representation of the people."

The U.S. Constitution of 1787 specifically bypassed direct citizen input on policy at the federal level. U.S. policies were to be determined by the people's representatives, with even most of those representatives to be chosen on the citizens' behalf rather than by the citizens themselves. For example, while members of the U.S. House of Representatives were originally to be chosen by eligible voters within the designated House districts (i.e., free white men, typically property holders within their respective states), even voters were excluded from the selection of other federal decision makers. While U.S. senators have been chosen directly by voters in the respective states since ratification of the Seventeenth Amendment in 1913, American voters are still separated from the selection of their president by the Electoral College and from the selection of federal judges. Further, federal voters today still have no direct mechanism by which to weigh in on specific policy debates.

Instead, we must look to the state and local levels to investigate opportunities for direct democracy. Direct democracy at the state and local levels in the United States captured a foothold near the turn of the 20th century, with American interest in greater direct democracy drawing heavily from the Swiss example. Most early support in the United States came from the Socialist Party and other labor organizations, and support later grew within the Populist movement, which also sought to give greater power to everyday citizens at the expense of business interests and concentrated wealth. South Dakota broke new ground in 1898 by incorporating options for the "initiative" and "referendum" processes on a statewide level, and a few more western states followed suit shortly thereafter. However, as Thomas Cronin argues, direct democracy proposals typically gained only limited traction while their support was drawn primarily from these more politically radical figures and organizations. Instead, he adds, it was ultimately support from leaders of the Progressive movement in taking on parts of the Populist agenda early in the 20th century which led to the enactment of direct democracy reforms in many states.

As noted in 2009 by the Initiative and Referendum Institute, a university-affiliated research center devoted to studying and promoting mechanisms of direct democracy, the use of direct democracy at the statewide level dropped precipitously from the 1940s through the 1960s. However, the late 1970s witnessed a resurgence that has continued to the present day. The writing, circulation, and passage of California's "Proposition 13" initiative in 1978 proved critical to this resurgence. Proposition 13 was promoted as a citizen-generated measure to curb escalating property taxes throughout California and to limit future tax measures in the state legislature. The passage of this initiative proved stunning both in its effect on tax policies across the country and in its effect on popular support and utilization of the initiative process. The Initiative and Referendum Institute has asserted that utilization of the initiative process has grown dramatically since the passage of Proposition 13. The initiative continues to be regarded as the most popular and significant of the contemporary direct democracy measures available today.

The major mechanisms of direct democracy available at the state and local levels today are the initiative, the referendum, and the recall. The preeminent form of direct democracy available today is the initiative. The initiative process is a mechanism by which citizens themselves write and vote on matters of local or state law. Through this process, citizens themselves can draft proposals and circulate their measures for signatures among registered voters; if enough signatures can be obtained, the measures are presented directly to the voters. Depending on the procedures laid out in respective state constitutions or local charters, an initiative can be passed into law as the equivalent to a policy passed by a legislative body (known as a "statutory initiative"), or an initiative measure can itself in certain instances even amend the state's very constitution (known as a "constitutional initiative"). The Initiative and Referendum Institute puts the current number of states with the statewide initiative option available to their citizens at 24, with voters in 18 of these states having the initiative available as an option for instituting constitutional amendments. Another form of initiative available in some jurisdictions is the "indirect initiative," whereby an initiative measure, upon collection of signatures, is forwarded for possible action by the state legislature before the voters have an opportunity to cast ballots on it. If the legislature does not act upon the proposal, the voting public then has an opportunity to enact the measure absent the legislature's support.

Unlike an initiative, a referendum asks voters to respond directly to a measure already passed by a state's legislature or a local governing body. According to the Initiative and Referendum Institute, all states currently allow for the option of statewide "legislative referendum," by which the legislature submits a measure for direct voter consideration. These are used in many states for some funding measures and/or approving amendments to state constitutions. In some states, local legislative referendums are common and can be essential in providing financing for local schools or other local bodies. Alternatively, according again to the Initiative and Referendum Institute, voters in 24 states can invalidate legislatively passed measures that run contrary to popular will via a "popular referendum" (also sometimes known as a "petition referendum"). Here, if enough valid signatures can be secured in opposition to a legislatively passed measure, the measure is put directly before the voters, and the legislature's decision can be thwarted by the public vote.

A final mechanism of today's direct democracy is the recall, which is available to voters in 15 states and in numerous cities across the nation. By this mechanism, voters can remove an officeholder at any time during his/her term in office with no provocation or wrongdoing, assuming simply that a sufficient number of signatures can be gathered to trigger a special recall election and that the official fails to win sufficient public support in the recall election. Perhaps the most famous example was California's 2003 recall of Democratic governor Gray Davis, when Davis was removed in an election that put Republican and Hollywood icon Arnold Schwarzenegger into office as his replacement. While extremely rare at the statewide level, recall campaigns have been used more frequently against local officials. Cronin traces the recall within the United States to at least 1780 in Massachusetts, and he also asserts that a form of recall was debated at Philadelphia's constitutional convention in 1787, though it was ultimately omitted from the final document.

Each state or local government that incorporates direct democracy provides its own rules and procedures for utilizing these mechanisms. One common restriction on initiatives is the so-called single subject rule, which requires that any single ballot measure can address only one issue. Another requirement common to all initiative states is that initiative ballot measures can be placed on the ballot only upon collection of sufficient numbers of signatures of registered voters to demonstrate a substantial public interest in the particular measure, though requirements on numbers of signatures vary. Many states require that some state officials, such as the secretary of state and/or attorney general, play roles in the process, such as verification of signatures for validly registered voters or some review of proposed ballot measures before they go before the voters. However, M. Dane Waters insists that only a few states allow elected officials to exert significant influence over proposed ballot measures. Waters provided some examples of such exceptions when he notes that "in Arkansas, the Attorney General has authority to reject a proposal if it utilizes misleading terminology. In Utah, the Attorney General can reject an initiative if it is patently unconstitutional, nonsensical, or if the proposed law could not become law if passed . . . and in Florida, the State Supreme Court—during its mandatory review—can stop an initiative if it is unconstitutional or violates the state's very strict single subject requirement for initiatives." On the other hand, it is commonly understood that California, a state that makes heavy use of the initiative process, is somewhat unusual in that its initiative process does not allow the state's legislature *any* independent mechanism by which to alter policies passed via an initiative.

How significant a role does direct democracy play in state-level policy making and politics in the United States? While asserting that most proposals never reach the ballot for lack of signatures, Waters estimates that voters were presented with an average of 42 statewide initiative ballot measures per election cycle from 1904 to 2000, with the average for 1991–2000 reaching 73 statewide initiative ballot measures per election cycle. Use of the initiative varies significantly among the states that allow for it, with the Initiative and Referendum Institute ranking the top five states for all initiative use, in order, as Oregon, California, Colorado, North Dakota, and Arizona. As of February 2009, the institute estimated that the successful passage rate of the 2,305 statewide ballot measures placed before the voters from 1904 through the 2008 election was approximately 41 percent.

While the initiative process remains popular among Americans and has been utilized by activists and interests of all ideological persuasions, many early debates over the pros and cons of direct democracy continue to play out even today. For example, early critics of direct democracy expressed concerns about whether voters would be sufficiently equipped to make direct policy decisions and to sift through information (including potentially manipulated messages) to make reasonable policy decisions for themselves. And even today, how well equipped are voters to make policy decisions on such intricate matters as tax policy and budgeting? While Cronin ultimately concedes that voters' information can often be incomplete, his reading of available literature leads him to credit voters with being able to make reasonable assessments of the measures before them.

Some critics of direct democracy processes, including prominent law professor Derrick Bell, have focused criticisms particularly on the damage that direct democracy procedures can inflict on the interests and even the basic rights of minority populations. Recent examples of direct democracy measures that have hurt minorities range from attacks on affirmative action in various states to a slew of measures beginning in the 1990s to deny same-sex couples access to marriage. However, while Cronin acknowledges instances in which popularly enacted measures have hurt the interests of minorities, he ultimately insists that the voters' record of injuring minorities via direct democracy policy opportunities has hardly been worse than that of the state legislatures. In short, Cronin and other supporters of direct democracy maintain that its mechanisms themselves should not receive disproportionate blame for American policies attacking minorities.

To what extent does the opportunity for citizens to engage policy decisions affect the voters and the political system? One criticism of the initiative process is that it can simply exhaust voters and can thus drag down voter participation; however, Professors Daniel A. Smith and Caroline J. Tolbert find just the opposite. Utilizing sophisticated statistical analyses that controlled for a host of possible alternative explanations of election participation from 1970 to 2002, Smith and Tolbert conclude that states placing more policy measures directly before the voters actually witnessed greater voter participation, particularly in "off-year" (nonpresidential) elections.

An additional controversy surrounding the use of direct democracy involves the role of money in ballot measure campaigns. Based on his reading of available literature, Cronin labels money as "other things being equal, the single most important factor determining direct legislation outcomes." Multiple efforts at restricting the influence of money in political campaigns have been rejected by the U.S. Supreme Court as violations of the First Amendment. For example, in such cases as *First National*

Bank of Boston et al. v. Bellotti (1978) and *Citizens Against Rent Control v. Berkeley* (1981), the U.S. Supreme Court used the First Amendment to invalidate various limits on campaign spending, including those related to certain ballot measure campaigns. Money is often a prerequisite to a successful ballot measure campaign, as money to pay workers to gather signatures of qualified voters can be a critical factor in getting measures qualified for ballots in the first place. In 1988, in *Meyer v. Grant*, the U.S. Supreme Court unanimously invalidated on First Amendment grounds several states' policies that banned paying individuals to collect signatures for ballot measures.

Ballot measure campaigns can often result in litigation, before or after passage of a controversial measure. Even initiative measures purporting to alter their states' constitutions can be found constitutionally invalid on a host of grounds, depending upon each state's respective law. Kenneth P. Miller states the matter rather bluntly: "Citizen lawmakers can bypass legislatures and other institutions of representative government to enact 'the will of the people,' but they cannot bypass the courts. Courts are the one institutional check on the people's initiative power." While measures can be challenged in some jurisdictions before going to the voters, legal challenges to initiative measures often follow after a measure's passage. Miller's research has shown that a majority of initiatives passed in several states making heavy use of the initiative have been the targets of judicial challenges; approximately half of those challenges ultimately resulted in judicial nullification of at least some portion of the challenged provisions. One example Miller provides of a nationally popular initiative drive that was derailed by the judiciary was congressional term limits: The U.S. Supreme Court negated the democratically enacted term limit measures of multiple states in *U.S. Term Limits, Inc. v. Thornton* (1995).

Authors often refer to mechanisms of direct democracy as a "safety valve," a voice for frustrated voters displeased by the operations of, and policy results produced by, elected officials. Direct democracy, particularly the initiative mechanism, remains a popular outlet for voters in a number of the states where it is available to them. However, as noted above, controversy remains regarding many aspects of the implementation of direct democracy, including how well equipped voters are to decide policy matters directly, how fair direct democracy mechanisms are to minority populations, and the role of money in direct democracy campaigns. Additionally, it must always be remembered that even successful initiative campaigns can end in a loss if a measure is invalidated in court.

Although expansion of direct democracy to the national level is unlikely, particularly given the difficulty of amending the U.S. Constitution, direct democracy remains a vital, if controversial, force in state and local politics and is likely to remain so into the foreseeable future.

Further Reading:

Bell, Derrick A., Jr. "The Referendum: Democracy's Barrier to Racial Equality." *Washington Law Review* 54 (1978): 1–29; Cronin, Thomas E. *Direct Democracy: The Politics of Initiative, Referendum, and Recall.* Cambridge, Mass.: Harvard University Press, 1989; Initiative and Referendum Institute. Available online. URL: http://www.iandrinstitute.org/. Accessed June 13, 2009; Miller, Kenneth P. "The Courts and the Initiative Process." In *Initiative and Referendum Almanac*, edited by M. Dane Waters. Durham, N.C.: Carolina Academic Press, 2003; Smith, Daniel A., and Caroline J. Tolbert. *Educated by Initiative: The Effects of Direct Democracy on Citizens and Political Organizations in the American States.* Ann Arbor: University of Michigan Press, 2004; Waters, M. Dane. *Initiative and Referendum Almanac.* Durham, N.C.: Carolina Academic Press, 2003.

– *Staci Beavers*

redistricting

John Engler, the former governor of Michigan, once claimed that redistricting is one of the purest actions a legislative body can take. Academicians and political leaders alike, however, have regularly debated the ideal way by to redistrict national and state legislatures. Rather than being the pure process that Governor Engler envisioned, redistricting has led to repeated court battles waged on such traditional democratic values as one person, one vote and minority rights. The following article includes an examination into the problems and politics associated with the redistricting process in the United States, the policies and decisions that have already been made, the effects of said decisions, and ultimately the ongoing controversies and key questions to consider related to the redistricting process.

When an individual attempts to remodel a house, the ultimate success of the project is oftentimes tied to his or her understanding of the original structure; likewise, before we are able to effectively navigate the muddy waters of redistricting, we must return to the original premise of districting national and state legislatures beginning with the nation's founders. As decided in the Great Compromise in 1787, each state would have two senators (elected via the state legislatures until the passage of the Seventeenth amendment) and then the seats for the House of Representatives would be allocated according to the population of each state.

Per the United States Constitution (Article I, Section 2, clause 3): "Representatives and direct Taxes shall be apportioned among the several States which may be included within this Union, according to their respective Numbers, which shall be determined by adding to the whole Number of free Persons, including those bound to Service for a Term of Years, and excluding Indians not taxed, three fifths of all other Persons." Further, Article I states that "the Number of Representatives shall not exceed one for every thirty Thousand, but each State shall have at Least one Representative." Using the founders' writings, the initial House of Representatives contained 59 seats in 1789. Each state today is apportioned a number of seats that approximately corresponds to the state's percentage of the entire U.S. population (minus the District of Columbia and other federal territories). The Constitution does not specify how members of the House are to be elected once they are apportioned to a state. Within this historical framework, the process of districting—and redistricting—begins.

Redistricting is the redrawing of district lines in states that have more than one member of the House of Representatives. In states that do not reach the population deemed necessary for multiple representatives, the entire state serves as the congressional district (which applied to Alaska, Delaware, Montana, North Dakota, South Dakota, Vermont, and Wyoming after the 2000 decennial census). The actual process by which states redistrict varies by state. In many states, the state legislature shapes the process, while in others the task falls to independent commissions that are empowered by the state legislatures or some hybrid combination of the legislature and commissions. The process of redistricting can have major political stakes given that it can shape who has, gets, and keeps power within a state.

Before concerning ourselves with how states choose to determine the boundaries of districts, we first must more fully examine how it is determined how many seats each state shall possess. Per the constitutional mandate above, 50 seats are automatically apportioned given the requirement that each state have at least one member in the House. The provision that seats are to be apportioned among the several states according to their numbers ultimately leaves all seats above the required one per state ambiguous in nature. Throughout its history, the United States has utilized five different mathematical appropriation methods—currently operating with the Method of Equal Proportions. Operating under the principle that proportional differences in the number of persons per representative should be kept to a minimum and near equal, the mathematical method creates a priority scale for each seat after the first 50 are automatically assigned, which shows the state most deserving of the next allocatable seat. Deservedness is determined by which state needs the seat most to allow for near equality in representation for all citizens of the United States.

Every 10 years when the census is taken, congressional seats are reapportioned based on population gains and losses. Public Law 62-5 in 1911 set the number of members of the House of Representatives at 433, while also allowing for the addition of two seats when New Mexico and Arizona were formally admitted to the Union in 1912; the Reapportionment Act of 1929 formally capped the number of seats in the House of Representatives at 435. Despite leading to more constituents per representative (in violation of the ideal view of the founders of 30,000 constituents per representative), Congress determined that 435 was the maximum efficient working number for the national legislature. This cap can be reviewed and adjusted by any Congress that deems it necessary to make an adjustment. Currently, the Voting Rights Act of 2007 attempts to add two new voting districts (one for the District of Columbia and one for Utah). Recent trends have demonstrated states in the Sun Belt (in the South and Southwest) have been gaining seats as citizens have migrated to these regions, ultimately costing Rust Belt states (the Northeast and Midwest) congressional seats. The average House district in 2000 contained 646,952 voters.

Politicians, citizens, or scholars have not always viewed the apportionment process positively. Charges of malapportionment have been levied after most census tabulations occur. Prior to the 1960s, many districts were uneven with regard to population—as high as 8 to 1 in some states. Yet ultimately, many of the issues have arisen due to the devolution of districting powers to state governments, who are able to apportion districts within their borders as they see fit. Gerrymandering has become another political buzzword emerging from the redistricting process. Originating in the *Boston Gazette* in 1812 in response to the actions of Massachusetts governor Elbridge Gerry when creating a salamander-shaped district within the state to benefit the Democratic Party, the term signifies the decision to draw district lines to directly benefit one group or another. Gerrymandering is often noticed due to the oddly shaped districts that emerge from the process.

Gerrymandering occurs through one of two techniques: cracking or packing. When cracking a district, an area of partisan strength is split into other districts to dilute the buildup of power and influence. This method denies a group a sufficiently large voting bloc in any district. Packing, on the other hand, involves combining as many of one party's voters as possible into one district, attempting to ensure electoral success. While there are two main techniques to gerrymander, three different types of gerrymandering tend to occur. Pro-incumbent gerrymandering occurs when a state legislature is closely divided and unable to give an advantage to one party or another. In this case, the members instead move to protect their own self-interest by reinforcing the present power structure. Second, with partisan gerrymandering we find redistricting efforts that attempt to maximize the possible seats that the party in power could win. This may involve splitting a traditionally conservative district into two weak conservative districts, for example. Lastly, racial gerrymandering occurs when district lines are drawn to favor or disadvantage a racial or ethnic group. Again, this could involve either packing all members of a group into one district or spreading them out so thinly that they may not receive representation.

Given that redistricting ultimately occurs as a result of reapportionment, which is based on the decennial census, it should come as no surprise that political actors have debated how to conduct the census. While Census Bureau statisticians are largely recognized as being nonpartisan, many political actors (particularly of the nonpresidential party) note that they are controlled by the extremely political Commerce Department. Per the Constitution, the census is supposed to be an "actual enumeration." Yet it is impossible to actually count every member of such a diverse and large population. While accountants use methodologies that they believe do the best job possible at properly counting the population, after the 1990 count the bureau found through a recount that their initial estimations had missed nearly 5 million residents (2.1 percent of the entire population). More troubling, however, was that a majority of these individuals were minorities from low-income areas and that the Republican secretary of commerce ultimately decided to use the original census numbers—effectively determining that 2.1 percent of the population did not exist. Sampling techniques became a major point of contention during the 2000 census as Democrats called for a method that would allow statisticians to better estimate hard-to-count populations, such as the homeless, less wealthy, immigrants, and transients—all who tend to be Democratic voters.

"The Gerry-Mander," a cartoon by Gilbert Stuart, refers to the event that led to the coining of the term *gerrymander*. The district depicted in the cartoon was created by the Massachusetts legislature to favor incumbent Democratic-Republican Party candidate Governor Elbridge Gerry over his Federalist opponent in 1812. *(Library of Congress)*

Ultimately, the census estimated that it missed 6.4 million individuals and double counted 3.1 million. As in previous attempts, blacks and Latinos were most likely to be undercounted while non-Latino whites were most likely to be overcounted. Ultimately, in *Department of Commerce v. U.S. House of Representatives* (1999), the Supreme Court found that statistical estimates could not be utilized, even if they allowed for a more accurate count, given that the Constitution clearly calls for an actual enumeration. Thus, if Democrats wish to see their voting blocs more accurately counted to allow for potentially more representatives in states where they constitute a higher percentage of the population, they will need to help statisticians determine ways to better achieve higher count rates in these areas.

Moving from concerns on how the way the population is counted plays a role in districting, we turn toward the history of policy and court decisions related to the process of reapportionment. Most policies that have been enacted related to apportionment focus on attempting to assure that malapportionment does not occur or is corrected. Congress began regulating House districts as early as 1842, when it added a requirement that representatives should come from districts composed of contiguous territory and that each district should elect one representative only. The 1872 Reapportionment Act added even finer language, claiming that districts should be as close to equal in regards to population as possible. These two clauses were eventually combined in 1901 when the Apportionment Act stated that districts were to be made of contiguous and compact territory and should consist of an equal number of citizens. This clause was last included in the Reapportionment Act of 1911.

All of these previous laws, however, would lapse and not be included in the Reapportionment Act of 1929, which has become the permanent reapportionment bill thus far in America's history. To place the 1929 act in context, we must revert to 1920 when Republicans retook the House from Democrats. After gaining power, Republicans violated the Constitution and refused to reapportion the House on the standards of equally populous, contiguous, and compact districts given that many of the newly elected representatives were aware that they would have been redistricted out of their current seats. Motivated purely by self-interest, the Reapportionment Act of 1929 ultimately did away with the provision for districts—allowing the parties and the representatives (in this case Republicans) to elect representatives at large or to draw districts in politically beneficial shapes and sizes. At this point in history, political parties in control of the state legislatures were able to draw districting lines at will.

The Supreme Court, in *Wood v. Broom* (1932), acknowledged that the provisions last stated in the 1911 act had immediately expired in 1912, given that the provisions of each apportionment act were valid only for the apportionment for which they were written. After 1929, not until 1941, when Congress enacted a law for redistricting contingencies if states failed to redistrict in a timely manner after a census, did the United States have any national standards for redistricting. Aside from the *Wood* decision, the Supreme Court avoided an active role in districting and apportionment; but in 1962, in *Baker v. Carr*, the Warren Court opted to overturn *Colegrove v. Green* (1946) and declare reapportionment issues to be judicial questions, not merely political, in a wrenching case that involved one justice abstaining based on his inability to decide and two other justices altering their decisions at the last minute.

While many questioned the Court for potentially violating the separation of powers and becoming entwined with legislative power, cases began to appear on the docket only two years after the *Baker* decision. At this point in history, districts of grossly unequal sizes and populations often existed side by side. Since the 1929 Reapportionment Act, states had been free to do as they pleased, allowing inequality to flourish. Take for example the state of Vermont, where one district had 36 people while another had over 35,000 (a ratio of roughly 1,000 to 1). In 1964, the Court ruled on its first apportionment case, finding in *Reynolds v. Sims* that state districting schemes that fell short of assuring Fourteenth Amendment protections of equality within state legislatures were unconstitutional as they were unrepublican in bicameral states, thereby violating the Article IV, Section 4, constitutional requirement that states have republican governments. From this point forward, districts would need to be roughly equal in population. That same year, the Warren court in *Wesberry v. Sanders* extended the principle of one person, one vote to the U.S. House by highlighting the intentions of Article I, Section 2, of the Constitution. Hugo Black, writing for the majority, reminded states that as nearly as practical, one person's vote in a congressional election should be worth as much as someone else's, regardless of the state in which they live. While asking for equality in district populations was easily done, achieving equality has proven to be much more difficult. Consider the 1983 Supreme Court case *Karcher v. Dagger*, in which the Court struck down a New Jersey plan in which districts were not permitted to vary in size by more than one-seventh of 1 percent. William Brennan, in the majority opinion, noted that allowing for any variance in district size would ultimately go against the Constitution's idea of equal representation.

To fully understand the policy influence the Court has had since its decision in 1962 to enter the quandary, we need to more fully examine the three types of gerrymandering mentioned earlier. The most common form of gerrymandering is partisan in nature. This variety can occur only when one party controls the process within a state. While the goal is to pad the numbers for a particular party statewide, scholars Bruce Cain and David Butler have found the process to be an inexact science. Ultimately, the net effect nationwide tends to be a wash as different parties control redistricting in different states at different times. The Supreme Court has not been overly active with regard to partisan gerrymandering—in many cases viewing the right to partisan gerrymander as a spoil of electoral victory. In *Davis v. Bandemer* (1986), however, the Supreme Court did determine that gerrymandering was a judiciable issue when the gerrymandering was substantial, long-standing, and harmful to the political minority. To the present day the Court is yet to hear a case based on the problem of measuring partisan inequities, however, and in *Hunt v. Cromartie* (1999), it went as far as to allow states to engage in constitutional political gerrymandering. By 2004, in *Vieth v. Jubelirer*, the Court claimed that partisan gerrymandering claims were nonjusticiable because there was no discernable and manageable standard for adjudicating such cases. Ultimately, representatives are allowed to choose their constituents.

Another area of gerrymandering that the courts have largely left untouched revolves around pro-incumbent gerrymandering—often referred to as sweetheart gerrymandering. In these circumstances lines are redrawn to protect incumbent legislators. Typically this occurs in split-party states where partisan gerrymandering is out of the question so legislators instead opt to protect their own. With gains and losses split fairly evenly among both parties, there is considerably less resistance to this method of gerrymandering. In the aftermath of reapportionment in 2000, large states such as California, Ohio, Illinois, New York, and Texas all protected the present legislature through pro-incumbent gerrymandering. Again, the Supreme Court has stayed away from intervening with pro-incumbent gerrymandering.

While the Court has steered away from the first two forms of gerrymandering, it has been extremely active in attempting to assure equality for all ethnic and racial groups by curbing the practice of racial gerrymandering. Throughout history, the Deep South has drawn district lines to ensure that African Americans could not get a majority in any district and consequently could not send a representative to Congress. Not till long after the passage of the Fifteenth Amendment did the Supreme Court step in to assure equality for African Americans, however. In the *Gomillion v. Lightfoot* (1960) case, the Court found that the 28-sided boundary of Tuskegee designed to exclude African Americans was unconstitutional and in violation of the Fifteenth Amendment. With this decision, the Supreme Court had inserted its foot into a political battle that continues to this day.

The Voting Rights Act of 1965—and its subsequent amendments—has done much to protect minority voting rights. The original act barred districting plans that intentionally or inadvertently dilute the voting power of racial minorities—in short preventing the cracking of districts. Since the 1982 amendments were added, states have been encouraged to pack districts to ensure the election of minority officeholders through so-called majority-minority districts. In 1986, the Court determined (through its decision in *Thornburg v. Gingles)* a set of questions to help ascertain whether a minority group's ability to select representation had been violated. The Court would look at whether the group was large enough, compact enough, and cohesive enough to select a representative if they were put into one district and if evidence of racially polarized voting by the majority existed when determining if a redistricting plan was constitutional. The Voting Rights Act went so far as to require particular states to submit their redistricting plans to Bush's Department of Justice in 1990 or a federal district court to assure compliance given their particularly discriminatory past. Ultimately, many of the districts drawn to assure majority-minority outcomes became the most blatant cases of intentionally manipulated, discontinuous boundaries recorded in American electoral history.

Throughout the 1990s, the Supreme Court has heard numerous cases and ultimately presented two main guidelines for states to follow when navigating through the redistricting process with race in mind. First, the Court found that race cannot be the predominant factor in districting, unless a compelling reason can be shown for this decision. As a suspect classification, race-based districting is subject to strict scrutiny when used to treat citizens differently. As such, laws that relate to the subject matter must fulfill a compelling state purpose, be narrowly tailored to fulfill that purpose, and be the least restrictive means to fulfill that purpose. In *Shaw v. Reno* (1993), the Court ruled that nonminority citizens had legal standing to sue a state over racial gerrymandering. The *Shaw* case dealt with the 1st and 12th districts in North Carolina, which white citizens claimed were so blatantly gerrymandered that it violated their own right to equal protection by diluting voters. Likewise, in *Miller v. Johnson* (1995), the Court rejected two districts in Georgia due to race being the predominant factor. To challenge districts on racial grounds, the majority of the Court found that the plaintiff must show that race was the predominant factor in placing individuals either in or out of a district and that race-neutral means of redistricting, such as contiguity and compactness, were ignored. In response to the *Miller* decision, at least 10 districts were found to be unconstitutional and sent states back to the drawing boards.

While saying that race could not be the sole factor in districting, the Court did leave open the possibility that race could be used as one of many factors. In *Hunt v. Cromartie* (1999), the last redistricting case of the 20th century, the majority found that where black voters tend to be Democrats, it is extremely difficult to separate race from politics, consequently allowing race to be a legitimate concern with redistricting. This decision was upheld by *Easley v. Cromartie* (2001), which more directly stated that race often correlates with political behavior.

As an ending reminder, it is important to remember that every state handles districting in its own manner. While districting state legislatures, many of the same topics—particularly gerrymandering—arise and need to be handled at the state level. Given the scope of this article, however, it proves impractical to discuss the varying methods that states utilize when districting their state legislatures.

When looking at the effects of redistricting, numerous topics immediately emerge as powerful consequences of the procedures employed to draw districts. First, we must note that partisan gerrymandering in particular has reduced competition, increased the incumbency advantage, and reduced voter turnout in many areas across the country. Ultimately, the individuals who are playing the game make the rules while they are still playing. Second, we have witnessed prolonged court battles as a direct result of the districting decisions of states. As the previous discussion demonstrated, the Supreme Court decided in 1962 that districting was a justiciable issue and, ever since, it has been an active player in the legislative task of redistricting. At times the Court has been extremely active in its approaches, while preferring at other times to be more permissive and hands-off. It appears that many Courts have borrowed Potter Stewart's take on pornographic materials and claim to simply know bad districts when they see them. Given the rash of 5-4 decisions, it should be clear that redistricting will not be leaving the Court's docket anytime soon. Lastly, we have seen redistricting in recent years benefiting the Republican Party. Migration patterns have led to a loss of seats for traditional Democratic areas (the Northeast and Upper Midwest) while the Republican-leaning South and Southwest have seen an increase through apportionment. Through Republican control in the past decade we have also witnessed the stacking of minorities in safe districts as Republicans have attempted to assure victories for themselves in outlying areas. Racial redistricting itself helped contribute to the GOP domination of the South that emerged throughout the 1990s. With such effects present, numerous questions exist as we move forward toward the 2010 decennial census and the assuredly contentious reapportionment and redistricting that will follow.

First, we must look at what the main goal of redistricting should be: providing equality or maintaining political and geographic boundaries. Gaining equality in number has led to the violation of political divisions, city and county lines. The districts that ultimately emerge are merely artificial creations that lack, as Alan Ehrenhalt explains, any sense of geographical community. Equality in number leads to less descriptive representation. What needs to be determined is what we view as more important to assure proper, equal representation. Is my voice heard louder and counted any more or less if all districts are equal in size or if the boundaries of my geographical community are respected and maintained?

Second, we again have to determine the best way to handle minority rights. Are we better off assuring minority voting rights through majority-minority districts or through influence districts? While majority-minority districts assure representation for minorities, it has led in many ways to a paradox of representation, according to David Lublin. There are more minority lawmakers, but at the same time it makes it so that surrounding legislators have fewer minorities in their districts, making them less likely to consider minority needs and wants when considering policies. Ultimately, majority-minority districts increase descriptive representation but evaporate minority leverage over legislative outcomes. An alternative that has been suggested involves the creation of influence districts, which would consist of substantial minority members, but not quite a majority. By doing so, minorities would have a higher chance of seeing a minority elected, but they would not sacrifice their say in numerous other districts to simply gain one representative. Once again, the Courts will need to ascertain opinions on determining how minority voting rights and representation can best be served as cases continue to appear on the docket.

Two changes occurred in the latter half of the first decade of the 21st century that may change the lay of the land for redistricting in the future. First, in 2006, the Supreme Court held in *League of United Latin American Citizens v. Perry* that states were free to mid-decade redistrict as often as they please. As a consequence, the door is now open for parties to begin redistricting procedures as soon as they take control of a legislative chamber. In reality, states could find themselves being redistricted in a partisan fashion up to five times a year depending on electoral outcomes. Whether states would ever choose to redistrict more regularly than once a decade is a question that is yet to be answered. Second, the District of Columbia Voting Rights Act of 2007 passed the House and only failed in the Senate due to Republicans utilizing a filibuster despite Democrats having 57 votes in favor of the bill. With Democrats in control of Congress and President Obama stating he would sign the bill, it is possible that the size of the House will move from 435 to 437. The District of Columbia would receive a voting seat in the House while a second seat would go to Utah (which is the next state in need according to the Method of Equal Proportions).

The larger question remains as to whether state legislatures should follow states such as Iowa and pass the process of redistricting off to independent commissions. The rationale is that issues arise when players create the rules to a game that they are already playing. Independent commissions have been shown to create more contiguous, equal districts that respect traditional political, city, and demographic geographies than state legislatures. The end result seems to be better representation for citizens, which is the ultimate goal of the apportionment and districting process.

As we move closer to the 2010 census and the apportionment and districting battles that will ensue, we find ourselves in an unfamiliar territory from past years. Democrats control Washington, D.C., and more states than many believed they would a few years ago at this time. The Supreme Court has confirmed the right of states to redistrict mid-decade as much as they please. And a bill that would alter the size of the House is likely to pass and be signed when it sees the floor of Congress again. With the economy continuing to slow and unemployment rates rising in many areas, the potential exists for significant population shifts prior to the completion of the census—leading to changes in state populations along with opening up additional questions of methodology. Ultimately, what is about to occur is best described by Justice Ginsburg writing for the minority in *Miller*: "Legislative districting is a highly political business . . . . Apportionment schemes, by their very nature, assemble people in groups." As students of political science, it will be an exciting time as census figures are released and states begin the process of assigning representation.

Further Reading:

Baker, Gordon E. *The Reapportionment Revolution: Representation, Political Power, and the Supreme Court.* New York: Random House, 1966; Brunell, Thomas. *Redistricting and Representation: Why Competitive Elections Are Bad for America.* New York: Routledge, 2008; Cain, Bruce E. "Assessing the Partisan Effects of Redistricting." *American Political Science Review* 79 (1985): 320–333; Cain, Bruce E., and David Butler. "Redistricting Myths Are at Odds with Evidence." *Public Affairs Report* 32 (1991): 6; Clayon, Dewey M. *African Americans and the Politics of Congressional Redistricting.* New York: Routledge, 1999; Davidson, Roger H., and Walter J. Oleszek. *Congress and Its Members* 12th ed. Washington, D.C.: CQ Press, 2009; Ehrenhalt, Alan. *The Lost City: The Forgotten Virtues of Community in America.* New York: Basic Books, 1996; Lublin, David. *The Paradox of Representation: Racial Gerrymandering and Minority Interests in Congress.* Princeton, N.J.: Princeton University Press, 1997; Rush, Mark E. *Does Redistricting Make a Difference? Partisan Representation and Electoral Behavior.* Lanham, Md.: Lexington Books, 2000; Thernstrom, Abigail M. *Whose Votes Count? Affirmative Action and Minority Voting Rights.* Cambridge, Mass.: Harvard University Press, 1987; Winburn, Jonathan. *The Realities of Redistricting: Following the Rules and Limiting Gerrymandering in State Legislative Redistricting.* Lanham, Md.: Lexington Books, 2008.

– William J. Miller

term limits

Term limits are the restrictions placed on the length of service for elected officials such as governors, presidents, and legislators. Term limits exist at the local, state, and federal levels of government. Currently, the president of the United States is the only federal government office holder to be limited to two terms in office due to the Twenty-second Amendment to the U.S. Constitution. Fifteen states currently have term limits on their state legislators, and 37 states have term limit restrictions on their governors and other state constitutional offices. Cities such as New York, San Francisco, Los Angeles, Philadelphia, Dallas, San Antonio, and Fort Collins have term limitations on their mayors and/or their city councils. Chicago is the only major city in the United States without term limits on its mayor or city council.

While the idea of term limits for our elected representatives has existed since the Articles of Confederation—our first government in 1781—efforts to implement term limits at the state and federal levels of government gained real momentum during a term limits movement in the late

1980s. According to the termlimits.org Web site, "Over the last twenty years, term limits has become one of the most widely debated issues across the nation. Americans have become sick of their local politicians who are seeking nothing more than to hold a seat for twenty years, until they have a shot at running for Congress." The impetus for term limits can be summed up by Mark P. Petracca, a political scientist, who stated, "When a legislative body has a near-perfect reelection rate and no significant turnover, elections lose their meaning as a device to assure political accountability, discouraging citizen participation as a further consequence."

To more fully understand term limits as a public policy, this article will examine the history of term limits, investigate the problems that led to the term limit movement, evaluate the term limits imposed by the states and federal government on elected officials, and finally, measure the effects of term limits at the state level and the implications for the future of term limits in the U.S. federal government.

Limiting our elected officials to a specified time in office is an idea that has been around since before the Articles of Confederation. Ancient and classical political writers such as Aristotle, Cicero, John Locke, John Milton, and others argued the principle of rotation in office is an important attribute of democratic republican government. Mark Petracca notes that the "rotation in office" concept was defined in Aristotelian terms as reciprocity "of ruling and being ruled by turn." Many of the American colonial governments, such as Pennsylvania, Maryland, and Virginia, had constitutions calling for rotation in office. The Maryland Declaration of Rights in 1776, for example, declared, "That a long continuance in the first executive departments of power or trust, is dangerous to liberty; a rotation, therefore in those departments, is one of the best securities of permanent freedom." Rotation in office was heralded by many classical thinkers because it was thought to check the abuse of power by returning the elected officials back to their private lives, provide opportunities for others to participate in elective office, and foster a steady relationship and trust between the rulers and the ruled. The American political tradition of term limits was recognized at the national level for the first time by the Articles of Confederation. Article V of the Articles of Confederation limited the state delegates to the Continental Congress to terms not to exceed three years. However, due to the myriad of other, more daunting problems facing the United States under the Articles of Confederation, this term limit requirement was rarely enforced on the state delegations.

Term limits were omitted from the U.S. Constitution, despite the deeply held rotation-in-office principle and the desire for a citizen legislature. Scholars have provided several reasons for not including term limits in the Constitution. First, the founders realized that imposing more requirements on the states could threaten the support for the new Constitution. A second reason given is because the Constitution was meant to be a short document, and including term limits would insert too much detail into the founding document. Third, the founders believed that a sufficient number of checks already existed in the Constitution, such as the separation of powers and federalism, to prevent any one branch of government from becoming too powerful. Fourth, the terms of office were already short—two years for members of the House and six years for senators. The founders believed it would be too much of an inconvenience for legislators to continually run for reelection so they would stay in office for a short period of time. Finally, voluntary rotation among the elected representatives in Congress was an accepted norm at the time that did not require a formal constitutional directive. Petracca points to George Washington's First Inaugural Address as evidence of the idea that representatives and senators should serve short stints in Congress to avoid corruption. President Washington declared, "Nor can the members of Congress exempt themselves from unjust and tyrannical acts which they may impose upon others. For in a short time they will mingle with the mass of people. Their interests must therefore be the same, and their feelings in sympathy with those of their constituents." Furthermore, Kernell suggests that serving in Congress was merely a stepping stone to other political offices, which is why there was significant turnover in the House and Senate during the first 100 years or so of American history. So, members of Congress would serve for a brief time before either moving on to the Senate or to run for governor. Following the constitutional convention in 1787, the most repeated criticism from the Anti-Federalists, those who opposed the ratification of the Constitution, was the fear of perpetual reelection of representatives in the new government. The Federalists, those who supported approval of the U.S. Constitution, argued against term limits in Federalist Paper no. 62, holding that those serving in the legislature and executive offices should stay in office long enough to achieve the best government.

Most scholars agree that, with some exceptions, voluntary rotation in office was the norm in American politics throughout most of the 18th and 19th centuries. However, various factors fueled the effort to limit the amount of time legislators can hold office during the latter half of the 20th century. The initiative behind limiting the president's time in office resulted from largely political forces. In reaction to Franklin Roosevelt's unprecedented election to four terms of office, Congress proposed, and the states ratified, the Twenty-second Amendment to the Constitution in 1951, limiting the president to a maximum of 10 years or two four-year terms of service. Several scholars argue that the Twenty-second Amendment was passed largely due to the violation of the traditional two-term voluntary limit for presidents set by George Washington. The second reason Congress acted to propose the formal limit on the president's terms of office was due to political reasons. Franklin Delano Roosevelt, a Democrat, defeated the Republican candidate for president in four straight elections. A *Washington Post* article described the Twenty-second Amendment as "the subject of a sharp controversy for the 80th Congress." Congress considered two proposals in 1947 to limit the president's tenure in office. The first proposed amendment would have limited the president to one six-year term, and the second proposal, the one that would later become the Twenty-second Amendment, limited the president to two four-year terms in office.

Efforts to limit the service of members of Congress began in earnest in the 1940s, although the idea would not receive any traction until the late 1980s and early 1990s. A few members of Congress felt very strongly about term limits for Congress between the 1940s and 1980s. Each congressman consistently reintroduced measures throughout their long tenure of office to limit the service for those in Congress. Representative Samuel Washington ("Wat") Arnold, a Republican representing Missouri's First Congressional District, introduced a constitutional amendment in 1944 that would have limited members of the House, Senate, and the president to six years in office. When asked about running for a fourth term of office in 1947, essentially violating his own proposed amendment, Washington said that his idea of limiting congressmen to three terms, "was all a mistake . . . it takes three terms before a congressman gets enough seniority to be of much benefit to his district." Thomas B. Curtis, also a Republican representative from Missouri, introduced a proposal nine times during his 18-year career as a member of Congress that would limit members of Congress to 12 consecutive years. Curtis's proposal called for a "two-year sabbatical" during which the member of Congress would sit out a term and then would become reeligible to run again. When he introduced his bill in 1965 he noted with dismay that term limits were essential to ease "the detrimental aspects of the seniority system" and give representatives a chance to "mix" with the people they represent. Finally, Representative Bill Frenzel, a Minnesota Republican who served in Congress from 1971 to 1991, introduced an 18-year term limit in each of the 10 Congresses he served. Toward the end of his lawmaking career in Washington, D.C., Frenzel noted that the press and his constituents never really paid attention to his term limit proposal, nor held him accountable to it.

In the late 1970s, following the Watergate scandal, efforts to implement term limits on Congress slowly began to emerge. Senators Dennis DeConcini (D-AZ) and John C. Danforth (R-MO) and Representatives John W. Jenrette (D-SC) and

Robert W. Kasten (R-WI) became the directors of the Foundation for the Study of Presidential and Congressional Terms. The foundation represented a grassroots effort to bring public pressure on Congress to enact term limits. DeConcini and his congressional colleagues became frustrated with trying to debate term limits in Congress so they appealed to the public through a series of public forums that included debates and essay contests. The foundation sought to put term limits as questions to the voters on ballots in eight to 10 states in 1978, but it failed to do so. By 1981, the foundation was no longer in operation. The board of directors for the foundation in 1980 included former Carter administration officials Griffin Bell and Cyrus Vance, along with former representative Thomas B. Curtis. Senator Dennis DeConcini held a hearing on term limits before his subcommittee on the Constitution in 1978. In his opening statement, DeConcini explained the need for term limits to provide the American people with new alternatives and stated that the current system provided for an increased "rigidity in government." The hearing produced no concrete results. Since the passage of the Twenty-second Amendment in 1951, no real efforts to limit the terms of federal lawmakers were made until the early 1990s with the birth of the state term limit movement in 1990 and the Republican "Contract with America" in 1995.

The heart of the term limit movement lies with the American people and the states, which is where we now turn. John David Rausch, Jr., explains the term limits movement in three phases—emergence, nationalization, and maintenance. The term limits movement began in 1990 when voters in Oklahoma, California, and Colorado approved ballot initiatives to limit the terms in office of their legislators. Colorado's term limit law limited its federal lawmakers as well as members of the state legislature. A Tulsa, Oklahoma, oilman by the name of Lloyd Noble was largely responsible for financing the term limit initiative that appeared on the ballot in Oklahoma in September 1990. Noble is quoted in a September 18, 1990, *New York Times* article explaining his support for term limits. "All our legislators talk about cutting waste, but they don't cut any waste that gets them elected. It's politicians perpetuating themselves at taxpayer expense." Fourteen additional states, including California, Michigan, Florida, Ohio, and Washington, approved term limits initiatives, primarily aimed at restricting the service of their congressional delegations in the November 1992 elections. By 1994, according to Rausch, nine states that did not previously limit congressional terms had term limit questions on their ballots. In a span of five years, more than half of the states in the Union had either voted on or approved term limits for their state and federal legislators. U.S. Term Limits (USTL), formed in 1991 by New York businessman Howard Rich, was the organization primarily responsible for the nationalization of the term limits movement. Rich managed the Libertarian Party's presidential campaign in 1980, successfully putting the Ed Clark/David Koch ticket on the ballot in every state. He worked for the Pete du Pont campaign in 1988 and was a cofounder of the Cato Institute. USTL controlled the assets of other pro–term limits groups such as Citizens for Congressional Reform (CCR) and Americans for Limited Terms (ALT). During the nationalization phase of the term limits movement, U.S. Term limits provided funding and manpower to help state activists circulate petitions and mobilize the public for term limits. USTL would get involved, however, only after the local organization would experience difficulty with circulating petitions in its state. In 1995, USTL was a party to the U.S. Supreme Court case *U.S. Term Limits v. Thornton,* in which the Court struck down an Arkansas state constitutional limitation on the terms of federal lawmakers, banning term limits for all members of Congress. As of 2000, U.S. Term Limits is the only interest group fighting for term limits. U.S. Term Limits maintains an Internet Web site (www.termlimits.org) with information about the movement and news releases on current term limit legislation around the country, in which it provides the public with an opportunity to sign a petition supporting term limits for members of Congress. The state organizations pushing for term limits no longer exist. Following the *U.S.*

Term Limits v. Thornton decision in 1995, the term limit movement largely came to a standstill.

The last major effort to limit federal lawmakers came about after the 1994 congressional elections. The Republican Party swept into majority status in 1994 bringing with them their "Contract With America." The contract constituted a list of reforms Congress promised to pass within the first 100 days of the 104th Congress. The Republican-led Congress failed to gather the necessary two-thirds majority vote to propose one of two potential constitutional amendments. Both proposed amendments limited Senators to no more than two terms of office. One proposal limited service in the House of Representatives to six terms and the other limited the membership in the House to three terms. Generally speaking, there were no organized groups working against term limits or USTL. Rather, the "opponents" of the USTL are mostly state and federal legislators who refuse to consider term limits legislation, turn back term limits laws that have been passed by initiative, or ask the courts to invalidate these statutes.

Why term limits? Making government accountable to the people is the centerpiece of the term limit movement. The classic debate within the term limits controversy is between making the government accountable to the people versus allowing people to have the freedom of choice and keeping long-serving legislators with policy expertise in office. Efforts to repeal the Twenty-second Amendment in the mid-1980s appeared soon after the reelection of President Ronald Reagan, one of the most popular presidents in the past 50 years. President Reagan publicly stated that while he was not interested in running for a third term, he thought that future presidents should have that option if the American people demand it. At least one proposed amendment to repeal the Twenty-second Amendment has been put forth in every Congress, starting with the 99th Congress in 1986 through the present Congress. Arthur M. Schlesinger, Jr., the former speech writer for President John F. Kennedy, argued that the Twenty-second Amendment is "undemocratic" and makes presidents less accountable to the people. "Nothing makes a president more attentive to popular needs and concerns than the desire for re-election." Several public opinion polls during the 1980s showed that more than one-third of Americans supported repealing the Twenty-second Amendment because of the popularity of President Reagan. While the debate rages on whether the Twenty-second Amendment was a good idea, Americans have several reasons to consider term limits as a viable solution to perceived problems with our current government.

Supporters of term limits argue they are necessary to make elections competitive again and to "restore a citizen legislature." Reelection rates for members of Congress remain staggeringly high. In 1990, for example, 96 percent of the incumbents seeking reelection were returned to Congress. With the exception of 1992, incumbents in the U.S. House of Representatives have been reelected at a greater than 90 percent rate. With the exception of 1992, U.S. senators have been reelected by a 90 percent margin or higher through the 1990s. Since 2000, however, the Senate has seen a reelection rate hovering around 80 percent. There is very little turnover in Congress. Paul Jacob points out that "incumbents have all of the advantages." More specifically, members of Congress have access to a war chest of donations from interest groups, free mail with the franking privilege, a television studio, congressional staff for casework, and favorable campaign finance laws. They can use all of these attributes of office to withstand challenges to their seat, perpetuating their professional career as a member of Congress. Even though the voting public has a choice on election day, challengers are at a severe disadvantage with regard to name recognition and financial resources. Term limits will allow for more electoral competition, inviting more qualified candidates to run for office who may otherwise be intimidated from running.

Scandals, such as the House Bank scandal of 1992 or the Jack Abramoff lobbying scandal of 2006, have led many to believe that members of Congress must be limited in their time on Capitol Hill. Term limits would cure the problem of corruption and scandal in politics by limiting the amount of time representatives can serve in office, proponents of term limits argue. Term limits could potentially break the cycle of organized interests and the appearance of overwhelming influence of political action committees over members of the legislature. Members of Congress will not be in politics to push their own professional interests. Instead, term-limited legislators would have the best interests of the people at heart, rather than their own careers.

Fourth, the American people have always supported term limits. On November 4, 1992, the *Washington Post* reported that term limits won in every state where such proposals were on the ballot and in virtually every one of the hundreds of cities, counties, and other jurisdictions where citizens had a chance to vote on the issue. Term limits are still popular with the American people.

The opponents of term limits make strong arguments against term limits. One of the concerns voiced by opponents to term limits is that power will shift to the legislative staff, unelected bureaucrats, and the executive branch because these officials would maintain an information advantage over the newer members of the legislature. Another objection to term limits is that the institution would lose members with policy expertise. As soon as members become familiar with the legislature it will be time for them to retire. Most importantly, term limits, according to opponents, are undemocratic in nature and run counter to the American political tradition.

The Twenty-second Amendment was proposed by a Republican Congress following four straight defeats of the Republican candidate by Franklin Roosevelt, but it also passed the requisite three-fourths of the state legislatures to become law. Interestingly, the government decisions regarding term limits have mostly come from the U.S. Supreme Court and other state legislatures. The people in many states passed a law or constitutional amendment through initiative proposals, and the state supreme court has invalidated these statutes. In many ways, the courts have acted in a countermajoritarian fashion with regard to term limits.

The two most important Supreme Court cases dealing with legislative term limits, *Powell v. McCormack* (1969) and *United States Term Limits v. Thornton* (1995), concern restrictions placed on candidates for the U.S. House and U.S. Senate by the states themselves, or by the people of the state through referendum or initiative. In *Powell v. McCormack* (1969), Adam Clayton Powell was duly elected a U.S. representative by the residents in the 18th Congressional District of New York in November 1966. Prior to Powell taking the oath of office in January 1967, the House of Representatives passed a resolution prohibiting Powell from being seated as a member of the new Congress because of his behavior as the chair of the Committee on Education and Labor. An investigation concluded that Powell had deceived the committee by using illegal travel money and making salary payments to his wife, at Powell's direction. By an 8-1 vote, the Supreme Court ruled that Congress cannot add to or change the Constitution's qualifications to hold federal office. Earl Warren wrote, "Therefore, we hold that, since Adam Clayton Powell, Jr., was duly elected by the voters of the 18th Congressional District of New York and was not ineligible to serve under any provision of the Constitution, the House was without power to exclude him from its membership." The important element of the Constitution in this case is found under Article 1, Section 2, Clause 2 of the Constitution, which states, "No person shall be a Representative who shall not have attained the Age of Twenty-five years and been seven Years a Citizen of the United States, and who shall not, when elected, be an inhabitant of That State in which he shall be chosen." In other words, the Court decided that Congress may not add to the minimum qualifications to serve in the House of Representatives. Article 1, Section 3, Clause 3 of the Constitution establishes the requirements for senators to be at least 30 years old and have been a citizen of the United States for nine years. *Powell* constitutes a critical decision for term limits because it set the stage for the Court to overturn term limits enacted by 17 states for federal officeholders in *United States Term Limits v. Thornton* (1995). The most recent federal decision regarding term limits concerned an actual challenge to term limits enacted by several states during the early 1990s.

In 1995, the Supreme Court heard arguments in the case of *United States Term Limits v. Thornton*. On November 3, 1992, the people of Arkansas adopted a term limit amendment, Amendment 73, to their state constitution. The amendment placed term limits on both members of the state government and on members of the state's congressional delegation. More specifically, it limited members of the state House of Representatives to no more than three two-year terms and members of the State Senate to no more than four two-year terms. Regarding the congressional delegation, the amendment stated that "(a) Any person having been elected to three or more terms as a member of the United States House of Representatives from Arkansas shall not be certified as a candidate and shall not be eligible to have his/her name placed on the ballot for election to the United States House of Representatives from Arkansas. (b) Any person having been elected to two or more terms as a member of the United States Senate from Arkansas shall not be certified as a candidate and shall not be eligible to have his/her name placed on the ballot for election to the United States Senate from Arkansas." The Court relied on the *Powell* holding that Congress may not add qualifications to the already set constitutional qualifications to hold public office, declaring that states also may not add qualifications for office. Furthermore, Justice Stevens, in the majority opinion, argued that electing members of Congress constituted a new right granted to the states by the Constitution. States cannot place additional qualifications on candidates for federal office because, as Stevens reasoned, "Any state power to set the qualifications for membership in Congress must derive not from the reserved powers of state sovereignty, but from the delegated powers of national sovereignty." The Supreme Court, in essence, found the reserved powers under the Tenth Amendment did not allow states to change the requirements for candidates for federal office. Term limits on state officeholders are still permissible. Lloyd Cutler, legal counsel to Presidents Carter and Clinton, agrees with the Court's decisions in this area because the "overwhelming historical evidence of the Founder's intent" supports the majority opinion.

A major study on the effect of term limits at the state level was released in a 2007 book, *Institutional Change in American Politics: The Case of Term Limits*, edited by Kurtz, Cain, and Niemi. The study involved a collaborative effort by representatives from the National Conference of State Legislatures, the Council of State Governments, and the State Legislative Leaders Foundation. The project came to be known as the Joint Project on Term Limits (JPTL). The JPTL study took place from 2001 to 2004. The results of this study are the most complete and updated empirical study of term limits that have been in place at the state level for some time. In their introduction, Kurtz, Cain, and Niemi note that "one of our key findings in this book is that the impact of term limits on legislatures is greatly affected by two factors: the degree of professionalism of the legislature and the restrictiveness of the term limit." What are their findings? Term limits do "sweep out the old politicians" in government. However, term limits do not invariably increase the number of women, minorities, or people with different backgrounds. There is also no significant difference between the age of legislators with or without term limits. Interestingly, term limits do not have any effect on political ambition. Candidates who are term-limited out of office will most likely run for another post.

Term limits have changed the relationships legislators have with their constituents. Surveys of state legislators with term limits demonstrate that they spend less time discussing issues with their constituents and solving individual problems. These representatives are more likely to adopt a "trustee" model of representation in which they vote according to what they think is best for their electoral district. This model of representation means that members of the state legislature will spend less time on campaign and reelection activities and more time working on the people's business. On the other hand, since legislators are in office for a shorter period of time, the constituents have less of an opportunity to become familiar with their representative. Term-limited state representatives also tend to be less educated about statewide issues and less effective in dealing with legislative procedures.

The Joint Project on Term Limits also considered the effect of term limits on the elected leaders of the legislatures. The literature confirms what seems intuitive with regard to term limits and leaders. The leadership in term-limited state legislatures has less experience and less time to hone their leadership skills. They spend "more time educating and leading legislators and expend more effort on candidate recruitment, training, and fundraising than did their predecessors or than do most of their counterparts in other legislatures." Leaders obviously have less long-term impact on public policy and less control over the legislative agenda than nonterm-limited legislative leaders. The authors of the study found no real differences in the behavior of legislative committees.

Term limits have an impact on the legislative staff of a term-limited state. Both the partisan and nonpartisan staff members take on the extra burden of becoming teachers and coaches for the less-experienced members of the legislature because the staff is career-oriented and will outlast the tenure of the lawmakers. More precisely, the JPTL stated, "These new roles suggest a new level of importance for staff in term-limited legislatures. No legislature can operate without staff, and term limits make their work even more crucial—and not necessarily in ways that circumvent the prerogatives of the elected membership."

Finally, the Joint Project on Term Limits evaluated the impact on the overall legislative climate and on the various institutional relationships in government. Term limits, after all, increase turnover among members, which hurts levels of experience and knowledge in the state legislature. More importantly, term limits destroy social networks. Regarding the legislative climate, surveys suggest legislators in term-limited states are less attached to the legislative norms of civility, specialization, and apprenticeships. Members of the legislature are also less likely to follow their legislative leaders and are more likely to act hurriedly. Term limits have altered the behavior of lobbyists in term-limited states. The research indicates that while lawmakers are increasingly relying on lobbyists for information, lawmakers are more suspicious of them. Also, as a result of the increased turnover in the legislatures, lobbyists are forced to work harder to make contacts each year with the newer members. The Kurtz, Cain, and Niemi study declares, "Overall, these effects on lobbying may be helping change term-limited legislatures into policy environments that are not just more hectic and less congenial but fairer and more open than they were before term limits." Lobbyists have become more active players in policy making with term limits at the state level. Powell's chapter in the Kurtz study finds term limits to have shifted the power and influence in state legislatures to the governors and executive branch at the expense of the legislatures. As mentioned earlier, the legislative staff and executive bureaucrats "have an informational advantage" over members of the legislature. The implication of this finding is that the power in term-limited state governments has shifted from the elected representatives to the unelected bureaucrats. Thad Kousser and John Straayer, also contributors to the JPTL investigation, argue that novice citizen-legislatures lack the knowledge required to put together state budgets and spending plans or even how to negotiate with others over the differences with others over the budget. Kousser and Straayer describe term limits in these states as making "their policy-making processes more chaotic and confrontational, and eroded their already-weak capacity to oversee the implementation of their policies. This is hardly a positive finding for the supporters of term limits."

John David Rausch, Jr., a longtime scholar in the field of term limits, has described the term limits movement in 2008 as being in a "holding pattern." The United States Term Limit organization is trying to maintain or expand the current term limits at the local and state levels at this point. A September 10, 2008, *New York Times* article reported how many cities and states with term limits are now trying to extend the number of terms council members and state legislators may now serve. "A decade after communities around the country adopted term limits to force entrenched politicians from office, at least two dozen local governments are suffering from buyer's remorse, with legislative bodies from New York City to Tacoma, Washington, trying to overturn or tweak the laws." The lame-duck mayor of San Antonio, Phil Hardberger, told the *New York Times*, "The learning curve of how city government works and how to get things done is steep, but when you keep putting people in, and throwing them out, there is very little accountability . . . . We do a lot of churning here, but we don't produce a lot of butter." Connie Ladenburg, a Tacoma, Washington, council member who is at the end of her term-limited second four-year term, pushed to get a term limits question on the Washington ballot to outlaw them. "That is when I thought, 'This is crazy.' If I go away, and it's not completed, what will happen?" She said she did not have enough time to construct a $2-million pedestrian and bike trail. "The public wonders why we don't get things done. Well, you have to be there a while to get things done." In the November 2008 elections there were referenda in nine cities and states throughout the country to eliminate or modify existing term limits. In every referendum, term limits gained a wide majority of the vote. In South Dakota, residents defeated Proposition J to repeal limits on the state legislature by a 75 percent to 25 percent margin. Likewise, Memphis, Tennessee, voted 78 percent to 22 percent to place a maximum of two terms on members of the city council, the mayor, and other constitutional offices. The residents of Shelby County, Tennessee, San Antonio, Texas, and State College, Pennsylvania, among other localities, all chose to keep or add term limits to their local officials.

The American people support term limits when given the chance to vote on them. The results of a Pulse Opinion Research National Survey in October 2008 indicated that 83 percent of the American people "believed elected officials should have their terms of office limited, while only 12 percent responded that "they should be allowed to hold office as long as they like." While the American people support term limits, there has been some recent skepticism about term limits.

Despite outrage among many New Yorkers, in November 2008, the mayor of New York City signed legislation he pushed through city council that would allow the mayor and members of city council to run for a third term in the 2009 city elections. The legislation signed by Michael Bloomberg essentially overturned two previous referenda. Bloomberg stated that the reason he wanted to extend the number of terms he could serve was so that he and the city council could tackle the current economic crisis. The expanded term limits for city officials in New York is telling because it was changed by the city council and mayor, and not decided by the people. This could be seen, perhaps, as a minor blip on the radar screen against term limits.

History has demonstrated that the American people largely support term limits. So far, the public has voted for almost every term limit proposed in state referenda going back to 1990. The polls show that an overwhelming majority of Americans prefer term limits. Term limits have been blocked by the people's representatives, whether they are local, state, or federal lawmakers. Term limits have also been blocked by the courts. The biggest challenge for term limit supporters to get restrictions on service at the federal level is Article 5 of the U.S. Constitution. The decision in *U.S. Term Limits v. Thornton* (1995) forces proponents to enact a constitutional amendment to overturn this decision. Amending the Constitution is a difficult process, as thousands of amendments have been introduced but only 27 have been ratified. Amending the Constitution to provide for term limits will be even more difficult because the people must either go through their state legislatures or through Congress, the people most likely to resist the effort.

Two joint resolutions were introduced during the 110th Congress (2007–2008) proposing constitutional amendments limiting the terms of members of Congress. On December 18, 2007, Representative Tom Price (R-GA) proposed an amendment (H.J. Res 71) that would limit members of the House and Senate to 18 years. It was referred to the House Judiciary Committee and then to the House Subcommittee on the Constitution on January 14, 2008, where it died in committee. Most recently, Representative Randy Kuhl (R-NY), on September 18, 2008, introduced a constitutional amendment (H.J. Res 98) that would impose term limits of six terms on representatives and two terms for senators. Neither of these bills had cosponsors and neither will be passed by this Congress, let alone voted on. For now, term limits exist primarily at the state and local levels of government.

Further Reading:

Carey, John M., Richard G. Niemi, and Lynda W. Powell. *Term Limits in the State Legislatures.* Ann Arbor: University of Michigan Press, 2000; Crane, Edward H., and Roger Pilon, eds. *The Politics and Law of Term Limits.* Washington, D.C.: Cato Institute, 1994; Farmer, Rick, John David Rausch Jr., and John C. Green, eds. *The Test of Time: Coping with Legislative Term Limits.* New York: Lexington Books, 2003; Kernell, Samuel. "Toward Understanding 19th Century Congressional Careers: Ambition, Competition, and Rotation." *American Journal of Political Science* 21 (1977): 669–693; Kurtz, Karl T., Bruce Cain, and Richard G. Niemi, eds. *Institutional Change in American Politics: The Case of Term Limits.* Ann Arbor: University of Michigan Press, 2007; Petracca, Mark P. "Rotation in Office: The History of an Idea." In *Limiting Legislative Terms,* edited by Gerald Benjamin and Michael J. Malbin. Washington, D.C.: CQ Press, 1992; Rausch, Jr., John David. "The Elite in the Term Limit Phenomenon." Ph.D. diss., University of Oklahoma, 1995; Sarbaugh-Thompson, Marjorie, et al. *The Political and Institutional Effects of Term Limits.* New York: Palgrave Macmillan, 2004.

– Harry C. "Neil" Strine IV

voting rights

Four large themes, or propositions, run through the history of minority voting rights in America. First, it has been laws and court decisions, not extralegal behavior or social attitudes or abstract philosophical positions, that have primarily formed and re-formed minority political rights. When rights are at stake, the law matters more than anything else. Second, minority rights have always been and they continue to be insecure, rising and falling in short bursts of progress and regression and, just as importantly, in long periods of incremental change in both directions. It is not a story of ever-increasing progress or of a dark age followed by one of fortunate enlightenment. Third, the effective exercise of minority rights has been largely determined by laws that govern the conditions in which voting is exercised, how votes are aggregated, and how the power of elected officials is allocated and constrained. The simple right to vote is anything but simple. Fourth, advances and declines in minority political rights have always been connected with struggles for political power, usually partisan conflicts, within the majority group. Racial politics is part of a larger series of stories, often brutally partisan ones. In sum, minority voting rights have been legally determined, variable, complex, and partisan.

During the colonial era and the early period of nationhood, America had the broadest suffrage and, not long after the Constitution was ratified, the best developed mass political parties in the world. The relatively small percentage of African-American male adults who were free were generally allowed to vote, if they could meet property or taxpaying qualifications, in the North and even in the southern states of Maryland and North Carolina. In many states, men had to own at least some property to be able to vote—land or houses that would rent for 40 shillings a year was often carried over as a requirement from Britain—but cheap land and loose enforcement of property qualifications made franchise rights for white men much more widespread than in Britain or anywhere else. Estimates of the proportion of white adult males eligible to vote in various states during the late 18th century range from 50 to 97 percent.

As the remaining property qualifications for white men were abolished in the first part of the 19th century, African Americans were often simultaneously disfranchised or subjected to racially defined property qualifications. In Maryland in 1802 and in North Carolina and Tennessee in 1834–35, for instance, voting rights were extended to all white adult males, while all blacks were excluded from the electorate. Connecticut in 1818 introduced the first version of what would later be known as the "grandfather clause" by allowing all African Americans then qualified to vote to continue to be able to exercise that right, but denying it to all other members of their race in the future.

In the best-studied instances, black disfranchisement has been shown to have been a partisan issue, most notoriously in New York State, where Democrats led by future president Martin Van Buren abolished the property qualification for whites, but raised it to $250 for blacks, in the state's 1821 constitutional convention. By 1825, only 68 of the total population of 12,559 African Americans in New York City remained eligible to vote.

Everywhere, blacks usually voted the Federalist ticket, and later the Whig and Republican tickets, a fact that intertwined partisanship with racism as motives for Democrats to favor black disfranchisement. Thus, Pennsylvania Democrats, reacting to a local election in Bucks County in 1837 in which black votes had likely provided the margin for Whig candidates, drove a black disfranchisement amendment through the 1837–38 constitutional convention at a time when the brilliant and staunchly antiracist leader of the opposition to the Democrats, Thaddeus Stevens, had to return temporarily to his seat in the state legislature. Stevens would later become one of the principal Radical Republican leaders and a staunch proponent of black suffrage nationally during Reconstruction. Democratic delegates in Pennsylvania in 1838 voted 58-3 to disfranchise blacks; the "Coalition" opposing the Democrats supported black suffrage 45-19.

In Rhode Island, African Americans were disfranchised in 1822 and reenfranchised in 1843, the renewal of their right a consequence of their support for the Whiggish "Law and Order Party" that had been formed to oppose Thomas Dorr's rebellion against the legally constituted government of the state. New states west of the Appalachians almost uniformly excluded blacks from voting at their initial constitutional conventions. By the Civil War, only Massachusetts, Rhode Island, New Hampshire, Vermont, and Maine allowed all black male adults to vote, and the black-only property qualification in New York had survived attempts to abolish it by referendum in 1846 and 1860.

The United States was the only country to grant ex-slaves the right to vote quickly after emancipation, but enfranchisement was difficult, bitterly controversial, and incomplete. Black suffrage faced opposition from Democrats and conservative Republicans in the North. In fact, from 1865 through 1869, majorities of only three of the 13 northern states that voted on the issue favored it.

But white southerners overreached. In the immediate aftermath of a Civil War in which 180,000 blacks served in the Union army and navy, all-white legislatures in the South passed "Black Codes" that denied African Americans such rights as to buy or lease real estate, to refuse to sign yearly labor contracts, to serve on juries, to testify against whites in court, and to vote. Blacks were excluded from public schools, black orphans were "apprenticed" to their former owners, and black "servants" were required to labor from sunup to sundown for their "masters." White southerners also demanded that a delegation of former Confederate officers and politicians be immediately seated in Congress; they aligned themselves with the racist president Andrew Johnson, successor to the martyred Lincoln, in the 1866 elections; and they met efforts by southern black and white Republicans to organize politically with shocking violence in New Orleans, Memphis, and elsewhere.

The outraged northern electorate responded by giving Radical Republicans a two-thirds majority in Congress, and the Republicans stripped Johnson of most of his powers and put the South temporarily under military control. Under the Military Reconstruction Acts of 1867, former Union generals dissolved the existing southern governments, established new ones after elections in which African Americans, but not all former rebels, could vote, and oversaw the drafting of new, much more egalitarian southern constitutions. Even before the 1866 election, Congress had passed the Fourteenth Amendment, which not only mandated "equal protection of the laws," but also threatened to reduce the congressional representation of any state that denied or abridged the suffrage to a substantial number of male citizens above 21 years of age, an obvious reference to black disfranchisement. Although probably drafted with the New York property qualification for blacks in mind, the "abridge" language, inserted in the Fifteenth, as well as in the Fourteenth Amendment, has been interpreted much more broadly.

To guard voting rights more securely, the Republican Congress in 1869 and Republican-dominated state legislatures in 1869 and 1870 quickly ratified the Fifteenth Amendment, which explicitly and absolutely banned the denial or abridgement of the suffrage in any American election on account of race, color, or previous condition of servitude. To make the amendment effective, Congress in 1870–71 passed sweeping Enforcement Acts, which sought to protect the right to vote and also prohibited any group or conspiracy from denying citizens "any right or privilege granted or secured" by the Constitution or by any federal law.

White southerners responded to black suffrage with a level of violence without precedent in American peacetime history. Louisiana led the way. When Philip Sheridan proved too protective of African-American rights as the military governor of the Reconstruction district overseeing Louisiana and Texas, President Johnson replaced him with Winfield Scott Hancock, a Democrat. Hancock then ensured his political future (he was the almost-successful Democratic nominee for president in 1880) by conciliating white southerners and refusing to prevent or prosecute the assassinations of 1,081 black and white Republicans in Louisiana in the six months from May to November, 1868—20 times the number of activists killed during three decades of the modern Civil Rights movement in the South.

Yet even after such violence, African Americans and their white Republican allies persisted, often turning out to vote at rates of 70 to 80 percent in Louisiana and elsewhere in the South. Reconstruction Republicans organized governments and passed laws and constitutions that launched statewide education systems, encouraged railroads, sought to guarantee civil rights, and protected the rights of laborers, renters, and small farmers. Even after the Reconstruction governments fell, blacks continued to enjoy the rights to legally marry, to worship as they wished, to form private clubs, to receive (usually inferior) educations at public expense, and often, to patronize public accommodations such as restaurants, theaters, streetcars, and railroads, on a nonsegregated basis, if they could afford to pay. Absolute segregation of public places in the South arrived only toward the turn of the 20th century, and it was a matter of law, not of custom.

Blacks were also not eliminated from politics after 1877. In fact, the number of African Americans elected to legislative office from the South was higher in 1882 than in any subsequent year until 1974, and from 1878 to 1890, the decline in black officeholders was palpable, but gradual. Moreover, even where they could not elect black candidates, which was usually their first preference, blacks could often still vote for sympathetic whites. In 1880, three years after President Rutherford B. Hayes symbolically confined U.S. troops to their barracks in the South, an estimated two-thirds of the adult male blacks were recorded as voting, and two-thirds of *those* managed to have their votes recorded for Republican James A. Garfield, whom they had nearly all, no doubt, supported for president against Hancock.

The high black turnout in the 1880 election, which was greater than overall national participation a century later, was fairly typical of state, as well as of presidential, elections in the South during the following decade. An average of six out of 10 African Americans voted in the most heavily contested gubernatorial races in each of the 11 ex-Confederate states during the 1880s, despite the fact that none of these elections took place on the same day as voters balloted for president. Of those blacks who voted, at least 60 percent supported the Republican, Greenback, or other anti-Democratic candidates in each state. Even in the 1890s, after several states had restricted the suffrage by law, nearly half of the blacks are estimated to have voted in key gubernatorial contests, although the Populist-Democratic battles were sufficiently severe that Democrats pushed fraud to new levels.

Five principal tactics were used to reduce, and finally to eliminate, black political strength, none sufficient by itself, all working together, but, roughly speaking, following a predictable developmental sequence: violence, fraud, structural discrimination, statutory suffrage restriction, and constitutional disfranchisement. Corresponding to these tactics were four approximate stages in the attack on black voting rights after Reconstruction: the Klan stage, in which fraud and violence predominated; the dilution stage, characterized by structural legal changes; the disfranchisement stage, where the last legal underpinnings of the real "Solid South" were put into place; and the lily white stage, the aim of which was to crush any elevation of blacks above the distinctly secondary political status into which the disfranchisement measures had forced them, and to reduce, from very slim to none, any chances of blacks being elected or appointed to office or exercising any political muscle whatsoever.

Violence was not only a dangerous weapon for a conservative establishment to use, for it invited retaliation from desperate victims, but it was also less effective than fraud perpetrated by election officials and their superiors. Southern election fraud in the late 19th century, as often a matter of boasting in the South as it was a matter of outrage in the North, far surpassed voting fraud at any other time or place in American history. For instance, Louisiana senator and former governor Samuel D. McEnery stated in 1898 that his state's 1882 election law "was intended to make it the duty of the governor to treat the law as a formality and count in the Democrats." William A. Anderson, author of the 1894 election law in Virginia, admitted that elections under his law were "crimes against popular government and treason against liberty."

A delegate to the 1901 Alabama constitutional convention reported that "any time it was necessary the black belt could put in ten, fifteen, twenty or thirty thousand Negro votes"—enough to decide most statewide elections in the period in the state. A leader of the 1890 Mississippi constitutional convention declared that "it is no secret that there has not been a full vote and a fair count in Mississippi since 1875," which was the last election until 1967 in which African Americans voted at all freely in the state. Like violence, fraud was most potent if ramped up during crucial elections, for instance, referenda on ratifying discriminatory amendments to state constitutions, as in Alabama in 1901, where, according to the official returns, nearly 90 percent of all adult males in counties with black populations of at least 70 percent supported a new constitution whose advertised purpose was black disfranchisement.

Supplementing fraud were structural changes in election laws, such as gerrymandering election district boundaries; drawing election districts with very different population sizes; switching from district to at-large elections, which made it more difficult to elect members of groups that formed a majority in a part of a city, but only a minority in the whole city; abolishing local elections entirely; annexation or deannexation of territory to add white or subtract black areas from a jurisdiction; requiring officeholders to post bonds too high for anyone who lacked wealthy friends to meet; shifting or consolidating polling places to confuse voters or require them to travel miles and miles to the polls; and impeaching Republican or other anti-Democratic officials, often on transparently specious grounds. All of these measures cut black and Republican officeholders at the local, state, and national levels without actually disfranchising voters.

Other statute laws did reduce individual voting: Poll taxes, which in some states had to be paid for every year after a person reached 21 years of age before one could vote, discouraged the poor of both races from voting, but especially the generally poorer blacks. Registration laws could be devised to prune the electorate by compelling registration months before every election, especially at a central location during working hours; demanding copiously detailed information, which sometimes had to be vouched for by witnesses, before a voter could register; allowing registration boards sufficient discretion to enable them to pad or unfairly purge the rolls; representing Democrats disproportionately on such boards; requiring voters unaccustomed to keeping records to produce registration certificates at voting places; or permitting widespread challenges to voters at the polls.

The then-infamous South Carolina "Eight-Box" law of 1882 required election officials to shift separate ballot boxes for each of eight offices around during the voting to make it impossible for a literate friend to put an illiterate's tickets in the correct order before he entered the polling place and prohibited anyone but the election officers, all but one or two of whom in the entire state seem to have been Democrats, from assisting unlettered voters. After 1888, when states began to require ballots to be supplied only by governments, secret ballot laws, employed in eight southern and many northern states with the intent and effect of disfranchising illiterates, could be designed to be so long and complex as to disfranchise all but the well-educated and those whom the election officials chose to help.

Along with violence, fraud, and structural measures, such laws reduced Republican, and inhibited Populist, representation enough to create legislative majorities in favor of state constitutional disfranchisement. Conventions or referenda then wrote into more permanent form poll taxes and literacy or property tests for registration, often with temporary exemption clauses to allow illiterate (white) voters to register if they could demonstrate to a registrar's satisfaction that they understood parts of the Constitution or laws when read to them; or if their ancestors could have voted before 1867 (before southern blacks were enfranchised); or if they or their ancestors had served in the military, including, of course, the Confederate army, which were referred to as the "grandfather" and "fighting grandfather" clauses. Constitutional disfranchisement effectively moved fraud one step back, delegating it to registration officials, instead of to those at the polls. It also reduced the widespread unfavorable publicity about southern Democratic election cheating and made legal attacks on white electoral supremacy more difficult to mount.

The Solid South created by disfranchisement laws—effectively outlawing political party competition, almost entirely excluding southern African Americans from political participation, proudly starving governmental services for poor people—lasted for a half-century. The legal disfranchisement of southern African Americans succeeded for three reasons: partisanship, the filibuster, and adverse decisions by the Supreme Court.

Since African Americans remained almost unanimously committed to the Republican Party—the party of Lincoln, emancipation, and Reconstruction—until well after disfranchisement, northern Democrats opposed any efforts to guarantee southern blacks the right to register, vote, and have their votes counted as cast. If southern blacks could vote freely, the fortunes of the Democratic Party nationally were likely to be permanently depressed. Accordingly, not a single Democratic member of Congress voted for any civil or voting rights measure from 1865 through 1900. That this pattern was motivated by partisanship, and not merely by racial animosity, is shown by the fact that an appreciable number of Democrats in northern state legislatures supported the school integration and public accommodations bills that became law in all but two northern states where the black population exceeded 1 percent in the late 19th century.

Rabid Democratic partisanship was especially on display in the bitter struggles over the national election bills in 1875 and 1890, when they relentlessly talked to death measures to protect individuals while voting, as well as to oversee registration, voting, and vote counting. Guarding the fundamental right to vote from violence, intimidation, and fraud amounted, the Democrats and much of the nation's press shrieked, to "force bills." Largely to counter these "filibustering" tactics, Republicans in the House changed the body's rules in 1889–90 to end unlimited debate, and these "Reed Rules" not only facilitated the passage of the Lodge Elections Bill in that branch of the national legislature, but they also fundamentally changed the nature of the House forever. Never again would a minority of the House be able to block the chamber's business until the majority gave up and dropped a bill or severely compromised it.

Yet the Senate during that same congressional session failed to adopt a proposal by Senator

Nelson W. Aldrich (R-RI) that was similar to the Reed Rules, Democrats filibustered the Lodge Bill for 33 days, the longest filibuster in history up to that time, and the bill was finally set aside by a single vote. Because the Senate has not yet followed the House's lead on antifilibuster rules, every civil rights or voting rights proposal through the 1960s has had to face the prospect or reality of having to break a filibuster to pass the Senate. As a consequence, between 1875 and 1957, not a single civil rights or voting rights bill passed Congress.

Disfranchisement was also facilitated by the zigzag course of the Supreme Court from 1876 through 1935. Endowed with life tenure to ensure the greatest possible independence from the pressures of partisan politics or public opinion, the Supreme Court during this period repeatedly wavered in protecting or allowing Congress to protect African-American political rights. In two opinions in 1876—*U.S. v. Reese*, a discriminatory poll tax case, and *U.S. v. Cruikshank*, an effort to punish the perpetrators of a brutal racial mass murder growing out of a local Louisiana election—Chief Justice Morrison R. Waite ruled provisions of the 1870–72 Enforcement Acts unconstitutional or largely unenforceable. Ignoring the Fourteenth Amendment, which does not mention race and which was repeatedly invoked during congressional debates as a basis for the Enforcement Acts, Waite declared that the only constitutional justification for the acts was the Fifteenth Amendment, and that either the acts or the indictments pursuant to them were insufficiently direct in their references to race to satisfy the Fifteenth Amendment.

But although the decisions in *Reese* and *Cruikshank* severely weakened existing federal voting rights enforcement machinery, nothing in them prevented Congress from passing new laws that made the connection between racial discrimination and the protection of voting rights more explicit, and later Court decisions viewed the Fourteenth Amendment's equal protection and privileges and immunities clauses more expansively, allowing Congress to guard the fundamental rights of citizens in instances when the states did not.

Just as northern legislatures and courts became much more sympathetic to African-American rights during the decade after the supposed end of Reconstruction, Supreme Court decisions of the 1880s seemed to invite a renewed movement for racial reform. In *Ex parte Siebold* (1880), *Ex parte Clarke* (1880), and *Ex parte Yarbrough* (1884), the high court interpreted Congress's plenary power under Article I, Section 4, to regulate the "times, places and manner of holding elections" to Congress broadly enough to allow it to guarantee peaceable assembly and restrict fraud and violence. These decisions inspired Republicans to frame the 1890 Lodge Bill without fear that it would be declared unconstitutional.

Equally importantly, in the 1880 jury exclusion case of *Strauder v. West Virginia* and the 1886 Chinese laundry case of *Yick Wo v. Hopkins*, the Supreme Court struck down racially discriminatory laws not related to voting in such expansive language as to suggest that the justices had not entirely forgotten the original purposes of the Reconstruction amendments, after all. Despite the Court's narrow construction of the powers of the federal government in *the Civil Rights Cases* (1883), the other, more moderate decisions allowed some scope for national action to protect minority rights if Republicans took firm control of the government again, as they did in 1889 for the first time since 1875.

After the failure of the Lodge Bill, however, the Supreme Court shifted direction again. In *Williams v. Mississippi* in 1898, the Court denied disfranchised blacks a remedy by requiring that they show that the state legislature's intent to disfranchise them was actually carried out (as everyone knew it had been). Yet when Wilford H. Smith, an African-American lawyer representing disfranchised Alabama blacks in *Giles v. Harris* (1903), presented extensive evidence of the new state constitution's discriminatory effects, as well as its intent, the Court, in a decision written by the "liberal" Oliver Wendell Holmes, Jr., declared that the judiciary could do nothing, because suffrage was a "political question."

Once southern blacks were safely disfranchised, the Court reversed itself once more, entirely ignoring *Williams* and *Giles* in its ruling in *Guinn and Beal v. U.S.* (1915) that the Oklahoma grandfather clause was unconstitutional. Chief Justice Edward Douglass White, a former member of the "conservative" faction of the Democratic Party in Louisiana, which had opposed the grandfather clause in that state's constitutional convention in 1898, did not endanger white supremacy directly in *Guinn*, because eliminating the escape clause for Oklahoma whites did not thereby actually allow any African Americans to vote.

A dizzying series of decisions on the white primary by the Supreme Court from 1927 through 1944 illustrated white southern ingenuity in circumventing attacks on white supremacy and the necessity of clear national laws to protect minority voting rights. The white Democratic primary did not disfranchise anyone. Any black could still vote in the general election. But in the dominant-party South, the Democratic nomination was tantamount to election, and an electoral rule that prohibited blacks from a crucial part of the electoral process would seem clearly to have abridged the suffrage because of race. Accepting this reasoning and dismissing the contention that the case involved a "political question" that courts ought to leave to Congress and the states, Justice Holmes—who had termed suffrage a political question 25 years earlier in *Giles*—ruled the Texas white primary unconstitutional as a violation of the Fourteenth Amendment.

But Holmes's brief opinion for a unanimous Court in *Nixon v. Herndon* (1927), the first of several NAACP challenges to the discriminatory practice, was quickly circumvented. Texas repealed its explicit racially restrictive primary law and delegated the setting of primary participation standards to the State Democratic Executive Committee, contending that the discrimination thereby became purely private, and not an action of the state. The Supreme Court struck down that subterfuge, too, in *Nixon v. Condon* (1932), but this time Justice James McReynolds, joined by the other three extreme conservatives on the Court, dissented. According to the Tennessean McReynolds, all-black, all-white, all-male, or all-female political parties were perfectly constitutional, even if a state extensively regulated the party's activities. Three years later, in 1935, a unanimous Court sidestepped the *Nixon* cases, ruling in *Grovey v. Townsend* that a state party convention could authorize an all-white primary, even if a state or a party executive committee could not.

Between 1935 and 1944, however, the Supreme Court itself underwent a revolution. First, a slim majority of the Court, often including only five of the nine justices, invalidated much of the New Deal's program. Then, after his landslide 1936 reelection, President Franklin D. Roosevelt proposed to "pack" the Court with up to six new members. Although that plan failed in the Senate, the most conservative justices quickly began to resign. Roosevelt replaced them with liberals and many of the Court's earlier decisions were overruled. By 1944, only two justices, Owen Roberts, who had written *Grovey*, and Harlan Fiske Stone remained from the 1935 Court, and the new majority, over only Roberts's dissent, repudiated *Grovey* in a fourth Texas case, *Smith v. Allwright*.

All across the Upper South, and even in Deep South states such as Georgia, African Americans began to register to vote in numbers not seen for nearly half a century. Thus, the Supreme Court finally rediscovered the original intent of the framers of the Fourteenth and Fifteenth Amendments, setting in motion events that would doom the Solid South and usher in a second period of racially egalitarian reform.

But the white primary was only one of many types of laws and practices that kept the 70 percent of African Americans who lived in the South in the mid-20th century from exercising political power. Although blacks could vote freely in the North after 1870, reenfranchising southern blacks would require action by the executive and legislative, as well as the judicial branch of the national government. Congress acted first by passing the 1957 Civil Rights Act, an extremely mild law that principally authorized a Civil Rights Division in the Department of Justice to sue southern governments that engaged in unconstitutionally biased electoral practices and a Commission on Civil Rights to study discriminatory actions by governments in elections and other public activities. In a larger sense, the significance of the 1957 law, guided through the Senate by Majority Leader Lyndon B. Johnson (D-TX) with the help of the Eisenhower administration, was to serve as proof that the southern Senate filibuster that had prevented any civil rights bill from passing for 82 years could finally be broken. Three years later, Congress in the 1960 Civil Rights Act added more power to the Justice Department and the Civil Rights Commission. These landmark laws marked the first time in American history that majorities of both major political parties had backed national action on a law designed to further racial equality.

The most significant of 70 lawsuits brought by the Justice Department under the 1957 and 1960 Civil Rights Acts was the famous "Tuskegee Gerrymander Case," *Gomillion v. Lightfoot* (1960). Despite the crafty intransigence of white officials in 84 percent black Macon County, the nation's most heavily black county, enough African Americans managed to register to vote to threaten white control of the town of Tuskegee, home of historically black Tuskegee Institute. The Alabama legislature therefore grotesquely reshaped the boundaries of Tuskegee to make it an almost wholly white town. Although no individual had her right to vote taken away—she could still vote in county, state, and federal elections—the blatant racial gerrymander preserved white power in the most important local decisions, those made by the city government.

In a decision that opened the way for the Supreme Court's plunge into the "political thicket" of reapportionment, as well as its consideration of racially discriminatory electoral structures, Justice Felix Frankfurter put *Giles*'s "political question" dodge to rest. Shocked by the "strangely irregular 28-sided-figure" drawn to "fence out" blacks from Tuskegee, Frankfurter and concurring justices held that a lack of equal protection through a racially discriminatory electoral structure was also a denial or abridgment of the right to vote guaranteed by the Fifteenth Amendment. Implicitly, the case also ruled that a racially discriminatory intent could be proven by evidence of its effect alone, since no direct evidence of the legislators' motives was presented. In voting rights, as in school integration cases, the U.S. Supreme Court began the Second Reconstruction much more favorably disposed than it had been during the First Reconstruction.

Yet weak laws and limited, place-specific court decisions fulfilled the constitutional promise of equal rights only slowly and partially. The experiences of civil rights workers during frustrating and often brutally suppressed campaigns to register black voters in the Deep South, the frustrations of Justice Department lawyers in trying to litigate voting rights cases, and the hearings and reports of the Civil Rights Commission taught four major lessons for public policy: First, discriminatory administration, especially of registration and literacy tests, was the chief barrier to qualifying more African-American voters. Second, bringing individual suits against registration officials before southern federal judges was a painfully slow and ineffective means of adding to the suffrage rolls. Third, southern jurisdictions were so adept at adding ingenious subterfuges to replace more obvious means of discrimination that a flexible administrative procedure was needed to stop discriminators from circumventing the effort to give black citizens equal political rights. And fourth, decisive action by the federal government was necessary to convince southern officials to comply with the Fifteenth Amendment and to persuade potential African-American voters that it was safe to take part in politics. The result, made possible by the Democratic landslide in the 1964 national elections and catalyzed by the 1965 Selma March, was the Voting Rights Act (VRA).

Section 2 of the act, which was permanent and applied nationally, prohibited any "voting qualification or prerequisite to voting, or standard, practice, or procedure" that denied or abridged the right to vote on the basis of race or color. Section 4, which was initially imposed for only five years, suspended any "test or device" imposed as a voting prerequisite in jurisdictions, all in the Deep South, that had especially low political participation. Section 5, by implication set to expire in 1970, required that every state or local government subject to Section 4 submit all changes in election laws to the Department of Justice or the federal district court of the District of Columbia before putting them into effect. If a law was disallowed by the Justice Department, the jurisdiction could sue in District of Columbia district court, not in the often much more racist southern federal courts, to overturn the Justice Department ruling. Section 6 authorized the appointment of federal voting registrars if local registrars continued to discriminate.

Within two years after the passage of the VRA, African-American registration in the Deep South surged. Most dramatic were the increases from 19 percent to 52 percent in Alabama and from 7 percent to 60 percent in Mississippi. But, as the Civil Rights Commission brought to the attention of Congress and the public, these and other states responded by erecting structural barriers to black power—gerrymandering, changing from single-member-district to at-large elections, prohibiting "single-shot" voting in multimember district contests, and making elective offices appointive. Contending that none of these laws denied anyone the right to vote, and that the VRA was not concerned with such structural changes, the covered southern jurisdictions generally did not submit these statutes for preclearance. Reasoning that it was exactly such circumventions that Section 5 was intended to preclude, black plaintiffs sued in *Allen v. Board of Elections* (1969).

In his opinion in *Allen*, Chief Justice Earl Warren, referring extensively to the congressional hearings and debates on the VRA, held that Section 5 applied to election laws in Virginia and Mississippi even if those laws had no direct connection with voter registration or casting a ballot. To have ruled otherwise would have opened a huge loophole for every state. A year later, over the noisy opposition of the Nixon administration, Congress extended Section 5 for another five years, endorsing the *Allen* decision by repeatedly mentioning it favorably in the extensive hearings and the committee reports on the law in both houses.

Where Sections 4 and 5 did not apply, minority plaintiffs in the 1960s and 1970s usually relied on the Fourteenth and Fifteenth Amendments, but as the major vote dilution case of the period, *White v. Regester* (1973), showed, legal standards under the Constitution and the VRA intermingled. Because Texas set up multimember legislative districts in Dallas and San Antonio and powerful "slating groups" (unofficial organizations that circulated lists of candidates whom they endorsed) rarely included black or Latino candidates on their lists, few or no minority candidates could hope to be elected from those cities. In a unanimous decision, Justice Byron White ruled that at-large elections violated the equal protection clause of the Fourteenth Amendment when an analysis of "the totality of the circumstances" indicated that jurisdictions that used the device denied minorities an "equal opportunity to participate in the political processes and to elect legislators of their choice." The emphasis on an equal chance to *elect* candidates, and not just to vote, practically wrote *Allen* into the Constitution, and the "totality of the circumstances" test was applied in cases brought under the VRA and served as the basis for the congressional amendments to the VRA in 1981–82.

Congress extended Sections 4 and 5 for a seven-year period in 1975, and, following the recommendations of the Civil Rights Commission and the federal courts' findings in *White v. Regester*, Congress took notice of discrimination against Latinos and explicitly added "language minorities" (chiefly Latinos, Native Americans, and recent Asian immigrants) to the VRA's coverage. But in *Beer v. U.S.* (1976), the Supreme Court reined in Section 5, construing its impact on electoral structures narrowly by holding that it prevented only "retrogression." If the New Orleans City Council before redistricting had one black-majority district, then the Justice Department, the Court said, could not reject a plan containing only one such district, even if more generous plans could have been drawn and even if the scheme, in the presence of racial bloc voting (where the voting patterns of two or more ethnic groups differ markedly), gave whites more than their proportional share of seats. Four years later, in *Mobile v. Bolden* (1980), the Court constrained Section 2 of the VRA, as well, a four-person plurality led by Justice Potter Stewart requiring proof of an intent to discriminate, rather than just evidence of a discriminatory effect.

Congress took the opportunity of the scheduled expiration of Section 5 in 1982 to try to reverse the Supreme Court's decisions in *Bolden* and *Beer*. Over the rather inept opposition of the Reagan administration, Congress amended Section 2 explicitly to overturn *Bolden* by making it clear that it applied to any law that had the *effect* of discriminating, whether or not judges would accept the contention that the law was passed with a discriminatory *intent*. Less clearly, in a footnote to the Senate report on the bill, Congress made an effort to overturn *Beer*, seeking to ban any law or practice that damaged minorities in politics, not just those that made them worse off than they already were. It also extended Sections 4 and 5 for 25 more years. Coincidentally, just two days after President Reagan signed the revised VRA, the Supreme Court handed down *Rogers v. Lodge*, which gingerly sidestepped *Bolden* and echoed Congress's actions. In his opinion for a 6-3 majority, Justice White, who had dissented in *Bolden*, merged the effect-based standards of *White v. Regester* with the intent notions of a series of Fourteenth Amendment cases. Thereafter, to prove intent, plaintiffs could use many of the same sorts of evidence that would previously have been considered indicative of effect.

Four years later in *Thornburg v. Gingles*, Justice William Brennan sustained the amended VRA and reinterpreted the standards for proving a Section 2 violation. The three-part *Gingles* test required plaintiffs to show that the minority group was sufficiently large and geographically compact to form a majority of a district in the governmental body at issue, that voting was racially polarized, and that minority candidates generally lost in contests for those offices. Brennan also rejected an attempt to make it much more difficult to prove that voting was racially polarized. Plaintiffs did not have to demonstrate that racism was the sole or most important *cause* of differences in voting patterns, but only that the electorate *did*, as a matter of fact, split along racial lines. Even though four justices disagreed with parts of the Court's reasoning, all nine agreed that Section 2 did not merely bar discrimination against individuals' exercise of the franchise, but also prohibited vote dilution.

The *Gingles* test led to the largest increase in the number of minorities elected to Congress from the South since the First Reconstruction and, subsequently, to the strongest judicial backlash against black political rights since *Cruikshank* and *Giles*. Justice Brennan's seemingly clear, simple criteria enabled civil rights lawyers to win case after case during the late 1980s. These victories warned state and local governments that if they discriminated against minorities during the 1990s round of redistricting, as they always had in past redistricting, they were likely to suffer expensive losses in federal courts. The Justice Department also interpreted the 1982 VRA amendments as barring preclearance under Section 5 if a redistricting would violate Section 2 or the U.S. Constitution. Accordingly, the department pressured state and local jurisdictions that were covered by Section 5 (mostly in the Deep South) to draw election districts in which African Americans or Latinos would have good opportunities to elect candidates of their choice.

The districts drawn in 1991–92 had the predicted effects, raising the number of African Americans in Congress from the South from five in 1990 to 17 after the redistricting in 1992. The comparable increase in state legislatures was from 235 to 274. Hispanic-majority congressional districts in Florida and Texas rose from 6 to 9 and those in the two states' legislatures, from 43 to 49.

Several of the redistricting plans that had led to the election of more minority candidates were struck down by a five-person majority of the U.S. Supreme Court, all appointees of Presidents Ronald Reagan and George H. W. Bush, in *Shaw v. Reno* (1993) and subsequent cases. Antiblack racial gerrymandering from 1872 until 1900 had confined a large portion of the blacks in North Carolina to the heavily packed "Black Second" congressional district, which usually elected an African-American representative. After mass African-American reenfranchisement in the state in 1965, antiblack racial gerrymandering had repeatedly split the black population to prevent blacks from dominating even a single congressional district.

Yet when the state legislature, under pressure from the Justice Department, drew two ungainly districts in which blacks constituted slight majorities of the registered voters in 1991–92, Justice Sandra Day O'Connor and her four conservative colleagues in *Shaw* bitterly condemned the most racially balanced districts in the state in a century as an effort "to segregate the races for purposes of voting . . to classify and separate voters by race . . . [to] balkanize us into competing racial factions . . . political apartheid." Although three months earlier, in *Voinovich v. Quilter*, she had praised a pro-Republican racial gerrymander in Ohio that had packed blacks into as few state legislative districts as possible, O'Connor asserted that the North Carolina districts, drawn by Democrats, would reinforce racial stereotypes, "exacerbate . . . patterns of racial bloc voting," and cue legislators elected from those districts to pay attention to only the black part of their constituencies. The "bizarre" challenged districts, the justice concluded, violated such "traditional districting principles" as compactness—principles, she neglected to note, that North Carolina and many other states had previously ignored if they got in the way of partisan or white supremacist purposes.

In *Miller v. Johnson* (1995), the same five justices as in *Shaw* ruled that district shape was only one indication of whether race had been "the predominant factor" in the Georgia legislature's "decision to place a significant number of [minority] voters within or without a particular district," which, they ruled, was unconstitutional. Seeming to put legislative and municipal districts throughout the country at risk, *Miller* also held that it was unconstitutional for redistricters to use "race as a proxy" for partisanship or incumbency protection and implied that the public participation of African Americans in framing redistricting plans itself made those plans suspect.

In *Shaw v. Hunt* and *Bush v. Vera* in 1996, the five justices dismissed contentions that North Carolina and Texas had acted to remedy past anti-black and anti-Latino gerrymandering, to comply with the VRA, or to preserve the seats of white Democrats, as insufficient to justify letting legislators take race into account in redistricting. All the VRA required, the justices held, was that the states not actually reduce the number of minority opportunity districts—an interpretation that could have kept southern political offices almost all white if it had been invented in 1965, instead of 30 years later. Strong dissents by the four moderates on the Court in all of these cases accused the majority of setting up a series of racial double standards, and the moderates graphically illustrated their point with maps of peculiarly shaped overwhelmingly white, safely Republican districts, which the Court's majority did not consider "segregated" and specifically ruled constitutional.

Two Supreme Court decisions in 1997 and 2000 in the same litigation, *Reno v. Bossier Parish*, severely weakened the Justice Department's role in overseeing redistricting. A Louisiana parish (county) with a history of violence notable even in that state, Bossier Parish had an all-white, 12-member school board that had only recently given up the fight for segregated schools when it drew 12 new majority-white election districts in 1991. The NAACP, which had presented a plan with two black-majority districts in the 20 percent black parish, convinced the Justice Department to deny preclearance to the plan under Section 5 of the VRA on the grounds that the black vote had been diluted.

In the first round of the Bossier Parish case, Justice O'Connor ruled that the Justice Department could not use vote dilution, as defined in Section 2 of the VRA, as a reason for denying preclearance under Section 5. After further action in a lower federal court, Justice Antonin Scalia of the Supreme Court declared that the department had to preclear any plan, even if the plan was clearly unconstitutional, unless it had a "retrogressive intent" or a retrogressive effect. Mere intentional discrimination did not violate Section 5, in other words, unless the intention was to make minorities worse off than they already were and the redistricting authority failed to carry out its purpose—"malevolent incompetence," in Justice Scalia's taunting phrase.

Shaw, *Miller*, *Bossier*, and the other "racial gerrymandering" decisions deactivated the Justice Department during the post-2000 round of mandatory redistricting, and, as a consequence, there were many fewer new black or Latino members of Congress or state legislatures elected in 2002 than there had been in 1992. In Georgia, where the Republican Party was surging, blacks and their white allies sought to preserve Democratic control of the state senate by reducing the black percentages of some overwhelmingly black districts. Spreading loyally Democratic black voters somewhat more evenly would increase the number of districts in which African Americans were numerous enough to make it likely that a Democrat of one race or the other would be elected. The Justice Department, which believed that black percentages in three senate districts had been reduced too far for black candidates to be able to carry them in the state's always racially polarized elections, refused to preclear the Democratic plan. The state's Republican Party, which wanted blacks to be packed into fewer districts so that the GOP could win more seats, intervened in the subsequent lawsuit.

In *Georgia v. Ashcroft* (2003), her last major voting rights opinion, Justice O'Connor surprisingly sided with the Democrats, ruling that to decide whether a redistricting plan as a whole had a retrogressive effect, the Justice Department had to take into account not only the number of districts in which minorities composed a *majority* of a district, but also the number of minority "influence districts"—those in which a minority group could coalesce with enough whites to elect a candidate that both could agree on, usually a white Democrat. Explicitly recognizing that contemporary southern white Republicans were much less responsive to the interests of blacks than white Democrats were, O'Connor's very race-conscious opinion frightened both civil rights groups and Republicans. Both worried that Democratic politicians would dilute the black vote, as they had before *Gingles*, to elect more Democrats.

The Supreme Court's opinions beginning with *Shaw v. Reno* slowed the racially egalitarian advances of the Second Reconstruction to a crawl, even if they did not reverse them entirely. They were also mutually contradictory, some seeming to stress district appearance, while others ignored it; some seeming to deny that race could constitutionally play any role in political decisions, while others recognized that it usually did; some encouraging political bargaining, while others professed to be shocked by its existence; some co-opting the rhetoric of the Civil Rights movement to undermine the movement's aims, while others recognized that it was necessary to be race conscious now in order ever to be able to transcend racial lines. Such contradictions reduced the influence of these decisions and made them murky, moving targets for critics and difficult to overcome through legislation. As Section 5 of the VRA approached the date of its expiration in 2007, the civil rights forces focused on overturning only Justice Scalia's opinion in *Bossier* and Justice O'Connor's in *Georgia v. Ashcroft*.

By 2006, the Voting Rights Act, termed by a leading conservative commentator "the twentieth century's noblest and most transformative law," had attained such symbolic stature that not even the Republican majorities in both houses of Congress or the George W. Bush administration dared oppose it openly. On the other side, civil rights organizations and their usual Democratic allies felt much too weak to sponsor major amendments to the act or to reform its administration. The consequence of timidity on both sides was a tepid compromise that only restored the VRA to its pre-*Bossier* vigor and that left to the courts the major issue of whether the geographical and ethnic focus of Section 5 should be updated.

Critics of the continuation of Section 5 and other parts of the act, such as Dr. Abigail Thernstrom, vice chair of the Civil Rights Commission, contended that African Americans no longer needed the law because they were registered in percentages comparable to whites, because many blacks had been elected to public office, and because the number of Justice Department objections to discriminatory laws had declined to a relative handful. Latinos and Asians, the other large minority groups, had, in Thernstrom's view, never suffered enough discrimination in politics to deserve legal protection. The act should be repealed or sections of it allowed to expire, the critics asserted, because it infringed on the prerogatives of state and local governments under traditional federalist principles. In response, VRA proponents marshaled voluminous specific examples of discrimination since the 1982 renewal of the act from legal cases and Justice Department preclearance files, and they maintained that if Section 5 were repealed, white politicians' self-interest and lingering bias would increase discrimination once again. They also pointed out that compliance with the preclearance requirement had become a simple, inexpensive matter of bureaucratic routine that states and localities now carried out without difficulty or protest. Because both sides knew that political pressures to renew the act were overwhelming, these arguments and supporting evidence were in reality directed toward the inevitable legal challenges to the act's renewal.

Fearing that the renewal bill would be stalled if the pro-VRA Republican chairman of the House Judiciary Committee, James Sensenbrenner, was replaced as chairman, as he was scheduled to be in 2007, by Lamar Smith, a Republican VRA opponent, civil rights forces pushed the bill early, so that it was actually passed in 2006, instead of 2007. Only three significant amendments to the original VRA were introduced in the original bill, and all other amendments on the floor of the House failed. None was even offered in the brief, one-day consideration of the bill in the Senate. The three amendments made clear that, contrary to Justice Scalia's opinion in *Bossier*, the Justice Department should refuse to preclear laws or regulations that had any discriminatory intent, not just a retrogressive intent; more equivocally countered Justice O'Connor's sanction of influence districts in *Georgia v. Ashcroft*; and renewed Section 5 for another 25 years. Despite warnings in the congressional hearings and in scholarly debates that a failure to update the criteria for designating areas that were covered under Section 5, and which therefore had to obtain Justice Department preclearance for all changes in their election laws, would put the law's constitutionality at risk in the Supreme Court, Congress voted not to make any such changes. Covering new areas might lose the votes of too many members of Congress. In this uncontroversial form, the law passed the House, 390-33, and the Senate, 98-0.

The desire to avoid a partisan conflict that might slow or preclude the renewal of the VRA left open several pressing questions that had potentially momentous consequences for minority voting rights: First, approximately 5 million people, who were overwhelmingly African-American and Latino men, had lost their right to vote because they had once been convicted of a crime. The states' rules on how and under what conditions these persons who were no longer imprisoned could get their rights restored varied widely and were often bureaucratic mazes. Studies showed that voting registrars throughout the country rarely understood the regulations on the reenfranchisement of prisoners much better than the former prisoners did. Did the racially disproportionate effects of criminal disfranchisement laws, as administered, make them violations of the VRA or the Fourteenth or Fifteenth Amendments, and, if they did not, should the laws be changed?

Second, in what has been advertised as an effort to prevent in-person vote fraud, many states have considered, and some have adopted, laws requiring that voters who appear at the polls provide photo identification on government-issued cards or badges. Despite a barrage of rumors and vague charges of wrongdoing, intensive searches by Republican legal authorities throughout the country during the administration of George W. Bush turned up only a couple of dozen instances of such fraud among hundreds of millions of votes cast in a variety of recent elections. Yet legislatures with Republican majorities in Georgia, Indiana, and Missouri dismissed Democratic evidence showing that substantial proportions of disproportionately black and Latino citizens had no drivers' licenses and that obtaining official identity cards often posed financial and/or logistical hardships for poor people. The episodes reminded some historians of the late-19th century charges of fraud, which were used to justify stringent registration and secret ballot laws that often had the intent and effect of disfranchising the partisan or racial opponents of the parties in power, particularly in the South. If the effect of "voter identification" laws is as racially discriminatory as the earlier quasi-literacy tests have been demonstrated to be, should Congress ban them?

Third, some of the areas now covered by Section 5 of the VRA have witnessed few or no documented instances of racially discriminatory voting regulations in decades, while some areas now exempt from preclearance requirements increasingly suffer from just the sort of combination of racial bloc voting and election laws that disadvantage minority groups that have been held to violate Section 5. The newer areas of discrimination usually contain fast-growing Latino populations. If the Supreme Court overturns the Section 5 coverage formula, should Congress rewrite it, and if so, how?

Or has America, as critics like Thernstrom contend, at long last overcome its history of racial antagonism and discrimination? Should courts and legislatures now assume that the legacy of slavery, segregation, disfranchisement, and structural discrimination has been so attenuated, so divorced, for the first time, from partisan advantage, so foreign to our enlightened political culture, that the intricate mechanisms devised to protect minorities against majority bias may safely be dismantled? America was the first large country in the world to frame a republican constitution and to introduce mass politics structured by political parties. Have we become the first country in the world to attain color blindness?

These questions were sharply put into focus by the election in November 2008 of the nation's first president of African descent, Barack H. Obama, and the Supreme Court's curious decision in June 2009, in the *NAMUDNO* Case (*Northwest Austin Municipal Utility District Number One v. Holder*). Those who professed a belief in an American racial transfiguration trumpeted the election of the son of a Kenyan economist as absolute proof that the only vestige of racial discrimination consisted of government programs, such as the VRA and local efforts to integrate public schools, that were motivated by a desire to improve opportunities for members of disadvantaged ethnic minority groups. They dismissed five exceptional circumstances of the 2008 election: First, two months before election day, the U.S. economy plunged into its worst recession in 70 years, and, since 1837, American voters have regularly punished parties in power at the time of economic downturns. Second, President George W. Bush, mired in an unpopular war and blamed for disastrous responses to Hurricane Katrina and other crises, was experiencing the lowest presidential approval ratings in public opinion polls since Richard Nixon had been forced to resign in 1974. Third, the deeply split Republican Party nominated the oldest first-time presidential candidate ever to be named by a major political party in American history, and one who was firmly identified with the Iraq War; further, McCain hurriedly chose as a vice presidential candidate a previously unknown governor, Sarah Palin, whose televised interviews showed her to be unprepared to assume the presidency, in the eyes of analysts across the political spectrum. By contrast, the Democratic Party, united after a long primary campaign that introduced the one-term senator from Illinois to the American public, selected for its vice presidential candidate a well-known senator, Joseph Biden, whose foreign policy experience complemented Obama's domestic proficiency. Fourth, Obama proved superbly eloquent and, unlike John McCain, manifestly steady in the face of adverse events during the campaign and the economic turbulence, and his program of specific, moderate changes energized an unprecedented number of volunteer campaign workers and small-scale donors. Fifth, the Democrats were riding a wave of electoral success that in 2006 gave them their first majority in both houses of Congress since 1994. Many observers believed that in the conditions of the 2008 general election, the landslide victory of a candidate with Obama's personal magnetism and remarkable campaign staff would have seemed inevitable long before it took place—if only he had been white.

Yet even assuming that Obama's election proved white voters less racially antagonistic to African Americans than they had been in previous elections, did it show that they were *everywhere* color-blind? There is reason to doubt the proposition. First, in the general election, exit polls showed Obama receiving only 17 percent of white votes in the five states traditionally denominated the "Deep South." Voting was starkly polarized. In every state across the country where exit poll results by race are available, Obama attracted the support of more than 90 percent of African Americans. Second, in the states wholly covered by Section 5 of the VRA (including the Deep South states), Obama received the same percentage of the white vote as losing Democratic presidential candidate John Kerry had in 2004, while in the rest of the states, Obama surpassed Kerry by four percentage points among whites. Throughout the country, Obama scored gains of from 9 to 13 percentage points among blacks and Latinos. Overall, in the general election, Obama received 48 percent of the white vote in states not wholly covered by the VRA, but only 26 percent in the covered states. If the country's electorate had been entirely white, in other words, Obama would have lost the national popular vote badly; in the states covered by the VRA, he would have lost by the staggering margin of 3 to 1. Third, during the Democratic primaries between Obama and Senator Hillary Clinton (D-NY), when partisanship could not have been a factor in voters' choices, exit polls showed that Obama received less than 30 percent of the white Democratic vote in the Deep South. In the core of the states covered by Section 5 of the VRA, racism was still surprisingly overt: Of the 24 percent of white voters in Mississippi who admitted to pollsters that race was an important factor in choosing between Obama and Clinton, only 10 percent chose Obama; in Louisiana, the analogous figures were 22 percent and 12 percent; in Alabama, 20 percent and 18 percent.

There is one more consideration: The election of a president is much different from elections for local or state officials, or even for members of Congress. Presidential candidates are much better known, conduct high-level debates about great national and international issues, and amass huge staffs of strategists, speech writers, and coordinators of every detail. Candidates for lower offices are often nearly invisible; their issue positions are often quite vague; and are publicized only in easily ignored campaign flyers; and local contacts in a still-segregated society tend to be more influential in voters' decisions than in national contests. The first and perhaps the only information many voters have about candidates in subnational elections may be their race. It is therefore problematic to generalize from the degree of white color-consciousness in national elections to that which might determine their choices in local elections. Obama's election, then, failed, by itself, to prove that the VRA is no longer necessary or appropriate in any county, in any state, at any level of election.

Opponents of continuing the VRA and several members of the U.S. Supreme Court, however, seemed to accept the racial transfiguration thesis. As Gregory Coleman, the attorney challenging the VRA in the *NAMUDNO* case, put it in a brief a month after the 2008 election, "The America that has elected Barack Obama as its first African-American president is far different than when Section 5 was first enacted in 1965. [Proponents of the VRA] barely acknowledge the deep-rooted societal change. . . ." During the oral arguments of the *NAMUDNO* case, on April 29, 2009, Chief Justice John Roberts asked Debo Adegbile, the lawyer for the NAACP Legal Defense Fund, "Is it your position that today southerners are more likely to discriminate than northerners?" Dismissing the contention that Section 5 deterred covered jurisdictions from passing racially discriminatory election laws as "silly," the chief justice and his four fellow conservatives, including key swing justice Anthony Kennedy, condemned Section 5's concentration on the South as unfair, an example of "disparate treatment," an attack on the "equal sovereignty" of each state. The formula for determining which local and state jurisdictions had to get Washington's permission before putting new election laws into effect, the conservative justices seemed to imply, was unconstitutional.

For several years before Congress voted to renew the VRA in 2006, proponents had worried about just this possibility, because the Supreme Court in 1997 had issued a new standard for the constitutionality of laws of Congress. Such laws, a 5-4 conservative majority of the Court announced in *City of Boerne v. Flores*, had to be "congruent and proportional," in the opinions of the justices, to a problem or evil that the constitution gave Congress the power to regulate. Accordingly, VRA supporters in and outside of Congress produced a mass of evidence—21 congressional hearings at which 86 witnesses presented 15,000 pages of testimony and reports on the question of whether Section 5 was still needed in the areas where it applied—which showed, for example, that, since 1982, Section 5 had directly prevented more than 2,400 discriminatory changes from taking effect. As the *NAMUDNO* case, filed just eight days after President George W. Bush signed the renewed VRA, moved through the courts, supporters repeated the massive pile of facts gathered for congressional consideration in each round of legal briefs. Yet at oral argument in the Supreme Court, those facts appeared to make little impression on the conservative majority, and VRA backers awaited the Court's decision with considerable trepidation.

On June 22, 2009, Chief Justice Roberts surprised all sides by issuing an opinion that at least temporarily put off a decision on the adequacy of Section 5's coverage scheme and, therefore, on the constitutionality of the VRA. In a strained interpretation of the wording of the VRA that contradicted earlier opinions of the Supreme Court, the chief justice allowed the tiny utility district, one of 105 local jurisdictions in Travis County, Texas, to apply to the Justice Department separately from the county to be released from the necessity of complying with Section 5. Although the likelihood of a harsh backlash against conservative judicial activism may have inhibited the majority of the Supreme Court, and especially Justice Kennedy, from declaring the VRA unconstitutional in this case, the chief justice ended his opinion with what sounded like a threat if Congress does not change the coverage scheme: "We are now a very different Nation. Whether conditions continue to justify such legislation is a difficult constitutional question we do not answer today."

Equal political rights for minorities hang in the balance today, as they have throughout the country's history, dependent on the legal actions of major political institutions. Whether Congress will update the VRA's coverage scheme and whether the Supreme Court will continue to sustain the act's constitutionality, even if Congress does update it, is a matter for a future entry in another volume, a sequel in the never-finished history of equal rights.

Further Reading:

Clarke, Kristen. "The Obama Factor: The Impact of the 2008 Presidential Election on Future Voting Rights Act Litigation." *Harvard Law and Policy Review* 3 (2009): 201–227; Davidson, Chandler, and Bernard Grofman, eds. *Quiet Revolution in the South: The Impact of the Voting Rights Act, 1965–1990.* Princeton, N.J.: Princeton University Press, 1994; Foner, Eric. *Reconstruction: America's Unfinished Revolution, 1863–1877.* New York: Harper & Row, 1988; Gans, David H., and Douglas T. Kendall. *The Shield of National Protection: The Text and History of Section 5 of the Fourteenth Amendment.* Washington, D.C.: Constitutional Accountability Center, 2009; Keyssar, Alexander. *The Right to Vote: The Contested History of Democracy in the United States.* New York: Basic Books, 2000; Kousser, J. Morgan. *Colorblind Injustice: Minority Voting Rights and the Undoing of the Second Reconstruction.* Chapel Hill: University of North Carolina Press, 1999; ———. *The Shaping of Southern Politics: Suffrage Restriction and the Establishment of the One-Party South, 1880–1910.* New Haven, Conn.: Yale University Press, 1974; ———. "The Strange, Ironic Career of Section Five of the Voting Rights Act, 1965–2007." *Texas Law Review* 86 (2008): 667–775; Lawson, Steven F. *Black Ballots: Voting Rights in the South, 1944–1969.* New York: Columbia University Press, 1976; Malone, Christopher. *Between Freedom and Bondage: Race, Party, and Voting Rights in the Antebellum North.* New York: Routledge, 2008; Manza, Jeff, and Christopher Uggen. *Locked Out: Felon Disfranchisement and American Democracy.* New York: Oxford University Press, 2006; McCool, Daniel, Susan M. Olson, and Jennifer L. Robinson. *Native Vote: American Indians, the Voting Rights Act, and the Right to Vote.* New York: Cambridge University Press, 2007.

–J. Morgan Kousser

Government Operations

budget process

Government budgets determine on what basis shall it be decided to allocate X dollars to activity A instead of activity B. Budgeting is the allocation of financial resources, mandated by the fact that wants are greater than resources. The national budget has increased greatly in size and complexity in the last few decades. Even when inflation had been taken into account, the national budget has more than quadrupled since 1960. The changes in the composition of the budget reflect changes in national priorities. Even in an age of trillion-dollar budgets, money is insufficient to meet all demands. The budget is not simply a financial statement; it is also a statement of policy. Conflicts over money are in reality conflicts over policy.

A government budget has three goals. First, budgets provide accountability. Where did taxpayer funds go? Where did it come from? Second, budgets help to plan for the future. Government expenditures on defense, public works, social insurance, and so forth require planning. People plan their lives around what they think government is going to do. Third, budgets play an important role in managing the economy. Governments want to keep the economy on an even keel; poor economic performance ruins political lives.

Traditionally, budgeting in the United States has been seen as an incremental process. That is, except in extraordinary times (war, depression), budgetary changes were small and at the margins. Incrementalism reduces the chance of unexpected surprises, and even though it does not rule out the possibility of major changes, it prevents major alterations in the budget from occurring quickly. The largest determining factor of this year's budget is last year's budget. Many items are standard and simply renewed every year unless a special reason exists to challenge them. Thus, a budget is based on the previous budget, with special attention given to a small range of increases or decreases. The base is some version of what you are getting now, and is the general expectation that programs will continue to receive an amount close to what they are currently receiving. The baseline, therefore, assumes that existing programs will continue without major policy change. It adjusts projected expenditures for estimated inflation and required workload changes.

To provide for responsible government, budgeting is geared to a cycle. The cycle allows the system to absorb and respond to new information and thus allows government to be held accountable for its actions. The budget cycle has four phases. First, the executive branch prepares the budget and submits the budget to Congress. The budgetary blueprint thus starts in the White House. Most of the day-to-day work in developing the budget is handled by the Office of Management and Budget (OMB) and the executive departments and agencies. The budget sent to Congress reflects the president's decisions and priorities on such matters as: (1) its overall size, (2) possible effects on the economy, (3) major directions in public policy, and (4) allocation of funds among the major agencies and programs. Second, the budget must be passed by Congress. Third, government agencies are responsible for the execution of the budget.

The obligation and actual expenditure of funds rests with the various departments and agencies. Finally, the government audits the budget that has been put into effect. This evaluation of the budget is done by the General Accountability Office (GAO).

Ideally, the budget timetable is the following:

October 1: Beginning of the new fiscal year. All action concerning the budget is to be completed.

February: The president submits his budget.

April 15: Congress is required to pass its budget resolution.

June 30: All 13 appropriations bills should have been passed by the House; this rarely happens.

September 30: Congress is supposed to have finished its budget work for the fiscal year that is supposed to start; it rarely does. The result is a series of continuing resolutions until the budget is finally passed.

Traditionally, the federal fiscal year began on July 1. In previous eras when government was small and relatively uncomplicated, Congress would have adjourned by summertime. Congress found this deadline more and more difficult to meet as budgeting became more complex, and finally in 1974 the fiscal year was shifted to October 1, giving Congress three additional months for its annual budget work. These three extra months, however, have often not been long enough as Congress has on numerous occasions found itself unable to agree to a budget by October.

Prior to 1921 the president was only marginally involved in the budget process. This changed with the Budget and Accounting Act of 1921, which made it a legal requirement for the president to submit a budget to Congress. Before 1921, if agencies wanted money, they went directly to Congress. Congress, unable to cope with the new budgetary environment and realizing that more centralization was needed in the budget process, was forced to forfeit some of its power of the purse to the president in 1921. The Budget Act of 1921 required the president to send an annual budget plan to Congress, created the Bureau of the Budget (later Office of Management and Budget) to help the president in his new budgetary role, and formalized a new budget process that divided labor among the branches. The basic provisions of the 1921 Budget Act remained intact until the process finally broke down during the Nixon administration as the deficit skyrocketed. Congress reacted by overhauling the budget process with the Budget and Impoundment Control Act of 1974.

As dictated by the Budget and Accounting Act of 1921, the president initiates the budget process by submitting a budget to Congress within 15 days of the start of the legislative session. Congress then follows the procedures set forth by the Budget and Impoundment Control Act of 1974. After the president submits the budget to Congress, congressional committees hold hearings that revolve around testimony from the various executive departments. After the hearings, Congress passes a budget resolution that lays out its taxing and spending priorities for the next fiscal year. The targets of the budget resolution become guidelines for the various authorizing and appropriating committees that write specific taxing and spending bills.

Following passage of the budget resolution in the spring, subcommittees of the appropriations committees consider specific appropriation bills, and the revenue committees consider their portion of the budget, with the appropriation subcommittees supposedly staying within the budget resolution. The budget committees serve as watchdogs, making sure that legislation is not substantially at variance with the resolution, although the budget committees lacked authority to override other committees.

The budget resolutions adopted by Congress each year constitute the heart of the budget process, expressing congressional decisions of fiscal policy by defining the balance between total spending and revenue. The breakdown of total spending by functional categories represents congressional priorities. Budget resolutions do not impose fixed limits on spending because the ceilings imposed can always be raised. The resolution is only a congressional declaration of budgetary goals, not a statute. As a result, it cannot make or change laws. The resolution sets forth spending totals and broad priorities but it does not identify specific programs. Thus, it can reduce overall spending levels but it cannot actually cut programs out of the budget.

Unlike the budget resolution, the budget reconciliation process is actually designed for Congress to make specific program cuts. Reconciliation is the process by which Congress tries to bring revenue and spending under existing laws into conformity with the levels set in the budget resolution. Enactment of a reconciliation bill changes revenues or spending laws. Reconciliation is an optional process that is not activated every year. It is most likely to be used if the president's budget recommends spending cutbacks and if Congress wants to take active steps to reduce spending. Major budget shifts today tend to take place through the reconciliation process, and it has evolved into the principal means by which Congress enacts deficit reduction legislation. The major budget shifts of 1981, 1990, 1993, and 2001 were all enacted through the reconciliation process.

The reconciliation process has generally made the budget process much more complicated. In one area, however, the reconciliation process brought about a significant change that has made budgetary politics easier: The reconciliation bill cannot be filibustered in the Senate. Given the complexity of omnibus budget packages and the reconciliation process, senators agreed that no filibusters would be allowed during reconciliation. Since the president still has veto power over the budget, however, this rule has worked to enhance the president's budgetary powers. While the president needs to muster only a majority of Congress to support his budget proposals, Congress would have to muster a two-thirds majority in both houses to pass the budget without presidential approval.

A whole range of committees deal with taxing and spending; no single focal point exists in the budget process. The major players in the committee organization relevant to the budget include the House and Senate Budget Committees, the House and Senate Appropriations Committees, the House Ways and Means Committee and Senate Finance Committee, and the authorization committees. The authorization committees set policy; the appropriation committees determine the levels and distribution of discretionary spending; and the taxation committees determine the volume of revenues and the distribution of the tax burden. All of these activities are supposed to be coordinated by the budget committees, so that Congress can meet its policy obligations and budget targets.

No appropriation can be made without authorization. Authorizations are the official expressions of the interests of Congress. The authorization requirement serves to highlight the fact that the primary responsibility of Congress is to provide services, not to make budgetary decisions. The authorization committees are organized according to governmental function. In the House, a total of 18 committees share some authorization responsibility.

Appropriations committee members traditionally see themselves in the role of watchdog of the budget process. The appropriation committees traditionally scrutinize presidential budgetary actions and compare them to authorization requests. If authorization requests are much different from the president's requests, appropriations will often side toward the president's position. For most annual authorizations, however, the amount appropriated is more than 90 percent of the authorized level. Authorizations and appropriations, however, will usually diverge when the committees do not share the same attitudes toward a program.

The Ways and Means Committee in the House and the Finance Committee in the Senate create the legislation that generates the revenue for the federal government. In addition to being responsible for tax legislation, the committees are responsible for trade and many of the largest spending programs in the budget, including Social Security and Medicare. As a result, not only do the Ways and Means and Finance Committees have control of 100 percent of taxes, but they have control of more than half of the federal government's spending as well. Since the tax-writing committees have almost complete control of the revenue side of the budget, control a good portion of the spending, and have jurisdiction over both the deficit and the national debt, some observers of Congress have argued that they have excessive control.

The balancing of congressional interests begins in the Budget Committees, which were created in 1974. Until the 1970s, Congress often made important economic decisions, but it had no means to make separate decisions on overall levels of taxing and spending. By 1974, Congress had become more concerned about fiscal policy overall and it adopted reforms to improve its ability to engage in macrolevel decision making. The Budget Act of 1974 constituted an attempt by Congress to reassert its intention to govern the country amid increasing indications that it could no longer do so. It created the modern congressional budget process. The act established standing House and Senate Budget Committees and adjusted the budget timetable. It did not change the authorization or appropriations processes, tax policy, or committee jurisdictions. The House Budget Committee was designed so that the Ways and Means Committee and the Appropriations Committee both held 10 seats on the committee, and tenure was limited (two terms until 1979, three terms since). The Senate Budget Committee, on the other hand, has no membership or tenure restrictions. This difference has played an important role in the dynamics of the budget process.

Although they can take a hard line and try to block legislation that does not meet their rules, the Budget Committees try to accommodate the budget process to the diverse legislative interests of other committees, especially those of Appropriations and Ways and Means/Finance. The dilemma for the Budget Committees is to accommodate without giving up all meaningful enforcement. The Budget Committees, however, are largely unable to prevent other committees from doing what they want to do. Both Budget Committees can be said to be "adding-machine" committees that gather the demands of the spending committees and impose as much restraint on them as the current congressional mood allows. Neither Budget Committee has the authority to act as the sole interpreter of congressional preferences, greatly weakening their designated role as guardians of the budget process.

The Budget Act of 1974 was the result of the political conflicts of the time. After the 1972 election, Nixon decided to impound—refuse to spend—billions of dollars in appropriations that he did not like. This rallied liberals around the concept of budget reform, while conservatives wanted reform to balance the budget. The bitter battles with Nixon over the budget and impoundment led Congress to enact this compromise measure, with conservatives supporting the budget reform measures, including an increase in centralization, and liberals liking the anti-impoundment measures. Mistrust of the White House can be seen in the act's creation of the Congressional Budget Office (CBO), which was envisioned to be the independent "scorekeeper" of Congress, charged with giving a nonpartisan accounting of the numbers in the legislation that moves through Congress every year. Today, CBO's numbers can make or break proposed legislation. The Budget Act of 1974 represented a radical new approach because Congress would now make programs fit fiscal policy—the parts would now fit the whole. Congress, it was hoped, would now make a budget. As it turned out, however, the act only made the process even more complex and cumbersome, leading to an even more dominant role of the president. The major budget shifts since 1974—the budgets of 1981, 1990, 1993, and 2001—were all initiatives led by the White House.

Ronald Reagan was elected president promising significant tax cuts, and his campaign pledge was fulfilled only eight months after he assumed office with the passage of the sweeping Economic Recovery Tax Act of 1981 (ERTA). Among the significant features of ERTA were: (1) tax cuts that ultimately equaled about one-quarter of tax brackets for personal income taxes were phased in over two years; (2) income tax brackets and exemptions were indexed for inflation, eliminating so-called bracket creep; (3) the top marginal tax bracket was reduced from 70 percent to 50 percent; and (4) a generous set of depreciation schedules (called the Accelerated Cost Recovery System) was initiated for businesses.

ERTA was an era-defining legislative drive that, according to one political scientist, ranks behind only the Civil Rights Act of 1964 as the most significant legislative drive during the past half-century. The 1981 tax cuts were the largest in history at the time, at a bit more than 2 percent of the gross domestic product (properly adjusted, the George W. Bush tax cuts in 2001 were about as large as the net tax cut created by the Reagan tax cuts). The Reagan tax cuts were guided by an unusually coherent political and economic ideology. Reagan's philosophy regarding the size and scope of government has set the tone for budget politics to this day.

The primary theoretical support for the Reagan tax cuts was provided by supply-side economic theory. Early supporters of the Reagan plan were strong adherents of this economic theory. According to supply-side theory, in a market economy where productivity is based upon the incentives of the private sector, excessively high tax rates discourage investment and innovation. Why work hard if the rewards are to be taxed anyway? High taxes, according to supply siders, arrest economic growth, reducing the growth rate of income and thus the tax base. If tax rates were cut, therefore, the economy would flourish and income would grow, increasing tax receipts.

Using supply-side economic theory as a guide, Reagan argued that economic stimulus resulting from a tax cut would result in an increase of governmental revenues even though economists overwhelmingly rejected this argument. Reagan's tax revolution turned FDR's New Deal on its head; instead of promising more benefits, the strategy became to promise to cut taxes and stay relatively quiet on benefits. Supply-side supporters of Reagan's radical tax cuts justified the tax cuts by arguing that deficits would not be a problem; in fact, it was argued by many in the Reagan administration that deficits would even be reduced.

The experiences of the early 1980s taught the Republicans that opposing taxes was good politics, but assailing popular domestic programs was not. Deficit levels, however, increased dramatically during the Reagan administration, eventually becoming too much for federal policy makers to tolerate. As a result, George H. W. Bush, Reagan's Republican successor, was finally forced to try to come to grips with record deficits. In the end, the tax debate in 1990 shifted to the Democrats' position. Despite having campaigned in 1988 on a pledge of "read my lips, no new taxes," Bush reluctantly agreed in a budget summit to a deficit reduction package in the Budget Enforcement Act of 1990 that raised taxes and imposed new user fees in return for cuts in entitlement programs and future limits on discretionary spending.

A number of factors accounted for the Republicans losing control of the tax issues as the parties maneuvered through 1990. The Bush administration, concerned that a soaring deficit could severely damage the economy and hurt Bush's reelection chances, sought Democrats' help to work out a bipartisan deficit-reduction deal and, in June, Bush issued a statement that "tax revenue increases" would have to be part of any package. With Republicans deeply split over Bush's tax shift and polls indicating a growing public perception that the Republican tax policies had favored the wealthy, Democrats seized the issue of tax equity and made it the focus of the tax debate. Democrats argued that tax changes made during the 1980s had largely benefited the wealthy and that this direction needed to be reversed.

When Republican and Democratic leaders originally unveiled a final budget package, strong opposition from rank-and-file members on both sides prevented the package from advancing. Congressional Democrats criticized the original package as imposing too much of the burden on low- and middle-income taxpayers and not enough on the wealthy. Congressional Republicans complained that the package would impede economic growth by calling for too many new taxes and too few breaks for investors. Rejection of the package by Congress forced the Bush administration to negotiate on the Democrats' terms. The result was a set of tax provisions in the reconciliation bill that not only raised the top income tax rate from 28 percent to 31 percent but also imposed other changes designed to shift the tax burden to the wealthy. The tax distribution was significantly different from that of the budget-summit package, which would have given relatively smaller increases to those with higher incomes. As they negotiated for a compromise that would make the tax system more progressive without imposing a visible surcharge on the wealthy, Congress and the Bush administration added new complexity to the tax system that was supposed to be simplified by the 1986 tax reforms.

Congressional discontent with the large deficits of the Reagan and Bush administrations led increasingly to calls to force the federal government to produce balanced budgets by amending the Constitution to force Congress to enact balanced budgets. In the 1980s and 1990s there were five votes on a Balanced Budget Amendment in the House and seven in the Senate. Though the details of the amendments sometimes varied (usually with exceptions for time of war or a change in economic conditions), the overall goal of supporters of a Balanced Budget Amendment was to constitutionally require the federal government to produce a balanced budget. The debate over the Balanced Budget Amendment, however, may have been more symbolic than practical. For one, it is unclear what the practical effects of such an amendment would be. Balanced Budget Amendment votes have been criticized by many as being purely symbolic, since they deal with the process, not tangible outcomes. Also, even if a Balanced Budget Amendment were enacted, it remains unlikely that the federal government could balance the budget year-in, year-out even if it wanted to. Producing a balanced budget requires accurate forecasting of revenues and expenditures. These forecasts depend upon accurate prediction of economic conditions, which is an inexact science to say the least. Inaccurate forecasts can play an important role in increasing the deficit. Deficit estimates are almost inevitably subject to seemingly large swings, even when they are made only a month before the end of the fiscal year.

Despite the fact that it was not an issue that he emphasized while running for the presidency in 1992, Bill Clinton demonstrated an early effort to reduce the deficit once he was elected president. Surprising many, Clinton showed a willingness to expend his own popularity once elected by proposing a politically risky budgetary blueprint that relied heavily on increased taxes. One month after his inauguration in 1993, President Clinton unveiled a proposed budget that included significant tax increases to bring the deficit downward.

Altogether, Clinton's deficit-cutting plan proposed generating $246 billion from tax increases over four years. Clinton's call for a tax increase was a direct repudiation of the economic philosophies of his two Republican predecessors. Clinton's proposals implied that the tax policies of Ronald Reagan and George H. W. Bush came at the price of high deficits. Clinton hoped that he could convince the American public that the economic expansion of the 1980s held negative consequences in the long run. The fact that the tax increases were disproportionately on upper incomes marked a return to traditional Democratic-style budgets of the post–New Deal era. Though the two new tax brackets that were created—36 percent and 39.6 percent—were much smaller than the highest tax brackets of the previous Democratic presidencies since the New Deal, the return to a more progressive income tax marked a significant shift from the tax policies of Reagan and Bush. Overall, more than half of the new taxes were projected to fall on families making more than $200,000 a year. By raising taxes in the name of deficit reduction, the Clinton administration hoped that the public now believed that large budget deficits were problematic and that they were now more supportive of tax increases than was the case during the Reagan years.

President Clinton's proposed budget, what ultimately became the Budget Reconciliation Act of 1993, emerged victorious, though just barely. It was approved in August 1993 without a single vote to spare in either chamber: 218-216 in the House and 51-50 in the Senate (Vice President Al Gore again made the tie-breaking vote). The measure passed without any Republican votes; with the Republicans unwilling to compromise and unable to drive the process themselves, the struggle to get the antideficit package through Congress was exclusively one of rounding up enough Democrats. This was the case even though the proposal had something to offend almost every Democrat;

conservatives were uncomfortable with the entire range of tax increases, and liberals were uncomfortable with some of the $87 billion in cuts over five years in entitlement spending programs such as Medicare and Medicaid as well as the $102 billion in cuts over five years in appropriated spending. Liberals and the Congressional Black Caucus, however, endorsed the bill early on, making moderates and conservatives the critical swing votes.

Overall, the Budget Reconciliation Act of 1993 was expected to shrink, but not eliminate, the deficit. Annual deficits, however, declined dramatically after the measure was enacted; indeed, they declined much more than anyone predicted. In a development that would have been thought impossible in the early 1990s, there were budget surpluses from 1998 to 2001, the first years since 1969 that the federal government did not run in the red. In 2000, the federal government had a surplus of a staggering $236 billion, the eighth consecutive year with a declining deficit or increased surplus, a postwar record. The situation changed with staggering speed. To illustrate how much the budgetary picture changed, in 1993 the Congressional Budget Office projected a fiscal 1998 deficit of $357 billion; the actual 1998 fiscal budget had a surplus of $69 billion. Liquidating the deficit ranks as one of the supreme budgetary accomplishments in American history and completely changed the dynamics of the federal budget process. The deficit-reducing conventions of the 1980s and early 1990s were replaced by a new set of ideas for fiscal policy. By the end of the Clinton presidency, surpluses had become an accepted part of the vocabulary and arithmetic of federal budgeting.

The success of the 1993 budget at bringing in more revenue was the most important reason for the elimination of the budget deficit. The reason for the significant increase in revenues after 1993 was the combination of the progressive nature of the tax increases—they raised taxes on upper incomes—coupled with a very strong economy. Those making relatively high incomes did particularly well in the economic environment of the late 1990s, and as a result they paid more federal taxes at a higher tax rate. After 1992, the last year the highest income tax rate was 31 percent, the federal government gained substantially more revenue from those with higher incomes. Because of the widened income gap between low and high earners, the federal government took in much more revenue than it would have without the 1993 tax increases.

George W. Bush decided to make cutting taxes the number one priority of his administration after he was inaugurated. The passage of significant tax cuts after Bush was elected president in 2000 was the culmination of years of debate over whether the nation could afford a substantial tax reduction at a time of large and growing federal budget surpluses. Bush's tax cuts represent a dramatic change in American tax policy and fundamentally reshaped the nation's fiscal landscape.

Bush's emphasis on tax cuts over deficit reduction marked a radical departure from the budgetary strategy of Clinton. After the 2000 elections, Republicans controlled both the White House and Congress for the first time since the Eisenhower administration and the Republicans were free to dictate the budget process. Despite the popularity of Ronald Reagan as president, the political as well as policy success of supply-side economics was still very much in doubt until the election of George W. Bush. With the election of Bush, however, the Republicans once again embraced supply-side economics as a justification for lowering taxes.

The Economic Growth and Tax Relief Reconciliation Act of 2001 consisted of a tax reduction package of $1.35 trillion. At $875 billion through 2011, the cuts in income taxes were by far the most expensive part of the bill, accounting for 65 percent of the package's total. Income tax rates were reduced to rates ranging from 10 percent to 35 percent, replacing the rates that had been in effect since 1993, which ranged from 15 percent to 39.6 percent.

An extraordinary provision in the 2001 tax cut package was the final one slated to take effect: the repeal of the entire measure at the end of 2010. Much of the 2001 tax cut package was not set to take effect until the second half of the decade, after the next presidential election. As a result of the sunset provisions, revenues were projected to increase sharply in 2011 when statutory tax rates would rise. The sunset provisions were necessary for the legislation to comply with the requirement that limited the cost of the tax cuts to $1.35 trillion through 2011. The Bush administration, however, was confident that the sunset would never happen because a future Congress would agree to extend the provisions of the 2001 law. Three-fifths of the package's cost came after 2006. To critics, the measure's back-loaded nature and limited duration allowed Bush and congressional Republicans to grossly underestimate the true cost of the tax cuts.

President Bush made making the tax cuts permanent a major priority after winning reelection in 2004, claiming that his election was a "mandate" to have Congress make the tax cuts passed in 2001 permanent. Bush's proposal to make the tax cuts permanent would have had major implications for projected long-term deficit levels. If all the tax provisions that are set to expire in 2011 were extended, the budget outlook for 2016 would have changed from a surplus of $67 billion to a deficit of $584 billion. Overall, projected revenues would be reduced by about $2.64 trillion from 2011 to 2016 if the tax cuts were made permanent.

Discussions of the federal budget process usually look at taxing and spending decision in tandem. A problem with this approach is that it underestimates the degree to which the political dynamics of taxing is different from the political dynamics of spending. The decision-making process for taxes, simply put, is considerably different from that for spending. Ultimately, the disconnection between taxing and spending is problematic for the federal government because spending levels tend to be consistently higher than tax revenues. Chronically large deficits are the obvious indicator that the budget process has gone awry.

Tax policy in the United States is largely one of inertia. It is extremely difficult to alter tax policy to changing needs and circumstances. Since it is politically much easier to cut taxes than to raise taxes, if tax policy is altered at all it tends to be downward. Good economic and political arguments may exist for reducing taxes, but without simultaneous spending reductions, tax cuts will result in larger budget deficits. Spending policy, on the other hand, is made piecemeal, with little regard to how spending affects the budget. The separation of taxing and spending policy encourages higher expenditure levels relative to revenues, leading to deficit-plagued budgets.

Unlike the federal government, all states with the exception of Vermont are legally required to produce balanced budgets. The requirements vary in rigidity from state to state, though no state imposes legal penalties for failure to produce a balanced budget. State balanced budget requirements, however, in practice refer to operation budgets and not to capital budgets. "Balancing the budget," therefore, refers to the general state fund, though general fund expenditures compose only 50 percent to 60 percent of total state spending. Though the dynamics of state budgets are considerably different from those of the federal government, state taxing and spending decisions inevitably influence federal budget priorities. The modern tax cut movement, for example, is often said to have started in 1978 with the passage of Proposition 13 in California, which dramatically lowered property taxes. Immediately after the success of Proposition 13, tax reduction referenda succeeded in a number of other states, including Illinois, Massachusetts, and Michigan.

As the major budget shifts over the past three decades—those of 1981, 1990, 1993, and 2001—demonstrate, the federal budget process system is simply not designed in a way that makes producing a comprehensive budget easy. The Budget Acts of 1921 and 1974 have created a budget process that is extremely complex and cumbersome.

Further Reading:

Bartels, Larry M. *Unequal Democracy.* New York: Russell Sage, 2008; Brownlee, W. Elliot. *Federal Taxation in America: A Short History.* 2d ed. New York: Cambridge University Press, 2004; Farrier, Jasmine. *Passing the Buck: Congress, the Budget, and Deficits.* Lexington: University of Kentucky Press, 2004; Fisher, Patrick. *The Politics of Taxing and Spending.* Boulder, Colo.: Lynne Rienner, 2009; Hacker, Jacob S., and Paul Pierson. "Abandoning the Middle: The Bush Tax

Cuts and the Limits of Democratic Control." *PS: Perspectives on Politics* 3 (2005): 33–53; Ippolito, Dennis S. *Why Budgets Matter: Budget Policy and American Politics.* University Park: Pennsylvania State University Press, 2003 ; Kettl, Donald F. *Deficit Politics.* 2d ed. New York: Longman, 2003; Nice, David. *Public Budgeting.* Belmont, Calif.: Wadsworth, 2002; Schick, Allen. *The Federal Budget Process: Politics, Policy, Process.* Washington, D.C.: Brookings Institution Press, 1995; Wildavsky, Aaron, and Naomi Caiden. *The New Politics of the Budgetary Process.* 5th ed. New York: Longman, 2004.

– *Patrick Fisher*

civil service

The U.S. Constitution created a powerful framework for our federal government. However, one of the characteristics that makes the Constitution both inspired and enduring is that it avoids excessive detail. The Constitution is a very concise document and many elements that now seem essential to our federal government are never mentioned. One notable omission is that the Constitution provides very limited direction regarding a federal bureaucracy—essentially, the federal workforce.

The federal workforce did not spring up fully formed upon President Washington's earliest appointments. Rather, the bureaucracy has evolved over the course of more than 200 years, influenced by the leaders, politics, and events of the day. This article entry details the development of the bureaucracy under the early presidential administrations, the growth of a "spoils" system and the resulting Pendleton Act reforms, the expansion of the federal workforce throughout the 20th century, and the efforts at reform attempted over the past three decades. For this discussion, the civil service will be defined as the unelected members of the federal government workforce who are selected and managed according to a system based on merit. The Pendleton Act of 1883 (discussed later) established the first federal civil service.

The first presidential administration began with no federal government workforce. Without a workforce in place, President George Washington was free to appoint employees for the federal government without removing existing employees. Further, Paul van Riper points out that federal politics during the first presidential administrations can best be described as a one-party system. This lack of political opposition raised the expectation that a federal employee would retain his position when a new president came to office. Accordingly, positions in the earliest administrations were characterized by an expectation of long tenure. However, the lack of political adversaries did not mean that appointments were nonpolitical during the first few administrations. In fact, holding a sympathetic political opinion was a necessity for an appointment by Washington or by Adams.

When Thomas Jefferson came to office, his presidency marked the first transfer of executive power from one political party, the Federalist Party, to another, Jefferson's Democratic-Republican party. This shift in political authority raised the question of how to remove employees appointed by the previous administration to fill the vacant positions with like-minded political supporters. Jefferson's efforts to answer that question constitutes some of the earliest examples of federal human resources reform. Van Riper notes that Jefferson argued for the equal division of all personnel between the parties. Such an allotment would provide a continuing staff who were equally loyal to whomever held the office of president. In the process of implementing this balance, Jefferson started slowly, then moved to replace many more employees than Washington and Adams had combined. Because Jefferson removed personnel appointed by the Federalist presidents and replaced them with supporters of his Democratic-Republican Party, Van Riper argues that Jefferson is the true initiator of the "spoils" system in the United States.

The term *spoils* is used to describe appointments made to reward political supporters for their assistance. The supporters gain lucrative positions in the government and the president gains a workforce of loyal supporters. Riccucci and Naff observe that the term *spoils* stems from a statement by Senator William Marcy made during an 1832 political debate. Marcy argued that politicians "see nothing wrong in the rule that to the victor, belong the spoils of the enemy." Marcy's description stuck, and it is regularly used to describe the practice of a newly elected official filling government offices with like-minded supporters as payment for their assistance.

Although Jefferson replaced many more federal employees than his predecessors, the extent of spoils politics was still fairly limited at the federal level during the early 1800s. Rather, the practice of spoils grew first in state and local politics. Van Riper attributes this "bottom-up" expansion to the greater significance of political parties at the state and local levels. As the party system grew in the states and localities, spoils appointments were used to reward supporters who fueled the financial and organizational growth of the parties. Essentially, the spoils system was necessary to the growth of party politics. Spoils enabled party leaders to secure financial and personal support with the promise of a lucrative government job as payment.

In 1820, the passage of the Four Years Law made a significant impact on the practice of federal spoils appointments. The statute set a maximum term of four years in office for numerous positions with fiscal responsibility. The consequence was that numerous positions were automatically vacated every four years, enabling the party in power to reward many supporters. Secretary of the Treasury William H. Crawford led the push for the Four Years Law, though it is not clear whether the secretary was seeking better fiscal accountability or an opportunity to make his own patronage appointments if he won the presidency in his later campaign.

The spoils system came to the forefront of federal politics with the 1829 inauguration of President Andrew Jackson. Jackson had campaigned on a populist platform, and his populist policies included opening government jobs to applicants outside of the upper class. Jackson's supporters expected the middle and lower classes to acquire a stake in the new government. The president addressed these public concerns during his first inaugural address, stating the need to reform the federal bureaucracy to make it both more representative of the people and smaller in size. Although Jackson did not fire a majority of the federal workforce and replace them with his supporters, Riccucci and Naff note that he solidified the federal spoils system with his speeches arguing for a more democratic federal government workforce.

Spoils practices grew for the next three decades, with the high point of politically motivated appointments coming during the first term of President Lincoln. With the fate of the country at stake, Lincoln had to ensure that all federal employees were working together to support the preservation of the Union, so he fired many office-holders and hired politically loyal replacements. Over the 15 years following the Civil War, spoils appointments grew, as did the opposition to spoils, which centered mainly on moral grounds. The moral argument reached a tipping point in 1881 when newly elected President Garfield was assassinated by a disgruntled applicant for a federal job. Advocates for reform argued that little could be more immoral than a system of spoils that led to the murder of the president. Garfield's death catalyzed the antispoils movement, and the resulting public outcry motivated the 1883 passage of the first, major civil service development, the Pendleton Act.

The events that led up to the Pendleton Act's passage created a fervor of support for reform. Public opinion shifted toward the reformers, who continued to advocate that throwing people out of office to reward others' political contributions was morally wrong, while hiring based solely on the consideration of an applicant's merit was plainly good. Democrats generally supported reform, and the party, including Senator Pendleton (D-OH), capitalized on the public zeal.

Although the Republicans were still in the majority in Congress, they had suffered significant defeats during the fall 1882 midterm elections. The Republican support that helped to pass the bill grew out of a recognition that public enthusiasm for reform could hurt them at the polls, and a desire to prohibit spoils appointments before the

Democrats won back the White House and removed Republican appointees. In the House of Representatives, where members were motivated by facing the reform-minded voters in two short years, the legislation was approved without debate, by acclamation. Despite lengthy debate in the Senate, little action was taken to thwart passage.

As Mosher observes, the Pendleton Act was based on an earlier reorganization of the British civil service system. The Pendleton Act created a federal civil service system founded on three principles derived from the British. The American version relied on the British standards of: (1) open, competitive examinations; (2) relative security of tenure; and (3) political neutrality. However, Van Riper notes that the resulting reform is a distinctly American creation.

Several elements of the Pendleton Act contrast with the British system. In one example, American lawmakers mandated examinations based on the practical requirements of the job rather than following the British reliance on theoretical examinations. Furthermore, the Pendleton Act did not provide officeholders with life tenure. The American federal civil service instead includes relative security of tenure, but personnel can be removed from office. Moreover, the British civil service required that all new applicants join government employment at the entry level, no matter their previous expertise. The American system does not restrict entry in this manner.

The central component of the Pendleton Act was the creation of a three-member Civil Service Commission to administer competitive employment examinations and to investigate violations of the new civil service law. Commission members were appointed and removed by the president with the advice and consent of the Senate. Importantly, the commission had to be bipartisan, with no more than two of the three members affiliated with the same party. The commission was required to develop and oversee all examinations for the federal civil service, and Congress unambiguously made technical expertise the focus for these hiring tests. The new law required practical exams to test applicants' ability to succeed at specific tasks.

As the Civil Service Commission developed during the first half of the 20th century, world events and presidential politics made a noteworthy impact on the growth of the federal civil service. The American involvement in World War I generated a need for both military and civilian personnel, and the Civil Service Commission bore responsibility for the thousands of new civil service appointments. During this period of World War I growth, the Civil Service Commission did have its detractors. Van Riper describes criticism by the National Civil Service Reform League charging that the Civil Service Commission issued exceptions to its rules to conceal a failure to certify a sufficient number of eligible employees.

Following World War I, the 1920s were marked by a period of business growth and a related focus on economic efficiency. The Civil Service Commission had developed over more than three decades of experience, and Van Riper records that private business recognized the government's success in recruiting personnel. The civil service examinations themselves offered a point of connection between business and public administration. Experts in business management were surprised, but notably impressed with the quality of the Civil Service Commission examinations, Van Riper notes.

The Great Depression and President Franklin D. Roosevelt's New Deal policies made a significant impact on the growth of the federal civil service. Most significantly, the increase in the sheer size of the federal government workforce under Roosevelt occurred outside of civil service regulations and protections. In short, the number of federal employees grew, but the number of those selected by Civil Service Commission examinations and protected by civil service rules did not increase apace. Aside from the increase in the number of federal employees under New Deal programs, Mosher reflects that the Roosevelt administration's response to the depression also shifted the government personnel objective from determining the most efficient performance of a task to the politically charged goals of creativity, ambition, and determination.

The rise of the cold war also brought changes to the federal civil service. Fear of communism was widespread in America, and individuals charged with communistic political ideals were thrown out of jobs in various sectors of employment. The Civil Service Commission had dealt with questions of personal loyalty during earlier conflicts, and it instituted harsh measures during the cold war as well. A World War I-era executive order from President Wilson permitted removal of employees believed to sympathize with enemies of the United States. This presidential action offers an example of discarding traditional civil service principles such as neutral competence to allow the firing of civil service members based on political ideals. Later, in the late 1940s, President Truman issued a sweeping executive order calling for investigation of all civil service applicants as well as current employees. The executive order did provide those accused of disloyalty with the right to a hearing and to be accompanied by legal counsel, but Van Riper argues that the invasive loyalty policy led to a drop in morale among federal civil service employees.

Following World War II, former president Herbert Hoover was named to lead a commission designed to study policy changes that would enhance the administration of the federal civil service. The first, and later a second, Hoover Commission sought to balance the civil service objectives of responsiveness to the elected representatives of the public, and a continuous presence of competent personnel who were politically neutral. The first Hoover Commission's recommendations included shifting the role of the Civil Service Commission to one of collaboration with, rather than supervision over, the federal agencies. The second Hoover Commission proposed to create a cadre of senior administrative officers who would remain outside of civil service regulations and would serve the federal government by shifting positions among the federal agencies as needed.

The Hoover Commission proposed policies to correct laws in the federal civil service system, but, after 95 years, many called for a complete overhaul. Riccucci and Naff detail pressure to increase the president's managerial authority, a frustration with rigid regulations that inhibited efficient personnel discipline, and a growing push for equal employment opportunity for minorities and women. These concerns and others created a climate of reform, and the response was the Civil Service Reform Act of 1978 (CSRA).

The CSRA implemented a sweeping reform of the federal civil service including: mandating key merit values, creating several new agencies to oversee the civil service, and establishing a Senior Executive Service on the lines of the second Hoover Commission's recommendations. Perry observes that the CSRA marked the first time that federal merit principles and prohibitions were codified as statutory requirements rather than mere suggestions for personnel administration. The CSRA included merit principles designed to expand federal civil service recruitment; ground employee selection and promotion in knowledge, skills, and abilities; ensure nondiscrimination; highlight the need to protect employees' constitutional rights; guarantee equal pay for equal work; mandate ethical behavior and concern for the public interest; require efficiency; and establish a system of retention, correction, and separation as employee performance warranted. Additionally, the CSRA established prohibitions against arbitrary employment actions, political coercion, and retaliation for whistle blowing. By including these standards in the text of the CSRA legislation, Congress ensured that they were hard and fast rules rather than mere suggestions for personnel management.

Moreover, the CSRA established a series of new federal agencies designed to administer, adjudicate, and safeguard the federal civil service. Among these, the Office of Personnel Management (OPM) and the Merit Systems Protection Board (MSPB) warrant special note. OPM took over administration of the federal workforce. The president was authorized to appoint the OPM director, and the agency became the federal government's central personnel office. The OPM was tasked with both administering the civil service and assisting agencies in their human resource management. Alternatively, the authority to protect against political persuasion and to adjudicate employee claims of improper treatment shifted from the Civil Service Commission to the new MSPB. With the creation of the MSPB, the power to bar those politically motivated personnel actions that had spurred the initial Pendleton Act reform was now embodied in an independent agency designed for the primary purpose of hearing employee appeals.

Pressure from civil rights groups led to the CSRA provision that shifted responsibility for claims of employment discrimination from the Civil Service Commission to the Equal Employment Opportunity Commission, according to Riccucci and Naff. Further, Riccucci and Naff note that labor organizations were frustrated by the limited right to collective bargaining in the federal civil service. Consequently, the CSRA also moved the role of labor arbiter to the independent Federal Labor Relations Authority.

As external events influenced changes in the civil service system through the first half of the 20th century, international governments set the stage for more recent civil service reform endeavors in the United States. Condrey and Maranto note that both Britain and Canada have considered modern civil service reform and that New Zealand implemented substantial changes to its civil service. In addition to these countries that offered models for possible reforms, world events also propelled the United States toward a new concept of federal civil service. Condrey and Maranto observe that the fall of communism solidified U.S. confidence in market-based systems and precipitated the push to make the civil service function more like human resources in private businesses. Accordingly, the Clinton and George W. Bush administrations undertook extensive programs to examine the benefits of reforming the federal civil service.

The National Partnership for Reinventing Government constituted the Clinton administration's expansive study of federal civil service reform. Vice President Al Gore led the ambitious project to create a civil service for the information age, which concluded with a series of wide-ranging management recommendations. Pfiffner describes the rationale behind the recommendations as an effort to shift the government role from that of service provider to coordinator and enabler of service production and delivery. The George W. Bush administration expanded the concept of government directing, rather than producing. Bush's Presidential Management Agenda included a strong emphasis on contracting out services originally produced by the workforce of the federal civil service. Far-reaching as the Clinton and Bush efforts seemed, they paled in comparison with the radical reform taking place at the state level.

While the federal civil service has been the subject of a myriad of reports, studies, and reviews to examine the efficacy of reform on a business sector model, Hays and Sowa found that several states have led the way with radical reform of their civil service systems. As Condrey and Battaglio discuss, radical reform along the lines of fully dismantling civil service protections to create a decentralized, flexible, businesslike system has spread across state and local governments. Radical reform efforts in some states have removed the Pendleton Act's principle of relative security of tenure and have dismantled traditional, centralized civil service offices. Examples from Georgia, Florida, and Texas will provide continuing insight into the practical outcomes of radical civil service reform.

Much has changed from the earliest days of the U.S. government, and the expansion of the federal workforce has been fundamental to those changes. What began as a small group limited to upper-class, white gentlemen has grown to 2.6 million employees with representatives from across the U.S. population. The federal civil service is selected by, managed by, and protected by the merit principles established in the Pendleton Act and codified in the CSRA. As the federal civil service works to meet the needs of an increasingly complex society, merit principles will evolve in response.

Current events have driven, and will continue to drive, significant changes in civil service at the federal and state levels. In the federal government, new national security needs led to the creation of the Department of Homeland Security and an accompanying new, flexible personnel system. Correspondingly, the Department of Defense has implemented significant changes to personnel policies designed to help the agency to meet current national security needs. At the state level, the focus on efficiency has motivated substantial reforms, shifting employees from civil service systems to employment at will. Although it is impossible to predict future changes to the American civil service, it is safe to assume that the two key concerns of national security and greater efficiency will continue to influence the shape of civil service.

Further reading:

Condrey, Stephen E., and R. Paul Battaglio. "A Return to Spoils? Revisiting Radical Civil Service Reform in the United States." *Public Administration Review* 67 (2007): 425–435; Condrey, Stephen E., and Robert Maranto. *Radical Reform of the Civil Service.* Lanham, Md.: Lexington Books, 2001; Hays, Steven W., and Jessica E. Sowa. "A Broader Look at the 'Accountability' Movement." *Review of Public Personnel Administration* 26 (2006): 102–117; Mosher, Frederick C. *Democracy and the Public Service.* 2d ed. New York: Oxford University Press, 1982; Perry, James L. "The Civil Service Reform Act of 1978: A 30-Year Retrospective and a Look Ahead." *Review of Public Personnel Administration* 28 (2008): 200–204; Pfiffner, James P., and Douglas A. Brook. *The Future of Merit: Twenty Years after the Civil Service Reform Act.* Washington, D.C.: Woodrow Wilson Center Press, 2000; Riccucci, Norma, and Katherine C. Naff. *Personnel Management in Government: Politics and Process.* 6th ed. Boca Raton, Fla.: CRC Press, 2008; Van Riper, Paul P. *History of the United States Civil Service.* Evanston, Ill.: Row, Peterson, 1958.

– *Christine Ledvinka*

---

freedom of information

Governmental transparency is the degree to which access to government information is available. One way to gain access to government information is by utilizing freedom of information laws. Freedom of information laws are sometimes referred to as "right to know" or "open public records" laws. These laws allow for government records to be requested, and unless specifically exempt, to be released to the public. The U.S. federal government operates on the basis of the Freedom of Information Act (FOIA), and all 50 states have a similar law on the books.

Over 80 countries now have some form of freedom of information law or regime. Of note is that more than half of these laws are new within the last decade. The United States was a relatively early adopter. It initially passed its FOIA in 1966. Many of the U.S. state laws actually predated the U.S. federal FOIA. The adoption of new national freedom of information laws is one outcome of the concerted international right-to-know movement. In the United States, this movement has established the National Freedom of Information Day, which falls every year on or near the birthday of James Madison—March 16. (James Madison himself was an early proponent of access to government records.) The International Right to Know Day was first celebrated in 2003 and is commemorated yearly on September 28. The international right-to-know movement gained momentum after a 2006 ruling by the Inter-American Court of Human Rights. The court found in the case of *Claude Reyes et al. v. Chile* that access to government information is a fundamental human right.

The U.S. federal Freedom of Information Act, enacted in 1966, amended the public records section (section 3) of the Administrative Procedure Act of 1946. A series of amendments modified the act. The FOIA is based on the concept of open government and that citizens should have access to documents held by executive branch agencies. An agency may withhold requested information pursuant to nine exemptions listed in the act and may charge fees for processing and producing of such material. The release of documents is based on the nature and content of the material, not who the requester is or the intended purpose of the material once received.

One of the first major federal statutes that dealt with the right of individuals and groups to access government information was the Administrative Procedure Act (APA) of 1946. The legislative intent of the APA was to make government more open and to increase accountability. Ultimately, though, the APA was ineffective, largely due to ambiguous language, for those seeking access to government information.

The issue of governmental transparency first made its way into the Democratic Party's platform in 1952, and the term *freedom of information* was first explicitly used in 1956. The Democratic Party platform of 1956 stated:

> During recent years there has developed a practice on the part of Federal agencies to delay and withhold information which is needed by Congress and the general public to make important decisions affecting their lives and destinies. We believe that this trend toward secrecy in Government should be reversed and that the Federal Government should return to its basic tradition of exchanging and promoting the freest flow of information possible in those unclassified areas where secrets involving weapons development and bona fide national security are not involved. We condemn the Eisenhower Administration for the excesses practiced in this vital area, and pledge the Democratic Party to reverse this tendency, substituting a rule of law for that of broad claims of executive privilege. We reaffirm our position of 1952 "to press strongly for world-wide freedom in the gathering and dissemination of news." We shall press for free access to information throughout the world for our journalists and scholars.

Senator Thomas C. Hennings Jr. (D-MO) was an early advocate of freedom of information laws and dissemination of government information. Early freedom of information legislation dealt with amending the Housekeeping Statute, a law which deals with federal agencies. On August 15, 1958, President Eisenhower signed into law an amendment to the Housekeeping Statute. This legislation also proved too ambiguous to be effective.

The amendment to the Housekeeping Statute had little substantive effect but gave momentum to freedom of information laws. Among the proponents for the passage of the Freedom of Information Act were Ralph Nader and a coalition of newspaper editors. After more than a decade of debate, the Freedom of Information Act was passed. President Lyndon B. Johnson signed the bill on July 4, 1966, while at his Texas ranch. Johnson chose not to have a signing ceremony for the bill and the signing statement was not released until later. In the signing statement, Johnson wrote:

> This legislation springs from one of our most essential principles: A democracy works best when the people have all the information that the security of the Nation permits. No one should be able to pull curtains of secrecy around decisions which can be revealed without injury to the public interest.

It should be noted that Johnson, in his statement, also stipulated that some information needs to be kept secret for security reasons and individual protections. Johnson's signing statement helped confuse implementation of the new law by sending mixed signals to his attorney general, Ramsey Clark, who was charged with implementing the law.

By 1974, it became clear that the FOIA was not working as intended. Long delays were reported in obtaining records, and exorbitant charges (up to $1 per page) were set for copies of documents. In *EPA v. Mink* (1973), the Supreme Court had narrowly interpreted the Court's role in reviewing exemption 1, which deals with "secret" and "top secret" material exempt from the FOIA that is properly classified under the terms of a prevailing executive order concerning classification policy and practice. Justice Potter Stewart's concurring opinion in the case pushed Congress to rewrite parts of the act. He stated that Congress has "built into" the FOIA an exemption that provided "no means to question an Executive decision to stamp a document 'secret,' however cynical, myopic, and even corrupt that decision might have been."

Extreme dissatisfaction with the FOIA was brewing in Congress. The Supreme Court's decision in *EPA v. Mink* only exasperated this sentiment. On top of the already growing groundswell for FOIA reform, Watergate stunned Washington and the nation. The FOIA amendments were pushed through both houses of Congress only to be vetoed by President Gerald Ford. President Ford's stated chief objections to the amendment were over military and intelligence secrets and diplomatic relations, confidentiality and law enforcement files, and the length of time afforded to the agencies to complete the requests. In the end, Congress overrode President Ford's veto, and the FOIA became law.

In 1986, Freedom of Information Act revisions were introduced as an amendment to the Omnibus Anti-Drug Abuse Act of 1986 with no public hearings or committee reports. The amendments created three categories of requesters. Prior to 1986, requesters were viewed as one undifferentiated group. The 1986 amendments made it more difficult to receive a fee waiver. One of the more controversial sections of these amendments addressed exemption 7, which deals with law enforcement records. The exemption was broadened to include "records or information compiled for law enforcement purposes," thus limiting access to these records and raising questions of government accountability.

The 1996 amendments, the Electronic Freedom of Information Act (EFOIA), ensured that individuals have access to government records regardless of format, including electronic. The EFOIA made it easier both to learn which records an agency had and to access these records electronically. If a record was requested and likely to be requested again, the law stated that the agency had to post it electronically and publish an index of such documents. Agencies were required to submit annual reports on FOIA activities, including information on the total number of FOIA requests, the number of requests processed, the median processing time, the number of staff assigned to FOIA activities, and the total amount expended by the agency for processing these requests.

The latest round of reforms came in 2007. The OPEN Government Act of 2007 is intended to fix some of the perceived problems with implementation of the law, namely, excessive delays in receiving requests, unresponsiveness of the federal agencies, and problems with litigating FOIA cases. Notably, the amendments required an Office of Government Information Services to be based at the National Archives. The Office of Government Information Services will mediate FOIA conflicts and review agency performance.

The authors of the original statute and the 1974 amendments viewed the exemptions to the FOIA as "permissive and not mandatory." Now, however, many agency FOIA offices interpret these exemptions as mandatory and will not release information covered by them. The federal FOIA contains nine broad document exemptions. The exemptions are for documents that deal with national security information; internal personnel rules and practices; information exempt under other laws; confidential business information; inter- or intraagency communication that is subject to deliberative process, litigation, and other privileges; personal privacy; law enforcement records; financial institutions; and geological information. Each state's freedom of information law has a series of exemptions that also remove some material from release.

The Homeland Security Act of 2002 includes a provision that relates to the FOIA. The act now operates as a statute covered by exemption 3 of the FOIA. "Critical infrastructure information" that is voluntarily submitted to the Homeland Security Department is extended protection by this statute. The exemptions that are most frequently used to withhold documents are related to personal privacy concerns.

Much of the information that individuals and businesses want from government is not at the federal level but closer to home. State and local freedom of information laws provide access to a significant amount of information that people are concerned about, including their municipal government's budget, teacher salary information, police records, environmental information, and state contractor records. Considerable variation exists among the state freedom of information laws. While all states have a freedom of information law, the provisions included within those laws vary widely, as does their implementation. Florida is known to have a very progressive public records law that allows for a relatively high amount of access to government records. Some states, such as Connecticut, have quasi-judicial bodies set up to facilitate access disputes, while others have ombudsmen designated to oversee freedom of information requests.

The kind of information that is released through freedom of information laws depends largely on the level of government and the type of agency from which records are requested. For example, the U.S. Department of Veterans Affairs receives a large number of requests from former military personnel looking for their own files. The U.S. Department of Justice receives a great number of requests from prisoners. Information on the environment, salary data, police records, and schools are all popular subjects for requests by individuals. Individuals are not the biggest users of freedom of information laws though. While it is hard to say for certain, businesses, including law firms, appear to be the biggest users of freedom of information laws. These private organizations request information that can help their businesses in some way. They may ask for information on their competitors, request government databases, or even seek lists of individuals given speeding tickets. (The latter is then used as a mailing list to solicit clients for legal services.)

In practice, constant tension arises between access to government information and concerns for efficiency, privacy, and security. The U.S. Department of Justice estimates that, in 2007, more than 21 million FOIA requests were filled by the equivalent of more than 5,000 federal employees at an approximate cost of $370 million. Finding, processing, and releasing government documents are expensive and lengthy processes. The counterargument is that the information released through these freedom of information requests can spotlight corruption and administrative malfeasance, which, when corrected, saves money. Privacy is also an ongoing concern. Government documents have personal information on government employees and others who interact with them. Freedom of information laws have some provisions written into them that limit the release of documents containing personal information. Similarly, the inappropriate release of information in government documents that relates to law enforcement, homeland security, or national security is a concern of governments. Freedom of information laws include a range of provisions to safeguard against the inappropriate release of security information.

The experiences of other countries may influence the future of freedom of information policy and practice in the United States. Technology has been embraced as a tool to facilitate request for and release of documents. Mexico has a particularly advanced Web-based freedom of information requesting system. In Mexico, individuals can anonymously request and receive documents via an online portal. The online systems not only have the advantage of making requests easier to make, but they also allow for truly anonymous requests, which are in fact impossible with in-person filings. Countries such as India and South Africa have shown freedom of information laws can be expanded to cover private organizations working on behalf of government. These laws allow for greater access to documents produced by private organizations working in the public interest or on behalf of governments. Increasingly, nongovernmental actors are providing services that were historically offered directly by governments. These expanded laws enable access to documents held by private organizations performing services done on behalf of the government. Countries that have newer freedom of information laws also have some of the most liberal laws. It may be that the United States will look abroad when considering further future revisions to the U.S. FOIA.

Further Reading:

Foerstel, Herbert. *Freedom of Information and the Right to Know: The Origins and Applications of the Freedom of Information Act*. Westport, Conn.: Greenwood Press, 1999; Johnson, Lyndon B. Statement by President upon Signing "Freedom of Information Act" on July 4, 1966, Washington, D.C., in *American Reference*

Library. Chicago: Western Standard Publishing Company, 1999; Office of Information and Privacy, U.S. Department of Justice. "Summary of Annual FOIA Reports for Fiscal Year 2007." Available online. URL: http://www.usdoj.gov/oip/foiapost/2008foiapost23.htm. Accessed November 30, 2008; Piotrowski, Suzanne J. *Governmental Transparency in the Path of Administrative Reform*. Albany: State University of New York Press, 2007.

– *Suzanne J. Piotrowski*

governmental ethics

"Just do the right thing!" might seem to be the principle that should guide governmental ethics. But that principle is insufficient. What the "right thing" is actually often constitutes the subject of intense disagreement and debate. For example, is "enhanced interrogation" necessary to obtain information that can protect national security, or is it "torture" that violates the law and shocks the conscience? Are campaign contributions a form of free speech or a legalized form of bribery? Given the disagreements about the nature of the "right thing," the evolution of governmental ethics has not been a smooth, steady, and predictable progress toward moral improvement. Instead, the development of government ethics has followed a more normal path of public policy making in the United States. Ethical reforms are usually precipitated by some triggering event (e.g., a scandal). Ethical reforms often have partisan components, with each party seeking to gain political advantage over the other, even as politicians seek to do the right thing. Ethical reforms have tended to create floors ("don't do the wrong thing") rather than raise ceilings ("do the right thing"), and so generally they have focused on avoiding scandals rather than producing virtue. Ethical reforms often have unintended consequences that may actually weigh against the public interest.

What, exactly, is ethics reform? There is no simple answer to that question. The most important ethics reforms in our nation's history arguably include such constitutional matters as protecting the freedom of speech and religion, enhancing due process, or expanding civil rights. But these are almost never considered "ethics" reforms. Other legislation clearly has ethical components—say, in guaranteeing income support and health care to the elderly through the Social Security and Medicare programs—but, again, such legislation is not usually seen as "ethics" reform. Instead, ethics reform most commonly is seen as the laws, rules, and regulations more narrowly tailored to reduce corruption—especially regarding financial conflicts of interest—or at least the appearance of it.

In constructing our nation, our founding fathers clearly recognized two things: Strong ethical values were essential for a thriving democracy, and humans do not always possess these characteristics. President George Washington, in his farewell address to the nation, argued for the first proposition in saying that "it is substantially true that virtue or morality is a necessary spring of popular government." James Madison, perhaps more pragmatically, wrote in Federalist 51, "If men were angels, no government would be necessary. If angels were to govern men, neither external nor internal controls on government would be necessary. In framing a government which is to be administered by men over men, the great difficulty lies in this: you must first enable the government to control the governed; and in the next place oblige it to control itself. A dependence on the people is, no doubt, the primary control on the government; but experience has taught mankind the necessity of auxiliary precautions." Although both perspectives—the need to promote virtue and the need to control the harm from those lacking virtue—have guided governmental ethics reforms since our nation's inception, by far greater emphasis has been placed on the latter. The Constitution itself deliberately manifests this through democratic elections, the separation of powers, federalism, and the Bill of Rights—in each case, the goal was to prevent the government (and, by inference, the individuals working in the government) from creating moral harm. The Constitution does not seek to promote good behavior so much as it seeks to limit the negative consequences of bad conduct. If constitutional strictures did not prevent wrongdoing, the democratic solution was to vote the rascals out.

The Constitution marked only the beginning of a long national debate over the ethics that are appropriate for governmental officials. To improve the ethics of governmental officials, the 20th century contains a long record of legislation, executive orders, rules, and codes of conduct.

Among the most important "ethics" laws of the modern era are:

1. The Hatch Act of 1939;
2. The Administrative Procedure Act of 1946;
3. The Code of Ethics for U.S. Government Service, 1958 (not actually a law, but instead a congressional resolution);
4. The Freedom of Information Act of 1967;
5. The Ethics in Government Act of 1978;
6. The False Claims Act of 1986;
7. The Whistleblower Protection Act of 1989.

These acts in general seek to reduce corruption, or the appearance of it, by setting standards for impartiality and transparency, by limiting the potentially corrosive impacts of partisanship and electoral activities, and by reducing conflicts of interest.

The Hatch Act (formally known as "An Act to Prevent Pernicious Political Activities"), and its modification over the years, has sharply limited the ability of federal employees to engage in partisan political activity. While this might seem—and it is—a limitation on citizen rights of free speech, it was primarily intended to prevent federal workers from using their legal authority or federal dollars to induce or coerce (through pledges to hire, promote, or fire; to offer or withhold contracts or funding; etc.) individuals to support or oppose particular candidates. The act was instigated by wide-ranging allegations by Republicans that Works Progress Administration (WPA) funds were being misused to support Democratic congressional candidates throughout Appalachia and other regions in 1938. Of course, during the Great Depression—and throughout every campaign season since then—it should not be surprising that federal programs supporting local economies actually do serve the political purpose of bolstering support for the party of the current administration. The Hatch Act hardly ended the use of federal power and money for electoral purposes, although it did seek to restrain the most abusive forms of this. Nonetheless, accusations of Hatch Act violations continue to crop up.

The Administrative Procedure Act of 1946 (the APA) was enacted to establish standards by which federal agencies propose, adopt, and adjudicate regulations. To ensure that agencies did not abuse the public trust, the APA required them to notify the public about their organization, procedures, and rules; to provide the public opportunities to participate in the rule-making process; and to establish uniform standards for conducting rule making and adjudication, among other purposes. But the development of the APA over an extended 10-year period was not simply an exercise in "good government." President Roosevelt's New Deal dramatically expanded the role of government, and opponents were concerned that this could lead to central planning at best and tyranny at worst. For its part, the Roosevelt administration wanted to establish procedures that would make it difficult for future administrations to easily disband its programs. The compromise that was the APA does serve to protect the public from administrative abuses, although it did not entirely level the regulatory playing field: Special interests are far more involved in regulatory proceedings than is the general public.

The Code of Ethics for U.S. Government Service was adopted in 1958 through resolutions by both the House and the Senate. Its "ten commandments" provide the most direct statement of the ethical obligations of federal employees:

1. Put loyalty to the highest moral principles and to country above loyalty to government persons, party, or department.
2. Uphold the Constitution, laws, and legal regulations of the United States and of all governments therein and never be a party to their evasion.

3. Give a full day's labor for a full day's pay; giving to the performance of his duties his earnest effort and best thought.
4. Seek to find and employ more efficient and economical ways of getting tasks accomplished.
5. Never discriminate unfairly by dispensing special favors or privileges to anyone, whether for remuneration or not; and never accept for himself or his family, favors or benefits under circumstances that might be construed by reasonable persons as influencing the performance of his governmental duties.
6. Make no private promises of any kind binding upon the duties of office, since a government employee has no private word that can be binding on public duty.
7. Engage in no business with the Government, either directly or indirectly which is inconsistent with the conscientious performance of his governmental duties.
8. Never use any information coming to him confidentially in the performance of governmental duties as a means for making private profit.
9. Expose corruption wherever discovered.
10. Uphold these principles, ever conscious that public office is a public trust.

Alas, the code contains neither investigatory nor enforcement mechanisms; it is purely aspirational, not operational.

The Freedom of Information Act of 1967 (FOIA), like the APA, was intended to protect the public from governmental abuses by granting individuals access to previously unreleased governmental information. The FOIA specifies what records are subject to disclosure, defines the process for disclosing information, and details the exceptions to the disclosure requirements.

The FOIA has been repeatedly modified since its enactment, and it continues to be a source of dispute. After Watergate, the Congress approved the Privacy Act Amendments of 1974. President Ford, advised by his staff that the law would encourage leaks, vetoed the bill, but Congress overrode the veto. This act specified individuals' access to records containing information about them. The FOIA was modified again in 1976 by the government in the Sunshine Act. Presidents Reagan and George W. Bush dramatically limited FOIA's reach by executive order; Presidents Clinton and Obama both expanded the reach of FOIA. Further amendments have dealt with electronic information and access to intelligence information. The ethical dilemmas that continue to be controversial center on the balance between the public's right to know and the government's desire to maintain sensitive records.

New Mexico Democratic senator Carl Hatch, for whom the Hatch Act is named, in Washington, D.C., July 1939; photo by Harris & Ewing *(Library of Congress)*

The Federal Election Campaign Act (FECA) of 1974 ended the era of unregulated campaign contributions, in which wealthy individuals often donated large sums to candidates. In 1972, however, corporations secretly channeled massive amounts of money into the Nixon campaign with the funds used, in part, to finance the activities that led to the Watergate scandal. (Corporate contributions to campaigns had already been outlawed in 1907 by the Tillman Act, and other laws were adopted over the interim to limit the influence of special interests on campaigns.) The major features of FECA included limits on the amounts that individuals could give directly to presidential and congressional campaigns; disclosure of the sources and amounts of contributions from individuals and political action committees (PACS); public financing of presidential campaigns; and the creation of the Federal Elections Commission (FEC) to regulate the financing of campaigns. The hope was that, by limiting the influence of money on campaigns, the corrupting power of money on political campaigns would be diminished.

FECA has been only partially successful, however: Given the stakes of elections, constitutional strictures, the importance of government in the economy, and the wealth of potential donors, vast sums continue to flow to political campaigns. FECA has subsequently been modified several times. The Supreme Court ruled parts of FECA unconstitutional in *Buckley v. Valeo*, and the act was amended in 1976 to address this ruling. In *Citizens United v. FEC* (2010), the Supreme Count ruled that corporate funding of independent political broadcasts could not be prohibited under the First Amendment; however, the Court did not address the general ban on corporate contributions to political candidates or parties. In 1979, the act was again amended to allow parties to spend unlimited amounts of "hard" (i.e., regulated) money on party-building and voter turnout activities. In 1979, the FEC ruled that parties could spend "soft" (i.e., unregulated) monies on party-building activities, but this money was often used for candidate-related "issue ads"; as a result, Congress enacted the Bipartisan Campaign Reform Act (BCRA) of 2002, which banned such expenditures. Various elements of BCRA have been struck down by the Supreme Court, and other issues continue to be to litigated. As importantly, the flow of money into political campaigns remains unabated, with (for example) the Obama campaign raising a record $750 million in 2008.

The Ethics in Government Act (EGA) of 1978 was one of several laws enacted after the Watergate scandals. This law requires public officials in the higher levels of all three branches of government to report the sources and amounts of all outside income and also to report any nongovernmental positions or offices they hold. It also sought to close the "revolving door" by restricting the ability of those in the executive branch to lobby their former agency—or any agencies—for a period of time after they leave office. A principal purpose of the legislation was to prevent public officials from using their inside knowledge for private gain when leaving office. This act has been repeatedly amended over the years (in 1979, 1983, 1988, 1989, 1990, and 1991). The most important reforms came in 1989 with the Ethics Reform Act, which was largely based on the recommendations of the President's Commission on Federal Ethics Law Reform and the report of the House Bipartisan Ethics Task Force. The Reform Act further tightened postemployment restrictions, financial disclosure requirements, and rules on accepting gifts for all three branches; it also amended the criminal ethics provisions.

The EGA also created the Office of Government Ethics (OGE). Initially, the OGE was located in the Office of Personnel Management, but it became a separate agency as part of the Government Ethics Reauthorization Act of 1988. Although its mission is to foster "high ethical standards for employees and strengthen the public's confidence that the Government's business is conducted with impartiality and integrity," in practice the OGE focuses primarily on conflicts of interest. Its jurisdiction is limited to executive branch employees, and it is an advisory and neither an investigatory nor enforcement agency. If allegations of misconduct occur, the inspector general of the respective agency typically leads the investigation, although the FBI is called in if necessary. The Department of Justice, through its Public Integrity Section of the Criminal Division, is responsible for prosecuting alleged criminal conduct concerning conflicts of interest.

The False Claims Act of 1986 strengthened one of the oldest ethics laws in the United States (indeed, when the law was first enacted in 1863, it became known as the "Lincoln Law"). The law allows individuals ("whistleblowers") to file suit on behalf of the government against fraudulent contractors and to receive a share of the award. The law was amended in 1943 (which relaxed the law) and again in 1986. The 1986 revisions were largely at the instigation of President Reagan, who proclaimed that vast amounts of federal dollars were being wasted in a time of rising deficits. The 1986 amendments made it easier for whistleblowers to win suits (on a "preponderance of evidence" basis) and offered higher rewards to successful claimants.

The Whistleblower Protection Act of 1989 protects federal employees who report agency misconduct from retaliation by their agencies so long as the employee "reasonably" believes that the agency is committing waste, fraud, abuse, or other illegal activities. The law created the Office of Special Counsel, which was responsible for investigating complaints from federal employees who believed they faced reprisals.

No president ever lost votes by siding with ethics reforms: All presidents want to argue that their administrations will have the highest ethical standards. Typically, however, there are partisan differences, with Democrats generally more concerned about closing the "revolving door" and Republicans more worried about having conflict of interest rules that are so restrictive that they limit their the ability to recruit (affluent) individuals.

In response to perceived ethical lapses regarding the influence of lobbyists during President Bush's administration, on his first full day in office President Obama issued his first executive order (EO 13490) to tighten ethical standards within the White House and for all political appointees throughout the federal government. The order required all executive branch political appointees to sign a contractually binding pledge to uphold a specific set of obligations regarding lobbying. In particular, the order prohibits political appointees from receiving any gifts from lobbyists or lobbying organizations and from participating in any matters directly related to previous lobbying activities for two years after their appointment, if they had been a registered lobbyist within two years of their appointment date. Finally, the order bars political appointees from lobbying the administration after leaving federal service. The latter two provisions essentially prevent lobbyists, or future lobbyists, from working for the Obama administration. To enforce the order, each agency was directed to develop, in coordination with the Office of Government Ethics, rules, monitoring programs, and enforcement strategies. The order is also explicit: It does not repeal previous executive orders, but it is enforceable on top of them. That same day President Obama issued another executive order designed to increase transparency in government by overturning a previous EO issued by President George W. Bush that had sharply limited access to presidential records.

Other presidents had issued executive orders concerning governmental ethics. President Clinton, also on his first day in office in 1993, issued Executive Order 12834 to remedy the perceived ethical abuses of the Reagan/Bush administrations. Like Obama's, this EO also focused on the "revolving door," but only on its exit. The Clinton EO barred senior political appointees from lobbying the executive branch for five years after their departure. President George H. W. Bush waited four full days before issuing Executive Order 12668 on ethics, which created the President's Commission on Federal Ethics Law Reform to "review Federal ethics laws, Executive orders, and policies and . . . make recommendations to the President for legislative, administrative, and other reforms needed to ensure full public confidence in the integrity of all Federal public officials and employees." The recommendations of this commission helped serve as the basis for the Ethics Reform Act of 1989. In 1988, President Bush also issued an executive order containing 14 principles of ethical conduct for the executive branch, guided in part by the Republican philosophy that "we cannot afford to have unreasonably restrictive requirements that discourage able citizens from entering public service."

President Reagan's Executive Order 12301 on ethics did not concern itself with the pre- or postgovernmental service of political appointees, but instead emphasized "fraud and waste" in governmental programs. Surprisingly, in the wake of Watergate, President Carter issued no executive orders targeted specifically to ethics reform. President George W. Bush, notably, did not issue an executive order on ethics.

Congress is fraught with ethical dilemmas, and the solutions are equally fraught. The potential for electoral defeat has not proven to be a sufficient constraint on congressional behavior, for several reasons. First, given the powers of incumbency, even those accused of serious ethical violations are sometimes returned to office by the voters (most recently, Congressman William Jefferson, who was reelected even after the FBI raided his office on suspicion of bribery, although he lost his subsequent reelection bid after a jury indicted him on 16 counts of corruption). Second, the public *expects* members of Congress to act ethically and to be held to higher standards than if they worked in the private sector.

But the political system dictates that members of Congress are often on the ethical edge, because their electoral incentives induce them to seek favors (e.g., campaign contributions and other campaign support) and to deliver them (especially through earmarks, appointments, and other funding opportunities). So the critical question has been: What forms of favor are acceptable?

Bribery involves an explicit quid pro quo, and it has long been illegal. Accusations (and convictions) have been fairly rare, and they are always scandalous when they occur. Yet three other forms of what some consider "bribery" merit attention. The first involves campaign finance; critics of privately financed campaigns argue that it by definition creates conflicts of interest because major donors understandably expect to receive preferential treatment. The second concerns earmarks, typically funds dedicated to a specific project in a specific district anonymously slipped into legislation without public hearing or review. Critics of earmarks argue that they do not so much fulfill public purposes as allow members of Congress to reward supporters without accountability or transparency. A final form is "vote trading" ("If you vote for my bill, I'll vote for yours."), which appears to meet the quid pro quo standard of bribes.

In addition to the campaign finance laws, Congress has developed detailed ethical standards, primarily to reduce the actuality or the perception of conflicts of interest. The "House Ethics Manual" runs well over 400 pages; the "Standing Rules of the Senate" (especially Sections 34 through 42) cover the same material more briefly. These formal rules are relatively new, however, as the House did not develop its first Code of Official Conduct until 1968. Over the years, the rules have gradually become more specific and more constraining. For example, the initial rules prohibited gifts to representatives from persons with direct business before Congress. This proved unworkable, as almost everyone has, or potentially has, interests affected by legislation, and so the rules have increasingly prohibited members and their staffs from receiving anything of value from virtually anyone. House and Senate rules specify prohibitions or limitations regarding outside income, gifts, investments, travel expenditures, disclosures, lobbying after leaving office, family members who are lobbyists, and so forth (some, but not all, of these rules were imposed through the Ethics Reform Act).

Despite the substantial progress in this area, critics remain. Governmental ethics reforms have moved the country far from the days of open graft and favor trading. Ethics reforms have tended to focus much more on process than on outcomes, not least because as difficult as it is to agree on what an "ethical" process is, it is much more difficult to agree on what an "ethical" outcome is. They remain open to substantial criticism, on several levels. A first is that they focus more on petty matters than on weighty ones. For example, interest groups can spend practically unlimited amounts to influence legislation and promote candidates, although they cannot legally buy congressional staffers a pizza. A second critique is that, although the ethics laws, rules, and regulations are extensive, enforcement can be sporadic, at best. This claim is especially directed toward Congress, as the members themselves are charged with enforcing their rules and incentives to enforce them are, to put it charitably, modest.

A third criticism concerns the unexpected (or perverse) consequences of reform. Whatever good reasons President Obama had for prohibiting lobbyists for working in his administration, this does diminish his ability to hire talented, knowledgeable staff. A final critique of ethics reforms is that they have often taken a "legalizing" approach that, while potentially limiting unethical behavior, has little promise of enhancing ethical behavior. The reason for this is that, for laws to be enforceable, they need to draw relatively bright lines between what is permissible and impermissible. The laws cannot meaningfully say "Do the right thing" but they can say "Don't do a specific X." If "X" is not done (or cannot be proven), the public official can say with a straight face: "I violated no ethics law," which is quite different from "I acted ethically."

Of this we can be sure: Problems with governmental ethics will continue, as will ethics reforms. The federal government's powers are so vast, and its interventions into the economy so substantial, that the temptation to misuse public power for private gain has never been larger. Humans, meanwhile, remain less than angels.

Further Reading:

Douglas, Paul H. *Ethics in Government.* Boston: Harvard University Press, 1952; North, Robert. *Ethics in U.S. Government: An Encyclopedia of Investigations, Scandals, Reforms, and Legislation.* Santa Barbara, Calif.: Greenwood Press, 2001; Painter, Richard W. *Getting the Government America Deserves: How Ethics Reform Can Make a Difference.* New York: Oxford University Press, 2009; Roberts, MacKenzie, G. Calvin, and Michael Hakfen. *Scandal Proof: Do Ethics Laws Make Government Ethical?* Washington, D.C.: Brookings Institution Press, 2002.

– Mark Carl Rom

lobbying

In essence, lobbying consists of all those activities undertaken by "outsiders" to obtain a particular result (generally a specific policy) from the decision-making process of a particular governmental entity. One of the most common images of the lobbyist is the lawyer working on behalf of a company or trade association seeking or opposing a governmental program under consideration by a legislature or an administrative agency. (In fact many lobbyists are lawyers, but the profession includes many nonlawyers.) However, it would equally constitute lobbying for a member of the executive, or even the judicial, branch of the government to seek action by the legislative branch on a favored topic (e.g., pay increases for executive or judicial branch employees). The methods of lobbying are numerous, including face-to-face discussions, telephone calls, e-mails, and even demonstrations of support evidenced in public parades or "blasts" of letters or e-mails from members of the public encouraged to express their views to legislators or administrators by the person or entity leading the lobbying campaign. The method last mentioned is known as "grassroots" lobbying.

The public perception of the lobbying process is often not flattering to the lobbyists involved: "Influence-peddling" or even more sinister descriptions are routinely invoked. Indeed, public scandals involving lobbyists seeking improperly to influence governmental decision making have periodically erupted. Most recently, 2004–06 turned out to be watershed years for lobbyists seeking to influence the federal government. The lobbying activities of Jack Abramoff, including his relationship to former House majority leader Tom DeLay (R-TX), captured national headlines. Among other exploits, Abramoff arranged lavish trips to the United Kingdom and the South Pacific for DeLay. One such outing involved an outlay of $70,000 to pay for DeLay, his wife, and two aides to visit Scotland and play golf at the famous St. Andrews links. Abramoff also allegedly enriched himself at the expense of various Native-American tribes he represented; at one point he worked both for and against a tribe with regard to approval for reopening a gambling casino. The unsavory portrayal of the uses and abuses of money and influence by lobbyists and legislators alike resulted in an avalanche of proposals for reform of statutory restrictions and congressional rules. The scandal (really a series of scandals involving far more than Abramoff's activities) ultimately resulted in the enactment of the Honest Leadership and Open Government Act of 2007, a dramatic expansion of regulation of lobbying and related activities at the national level.

Despite the often unsavory public perception of lobbyists, their activities—shorn of attempts at bribery and other forbidden practices—are the very embodiment of the First Amendment's guarantee of "the right of the people peaceably to assemble, and to petition the government for a redress of grievances." Indeed, it would be very unusual to find a group in the general population whose interests (or, at least, some of whose interests) are not represented by lobbyists in Washington and the various state capitals. It is not far-fetched to claim that lobbyists are a crucial component of the democratic process as we know it: They bring the needs of the public to the attention of elected and appointed officials along with information essential for good decision making that might not otherwise be available.

In essence, the history of lobbying law involves changing balances struck between, on the one hand, the constitutional interests represented by the First Amendment's right to petition and, on the other, the need to protect against public corruption and the adverse effects that may flow from a lack of transparency in governmental decision making. The rationales for lobbying regulation have varied over time. Today the emphasis at the national level is primarily on the ability of the public to know about the potential influence of lobbyists, thereby facilitating its ability to hold public officials accountable. Accordingly, the law focuses on disclosure of who is doing the lobbying, on what issues, how much is being spent or earned, and who (or what institution of government) is being contacted by lobbyists. More recently, an emphasis has been placed on disclosure of campaign fundraising done by lobbyists and on whether lobbyists are complying with gift and travel rules applicable to Congress and the executive branch. State laws share many of these characteristics, though some have been more aggressive (e.g., banning lobbying entirely or taxing lobbying expenditures). Lobbying reform can present difficult choices for legislators: The adverse political consequences of unqualified opposition in the face of lobbying scandals may push in the direction of bipartisan support for reform, and yet disclosure can impinge on important political interests (e.g., impair grassroots work by certain groups that are likely to support the election of the representatives favoring reform).

At the federal level, Congress could not forge a winning coalition on lobbying reform until after World War II. Since then, two general federal lobbying disclosure schemes have been in effect:

1. the Federal Regulation of Lobbying Act (FRLA) of 1946, which was narrowly construed by the Supreme Court in its one decision (to date) dealing with the constitutionality of lobbying law, *United States v. Harriss* (1954), handed down more than half a century ago; and
2. the Lobbying Disclosure Act of 1995, which replaced the FRLA, expanded lobbying disclosure to attempt to influence not just members of Congress, but also congressional staff and the executive branch of government, and was itself significantly strengthened by the 2007 Honest Leadership and Open Government Act that also integrated, to some degree, the disparate laws and rules governing lobbying disclosure, political contributions, and gift and travel for members of Congress and their staffs.

As it exists today, the body of legal rules and other restrictions that apply to lobbying is detailed and complex, involving among other things: disclosure of lobbying activities (whether by domestic or by foreign interests); use of public monies for lobbying by both nongovernmental interests and governmental entities; the treatment of lobbying entities under the Internal Revenue Code; federal election law; congressional and executive branch gift and travel rules; restrictions on employment of former government officials as lobbyists; illegal gratuities and bribery of public officials; and ethical codes applicable to lawyer and nonlawyer lobbyists. For simplicity, the following discussion will focus on lobbying disclosure legislation, particularly at the national level.

Not surprisingly, lobbying the U.S. government to obtain favors or in self-defense is as old as the Constitution of 1787. For example, during the First Congress, Pennsylvania senator William Maclay noted in his diary that New York merchants employed "threats, dinners, [and] attentions" to help delay passage of a tariff bill. Likewise, legislative "fixes" to deal with lobbying go back as far. In April 1798, a committee of Philadelphia citizens personally presented a petition on the Senate floor seeking to support the government's policies toward France. In reaction to what was apparently viewed as a disruptive procedure, the Senate passed a resolution barring such direct exercises of the First Amendment's "right to petition."

As the 19th century progressed, Congress acted in other ways to deal with the increasing complaints regarding the activities of lobbyists. In 1852, the House of Representatives barred newspapermen from the floor when acting as agents to "prosecute a claim pending before Congress." Two years later, the House established a select committee to investigate whether or not its members had been bribed or otherwise improperly influenced to vote for or against legislation.

The targets for lobbyists expanded exponentially with the increase in the scope of the national government following the Civil War, and particularly its ability and willingness to dispense direct and indirect subsidies of various types. The Credit Mobilier scandal of 1872–73 was a showcase for bribery and other unsavory practices by railroad lobbyists seeking participation in the transcontinental railroad project of the Union Pacific. Yet, despite the public outcry against such abuses, during the last quarter of the 19th century only one effort at the national level to regulate lobbying occurred that compares favorably to the law of today: It was a registration requirement for lobbyists that was effective for only part of the 44th Congress (1876) and only in the House of Representatives. On the state level, however, more aggressive efforts were made to deal with lobbying abuses: The 1877 Georgia Constitution outlawed lobbying altogether (a technique of doubtful constitutionality under the U.S. Constitution) and, in 1890, Massachusetts required lobbyists to both register and disclose expenses, a model followed in other states and ultimately at the federal level.

Concerns with regard to the influence of lobbyists continued to multiply with the number of lobbyists. In 1913, President Wilson was quoted to the effect that "Washington was full of these representatives of special interests and that 'a brick couldn't be thrown without hitting one of them. And I certainly feel like throwing some bricks.'" He denounced business lobbyists' opposition to the Underwood tariff bill of that year. The Senate soon thereafter conducted a special investigation of the tariff lobby. Also in 1913 the House launched an investigation of lobbying by the National Association of Manufacturers (NAM), uncovering instances of NAM's control of committee appointments and its monitoring of private conversations of House members. Thereafter, and continuing into the 1920s, various lobbying reform proposals were introduced; none were enacted.

The utility lobby's attempt in the mid-1930s to block regulation of public utility holding companies was investigated in the Senate by a committee headed by Senator (later Supreme Court Justice) Hugo Black (D-AL). As it turns out, the utility companies employed what today would be called grassroots lobbying—that is to say, generating hundreds of thousands of expressions of opposition from purportedly interested members of the public, though in this case the "spontaneous" outpouring was not what it seemed, given the generous amount of forgery of signatures that was involved. In the end, Congress enacted a regulatory scheme in 1935 governing holding companies and, for good measure, included a lobbying registration and reporting requirement that existed until its repeal in 2005.

At the same time, both the Senate and the House passed bills to more broadly regulate lobbying the federal government. While the right of citizens to make themselves heard on legislative matters was clearly acknowledged, so was Congress's and the public's right to know who made appeals for protection or assistance, who paid for those appeals, and how the money was spent. As it turns out, these themes have dominated the debate on lobbying regulation to the present day. A House-Senate Conference Committee proposed a registration and disclosure bill in 1936 that extended not simply to legislative lobbying, but also to lobbying federal agencies. But the attempted compromise proved to be too ambitious and failed to pass the House.

Ten years later, in 1946, a general lobbying disclosure bill modeled on the unsuccessful 1936 compromise was enacted as part of the much larger Legislative Reorganization Act, but without specific hearings on the topic of lobbying or fanfare. Complaints made to the Joint Committee on the Organization of Congress with regard to the influence of organized groups on the legislative process were enough to prompt the committee to direct the drafting of what was to become the Federal Regulation of Lobbying Act. While significant, and perhaps successful, opposition might have been presented to a stand-alone lobbying bill, the perceived need to adopt the legislative reforms found in other parts of the broader reorganization legislation carried the day.

As it turns out, the inconspicuous origin of the Federal Regulation of Lobbying Act of 1946 (FRLA) foreshadowed its irrelevance to effective lobbying regulation. While the FRLA borrowed heavily from the proposed 1936 legislation, it did not extend coverage to lobbying the executive branch. The pivotal disclosure provisions of the statute were Sections 305 and 308, which served distinct purposes, despite the fact that their requirements overlapped to some degree as a practical matter.

Section 305 required that every person receiving contributions or making expenditures for the purpose of influencing the enactment or defeat of legislation by Congress file with the clerk of the House of Representatives quarterly reports of (1) total contributions received (cumulatively for the year), along with the names of contributors of $500 or more, and (2) total expenditures (also cumulative for the year) for the identified purpose, along with the names of each person to whom an expenditure of $10 or more was made, together with the amount, date, and purpose of the expenditure. In short, the intended effect of Section 305 was to give both an overall and a detailed sense of the amount of money raised and expended for lobbying Congress on behalf of a particular entity.

Section 308, on the other hand, was intended to elicit specific information with regard to the persons who were paid to be lobbyists. They were required to register with the clerk of the House and the secretary of the Senate and, in addition to identifying themselves, identify their client(s), the compensation paid for their services, and the amount of expenditures related to their work paid by the client(s). Quarterly reports by registered lobbyists were intended to reveal how closely the estimates of compensation and expenses contained in the initial registrations reflected actual experience. Accordingly, those reports were to reflect money paid to or expended by the lobbyist in his or her work for the client during the covered period, to whom money was paid and for what purposes, and what specific legislation served as the focus of lobbying efforts. Congress provided several exceptions from the registration provision, including ones for congressional testimony, for public officials, and for newspapers and magazines publishing comments, advertisements, and other material advocating the passage or defeat of legislation.

The FRLA provided for two types of penalties. A violation of the act was a misdemeanor punishable by fine and imprisonment. In addition, conviction for violation resulted in a three-year prohibition on lobbying by the defendant.

Very few prosecutions for noncompliance were brought by the Department of Justice even in the early years of the FRLA's history. One of those cases resulted in a significant narrowing of the act; it involved an attempt to influence Congress with regard to commodities prices undertaken by several commodities traders, various state officials, and a "national committee" purportedly acting on behalf of farmers. When a district court dismissed the information based on the unconstitutionality of the FRLA, the government took a direct appeal to the Supreme Court, which split five-to-three in upholding the statute through a tortured reading that left the act, according to dissenting Justice Jackson, "not much like any Act passed by Congress."

In this case, *United States v. Harriss*, decided in 1954, the Court confronted three facial challenges to the act: that it was too vague to meet the requirements of the due process clause of the Fifth Amendment; that the disclosure provisions violated the First Amendment's guarantees of freedom of speech, press, and the right to petition the government; and, finally, that the penalty provision imposing a three-year ban on lobbying by anyone convicted of violating the FRLA unlawfully interfered with the right to petition.

The Court did not resolve the third challenge on the basis that the sanction had yet to be invoked. It disposed of the other two by construing the FRLA as extending only to persons who (1) "directly" communicated with members of Congress on pending or proposed federal legislation (2) where influencing the passage or defeat of federal legislation was one of the "main purposes" of such persons or the money solicited or received by them. In reading out of the act its explicit coverage of "indirect" communications with Congress, finding coverage in that regard to extend no farther than "*artificially stimulated* letter campaign[s]," the Court implied that lobbying disclosure raised serious constitutional problems if it applied to attempts to influence ("propagandize") the general public to communicate its wishes to Congress ("grassroots lobbying"). In the end the Court found that the statute, as narrowly construed, did not violate the First Amendment, noting:

> Present-day legislative complexities are such that individual members of Congress cannot be expected to explore the myriad pressures to which they are regularly subjected. Yet full realization of the American ideal of government by elected representatives depends to no small extent on their ability to properly evaluate such pressures. Otherwise the voice of the people may all too easily be drowned out by the voice of special interest groups seeking favored treatment while masquerading as proponents of the public weal.

The majority's "interpretation" of the FRLA did not satisfy Justices Douglas, Black, or Jackson. While accepting that some type of lobbying disclosure legislation could pass constitutional muster, they all viewed the statute as written to impinge on First Amendment rights and so vague that any attempted judicial limitation was inherently arbitrary. Justice Jackson concluded by observing that "to reach the real evils of lobbying without cutting into the constitutional right of petition is a difficult and delicate task for which the Court's action today gives little guidance." The dilemma thus so succinctly described and the uncertainties created by *Harriss* have bedeviled reformers seeking effective lobbying regulation.

One of the immediate effects of *Harriss* was to render the FRLA grossly underinclusive as a lobbying disclosure scheme. For example, a huge automobile corporation could spend millions of dollars on a lobbying campaign and not have to register; since the "main" purpose of the corporation was not to influence the passage or defeat of legislation. Moreover, the Department of Justice (DOJ), whose enforcement efforts had been anemic at best prior to *Harriss*, simply abandoned prosecution as a means of insuring compliance, declaring the statute to be "ineffective, inadequate, and unenforceable." The statute, even as construed by the Supreme Court, exhibited significant vagueness, making successful prosecution a matter of doubt in some, perhaps many, cases. DOJ's avoidance of aggressive enforcement, whether justified or not, itself played a role in insuring the act's ineffectiveness.

By 1991, the General Accounting (now Government Accountability) Office (GAO) reported to Congress that only about 6,000 individuals or organizations were registered under the FRLA, a fraction of the number of lobbying entities thought to be subject to the statute. Moreover, even among registered entities, required reports were often submitted late (62 percent) and, when submitted, were often incomplete (in excess of 80 percent).

The 1950s through the mid-1980s witnessed congressional interest in lobbying reform waxing and waning, in large part in reaction to various scandals involving the national government.

The impetus for reform never, however, became irresistible during those years. If legislation actually emerged from a committee in the House or Senate, it died on the floor or, alternatively, was met by inactivity in the other chamber. Only once during this period did lobbying reform bills pass both chambers, but then securing compromise on the differing bills proved to be impossible. Not surprisingly, it was during the twilight of the Watergate era (in 1976) that the reform effort came tantalizingly close to a successful conclusion. The lobbying reform bills that were introduced during this period differed significantly in their details, but they attempted to grapple with the same basic issues: the definition of covered activities, the scope of mandated disclosure, and the mechanism(s) for enforcement.

In 1987, a congressional investigation revealed that a corporation had hired lobbyists, including former members of Congress, who allegedly obtained lucrative government contracts for their client by improper means; none of the activity had been reported under the lobbying law. The patent inadequacies of the FRLA were again highlighted, and the effect on the political climate of this scandal was magnified by others, along with the presidential campaign of 1992, during which H. Ross Perot, as a surprisingly strong third-party candidate, focused on the allegedly baneful influence of lobbyists. The first version of what was to become the Lobbying Disclosure Act of 1995 (LDA) was introduced by Senator Carl Levin (D-MI) in 1992. Congress almost enacted a revised version of the bill in 1994, but the bill was filibustered and died in the Senate, with various senators contending that it would require grassroots organizations, including some religious groups, to disclose information relating to their contributors. The midterm elections of 1994 turned over the control of Congress to the Republicans, who had campaigned on the theme of reforming that institution. It was no surprise, therefore, that a bipartisan coalition finally came together to enact the LDA in November 1995. Crucial to its enactment were a variety of changes from prior proposals, including the deletion of any coverage of grassroots lobbying and vesting administrative duties in the secretary of the Senate and the clerk of the House of Representatives rather than in a typical administrative agency free of direct congressional control. Various technical amendments to the act were adopted in 1998.

A short six-year respite from lobbying disclosure reform followed. But the series of scandals commonly associated with Jack Abramoff, a Republican lobbyist, erupted in 2004 and continued to grab headlines into 2006. Not surprisingly, the first efforts to strengthen the LDA began largely as a Democratic initiative. After years of seemingly fruitless challenges to the Republican control of government, the "loyal opposition" had finally found an issue that would resonate with the electorate and lead to increasing political support for Democratic candidates for national office. By the end of 2005, even prominent Republicans were joining in the chorus for lobbying and congressional reform. In the end, the gathering "perfect storm" did not result in final legislative action during 2006.

But, when the midterm elections of 2006 shifted control of Congress to the Democrats, the majority party immediately proposed a series of significant changes with regard to lobbying disclosure and congressional gift and travel rules, among other areas involving the activities of lobbyists. Mandatory disclosure of some grassroots lobbying, which was initially contained in the Senate bill, went down to early defeat due to First Amendment concerns, the same fate it suffered in conjunction with the enactment of the LDA. However, by the summer of 2007, the Democratic leaders in the House and Senate brokered a deal that resulted in the largely bipartisan enactment of the Honest Leadership and Open Government Act of 2007 (HLOGA), which was signed into law by President George W. Bush on September 14, 2007, and that amended various provisions of the LDA (among other things).

As federal lobbying disclosure law now stands, the stated purpose is different from the one relied upon in *Harriss* to sustain the FRLA; rather, it is to help insure public, not necessarily congressional, awareness of the efforts of lobbyists and, thereby, contribute to accountable government. The LDA does not, however, cover the efforts of unpaid lobbyists, nor does it extend to persons who: have less than two contacts with congressional and certain high level executive branch officials on behalf of a particular client; *or* spend less than 20 percent of their time on lobbying for that client during a quarterly period; *or* earn $6,000 or less during a quarterly period from the client or expend $10,000 or less during that period on lobbying activities for the client. (These monetary amounts are adjusted every four years based on changes in the Consumer Price Index.) Covered lobbying entities are known as "lobbying firms" (those who lobby for others) and self-lobbying organizations (those who lobby on their own behalf, such as corporations, trade associations, and various nonprofit groups). Both must register with the secretary of the Senate and the clerk of the House of Representatives and disclose the name of the client represented; the names of employees who qualify as lobbyists under the statute; the issues as to which lobbying will be directed; the names of organizations that both provide more than $5,000 in financial support for the client's lobbying activities during the quarterly period and also "actively participate" in the planning, supervision, or control of those lobbying activities; and, finally, the names of foreign entities with certain relationships to the registrant's client. Each registrant must file a quarterly report of its lobbying activities to include the income earned or expenses incurred; the general issue areas (e.g., tax) with regard to which lobbying has taken place during the period along with the "specific" issues on which lobbying has focused; whether the House, Senate, or a particular federal agency was contacted by a lobbyist employed by the registrant (but not the name[s] of the committee or particular individual who was contacted or what was said); the interest of any foreign entity in the issues lobbied; and, finally, an update of information contained on the initial registration form. In actual practice, the nature of the disclosures and how they appear on quarterly reports offer only a very general sense of the contours of specific lobbying campaigns.

As a result of HLOGA, both LDA registrants and lobbyists listed on registration statements and quarterly reports must semiannually report to the secretary and clerk with regard to various contributions (including campaign contributions) and disbursements made by them or their political action committees (PACs) to or on behalf of various federal candidates and congressional and executive branch officials. Filers must certify that they have not given a gift that violates the House or Senate's gift and travel rules. Indeed, giving such gifts is itself a violation of the LDA, which is subject to the civil and criminal penalties that apply to all LDA violations. Finally, political committees that receive large contributions that have been gathered ("bundled") by LDA registrants and listed lobbyists must publicly report those payments.

All of the reports required under the LDA must be filed electronically and posted on the Internet as soon as practicable. Their content must be fully searchable on the Internet. These improvements in past practice help to ensure that the public can, if it wishes, easily obtain at least a general picture of the nature and scope of federal lobbying activity.

The increased stringency of lobbying disclosure requirements triggered the first constitutional challenge to federal lobbying legislation since the Supreme Court's *Harriss* decision in 1954. In *National Association of Manufacturers v. Taylor* (2008), the federal district court for the District of Columbia rejected contentions that the LDA's requirement (as revised in HLOGA) that organizations contributing to lobbying campaigns be disclosed in registration statements was an unconstitutional abridgment of First Amendment rights and was void on vagueness grounds. (At the time of this writing, the appeal of this case remains to be decided.)

Finally, it is important to note that, as in the case of federal law, state lobbying law has undergone significant development over the last century and, today, continues to change. Indeed, the Jack Abramoff controversy ignited reform efforts outside the national capital. The diversity of state law today defies detailed treatment here. All states have laws governing lobbying the state legislature, and most also cover efforts to influence at least some executive branch actions. While generally, local law governs the lobbying of local officials, some state laws also apply at that level. Unlike federal law as it stands today, a majority of states include grassroots lobbying in their registration and disclosure schemes. Political contributions by lobbyists are prohibited in some states; many explicitly prohibit lobbyists from "deceiving" public officials. In the end, however, the heart of state lobbying law, like federal, is lobbyist registration and disclosure, though the variation among state laws is significant. For example, in some states only lobbyists must register; in others their employers must also register or at least certify lobbyist registrations. Some states even require lobbyists to carry identification cards. The content of required disclosure varies, but often includes the income earned from and expenses incurred for lobbying, matters lobbied, campaign contributions, and gifts paid to public officials.

The trend in recent years has been in the direction of increased regulation of lobbying activities. It is likely that that trend will continue, including more integration of reporting of campaign and lobbying activities. It remains unclear today whether existing public disclosure of the nature of specific lobbying efforts can effectively contribute to a policy-making process that is faithful to democratic ideals. The periodic revelation of lobbying abuses, while it has been the historic engine of reform, is not always—or perhaps ever—an adequate indication of whether existing lobbying law is up to the task given it, since even an effective system cannot eliminate all problems. Rather, only sustained and detailed empirical study can shed significant light on whether the practice of lobbying and good government are, more often than not, existing in harmony with one another.

Further Reading:

Byrd, Senator Robert C. "Lobbyists." In *The Senate, 1789–1989: Addresses on the History of the United States Senate*. S. Doc. No. 100-20, edited by Mary Sharon Hall, 1989. Available online. URL: http://www.senate.gov/legislative/common/briefing/Byrd_History_Lobbying.htm. Accessed July 10, 2009; Goldstein, Kenneth M. *Interest Groups, Lobbying, and Participation in America*. New York: Cambridge University Press, 1999; Levine, Bertram J. *The Art of Lobbying: Building Trust and Selling Policy*. Washington, D.C.: CQ Press, 2008; Luneburg, William V., Thomas M. Susman, and Rebecca H. Gordon, eds. *The Lobbying Manual: A Complete Guide to Federal Lobbying Law and Practice*. 4th ed. Chicago: American Bar Association, 2009.

– William V. Luneburg

security classification

The question of finding the correct balance between the public's right to know of the actions and policies of their government and the government's legitimate need, especially during times of war or transnational terrorism, to protect vital assets and conduct foreign relations, is central to the U.S. concept of democracy. As President James Madison, the framer of the U.S. Constitution, wrote in 1822, "A popular Government without popular information or the means of acquiring it is but a Prologue to a Farce or a Tragedy; or perhaps both. Knowledge will forever govern ignorance; And a people who mean to be their own Governors, must arm themselves with the power which knowledge gives."

Security classification can be described as the process of identifying the specific information that requires protection in the interest of preserving national security. Although classification has been a part of the art of war since ancient times, formal government-wide frameworks for classification policy have existed in the United States only since March 1940, when President Franklin D. Roosevelt issued Executive Order (EO) No. 8381, "Defining Certain Vital Military and Naval Installations and Equipment." This order provided: "1. All military or naval installations and equipment which now are classified, designated and marked under the authority or at the direction of the Secretary of War or the Secretary of the Navy as 'secret,' 'confidential,' or 'restricted,' and all military or naval installations and equipment which hereafter be so classified, designated, and marked with the approval of or at the direction of the President."

Prior to this EO, the military departments and the Department of State had regulated classification policies as internal "housekeeping" matters. The rather unusual title of the EO reflects one of the first classification policy issues: What authority does the president have to set classification policy and authorize the classification of executive branch information? President Roosevelt used an act of January 12, 1938—that established a punishment by a fine of no more than $1,000 or imprisonment for not more than one year, or both, for failure to obtain advance permission to make any graphic image of vital installations and equipment—as the sole authority for issuing the EO. President Harry S. Truman's first executive order revised EO 8381 to reflect the new organization of the defense establishment, again citing the same specific legislation. All subsequent executive orders on National Security Information (NSI), including President Truman's second executive order, have cited a much broader "authority vested in me by the Constitution and statutes. . . ."

When one mentions "security classification," most citizens immediately think in terms of the National Security Information (NSI) framework, and the now traditional categories of "top secret," "secret," and "confidential." Two other frameworks emerged during the post–World War II years: (1) the nuclear weapons and atomic energy framework created by the Atomic Energy Act (AEA) of 1946; and (2) the Sensitive Compartmented Information (SCI) framework rising from the establishment of the Central Intelligence Agency, authorized by executive action. All "Restricted Data" (RD) and "Formerly Restricted Data" (FRD) classified under the AEA of 1946 and 1954 are "born classified," and are also considered as NSI under the appropriate executive orders. While SCI must be classified to specific "code words" by an authorized original classification authority, all SCI is also classified as NSI. However, vast quantities of NSI are not classifiable under the AEA or SCI frameworks. All three of these frameworks now formally address declassification or "downgrading," and contain a formal review requirement.

Several concepts are shared by these three formal frameworks. All require that, before an individual can have access to classified information, a determination must be made that access at a specific level is required by a recurring mission responsibility of their position. Once this basic requirement is met, the individual is subject to one of four levels of background checks, ranging from the relatively quick "National Agency Check" with credit check and local agency (police records) check required for access to confidential information; the "Single Scope Background Investigation" required for access to top secret information, which includes a full field investigation, personal interviews, and confirmation of all education beyond high school and all residences and work experience for the past 10 years; to the additional requirements for "lifestyle polygraphs" or "counterintelligence polygraphs," or even "full-scope polygraphs." Once the investigation is complete, an authorized personnel security officer must make an adjudication that the individual meets the requirements for that level of access. After a vetting process that can take from as little as several weeks (for confidential access) to well over a year for SCI or RD access, the individual must sign the appropriate nondisclosure statement and receive a security briefing before the clearance is granted. These frameworks also share a "pull' rather than a "push" distribution model, where one must determine which organization might have the information needed, then convince the holder of the information that they have a "need to know" before access to any specific classified information can be provided.

The fourth security classification framework, just recently (May 9, 2008) named "Controlled Unclassified Information" (CUI), has existed since the beginning of the republic under various names, but it has never before been officially authorized for use across the executive branch. Various studies in recent years have estimated that over 50 different markings, including the more common terms of "For Official Use Only," "Sensitive But Unclassified" (SBU), "Limited Official Use," etc., have been used throughout the executive branch. While the AEA framework specifically defines RD and FRD, and the NSI framework limits original top secret classification authority to a relatively small number of very senior officials, virtually any executive branch employee, member of the military, or even any federal contractor could, and many did, apply SBU markings. Once marked, SBU was rarely reviewed for unmarking.

Access to CUI generally does not require any additional vetting than is required for federal employment, and there is no equivalent to a clearance for access. However, until the formal establishment of the "Information Sharing Environment" (ISE) (December, 2005), access to SBU still generally followed the "pull" model. In a Memorandum for the Heads of Executive Departments and Agencies, President George W. Bush directed the development of a common framework for sharing information between and among the executive departments and state, local, and tribal governments, law enforcement agencies, and the private sector, essentially moving the "pull" model to a "push" model, where sensitive information would be distributed on a role- and event-based access model (sometimes referred to as "Right-to-Know").

In addition to the four frameworks introduced above, the federal government has also restricted access to wide ranges of information that are not associated with even the broadest definition of NSI. See for example the Privacy Act, the Freedom of Information Act (FOIA), and other specific legislation restricting access to individually-identifying census data or IRS records.

National Security policies have developed incrementally, mainly by presidential orders. President Roosevelt's very brief (under three full pages) EO in March 1940 formalized and provided a legislative authority for the existing classification systems then being used by the army and the navy. This EO was issued while the United States had not yet formally joined the Allied effort in World War II, but the United States was already providing Lend-Lease assistance to Great Britain. Under its very broad definitions, essentially all information pertaining to the military, its facilities, equipment, and plans could be classified, including information relating to commercial production facilities. Under the initial order, technically any member of the military and any civilian employee in the military departments held original classification authority, though in practice this authority was more limited. A September 1942 Office of War Information (OWI) classification regulation substantially expanded the types of information that could be classified, including any information "which could endanger national security, impair the prosecution of the war, or should be limited for administrative privacy could be classified." EO No. 8381 provided for three classification levels: Secret, Confidential, and Restricted. The first EO on National Security Information must be viewed in the context of World War II in Europe, and OWI regulation in the context of the active entry by the United States into World War II.

President Truman's February 1950 EO on NSI was essentially a housekeeping measure that recognized the reorganization of the military departments into the Department of Defense. Its only substantive change was to add a new level, Top Secret, to the existing three levels of Secret, Confidential, and Restricted.

President Truman's September 1951 EO on NSI significantly expanded the classification systems to grant Original Classification Authority (OCA) to the heads of all executive agencies, with the authorization to delegate this authority with the agency. It clearly established the principle that the number of OCAs at the Top Secret level should be significantly fewer than at the Secret level, and so on down to OCA at the Restricted level. While retaining the four existing classification levels, this order was the first to specifically require that NSI be classified at the lowest level consistent with national security. It also introduced for the first time a requirement that, to the maximum extent possible, the OCA, at time of initial classification, provide a specified event or date for automatic downgrading and/or declassification. The EO also required "every government official to keep classified security information in his custody constantly under review, and initiate action towards downgrading or declassification as soon as conditions warrant." Restricted data under the AEA of 1946 was specifically exempted for all provisions of the order.

Developed within the context of the ongoing Korean conflict and the cold war in Europe. This EO contained for the first time formal policy that at least nominally advocated "minimizing" classification both by levels and by duration, but these features did not protect the order from widespread criticism in Congress and the press over a concern that expansion of classification authority at all executive agencies was far too inclusive.

President Eisenhower's December 1953 EO on NSI responded to the criticism against Truman's EO by significantly reducing the number of agencies that were granted Original Classification Authority, with OCA totally removed from 28 agencies, and OCA limited to the head of agency for 17 additional agencies. The order also eliminated the Restricted level. It retained the requirement that information be classified at the lowest practical level, and contained the requirement that the initial classifier specify a date or event for automatic declassification whenever possible. Section 10 of the order required that each agency originating or handling classified defense information "shall designate experienced persons to coordinate and supervise the activities applicable to their departments or agencies under this order."

President Kennedy's September 1961 EO retained most of the requirements of EO No. 10501, and it recognized Formerly Restricted Data under the AEA of 1954. The order required the OCA to categorize classified information into one of four groups. Group 1 included all information required by law or treaty to remain classified (including RD and FRD), and "information requiring special handling, such as intelligence and cryptography" and is excluded from automatic downgrading or declassification. Group 2, also exempt from automatic downgrading and declassification, was limited to "extremely sensitive information . . . which the head of the agency or his designee exempt, on an individual basis." Group 3 included information "that warrants some degree of classification for an indefinite period. Information in this group would be automatically downgraded at 12-year intervals, but not below Confidential. Group 4 contained all information that does not qualify for one of the first three groups. "Such information shall be downgraded at three-year intervals until the lowest classification is reached, and shall be automatically declassified twelve years after the date of issuance."

President Nixon's March 1972 EO must be viewed in the context of the continuing controversy over misclassification and the publication of the Pentagon Papers. It significantly increased the emphasis on downgrading and declassification by establishing a presumption for automatic downgrading and ultimately declassification unless the information qualified for a limited number of specific exemptions for automatic declassification. Top Secret would automatically be downgraded to Secret after two years; Secret would downgrade to Confidential after two years; and Confidential would be declassified after six years, effectively setting 10 years as the default for declassifying Top Secret data.

The order was the first to specifically prohibit certain classification actions: "In no case shall information be classified in order to conceal inefficiency or administrative error, to prevent embarrassment to a person or department, to restrain competition or independent initiative, or to prevent for any other reason the release of information which does not requires protection in the interest of national security." Two other innovations, the establishment of mandatory review procedures and the requirement to "portion mark" all classified documents, also emphasized the order's bias toward declassification. Prior to this order, the standard practice had been to mark the entire document at the highest level of classification of any information it contained. Under Nixon's order, each paragraph had to be marked with its own level of classification.

Marking portions therefore made reviewing of lengthy documents much easier.

President Carter's June 1978 EO continued the trend to reduce classification. His order restricted the use of Confidential unless the OCA could cite "identifiable damage." The order slightly modified President Nixon's prohibitions on classification by adding violation of law and misconduct to the list of prohibited items. The order introduced the balance test: Does public interest outweigh any possible damage? The order also mandated a policy to use the less restrictive designation if in doubt.

The order also established an independent Information Security Oversight Office to provide governmentwide implantation instruction, monitor agency classification actions, and report misclassifications to the White House.

President Reagan's April 1982 EO slightly shifted the emphasis back in favor of more restrictive classification policy, by deleting the requirement for "identifiable damage" and changing the policy to favor the more restrictive classification if in doubt. While the previous executive orders had presumed that once information had been officially declassified it would remain declassified, the Reagan order permitted reclassification of NSI under limited conditions.

President Clinton's April 1995 EO returned the emphasis toward access, including restoring the "identifiable damage" test. The order reduced the list of types of information that could be classified to seven by including cryptology with the intelligence grouping, placing confidential sources with the foreign relations group, and eliminating the final catch-all group.

The major change in policy occurred in the declassification area. The Clinton order established automatic declassification times for NSI designated as having permanent value. At the time of original classification, the OCA must attempt to establish a specific date or event for declassification, not to exceed 10 years, or to specifically identify a reason why it should be exempt from automatic declassification. All previously classified information would be automatically declassified on December 31, 2000, unless it was determined that the release could reasonably be expected to cause extreme harm under one or more of the eight specific categories listed in the EO.

Clinton's order also established the Interagency Security Classification Appeals Panel (ISCAP). Since the panel's startup in May 1996 through September 2007, it has reviewed 679 documents and declassified in full 138 documents (20 percent); declassified in part an additional 279 documents (41 percent); and affirmed the classification of 262 documents (39 percent).

President George W. Bush's March 2003 EO was initially perceived as favoring secrecy over access, as it further delayed the automatic declassification of historically significant records over 25 years old to December 31, 2006, for most records, and provided agencies an additional five years to review nontextual records requiring extra processing time and also provided an additional three-year grace period for textual records that require multiple agency review. As the anticipated December 31, 2006, date was in fact maintained, most of the original critics began to recognize that the delays provided for in the order simply matched the fact that the time extension was in fact necessary.

Set against the background of the active wars in Iraq and Afghanistan, and the "Global War on Terror," and as could be expected with the change from a Democratic administration to a Republican administration, the "if in doubt, use less restrictive classification" language was deleted, and the new order was also less restrictive on reclassification issues. The order added one additional type of information, weapons of mass destruction, to the list of classifiable information, and it added language to specifically include "defense against transnational terrorism" as part of national security.

As of fall 2009, President Obama has not issued an EO on NSI, but the administration has signaled its intention to revise the previous policies in a manner that will further reduce the amount of information that is classified. While not directly impacting NSI, one of President Obama's first

EOs directed a return to a more open government information policy with regard to FOIA review and release. In May 2009 Obama issued a memo directing his administration to conduct a review of classified information policies. His administration's support for the creation of a National Declassification Center, under the supervision of the archivist of the United States, further signals the administration's intentions.

Although presidents have been the major force behind the development of classification policy, Congress has occasionally responded. Since the mid-1950s Congress has held many hearings and issued numerous reports, but it has consistently refused to independently legislate classification policy (the Atomic Energy Act was requested by the administration to handle a new scientific development that the Constitution could not have foreseen). Regardless of the party in power, the general thrust of the congressional reports has been that too much information was being classified at too high a level, while important information was being leaked or stolen. Senator Daniel Patrick Moynihan's (D-NY) 1997 *Report of the Commission on Protecting and Reducing Government Secrecy* is one of the most comprehensive (although hardly neutral) discussions of the history of overclassification, and it argues that the policies ironically fail to protect adequately the genuinely important secrets. Nevertheless, over the years the courts have consistently displayed great deference to the executive branch in matters of classification policy, refusing to substitute their judgment on the validity of a classification action.

The most famous secrecy debate occurred in 1971 when the Nixon administration attempted to enjoin the publication by the *New York Times*, and subsequently, the *Washington Post*, of a history of the Vietnam War compiled by the Department of Defense, which became known as "the Pentagon Papers." Although the documents were historical and lacking any operational value, they were classified Top Secret. The Supreme Court did not rule on the issue of the proper level of classification (if any) of the Pentagon Papers. However, the actual publication of the papers caused many, both within government and in advocacy organizations, to cite the papers as definitive proof of mindless overclassification. In its decision, the Supreme Court concluded that it had no constitutional or legislative authority to enjoin the publication of classified NSI. By their very nature, executive orders apply solely to executive departments and agencies and their employees, and not to the general public. If the publication of NSI were to separately constitute a violation of one of the espionage laws, the administration could subsequently bring action.

In October 1985, Samuel Loring Morison, a civilian analyst with the Office of Naval Intelligence, became the first, and only, person convicted under the Espionage Act for the unauthorized disclosure of classified defense information to the press. His conviction was upheld in 1988 and the Supreme Court declined to hear the case. Morison supplied a classified photograph of a Soviet nuclear-powered carrier under construction to *Jane's Defense Weekly*, which subsequently published the photo.

It has long been considered an axiom that, in the politically charged culture of Washington, secrets are hard to keep secret. Politicians who are in power have repeatedly selectively declassified information that would support their particular causes, while withholding other documents from the same file that would question their causes. Politicians who were out of power would simply leak classified information that supported their views to the ever-hungry media corps. In addition to the political use of leaks, the career bureaucrats also know how to play the game, to defend their own organization against a rival organization.

OpenTheGovernment.org is a coalition of the major groups that have generally argued against excessive secrecy and that promote openness. The organization includes private groups that not only advocate for openness, but also collect and publish formerly classified information (e.g., Federation of American Scientists, National Security Archive, and Electronic Frontier Foundation) as well as less agenda-focused organizations (American Association of Law Libraries,

Society of Professional Journalists). Its annual *Secrecy Report Card* is normally published in the early fall. Its fundamental argument is that making the federal government a more open place will make the citizens safer, strengthen public trust in government, and support democratic principles.

Restricted data is defined by the Atomic Energy Act of 1946 as "all data concerning the manufacture or utilization of atomic weapons, the production of fissionable materials, or the use of fissionable material in the production of power, but shall not include any data which the Commission from time to time determines may be published without adversely affecting the common defense and security." The definition was broad and encompassed all information dealing with atomic power. Any information that fits into the definition of RD is considered to be classified by the act upon its generation. This is generally referred to as being "born classified." Although the act has been amended several times over the years, unlike the other frameworks, it has been relatively free from controversy.

On October 16, 2001, just over a month after the attacks of September 11, President George W. Bush issued an EO regarding the protection of critical infrastructure. This EO formally recognized that information and systems operated and maintained by the private sector were critical to homeland security and national defense.

While the critical infrastructure sectors—telecommunications, energy, financial services, manufacturing, water, transportation, health care, and emergency services—are regulated, and in some cases are partially funded, by the federal government, *none* of these sectors is actually under the operational control of the federal government. The terrorist attacks of 9/11 were not specifically targeted against any particular critical infrastructure sector, but they had significant impact on various critical infrastructure sectors. The telecommunications sector, particularly in the mid-Atlantic and Northeast, was severely disrupted for several hours until work-around capabilities could reduce the massive overload on the land-line and cellular telecommunications networks. As New York City is one of the primary hubs of the financial services sector, the damage ranged from momentary (for the best prepared corporations that maintained remote "hot sites" with mirror backup systems) to long-term disruptions and even bankruptcy for the least prepared corporations. The civil aviation portion of the transportation sector was totally out of operation for several weeks, and many operators never recovered from the loss of traffic that lasted for many months. The emergency services sector, and, in particular, the "blue light" forces (police, fire, and emergency medical services), relies primarily on local government resources, supplemented by mutual aid resources.

Protecting the physical assets and operational capabilities of the critical infrastructure sectors requires the full exchange of threat information from the federal government to both state and local governments and to the private sector organizations that actually operate the assets. The federal government needs to receive risk, vulnerability, and operational information from the corporate sectors. Private sector operators must be able to share operational information with their corporate competitors to prevent system meltdowns. None of the necessary vertical or horizontal information flow will occur unless all parties have a reasonable expectation that their data will not be misused or left without proper protection.

Security classification, defined broadly, is essential in the vertical flow of information in both directions. Unfortunately, no overall framework existed in the post-9/11 environment to address this problem. The National Security Information framework could not be used for a variety of reasons. First, the NSI framework applies only to "information ... owned by, produced by or for, or is under the control of the United States Government," and thus it cannot be used to protect information that is voluntarily provided by the private sector, which blocks the upward flow of information. The second problem is that no one may have access to classified information unless "a favorable determination of eligibility has been made by the agency head or the agency head's designee." Just within the emergency services sector, it would be impossible to subject the hundreds of thousands of local and state police officers, firemen, and EMTs to such strict scrutiny. The same executive order contains an emergency clause: "In an emergency, when necessary to respond to an imminent threat to life or in the defense of the homeland, the agency head or any designee *may* [emphasis added] authorize the disclosure of classified information to an individual or individuals who are otherwise not eligible for access [the clause goes on at great length to add conditions and restrictions]." There have been no reported incidents where this has actually occurred.

Even before the terrorist attacks of September 2001 and the actions taken by the White House during 2001 and 2002 to safeguard what was then termed "sensitive but unclassified" information, federal agencies had implemented a variety of procedures to safeguard information. According to a report of the Commission on Protecting and Reducing Government Secrecy, 1997, "at least 52 different protective markings [are] being used on unclassified information, approximately 40 of which are being used by departments and agencies that also classify information." These markings include the most familiar: "Sensitive But Unclassified" (SBU), "Limited Official Use," "Official Use Only," and "For Official Use Only" (FOUO).

Prior to the May 9, 2008, Memorandum for the Heads of Executive Departments and Agencies, there was no uniformity in federal agency definitions, or rules to implement safeguards for "sensitive but unclassified" information.

Unlike the NSI framework, where information could be originally classified only by designated OCAs, who had to be personally identified by name or personal identifier and job title, virtually any member of the military, civilian employee of the federal government, or government contractor could stamp SBU or FOUO on a document anonymously, and without stating the reason or the duration for the marking. While the framework for NSI provided for mandatory review of classification action, automatic declassification, and a formal appeals process within the executive branch to the Interagency Security Classification Appeals Panel, a citizen who was denied access to SBU could only file suit under the Freedom of Information Act.

The Freedom of Information Act (see separate entry) creates a balancing test between the public's right to be informed and the government's legitimate needs to protect sensitive information. FOIA lists specific categories of information that may be withheld from release. CUI may or may not fall under one or more of these exempt categories. FOIA places the burden on the government to prove why any particular information should not be released, and the simple marking of that information as CUI or SBU does not in itself justify withholding that information.

Formal CUI policy is both very recent and highly evolving. The developing CUI framework closely parallels the NSI framework, with one significant exception: CUI does not yet have an automatic or mandatory review structure. The establishment of the Controlled Unclassified Information Office within the National Archives and Records Administration may eventually lead to an executive branch alternative to the FOIA as a means to compel review of CUI.

Classification policy is very likely to remain the exclusive domain of the executive branch, as for the past nearly 60 years Congress and the courts have been very reluctant to impose their will over that of the president. As classification policy is expressed via executive orders, the one sure conclusion is that the policies will change over time with the changing fundamental political philosophies of each new administration and external events. In the past, absent a significant external cause (e.g., the Pentagon Papers and Nixon), a general trend has developed whereby Democratic administrations tend to emphasize a bias toward release and Republican administrations tend to emphasize "when in doubt, restrict."

Further reading:

Gansler, Jacques S., and Willian Lucyshyn. "The Unintended Audience: Balancing Openness and Secrecy: Crafting an Information Policy for the

21st Century." Center for Public Policy, University of Maryland, September 2004. Available online. URL: http://www.cpppe.umd.edu/Bookstore/Documents/UnintendedAudience_3.05.pdf. Accessed September 20, 2009; U.S. Senate. "Report of the Commission on Protecting and Reducing Government Secrecy." 103rd Cong. S. Doc. 105-2. Washington, D.C.: GPO, 1997. Available online. URL: www.fas.org/sgp/library/moynihan/. Accessed September 20, 2009. See also various executive orders, including 8381 (March 22, 1940); 10104 (February 1, 1950); 10290 (September 24, 1951); 10501 (December 15, 1953); 10964 (September 20, 1961); 11653 (March 8, 1972); 12085 (June 28, 1978); 12356 (April 2, 1982); 12958 (April 16, 1995); and 13292 (March 25, 2003). All available online at the American Presidency Project. URL: http://www.presidency.ucsb.edu/executive_orders.php. Accessed September 20, 2009.

– Stephen Hannestad

Immigration and Naturalization

border security

International borders between nation-states continue to be transformed in an era marked by globalization and new security threats such as transnational terrorism, organized crime, and disease. This is no less the case for the land, air, and sea boundaries of the United States. These borders remain key focal points in the wide policy effort to regulate the flows of goods and individuals in and out of the country; they also retain their role as traditional markers of state sovereignty and territoriality. The security policies deployed at U.S. borders have shifted over time as a result of defined threats, economic interests, and political priorities. They have had mixed results in terms of effectiveness. And while control of entry into the United States remains largely a federal matter, regional, state, and local authorities play an important, and often interinstitutional and interjurisdictional function, in U.S. border security policy, particularly for law enforcement and disaster response.

This article will trace some of the key dimensions of U.S. border security policy, operating first from a geographical and historical perspective and then moving to a discussion about key contemporary institutions, policies, and issues in the 1986–2001 period and then the post-September 11, 2001, era. The focus here is largely on federal government actions.

The borders of the United States have undergone several periods of change since the nation's founding in 1776. The southern border with Mexico has been largely fixed since the Treaty of Guadalupe Hidalgo ended the controversial Mexican-American War (1846–48). The treaty acknowledged acquisition by the United States of much of then northern Mexico, including present-day California, Arizona, New Mexico, Texas, Nevada, Utah, and parts of Wyoming, Colorado, and Oklahoma. The southern border was finalized through the Gadsden Purchase in 1853.

In the north, the U.S.-Canada border was settled by terms of the Treaty of Paris in 1783, which recognized the independence of the original 13 colonies and established the boundaries between the United States and British North America. In 1803, the Louisiana Purchase between the United States and France continued the country's territorial expansion to include the states, in the Midwest, including Minnesota, North Dakota, and Montana, and setting the northern boundary; the Treaty Line of 1818 eventually established the formal boundary between those states and British Canada. Finally, under terms of the Oregon Treaty of 1846, the remaining present-day territory of the Pacific Northwest was acquired. U.S. border coastlines include the Atlantic-Caribbean in the east and the Pacific coast in the west. In total, the border consists of 95,000 miles of coastline, 26,000 miles of navigable inland rivers and waterways, and 6,500 miles of land borders, divided roughly as the 4,500 mile border between the United States and Canada and the 2,000 miles of the U.S.-Mexico border. According to the U.S. Customs and Border Protection (CBP) Agency, there are currently 327 official ports of entry (land, air, and sea) in the United States and 15 preclearance offices.

The varying geographical and climactic features of U.S. borders—ranging from deserts to forest to sea coasts—have dictated various degrees of security considerations and measures; hence, different U.S. border security policies have emerged and evolved over time. Nonetheless, as discussed below, scholars generally accept that meaningful land border security efforts were not deployed until late in the 20th century.

Millions of people and goods travel across U.S. borders every day through both formal and informal entry points. U.S. CBP estimates that formal ports facilitate the entry of approximately 1.1 million international travelers via land, air, and seaports on a typical day; $2 trillion in legitimate trade entered via the same ports in 2008; 11 million cargo containers enter through U.S. seaports annually. The United States is the most important trading partner—both for imports and for exports—for Canada and Mexico, respectively. According to the U.S. Bureau of Transportation Statistics, in 2007, $511 billion of surface transportation trade occurred between the United States and Canada; and $286 billion between the United States and Mexico.

Between these formal points of entry, however, the movement of unauthorized people and goods into America's national territory is also constant, albeit to a lesser extent, with a rough approximation of 500,000 people entering annually. Critical to note is that unauthorized immigrants are made up of those who enter illegally through both formal and informal channels, and those who enter legally into the United States but remain in the United States beyond their legal visit, e.g., overstay their visas, as demonstrated by the 19 terrorists who executed the September 11, 2001, attacks. The numbers of people and amounts of goods that cross U.S. borders on a daily basis require massive resources and attention to manage and secure these entries. The problem of facilitating licit trade and interaction while screening out illicit goods and individuals is the central policy challenge for U.S. policy makers.

The next section will discuss the key border security institutions that deal with this challenge. The discussion then moves into several key policy and political issues, both pre- and post-9/11, that have dominated life and policy on U.S. borders.

Through the nation's history, different security institutions have operated on American frontiers. The United States began regulating mass immigration in significant ways only by late in the 19th century; at that time, government institutions were created, such as the U.S. Bureau of Immigration, to manage these legal entries through access points such as Ellis Island, New York. At the land border, mounted patrols by the U.S. Immigration Service began in 1904. Since that time, a complex and overlapping web of multiple federal government agencies (chief among them the Immigration and Naturalization Service [INS]), were created and reformed in accordance with wide changes in U.S. border security and immigration policies; these policies tend to reflect the general ambivalence the country has had toward its immigrants and its borders at different points in its history. Hotly debated even today, the 1965 Immigration and Nationality Act, for instance, moved the country from a national origins quota system to a structure that gave priority to family reunification; this change altered the nature of immigrant flows into the United States. Proponents saw the act as a means to revise a racially inspired policy tradition of favoring immigrants from Europe; opponents predicted social and cultural fragmentation.

The terrorist attacks of September 11, 2001, prompted a dramatic shift in U.S. border policies and institutions. Formed in response to the incidents, the National Commission on Terrorist Attacks Upon the United States (the 9/11 Commission) highlighted the problem of information sharing among desperate security agencies as a key factor that contributed to government's failure to prevent the attacks. Explicit in this critique were the nation's border and immigration agencies. In 2002, President George W. Bush proposed a massive reorganization of the federal government that included these institutions: The proposed Department of Homeland Security (DHS) would combine 22 agencies—creating, among other things, "One Face at the Border"—into one institution with approximately 200,000 employees. With wide majorities from both Democrats

The towns of Nogales, Arizona, left, and Nogales, Mexico, are separated by a concrete and steel fence. Despite the existence of a legal crossing point, enough illegal crossings occur to warrant 24-hour Border Patrol operations here. *(U.S. Army)*

and Republicans, Congress passed the Homeland Security Act of 2002, and the president signed the legislation into law on November 25, 2002.

While multiple agency components are now responsible for different aspects of border security, the lead agency is U.S. Customs and Border Protection (CBP). In early 2009, there were approximately 24,000 CBP employees, roughly divided among 19,000 CBP officers in field operations, 2,200 agricultural specialists, and 3,000 in administrative positions. At formal ports of entry, CBP personnel are responsible for enforcing import and export laws and federal regulations, implementing immigration and trade policies, and conducting agricultural inspections. In addition to authorizing the entry of individuals and goods, a primary responsibility of CBP personnel is to detect unauthorized entries and/or potential harm, in the form of persons, goods, and/or animal or plant pests and/or diseases that enter the United States via formal channels. The Border Patrol is the primary agency responsible for securing informal channels of entry on land between the ports of entry, where all entries are unauthorized. A primary duty of a Border Patrol agent is what is known in the field as "line watch," that is, maintaining round-the-clock surveillance of the land border for detection, prevention, and apprehension of unauthorized persons and illegal contraband by using intelligence, technology, and law enforcement operations.

Interdiction of unauthorized entry by air remains under the official jurisdiction of the Department of Defense. Along the shores it is the responsibility of the U.S. Coast Guard (although the Border Patrol assumes certain responsibilities in some locations along the Caribbean border). As noted below, the military performs some support roles on U.S. borders.

As noted above, the trajectory of U.S. border security policy has followed different cycles over time, in response to differently defined threats and different political priorities. For the purposes of this article, we consider contemporary policy issues and responses, and, in doing so, divide them into two broad periods: 1986–2001 and 2001–08.

The first contemporary period is characterized by two major policy problems, particularly (but not exclusively) focused on the southwest border with Mexico: unauthorized immigration and illicit narcotics trafficking. The major policy response to these two defined threats was new security tactics and resources, largely directed on the U.S.-Mexico frontier.

As noted above, U.S. borders are gateways for both authorized and unauthorized individuals. Responding to basic economic laws of supply and demand, both documented and undocumented workers (approximately 60 percent of whom are Mexican nationals) have provided a substantial, and arguably a necessary, workforce in the United States. Immigration, however, is also a chronic source of contention for the United States and Mexico that has at times raised animosity at the political and social levels. Indeed, in response to a number of national political, social, and economic factors in the mid-1980s to the mid-1990s, border control came to be cast as a security issue as politicians responded to constituent perceptions about "illegal aliens" and an "open border." This formulation was particularly powerful among conservatives and even some Democrats who were concerned about perceptions of being "soft" on security issues. In 1986, President Reagan signed into law the Immigration Reform and Control Act (IRCA), which expanded funding for the U.S. Border Patrol as well as tightened immigration laws. Subsequent legislation in this period resulted in bolstering funding and political support for U.S. border operations.

The general bipartisan support for enhanced border enforcement continued into the 1990s. Early in President William J. Clinton's administration, for instance, the Border Patrol began a new tactic of line-watching at the southwestern frontier, designed to "prevent [entry] through deterrence" by deploying agents to within line-of-sight of one another. The strategy proved attractive politically and became the centerpiece of the agency's national strategy. Additional resources for manpower and technology flowed to the border; between 1986 and 2002, the number of Border Patrol officers tripled. In 1994's "Operation Gatekeeper," surveillance equipment was deployed by the Border Patrol alongside a new 18-mile physical barrier in the San Diego/Tijuana area. Finally, the 1996 Illegal Immigration Reform and Immigrant Responsibility Act (IIRIRA) consolidated the new enforcement regime, providing funding for additional border agents, fencing, and stricter immigration penalties.

As a component of the American government's "War on Drugs," declared as early as 1971 by President Richard Nixon, the effort to interdict drug shipments to the United States was located in large part at the southwestern border with Mexico and at sea routes to Florida. Driven by massive economic incentives—the U.S. market for drugs is estimated to be worth at least $25 billion annually—as well as the geographic opportunity a long, relatively open land border with millions of annual crossings affords, drug cartels have long operated along and across the U.S.-Mexico border. U.S. drug policy has long been weighted in favor of interdiction, so the border has, over the past three decades, been a primary site for operations designed to counter this defined policy problem. Multiple federal agencies, including the Drug Enforcement Agency, the Federal Bureau of Investigation, CBP, and even the U.S. military were involved in counternarcotics activity during the 1981–2001 period. Most notably, but not without controversy, the U.S. military has offered logistical support, surveillance, reconnaissance, and intelligence gathering to law enforcement, principally in the form of "Joint Task Force-6," (now known as "Joint Task Force North"), which is based at Fort Bliss, Texas. The use of the military at the border was, and continues to be, a flash point politically for those in civil society concerned about the "militarization" of the border, with occasional protests about human rights concerns.

Public policies may be evaluated in terms of their intended and unintended consequences. In this period, new resources flowed to border security, as illustrated by the growth of Border Patrol alone; the force increased from 3,965 agents in 1993 to 9,651 in 2001. The vast majority of these agents were stationed at the U.S.-Mexico border. As defined by Border Patrol's national strategy, their job was to deter illicit crossings and interdict drug shipments. While U.S. policy has, at times, attempted to address the supply side as well as the demand side of the drug and immigration issues, the overwhelming emphasis has been on the former. Public and political support for these policies has generally remained strong.

Policy analysts have generally offered mixed assessments of the success of these strategies. The social science literature on the effect of increased border enforcement on illegal movement, for instance, shows varied results. Some studies suggest interdiction and deterrence did impact the illegal flow of individuals into the United States. Other research, however, indicates that additional manpower, technological, and physical resources (such as border fences) produce a negligible impact on illegal migration (but may offer attractive and symbolic political value). In terms of illegal narcotics, research indicates that the general levels of drug use in the United States that have not decreased at the same rate interdiction and eradication efforts have increased.

A number of important unintended consequences emerged from U.S. border policy in this period. Because of increased enforcement at urban areas, displacement of migratory flows along the border occurred—increasingly forcing migrants into desolate and inhospitable areas of the desert southwest. There, hundreds of migrants die annually due to exposure; deaths at the border increased from fewer than 10 per year during the 1980s to at least 475 in FY2005, before falling back to fewer than 400 in FY2008. Civil society groups in the border region have highlighted these tragedies as an important political issue. Because of the border buildup, migrants have increasingly turned to smugglers (whose fees have rapidly increased) and false documents for entry at ports. Finally, state and local governments are left to deal directly with the unintended consequences of federal policy. These include significant economic costs in areas such as health care and education.

As in other dimensions of U.S. governance, the events of September 11, 2001, prompted both change and continuity in the domain of U.S. border policy. The initial response to the attacks was clearly manifest at U.S. borders and ports of entry; U.S. Customs agents were put on high alert and the U.S. National Guard was deployed to border and airport locales. Tight inspections and uncertainty at U.S. borders resulted in significant delays to U.S.-bound traffic; waits of up to 11 hours were reported in the immediate post-9/11 period. New security measures resulted in major socioeconomic impacts, including added transaction costs to trade and curtailed cross-border interaction; the full impact of these measures remains under evaluation. Additional terrorism in the United States would likely reinforce and expand the current security dynamics at the nation's borders.

Although it eventually became clear that none of the 9/11 terrorists entered the country illegally or via the U.S.-Mexico or U.S.-Canada borders, an important shift in policy quickly emerged: The detection and apprehension of terrorists and terrorist weapons, also known as weapons of mass destruction (WMDs), became the primary focus of U.S. border security policy. Supported by strong public opinion, bipartisan political majorities backed this new focus on counterterrorism. Border security agents and agencies also readjusted their priorities to this new mission, with official statements indicating their paramount goal role of "protecting the homeland." Counterterrorism and risk management strategies became hallmarks of U.S. border policy in this period.

In accordance with this shift, a variety of additional surveillance measures for both goods and people were gradually introduced at U.S. borders and ports of entry. For cargo entry, these included, among other measures, personal and fixed radiation detectors, vehicular scanning equipment, and airline baggage screening. Through legislation such as the Bioterrorism Act of 2002, new regulatory regimes to screen imports of commodities such as food as well as consumer goods were introduced. Importing companies, for instance, now need to provide the government "advance notice" of their shipments before arrival at U.S. ports; this information is evaluated using risk assessment methodologies. While these new surveillance mechanisms have been introduced by federal law enforcement and intelligence agencies, it is important to note that given the large scope of all international conveyances—and the need to maintain efficient trade—relatively small numbers of shipments are physically inspected by border agents.

Within the counterterrorism rubric, for individual travelers, a number of new screening systems and procedures have been gradually rolled out at U.S. ports of entry. These include new document requirements, integrated intelligence and law enforcement databases (such as terrorist watch lists), and surveillance mechanisms. They include systems such as the United States Visitor and Immigrant Status Indicator Technology (U.S.-VISIT), which is an immigration and border management system designed to track the entries and exits of individuals to and from the United States. U.S.-VISIT collects biometric information to authenticate travelers. Entry screening using U.S.-VISIT is now active in all U.S. airports and seaports receiving international passengers; it is also in place at secondary screening sites on U.S. land borders. It has yet to be fully implemented to deal with all land entries nor for air, land, or sea departures.

In addition to U.S.-VISIT, a contentious document requirement protocol known as the Western Hemisphere Travel Initiative (WHTI) was developed in this period. Mandated by the 2004 Intelligence Reform and Terrorism Prevention Act of 2004 (IRTPA), WHTI sharply changes the entry requirements at land, air, and sea entry points for individuals traveling to the United States from countries in the Western Hemisphere, including Canada and Mexico; such individuals now require passports or similar documents for admission to the United States. Previously, individuals arriving from these countries needed to show only unsecured documents such as birth certificates, or in some cases, simply make an oral declaration of citizenship. WHTI encountered resistance among some members of the U.S. Congress from border districts concerned about negative impacts on trade and tourism.

Between ports of entry, concerns about terrorist incursions surfaced in the media, government agencies, and Congress, including at the still relatively open and insecure U.S.-Canada frontier. Policy direction on this question from the U.S. Congress and the George W. Bush administration included new resource allocations, discussed below, as well as two new initiatives involving both physical and "virtual" border fencing. While consolidating some extant efforts, many of these programs fall within the 2006 Secure Border Initiative (SBI). Through SBI, DHS has set out an integrated and comprehensive plan for border security that involves technology, manpower, enforcement, and legal elements.

Physical fencing is perhaps the most visible manifestation of border security policy in the post–September 11 period. The construction of border fencing, which includes a mix of vehicle and pedestrian barriers, along the U.S.-Mexico frontier was facilitated by the passage of the Secure Fence Act of 2006; the act instructed DHS to construct 670 miles of fence by the end of 2008. As of January 2009, 601 miles of fencing had been completed. In addition to physical fencing, SBI's "virtual" fence project—known as SBInet—is a highly touted and expensive Boeing Corporation–led test project involving camera and radar towers along a 28-mile stretch of border in Arizona. Testing has indicated the system is less effective than anticipated, and the project is under review and congressional scrutiny. Despite some vocal opposition from border civil society groups, private landholders, and several key members of Congress, the body has appropriated $2.7 billion for both physical and virtual fencing since 2006.

These new security regulations, which target unauthorized migrants, cargo, and travelers, have indeed not gone uncontested politically or socially; concerns about insufficient border infrastructure, impacts on tourism and spending, as well as foreign relationships have resulted in significant political battles within and between Congress, the executive branch, and stakeholder groups. Border fencing, in particular, is a highly controversial measure in some communities and in Mexico. The policy trajectories discussed here also test the limits of technological solutions to policy problems such as border security.

In addition to this sharp change in policy focus, major continuities in border policy persisted. The United States has still maintained its concentration on mass unauthorized immigration control and narcotics interdiction, with these two duties occupying the vast majority of time and resources of border agencies. And, like the previous period, in response to the new post-9/11 security agenda, federal border agencies have enjoyed significant resource boosts. The CBP budget, for instance, jumped in a relatively uncontested way from approximately $5 billion in 2002 to $9.3 billion in 2008. The Border Patrol has rapidly increased to over 18,000 agents, making it the largest law enforcement agency in the country. Critics have raised concerns over the swift buildup of the Border Patrol, citing recruiting and training issues.

The security policies of the 2001–08 period described here have unfolded within the early development of the Department of Homeland Security. This process has not been unproblematic. Allegations of waste, inefficiency, and questions of efficacy remain constant elements in the border security policy dialogue. Unauthorized flows of immigrants and drugs to the United States continue, according to some scholars, at levels consistent with earlier periods. It is difficult to authoritatively and objectively assess whether changes in U.S. border policy are responsible for the lack of terrorist incidents on U.S. soil since 9/11. What is certain is that the central dilemma of border policy—facilitating legal entries into the United States while screening out illicit goods, weapons, and people—remains unresolved and, at best, only mitigated.

The challenge of controlling drug flows across U.S. borders, as noted above, has been a longstanding component of U.S. policy. In recent years, however, the impact of the drug trade has reached alarming levels on the border and within Mexico. Mexican president Felipe Calderón began an aggressive effort in 2006 to crack down on narcotraffickers in Mexico. Drug trafficking cartels in Mexico have grown even stronger in recent years, taking advantage of a decline in Colombian drug trafficking organizations and responding to steady demand in the United States and, increasingly, in Mexico itself. In addition, U.S. efforts to seal off drug smuggling in the Caribbean region have created additional incentives to transit drugs through Mexico. In 2008, for example, approximately 90 percent of the cocaine consumed in the United States entered through Mexico. Mexico remains the largest supplier of marijuana and methamphetamine to the U.S. market.

The lucrative market for drugs and cross-border smuggling routes is highly contested. President Calderón's crackdown on the cartels that thrive on these markets and pathways has resulted in an explosion of violence in Mexico, particularly along the border. The number of drug-related killings in Mexico has steadily increased; in 2008, over 6,000 individuals were killed, largely in cartel-related violence. The Mexican border city of Ciudad Juárez—across the Rio Grande River from El Paso, Texas—is the epicenter of the carnage, with approximately 1,600 killings in 2008 alone. To deal with the problem, in 2008 and early 2009 the Mexican government ordered 7,000 soldiers to the city.

The deep influence of drug profits, endemic corruption, systemic impunity, readily available weapons (most of which are smuggled across the border from the United States), and the weakness of the Mexican state have all combined to create a toxic and extremely serious crisis. Some analysts and officials within the U.S. government have discussed the possibility that Mexico will turn into a "failed state" or, at the minimum, an undermined regime. Spillover violence into the United States has occurred and has the potential to increase, with numerous kidnappings and cartel penetration extending well into the interior United States. This has raised political calls for yet additional security measures such as fencing. Cross-border trade and tourism are significantly down. The U.S. policy response to the Mexican cartel violence has largely been in the form of the Merida Initiative, President George W. Bush's multibillion-dollar plan to provide military, police, and judicial assistance to Mexico. The plan enjoyed relatively strong support in Congress. The results of this policy remain to be seen, but the crisis threatens to dominate and destabilize the U.S.-Mexico border region for some time to come.

Further Reading:

Ackleson, Jason, and Josiah McC. Heyman. "U.S. Border Security after 9/11." In *Transforming Borders in the Al Qaeda Era*, edited by John A. Winterdyk and Kelly W. Sundberg. London: Ashgate, 2009; Andreas, Peter. *Border Games: Policing the U.S.-Mexico Divide.* Ithaca, N.Y.: Cornell University Press, 2000; Cornelius, Wayne A. "Death at the Border: Efficacy and Unintended Consequences of U.S. Immigration Control Policy." *Population and Development Review* 27 (2001): 661–685; Dunn, Timothy J. *The Militarization of the U.S.-Mexico Border, 1978–1992: Low-Intensity Conflict Doctrine Comes Home.* Austin: CMAS Books, University of Texas at Austin, 1996; Ganster, Paul, and David E. Lorey. *Borders and Border Politics in a Globalizing World.* Boulder, Colo.: SR Books, 2005; Heyman, Josiah McC. "Why Interdiction? Immigration Law Enforcement at the United States-Mexico Border." *Regional Studies* 33 (1999): 619–630; Lorey, David. *The U.S.-Mexican Border in the Twentieth Century.* Wilmington, Del.: Scholarly Resources, 1999; Massey, Douglas S., Jorge Durand, and Nolan J. Malone. *Beyond Smoke and Mirrors: Mexican Immigration in an Era of Economic Integration.* New York: Russell Sage Foundation, 2002; Meyers, Deborah Waller. "Does 'Smarter' Lead to Safer? An Assessment of the U.S. Border Accords with Canada and Mexico." *International Migration* 4 (2003): 5–44; National Commission on Terrorist Attack. *The 9/11 Commission Report.* New York: W.W. Norton, 2004; Nevins, Joseph. *Operation Gatekeeper: The Rise of the "Illegal Alien" and the Making of the U.S.-Mexico Boundary.* New York: Routledge, 2002.

–Jason Ackleson and Rose Ann Vasquez

immigration and citizenship

The politics of immigration has become one of the most contentious public policy issues of recent times. Driving the issue are unprecedented levels of legal and illegal immigration, which increasingly pose new challenges for citizens and elected officials, who are forced to confront trade-offs between the nation's legacy as a haven for immigrants and its responsibilities for ensuring public safety and a decent standard of living for its native-born citizens who face new challenges in the global economy.

Immigration occurs when people voluntarily leave their native land to claim residency in a new country. In the United States of America, immigrants fall into one of several categories: legal temporary, legal permanent, illegal alien, refugees, asylees, and nonimmigrants. These categories help us understand the complexity of the situation that immigrants and policy makers confront when dealing with government agencies. Legal temporary immigrants include students, visitors, and guest workers with proper documentation. The legal permanent immigrants consist of long-term residents who have not yet naturalized. Illegal aliens are often called undocumented persons, which refers to their lack of proper paperwork. Refugees consist of people forced to leave native countries because of a documented fear of persecution or physical harm from a political regime; a category that can include women fleeing spousal abuse. If an individual meets the criteria of refuge, and is living in the country, the person becomes an asylee. It is the physical location of the applicant that determines whether the person is classified as a refugee or an asylee: a classification that can become a critical distinction when it comes to the allocation of federal dollars for resettlement. More generous resources are allocated for those holding the status of refugee. In many ways, the amount of sympathy immigrants receive from native-born citizens depends on the classification of the individual. Undocumented immigrants receive the least amount of sympathy from native-born citizens.

Much of the controversial aspects of the debate concern whether to deport or grant amnesty to the millions of immigrants who lack proper paperwork and therefore reside in the country illegally. In 2009, the federal government estimated an undocumented population of 12 million people, with roughly 8 million working in the labor force. But some organizations have given a range of 12 to 20 million undocumented persons. According to the Pew Hispanic Center, 76 percent of illegal immigrants are Hispanics, with the majority (59 percent) coming from Mexico, a country sharing a contiguous border with the United States. Although the majority of the undocumented immigrants entered the country illegally, others fell into this category deliberately or accidentally by overstaying their student or tourist visas. In fact, it is estimated that 40 percent of the illegal population are visa overstayers.

After five years of legal permanent residency, an immigrant can apply for naturalization. Naturalization requires the applicant to pass an English language test, take an oath of allegiance, and pay a small fee to become a naturalized citizen with full rights of membership, including voting and running for and serving in political office. California governor Arnold Schwarzenegger, elected in 2003, is one of the most visible naturalized officeholders. Only the presidency of the United States is barred from the reach of a naturalized citizen. The naturalized citizen is eligible to bring in family members under provisions of the Family Reunification Act currently a part of U.S. immigration law.

The Department of Homeland Security (DHS) and the Census Bureau track the numbers of foreigners residing in the United States. As of 2008, the DHS estimated that the foreign-born population stands at approximately 18.8 million people. This population includes authorized immigrants who have been awarded legal permanent residence status (otherwise known as green card holders). In 2007, the United States awarded legal permanent resident status to 1,052,415 people. This population includes those persons who were immediate relatives of U.S. citizens (494,920), family-sponsored immigrants (194,900), persons sponsored by employers (162,176), and those considered refugees or those seeking asylum (136,125). Since 2000, approximately 8 million people have been awarded legal permanent residence.

Though the influx of immigrants into the United States has been widespread, it is important to note that a few states have seen much higher immigration than others. In 2007, 90 percent of states experienced higher levels of legal immigration than in 2000, but over half (54 percent) of those immigrants receiving legal permanent status in 2007 were situated in California, Texas, New York, and Florida. Since 1998, over 9 million immigrants have been awarded legal permanent residence and over half have been situated in the aforementioned states.

According to Census Bureau and DHS statistics, the two largest groups of immigrants hail from Asia and Latin America. In 2007, immigrants from Latin American countries accounted for approximately 40 percent of people receiving legal status. Immigrants from Asian nations accounted for about 36 percent of legal immigrants. Chinese immigrants make up the largest nationality of Asian immigrants and, in 2007, they accounted for 7 percent of total American immigrants. Mexico is the largest sender of Latin American immigrants and, in 2007, accounted for 14 percent of all immigrants. Currently, it is documented that 11 percent of the Mexican population resides in the United States.

The specific influx of Latin American immigrants has received the most media and political attention. According to the 2000 census, the majority of *naturalized* immigrants born in Latin America typically arrived prior to 1980, with only 4.2 percent entering between 1990 and 2000. The 2000 census estimated that approximately 70 percent of people living in the United States who were born in Latin America were *not* U.S. citizens and that the majority of that population had arrived in the United States between 1990 and 2000. The Census Bureau has forecasted that the trend in an increasing Hispanic population is not an aberration in immigration, but rather one that will continue well into the future.

For the first time in the history of the United States, minorities, boosted by the influx of immigrants, are poised to overtake the non-Hispanic, single-race white majority by 2042. The Census Bureau estimates the nation will be 54 percent minority by 2054. During this same time period, the Hispanic population is expected to triple by 2050 and double in proportion to the total population, from 15 to 30 percent. The Census Bureau has also published data that reveal that, in the year 2028, net international migration into the United States will be a larger factor in population change in the United States than net births.

Immigrants come to the United States for many different reasons. It is easy to identify some of the "push" and "pull" factors that apply to immigration in general. Some of the most important "push" factors compelling immigrants to leave their native country (or current country of residence) include poverty, war, natural disaster, overpopulation, persecution, or evasion of criminal prosecution. In addition, there are "pull" factors characteristic of destination countries that signal the opportunity for a better future. These pull factors include the appearance of job availability, family reunification, expanded educational opportunities (including opportunities for international students), as well as retirement.

Not surprisingly, it is not the poorest of the poor who immigrate to the United States. Those who make the decision to leave their home country are usually connected to social networks within the United States. Social networks are linkages of family, friends, and associates that provide immigrants with vital information about jobs, housing, and resources necessary to successfully establish themselves within a community.

Immigration scholars such as Princeton University's Doug Massey have made a compelling argument that increases in the Latin American population can be directly linked to U.S. politics and policies set in motion in the middle of the 20th century. Prior to World War II, Mexican immigrants were lured to the United States because of ample job opportunities available in California's agricultural industry. In hopes of alleviating wartime labor shortages, the government passed legislation in 1943 creating what was known as the "Bracero" program. Although this was not the first time the federal government had allowed temporary workers from Mexico into the United States, the Bracero program was important because it mandated competitive wages for the guest workers. The Bracero program was reauthorized by Congress until 1964, when it failed to pass in the Senate by one vote.

While the Bracero program invited laborers to the United States during World War II, the vast majority of immigrant workers came after the war had ended. Between 1950 and 1959, approximately 3.2 million workers were admitted, 96 percent of them Mexican. According to Douglas Massey, the program ended due to pressure from labor groups advocating an end to special treatment for imported labor. By the time the program ended, 4.9 million workers had been admitted to the United States, and 4.6 million were Mexican.

The failure of the Bracero program's extension in 1964 paved the way for passage of legislation in 1965 that completely changed the face of American immigration policy. In a series of amendments to the 1952 Immigration and Nationality Act, Congress abolished the previous practice of admitting immigrants from different countries according to quotas. Instead, the legislation allocated 290,000 visas yearly according to a set of preferential categories, not immigrant nationality. The visas allocated were originally capped at hemispheric limits. But in 1976, the hemispheric cap was replaced with global limits and national caps of 20,000 immigrants per country.

The 1965 law continued the process of exempting caps on spouses, unmarried minor children, and parents established in 1952, and expanded preferential treatment for more family categories such as brothers and sisters of adult U.S. citizens and unmarried adult children of permanent legal residents. This new emphasis on family reunification created an unwieldy chain migration. After a five-year waiting period, immigrants could then begin to sponsor not only the capped categories of immigrants but the uncapped as well. By the 1970s, yearly averages of legal immigration were approximately 450,000 and, by 2000, they exceeded 700,000.

In 1981, the Select Commission on Immigration and Refugee Policy found that illegal immigration was the most pressing issue affecting immigration policy. In 1986, after much debate and negotiation in Congress, the Immigration Reform and Control Act (IRCA) was passed, granting amnesty to unauthorized immigrants living in the United States. The legislation essentially had two parts: one mandating employer sanctions and border control and the other expanding legal immigration. The tougher part of the IRCA was aimed at punishing employers of unauthorized aliens as well as increasing security along the border. Unfortunately, the enforcement of employer sanctions was soon gutted, leading some of its supporters to cry foul.

The transformational part of the legislation was the "legalization of status" or amnesty provision. The amnesty provision constituted a year-long window in which unauthorized immigrants who had been in the country since January 1, 1982, were allowed to register for legal permanent residency. Approximately 1.7 million immigrants signed up for the amnesty. The legislation also provided an amnesty program for seasonal agricultural workers, which allowed workers who had been employed in the agricultural industry for 90 days between May 1985 and May 1986 to apply for regularization of status. The IRCA eventually granted an additional 1.3 million visas to seasonal workers.

The IRCA was followed four years later by the Immigration Act of 1990, legislation that raised the caps on all preferential categories of immigrants. It expanded the overall visas issued to 700,000 in the years 1992–94, and thereafter reduced the level to 675,000 a year. At the 675,000 visa level, approximately 70 percent were allocated to family-sponsored immigration and 20 percent were allocated to employer-based immigration, which included four new temporary visa categories. The Immigration and Naturalization Service estimated that, in 2000, employer-based immigration had grown to 1.2 million immigrants.

Since 1990, the legislative landscape has been focused on increasing penalties for illegal immigrants, lengthening reentry waiting periods (after being caught in the United States for being here illegally), and increasing border security. For example, in 2005, the 109th Congress passed the REAL ID Act, which mandated increased minimum standards for state-issued drivers' licenses and ID cards as well as increased technology along the Mexican-American border to facilitate better information-sharing among enforcement agencies. In addition, in 2008, President George W. Bush signed an executive order mandating all federal contractors to participate in the E-Verify program, which electronically verifies a laborer's identification documents and work permits. The program came up for reauthorization in 2008 and the House passed the necessary legislation, but the Senate has yet to do so. According to the DHS Web site, "E-Verify is an essential tool for employers committed to maintaining a legal workforce, and the number of registered employers is growing by over 1,000 per week."

The American-born children of illegal immigrants are automatically U.S. citizens. It is seen by many as a huge loophole in the system, one that has resulted in more than 3 million mixed-status families in which the children are legal, with parents subject to deportation if apprehended. The Fourteenth Amendment's equal protection clause is the basis for their legality. Originally adopted to overturn the dehumanizing effects of the infamous *Dred Scott* decision, which stripped native-born blacks of their citizenship rights, it is now a backdoor way for eventual citizenship. Likewise, the equal protection clause of the Fourteenth Amendment now forms the most basic underpinning of modern citizenship and immigration jurisprudence because it extends rights to all persons regardless of citizenship.

Within 30 years of the Fourteenth Amendment's passage, the Supreme Court upheld the *jus soli* aspect of American immigration and citizenship. Borrowed from English common law, the policy of *jus soli* is fundamentally based upon the idea that birth within a specific jurisdiction or nation is sufficient for citizenship and allegiance (see *United States v. Wong Kim Ark* [1884] and *Elk v. Wilkins* [1898]). It is through these cases that the Court affirmed the ineligibility of foreign diplomats and their children as well as hostile occupying forces for U.S. citizenship. Though the

Court did not address the status of children born to illegal immigrants, the Court in more modern times has implied that children born to illegal aliens are definitely citizens. Other individuals concerned about the growth of illegal immigration and the rise in the number of mixed-status families argue that this is an unfortunate loophole that could be closed by legislative action.

The Court has also been active in establishing alienage laws, augmenting and defining what it means to be a legal resident in America. In 1886, the Supreme Court invalidated a San Francisco ordinance that burdened Chinese laundries and essentially prohibited them from doing business. The Court held that the ordinance overtly discriminated against the Chinese. For the unanimous court, Justice T. Stanley Matthews wrote:

> The fact of this discrimination is admitted. No reason for it is shown, and the conclusion cannot be resisted that no reason for it exists except hostility to the race and nationality to which the petitioners belong, and which, in the eye of the law, is not justified. The discrimination is, therefore, illegal, and the public administration which enforces it is a denial of the equal protection of the laws and a violation of the Fourteenth Amendment of the Constitution.

In fact, in *Yick Wo v. Hopkins* (1886) the Court held that: "The Fourteenth Amendment to the constitution is not confined to the protection of citizens. It says: 'Nor shall any state deprive any person of life, liberty, or property without due process of law; nor deny to any person within its jurisdiction the equal protection of the laws." These provisions are universal in their application, to all persons within the territorial jurisdiction, without regard to any differences of race, of color, or of nationality; and the equal protection of the laws is a pledge of the protection of equal laws."

During the modern postwar era, the Court has expanded the roots of alien rights established in *Yick Wo*. The mandatory evacuations of American citizens of Japanese descent along the West Coast during World War II led the court to rule that "all legal restrictions which curtail the civil rights of a single racial group are immediately suspect" and that they should be evaluated under strict scrutiny (*Korematsu v. United States* [1944]). In addition, the Court used the strict scrutiny approach when it struck down similar statutes in Arizona and Pennsylvania that denied welfare benefits to legal aliens (*Graham v. Richardson* [1971]). However, in *Foley v. Connelie* (1978), the Court held that a strict scrutiny test of all laws affecting aliens would inappropriately blur the line between citizens and alien. The Court noted that "the State need only justify its classification by a showing of some rational relationship between the interest sought to be protected and the limiting classification," and held that New York's law preventing aliens from holding police officer positions was constitutional.

Thus, the Supreme Court has carved out equal protection for alien residents, despite different degrees of applied scrutiny. However, the Court has been more silent on protections afforded those living in America illegally. In 1982, the Court ruled in *Plyler v. Doe* that a Texas statute that withheld state education funds to districts that enrolled students who were not "legally admitted" into the United States was unconstitutional. The Court denied the state's assertion that illegal aliens were not protected under the Fourteenth Amendment as they were not subject to the jurisdiction of the United States. The Court reasoned that because illegal aliens are subject to due process they are also subject to the protections afforded under the equal protection clause.

More recently, in another move to protect illegal aliens, the Court, in May 2009, unanimously rejected the government's argument that an aggravated identity fraud charge could be brought without proving the accused knowingly used a real person's identity documents. According to the *New York Times*, the threat of an aggravated identity fraud conviction (which results in a mandatory two-year sentence addition) would often allow prosecutors to get illegal immigrants to plead guilty to a lesser charge. The Court's finding that a common understanding of the English grammar of the statute did not support the government's position was significant, as it will limit the ability of immigration officials to bring criminal charges against those who work here illegally. In a concurring opinion, Justice Alito reasoned the statute's applicability was based on chance, as someone could falsify identity documents and be subject to the aggravated charge should they be unlucky enough to replicate a real Social Security number.

Comprehensive immigration bills have been debated in Congress for several years, but an inability to reach a consensus has derailed progress. Pieces of legislation, such as the Development, Relief and Education for Alien Minors (DREAM) Act, which would provide unauthorized immigrant high school students the ability to work toward legal citizenship, have died in Congress. Most recently, comprehensive immigration legislation was debated by the 110th Congress in summer 2007. Even with a bipartisan bill supported by the president, divisions followed predictable party lines. Democrats, anticipating the allegiance of millions of the undocumented immigrants, favored a comprehensive "pathway to citizenship." Whereas, many Republicans characterized the bill as undermining the rule of law by granting amnesty to lawbreakers. The 2007 bill never reached a final vote in the Senate. It fell short of the 60 votes needed to cut off debate, which would have cleared the path for a final vote. The 111th Congress has not yet begun to aggressively address immigration reform. In the meantime, the Department of Homeland Security is quietly reforming immigration by changing administrative rules and regulations.

In reality, party platforms are reflections of constituent and interest group desires. Some of the most vocal groups influencing the policy debate are business groups such as the U.S. Chamber of Commerce, which backed the compromise bill saying that the bill had "the contours of a sound compromise." Whereas the National Association of Homebuilders rejected the reform bill, saying that if enacted the bill "would do irreparable harm to America's small businesses," specifically provisions that would penalize employers for hiring undocumented workers. Immigrant Advocacy groups such as the National Council of La Raza universally support creating a comprehensive path to legal status for immigrant workers, even if not full citizenship, citing worker safety and family unification as primary goals. Labor groups such as the AFL-CIO, whose members have historically viewed immigrant labor as competition (unfair competition when the immigrants are working illegally), advocates for stricter visa and green card enforcement. And the Roman Catholic Church has also weighed in on the debate. The church has stated that it supports an "earned legalization" program for the country's undocumented workers and states as its primary concerns family reunification and safeguarding the human rights of immigrant workers. Lastly, U.S. Border Control, a lobby dedicated to ending illegal immigration, has stated on its Web site that the compromise bill, supported by George W. Bush, was an "amnesty bill" and "a betrayal of everything America stands for." Both the Republican and the Democratic policy positions are incarnations of the public policy preferences voiced by those who would work to secure each political party's reelection. And given the plethora of stated objectives, neither party has been able to craft legislation amenable to all of the interest groups.

The inability of federal legislators to craft consensual policy in regard to immigration has led state and local governments to initiate their own policy prescriptions, some of dubious constitutionality. States have recognized the effect of immigration on the distribution of social services such as public education, health care, and law enforcement, as well as the collection of tax revenue. In perhaps one of the most famous attempts to withhold taxpayer-funded services from illegal immigrants, the voters of California passed Proposition 187 in 1994. Proposition 187, signed into law by Governor Pete Wilson, was a law that withheld social services such as public education and nonemergency medical treatment from illegal aliens. Though it was quickly enjoined by a federal judge and later ruled unconstitutional, it spawned a national debate about the obligations of state government to all residents, including illegal aliens.

In December 2007, the Congressional Budget Office published an article that shed light on the actual expenses incurred by states for the services that were provided to illegal immigrants. In an attempt to synthesize 29 independent studies on the impact of immigrants on state and local budgets, the CBO found that finding an aggregate effect was difficult. However, the paper concluded that because of various federal and state statutes that mandate the provision of certain social services, it is very difficult for state and local governments to deny those services. As well, the actual amounts spent on providing services to the unauthorized population represent a very small percentage, typically less than 5 percent, of the whole budget for providing those same services to the rest of the population. In certain states, such as California, the percentage is larger, but even then, accounts for less than 10 percent of the state budget.

In addition to an aggregate impact on state budgets, many studies have shown the disparity between the tax revenue collected from unauthorized immigrants and the amount of services that they consume. For example, a study conducted by the state of Iowa estimated that illegal immigrants in Iowa paid between $45.5 million and $70.9 million in income and sales tax, but consumed approximately $107.4 million in state services. Other studies have shown that the taxes collected by the state for public education from unauthorized immigrants were more than the amount spent on providing educational service to the children of unauthorized immigrants. For example, a study on public education spending in New Mexico found that the taxes collected from unauthorized immigrants was $1 to $2 million more than the state spent on the education of those children. The CBO has determined that overall, the taxes collected from the unauthorized population do not cover the amount of services that they consume, but the net impact on state and local budgets is likely modest.

Nonetheless, the political pressure on lawmakers has been increasing, especially in states with large numbers of unauthorized immigrants. On both sides of the issue, core interests are at stake, and emotions run very high. With the widespread perception that the federal government is failing to address the issue adequately, states and localities have recently taken actions that illustrate the scope of the problem, as well as the challenges of finding an appropriate solution.

In April 2010, Arizona Governor Jan Brewer signed into law a highly controversial measure that requires noncitizens to carry their immigration papers at all times, and, further, requires police to request the documentation if there is "reasonable suspicion" that an individual may be an illegal alien. The law also penalizes employers who knowingly hire unauthorized immigrants and mandates fines for those who harbor or transport such individuals. Supporters argue that the new law is a modest step toward curtailing an escalating problem in the southwestern United States; some even claim that the law simply mirrors the (poorly enforced) federal policy. They point out that the measure is very popular, in Arizona and across the United States; roughly 70 percent of Americans expressed support for the measure in the months following its passage.

But if support ran wide, opposition ran deep. Critics of the measure demonstrated across Arizona and even initiated an economic boycott of the state. Their objections vary, but their major concerns involve the constitutionality of the measure. The lines of responsibility between the states and the federal government are well established in this area, and critics argue that this law amounts to a state seizing authority from the federal government. Moreover, the nature of the law invites the potential for racial profiling, and other civil rights violations, and may increase tensions between law enforcement officials and Latinos—citizens or otherwise. Notably, the chiefs of police of the two largest cities, Phoenix and Tucson, oppose the measure because it places officers in an impossible situation. President Obama seemed to have this concern in mind when he called the law "misguided," and added that it would "undermine basic notions of fairness that we cherish as Americans, as well as the trust between police and our communities that is so crucial to keeping us safe." In July 2010, a federal judge agreed and blocked enforcement of certain provisions on the somewhat narrow grounds that they would put an excessive burden on *legal* aliens to produce their papers at all times. The state of Arizona appealed the ruling, and the case remains active as of September 2010.

Just a few years before, a community in Pennsylvania took a similar approach to the problem. In 2006, the city of Hazleton passed an ordinance that would have made it illegal to rent property to or hire illegal aliens. The ordinance mandated employers and landlords to verify immigration status and threatened to revoke business licenses or impose fines on those found to be in business with illegal aliens. A federal judge eventually struck down the ordinance under the argument that the ordinance was in conflict with the federal immigration statutory scheme. Omar Jadwat, an immigration attorney for the ACLU, said in response to the ruling, "It's not up to the states to choose an iron fist where Congress has chosen a velvet glove." Other cities such as Nashville, Tennessee, Farmer's Branch, Texas, and Herndon, Virginia, have also considered similar measures.

The uniting element found in the measures considered at the local, state, and federal levels of government is dealing with the immigrant population already residing in the United States. In other words, the laws are primarily concerned with alienage or issues of citizenship. Legislation such as the REAL ID Act, the Arizona law, and the Hazleton city ordinance aims at curtailing work opportunities for unauthorized immigrants, rather than espousing a new immigration philosophy. Curtailing work opportunities to unauthorized immigrants reflects the concern of many Americans that unauthorized laborers take jobs away from native-born Americans with the lowest skill sets. Scholarship has documented that high levels of illegal immigration adversely impacts the wages of native-born workers. Given this pool of legally unrecognized labor, employers sometimes have little incentive to employ native-born workers who are protected by labor laws. Competition has not increased for all jobs, but is most intense among applicants for jobs that do not require higher education. According to the 2000 census, of all immigrants age 25 or older, 56 percent do not have a high school diploma. These immigrants often compete for the same jobs disproportionately desired by native blacks and Hispanics. In 2009, a detailed breakdown of U.S. Census unemployment data released by the Center for Immigration Studies revealed startling levels of unemployment for U.S.-born blacks and Hispanics without a high school education. Blacks had a 24.7 percent unemployment rate and Hispanics were at 16.2 percent. Meanwhile, the unemployment rate for legal and illegal immigrants without a high school education was 10.6 percent. One of the most effective federal programs for identifying undocumented workers is a voluntary program called E-Verify. It is run by the Department of Homeland Security, which allows employers to check Social Security numbers against a national database that has a 99.6 percent accuracy rate, yielding results in seconds.

It has been more than two decades since we have had a major overhaul of immigration policy. Although members of both political parties will agree wholeheartedly about an urgent need for reform, the politics surrounding the issue has made it difficult for Democrats and Republicans to reach a consensus. One contentious issue often not verbalized is about which political party is likely to benefit the most if illegal immigrants are given a pathway to citizenship; it is generally assumed that the Democrats would benefit more from mass legalization than would Republicans. Another sticking point has to do with temporary guest worker programs. Democrats tend to be more wary of guest worker programs than Republicans. In any event, recession and high unemployment among native workers in 2008–09 have complicated the situation and made it far more difficult to justify any importation of guest workers. The politics of immigration reform is also affected by the demographic changes discussed earlier, which are rapidly shifting the racial makeup of the country in ways that benefit nonwhites. Whether these issues are discussed overtly or not, rest assured that they do affect policy makers and how voters react to the issue. Until a broad consensus can be formed, we can expect a continuation of haphazard, piecemeal efforts of reform designed to address pressing issues.

Further Reading:
Daniels, Roger. *Guarding the Golden Door.* New York: Hill & Wang, 2004; Krikorian, Mark. *The New Case against Immigration: Both Legal and Illegal.* New York: Sentinel, 2008; Massey, Douglas S., Jorge Durand, and Nolan J. Malone. *Beyond Smoke and Mirrors: Immigration Policy and Global Economic Integration.* New York: Russell Sage Foundation, 2002; Portes, Alejandro, and Ruben G. Rumbant. *A Portrait of Immigrant America.* 3rd ed. Berkeley: University of California Press, 2006; Swain, Carol M., ed. *Debating Immigration.* New York: Cambridge University Press, 2007; Tichenor, Daniel J. *Dividing Lines: The Politics of Immigration Control in America.* Princeton, N.J. Princeton University Press, 2002; Wong, Carolyn. *Lobbying for Inclusion: Rights, Politics, and the Makings of Immigration Policy.* Stanford, Calif.: Stanford University Press, 2006; United States. Executive Office of the President. Counsel of Economic Advisors. *Immigration's Economic Impact.* Washington, D.C.: GPO, 2007; U.S. Congress. Congressional Budget Office. *The Impact of Unauthorized Immigrants on the Budgets of State and Local Governments.* Washington, D.C.: CBO, 2007.

– *Carol M. Swain and Jonathan Miller*

refugees

For reasons ranging from persecution to natural disasters to civil wars, people have fled their homelands en masse for thousands of years. Indeed, some of the earliest stories in Western civilization involve refugees—the book of Exodus in the New Testament tells of the displacement of the Jewish people from Egypt long before traditional recorded history. The modern concept of refugees is often traced to the reign of Louis XIV of France; from 1681 to 1720, approximately 200,000 Huguenots (French Calvinists) fled persecution in France for neighboring countries.

Until World War II, however, the definition of a refugee lacked clarity. In 1950, with the establishment of the United Nations High Commissioner for Refugees and the 1951 UN Convention Relating to the Status of Refugees, the definition of refugee would be settled. Article 1 of the 1951 Convention Relating to the Status of Refugees, as modified by the 1967 Protocol, defines a refugee as:

> A person who owing to a well-founded fear of being persecuted for reasons of race, religion, nationality, membership of a particular social group or political opinion, is outside the country of his nationality and is unable or, owing to such fear, is unwilling to avail himself of the protection of that country; or who, not having a nationality and being outside the country of his former habitual residence as a result of such events, is unable or, owing to such fear, is unwilling to return to it.

As a party to the 1967 Protocol, the United States government has adopted this language. The United States defines a "refugee" as a person who has suffered persecution or has a well-founded fear of persecution due to race, religion, nationality, membership in a particular social group, or political opinion. The U.S. government is bound under Article 33 of the Convention Relating to the Status of Refugees, which holds that states may not return refugees to countries where they may be at risk. While the United States adheres to this rule in its territory, the U.S. Supreme Court has held that this law does not apply to the high seas, or extraterritorial waters. That is, the United States may turn back refugees who are encountered before landing on U.S. territory.

The first action to aid displaced people on a wide scale began after World War I in Europe and Asia Minor. The League of Nations created the Nansen Office in 1930, named after the Norwegian explorer who led the Office of High Commissioner. It first served refugees from the Spanish Civil War and Jewish refugees suffering under the Nazis. Following the end of World War II in 1945, the United Nations Relief and Rehabilitation Administration (UNRRA) was formed specifically to work with war refugees.

The United States was not bound to the earliest forms of international legislation on refugees. As the U.S. Senate voted not to ratify the League of Nations Treaty, the United States instead created its own legislation to deal with immigrants and refugees. Prior to the 20th century, refugees and the larger immigrant population gained admission to the United States based on a quota system. Under the Immigration and Nationality Act of 1924 (National Origins Act), the U.S. government established quotas on how many immigrants would be allowed into the United States, subject to their percentage representation in the United States. This quota system would be the basis for much immigration legislation in the coming decades. This system led to a number of problematic outcomes; most notably, during World War II, many Jewish refugees were turned away because the quota for German immigrants was met.

Under Franklin Delano Roosevelt's administration, the United States became more involved in international refugee affairs. In 1938, 32 countries, including the Roosevelt administration, gathered to establish the Intergovernmental Committee for Refugees to help those fleeing Nazi persecution. Toward the close of World War II, the United Nations created an office called the International Refugees Organization (IRO). The United States assisted with the IRO's work up through its transformation into the United Nations High Commissioner for Refugees (UNHCR) in 1951. Today, the UNHCR remains the body responsible for handling refugee issues.

In 1948, the United States enacted the Displaced Persons Act. This act initially allowed entrance to over 200,000 displaced persons, specifically those who were concentration camp survivors. This decision grew out of the desire to welcome those Jews who had suffered under the Nazis. The Displaced Persons Act is important because it signified the first time that U.S. legislation had distinguished refugees as a separate group from the broad category of immigrants. Refugees were still subject to the requirements of the National Origins Act of 1924, but with certain distinctions. In 1953, Congress enacted the Refugee Relief Act (RRA), which authorized over 200,000 special, nonquota visas for refugees, allocated by ethnicity and country of origin. The RRA specifically aimed at helping refugees, escapees, and those expelled from Germany after World War II, as well as people escaping from communist countries. In 1956, the RRA was instrumental in providing relief to more than 38,000 Hungarians who fled that country's revolution. In a similar move, Presidents Eisenhower and Kennedy would authorize admittance to nearly a quarter of a million Cubans between 1959 and 1962.

The Fair Share Refugee Act of 1960 continued the specific allowance of refugees from communist and Middle Eastern countries. This differed from previous laws in that the U.S. government granted general admission to refugees over a period of time instead of granting admission based on a specific crisis or country of origin. However, the Refugee Fair Share Law was soon superseded by the 1965 Immigration and Nationality Act, which ended the national origins quota system and created a basic standard for refugee admission. The Immigration and Nationality Act Amendments of 1965 permanently abolished the national origins quota system, favoring instead a 20,000 limit for every Eastern Hemisphere country and an overall ceiling of 170,000 annually. The Western Hemisphere was limited to 120,000 total immigrants without specific country limitations.

Between 1948 and 1980, more than 2 million refugees arrived in the United States. Due to this influx, Congress passed the Refugee Act of 1980, which superseded the Immigration and Nationality Act of 1965. This Refugee Act set quotas on refugees for the first few years and then authorized the president to set annual quotas. It also accepted the UN's 1968 definition of a refugee as one who is unwilling to return to his home country due to persecution or a well-founded fear of persecution on account of race, religion, nationality, or memberships of a particular social group or political opinion.

At a time of increased concern over political enemies, the Refugee Act of 1980 allowed the president, in consultation with Congress, to set annual review of refugee quotas for each geographical area. The U.S. government could alter its number of admittances annually, allowing 50,000 refugees in 1980 and up to 110,000 by the mid-1990s. Under guidelines from the United Nations Protocol Relating to the Status of Refugees, the act also divided refugee and immigration policy. The act created the first permanent admissions procedure for refugee resettlement in the United States by eliminating refugees as a category from the general immigration preference system. The Refugee Act of 1980 also allowed refugees to gain permanent resident status after having lived in the United States for one year.

The Illegal Immigration Reform and Immigrant Responsibility Act of 1996 (IIRIRA) brought a new era to immigration and refugee policy. While focusing on increased restrictions against immigrants charged with crimes, the IIRIRA of 1996 also expanded the classification of a refugee to include anyone who was fleeing "coercive population control procedures." Aimed at China's reproductive policies, this regulation emerged as a response to a Board of Immigration decision that forcible sterilization constituted persecution (see *In Matter of Chang* [1989]). The new provision of the IIRIRA included regulations that a person who proves a well-founded fear of coerced abortion or sterilization may be included for asylum and refugee status.

China is not the only country that has been of particular interest to American policy makers. In fact, the recent history of political asylum in the United States can largely be told with stories of specific nations during periods of turbulence. For example, after the United States ended diplomatic relations with Cuba on January 3, 1961, Cuban refugees began arriving in massive numbers. Nearly 50,000 Cubans (mostly professionals) arrived in Miami in 1961 alone, as the Kennedy administration worked to develop the Cuban Refugee Program. The Cuban government supported the flow of refugees from its country. Starting in September 1965, the Cuban government opened the fishing town of Camarioca; for six weeks, boats took Cuban refugees to the United States. Shortly after, the U.S. government started the "Freedom Flights" operation during which, over a period of seven years, Cubans were transported to the United States. In 1980, Fidel Castro released 125,000 Cubans, many from prisons and mental hospitals, to seek refugee protection in the United States. Many Cubans benefited from the Refugee Act of 1980; for example, refugees from movements such as the Mariel Boatlift of 1980 formed part of the 130,000 Cubans granted refugee status. Even with this grant, President Reagan reduced total refugee admissions, continuing to favor those refugees who came from communist countries.

In the early 1980s, many Haitians attempted to flee to the United States claiming economic refugee status. They claimed that even though they fled due to poverty, returning to Haiti would cause them to be politically persecuted. In 1981, President Reagan authorized the U.S. Coast Guard to turn Haitian boats back to Haiti if they were caught bringing economic immigrants to the United States. Generally, when political refugees faced persecution in Latin America, the Reagan administration was reluctant to aid them, especially when those persons came from a friendly, noncommunist country. Reagan rejected political refugees from Guatemala and El Salvador, and later, George H. W. Bush refused Haitian refugees, despite the political troubles occurring in their countries. In *Matter of Acosta* (1985), the Board of Immigration denied the appeal of a taxi driver who had been persecuted by guerrillas in El Salvador, refusing to grant him asylum in the United States as he could not prove that his request for refuge was primarily motivated by fear.

Indochina was another geographical region of particular political interest to U.S. policy makers. In 1975, Congress created the Indochina Migration and Refugee Assistance Act, creating the Indochinese Refugee Assistance Program (IRAP), which provided funding to the states for assisting refugees. Shortly after, in 1979 and the early 1980s, Cambodian refugees formed a major part of the influx of refugees to the United States. In the aftermath of the Vietnam War, approximately 114,000 Cambodian refugees arrived in the United States.

Asylum seekers from troubled regions continue to dominate this policy area. One refugee group that received particular attention in the late 1990s and early 2000s was the Lost Boys of

Sudan. Originally a group of approximately 27,000 young refugees displaced by the Sudanese Civil War, these young people fled to countries such as Kenya. Eventually, the U.S. took in approximately 3,800 of these refugees.

Most recently, the U.S. government has also placed increased emphasis on helping refugees from Iraq. The increased focus has led to the resettlement approval of more than 25,000 Iraqi refugees as of February 2009. In January 2008, President Bush enacted the Refugee Crisis in Iraq Act within the Defense Authorization Act, giving new access categories to certain Iraqis. In addition, in fiscal year 2009, the United States allocated $90 million to the UNHCR for aiding displaced Iraqis.

Numerous organizations and agencies provide assistance to refugees. Before refugees are admitted to the United States, international organizations provide oversight for their well-being. For example, the United Nations High Commissioner for Refugees (UNHCR) and the International Organization for Migration (IOM) are the international institutions that provide care and administration of refugee camps. The United States provides funding for these international institutions and cooperates with them in the processing of refugees to the United States.

In the United States, the main oversight organization for all immigration is the Department of Homeland Security (DHS). DHS oversees Immigration and Customs Enforcement (ICE) and the U.S. Bureau of Citizenship and Immigration Services (USCIS). ICE enforces immigration and customs laws. USCIS adjudicates cases for refugee admission. The U.S. Department of State's Bureau of Population, Refugees, and Migration (PRM) administers the U.S. Refugee Admissions Program. The PRM works with refugees and conflict victims who are living in dangerous conditions, irrespective of a specific geographical focus. PRM contracts outside groups, such as the Overseas Processing Entity (OPE), to prepare cases for resettlement.

Refugees to the United States are admitted based on three priority levels. Priority 1 deals with individual cases based on need. Priority 2 operates for groups of individuals based on need. Finally, Priority 3 cases focus on individuals of specific nationalities who aim to reunite with anchor family members in the United States. Once a refugee arrives in the United States, the PRM provides funding to 10 voluntary agencies for initial resettlement. In addition, the Office of Refugee Resettlement (ORR), a branch within the Administration for Children and Families of the Department of Health and Human Services (HHS), also coordinates and funds assistance to refugees via state and nonprofit organizations. The ORR provides benefits to refugees for their first eight months in the United States, and the refugees may receive additional employment and support services for up to 60 months. Refugees may receive transitional assistance such as housing, medical attention, employment assistance, and medical assistance in the initial stages of their time in the United States from both public and private organizations. A refugee, once admitted to the United States, remains in refugee status for 12 months, during which time he or she may work. After 12 months, he or she may adjust to legal permanent resident, and after five years, he or she may apply for citizenship.

Although the number of refugees entering the United States declined during the first half of the 1980s, those numbers increased through the early 1990s. By then, the number of refugees entering the United States was rather high; over 114,000 were admitted in 1992 alone. However, that number steadily decreased and dropped sharply following the September 11 attacks; only 27,100 were admitted in 2002.

Currently, the executive branch, in consultation with Congress, sets a numerical limit as to refugee admissions based on geographical regions. Those limits are rarely reached. For example, in 2007, the U.S. government allocated 70,000 spaces for refugees, but fewer than 50,000 were actually admitted. Nonetheless, the allocated number has increased; the total ceiling for refugees for fiscal year 2009 is 80,000.

Refugee legislation continues to draw the attention of lawmakers in Washington. Several measures were active in 2009, including one that

A U.S. Coast Guard cutter that intercepted and transported Haitian refugees who fled the turmoil of their country in July 1992 at the port of the U.S. Naval Base at Guantánamo Bay, Cuba. More than 14,000 refugees attempted to reach the United States by boat and were picked up by the Coast Guard in international waters and transported to the base at Guantánamo Bay. *(U.S. Air Force)*

would push the United Nations to increase the accountability and transparency of the United Nations Relief and Works Agency for Palestinian Refugees (UNRWA) to ensure that terrorist groups are not receiving funding or employment through the organization. Another bill, known as the "Uniting American Families Act of 2009," would amend the Immigration and Nationality Act to allow permanent partners of U.S. citizens and lawful permanent residents to obtain lawful permanent resident status as a spouse would. Yet another (the "Iraqi Refugee and Internally Displaced Persons Humanitarian Assistance, Resettlement, and Security Act of 2009") would commit the U.S. government to lead funding assistance requests from the UNHCR pertaining to Iraqi refugees and to assist in resettling said refugees. It would allow for increased cooperation with some countries in the Middle East and raise the number of Iraqi refugees admitted into the United States.

Still, policy pertaining to refugees is incredibly complex and contentious, as it inevitably raises a host of considerations pertaining to national security, cultural issues, and delicate diplomatic issues, as well. But the 21st century is likely to see a large increase in the numbers of displaced persons, as conflicts become more destructive and natural disasters more common. As the numbers of refugees rise, the pressures on lawmakers to put up walls around the United States may rise as well. Addressing this issue may prove to be one of the greatest challenges to policy makers in the century ahead.

Further Reading:
Anker, Deborah E., and Paul T. Lufkin. *The Law of Asylum in the United States.* 3rd ed. Boston: Refugee Law Center, 1999; Bloemraad, Irene. *Becoming a Citizen: Incorporating Immigrants and Refugees in the United States and Canada.* Berkeley: University of California Press, 2006; Brownstone, David M., and Irene M. Franck. *Facts about American Immigration.* New York: H. W. Wilson, 2001; Gibney, Matthew, and Randall Hansen, eds. *Immigration and Asylum: From 1900 to the Present.* Santa Barbara, Calif.: ABC-CLIO, 2005; Goodwin-Gill, Guy, and Jane McAdam. *The Refugee in International Law.* 3rd ed. New York: Oxford University Press, 2007; Hathaway, James. *The Rights of Refugees under International Law.* Cambridge: Cambridge University Press, 2005.

– *Rebecca Bowman*

Miscellaneous Government Functions

census

The U.S. Constitution requires that a census of the population be taken at least every 10 years. In classic fashion, explained by James Madison in Federalist 54, the framers of the Constitution initially balanced a state's incentive to maximize the count, in order to increase representation, with a countervailing incentive to minimize the numbers and thus decrease potential tax burdens. Article I, Section 2 of the Constitution originally stated: "Representatives and direct Taxes shall be apportioned among the several States which may be included within this Union, according to their respective Numbers, which shall be determined by adding the whole Number of free Persons, including those bound to Service for a Term of Years, and excluding Indians not taxed, three fifths of all other Persons. The actual Enumeration shall be made within three Years after the first Meeting of the Congress of the United States, and within every subsequent Term of ten Years, in such Manner as they shall by Law direct." After the Civil War, the Fourteenth Amendment effectively replaced the three-fifths clause and stated, in Section 2, "Representatives shall be apportioned among the several States according to their respective numbers, counting the whole number of persons in each State, excluding Indians not taxed."

With the shift away from state-based direct taxes, the purpose of the census today is primarily its role as the basis for congressional apportionment. Over the years, though, the census count has come to be used for other important purposes. The U.S. Census is often used as one factor in determining the level of federal funding for programs and grants. Data from the census are used to evaluate concerns regarding discrimination, particularly in the area of voting rights.

Taking the census is a fundamentally political endeavor. Often misunderstood as a static and apolitical exercise, conducting a census requires individuals to craft and select (or exclude) categories for data collection and analysis, and it requires individuals to choose who to include or exclude in the count. For example, recent censuses have counted overseas members of the military, federal civilian employees, and their dependents, for purposes of apportionment, while excluding private citizens residing abroad. Prison populations present tricky issues, as well. The Census Bureau's "usual residence rule" counts people according to their usual residence, rather than their legal residence. An incarcerated offender legally resident in an urban area is likely to be counted where he or she is imprisoned. In many states, David Hamsher argues, this means a shift in population counts from urban areas such as New York City and Chicago to rural areas where prisons have been built to incarcerate growing numbers of prisoners. In addition to issues surrounding the counting of overseas personnel and domestic prisoners, choices need to be made about how to count—and how diligently to search for—populations such as migrant workers, the homeless, college students, and undocumented persons.

Any drawing of boundaries and categories around and among a population is, at its core, an initiative that cannot escape political questions and choices. Animated debates surround the questions of who to count, how to count, and how to utilize the data.

The census is conducted by the U.S. Census Bureau, which lies within the Department of Commerce. Congress authorizes the census, appropriates and allocates funds, and oversees activities during and between censuses. Presidents have used the Office of Management and Budget as a vehicle for monitoring and sometimes influencing census policy and decision making since the Reagan administration. Using constant dollars projected for 2010, the Government Accountability Office (GAO) in June 2008 assessed the cost of the 1990 census at $4.1 billion, or roughly $40 per housing unit, and the 2000 census at $8.2 billion, or roughly $70 per housing unit. The expected life cycle cost of the 2010 census may exceed $14 billion.

The Census Bureau uses a variety of data sources to identify and locate residences. To conduct the census, the bureau sends mail-out/mail-back forms to U.S. households, then sends enumerators to homes that fail to return the forms. The bureau also conducts a variety of follow-up measures and postenumeration surveys to account for nonresponse and to identify problems or inaccuracies.

Mail return is a critical component of conducting the census, but mail return rates have dropped in the last few decades. In 1970, the overall mail return rate was 87.0 percent. By 1980, the rate had dropped to 81.3 percent, and in 1990 and 2000 it dipped to 74.1 percent. Mail return rates vary: In the 2000 census, the return rate for whites was 77.5 percent, while the rate for blacks was 59.7 percent. Those reporting two or more races had an even lower return rate of 57.7 percent, and Pacific Islanders' rate was only 54.6 percent. The bureau has altered the instructions that come with the form, in hopes of improving the count's accuracy and increasing response rates. In 2010, the bureau plans to use the short form exclusively. The more extensive data collected on the long form in past censuses will now be collected via a rolling series of American Community Surveys.

One of the most significant aspects of the census process, and one that creates ongoing controversy, is the undercount. The undercount is the difference between the census count of the population and a 100 percent count of the population. The census generally undercounts the population as a whole, a finding determined by comparing the census result with other sources of data, including the census Bureau's own coverage measurement program and follow-up efforts. The 2000 census—for the first time in history, according to GAO—actually *over*counted the general population by approximately 0.5 percent, or about 1.3 million people.

The census undercounts blacks, American Indians, and difficult-to-count groups such as undocumented persons at a rate greater, typically, than it undercounts other populations. GAO reported in September 2008 that within the 0.5 percent net overcount in the 2000 census, the net overcount of non-Hispanic whites was 1.13 percent. By contrast, the net percent *under*count for black (non-Hispanic) was 1.84; for Hispanic origin, it was 0.71; and for Native American/Alaska Natives off reservations, it was 0.62. The fact that the census typically undercounts certain populations at a rate different than it undercounts (or overcounts) other populations is referred to as the "differential undercount."

If the undercount occurred equally across the country, regardless of race, region, or other factors, it might be less politically volatile. The existence of a differential undercount, however, leads to charges of knowing discrimination, unequal representation, and government callousness. Proposals for "adjusting" the census count—effectively bringing the official census count into line with what the government knows from other data—raise significant political issues.

Advocates of adjustment argue that the government has a legal obligation to get the count right. The argument for adjustment sometimes involves a reminder of the three-fifths clause cited above—a deep insult to many Americans that casts a long shadow over contemporary debates about the census, representation, and fairness. Other advocates for adjustment include representatives of congressional districts, cities, and states, who argue that undercounts will damage their interests, deprive people of full representation, and divert program funding from undercounted areas.

Opponents of adjustment argue that statistical adjustment does not necessarily lead to a "better" count because different methodologies may introduce more (or different) errors. Opponents also worry about the appearance (or reality) of politically driven statistical manipulation, as well as the ethics of statistically adjusting in order to count people who failed in their legal obligation to respond to the census. Further, opponents of statistical adjustments point to improvements over time: For example, the net percent undercount of American Indians/Alaska Natives on reservations went from 12.22 percent in the 1990 census to a 0.88 net percent overcount in the 2000 census. Finally, opponents of adjustment argue that statistical manipulation of the census count violates the Constitution's requirement of an "actual Enumeration" of the population.

A key legal ruling clarified at least one aspect of this debate in 1996. In *Wisconsin v. City of New York*, a unanimous U.S. Supreme Court found that the commerce secretary's discretionary authority included his decision *not* to adjust the 1990 census results based on a postenumeration survey.

According to a GAO report issued in April 2008, the Census Bureau "has no plans to use the results of its coverage measurement program to improve or adjust the 2010 Census count," a sentiment echoed by Commerce secretary nominee Gary Locke in 2009. The Census Bureau stated in a 2003 letter that adjustment would introduce as much or more error into the count as it was designed to correct. Moreover, the bureau reportedly has neither the time nor the technical capacity to adjust based on the coverage measurement program before the April 1, 2011, deadline for producing count data for redistricting. Even were the bureau able to produce adjusted national level data, a point of some debate, GAO writes that experts believe that the Census Bureau would have great difficulty offering adjusted counts for state and local levels.

Adjustment is the process of refining the results of the census to reflect more accurately what the government knows about the population from a variety of sources. In recent censuses, this has produced two numbers: a "traditional enumeration" and later, "adjusted" figures. Both sets of numbers are used by many public and private organizations for a host of purposes, including important decisions about grants and funding.

Some proposals in recent years have called for using statistical sampling methods to create a more accurate census count at lower cost. Before the 2000 census, for example, the Census Bureau planned to use "sampling for non-response follow-up": The bureau would have guaranteed a 90 percent response rate in each census tract, then used statistical sampling methods to draw inferences about leftover nonresponders. As a further check for missed populations and to increase the accuracy of the count, a postenumeration survey of 750,000 housing units would have been matched to questionnaires received during the enumeration and to the sampling for nonresponse follow-up. The bureau planned to integrate the traditional enumeration with its sampling for nonresponse follow-up and its postenumeration survey, resulting in a "one-number" census.

Using statistical sampling in the production of census numbers is very controversial, however, and the Census Bureau ultimately abandoned these plans for the 2000 census.

Opponents of sampling argue that using technically complex, mathematically intricate statistical techniques could introduce more errors into the census count, allow an essentially political endeavor more easily to masquerade as an apolitical and "scientific" exercise, and undermine public confidence in the accuracy and trustworthiness of the census. Opponents also suggest that use of statistical sampling techniques might reduce even further the public's declining participation in the census: In other words, they fear that if the census tally is crafted through statistical sampling techniques, the public might see little reason to participate in the traditional enumeration.

A key ruling addressed the issue of sampling in 1999. In *Department of Commerce v. United States House of Representatives*, a divided U.S. Supreme Court ruled that the Census Act prohibits the use of statistical sampling for the purpose of apportioning seats in the U.S. House of Representatives.

Proponents of sampling argue that statistical sampling might reduce costs and improve the census count generally and among traditionally undercounted populations and geographic areas. Proponents also argue that a variety of statistical techniques have historically characterized the census process. In *Utah v. Evans* (2002), for example, a divided U.S. Supreme Court condoned the use of a specific statistical procedure known as "hot-deck imputation" during the census in order to improve accuracy. In the wake of the 1999 case prohibiting sampling for the purpose of apportionment, the Court burrowed into the details of which specific techniques do or do not constitute prohibited statistical sampling. Ultimately, the Court sanctioned the use of hot-deck imputation in the census process—and simultaneously raised questions about which other techniques would or would not be acceptable, and for which purposes. Justice Stephen Breyer, writing for the Court, concluded: "We need not decide here the precise methodological limits foreseen by the Census Clause. We need only say that in this instance, where all efforts have been made to reach every household, where the methods used consist not of statistical sampling but of inference, where that inference involves a tiny percent of the population, where the alternative is to make a far less accurate assessment of the population, and where consequently manipulation of the method is highly unlikely, those limits are not exceeded." In dissent on this issue, Justice Sandra Day O'Connor wrote, simply, "I would find that the Bureau's use of imputation constituted a form of sampling and thus was prohibited by section 195 of the Census Act." The disagreement highlights the difficulty facing the Court, and the public, in evaluating the usefulness and constitutionality of highly sophisticated census-taking techniques.

The politics of sampling and adjustment are often oversimplified as a battle between Democrats and Republicans. In this formulation, Democrats are cast as proponents of sampling and adjustment because these are presumed to help Democrats by counting undercounted populations that traditionally align as Democratic voters: blacks, American Indians, urban residents, and so on. Republicans are seen as opponents of sampling and adjustment, on the belief that adjustment would help their rivals. There is some truth to this lineup, especially when looking at the positions of interest groups traditionally aligned with either party.

Yet the politics do not always break down cleanly along these partisan lines. The position a group or a jurisdiction takes on adjustment is often closely related to a calculation of narrow self-interest. Republican interests that foresee a gain from adjustment, politically or otherwise, may support adjustment, while Democrats who foresee losses may oppose it. After the 1990 census, for example, California would have gained a congressional seat had the census been adjusted. Political scientist Peter Skerry notes that the Republican governor of California, Pete Wilson, supported adjustment—even as national Republicans opposed it. At the same time, according to sociologist Harvey Choldin, Democrats in the Pennsylvania and Wisconsin congressional delegations—states that would have lost seats from an adjustment—joined with their Republican colleagues to *oppose* adjustment of the 1990 census. It is thus an oversimplification, and even inaccurate, to suggest that the battle over adjustment is a simple battle between Democrats and Republicans.

Finally, it should be pointed out that it is almost impossible to predict winners and losers from adjustment. If adjustment shifts a congressional seat from Pennsylvania to California, for example, is that a Democratic or a Republican victory? The answer will depend on state-level politics at a specific moment in time far more than it depends on the simple calculation that adjustment necessarily helps Democrats. Similarly, if adjustment means that New York City gains population but New York State loses, who benefits? And if adjustment reduces a particular minority group's undercount, but also reduces a different group's undercount by even more—who wins and who loses then? The answers to these questions depend on complex and changing calculations, not simple partisan assumptions.

What is perhaps most surprising about the census, though, is that the heat surrounding the politics of sampling and adjustment does not reflect the reality of the true impact of the census. Adjusting the census—however it's done—generally plays a much smaller and less predictable role in program funding and political representation than people often expect.

The significance of the census count in determining federal funding and grant awards is frequently overstated. In June 2006, the GAO examined the prospective impact of alternative population counts on Medicaid, the federal government's largest formula grant program, and on Social Services Block Grants, a program particularly sensitive to changes in population data. The impacts on these programs are much smaller than news media accounts of the relationship between the census and grant funding often suggest. For example, GAO found that adjustment of census data would have resulted in only 0.23 percent of Medicaid funds being shifted among different states, or $368 million out of a $159.7-billion program. GAO concluded that 22 states would have received additional Medicaid funding, with Nevada the largest gainer, with an increase of 1.47 percent of funding. Seventeen states would have received less funding, with Wisconsin losing the greatest percentage (1.46 percent). Eleven states and the District of Columbia would have received the same amount. In GAO's analysis of Social Services Block Grants, only 0.25 percent of funds would have been shifted using adjusted census data, or $4.2 million out of a $1.7-billion program. Twenty-seven states and the District of Columbia would have gained—and shared—$4.2 million, and 23 states would have shared the loss of $4.2 million. The largest gain, 2.05 percent (or $67,000), would have been seen by Washington, D.C.; the biggest loss would have been suffered by Minnesota, which would have lost 1.17 percent (or $344,000) of its funding.

Census data are less significant than people often think, when it comes to federal or other funding, for several reasons. Some programs do not use census data at all. Some programs, such as highway funding, only allocate small portions of the total program on the basis of census data. Some programs establish floors or caps for funding, meaning that beyond a certain point census counts have no effect; other programs use population data released between censuses, or rely on adjusted census data to begin with. Finally, federal funding awards are not necessarily in direct relation to population, such that population increases always lead to increased funding while population decreases lead to funding decreases. Some programs *decrease* funding when population goes up, under the theory that population increases reflect growth and thus less need for government aid.

In general, then, many programs use a variety of data sets to calculate funding, and so the census is often only one among many factors used in determining awards. Moreover, in many cases program use of the decennial census count could be changed to other sources of data through legislation. As Skerry points out, "Nothing prevents Congress from adjusting specific grant formulas to compensate for minority undercounts."

The federal funding question is thus more complicated, and generally less significant, than casual observers often recognize. Readers are encouraged to pursue approaches to these questions in the sources listed below. In particular, GAO's February 1999 study and its report of June 2006 are excellent examinations of the effect of statistical adjustment on federal grant programs.

The roles of the census in redistricting and political representation are similarly complicated and often misunderstood. The notion that census counts are the determining force in state redistricting, for example, overlooks the vast and powerful behind-the-scenes mechanisms that twist and tweak districts based on factors such as party alignments, voting patterns, individual funding, campaign contributions, and control of state legislative and executive offices. The claim that census counts determine state activity during redistricting also overlooks states such as Kansas that, according to David Hamsher's analysis, constitutionally mandate modifications to census data prior to apportionment and redistricting. Undercounts and adjustments are likely to have very limited effect on state and local districting issues.

The place of the census in political representation is also often overstated, sometimes through a facile equation of "being counted" and "being represented." Not being counted by the census does not necessarily translate easily into not being represented, or into being disenfranchised. Political organization and participation, voting, and other activities undertaken by people in a democratic republic bear as much, if not far more, effect on the relationship of individuals to the larger polity.

Peter Skerry concludes that much of the political activity around the census may be related to satisfying certain populations that demand action, even when those populations have miscalculated the stakes. In other words, even if city leaders or interest groups understand that adjusting the census has little effect on funding and other matters—and that that effect is unpredictable, besides—it is safer politically to be seen as defending those interests than it is to be seen as standing idly on the sidelines.

Race and ethnicity categories in the census have long been controversial, with opponents of the categories charging that inclusion of this data violates privacy, perpetuates invidious racial and ethnic distinctions, and fails to capture the nuances of a diverse and multicultural population.

Race and ethnicity questions have a long and imprecise legacy. The first census counted free and enslaved persons, and sought to distinguish between American Indians who paid taxes and those who did not. Over the years, a variety of categories have come and gone, including "free colored persons," "Mulatto," "Hindu," and "Mexican." Often blurring the lines of social categories such as race, ethnicity, religion, and national origin, the comings and goings of these classifications reflected developments in abolitionism, immigration, and prejudice. In *Who Counts? The Politics of Census-Taking in Contemporary America*, Margo J. Anderson and Stephen E. Feinberg offer a thorough discussion, including helpful tables, outlining the development of various categories in the history of the census.

The key moment in modern classification by race came in 1977, when the Office of Management and Budget issued Statistical Policy Directive 15. The directive instituted the use of four categories to be used by federal agencies in collecting data on race (American Indians and Alaska Natives; Asians and Pacific Islanders; Non-Hispanic Blacks; Non-Hispanic Whites) and one category on ethnicity (Hispanic). Directive 15 specified that "These classifications should not be interpreted as being scientific or anthropological in nature." Noting the use of these classifications throughout government, business, education, and research institutions, sociologist C. Matthew Snipp writes, "The impact of Directive No. 15 cannot be underestimated. In many respects, this standard established an official racial cosmology for the United States. . . . To the extent that sociological knowledge is conditioned by the extant data, Directive No. 15 had a tremendous impact in defining the known racial landscape of the United States in the late twentieth century."

Directive 15 was revised in 1997. The revisions specified five categories on race (American Indian or Alaska Native; Asian; Black or African American; Native Hawaiian or other Pacific Islander; White), and two categories on ethnicity (Hispanic or Latino; Not Hispanic or Latino). OMB states that the categories "provide a common language for uniformity and comparability in the collection and use of data on race and ethnicity by Federal agencies." The data are to be "used for all Federal administrative reporting or record keeping requirements that include data on race and ethnicity," including "for civil rights and other compliance reporting from the public and private sectors and all levels of government." The government uses the data to monitor "equal access in housing, education, employment, and other areas, for populations that historically had experienced discrimination and differential treatment because of their race or ethnicity."

Defenders of the race and ethnicity questions on the census point to the role of this data in identifying and combating discrimination. The race and ethnicity data collected by the census in accordance with OMB's categorization is used to identify and counter voting discrimination under the Voting Rights Act, for example.

The option for respondents to select more than one race on the census became available in 2000, a new development that former Census Bureau director Kenneth Prewitt called "the early tremor of an earthquake in political and social life" because it explodes the classic, discrete, and few race and ethnic categories into 126 race-ethnic groups.

The census is an important instrument for counting the nation's population and apportioning representatives. The information gleaned decennially from the census is an important component of a host of governmental activities, from illuminating society's choices about political inclusion and exclusion to contributing to decisions about federal grant funding. The nature and relevance of the census in any given political environment, though, is complicated. Easy rhetoric about the census as an apolitical endeavor, or suggestions that census counts alone determine (and *must* determine) billions of dollars in funding, or complaints that missed counts and undercounts easily and necessarily lead to political disenfranchisement or a lack of representation, reflect oversimplifications of the complex environment of the census and the complicated ways in which the census, and changes in the census from population shifts or methodological choices, influence political society.

Further Reading:

Anderson, Margo J., and Stephen E. Feinberg. "Census 2000 and the Politics of Census Taking." *Society* 39 (November/December 2001): 17–25; ———. *Who Counts? The Politics of Census-Taking in Contemporary America.* New York: Russell Sage Foundation, 1999; Choldin, Harvey. *Looking for the Last Percent: The Controversy over Census Undercounts.* New Brunswick, N.J.: Rutgers University Press, 1994; Hamsher, David. "Counted Out Twice—Power, Representation & the 'Usual Residence Rule' in the Enumeration of Prisoners: A State-Based Approach to Correcting Flawed Census Data." *Journal of Criminal Law & Criminology* 96 (Fall 2005): 299–328; Prewitt, Kenneth. "Racial Classification in America: Where Do We Go from Here?" *Daedalus* 134 (Winter 2005): 5–17; Skerry, Peter. "The Census Wars." *Public Interest* 106 (1992): 17–31; ———. *Counting on the Census? Race, Group Identity, and the Evasion of Politics.* Washington, D.C.: Brookings Institution Press, 2000; Snipp, C. Matthew. "Racial Measurement in the American Census: Past Practices and Implications for the Future." *Annual Review of Sociology* 29 (2003): 563–588; Numerous GAO publications on the census also provide essential information.

– *Stephen J. Rockwell*

emergency management

Ensuring the public's safety remains the number one responsibility of governments throughout the United States. It has become a more daunting challenge for governments at all levels—federal, state, local. Many are experiencing significant growth and population diversification. The list of hazards is ever-expanding, driven by technological, demographic, political, and even climate changes. And officials must maneuver in a media world with its 24/7 news cycle—hungry for drama and prone to treat every emergency event as a "mega-disaster."

Emergency management is a broad policy area that interfaces with virtually all government operations in a crowded intergovernmental landscape. By necessity, it involves working with people (management and rank and file) from the public, private, and nonprofit sectors. The field of emergency management has become much more professional in recent years, although in crisis situations, reliance on volunteers—neighbors, churches, and charities—is still significant.

Major changes in emergency management policies, including organizational restructurings, tend to come after a high-profile disaster, whether natural or human made. Policy shifts at the national level often reflect whether the dominant concern during a particular presidential administration is domestic or foreign policy or both. Whether a president has been a governor may also prompt changes in federal policies spelling out the relative responsibilities of the national government vis-à-vis those of states and localities in the emergency management system. But it remains a fact that significant policy redirections in the field of emergency management have occurred *after* catastrophic events. It is also true that executive officials at all levels—presidents, governors, mayors, county and city managers—are judged by their crisis management skills. Yet it is generally up to legislative bodies—Congress, state legislatures, county commissions, and city councils—to enact laws affecting every stage of the policy-making process.

The complexity of the environment in which emergency management takes place unavoidably produces some rather intense controversies both inside and outside government. Some of the perennial policy debates focus on: Who has responsibility to make decisions in times of crisis (who's in charge)? Who pays? What should be the right balance when it comes to the four phases of emergency management—mitigation, preparedness, response, and recovery—or in protecting people versus infrastructure? What organizational structure best promotes efficiency, effectiveness, and equity? Which disasters (natural versus human made) are more catastrophic and/or matter most? What methods are best at identifying risk factors and predicting/measuring vulnerabilities and postdisaster damages? Who determines inadequacies—malfeasance, misfeasance, and nonfeasance—in the delivery system? Often the debate boils down to one that has divided policy makers from the nation's inception—centralization versus decentralization—the role of the federal government versus that of states and localities.

These challenges, and their urgency, arguably have become more intense as the public's expectations of, and demands for, immediate government responses to all sorts of emergencies, disasters, and catastrophes have intensified in the post-9/11-Hurricane Katrina era.

Identifying community hazards is a critical component of emergency management because they are the sources of emergency and/or disaster events. A *hazard* is a potential source of danger that may result in harm to people, property, or the natural environment. *Emergencies* are crisis events that, when compared to a disaster, result in comparably fewer casualties or limited property damage. The term *disaster* is reserved for events that produce more losses in terms of life and property and a level of damage to the natural environment that is greater than a community can manage on its own. Such events require cross-jurisdictional support and most likely aid from the state and federal governments. Emergency management professionals at the local level often distinguish between emergencies and disasters by the length of forewarning, the magnitude, scope, and duration of their impact, and the predictability of the associated hazard. Others use slightly different classification factors: degree of uncertainty, urgency, consensus, involvement of citizens, de-emphasis on contractual and personal relationships, and the rapidity with which people and material converge at a scene.

Following 9/11, the National Response Plan/Framework created another type of incident even more serious than a disaster or emergency—the *catastrophic incident*—a natural or human-made incident, including terrorism, that results in an extraordinary level of mass casualties, damage, or disruption severely affecting the population, infrastructure, environment, economy, and national morale and/or government functions. The magnitude of this type of event usually necessitates federal aid, often over a prolonged period of time.

National Special Security Events (NSSEs) are nationally significant high-profile, large-scale events that present high probability targets. NSSE designation factors include: anticipated attendance by U.S. officials and foreign dignitaries, size of the event, and significance of the event. The president—or his representative, the secretary of the Department of Homeland Security (DHS)—has the authority to declare a

NSSE. Beginning in September 1998 through February 2008, 28 events have been designated as NSSEs. Some of these events have included presidential inaugurations, presidential nominating conventions, major sports events, and major international meetings. The U.S. Secret Service (USSS) is the lead federal agency responsible for coordinating, planning, exercising, and implementing security for NSSEs. A tremendous amount of advance planning and coordination is done in preparation for these events, particularly in the areas of venue and motorcade route security, communications, credentialing, and training. The Secret Service relies heavily on its established partnerships with law enforcement and public safety officials at the local, state and federal levels.

Hazard identification is central to emergency management. Localities must assess how big a risk each identified hazard poses to its people, infrastructure, environment, and economy. The all-hazards approach, part of the Integrated Emergency Management System (IEMS) established in the early 1980s, calls for a community to incorporate each hazard to which it is deemed vulnerable into its comprehensive emergency management plan. This comprehensive all-hazards approach is designed to enable a jurisdiction to make its emergency management system operate more effectively and efficiently.

Natural hazards. Natural hazards result from the natural environment. Not all natural hazards produce disasters, but all have the potential to produce catastrophic events. Natural hazards include floods, earthquakes, wildfires, hurricanes, tsunamis, storm surges, tornadoes, and volcanic eruptions as well as landslides, coastal erosion, severe winter storms, snow avalanches, droughts, and extreme heat. Even the common thunderstorm can present hazards in the form of heavy rains that cause flash flooding, strong winds, hail, or tornadoes.

Over time, more and more people are exposed to natural hazards. As the world's population has grown, increasing numbers of people live in flood plains, along seismic faults, near volcanoes, or on mountain slopes. Effective mitigation techniques, such as disaster-resistant building designs and materials, can reduce the impact of natural hazards. In addition, unlike technological or terrorist disasters, often there is advance warning of a natural hazard giving emergency managers time to evacuate people and protect property.

Technological hazards. Technological hazards are hazardous materials or chemical substances that, when released, pose health and environmental threats. Technological disasters generally involve some type of human error. A well-known technological disaster occurred in 1986 at the Chernobyl Nuclear Power Plant in Russia when a reactor exploded, unleashing unsafe levels of radioactivity into the atmosphere. Hazardous materials include explosives, flammable and combustible substances, poisons, and radioactive materials. An accident during transport or human error at a storage or usage site can cause a technological disaster as dangerous chemical materials come into contact with the environment and its people.

Deliberate human-made disasters (social hazards). Terrorist incidents (bombings, shootings, hostage taking, hijacking, weapons of mass destruction attacks), those involving crowds (riots, demonstrations, stampedes), and warfare are often labeled social hazards. Perpetrators often use the same materials involved in technological disasters. However, these events are not the result of human error; they are planned and deliberate acts designed to cause human casualties, property damage, and/or the disruption of services such as transportation, communication, and power. (The terrorist attacks of September 11, 2001, constituted that type of act.)

Weapons of mass destruction, such as biological, chemical, or nuclear weapons (as well as their conventional counterparts), constitute a grave danger should they fall into the hands of terrorists seeking to inflict mass casualties or massive physical destruction. Fears of this type of disaster have escalated in recent years, particularly as foreign nations gain the capacity to produce them.

Today's emergency managers must balance the demands of natural hazards with the urgency of preventing technological and terrorist disasters.

Estimating the likelihood of each (risk assessment) is extremely difficult and often provokes controversy when funds must be budgeted and personnel assigned accordingly.

Emergency management, as practiced in the United States, is based on the Comprehensive Emergency Management (CEM) concept. Under CEM, there are four phases of emergency management—mitigation, preparedness, response, and recovery.

Mitigation is defined as a *sustained* action to reduce or eliminate risk to people and infrastructure from hazards and their effects. The purposes of mitigation programs are to address the causes of disaster, reduce the likelihood of a disaster event, and minimize the impact of a disaster should one occur. In this manner mitigation offers long-term benefits by reducing the risks associated with disasters.

Members of the fire community were some of the first emergency management professionals to advocate for mitigation through their support for improved building codes, proactive code enforcement, and public education in schools. Through the processes of hazard identification and mapping, policy planners have information that can be used to guide decisions about design and building codes and land management (e.g., FEMA's detailed flood maps and the U.S. Geological Survey's earthquake and landslide surveys). Building codes and land use requirements can help protect communities from the impact of flooding, earthquakes, and wild fires—among other natural disasters. For example, strict building codes have made Florida's homes and businesses more resistant to the impact of hurricanes, and the use of dams and levees that confine floodwaters have protected communities in flood-prone areas.

Federal grant-in-aid and technical assistance programs now stress the importance of comprehensive mitigation plans. The Disaster Mitigation Act of 2000 directs federal resources at mitigation efforts and established a program of financial and technical assistance for predisaster mitigation efforts at the state and local levels. Based on the principle that mitigation produces more disaster resilient communities, the act requires states to prepare comprehensive mitigation plans to be eligible for these federal funds.

Whereas mitigation represents continuing efforts to lessen the impact of disasters, *preparedness* refers to the plans, procedures, and resources that will be used to support emergency response and recovery. Preparedness is an essential component of emergency management and it is cultivated through planning, training, first responder exercises, technical expertise, and coordination across first responder groups and local officials.

The first step toward disaster preparedness is creating an effective plan for responding to disaster events. Planning will require an assessment of the community's risks or hazards, including hazard exposure, physical/infrastructure vulnerabilities, and population vulnerabilities. Training will familiarize emergency management personnel with preparedness plans. Participation in exercises designed to test how well personnel are able to execute those plans will allow stakeholders to evaluate the quality of emergency management plans.

Most large-scale disasters will require coordination across jurisdictions, highlighting the importance of interoperable communication systems that allow various first responder groups to communicate in a timely and effective manner. Specialized equipment and technical expertise is also critical when faced with a human-made disaster involving the use of chemical, biological, radiological, and explosive weapons as well as in the context of cyber attacks.

Not all emergency operations plans are identical, but any basic plan will include the foundational plan itself, functional annexes that address issues that are specific to a single emergency response function, and hazard-specific appendixes that inform personnel how to respond to specific types of disasters. Well-designed and executed preparedness plans produce better emergency response and recovery functions.

Emergency response begins once a disaster event has occurred. The *response* function has three primary goals: protect the population, limit the damage from the primary impact of the disaster, and minimize damage from any secondary impacts from the event. Secondary impacts might include identifying contaminated water in the wake of flooding or fighting fires that result from earthquakes. Some disaster events, such as hurricanes and volcano eruptions, involve a certain degree of advance warning. Others, such as chemical spills and other human-made disasters, often occur without advance notice.

Local officials and first responders—law enforcement, fire, and emergency medical personnel—will be the first on the scene. If the magnitude of the disaster warrants additional assistance, a state's governor may offer resources such as the National Guard and state level emergency management personnel. If the size of the disaster exceeds the state's capacity to respond, the governor may make a formal request to the president for a federal disaster declaration. The state request is reviewed by the Federal Emergency Management Agency (FEMA) and a recommendation is forwarded to the president. If a presidential disaster declaration is forthcoming, FEMA then activates the National Response Plan/Framework, which triggers action by a broad spectrum of federal departments and agencies, including the Red Cross. A presidential disaster declaration also makes several sources of federal funds available to individuals and communities for recovery purposes.

As the response stage of emergency management concludes, recovery begins. Depending on the severity of a disaster event, recovery may take a few days, weeks, months, or years. The immediate goal of disaster *recovery* is to restore the infrastructure of the community, including electricity, water, telecommunications, transportation, and access to fuel and food. The process incorporates relief, rehabilitation, and reconstruction activities. Whereas the participants in the response phase of emergency management are largely emergency management personnel and first responder groups, the recovery process involves individuals, business groups, political leaders, community groups, and the state and federal governments.

The ultimate goal of recovery efforts is to rebuild the disaster-affected area—ideally into a community more robust than its predecessor. The reconstruction process will be used to build a more hazard resistant community, but may also include wholesale changes to the community landscape and/or improvements to existing residential or commercial areas. Recovery offers an opportunity for improvement.

The emergency management policy-making process is continuous. It is constantly evolving, often in response to changes in the political landscape—domestically and globally.

Historically, disaster relief has been considered primarily a local responsibility, with the federal government providing assistance only when state and local relief capacities are exhausted. Local officials and first responders are likely to be first on the scene of a disaster. They are largely responsible for emergency services in the immediate aftermath of a disaster. State governments generally act as coordinators, encouraging cooperation at the local level, promoting resource sharing, and providing technical and logistical support.

For many years, the federal government's role was largely limited to providing financial assistance in the event of major disasters or passing legislation dictating the creation of organizational structures at the state and local levels. But the 9/11-Hurricane Katrina megadisasters pushed the federal government to the forefront, radically restructuring the nation's emergency management system, and reigniting the age-old centralization-decentralization debate about the relative roles of the national, state, and local governments.

The Congressional Act of 1803, recognized as the first piece of disaster legislation, provided a New Hampshire town with fiscal assistance after an extensive fire. For many years, Congress continued to mete out financial aid on an ad hoc, case-by-case basis in response to hurricanes, earthquakes, floods, and other natural disasters. The prevailing view was that disaster relief was not the primary responsibility of the federal government.

The role of the federal government expanded in the wake of the Great Depression. With economic recovery as its primary aim, Congress passed legislation aimed at assisting state and local governments and putting people back to work. Clearly, domestic policy concerns dominated

President Franklin D. Roosevelt's early administrations. During this time, various federal agencies (the Reconstruction Corporation, Bureau of Public Roads, Works Progress Administration) were given authority to help fund the repair of disaster-damaged infrastructure across the nation. Congress passed the Flood Control Act of 1934 and created the Tennessee Valley Authority (hydroelectric power), making flood control a proper activity of the national government. These years saw the beginning of the intergovernmental grants-in-aid programs that have multiplied and evolved into key funding sources for emergency management.

The outbreak of World War II turned President Roosevelt's attention to foreign threats to the safety and security of U.S. citizens. On May 20, 1941, he created the Office of Civilian Defense and advised cities across the United States to organize their own "civil defense" systems. Literally thousands of local Civil Defense (CD) chapters were formed. While the Civil Defense system has subsequently undergone many organizational changes, some attribute the volunteerism that even today is such a central part of emergency management as having begun with the CD movement in the 1940s.

The cold war era of the 1950s kept attention focused on the possibility of an international security-related threat, namely, a nuclear attack by the Soviet Union and nuclear fallout. The escalation of the Korean War also kept the focus on security. Congress passed the Federal Civil Defense Act of 1950, creating the Federal Civil Defense Administration, which President Harry S. Truman placed in the Office of Emergency Management. Its purpose was primarily to promote and facilitate CD at the state and local levels. Those governments bore the bulk of the responsibility for CD, effectively maintaining a heavily decentralized, locally controlled, volunteer-heavy system. Congress also created the Office of Defense Mobilization in the Department of Defense, whose purpose was to mobilize materials if a war broke out. These two agencies were merged into the Office of Civil and Defense Mobilization in 1958 during the administration of President Dwight D. Eisenhower.

Ironically, the most significant emergency management-related legislation passed in the 1950s came in response to a domestic natural disaster (flooding in the Midwest). The Federal Disaster Relief Act of 1950 established three major principles: (1) federal authority for disaster-related action is ongoing; (2) presidents, rather than Congress, can declare when a disaster is deserving of federal assistance; and (3) federal aid can be used to supplement the efforts of others—state and local governments and nonfederal entities such as the American Red Cross. The act created little political controversy because nearly every member of Congress saw it as potentially benefiting his/her district. (Even the companion Civil Defense Act of 1950 was relatively noncontroversial for the same reason—federal funds for bomb shelter–building programs were spread around the states.)

Looking back, the general consensus is the Federal Disaster Relief Act of 1950, as amended, is still the most significant federal disaster assistance policy to date, even though at the time it was passed, it was not seen as precedent-setting. Many also believe today's complex intergovernmental emergency management system evolved from the more narrowly defined civil defense programs of the 1950s and 1960s.

A series of large-scale natural disasters (hurricanes, earthquakes, tsunamis, tornadoes) during the early days of the President John F. Kennedy administration prompted creation of an Office of Emergency Preparedness lodged in the White House. Major natural disasters also plagued President Lyndon B. Johnson (along with the Vietnam War) during his years in office. The plethora of disasters led Congress to pass new legislation expanding federal relief programs (Disaster Relief Act of 1966; National Flood Insurance Act of 1968, creating the National Flood Insurance Program). Nevertheless, civil defense remained the nation's top disaster priority and the responsibility of the Department of Defense and its surrogates during the Kennedy-Johnson years. The Cuban missile crisis (Kennedy years) and the Vietnam War (Johnson years) made it so.

Finding the right size and scope of the civil defense program was a policy issue debated among federal officials during the early 1960s. Many saw it as primarily a warning and shelter program that was underfunded (especially the shelter portion) and incapable of handling any missile or nuclear attack on U.S. soil. However, large-scale protests against nuclear proliferation and the Vietnam War made it politically impossible to substantially revamp the civil defense system. That did not happen until the mid-1960s.

Beginning in the mid-1960s, a policy known as "dual-use" began to emerge with passage of the Disaster Relief Act of 1966. Two significant natural disasters—the Alaska Earthquake (1964) and Hurricane Betsy (1965)—prompted Congress to expand the civil defense warning system to include natural disasters (dual-use) and to minimize the fallout shelter program.

In 1968, President Richard Nixon formalized the dual-use approach to emergency preparedness by issuing and implementing a National Security Decision Memorandum that recommended replacing the Office of Civil Defense with the Defense Civil Preparedness Agency and locating it in the Department of Defense. As structured, the dual-use policy allowed the president to concentrate federal resources on civil defense and national security while at the same time stretching those functions to fit preparedness for and response to natural disasters.

The "dual-use" policy continued into the early 1970s until Nixon's successor, President Gerald R. Ford, took office. An escalation in the cold war prompted Ford to revert back to a civil defense system more focused on nuclear attack preparedness. The back-and-forth nature of federal policy, along with the confusion and turf wars it created, were beginning to annoy officials at all levels. The disgruntlement helped President Jimmy Carter, elected in 1976, to make major changes in the purpose, structure, and operation of the emergency management system.

While passage of the Federal Disaster Relief Act of 1970 and its 1974 companion legislation marked the beginning of a process of centralizing emergency management functions at the federal level, it was not until FEMA's creation that disaster policy began to truly integrate natural hazards preparedness with civil defense.

A former governor, President Carter had witnessed firsthand the disjointedness of the nation's emergency management system and was knowledgeable of and sympathetic to the National Governors Association's call for centralization of federal emergency functions. In 1979, Carter used his executive reorganization powers to create FEMA. The agency absorbed a number of other federal agencies and was given primary responsibility for mobilizing federal resources, coordinating emergency management activities with state and local governments, and involving both the public and the private sectors in disaster-related recovery and response efforts. FEMA began developing the Integrated Emergency Management System (IEMS) with an all-hazards approach that included direction, control, and warning systems, which are common to the full range of emergencies from a small isolated event to the ultimate emergency—war. It would take another decade for the all-hazards approach to take hold.

President Ronald Reagan entered office with national security dominant. His defeat of President Carter in 1980 was in large part due to an international situation—the Iranian hostage crisis. Fears of a nuclear attack by the Soviet Union resurfaced. The Cuban Mariel boatlift sent immigrants pouring into the United States, as they fled a dictator's rule. Simply put, the presidency of Ronald Reagan marked a return to the prioritization of civil defense against nuclear attack at the expense of natural disaster policy. FEMA's role changed; federal funds to state and local governments declined; conflicts among all the stakeholders increased.

Nonetheless, President Ronald Reagan signed the Robert T. Stafford Disaster Relief and Emergency Assistance Act of 1988 (Stafford Act). It amended the Federal Disaster Relief Acts of 1970 and 1974 and marked a new era of national disaster management. The Stafford Act gives presidents the authority to issue disaster declarations in cases where an emergency event overwhelms state resources, to establish eligibility criteria for state and local recipients of federal aid, and to specify the type of assistance that the federal government can provide. After a formal declaration has been made at the federal level, all authority for disaster relief operations descends from the president, through FEMA, and down to state and local agencies engaged in relief operations. In the case of megadisasters, FEMA is responsible for coordinating relief efforts with state and local partners.

Major natural disasters, most notably the devastating Hurricane Andrew (1992), occurred during the last half of President George H. W. Bush's administration. Some scholars attribute his loss to Bill Clinton in 1992 partly to failures in the emergency management system, most notably in its leadership.

Under President Clinton, FEMA underwent a major reorganization, leadership choices were based on emergency management experience and professionalism, and a shift in focus occurred—from civil defense activities to core emergency management functions that serve both natural, technological, and deliberate human-made disasters. Under the leadership of James Lee Witt, an experienced emergency manager, FEMA sought greater coordination among federal, state, and local emergency management stakeholders. The all-hazards approach allowed state and local policy makers to address natural disasters more fully than under the narrower civil defense model.

While Clinton's FEMA advocated the all-hazards approach at the local level and pursued greater intergovernmental cooperation, terrorism began to emerge as an important disaster threat. The 1993 truck bomb attack on the World Trade Center in New York City and the 1995 bombing of the Murrah Federal Office Building in Oklahoma City rejuvenated the civil defense mission. Under President Clinton, FEMA began to explore its role in terrorism management. Terrorism would dominate the emergency management landscape following the events of September 11, 2001.

Under President George W. Bush, elected in 2000 and again in 2004, emergency management policies changed considerably in response to two megadisasters—the terrorist attacks of September 11, 2001, and Hurricane Katrina in 2005.

Following the 2001 terrorist attacks, FEMA was incorporated into a newly created Department of Homeland Security (2003). Previously an independent agency with cabinet-level status, the agency became a small part of a large department whose mission focus is counterterrorism. The creation of the Department of Homeland Security (DHS) during President George W. Bush's first administration entailed one of the largest bureaucratic reorganizations in American history. Twenty-two federal agencies, over 40 various federal organizations, and more than 180,000 employees were consolidated into the newly created entity. Debates about whether FEMA belongs within the framework of DHS have been ongoing since DHS's creation.

A series of homeland security presidential directives issued by President Bush during his tenure mandated major changes in emergency management policy, effectively centralizing decision making at the federal level, a significant change from the bottom-up approach that defined emergency management during previous administrations. The National Response Plan (NRP), adopted in 2004, was designed to align federal coordination structures, capabilities, and resources into a unified, all-discipline, and all-hazards approach. While recognizing that state and local governments have primary responsibility for disaster preparedness and response, the NRP makes it clear the federal government will step in if they cannot do the job. The plan established the National Incident Management System (NIMS) as the standard framework to be used by the public and private sectors at every level to manage incidents and synchronize responses. Federal grant money available to states and urban centers is contingent upon compliance with the guidelines and standards of NIMS.

The National Response Plan, reissued in 2008 as the National Response Framework, gives the secretary of DHS primary authority over the management of domestic disasters and asserts a more proactive role for the federal government in the emergency management process. The National Response Framework: (1) describes how communities, tribes, states, the federal government, private sectors, and nongovernmental partners work together to coordinate a national response; (2) identifies specific authorities and best practices for managing incidents; and (3) expands NIMS. This policy refinement came after a remarkably inept response from national, state, and local officials to the Katrina disaster.

Hurricane Katrina in 2005 highlighted the danger of overemphasizing counterterrorism at the expense of natural and technological disasters. Post–Hurricane Katrina analyses concluded that the reassignment of functions, resources, and responsibilities to entities other than FEMA and the emphasis on terrorist-caused incidents had diminished FEMA's capabilities. Passed in 2006, the Post-Katrina Emergency Management Reform Act reconfigured FEMA with consolidated emergency management functions, elevated its status within the DHS, and gave it greater organizational autonomy.

Terrorist-related concerns did not go away following Katrina. The ongoing war in Iraq, growing conflicts in Afghanistan, threats of Iran and North Korea developing nuclear arms, and the spread of radical Islamic fundamentalism, among other international security threats, meant that homeland security would continue to dominate concerns of the Bush administration until he left office.

President Barack Obama took office in January 2009. At the time, domestic concerns dominated, as the nation's economy teetered on the brink of another depression. At the same time, Obama was elected on a platform of redirecting America's disaster-management policies by revamping U.S. security-oriented policies (e.g., treatment of terrorist suspects at Guantánamo) and its natural disaster–related policies (e.g., perceived discrimination in Katrina evacuation priorities).

It is early in his administration, but his discussions about emergency management during his tenure have signaled the possibility of a change in policy regarding FEMA (its independence). Some have speculated that Obama will adopt a more balanced approach to managing the risks associated with terrorism with the more likely threat of natural and technological disasters. They point to the president's choice of Craig Fugate, the former director of Florida's Division of Emergency Management, as evidence of a desire for such a rebalancing. Fugate's selection was in large part due to Florida's experiences with both natural disasters (devastating back-to-back hurricane seasons) and terrorism-related incidents (anthrax deaths), and the state's ranking as the nation's best emergency management system.

As with other presidents, Obama's emergency management policies will inevitably be affected by the incidence of major "focusing events"—sudden, unexpected, high-profile events that capture the nation's attention, expose shortcomings of the emergency management system at all levels, and force major policy redirections.

The megadisasters of the early 2000s (9/11 and Katrina) laid bare many of the inadequacies of the nation's emergency management system. On the heels of these catastrophes, multiple task forces were formed, thousands of recommendations for change were made, millions of dollars were spent via new federal grants-in-aid programs, and significant organizational restructurings occurred at all levels. These have not come without controversy and extensive debate.

The terrorist attacks on the World Trade Center and the Pentagon in 2001 shook the nation and redirected attention away from natural disasters to deliberate human-induced catastrophes. Congress, at the urging of the president, rushed to create the massive Department of Homeland Security into which FEMA was folded. DHS issued mandates to state and local governments to revamp their emergency management systems, pay more attention to vulnerable populations and infrastructure, revise their preparedness standards, and rework their training exercises to include human-made disasters, to name a few. DHS created multiple grant programs aimed at strengthening these governments' capacity to deal with human-made disasters and to better communicate with each other via strengthened intergovernmental networks (regionalism).

Four years later, the disastrous Hurricane Katrina hit with its vengeful 145-mile-per-hour winds and 20-foot storm surge, literally devastating coastal properties in multiple southeastern states and flooding the city of New Orleans. The woefully inadequate responses of governments at all levels reopened many of the debates that followed 9/11 about the optimal organizational structure; preparedness; equity in emergency responsiveness to less mobile, more dependent populations (particularly the poor, racial/ethnic minorities, children, the elderly, and the disabled); and greater balance in funding priorities and grant-in-aid distributional formulae. It refocused attention on emergency management–related deterrents to intergovernmental cooperation and collaboration, particularly at the local level—political conflicts between jurisdictions, incompatible communication equipment, inadequate communication with local partners, bureaucratic red tape regarding cost-sharing agreements, and training and personnel qualification differences.

As of the late 2000s, disagreements remain intense over whether FEMA should again become a separate entity from the Department of Homeland Security. Proponents of an independent FEMA argue that DHS's dominant mission of national security makes it difficult to reach the right balance between terrorism and natural disasters. Opponents of an independent FEMA argue that it is more effective and efficient to include both broad types of disasters (natural; deliberate human made) in the same agency, since a certain degree of commonality exists in vulnerabilities and risks. Others see FEMA inside DHS as better enabling involvement of the U.S. military in the event of a large-scale megadisaster of any type. In summary, the "where-to-put-FEMA" argument is a classic example of the centralization versus decentralization debate.

This debate extends into arguments about the structure and priorities of large federal grants-in-aid, such as the extensive Homeland Security Grant Program created after 9/11 with its multiple parts, including the Urban Areas Security Initiative and the State Homeland Security Grant, Metropolitan Medical Response System, and Citizen Corps programs. These funding categories remain heavily oriented toward counterterrorism and homeland security. They are disproportionately targeted to large metropolitan-area governments (centralization) rather than spread more evenly across a wider range of jurisdictions (decentralization), as they would be if the focus were more on vulnerabilities to a broader range of hazards.

Money debates are not limited to federal grants-in-aid. There is considerable divergence across states as to whether Congress should create a national catastrophic fund. States highly susceptible to a wide range of commonly occurring natural disasters say "Yes"; others with lower levels of risk say "No." Proponents argue that the whole nation's economy is affected by major disasters and thus all the nation's taxpayers should share in funding the recovery costs. Opponents vehemently disagree. A similar debate frequently occurs when the National Flood Insurance Program goes under the microscope, although in that case it's more about whether the government or individual property owners should bear the fiscal consequences of building in high-risk disaster-prone areas.

Occasional debates also occur over whether the *true* purpose of a presidential disaster declaration is *economic* relief for the affected area (the intended purpose) or for the *political* benefit of the president, the state's governor, individual Congress members, and/or local officials. (Media coverage of these declarations often enhances a politico's reputation with constituents as being a good crisis manager.) Critics increasingly paint disaster declarations as pork barrel spending, while supporters point to their fiscal relief to the affected area/individuals. These debates have escalated in recent years due to legislation giving presidents more latitude to make such proclamations and a sharp increase in the number of such declarations.

The emergency management community is divided as to how to assess risks—identifying specific hazards; determining vulnerabilities to them; estimating the likely impacts on people, infrastructure, the environment, and the economy; and predicting the capacity of a community (or region) to react to a crisis. Even within the same locality, arguments routinely ensue across different types of public and private sector officials (management versus specialists) as to what methodologies to use—quantitative, qualitative, or both—or even something as basic as whether to measure disaster size by property damage cost (in dollars) or by the number of people affected.

Differences in governing philosophies create conflict over rankings emanating from such determinations, particularly when it comes to measuring people-oriented versus infrastructure-based vulnerabilities. It is far easier to estimate infrastructure-related hazards than it is people-related hazards and their relative fiscal impacts. Following 9/11, the pendulum swung more in the direction of assigning a higher priority to infrastructure; after Katrina, it moved back in the direction of people. However, differences in the incidence of highly vulnerable critical infrastructure (public and private) and in the composition of the resident population even within the same geographical area may yield vastly different risk assessments and emergency management priorities. Such a situation increases the likelihood of intergovernmental conflict rather than cooperation.

The public and professional emergency managers do not always see eye to eye on the role or impact of the media in emergency situations. The public expects to *see* (television) their elected officials "on the ground" examining damages, talking to everyday citizens, and being empathetic with them in the midst of their sufferings. Emergency management professionals worry that aggressive media will keep first responders from doing their jobs as expeditiously as possible and/or will misinterpret or misreport the facts. Fierce policy debates ensue when governments try to impose restrictions on media access to locations, people, or sensitive information.

The media's huge appetite for "breaking news" headlines has led to charges of sensationalism. The rapidity with which a single case of swine flu (H1N1) in Mexico escalated into worldwide fears of another flu pandemic such as the one in 1918 led some to criticize the media for frightening and provoking hysteria among the populace. Others saw it quite differently—as extremely helpful in prompting the public to exercise caution. Such frenzied coverage also opens up government officials to intense scrutiny and charges of overreacting. The reality is that they are subject to what some have labeled "The Katrina Effect"—the fact that when it comes to government agencies responsible for public health and safety having to decide whether to escalate warnings or not, they are "damned if they do, damned if they don't."

The expanding role of government in the emergency management policy area has reignited another perennial debate—individual versus societal rights. Antiprofiling proponents frequently conflict with those who argue that use of data-based statistical odds is enough to generate greater scrutiny of some individuals/groups to protect the nation from terrorism. And community law enforcement and emergency management officials often encounter individuals who refuse to evacuate even in the face of a mandatory evacuation order, thereby endangering others.

But nothing more reflects the individual rights versus societal rights debate than the USA Patriot Act, enacted after the September 11, 2001, terrorist attacks, then renewed in 2006. Proponents argue that the counterterrorism tools spelled out in the act for use by the government help keep Americans safe (societal rights). Opponents disagree; they believe that the legislation threatens individual constitutionally protected civil liberties, most notably the right to privacy. It is a debate watched around the world as security concerns escalate.

The basic objectives of emergency management—providing for the public safety of citizens and protecting property and the environment—have not changed. Policies for how to accomplish those goals have, most often in response to major focusing events. Emergency management as a field is constantly evolving.

The list of potential hazards continues to grow as new technological, demographic, economic, environmental, and political conditions surface in the United States and abroad. Disaster classifications are altered and new ones created, depending on prevailing circumstances. The likelihood of specific types of incidents (wildland and urban fires, floods, hazardous material spills, nuclear accidents, aircraft accidents, earthquakes, hurricanes, tornadoes, typhoons, acts of terrorism, war-related disasters) fluctuates and varies across different states and localities.

The relative emphasis on (and within) each of the four phases of emergency management—mitigation, preparedness, response, and recovery—shifts over time and across jurisdictions and is generally reflected in the structuring of federal grants-in-aid programs. The specific roles and responsibilities of the federal, state, and local governments, their interface with each other, and their interactions with the private and nonprofit sectors are constantly being debated. The search for the right balance in an all-hazards system between natural disaster–and national security–related dangers constitutes an ongoing challenge facing each new presidential administration and Congress.

At the same time that the field of emergency management has become more professional, it has also become more political. The media's spotlight on disasters and on those responsible for handling them has grown brighter with the advent of 24-hours-a-day coverage. Elected officials at all levels and their appointees know full well that the public expects its leaders to be effective crisis managers.

Public policy making in the field of emergency management is very difficult because of the degree to which the field overlaps with virtually every other governmental operation and involves the private and nonprofit sectors. It is an extremely complex policy area with life and death consequences in the United States and the world.

Further Reading:

Birkland, Thomas A. *Lessons of Disaster: Policy Change after Catastrophic Events.* Washington, D.C.: Georgetown University Press, 2006; Boin, Arjen, Paul 't Hart, Eric Stern, and Bengt Sundelius. *The Politics of Crisis Management: Public Leadership under Pressure.* Cambridge: Cambridge University Press, 2005; Bumgarner, Jeffrey B. *Emergency Management: A Reference Handbook.* Santa Barbara, Calif.: ABC-CLIO, Contemporary World Issues Series, 2008; Haddow, George D., Jane A. Bullock, and Damon P. Coppola. *Introduction to Emergency Management.* 3rd ed. New York: Butterworth-Heinemann, Elsevier; 2008; Lindell, Michael K., Carla Prater, and Ronald W. Perry. *Introduction to Emergency Management.* Hoboken, N.J.: John Wiley & Sons, 2007; Kettl, Donald F. *System under Stress: Homeland Security and American Politics.* Washington, D.C.: CQ Press, 2007; National Research Council of the National Academies. *Facing Hazards and Disasters: Understanding Human Dimensions.* Washington, D.C.: National Academies Press, 2006; Rubin, Claire B. *Emergency Management: The American Experience 1900–2005.* Fairfax, Va.: Public Entity Risk Management (PERI), 2007; Sylves, Richard. *Disaster Policy and Politics: Emergency Management and Homeland Security.* Washington, D.C.: CQ Press, 2008; Waugh, William L., Jr., and Kathleen Tierney, eds. *Emergency Management: Principles and Practice for Local Government.* 2d ed. Washington, D.C.: International City/County Management Association, ICMA Press, 2007.

– Susan A. MacManus and Kiki Caruson

---

postal service

The spare language of the Constitution's postal clause—that "Congress shall have the power to . . . establish Post Offices and Post roads"—provided authority for some of the federal government's most far-reaching enterprises. Postal policy created the nation's first communication network, one that has served individuals, businesses, the press, reform groups, retailers, political parties, and others since the beginning of the nation. Through most of U.S. history, the postal service's sprawling network made it the largest civilian employer and the only federal institution reaching into nearly every community. Because of the post office's ubiquitous presence, Congress used it for many purposes ancillary to moving the mails.

The U.S. postal system has operated under two regimes. From the adoption of the Constitution until 1971, Congress set postal policy and directly controlled postage rates as well as general levels of service, while the executive branch managed the department's affairs. Governed by politicians

The old Post Office Pavilion in Washington, D.C. Used only for a short time as an actual post office, the building, a fine example of Romanesque revival architecture, was completed in 1899. *(Photo by TCY/ Used under a Creative Commons license)*

during this regime, the post office elevated service to the public—and influential constituencies—over businesslike administration. The 1970 Postal Reorganization Act, however, rebalanced these priorities. With this law, Congress converted the Post Office Department into the quasi-corporate U.S. Postal Service (USPS), loosening politicians' grip on the postal system and mandating that the new institution operate more like a business. In 2006, Congress reinforced this mandate by repositioning the USPS to help it survive in a modern communication environment in which it competed with electronic message systems and private sector carriers.

From the adoption of the Constitution until 1801, the post office operated as a branch of the

Treasury and then became an independent unit. It slowly gained identity as the Post Office Department (POD) after President Andrew Jackson elevated the postmaster general to cabinet-level status in 1829. For the next 100 years and beyond, the postmaster general functioned as the "cabinet politician," the politico who controlled tens of thousands of jobs. POD resources, especially patronage appointments, were deployed to mobilize partisan forces on behalf of a candidate's election or reelection. Presidential and congressional politics thus continually intruded into post office affairs, but department administrators nonetheless developed considerable professional autonomy and management expertise by the early 20th century. Regardless of their politics, administrators supervised a nationwide system of offices, employees, and private transports; scholars have identified the post office as a key agent in the development of the federal government's administrative capacity before the New Deal.

For 180 years, Congress exercised its direct control over rates by engaging in endless debates over postage for different classes of mail, often dwelling on changes in a fraction of a cent. With legislative ratemaking, only letter mail and, later, parcel post consistently produced enough postage to cover their costs; other mail classes, especially the one for periodicals, were heavily subsidized, leading to long-running controversies about the government supporting the press, a powerful interest group. Lawmakers justified these cross subsidies (charging letter writers more to underwrite publishers' mail) by pointing to the societal value of widely disseminated print media. Policy makers also recognized the principles of network economics when they explained in 1845 how a nationwide system necessarily averaged costs from expensive-to-serve communities (mainly rural) with cheaper-to-serve areas (mainly urban). With a congressional commitment to maintain low postage while expanding operations, the post office consistently ran a deficit after 1830, which lawmakers covered in annual appropriations from the Treasury.

The very size and ubiquity of the post office prompted Congress to use it for sundry purposes secondary to moving the mails. Congress assigned some tasks to the POD simply because it was the only federal agency whose operations involved daily contact with citizens everywhere. Thousands of post offices sold savings bonds and migratory bird stamps, reported aliens' addresses, stored flags used at veterans' funerals, located relatives of deceased soldiers, displayed military recruiting materials and FBI-wanted posters, and distributed income tax forms in lobbies.

More ambitiously, Congress exploited the amorphous language of the Constitution's postal clause to launch federal initiatives that many regarded as intrusions on private sector prerogatives. Parcel post initially aroused opposition as unwarranted government competition with private package carriers. Similarly, bankers protested when Congress grafted banking functions onto the post office. From 1910 to 1966, postal savings banks provided a financial safety net first popular in rural America and then everywhere during the Great Depression. The most far-reaching proposals, repeatedly considered by Congress from the end of the Civil War to World War I, called for government to acquire the nation's telegraph and telephone networks and to operate them under the auspices of the post office—the arrangement followed in virtually every other nation. This initiative never succeeded and, by the mid-1950s, the first postal regime increasingly focused on cutting or at best protecting existing services rather than extending them.

Ever-mounting postal deficits, widely publicized breakdowns in mail delivery, and concerns about partisan meddling prompted Congress to abandon the first postal regime. The Postal Reorganization Act of 1970 loosened congressional control and replaced the POD with a government corporation, the U.S. Postal Service. The postmaster general, formerly a presidential cabinet officer, was now selected by a board of governors. A new independent regulatory body, the Postal Rate Commission, reviewed the board's requests for rate hikes. Rates were set after extensive commission hearings in which the lobbying that had characterized congressional ratemaking was forbidden by law. The Reorganization Act stipulated that rates reflect the costs of delivering each type of mail, though it retained some consideration for the social and cultural value of periodicals, media mail, and materials sent by nonprofit organizations. Challenges to the Rate Commission's decisions could be appealed to the courts (unlike congressional ratemaking).

Under this new regime, postage rose quickly, especially for classes of mail that had been heavily subsidized by Congress. The Postal Service tried, with modest success, to cut expenses by closing small rural post offices and contracting out services. With higher rates and more efficient operations, the Postal Service ended its reliance on the Treasury to cover revenue shortfalls. Streamlining Postal Service operations, however, did not address a threat to the mails that emerged in the 1990s—ever-growing electronic substitutes for hard-copy delivery. Although earlier technologies, especially the telegraph and the telephone, had diverted considerable business from the mails, the Internet presented more formidable competition. First-class mail—mainly letters and business correspondence (bills, remittances, quarterly statements, etc.)—provided the bulk of the Postal Service's revenue, and those very types of communications quickly migrated to the Internet.

To realign the Postal Service for this modern communication environment, Congress passed the 2006 Postal Accountability and Enhancement Act. The law allows the Postal Service to compete vigorously in some sectors so as long as it does not cross-subsidize those services with revenue from its monopoly or market-dominant offerings. Several provisions of the new law assure that the Postal Service cannot use its advantages as a government corporation or its legal monopoly over letter mail to compete unfairly with private carriers such as Federal Express and United Parcel Service. The Postal Service can now increase postage at the rate of inflation without going through the time-consuming hearings required under the 1970 law. For the first time in U.S. history, raising basic postage does not require a legislative debate (conducted by Congress before 1970) or a formal administrative hearing (conducted by the Rate Commission between 1971 and 2006). The 2006 law also converted the Postal Rate Commission into the Postal Regulatory Commission and gave it broader powers to oversee the USPS.

At its core, the post office provided a communication service—the nation's first. Shortly after the adoption of the Constitution, lawmakers exercised their authority to "establish Post Offices and Post roads" and then went further, crafting policies that committed the government to underwrite the cost of circulating public information over its network.

The 1792 postal law represented a striking counterpoint to the First Amendment, adopted the preceding year. The First Amendment's negative admonition—"Congress shall make no law abridging . . . the freedom of speech or of the press"—promised that the federal government would not meddle with the content of the press. The 1792 postal law committed the public posts to facilitate the dissemination of information, especially political news. Most notably, newspapers traveled at a fraction of the postage charged letters; for instance, a three-sheet letter mailed beyond 450 miles paid 75 cents while a newspaper the same size could be dispatched for 1.5 cents. This below-cost transmission of news continued well into the 20th century. The 1792 law also allowed editors to exchange newspapers free of postage. This policy enabled editors to obtain their out-of-town news by exchanging papers through the mails; they then simply copied articles from one another. Lawmakers ended postage-free exchanges in 1873; by then, the telegraph and wire services transmitted timely information for the press. Congress designed these earliest postal laws to promote the circulation of information that would foster political cohesion at a time of fragile nationalism.

Postal laws slowly extended mailing privileges from news narrowly defined as political intelligence to public information broadly conceived. Magazines, featuring social and educational information, were at first treated inhospitably by postal policy but attained mailing parity with newspapers in 1852. Bound books, considered too bulky for early transports and also slighted because they did not transmit timely news, were excluded from the mails until 1851. Postal law treated books as merchandise until President Franklin D. Roosevelt temporarily established a book rate in 1938; Congress made it permanent in 1942. Congress gradually extended special rates, that is, below the postage charged similar commercial mail, to other types of public information: library materials (1928) and films (1953). Nonprofit groups, notably educational and charitable organizations, won the right to send their magazines (1917) and promotional circulars (1951) at rates below that charged for similar commercial mail. These special rates survive today as categories for libraries, media mail, and nonprofit organizations.

Although promoting the circulation of public information in the form of print media could be justified by the general benefits it produced for society, deciding on the proper treatment of commercial information in the mail proved troublesome. Congress and postal administrators acknowledged the importance of market intelligence—prices for commodities and financial instruments—as early as the 1820s and 1830s, when the department began running special expresses to speed data about crop prices between agricultural regions and commercial centers. Advertising circulars, however, were treated as letters, subject to prohibitively expensive rates for large mailings. Not until 1928 did Congress create a rate class for bulk mailings of identical advertisements, popularly known as junk mail, that reflected the relatively low cost of handling them.

The emergence of mass circulation, general-interest magazines triggered a perennial debate about the proper policy treatment of magazines that commonly carried more advertising than editorial content. An 1885 postal law cut postage to 1 cent a pound for the circulation of newspapers and magazines anywhere in the nation. This opened a cheap distribution channel for a new breed of magazines, filled with ads for nationally available brand-name products, aimed at middle-class reader-consumers. Policy debates raged in and out of Congress until 1917, when lawmakers devised the solution still followed today: charge the advertising portion of magazines and newspapers more than the editorial content. The former enriches publishers and advertisers and thus its postage reflects the cost of service; editorial content, in contrast, enjoys lower rates to reflect its value to society.

Early postal laws discouraged letter writing. For the first 50 years, letter rates—much higher than those for newspapers—were scaled to distance and the number of sheets enclosed. This rate structure deterred casual letter writing by anyone other than political and business elites. Congress enacted a fundamental reform in 1845, modeled on a similar change in Britain, that drastically cut and simplified letter postage. For the first time, letter postage became affordable for many citizens. Policy makers continued to simplify letter postage, establishing a nationwide uniform rate in 1851.

The post office's role as the nation's largest carrier of printed information positioned it to become the nation's leading censor. During the early years of the nation, partisan postmasters sporadically interfered with opponents' newspapers. Censorship of the mails became a constitutional issue in the 1830s when southern states demanded that the federal government ban the circulation of antislavery material from the North to the South. Andrew Jackson's postmaster general could not find authority for such censorship, but he tacitly approved the actions of postmasters in the South who refused to deliver it. Southern mobs occasionally took matters into their own hands by burning sacks of abolitionist tracts removed from post offices.

After the Civil War, Congress approved more systematic postal censorship to stop the circulation of information about socially disapproved activities. Most notably, the 1873 Comstock Law criminalized the mailing of material deemed obscene. Obscenity was construed broadly and, until the mid-1900s, the post office prosecuted those who mailed information about sex education, birth control, and abortion, ensnaring such activists as Margaret Sanger and Planned Parenthood. Other laws kept prizefighting films and lottery promotions out of the mails. Mail fraud statutes have long extended federal jurisdiction to mundane offenses—illicit business schemes, consumer deception, and all manner of criminal activities—in which the mails played even an incidental role.

Postal censorship of allegedly radical publications prompted litigation that shaped modern First Amendment principles. During World War I, Congress empowered the post office to punish antiwar and seditious publications. Periodicals issued by pacifists, socialists, and many labor organizations were barred from the mails or denied the low postage rates that enabled them to reach subscribers. Many foreign-language newspapers ceased publication during World War I partly because of onerous postal rules. For the most part, courts upheld this early 20th-century postal crackdown on publications outside the political mainstream, viewing freedom of circulation as falling outside of core First Amendment protections. After mid-century, however, postal rules interfering with the circulation of sexually explicit periodicals and radical political material were successfully challenged in the Supreme Court.

Congress used the network of post offices and roads to directly foster the development of institutions that bound the nation together at a time of fragile nationalism and rapid national expansion. Moreover, the postal communication network undergirded the other networks—transportation, political, social, cultural, and marketing—that formed the connective tissue in an extensive, diverse nation.

After a burst of growth in the 1790s tied seaboard cities into a postal network, the post office turned inland. Congress, which directly controlled the establishment of new postal routes and offices, responded favorably to almost all petitions from citizens asking for the extension of service to newly settled areas. Through most of the 19th century, the network of post offices and post roads grew at a faster rate than the population.

Significantly, Congress used postal policy as a proxy for transportation policy for more than 150 years. With minor exceptions, the federal government did not directly develop roads or transports; instead, postal operations provided subsidies and incentives for others to do so. Through contracts to carry the mails, the post office helped develop the nation's transportation industry, first stagecoaches and then steamboats, railroads, and airlines. Government mail contracts were highly prized by transport firms, sustaining them when private customers were few, and, as a by-product, they improved service for passengers. Because the mails needed to be delivered on a regular basis, postal contracts compelled transport firms to follow fixed schedules. For instance, early airlines with sporadic service adopted precise timetables to qualify for mail contracts, benefiting passengers who sought predictable flight schedules. Postal policy similarly boosted the nation's road- and bridge-building efforts. Although the federal government rarely funded such infrastructures in the 19th century, the post office pressed states and communities to upgrade routes if they wanted improved mail service.

Lawmakers exploited the post office's assets to foster the nation's political development. To forge connections among the different levels of government, early Congresses took pains to authorize postal routes that linked the federal capital with state capitals and county seats. This infrastructure complemented the favored treatment enjoyed by newspapers laden with political news. Together, these policies facilitated the exchange of political information between the federal capital and the hinterlands and among the states, a policy Congress believed would cultivate a sense of national community at a time when citizens had few contacts outside their hometowns. As westward expansion multiplied the number of post offices, the department became the largest source of patronage appointments. Tens of thousands of postmasterships, often the only federal jobs in small towns, sustained party activists throughout the nation.

From its beginnings, the post office narrowed the gaps—economic, informational, and cultural—between urban and rural life, and, since the late 1800s, it has operated with an express mandate to boost rural America. Tests of rural delivery in the 1890s convinced Congress in 1902 to place Rural Free Delivery (RFD) on a permanent footing. RFD provided delivery services nearly equal to those enjoyed by city residents. Indeed, the language in current postal law that mandates universal postal service for the nation derives largely from a 1916 RFD statute.

Rural mail services, combined with parcel post, fostered the development of truly national retail markets. In the late 1800s, firms producing consumer goods penetrated markets throughout the nation by exploiting several postal services. The post office distributed ads for brand-name consumer goods on the pages of newspapers and magazines for negligible postage; mail-order merchandisers' catalogues paid higher but still modest rates. But until 1912, the post office could not deliver packages exceeding four pounds, leaving a gap in the postal marketing network. Parcel post, seemingly innocuous today, was a flashpoint in early 20th-century cultural battles. Small town merchandisers fought to protect their businesses from the incursion of big city retailers by mounting an offensive against the urban culture and production systems associated with mail-order marketing. Nonetheless, Congress raised the weight limit on parcels transported by mail, completing the suite of services that turned the postal network into a full-fledged adjunct of the nation's marketing system.

The postal system has long adapted to changes in technology and political culture, but the Internet is forcing unprecedented adjustments in the mails. Although the Internet creates a few new opportunities for the Postal Service, for example, delivering parcels for online retailers such as Amazon.com and eBay, it diverts more revenue-generating mail to electronic channels than it brings in. The 2006 Postal Accountability and Enhancement Act recognized this fundamental challenge and provides for adjustments in the government monopoly over key mail classes and the Postal Service's mandate to provide universal service.

From its beginnings, the postal service has jealously guarded its legally protected monopoly over the transportation of specified mail classes as a way to prevent cream-skimming—private firms delivering high-profit mail and leaving money-losing services to the government posts. But state postal monopolies around the world have been crumbling since the late 1900s, with some government mails partly or wholly privatized. Perhaps starting the United States down the same path, the 2006 law established a mechanism for introducing ever more competition into the carriage of mail. Congress directed the Postal Regulatory Commission to evaluate the necessity for the two legal bulwarks that protect the Postal Service's monopoly: statutory prohibitions against private carriers competing directly for first-class letter mail and a ban on private carriers' access to mailboxes.

If the Postal Service hemorrhages revenue to private carriers and electronic networks, will it have resources sufficient to maintain universal service for the nation? The 1970 Reorganization Act adopted universal service as the institution's overarching objective, though it had been the guiding principle at least since the advent of RFD if not much earlier. Policy makers in the 21st century are struggling to redefine universal postal service, or perhaps abandon it, in a communication environment with multiple competitors and substitutes for transmission by mail. Possible changes include cutting back service (less frequent delivery for rural areas or the entire nation), eliminating rate preferences long enjoyed by mail classes with high societal value (the editorial content of periodicals, media mail, materials sent by nonprofit groups), forging more partnerships with private firms (e.g., USPS now collaborates with Federal Express), and closing additional rural facilities. The government postal service, once the nation's only communication system, is now scrambling to find a new niche in an environment in which it is but one network among many.

Further Reading:

Desai, Anuj C. "The Transformation of Statutes into Constitutional Law: How Early Post Office Policy Shaped Modern First Amendment Doctrine." *Hastings Law Journal* 58 (March 2007): 671–727; Fuller, Wayne E. *The American Mail: Enlarger of the Common Life*. Chicago: University of Chicago Press, 1972; John, Richard R. *Spreading the News: The American Postal System from Franklin to Morse*. Cambridge, Mass.: Harvard University Press, 1995; Kielbowicz, Richard B. *News in the Mails: The Press, Post

Office, and Public Information, 1700–1860s. New York: Greenwood Press, 1989; ———. "Preserving Universal Postal Service as a Communication Safety Net: A Policy History and Proposal." *Seton Hall Legislative Journal* 30 (2006): 383–436; Paul, James C. N., and Murray L. Schwartz. *Federal Censorship: Obscenity in the Mail*. New York: Free Press of Glencoe, 1961; Rogers, Lindsay. *The Postal Power of Congress*. Baltimore: The Johns Hopkins University Press, 1916.

– Richard B. Kielbowicz

Selected Bibliography

Volume 1: Economic Policies

1. Agriculture

Conkin, Paul K. *A Revolution Down on the Farm: The Transformation of American Agriculture since 1929*. Lexington: University Press of Kentucky, 2008.

Evenson, Robert E., and Prabhu Pringali. *Handbook of Agricultural Economics: Agricultural Development: Farm Policies and Regional Development*. Maryland Heights, Mo.: North Holland Books, 2009.

Hamilton, David E. *From New Day to New Deal: American Farm Policy from Hoover to Roosevelt, 1928–1933*. Chapel Hill: University of North Carolina Press, 2009.

Hurt, R. Douglas. *American Agriculture: A Brief History*. Rev. ed. West Lafayette, Ind.: Purdue University Press, 2002.

Knutson, Ronald D., J. B. Penn, and Barry L. Flinchbaugh. *Agricultural and Food Policy*. 6th ed. Upper Saddle River, N.J.: Prentice Hall, 2006.

Richardson, Joe, Donna V. Porter, and Jean Yavis Jones. *Child Nutrition and WIC Programs: Background and Funding*. New York: Nova Science Publishers, 2003.

2. Commerce

Blair, John, and Michael Carroll. *Local Economic Development: Analysis, Practices and Globalization*. 2d ed. Los Angeles: Sage Publications, 2009.

Card, David, and Alan B. Krueger. *Myth and Measurement: The New Economics of the Minimum Wage*. Princeton, N.J.: Princeton University Press, 1995.

De Kluyver, Cornelis A. *A Primer on Corporate Governance*. Williston, Vt.: Business Expert Press, 2009.

Derthick, Martha, and Paul J. Quirk. *The Politics of Deregulation*. Washington, D.C.: Brookings Institution Press, 1985.

Gitterman, Daniel P. *Boosting Paychecks: The Politics of Supporting America's Working Poor*. Washington, D.C.: Brookings Institution Press, 2009.

Grace, Martin F., and Robert W. Klein, eds. *The Future of Insurance Regulation in the United States*. Washington, D.C.: Brookings Institution Press, 2009.

Halbert, Debora. *Resisting Intellectual Property*. London and New York: Routledge, 2005.

Hilton, Matthew. *Prosperity for All: Consumer Activism in an Era of Globalization*. Ithaca, N.Y.: Cornell University Press, 2009.

Hovenkamp, Herbert. *The Antitrust Enterprise: Principle and Execution*. Cambridge, Mass.: Harvard University Press, 2005.

Jackson, Thomas H. *The Logic and Limits of Bankruptcy Law*. 2d ed. New York: Beard Books, 2001.

Mann, Bruce H. *Republic of Debtors: Bankruptcy in the Age of American Independence*. Cambridge, Mass.: Harvard University Press, 2002.

Markham, Jerry W. *A Financial History of the United States*. Armonk, N.Y.: M.E. Sharpe, 2001.

Mishkin, Frederic S. *The Economics of Money, Banking, and Financial Markets*. 5th ed. The Addison-Wesley Series in Economics. Reading, Mass.: Addison-Wesley, 1998.

Palmiter, Alan R. *Securities Regulation: Examples and Explanations*. New York: Aspen Publishers, 2008.

Richardson, William D. *Democracy, Bureaucracy, and Character: Founding Thought*. Lawrence: University Press of Kansas, 1997.

Sell, Susan K. *Private Power, Public Law: The Globalization of Intellectual Property Rights*. Cambridge: Cambridge University Press, 2003.

Taylor, Robert V. *The Process of Change in American Banking: Political Economy and the Public Purpose.* Westport, Conn.: Quorum Books, 1990.

Wilson, James Q., ed. *The Politics of Regulation*. New York: Basic Books, 1980.

3. Consumer Safety

Foreman, Christopher H. *Signals from the Hill: Congressional Oversight and the Challenge of Social Regulation*. New Haven, Conn.: Yale University Press, 1988.

Hawthorne, Fran. *Inside the FDA: The Business and Politics behind the Drugs We Take and the Food We Eat*. Hoboken, N.J.: Wiley Press, 2005.

Hilts, Philip J. *Protecting America's Health: The FDA, Business, and One Hundred Years of Regulation.* Chapel Hill: University of North Carolina Press, 2004.

Mashaw, Jerry L., and David L. Harfst. *The Struggle for Auto Safety*. Cambridge, Mass.: Harvard University Press, 1990.

Norton, Peter D. *Fighting Traffic: The Dawn of the Motor Age in the American City*. Cambridge, Mass.: The MIT Press, 2008.

O'Reilly, James T. *Consumer Product Safety Regulation: Impact of the 2008 Amendments*. New York: Practising Law Institute, 2008.

4. Energy

Ayres, Robert U., and Edward H. Ayres. *Crossing the Energy Divide: Moving from Fossil Fuel Dependence to a Clean-Energy Future*. Philadelphia: Wharton School Publishing, 2009.

Laird, Frank N. *Solar Energy, Technology Policy, and Institutional Values*. New York: Cambridge University Press, 2001.

Lyon, Thomas, ed. *The Political Economy of Regulation.* Northampton, Mass.: Edward Elgar Publishing, 2007.

Mazuzan, George T., and J. Samuel Walker. *Controlling the Atom: The Beginnings of Nuclear Regulation, 1946–1962*. Berkeley: University of California Press, 1984.

Phillips, Charles F., Jr. *The Regulation of Public Utilities: Theory and Practice.* Vienna, Va.: Public Utilities Reports, 1993.

Samuels, Warren J., and Edythe S. Miller. *The Institutionalist Approach to Public Utilities Regulation.* East Lansing: Michigan State University Press, 2002.

Simon, Christopher A. *Alternative Energy: Political, Economic, and Social Feasibility*. Lanham, Md.: Rowman & Littlefield Publishers, 2007.

Stagliano, Vito A. *A Policy of Discontent: The Making of a National Energy Strategy*. Tulsa, Okla.: PennWell, 2001.

Vietor, Richard H. K. *Energy Policy in America since 1945: A Study of Business-Government Relations.* Cambridge: Cambridge University Press, 1984.

Walker, Samuel J. *Three Mile Island: A Nuclear Crisis in Historical Perspective*. Berkeley: University of California Press, 2004.

Weart, Spencer R. *Nuclear Fear: A History of Images*. Cambridge, Mass.: Harvard University Press, 1988.

5. Environment and Conservation

Aldy, Joseph E., and Robert N. Stavins, eds. *Architectures for Agreement: Addressing Global Climate Change in the Post-Kyoto World.* New York: Cambridge University Press, 2007.

Babcock, Richard F. *The Zoning Game Revisited.* Madison: University of Wisconsin Press, 1990.

Bailey, Christopher J. *Congress and Air Pollution: Environmental Policies in the USA*. Manchester and New York: Manchester University Press, 1998.

Burgess, Bonnie B. *Fate of the Wild: The Endangered Species Act and the Future of Biodiversity.* London: University of Georgia Press, 2001.

Colten, Craig E., and Peter N. Skinner. *The Road to Love Canal: Managing Industrial Waste before EPA*. Austin: University of Texas Press, 1996.

Easter, K. William, and Naomi Zeitouni. *The Economics of Water Quality*. Burlington, Vt.: Ashgate Publishing, 2006.

Eisner, Simon, Arthur Gallon, and Stanley Eisner. *The Urban Pattern: City Planning and Design*. New York: Van Nostrand Reinhold, 1993.

Favre, David. *Animal Law: Welfare, Interests and Rights*. New York: Aspen Publishers, 2008.

Glicksman, Robert L., and George Cameron Coggins. *Modern Public Land Law in a Nutshell.* St. Paul, Minn.: West Group, 2001.

Goklany, Indur M. *Clearing the Air: The Real Story of the War on Air Pollution.* Washington, D.C.: Cato Institute, 1999.

Graham, Mary. *The Morning after Earth Day: Practical Environmental Politics.* Washington, D.C.: Brookings Institution Press, 1999.

Hays, Samuel P. *Explorations in Environmental History.* Pittsburgh, Pa.: University of Pittsburgh Press, 1998.

Morag-Levine, Noga. *Chasing the Wind: Regulating Air Pollution in the Common Law State.* Princeton, N.J.: Princeton University Press, 2003.

Petersen, Shannon. *Acting for Endangered Species.* Lawrence: University Press of Kansas, 2002.

Plotkin, Sidney. *Keep Out: The Struggle for Land Use Control.* Berkeley: University of California Press, 1987.

Rabe, Barry George. *Statehouse and Greenhouse: The Emerging Politics of American Climate Change Policy.* Washington, D.C.: Brookings Institution Press, 2004.

Wilson, William. *The City Beautiful Movement.* Baltimore, Md.: The Johns Hopkins University Press, 1989.

Yaffee, Steven. *The Wisdom of the Spotted Owl: Policy Lessons for a New Century.* Washington, D.C.: Island Press, 1994.

6. Labor

Baumer, Donald C., and Carl E. Van Horn. *The Politics of Unemployment.* Washington, D.C.: CQ Press, 1985.

Blaustein, Saul J. *Unemployment Insurance in the United States.* Kalamazoo, Mich.: W.E. Upjohn Institute for Employment Research, 1993.

Chelius, James Robert. *Workplace Safety and Health: The Role of Workers' Compensation.* Washington, D.C.: American Enterprise for Public Policy Research, 1977.

Hawthorne, Fran. *Pension Dumping: The Reasons, the Wreckage, the Stakes for Wall Street*, New York: Bloomberg Press, 2008.

Hess, Benjamin. *Children in the Fields: An American Problem.* Washington, D.C.: Association of Farmworker Opportunity Programs, 2007.

Holley, William H., Kenneth M. Jennings, and Robert M. Wolters. *The Labor Relations Process.* Boston: South-Western/Cengage Learning, 2009.

Kearney, Richard C., and David G. Carnevale. *Labor Relations in the Public Sector.* New York: Marcel Dekker, 2001.

McGarrity, Thomas O., and Sidney A. Shapiro. *Workers at Risk: The Failed Promise of the Occupational Safety and Health Administration.* Westport, Conn.: Praeger Publishers, 1993.

Modigliani, Franco, and Arun Muralidhar. *Rethinking Pension Reform*, Cambridge: Cambridge University Press, 2005.

Noble, Charles. *Liberalism at Work: The Rise and Fall of OSHA.* Philadelphia: Temple University Press, 1984.

Riccucci, Norma M. *Managing Diversity in Public Sector Workforces.* Boulder, Colo.: Westview Press, 2002.

Thomason, Terry, Timothy P. Schimidle, and John F. Burton, Jr. *Workers' Compensation: Benefits, Costs, and Safety under Alternative Insurance Arrangements.* Kalamazoo, Mich.: W.E. Upjohn Institute for Employment Research, 2001.

Whittaker, William G. *Child Labor in America: History, Policy, and Legislative Issues.* Washington, D.C.: Congressional Research Service, Library of Congress, 2005.

7. Monetary Policy

Axilrod, Stephen H. *Inside the Fed: Monetary Policy and Its Management.* Cambridge, Mass.: MIT Press, 2009.

Livingston, James. *Origins of the Federal Reserve System.* Ithaca, N.Y.: Cornell University Press, 1986.

Meltzer, Allan. *A History of the Federal Reserve.* Chicago: University of Chicago Press, 2003.

Mishkin, Frederic. *Monetary Policy Strategy.* Cambridge, Mass.: MIT Press, 2009.

Rockoff, Hugh. *Drastic Measures: A History of Wage and Price Controls in the United States.* Cambridge: Cambridge University Press, 1984.

8. Taxation

Brunori, David. *State Tax Policy: A Political Perspective.* 2d ed. Washington, D.C.: Urban Institute Press, 2007.

Burke, Karen C. *Federal Income Taxation of Corporations and Stockholders in a Nutshell.* 6th ed. St. Paul, Minn.: West Publishing, 2007.

Conlan, Timothy J., Margaret T. Wrightson, and David Beam. *Taxing Choices: The Politics of Tax Reform.* Washington, D.C.: CQ Press, 1990.

Fisher, Glenn W. *The Worst Tax? A History of the Property Tax in America.* Lawrence: University Press of Kansas, 1996.

Graetz, Michael J., and Deborah H. Schenk. *Federal Income Taxation: Principles and Policies.* Westbury, N.Y.: Foundation Press, 2008.

Ingram, Gregory K., and Yu-Hung Hong, eds. *Fiscal Decentralization and Land Policies.* Cambridge, Mass.: Lincoln Institute of Land Policy, 2008.

Martin, Isaac William. *The Permanent Tax Revolt: How the Property Tax Transformed American Politics.* Palo Alto, Calif.: Stanford University Press, 2008.

Morone, James A. *Hellfire Nation: The Politics of Sin in American History.* New Haven, Conn.: Yale University Press, 2003.

Shaviro, Daniel N. *Decoding the U.S. Corporate Tax.* Washington, D.C.: Urban Institute, 2009.

Slemrod, Joel, and Jon Bakija. *Taxing Ourselves: A Citizen's Guide to the Debate over Taxes.* 3rd ed. Cambridge, Mass.: MIT Press, 2004.

9. Transportation

Adams, Alice. *Trucking Rules and Regulations.* Stamford, Conn.: Cengage Learning, 2004.

Black, William R. *Sustainable Transportation: Problems and Solutions.* New York: Guilford Press, 2010.

Button, Kenneth J., and Erik T. Verhoef, eds. *Road Pricing, Traffic Congestion and the Environment: Issues of Efficiency and Social Feasibility.* Northampton, Mass.: Edward Elgar, 1998.

Childs, William R. *Trucking and the Public Interest.* Knoxville: University of Tennessee Press, 1985.

Doganis, Rigas. *The Airline Business.* New York: Routledge, 2005.

Keeler, Theodore. *Railroads, Freight, and Public Policy.* Washington, D.C.: Brookings Institution Press, 1983.

Nice, David C. *Amtrak: The History and Politics of a National Railroad.* Boulder, Colo.: Lynne Rienner Publishing, 1998.

Oster, Clinton V., and John S. Strong. *Managing the Skies: Public Policy, Organization and Financing Air Traffic Management.* Aldershot, England: Ashgate Publishing, 2007.

Rose, Mark H. *Interstate: Express Highway Politics, 1939–1989.* Knoxville: University of Tennessee Press, 1990.

Shinar, David. *Traffic Safety and Human Behavior.* London: Elsevier Science, 2007.

Siggerud, Katherine. *Traffic Safety Programs: Progress, States' Challenges, and Issues for Reauthorization.* Washington, D.C.: U.S. Government Accountability Office, 2008.

Usselman, Steven. *Regulating Railroad Innovation.* Cambridge: Cambridge University Press, 2002.

Volume 2: Social Policies

10. Arts

Benedict, Stephen, ed. *Public Money and the Muse: Essays on Government Funding for the Arts.* New York: W. W. Norton, 1991.

Binkiewicz, Donna M. *Federalizing the Muse: United States Arts Policy and the National Endowment for the Arts, 1965–1980.* Chapel Hill: University of North Carolina Press, 2004.

Carter, Thomas L., and G. Edward Evans. *Introduction to Library Public Services.* Santa Barbara, Calif.: Libraries Unlimited, 2008.

Engleman, Ralph. *Public Radio and Television in America: A Political History.* Los Angeles: Sage Publications, 1996.

Levy, Alan Howard. *Government and the Arts: Debates over Federal Support of the Arts in America from George Washington to Jesse Helms.* Latham, Md.: University Press of America, 1997.

McCauley, Michael P., Eric E. Peterson, B. Lee Artz, and Deedee Halleck. *Public Broadcasting and the Public Interest.* Armonk, N.Y.: M.E. Sharpe, 2003.

U.S. Office of Education. *Public Libraries in the United States of America: Their History, Condition, and Management.* Ann Arbor: University of Michigan Library, 2006.

Usherwood, Bob. *Equity and Excellence in Public Libraries*. Burlington, Vt.: Ashgate, 2007.

11. Civil Rights

Anderson, Terry H. *The Pursuit of Fairness: A History of Affirmative Action*. New York: Oxford University Press, 2004.

Bowen, William G., and Derek Bok. *The Shape of the River: Long-Term Consequences of Considering Race in College and University Admissions*. Princeton, N.J.: Princeton University Press, 1998.

Carr, James H., and Nandinee K. Katty, eds. *Segregation: The Rising Costs for America*. New York: Routledge, 2008.

Colker, Ruth. *The Disability Pendulum: The First Decade of the Americans with Disabilities Act*. New York: New York University Press, 2005.

Fehrenbacher, Don E. *The Slaveholding Republic: An Account of the United States Government's Relations to Slavery*, edited by Ward M. McAfee. New York: Oxford University Press, 2001.

Foner, Eric. *Reconstruction: America's Unfinished Revolution*. New York: Harper & Row, 1988.

Ford, Lynne E. *Women and Politics: The Pursuit of Equality*. Boston: Houghton Mifflin, 2002.

Han, Lori Cox. *Women and American Politics: The Challenges of Political Leadership*. Boston: McGraw-Hill, 2007.

Hull, N.E.H., and Peter Charles Hoffer. *Roe v. Wade: The Abortion Rights Controversy in American History*. Lawrence: University Press of Kansas, 2001.

Klinkner, Philip A., and Rogers M. Smith. *The Unsteady March: The Rise and Decline of Racial Equality in America*. Chicago: University of Chicago Press, 1999.

Lindemann, Barbara T., and David D. Kadue. *Age Discrimination in Employment Law*. Portland, Ore.: BNA Books, 2003.

O'Meara, Daniel P. *Protecting the Growing Number of Older Workers: The Age Discrimination in Employment Act*. Philadelphia: University of Pennsylvania Press, 1989.

Padavic, Irene, and Barbara F. Reskin. *Women and Men at Work*. Thousand Oaks, Calif.: Pine Forge Press, 2002.

Rawls, James J. *Chief Red Fox Is Dead: A History of Native Americans since 1945*. New York: Harcourt Brace College Publishers, 1996.

Riggle, Ellen D. B., and Barry Tadlock. *Gays and Lesbians in the Democratic Process: Public Policy, Public Opinion, and Political Representation*. New York: Columbia University Press, 1999.

Rimmerman, Craig A., and Clyde Wilcox. *The Politics of Same-Sex Marriage*. Chicago: University of Chicago Press, 2007.

Rusco, Elmer R. *A Fateful Time: The Background and Legislative History of the Indian Reorganization Act*. Reno: University of Nevada Press, 2000.

Switzer, Jacqueline Vaughn. *Disabled Rights: American Disability Policy and the Fight for Equality*. Washington, D.C.: Georgetown University Press, 2003.

Tatalovich, Raymond. *The Politics of Abortion in the United States and Canada*. New York: M.E. Sharpe, 1997.

Thernstrom, Abigail, and Stephan Thernstrom. *No Excuses: Closing the Racial Gap in Learning*. New York: Simon & Schuster, 2003.

12. Education

Beatty, Barbara. *Preschool Education in America: The Culture of Young Children from the Colonial Era to the Present*. New Haven, Conn.: Yale University Press, 1995.

Belfield, Clive, and Henry M. Levin, eds. *The Price We Pay: Economic and Social Consequences of Inadequate Education*. Washington, D.C.: Brookings Institution Press, 2007.

Brisk, Maria E. *Bilingual Education: From Compensatory to Quality Schooling*. Mahwah, N.J.: Lawrence Erlbaum Associates, 1998.

Fuller, Bruce. *Standardized Childhood: The Political and Cultural Struggle over Early Education*. Palo Alto, Calif.: Stanford University Press, 2007.

Gallagher, James J. *Driving Change in Special Education*. Baltimore: Brookes Publishing Company, 2006.

Garcia, Ofelia. *Bilingual Education in the 21st Century: A Global Perspective*. Hoboken, N.J.: Wiley-Blackwell Press, 2008.

Heller, Donald E., ed. *The States and Public Higher Education Policy: Affordability, Access, and Accountability*. Baltimore: The Johns Hopkins University Press, 2001.

Howell, William G., and Paul E. Peterson. *The Education Gap: Vouchers and Urban Schools*. Washington, D.C.: Brookings Institution Press, 2006.

Kozol, Jonathon. *Savage Inequalities*. New York: Harper Perennial, 1991.

Orfield, Gary, Patricia Marin, and Catherine L. Horn, eds. *Higher Education and the Color Line: College Access, Racial Equality and Social Change*. Cambridge, Mass.: Harvard Education Press, 2005.

Price, Derek V. *Borrowing Inequality: Race, Class and Student Loans*. Boulder, Colo.: Lynne Rienner, 2004.

St. John, Edward P., and Michael D. Parsons, eds. *Public Funding of Higher Education: Changing Contexts and New Rationale*. Baltimore and London: The Johns Hopkins University Press, 2004.

Vinovskis, Maris A. *The Birth of Head Start: Preschool Education Policies in the Kennedy and Johnson Administrations*. Chicago: University of Chicago Press, 2005.

West, Martin R., and Paul E. Peterson, eds. *School Money Trials: The Legal Pursuit of Educational Adequacy*. Washington, D.C.: Brookings Institution Press, 2007.

Williams, Joe. *Cheating Our Kids: How Politics and Greed Ruin Education*. New York: Palgrave, 2005.

Yell, Mitchell L. *The Law and Special Education*. 2d ed. Upper Saddle River, N.J.: Prentice Hall, 2005.

13. Family Law

Carp, E. Wayne. *Adoption Politics: Bastard Nation and Ballot Initiative 58*. Lawrence: University Press of Kansas, 2004.

Cherlin, Andrew J. *The Marriage Go Round: The State of Marriage and the Family in America Today*. New York: Alfred A. Knopf, 2009.

Coontz, Stephanie. *Marriage, a History: From Obedience to Intimacy, or How Love Conquered Marriage*. New York: Viking, 2005.

Hoyano, Laura, and Caroline Keenan. *Child Abuse: Law and Policy across Boundaries*. New York: Oxford University Press, 2010.

Hunter, James Davison. *Culture Wars—The Struggle to Define America: Making Sense of the Battles over the Family, Art, Education, Law and Politics*. New York: Basic Books, 1991.

Nelson, Barbara. *Making an Issue of Child Abuse*. Chicago: University of Chicago Press, 1984.

Nerenberg, Lisa. *Elder Abuse Prevention: Emerging Trends and Promising Strategies*. New York: Springer Publishing, 2008.

Pertman, Adam. *Adoption Nation: How the Adoption Revolution Is Transforming America*. New York: Basic Books, 2000.

Schneider, Elizabeth M. *Battered Women and Feminist Lawmaking*. New Haven, Conn.: Yale University Press, 2000.

Summers, Randal W., and Allan M. Hoffman. *Elder Abuse: A Public Health Perspective*. Washington, D.C.: American Public Health Association, 2006.

Wallerstein, Judith S., Julia Lewis, and Sandra Blakeslee. *The Unexpected Legacy of Divorce: A 25 Year Landmark Study*. New York: Hyperion, 2000.

Whittier, Nancy. *The Politics of Child Sexual Abuse*. New York: Oxford University Press, 2009.

14. First Amendment Rights

Blanchard, Margaret A. *Revolutionary Sparks: Freedom of Expression in Modern America*. New York: Oxford University Press, 1992.

Fisher, Louis. *Religious Liberty in America: Political Safeguards*. Lawrence: University Press of Kansas, 2002.

Gilmore, Donald M. *Power, Publicity, and the Abuse of Libel Law*. New York: Oxford University Press, 1992.

Hamburger, Philip. *Separation of Church and State*. Cambridge, Mass.: Harvard University Press, 2002.

Hamilton, Marci A. *God v. the Gavel: Religion and the Rule of Law*. New York: Cambridge University Press, 2005.

Lewis, Anthony. *Freedom for the Thought We Hate: A Biography of the First Amendment*. New York: Basic Books, 2007.

Martin, Robert W. T. *The Founding of American Press Liberty, 1640–1880*. New York: New York University Press, 2001.

Stone, Geoffrey R. *Perilous Times: Free Speech in Wartime from the Sedition Act of 1798 to the War on Terrorism*. New York: Norton, 2004.

Tedford, Thomas L., and Dale A. Herbeck. *Freedom of Speech in the United States*. 6th ed. State College, Pa.: Strata, 2009.

Weaver, Russell L., Andrew T. Kenyon, David F. Partlett, and Clive P. Walker. *The Right to Speak Ill: Defamation, Reputation, and Free Speech*. Durham, N.C.: Carolina Academic Press, 2006.

15. Health Care

Angel, Ronald, and Jacqueline Angel. *Who Will Care for Us? Aging and Long-Term Care in Multicultural America*. New York: New York University Press, 1999.

Axinn, June, and Michael J. Stern. *Social Welfare: A History of the American Response to Need*. Boston: Allyn & Bacon, 2005.

Battin, Margaret, ed. *Physician-Assisted Suicide: Expanding the Debate*. New York: Routledge, 1998.

Behuniak, Susan M., and Arthur G. Svenson. *Physician-Assisted Suicide: The Anatomy of a Constitutional Law Issue*. Lanham, Md.: Rowman & Littlefield, 2003.

Frank, Richard, and Sherry Glied. *Better but Not Well: Mental Health Policy in the United States since 1950*. Baltimore: The Johns Hopkins University Press, 2006.

Merritt, David, ed. *Paper Kills: Transforming Health and Health Care with Information Technology*. Washington, D.C.: CHT Press, 2007.

Moon, Marilyn. *Medicare: A Policy Primer*. Washington, D.C.: Urban Institute Press, 2006.

Oberlander, Jonathan. *The Political Life of Medicare*. Chicago: University of Chicago Press, 2003.

Rosen, George. *History of Public Health*. Baltimore: The Johns Hopkins University Press, 1993.

Rosner, David, and Gerald Markcowitz. *Are We Ready: Public Health since 9/11*. Berkeley: University of California Press, 2006.

Sage, William M., and Rogan Kersh. *Medical Malpractice and the U.S. Health Care System*. New York: Cambridge University Press, 2006.

Satel, Sally. *When Altruism Isn't Enough: The Case for Compensating Kidney Donors*. Washington, D.C.: AEI Press, 2008.

Siplon, Patricia D. *AIDS and the Policy Struggle in the United States*. Washington, D.C.: Georgetown University Press, 2002.

Smith, David, and Judith D. Moore. *Medicaid Politics and Policy: 1965–2007*. New Brunswick, N.J.: Transaction Publishers, 2008.

Thaler, Richard H., and Cass R. Sunstein. *Nudge: Improving Decisions about Health, Wealth, and Happiness*. Rev. ed. New York: Penguin, 2009.

Thompson, Frank J., and John J. Dilulio, eds. *Medicaid and Devolution: A View from the States*. Washington, D.C.: Brookings Institution Press, 1998.

Washington Post. *Landmark: The Inside Story of America's New Health Care Law and What It Means for Us All*. New York: PublicAffairs Books, 2010.

16. Housing and Urban Policy

Burt, Martha, et al. *Helping America's Homeless: Emergency Shelter or Affordable Housing?* Washington, D.C.: Urban Institute Press, 2001.

Epstein, Richard A. *Takings: Private Property and the Power of Eminent Domain*. Cambridge, Mass.: Harvard University Press, 1985.

Hopper, Kim. *Reckoning with Homelessness*. Ithaca, N.Y.: Cornell University Press, 2003.

Marsico, Richard D. *Democratizing Capital: The History, Law, and Reform of the Community Reinvestment Act*. Durham, N.C.: Carolina Academic Press, 2005.

Massey, Douglas, and Nancy Denton. *American Apartheid: Segregation and the Making of the Underclass*. Cambridge, Mass.: Harvard University Press, 1993.

Paul, Ellen Frankel. *Property Rights and Eminent Domain*. Piscataway, N.J.: Transaction Publishers, 2008.

Retsinas, Nicholas P., and Eric S. Belsky, eds. *Low Income Homeownership: Examining the Unexamined Goal*. Washington, D.C.: Brookings Institution Press, 2002.

Reynolds, Susan. *Before Eminent Domain: Toward a History of Expropriation of Land for the Common*

Good. Chapel Hill: University of North Carolina Press, 2010.

Yinger, John. *Closed Doors, Opportunities Lost*. New York: Russell Sage Foundation, 1995.

17. Science, Communications, and Technology

Bell, Tom W., and Solveig Singleton. *Regulators' Revenge: The Future of Telecommunications Deregulation*. Washington, D.C.: Cato Institute, 1998.

Brock, Gerald W. *Telecommunications Policy for the Information Age: From Monopoly to Competition*. Cambridge, Mass.: Harvard University Press, 1994.

Crandall, Robert W. *Competition and Chaos: U.S. Telecommunications since the 1996 Telecom Act*. Washington, D.C.: Brookings Institution Press, 2005.

Dupree, A. Hunter. *Science in the Federal Government: A History of Policies and Activities to 1940*. Cambridge, Mass.: Belknap Press of Harvard University Press, 1957.

Foster, Lynn E. *Nanotechnology: Science, Innovation, and Opportunity*. Upper Saddle River, N.J.: Prentice Hall, 2009.

Handberg, Roger. *Reinventing NASA: Human Spaceflight, Bureaucracy, and Politics*. Santa Barbara, Calif.: Praeger Publishing, 2003.

Korobkin, Russell, and Stephen R. Munzer. *Stem Cell Century: Law and Policy for a Breakthrough Technology*. New Haven, Conn.: Yale University Press, 2007.

Levine, Aaron D. *Cloning: A Beginner's Guide*. Oxford: Oneworld Publications, 2007.

Sheehan, Michael. *The International Politics of Space*. New York: Routledge, 2007.

Zarkin, Kimberly A., and Michael J. Zarkin. *The Federal Communications Commission: Front Line in the Culture and Regulation Wars*. Westport, Conn.: Greenwood Press, 2006.

18. Morality Issues

Abbott, Karen. *Sin in the Second City: Madams, Ministers, Playboys and the Battle for America's Soul*. New York: Random House, 2007.

Brandt, Allan M. *The Cigarette Century: The Rise, Fall, and Deadly Persistence of the Product That Defined America*. New York: Basic Books, 2007.

Gerdes, Louise. *Prostitution and Sex Trafficking*. Chicago: Greenhaven Press, 2006.

Grinols, Earl L. *Gambling in America: Costs and Benefits*. Cambridge: Cambridge University Press, 2004.

Grittner, Frederick K. *White Slavery: Myth, Ideology, and American Law*. New York: Garland, 1990.

Hamm, Richard F. *Shaping the 18th Amendment*. Chapel Hill: University of North Carolina Press, 1995.

Laband, David N., and Deborah Hendry Heinbuch. *Blue Laws: The History, Economics, and Politics of Sunday Closing Laws*. Lexington Mass.: Lexington Books, 1987.

MacCoun, Robert J., and Peter Reuter. *Drug War Heresies: Learning from Other Vices, Times & Places*. Cambridge, Mass.: Cambridge University Press, 2001.

McGowan, Richard A. *Government and the Transformation of the Gaming Industry*. Cheltenham, England: Edward Elgar Publishing, 2001.

McGowan, Richard A. *Government Regulation of the Alcohol Industry: The Search for Revenue and the Common Good*. Westport, Conn.: Quorum Books, 1997.

Rabin, Robert L., and Stephen D. Sugarman, eds. *Regulating Tobacco*. New York: Oxford University Press, 2001.

Tate, Cassandra. *Cigarette Wars: The Triumph of "The Little White Slaver."* New York: Oxford University Press, 1999.

Wallenstein, Peter. *Blue Laws and Black Codes: Conflict, Courts, and Change in Twentieth Century Virginia*. Charlottesville: University of Virginia Press, 2004.

Zimring, Franklin E., and Gordon Hawkins. *The Search for Rational Drug Control*. New York: Cambridge University Press, 1992.

19. Welfare and Income Support

Amenta, Edwin. *When Movements Matter: The Townsend Plan and the Rise of Social Security*. Princeton, N.J.: Princeton University Press, 2006.

Béland, Daniel. *Social Security: History and Politics from the New Deal to the Privatization Debate*. Lawrence: University Press of Kansas, 2005.

Cammisa, Anne Marie. *From Rhetoric to Reform?: Welfare Policy in American Politics.* Boulder, Colo.: Westview Press, 1998.

DeWitt, Larry W., Daniel Béland, and Edward D. Berkowitz, eds. *Social Security: A Documentary History*. Washington, D.C.: Congressional Quarterly Press, 2008.

Gilens, Martin. *Why Americans Hate Welfare: Race, Media, and the Politics of Antipoverty Policy*. Chicago: University of Chicago Press, 1999.

Howard, Christopher. *The Welfare State Nobody Knows: Debunking Myths about U.S. Social Policy*. Princeton, N.J.: Princeton University Press, 2008.

Katz, Michael B. *The Price of Citizenship: Redefining the American Welfare State.* New York: Henry Holt, 2001.

Weaver, R. Kent. *Ending Welfare as We Know It.* Washington, D.C.: Brookings Institution Press, 2000.

Volume 3: Government, Law Enforcement, and Foreign Affairs

20. Crime

Acker, James R., Robert M. Bohm, and Charles S. Lanier, eds. *America's Experiment with Capital Punishment: Reflections on the Past, Present, and Future of the Ultimate Penal Sanction.* 2d ed. Durham, N.C.: Carolina Academic Press, 2003.

Banner, Stuart. *The Death Penalty: An American History.* Cambridge, Mass.: Harvard University Press, 2002.

Beckett, Katherine. *Making Crime Pay: Law and Order in Contemporary American Politics.* New York: Oxford University Press, 1997.

Cornell, Saul. *A Well-Regulated Militia: The Founding Fathers and the Origins of Gun Control in America*. New York: Oxford University Press, 2006.

Feld, Barry. *Bad Kids: Race and the Transformation of the Juvenile Court*. Oxford: Oxford University Press, 1999.

Goss, Kristin. *Disarmed: The Missing Movement for Gun Control in America*. Princeton, N.J.: Princeton University Press, 2006.

Jacobs, James B., and Kimberly Potter. *Hate Crimes: Criminal Law and Identity Politics.* New York: Oxford University Press, 1998.

Koenig, Thomas H., and Michael L. Rustad. *In Defense of Tort Law.* New York: New York University Press, 2002.

Lewis, Anthony. *Gideon's Trumpet*. New York: Random House, 1964.

Logweller, Cary, ed. *Identity Theft Breaches*. New York: Nova Science Publishers, 2009.

McNally, Megan M., and Graeme R. Newman, eds. *Perspectives on Identity Theft*. Monsey, N.Y.: Criminal Justice Press, 2008.

Paternoster, Raymond, Robert Brame, and Sarah Bacon. *The Death Penalty: America's Experience with Capital Punishment.* New York: Oxford University Press, 2007.

Ross, H. Laurence. *Deterring the Drinking Driver: Legal Policy and Social Control*. Lexington, Mass.: Lexington Books, 1984.

Rustad, Michael L. *Everyday Law for Lawyers*. Boulder, Colo.: Paradigm Publishers, 2007.

Spitzer, Robert J. *Gun Control: A Documentary and Reference Guide.* Westport, Conn.: Greenwood Publishing Group, 2009.

Spohn, Cassi, and Julie Horney. *Rape Law Reform: A Grass Roots Revolution and Its Impact*. New York: Springer Publishing, 1992.

Stone, Geoffrey R., et al. *Constitutional Law*, 5th ed. New York: Aspen Publishers, 2005.

Tanenhaus, David S. *Juvenile Justice in the Making*. Oxford: Oxford University Press, 2004.

Western, Bruce. *Punishment and Inequality in America.* New York: Russell Sage Foundation, 2006.

Winick, Bruce J., and John Q. LaFond, eds. *Protecting Society from Sexually Dangerous Offenders: Law, Justice, and Therapy*. Washington, D.C.: American Psychological Association, 2003.

21. Defense and National Security

Adler, David, and Larry George, eds. *The Constitution and the Conduct of American Foreign Policy*. Lawrence: University Press of Kansas, 1996.

Betts, Richard. *Enemies of Intelligence: Knowledge and Power in American National Security*. New York: Columbia University Press, 2007.

Birkland, Thomas A. *After Disaster: Agenda Setting, Public Policy, and Focusing Events*. Washington, D.C.: Georgetown University Press, 1997.

Burns, Richard Dean. *The Evolution of Arms Control: From Antiquity to the Nuclear Age*. Santa Barbara, Calif.: Praeger, 2009.

Ervin, Clark Kent. *Open Target: Where America Is Vulnerable to Attack*. New York: Palgrave Macmillan, 2006.

Fisher, Louis. *Presidential War Power*. 2d rev. ed. Lawrence: University Press of Kansas, 2004.

Flynn, Stephen. *America the Vulnerable: How Our Government Is Failing to Protect Us from Terrorism*. New York: HarperCollins, 2004.

Hinckley, Barbara. *Less than Meets the Eye: Foreign Policy Making and the Myth of the Assertive Congress*. Chicago: University of Chicago Press, 1994.

Hymans, Jacques E. *The Psychology of Nuclear Proliferation*. New York: Cambridge University Press, 2006.

Kriner, Douglas. *After the Rubicon: Congressional Constraints on Presidential Warmaking*. Chicago: University of Chicago Press, 2010.

Mettler, Suzanne. *Soldiers to Citizens: The G.I. Bill and the Making of the Greatest Generation*. Oxford and New York: Oxford University Press, 2005.

National Commission on Terrorist Attack. *The 9/11 Commission Report*. New York: W.W. Norton, 2004.

Shaffer, Donald R. *After the Glory: The Struggles of Black Civil War Veterans*. Lawrence: University Press of Kansas, 2004.

Zegart, Amy. *Spying Blind: The CIA, the FBI, and the Origins of 9/11*. Princeton N.J.: Princeton University Press, 2007.

22. Diplomacy

Armitage, Richard L., and Joseph S. Nye. *A Smarter, More Secure America*. Washington, D.C.: Commission on Smart Power, Center for Strategic and International Studies, 2007.

Bergsten, C. Fred. *The United States and the World Economy: Foreign Economic Policy for the Next Decade*. Washington, D.C.: Peterson Institute, 2005.

Buss, Terry F. *Haiti in the Balance: Why Foreign Assistance to Haiti Has Failed and What to Do about It*. Washington, D.C.: Brookings Institution Press, 2008.

Destler, I. M. *American Trade Politics*. 4th ed. Washington, D.C.: Institute for International Economics, 2005.

Friedman, Thomas L. *The World Is Flat: A Brief History of the Twenty-First Century*. New York: Farrar, Straus and Giroux, 2005.

Lancaster, Carol. *Foreign Aid: Diplomacy, Development, Domestic Politics*. Chicago: University of Chicago Press, 2007.

Picard, Louis A., Robert Groelsema, and Terry F. Buss, eds. *Foreign Aid and Foreign Policy: Lessons for the Next Half-Century*. Armonk, N.Y.: M.E. Sharpe, 2008.

Wolf, Martin. *Why Globalization Works*. New Haven, Conn.: Yale University Press, 2005.

23. Elections

Brunell, Thomas. *Redistricting and Representation: Why Competitive Elections Are Bad for America*. New York: Routledge, 2008.

Carey, John M., Richard G. Niemi, and Lynda W. Powell. *Term Limits in the State Legislatures*. Ann Arbor: University of Michigan Press, 2000.

Corrado, Anthony, Daniel R. Ortiz, Thomas E. Mann, and Trevor Potter, eds. *The New Campaign Finance Sourcebook*. Washington, D.C.: Brookings Institution Press, 2005.

Cronin, Thomas E. *Direct Democracy: The Politics of Initiative, Referendum, and Recall*. Cambridge, Mass.: Harvard University Press, 1989.

Davidson, Chandler, and Bernard Grofman, eds. *Quiet Revolution in the South: The Impact of the Voting Rights Act, 1965–1990*. Princeton, N.J.: Princeton University Press, 1994.

Farrar-Myers, Victoria A., and Diana Dwyre. *Limits and Loopholes: The Quest for Money, Free Speech, and Fair Elections*. Washington, D.C.: CQ Press, 2008.

Keyssar, Alexander. *The Right to Vote: The Contested History of Democracy in the United States*. New York: Basic Books, 2000.

Kousser, J. Morgan. *Colorblind Injustice: Minority Voting Rights and the Undoing of the Second*

Reconstruction. Chapel Hill: University of North Carolina Press, 1999.

Kurtz, Karl T., Bruce Cain, and Richard G. Niemi, eds. *Institutional Change in American Politics: The Case of Term Limits*. Ann Arbor: University of Michigan Press, 2007.

Lublin, David. *The Paradox of Representation: Racial Gerrymandering and Minority Interests in Congress*. Princeton, N.J.: Princeton University Press, 1997.

Manza, Jeff, and Christopher Uggen. *Locked Out: Felon Disfranchisement and American Democracy*. New York: Oxford University Press, 2006.

Matsusaka, John G. *For the Many or the Few: The Initiative, Public Policy, and American Democracy*. Chicago: University of Chicago Press, 2008.

Rush, Mark E. *Does Redistricting Make a Difference? Partisan Representation and Electoral Behavior*. Lanham, Md.: Lexington Books, 2000.

Sarbaugh-Thompson, Marjorie, et al. *The Political and Institutional Effects of Term Limits*. New York: Palgrave Macmillan, 2004.

Schultz, David, ed. *Money, Politics, and Campaign Finance Reform Law in the States*. Durham, N.C.: Carolina Academic Press, 2002.

Thernstrom, Abigail M. *Whose Votes Count? Affirmative Action and Minority Voting Rights*. Cambridge, Mass.: Harvard University Press, 1987.

Waters, M. Dane. *Initiative and Referendum Almanac*. Durham, N.C.: Carolina Academic Press, 2003.

24. Government Operations

Condrey, Stephen E., and Robert Maranto. *Radical Reform of the Civil Service*. Lanham, Md.: Lexington Books, 2001.

Farrier, Jasmine. *Passing the Buck: Congress, the Budget, and Deficits*. Lexington: University of Kentucky Press, 2004.

Fisher, Patrick. *The Politics of Taxing and Spending*. Boulder, Colo.: Lynne Rienner, 2009.

Foerstel, Herbert. *Freedom of Information and the Right to Know: The Origins and Applications of the Freedom of Information Act*. Westport, Conn.: Greenwood Press, 1999.

Goldstein, Kenneth M. *Interest Groups, Lobbying, and Participation in America*. New York: Cambridge University Press, 1999.

Ippolito, Dennis S. *Why Budgets Matter: Budget Policy and American Politics*. University Park: Pennsylvania State University Press, 2003.

Levine, Bertram J. *The Art of Lobbying: Building Trust and Selling Policy*. Washington, D.C.: CQ Press, 2008.

Luneburg, William V., Thomas M. Susman, and Rebecca H. Gordon, eds. *The Lobbying Manual: A Complete Guide to Federal Lobbying Law and Practice*. 4th ed. Chicago: American Bar Association, 2009.

North, Robert. *Ethics in U.S. Government: An Encyclopedia of Investigations, Scandals, Reforms, and Legislation*. Santa Barbara, Calif.: Greenwood Press, 2001.

Painter, Richard W. *Getting the Government America Deserves: How Ethics Reform Can Make a Difference*. New York: Oxford University Press, 2009.

Pfiffner, James P., and Douglas A. Brook. *The Future of Merit: Twenty Years after the Civil Service Reform Act*. Washington, D.C.: Woodrow Wilson Center Press, 2000.

Piotrowski, Suzanne J. *Governmental Transparency in the Path of Administrative Reform*. Albany: State University of New York Press, 2007.

Roberts, MacKenzie, G. Calvin, and Michael Hakfen. *Scandal Proof: Do Ethics Laws Make Government Ethical?* Washington, D.C.: Brookings Institution Press, 2002.

Schoenfeld, Gabriel. *Necessary Secrets: National Security, the Media, and the Rule of Law*. New York: W. W. Norton, 2010.

Wildavsky, Aaron, and Naomi Caiden. *The New Politics of the Budgetary Process*. 5th ed. New York: Longman, 2004.

25. Immigration and Naturalization

Andreas, Peter. *Border Games: Policing the U.S.-Mexico Divide*. Ithaca, N.Y.: Cornell University Press, 2000.

Bloemraad, Irene. *Becoming a Citizen: Incorporating Immigrants and Refugees in the United States and Canada*. Berkeley: University of California Press, 2006.

Goodwin-Gill, Guy, and Jane McAdam. *The Refugee in International Law*. 3rd ed. New York: Oxford University Press, 2007.

Hathaway, James. *The Rights of Refugees under International Law*. Cambridge: Cambridge University Press, 2005.

Krikorian, Mark. *The New Case against Immigration: Both Legal and Illegal*. New York: Sentinel, 2008.

Lorey, David. *The U.S.-Mexican Border in the Twentieth Century*. Wilmington, Del.: Scholarly Resources, 1999.

Swain, Carol M., ed. *Debating Immigration*. New York: Cambridge University Press, 2007.

Tichenor, Daniel J. *Dividing Lines: The Politics of Immigration Control in America*. Princeton, N.J.: Princeton University Press, 2002.

Winterdyk, John A., and Kelly W. Sundberg. *Transforming Borders in the Al Qaeda Era*. London: Ashgate, 2009.

Wong, Carolyn. *Lobbying for Inclusion: Rights, Politics, and the Makings of Immigration Policy*. Palo Alto, Calif.: Stanford University Press, 2006.

26. Miscellaneous Government Functions

Anderson, Margo J., and Stephen E. Feinberg. *Who Counts? The Politics of Census-Taking in Contemporary America*. New York: Russell Sage Foundation, 1999.

Birkland, Thomas A. *Lessons of Disaster: Policy Change after Catastrophic Events*. Washington, D.C.: Georgetown University Press, 2006.

John, Richard R. *Spreading the News: The American Postal System from Franklin to Morse*. Cambridge, Mass.: Harvard University Press, 1995.

Kielbowicz, Richard B. *News in the Mails: The Press, Post Office, and Public Information, 1700–1860s*. New York: Greenwood Press, 1989.

Rubin, Claire B. *Emergency Management: The American Experience 1900–2005*. Fairfax, Va.: Public Entity Risk Management (PERI), 2007.

Skerry, Peter. *Counting on the Census? Race, Group Identity, and the Evasion of Politics*. Washington, D.C.: Brookings Institution Press, 2000.

Sylves, Richard. *Disaster Policy and Politics: Emergency Management and Homeland Security*. Washington, D.C.: CQ Press, 2008.

Contributor List

Abolofia, Mitch (SUNY—Albany)
Ackelson, Jason (New Mexico State University)
Acker, James (SUNY—Albany)
Adams, Jason Michael (Arkansas State University)
Aguilera, Gabriel (California State University—Chico)
Allen, Sam (Virginia Military Institute)
Andrews, Christine M. (University of Chicago)
Anetzberger, Georgia (Cleveland State University)
Barr, Kathleen (Texas A&M University)
Beavers, Staci (California State University—San Marcos)
Beecher, Jan (Michigan State University)
Behuniak, Susan (LeMoyne College)
Belt, Todd (University of Hawaii)
Benton, Ed (University of South Florida)
Berkowitz, Ed (George Washington University)
Binkiewicz, Donna (California State—Long Beach)
Blakesley, Lance (Loyola Marymount University)
Blaser, Arthur (Chapman University)
Bosso, Christopher (Northeastern University)
Bow, Shannon (University of Texas)
Bowman, Rebecca (Luther College)
Buck, Stuart (University of Arkansas)
Buss, James (Oklahoma City University)
Buss, Terry (Carnegie Mellon University)
Cagle, M. Christine (Centers for Disease Control and Prevention)
Carpenter, Stephanie (Murray State)
Caruson, Kiki (University of South Florida)
Cheit, Ross (Brown University)
Chevrier, Marie (University of Texas—Dallas)
Choe, Gretchen (University of Texas—Dallas)
Cohen, Sally (University of New Mexico)
Cook, Karen (University of Louisiana—Monroe)
Cunion, William (University of Mount Union)
Cusick, Roger (Morehouse College)
DeLaat, Jacqueline (Marietta College)
DeVille, Kenneth (East Carolina University)
DeWitt, Larry (Social Security Administration)
Ditmore, Melissa Hope (independent scholar)
Durbin, Brent (Smith College)
Eijmberts, Hans (Northeastern University)
Elmendorf, William (Penn State University)
Farrar-Myers, Victoria (University of Texas—Arlington)
Finley, Jim (Penn State University)
Fishback, Price (University of Arizona)
Fisher, Patrick (Seton Hall University)
Galloway, Fred (University of San Diego)
Gaziano, Joe (Lewis University)
Geddes, Rick (Cornell University)
Gitterman, Daniel (University of North Carolina—Chapel Hill)
Griffin, O. Hayden (University of Southern Mississippi)
Groelsema, Robert (University of Pittsburgh)
Grogan, Colleen (University of Chicago)
Grosshuesch, Ariel (Appalachian State University)
Halbert, Debora (University of Hawaii at Manoa)
Han, Lori Cox (Chapman University)
Hannestad, Stephen (University of Maryland—College Park)
Hasecke, Edward (Wittenberg University)
Hassler, Gregory (East Carolina University)
Hayler, Barbara (University of Illinois—Springfield)
Hecht, Stacey (Bethel University)
Henderson, Robert (Northern Virginia Community College)
Henry, Jessica (Montclair State University)
Herbeck, Dale (Boston College)
Herian, Mitch (University of Nebraska)
Hindman, Hugh (Appalachian State University)
Hoffman, Steve (University of St. Thomas)
Hogen-Esch, Tom (California State University—Northridge)
Houston, David (University of Tennessee—Knoxville)
Huber, Walter (Muskingum University)
Hunter, Susan (West Virginia University)
Jasso, Sean (Pepperdine University)
Jones, Sheila (Broward College)
Kaneukis, Derek (University of Nevada—Reno)
Karch, Andrew (University of Minnesota)
Keel, Gina (SUNY—Oneonta)
Kelly, Christopher (Miami University)

Kemp, Donna (California State University—Chico)
Khey, David (Loyola University—New Orleans)
Kielbowicz, Richard (University of Washington)
Kilborn, Jason (John Marshall Law School)
Kochtcheeva, Lada (North Carolina State University)
Kole, Subir (University of Hawaii at Manoa)
Kousser, Morgan (Cal Tech)
Kraus, Jeff (Wagner College)
Kriner, Douglas (Boston College)
Kurlat, Pablo (Stanford University)
Lahey, Joanna (Texas A&M)
Lambert, Bart (St. Bonaventure University)
Law, Mark (University of Vermont)
Ledvinka, Christine (Cleveland State University)
Leitch, Richard (Gustavus Adolphus College)
Lencsis, Peter (Yeshiva College)
Levine, Aaron (Georgia Institute of Technology)
Liesen, Laurette (Lewis University)
Longo, Peter (University of Nebraska—Kearney)
Lukens, Jonathan (University of Pennsylvania)
Luloff, A. E. (Penn State University)
Luneburg, William (University of Pittsburgh School of Law)
MacDonald, Heather (University of Western Sydney)
MacManus, Susan (University of South Florida)
Manrique, Cecilia (University of Wisconsin—LaCrosse)
Maranto, Robert (University of Arkansas)
Martin, Janet (Bowdoin College)
Martinez, J. Michael (Kennesaw State University)
Mastrodicasa, Jeanna (University of Florida)
Matsuda, Kristy (University of Missouri—St. Louis)
McAllister, Caitlin (Product Stewardship Institute)
Mergner, Stephen (Georgetown College)
Miller, Jonathan (Vanderbilt University)
Miller, Will (Southeast Missouri State University)
Nice, David (Washington State University)
O'Donnell, Sean (Harvard University)
Oliver, Tom (University of Wisconsin)
Oster, Clint (Indiana University)
O'Sullivan, Daniel (Claremont)
Owens, Lori (Jacksonville State University)
Patton, Dana (University of Kentucky)
Percival, Garrick (University of Minnesota—Duluth)
Picard, Louis (University of Pittsburgh)
Piotrowski, Suzanne (Rutgers University)
Piskulich, Pat (Oakland University)
Pitney, John (Claremont McKenna College)
Plant, Jeremy (Penn State University—Harrisburg)
Pope, Daniel (University of Oregon)
Price, Derek (DVP-Praxis LTD)
Rao, Nirupama (Massachusetts Institute of Technology)
Riccucci, Norma (Rutgers University)
Rice, Laurie (Southern Illinois University—Edwardsville)
Richardson, Lilliard (University of Missouri)
Richardson, William (University of South Dakota)
Roberts, Patrick (Virginia Tech)
Robinson, Kent (Seattle University)
Rockwell, Steve (St. Joseph's College of New York)
Rom, Mark (Georgetown University)
Routh, Steve (California State University—Stanislaus)
Rozzi, Alan (Santa Clara University)
Rustad, Michael (Suffolk University Law School)
Rynerson, Steve (independent scholar)
Sack, Emily (Roger Williams University School of Law)
Sands, Eric (Berry College)
Schierling, Dan (Ohio University)
Schrad, Mark Lawrence (Villanova University)
Shepherd, Scott (John Marshall Law School)
Sherman, Daniel (University of Puget Sound)
Shughart, William (University of Mississippi)
Singh, J. P. (Georgetown University)
Sirgo, Henry (McNeese State University)
Smith-Heimbrock, Sydney (Office of Personnel Management)
Solomon, Phyllis (University of Pennsylvania)
Soma, John (University of Denver)
Spitzer, Robert (SUNY—Cortland)
Spitzer, Scott (Cal State—Fullerton)
Stockstill, Helen King (University of South Carolina)
Stoutenborough, James (University of Kansas)
Streicher, Jennifer (Washington State University)
Strine, Neil (Bloomsburg University)
Strong, John (College of William & Mary)
Studlar, Donley (West Virginia University)
Sutton, Thomas (Baldwin Wallace College)
Swain, Carol (Vanderbilt University)
Tadlock, Barry (Ohio University)
Taylor, Jami (University of Toledo)
Thelin, John (University of Kentucky)
Thompson, Robert (East Carolina University)
Tovino, Stacey (University of Nevada—Las Vegas)
Trish, Barbara (Grinnell College)
VanDerWerff, Jeff (Northwestern College)
Van Horn, Patrick (New College of Florida)
Vasquez, Rose Ann (University of New Mexico)
Vitello, Stanley (Rutgers University)
Weissert, William (Florida State University)
Ye, Lin (Sun Yat-sen University [China])
Zarkin, Michael (Westminster College)

Index

Note: *Italic* page numbers refer to illustrations. **Boldface** page numbers indicate main discussions.

J

O

Q

R